Lecture Notes in Computer Science 1710

Edited by G. Goos, J. Hartmanis and J. van Leeuwen

T0217355

Springer

Berlin
Heidelberg
New York
Barcelona
Hong Kong
London
Milan
Paris
Singapore
Tokyo

Ernst-Rüdiger Olderog   Bernhard Steffen (Eds.)

Correct
System Design

Recent Insights and Advances

 Springer

Series Editors

Gerhard Goos, Karlsruhe University, Germany
Juris Hartmanis, Cornell University, NY, USA
Jan van Leeuwen, Utrecht University, The Netherlands

Volume Editors

Ernst-Rüdiger Olderog
Fachbereich Informatik, Universität Oldenburg
Postfach 2503, D-26111 Oldenburg, Germany
E-mail: olderog@informatik-uni.oldenburg.de

Bernhard Steffen
Fachbereich Informatik, Universität Dortmund
Baroper Str. 301, D-44221 Dortmund, Germany
E-mail: steffen@cs.uni-dortmund.de

Cataloging-in-Publication data applied for

Die Deutsche Bibliothek - CIP-Einheitsaufnahme

Correct system design : recent insights and advances / Bernhard
Steffen ; Ernst-Rüdiger Olderog (ed.). - Berlin ; Heidelberg ; New
York ; Barcelona ; Hong Kong ; London ; Milan ; Paris ; Singapore ;
Tokyo : Springer, 1999
    (Lecture notes in computer science ; Vol. 1710)
    ISBN 3-540-66624-9

CR Subject Classification (1998): F.3, D.3, D.4, D, F.4.1, I.2.3, C.3

ISSN 0302-9743
ISBN 3-540-66624-9 Springer-Verlag Berlin Heidelberg New York

© Springer-Verlag Berlin Heidelberg 1999
Printed in Germany

Typesetting: Camera-ready by author
SPIN: 10705026   06/3142 – 5 4 3 2 1 0   Printed on acid-free paper

Preface

Computers are gaining more and more control over systems that we use or rely on in our daily lives. Besides the visible appearance of computers, for example in the form of PCs at home or at work, booking terminals in travel agencies, or automatic teller machines in banks, there is a growing demand for computers as invisible parts of systems in order to control their proper functioning. For example, computers inside washing machines or central heating systems should help in saving energy in our homes. Computer-controlled airbags in cars and automatic pilots in airplanes should bring more safety to the passengers. Computerised signalling systems should guarantee safe and efficient operation of railway traffic. Computer-operated telecommunication networks should bring individual services to their customers.

But despite all these successes of computer applications, the question is how much can we really rely on these systems? Every now and then we read about failures of computerised systems. It may only be annoying if the PC does not work as expected. More serious is a breakdown of a railway signalling system or an unwanted explosion of an airbag. Here the question of *correctness* of the system, of its software and hardware arises. In other words: does the computer system behave according to expectations and requirements?

This question is a challenge to software engineers and computer scientists: they need to understand the foundations of programming, need to understand how different formal theories are linked together, how compilers correctly translate high-level programs into machine code, why optimisations performed are justifiable. They need the intellectual power to understand all these aspects together in the framework of a suitable methodology for designing correct computerised systems. These are the questions this book is about.

The concern about correctness goes in fact back to the origins of computer programming. Already in 1949 Alan M. Turing posed in a conference paper entitled *"On Checking a Large Routine"* [1] the question: "How can one check a routine in the sense of making sure that it is right?" and went on to answer that "... the programmer should make a number of definite assertions which can be checked individually, and from which the correctness of the whole programme easily follows." In modern terminology, Turing proposes the "inductive assertion method" to prove program correctness, but the "large routine" considered in the report is in fact quite small: a flow chart program for computing the square root.

Where are we today, 50 years after Turing's pioneering paper? What is our current understanding of programming methodology, what has been achieved in automatic correctness proofs, how far are we with the production of correct compilers, what application domains of industrial relevance can be handled today? To answer these questions we invited 15 researchers to help us by explaining their current understanding and contributions to the issue of correct system design.

---

[1] A.M. Turing. *On Checking a Large Routine*. Report of a Conference on High Speed Automatic Calculating Machines, Univ. Math. Laboratory, Cambridge, pages 67–69, 1949. (See also: F.L. Morris and C.B. Jones, *An Early Program Proof by Alan Turing, Annals of the History of Computing 6*, pages 139–143, 1984.)

A Book Dedicated to Hans Langmaack

How did we select the authors? We took the opportunity of Prof. Dr. Dr. h.c. Hans Langmaack's retirement from his professorship at the University of Kiel on October 1st, 1999, in order to present the area closest to his heart from a personal perspective. The contributors are on the one hand prominent scientists who had or have some close scientific contacts with Langmaack and on the other hand some of his former students who directly contributed to the area of correct system design.

Hans Langmaack studied mathematics, physics, and logic at the Universities of Münster and Freiburg. After receiving his doctorate in mathematics he became the assistant of Klaus Samelson, who together with Friedrich L. Bauer, is one of the German pioneers in the area of computer science in general and compiler construction in particular. The assistantship brought Langmaack to the University of Mainz and the Technical University of Munich where he worked on the topics of programming languages, compiler construction and formal languages. This is where contacts to Gerhard Goos and David Gries were established. Langmaack wrote one of the first compilers for the programming language ALGOL 60. After a visiting assistant professorship at Purdue University, Lafayette, Indiana, he took positions as a full professor of computer science at the Universities of Saarbrücken and Kiel.

Hans Langmaack's scientific interest is motivated by his work on compilers and his pursuit of correctness. Among others, he investigated the procedure concept of ALGOL 60 and ALGOL 68, where procedures are allowed as untyped and typed parameters, and formalised the semantics of procedures in a partly operational style in terms of a copy rule. This formalisation allowed him to attack and solve decidability questions of so-called "formal" run time properties of ALGOL-like programs, i.e. where the data are left uninterpreted. These questions concerned the formal reachability of procedures, their formally correct parameter transmission, and the formal "most-recent" property. The last property is concerned with an error occurring in an implementation of recursive procedures by Edsger W. Dijkstra.[2] A major achievement was the decidability proof of the formal reachability of procedures within ALGOL 68 programs, which are typed in the sense of the Lambda calculus.

Due to Edmund M. Clarke's investigations on obtaining sound and relatively complete Hoare-like proof systems for programming languages with an ALGOL-like procedure concept, Langmaack's interest turned to the issue of program correctness in the sense of Hoare. This is where contacts to Krzysztof R. Apt came about. Very interestingly, it turned out that essentially the same proof techniques that had been used to prove the decidability or undecidability of formal procedure properties could also be applied to show the presence or absence of sound and relatively complete Hoare-like proof systems for programming languages with ALGOL-like procedures. This topic was pursued further by Werner Damm, Ernst-Rüdiger Olderog and Hardi Hungar.

---

[2] A minimal program violating the "most recent" property is shown on the cover.

Besides his theoretical investigations Hans Langmaack has always been involved in practical compiler projects. These projects were conducted in cooperation with industrial partners. A major concern of these projects was to lift the level of specification of the compiling function. Due to contact with and visits by Dines Bjørner, VDM was used as a specification technique. Work on optimisation techniques and their scientific foundation also started from these practical projects. This topic, comprising abstract interpretation and data flow analysis, was pursued further by Bernhard Steffen, Jens Knoop and Oliver Rüthing, and, focussing on functional and parallel languages, by Flemming Nielson, who, on the initiative of Hans Langmaack, was guest professor at the University of Kiel in 1992.

A major activity was the European basic research project ProCoS (Provably Correct Systems) founded by Tony Hoare, Dines Bjørner and Hans Langmaack. The project was conceived by Hoare in reaction to the so-called "CLInc stack", a multi-level verification task solved by Robert S. Boyer and J S. Moore. It defined the so-called "ProCoS tower" of language levels and was concerned with the correct links between these levels. In this project Hans Langmaack's group was responsible for correct compilers from an OCCAM-like programming language to transputer machine code. Martin Fränzle and Markus Müller-Olm earned their first scientific merits in this project. Anders P. Ravn and Hans Rischel at Lyngby, and Ernst-Rüdiger Olderog at Oldenburg also participated in ProCoS. The work of Langmaack's group on compiler correctness in the ProCoS project is currently continued in the project Verifix conducted by Gerhard Goos, Friedrich von Henke and Hans Langmaack.

Links to local companies in Kiel established contacts to Jan Peleska, who was rigorously applying formal methods in industry. Amir Pnueli brought "Turing power" to international meetings in Schleswig-Holstein.

Hans Langmaack has also been successful as a teacher and advisor to many students. About 170 students graduated with a Diplom (MSc) from his reseach group, 22 completed a doctoral dissertation (PhD) under his supervison and 5 finished the habilitation procedure to qualify for a professorship with his guidance. Being among his students, we have closely experienced his continuous engagement for the topic of "Correct System Design", in research, education and unforgettable grill parties. Here, Bengt Jonsson, who regularly visited Kiel, revealed unexpected talents, as an interpreter for both a Russian visitor and for Chopin at the piano.

Structure of this Book

This book consists of 17 chapters describing recent insights and advances in *Correct System Design*. They are grouped together under the five topics of methodology, programming, automation, compilation and application.

Methodology. Tony Hoare discusses in his paper *"Theories of Programming: Top-Down and Bottom-Up and Meeting in the Middle"* complementary approaches to describing the behaviour of programs. The top-down approach starts from a specification of the desired behaviour; the bottom-up approach from a collection of realisable components. A complete theory of programming will combine both approaches. Throughout the presentation Hoare stresses the advantages of algebraic laws in conveying the essence of both approaches.

Dines Bjørner illustrates in his chapter *"A Triptych Software Development Paradigm: Domain, Requirements and Software"* his view of software engineering by describing a three-step approach to rigorous software development. The approach comprises descriptions of the application domain, the requirements, and the software architecture. It is exemplified in terms of a decision support software for sustainable development.

Anders P. Ravn and Hans Rischel summarise in their chapter *"Real-Time Constraints Through the ProCoS Layers"* the results of the European research project ProCoS in which the Universities of Oxford, Lyngby, Kiel and Oldenburg collaborated. They concentrate on the main achievements of ProCoS in the area of real-time systems: the correct link between different layers of formal description ranging from requirements capture, through design and programming, down to machine code generation.

David Gries looks in his chapter *"Monotonicity in Calculational Proofs"* at logic formulae as a basic formalism for specifying systems. He is interested in a specific aspect that is of importance in the calculational manipulation of logic formulae: the monotonicity of positions where substitutions of formulae for variables are applied, and he presents a suitable metatheorem concerning monotonicity.

Programming. Krzysztof R. Apt and Andrea Schaerf explain in their chapter *"The Alma Project, or How First-Order Logic Can Help Us in Imperative Programming"* how a given imperative programming language like Modula-2 can be extended by concepts from the logic programming paradigm in order to raise the level of abstraction. As a result executable specification statements allowing bounded quantifiers can be formulated in the extended language. This leads to surprisingly clear and short programs.

Flemming Nielson and Hanne Riis Nielson show in their chapter *"Type and Effect Systems"* how static inference techniques can be used to ensure that the dynamic behaviour of a program satisfies the specification. To this end, the basic type information is extended by suitable annotations to express further intensional or extensional properties of the semantics of the program.

Automation. J S. Moore describes in his chapter *"Proving Theorems about Java-Like Byte Code"* how correctness theorems about Java programs compiled into code for a toy version of the Java Virtual Machine can be proved mechanically. The basis for this work is the mechanized logic ACL2 (A Computational Logic for Applicative Common Lisp) developed by Boyer and Moore.

Armin Biere, Edmund M. Clarke and Yunshan Zhu present in their chapter *"Multiple State and Single State Tableaux for Combining Local and Global Model Checking"* a new algorithm for the automatic verification of reactive systems specified in linear temporal logic. It combines the advantages of local and explicit state model checking with those of global and symbolic model checking.

Parosh A. Abdulla and Bengt Jonsson consider in their chapter *"On the Existence of Network Invariants for Verifying Parametrized Systems"* infinite classes of finite state systems consisting of an unbounded number of similar processes specified by a parametrised system. The aim is an inductive correctness proof of such systems using the notion of a network invariant. The paper presents sufficient conditions under which a finite-state network invariant exists.

Compilation. Gerhard Goos and Wolf Zimmermann report in their chapter *"Verification of Compilers"* on the results of a joint research project of the Universities of Karlsruhe, Kiel and Ulm. They discuss a suitable notion of correctness for compilers and how it can be verified exploiting the traditional compiler architectures involving certain intermediate languages. A main achievement is the use of program checking for replacing large parts of compiler verification by the simpler task of verifying program checkers. As semantic basis for the programming language abstract state machines are used.

Amir Pnueli, Ofer Shtrichman and Michael Siegel present in their chapter *"Translation Validation: From* SIGNAL *to C"* an alternative approach to compiler verification where each run of a compiler is considered individually and followed by a validation phase. This phase verifies that the target code produced on this run correctly implements the submitted source program. The authors address the practicality of this approach for an optimising, industrial code generator from SIGNAL to C.

Martin Fränzle and Markus Müller-Olm provide in their chapter *"Compilation and Synthesis for Real-Time Embedded Controllers"* an overview of two constructive approaches for the generation of hard real-time code from abstract specifications. The first approach starts from a real-time imperative programming language and pursues an incremental code generation. The second approach starts from formulae in a real-time logic and pursues a synthesis approach.

Jens Knoop and Oliver Rüthing investigate in their chapter *"Optimization Under the Perspective of Soundness, Completeness, and Reusability"* the code optimization technique PRE (partical redundancy elimination) in various programming paradigms: imperative, parallel, and object-oriented. For each of these paradigms the authors analyse whether PRE is sound (i.e. admissible) and complete (i.e. optimal).

Application. Tom Bienmüller, Jürgen Bohn, Henning Brinkmann, Udo Brockmeyer, Werner Damm, Hardi Hungar and Peter Jansen describe in their chapter *"Verification of Automotive Control Units"* the application of automatic verification (model-checking) tools to specification models of electronic control units for automotive applications. The approach is based on the use of the design tool STATEMATE for dealing with the discrete part of the models. For dealing with values ranging over continuous domains, the authors also present a new technique of first-order model-checking. The approach has been successfully applied in cooperation with the car manufacturer BMW.

Ernst-Rüdiger Olderog shows in his chapter *"Correct Real-Time Software for Programmable Logic Controllers"* how ideas from the theory of real-time systems can be applied to an area from industrial practice: the design of railway signalling systems to be implemented on PLCs (programmable logic controllers). The proposed approach comprises the levels of requirements, design specifications and programs for PLCs. Correctness between these levels is achieved on the basis of a real-time logic.

Jan Peleska and Bettina Buth summarise in their chapter *"Formal Methods for the International Space Station ISS"* the results and experiences obtained in a project in collaboration with DaimlerChrysler Aerospace. The aim of this project was to check a number of correctness requirements for a fault-tolerant computer to be used in the International Space Station ISS. To this end, a combination of formal verification, simulation and testing was applied. The formal verifcation relied on the careful use of Hoare's theory CSP (communicating sequential processes) and its associated model checker FDR.

Bernhard Steffen and Tiziana Margaria explain in their chapter *"METAFrame in Practice: Design of Intelligent Network Services"* how concepts from the theory of reactive systems, temporal logics, and model-checking can be applied to the area of intelligent networks. The problem considered is how to assist programmers in the correct design of new telecommunication services for customers. The approach, on the basis of the METAFrame environment, led to a product that has been adopted, bought, and marketed by Siemens Nixdorf Informationssysteme AG.

Acknowledgements

In the first stages of the book project Krzysztof R. Apt and David Gries were helpful. Alfred Hofmann from Springer-Verlag was supportive from the very first moment. Annemarie Langmaack kindly helped us to obtain a photograph of Hans Langmaack. We are particularly grateful to Claudia Herbers for her devoted support in the production of this book. Last but not least all contacted authors were very easy to motivate to contribute and in the end kept their promise. They also helped in the mutual refereeing process of the contributed papers.

Oldenburg and Dortmund   E.-R. Olderog and B. Steffen
July 1999

Prof. Dr. Dr. h.c. Hans Langmaack
Foto: Foto-Renard, Kiel

Table of Contents

Part I

Methodology

Theories of Programming: Top-Down and Bottom-Up and Meeting in the Middle

C.A.R. Hoare

Oxford University Computing Laboratory,
Wolfson Building, Parks Road, Oxford, OX1 3QD
tony.hoare@comlab.ox.ac.uk

Abstract. A theory of programming provides a scientific basis for programming practices that lead to predictable delivery of programs of high quality. A top-down theory starts with a specification of the intended behaviour of a program; and a bottom-up theory starts with a description of how the program is executed. The aim of both theories is to prove theorems (often algebraic laws) that will be helpful in the design, development, compilation,testing,optimisation and maintainance of all kinds of program. The most mature theories are those that are presented both in bottom-up and top-down fashion, where essentially the same laws are valid in both presentations.

1 Introduction

The goal of scientific research is to develop an understanding of the complexity of the world which surrounds us. There is certainly enough complexity out there to justify a wide range of specialist branches of science; and within each branch to require a wide range of investigatory styles and techniques. For example, among the specialists in Physics, cosmologists start their speculations in the vast distances of intergalactic space, and encompass the vast time-scales of the evolution of the stars. They work methodically downward in scale, until they find an explanation of phenomena that can be observed more or less directly by the naked eye. At the other end of the scale, particle physicists start with the primitive components of the material world, currently postulated to be quarks and gluons. They then work methodically upward in scale, to study the composition of baryons, hadrons, and leptons, clarifying the laws which govern their assembly into atoms and molecules. Eventually, they can explain the properties of materials that we touch and smell and taste in the world of every day. In spite of the difference in scale of their starting points, and in the direction and style of their investigations, there is increasing excitement about the convergence and overlap of theories developed by cosmologists and by particle physicists. The point at which they converge is the most significant event in the whole history of the universe, the big bang with which it all started.

The same dichotomy between top-down and bottom-up styles of investigation may be found among mathematicians. For example, category theorists start

E.-R. Olderog, B. Steffen (Eds.): Correct System Design, LNCS 1710, pp. 3–28, 1999.
© Springer-Verlag Berlin Heidelberg 1999

at the top with a study of the most general kind of mathematical structure, as exemplified by the category of sets. They then work downward to define and classify the canonical properties that distinguish more particular example structures from each other. Logicians on the other hand start from the bottom. They search for a minimal set of primitive concepts and notations to serve as a foundation for all of mathematics, and a minimal collection of atomic steps to define the concept of a valid proof. They then work methodically upward, to define all the more familiar concepts of mathematics in terms of the primitives, and to justify the larger proof steps which mathematicians need for efficient prosecution of their work. Fortunately in this case too, the top-down and the bottom-up styles of investigation both seek a common explanation of the internal structure of mathematics and clarification of the relationship between its many branches. Their ultimate goal is to extend the unreasonable power of mathematical calculation and make it more accessible to the experimental scientist and to the practicing engineer.

Computer science, like other branches of science, has as its goal the understanding of highly complex phenomena, the behaviour of computers and the software that controls them. Simple algorithms, like Euclid's method of finding the greatest common divisor, are already complex enough; a challenge on a larger scale is to understand the potential behaviour of the million-fold interlinked operating systems of the world-wide computing network. As in physics or in mathematics, the investigation of such a system may proceed in a choice of directions, from the top-down or from the bottom-up. In the following exposition, this dichotomy will be starkly exaggerated. In any particular scientific investigation, or on any particular engineering project, there will be a rapid alternation or mixture of the two approaches, often starting in the middle and working outward. A recommendation to this effect is made in the conclusion of the paper.

An investigation from the top-down starts with an attempt to understand the system as a whole. Since software is a man-made artifact, it is always relevant to ask first what is its purpose? Why was it built? Who is it for? What are the requirements of its users, and how are they served? The next step is to identify the major components of the system, and ask how they are put together? How do they interact with each other? What are the protocols and conventions governing their collaboration? How are the conventions enforced, and how does their observance ensure successful achievement of the goals of the system as a whole?

A top-down theory of programming therefore starts by modelling external aspects of the behaviour of a system, such as might be observed by its user. A meaningful name is given to each observation or measurement, so that the intended behaviour of the system can be described briefly and clearly, perhaps in a user manual for a product, or perhaps even in a specification agreed with the user prior to implementation. The set of observations is extended to include concepts needed to describe the internal interfaces between components of the system. The goal of the theory is to predict the behaviour of a complex assembly by a calculation based only on descriptions of the behaviour of its major components. The collection of formulae used for these calculations effectively constitutes a denotational semantics for the languages in which a system is specified, designed, and eventually implemented. The programming language used for ultimate implementation is defined by simply selecting an implementable subset of the mathematically defined notations for describing program behaviour. The correctness of a program simply means that all possible observations of its behaviour under execution are included in the range defined by its specification. The development of the theory starts from the denotational definitions and continues by formalisation and proof of theorems that express the properties of all programs written in the language. The goal is to assemble a collection of mathematical laws (usually equations and inequations) that will be useful in the top-down design of programs from their specifications, and ensure that the resulting code is correct by construction.

Investigation of a complex system from the bottom-up starts with an attempt to discover a minimum collection of primitive components from which it has been made, or in principle could have been. These are assembled into larger components by primitive combinators, selected again from a minimal set. The notations chosen to denote these primitives and combinators constitute the syntax of a simple programming language. Since programs are intended for execution by a machine, their operational meaning is defined by enumerating the kinds of primitive step that will be taken by the machine in executing any program that is presented to it. The theory may be further developed by investigation of properties of programs that are preserved by all the possible execution steps; they are necessarily preserved throughout execution of any program. The resulting classification of programs is presented as a set of axioms that can be used in proofs that a program enjoys the relevant property. The properties are often decidable, and the axioms can be used as a type system for the programming language, with conformity checkable by its compiler. In favourable cases, the type system allows unique or canonical types to be inferred from an untyped program. Such inference can help in the understanding of legacy code, possibly written without any comprehensible documentation describing its structure or purpose (or worse, the original documentation often has not been kept up to date with the later changes made to the code).

The benefits of a top-down presentation of a theory are entirely complementary to those of a bottom-up presentation. The former is directly applicable to discussion and reasoning about the design of a program before it has been written, and the latter to the testing, debugging, and modification of code that has already been written. In both cases, successful application of the theory takes advantage of a collection of theorems proved for this purpose. The most useful theorems are those which take the form of algebraic laws. The advantages of both approaches can be confidently combined, if the overlap of laws provided by both of them is sufficiently broad. The laws are a specification of the common interface where the two approaches meet in the middle. I suggest that such a convergence of laws developed by complementary approaches and applied to the same programming language should be a rigorous scientific criterion of the maturity of a theory and of a language, when deciding whether it is ready for practical implementation and widespread use.

2   Top-Down

A top-down presentation of a theory of programming starts with an account of a conceptual framework appropriate for the description of the behaviour of a running program as it may be observed by its users. For each kind of observation, an identifier is chosen serve as a variable whose exact value will be determined on each particular run of the program. Variables whose values are measured as a result of experiment are very familiar in all branches of natural science; for example in mechanics, x is often declared to denote the displacement of a particular object from the origin along a particular axis, and $\dot{x}$ denotes the rate of change of x. We will find that such analogies with the normal practice of scientists and engineers provide illumination and encouragement at the start as well as later in the development of theories of programming.

There are two special times at which observation of an experiment or the run of a program are especially interesting, at the very beginning and at the very end. That is why the specification language VDM introduces special superscript arrow notations: $\overleftarrow{x}$ to denote the initial value of the global program variable x, and $\overrightarrow{x}$ to denote its final value on successful termination of the program. (The Z notation uses x and x' for these purposes). Fragments of program in different contexts will update different sets of global variables. The set of typed variables relevant to a particular program fragment is known as its *alphabet*. In the conventional sequential programming paradigm, the beginning and the end of the run of a program are the only times when it is necessary or desirable to consider the values of the global variables accessed and updated by it. We certainly want to ignore the millions of possible intermediate values calculated during its execution, and it is a goal of the theory to validate this simplification.

A full understanding of a description of program behaviour requires prior specification of its alphabet, and agreement on the way in which the value of each variable in it can be determined by experiment. To interpret the meaning of a program without knowing its alphabet is as impossible as the interpretation of a message in information theory without knowing the range of message values that might have been sent instead. Not all the relevant parameters of program behaviour have to be directly observable from outside the computer; some may be observable only indirectly, by their effect on other programs. Actually, even the values of the program variables inside the computer are inaccessible to a user; they can be controlled or observed only with the aid of an input-output package, which is written in the same language as the program under analysis. The indirect observations are needed to make successful predictions about the behaviour of larger programs, based on knowledge of the behaviour of their components parts.

Successful termination is one of the most important properties of a program to predict, so we need a special variable (called $\overrightarrow{ok}$) which is true just if and when termination occurs. The corresponding initial variable $\overleftarrow{ok}$ indicates that the program has started. Of course a false value of $\overrightarrow{ok}$ will never be conclusively observed; but that doesn't matter, because the intention of the theorist and the programmer alike is to ensure it that $\overrightarrow{ok}$ is necessarily true, and to prove it. Such a proof would be vacuous if the possibility of its falsity were not modelled in the theory. In general, for serious proof of total correctness of programs, it is essential to model realistically all the ways in which a program can go wrong, even if not directly observable. In fact, the progress of science is marked by acceptance of such unobservable abstractions as force and mass and friction as though they were directly measurable quantities. As Einstein pointed out, it is the theory itself which determines what is observable.

In the interactive programming paradigm, the most important observable component of program behaviour is an interaction between the system and its environment. Each kind of interaction has a distinct name. For example, in the process algebra CCS[Milner] the event name *coin* may stand for the insertion of a pound coin in the slot of a vending machine, and the event name *choc* may stand for the selection and extraction of a chocolate bar by the user. The CSP[Roscoe] variant of process algebra allows the user to record a *trace* of the sequence in which such events have occurred while the machine is running; so ⟨*coin, choc, coin*⟩ is a value of *trace* observed in the middle of the second transaction of the machine; the empty trace ⟨ ⟩ is the value when the machine is first delivered. We also model the possibility of deadlock (hang-up) by recording the set of events currently offered by the machine's environment, but which it refuses to accept. For example, initially the machine refuses {*choc*} because it has not been paid (or perhaps because it has run out of chocolates). A deadlocked machine is one that refuses all the events offered by its environment.

Practical programming of useful systems will involve a combination of interactive and imperative programming features; and the relevant alphabet must include both internal variable names and external event names. The special variable $\overrightarrow{ok}$ should be reinterpreted as successful stabilisation, or avoidance of livelock (divergence). A new special variable $\overrightarrow{wait}$ is needed to distinguish those stable states in which the program is waiting for an interaction with its environment from those in which it has successfully terminated. An important achievement in the theory of programming has been to formalise separate models for sequential and for interactive programs, and then to combine them with only a minimum of extra complexity.

A top-down theory of programming is highly conducive to a top-down methodology for program design and development. The identifiers chosen to denote the relevant observations of the ultimate program are first used to describe the intended and permitted behaviour of a program, long before the detailed programming begins. For example, a program can be specified not to decrease the value of x by the statement

$$\overleftarrow{x} \leq \overrightarrow{x}$$

A precondition for termination of a program can be written as the antecedent of a conditional

$$(\overleftarrow{x} < 27 \wedge \overleftarrow{ok}) \Rightarrow \overrightarrow{ok}$$

The owner of a vending machine may specify that the number of *choc* events in the *trace* must never exceed the number of *coin* events. And the customer certainly requires that when the balance of coins over chocs is positive, extraction of a chocolate will not be refused. Explicit mention of refusals is a precise way of specifying responsiveness or liveness of a process, without appeal to the concept of fairness. But there is nothing wrong with fairness: it can be treated simply by allowing traces to be infinite. A fair trace is then one that contains an infinite number of occurrences of some relevant kind of event. It is not an objective of a programming theory to place finitary or other restrictions on the language in which specifications are written. Indeed, our goal is to place whole power of mathematics at the disposal of the engineer and scientist, who should exercise it fully in the interests of utmost clarity of specification, and utmost reliability in reasoning about correctness. We will therefore allow arbitrary mathematical statements as predicates: as in the mu-calculus, we will even allow the definition of weakest fixed points of monotonic predicate transformers.

In an observational semantics of a programming language, the meaning of an actual computer program is defined simply and directly as a mathematical predicate that is true just for all those observations that could be made of any execution of the program in any environment of use. For example, let x, y, and z be the entire alphabet of global variables of a simple program. The assignment statement $x := x + 1$ has its meaning completely described by a predicate stating that when it is started, the value of x is incremented, and that termination occurs provided the value of x is not too large. The values of all the other global program variables remain unchanged

$$\overleftarrow{x} < max \wedge \overrightarrow{ok} \Rightarrow \overrightarrow{ok} \wedge \overrightarrow{x} = \overleftarrow{x} + 1 \wedge \overrightarrow{y} = \overleftarrow{y} \wedge \overrightarrow{z} = \overleftarrow{z}$$

Similarly, the behaviour of the deadlock process in a process algebra can be described purely in terms of its trace behaviour – it never engages in any event, and so the trace remains forever empty

$$trace = <>$$

(Here and in future, we will simplify our treatment of processes by ignoring issues of divergence). This kind of definition of programming concepts enables us to regard both specifications and programs as predicates placing constraints on the range of values for the same alphabet of observational variables; the specification restricts the range of observations to those that are permitted; and the program defines exhaustively the full range of observations to which it could potentially give rise. As a result, we have the simplest possible explanation of the important concept of program correctness. A program P meets a specification S just if the predicate describing P logically implies the predicate describing S. Since we can identify programs and specifications with their corresponding predicates, correctness is nothing but the familiar logical implication

$$P \Rightarrow S$$

For example, the specification of non-decreasing x is met by a program that increments x, as may be checked by a proof of the implication

$$\overleftarrow{ok} \wedge \overleftarrow{x} < max \wedge x := x + 1 \quad \Rightarrow \quad \overleftarrow{x} \leq \overrightarrow{x} \wedge \overrightarrow{ok}$$

This simple notion of correctness is obviously correct, and is completely general to all top-down theories of programming. Furthermore it validates in complete generality all the normal practices of software engineering methodology. For example, stepwise design develops a program in two (or more) steps. On a particular step, the engineer produces a design D which describes the properties of the eventual program P in somewhat greater detail than the specification S, but leaving further details of the eventual program to be decided in later steps. The general design method is defined and justified by the familiar *cut rule* of logic, expressing the mathematical property of transitivity of logical implication

$$\frac{D \Rightarrow S \qquad P \Rightarrow D}{P \Rightarrow S}$$

In words this rule may be read: if the design is correct relative to the specification, and if the program meets its design requirement, then the program also meets its original specification.

The most useful method of constructing the specification of a large system is as the conjunciton of its many requirements. Programs and designs can also be combined by conjunction, provided that they have completely disjoint alphabets. In that case, the conjunction can generally be implemented by parallel execution of its operands. Such a parallel implementation is also possible when programs share parts of their alphabet, provided that these include observations of all the ways in which the programs can interact with each other during their execution. In these cases, the stepwise approach to implementation can be greatly strengthened if each step is accompanied by a decomposition of the design D into separately implementable parts D_1 and D_2. The correctness of the decomposition can be checked before implementation starts by proof of the implication

$$D_1 \wedge D_2 \Rightarrow D$$

Further implementation of the designs D_1 and D_2 can be progressed independently and even simultaneously to deliver components P_1 and P_2. When the components are put together they certainly will meet the original design requirement D. The proof principle that justifies the method of design by parts is just the expression of the monotonicity of conjunction with respect to implication

$$\frac{P_1 \Rightarrow D_1 \qquad P_2 \Rightarrow D_2}{P_1 \wedge P_2 \Rightarrow D_1 \wedge D_2}$$

An even more powerful principle is that which justifies the reuse of a previously written library component, which has been fully described by the specification L. We want to implement a program P which uses L to help achieve a specification S. What is the most general description of a design for P that will achieve this goal in the easiest way? The answer is just $S \vee \overline{L}$, as described by the proof rule

$$\frac{P \Rightarrow S \vee \overline{L}}{P \wedge L \Rightarrow S}$$

The Boolean term $S \vee \overline{L}$ is often written as an implication (e.g., $L \supset S$); indeed, the above law, together with the inference in the opposite direction, is used in intuitionistic logic to define implication as an approximate inverse (Galois connection) of conjunction. An implication is always a predicate, but since it is antimonotonic in its first argument, it will rarely be a program

The identification of programs with more abstract descriptions of their behaviour offers a very simple and general explanation of a number of important programming concepts. For example, a non-deterministic program can be constructed from two more deterministic programs P and Q by simply stating that you do not care which one of them is selected for execution on each occasion. The strongest assertion you can make about any resulting observation is that it must have arisen either from P or from Q. So the concept of non-determinism is simply and completely captured by the disjunction $P \vee Q$, describing the set union of their observations. And the proof rule for correctness is just the familiar rule for disjunction, defining it as the least upper bound of the implication ordering

$$\frac{P_1 \Rightarrow D \qquad P_2 \Rightarrow D}{P_1 \vee P_2 \Rightarrow D}$$

In words, if you want a non-deterministic program to be correct, you have to prove correctness of both alternatives. This extra labour permits the most general (demonic) interpretation of non-determinism, offering the greatest opportunities for subsequent development and optimisation.

Existential quantification in the predicate calculus provides a means of concealing the value of a variable, simultaneously removing the variable itself from the alphabet of the predicate. In programming theory, quantification allows new variables local to a particular fragment of program to be introduced and then eliminated. In a process algebra, local declaration of event names ensures that the internal interactions between components of an assembly are concealed, as it were in a black box, before delivery to a customer. Observations of such interactions are denoted by some free variable, say x occurring in the formula P_x ; on each execution of P_x this variable must have some value, but we do not know or care what it is. The value and even the existence of the variable can be concealed by using it as the dummy variable of the quantification $(\exists x . P_x)$.

An important example of concealment is that which occurs when a program component P is sequentially composed with the component Q, with the effect that Q does not start until P has successfully terminated. The assembly (denoted $P; Q$) has the same initial observations as P, and the same final observations as Q. Furthermore, we know that the initial values of the variables of Q are the same as the final values of the variables of P. But in normal sequential programs we definitely do not want to observe these intermediate values on each occasion that execution of the program passes a semicolon. Concealment by existential quantification makes the definition of sequential composition the same as that of composition in the relational calculus

$$(P; Q) =_{df} \exists x.\, P(\overleftarrow{x}, x) \wedge Q(x, \overrightarrow{x})$$

Here we have written x and its superscripted variants to stand for the whole list of global variables in the alphabet of P and Q. In a procedural programming language sequential composition is the commonest method of assembling small components. The definition given above shows that the properties of the assembly can be calculated from a knowledge of its components, just as they can for conjunction.

Surprisingly, sequential composition is like conjunction also in admitting an approximate inverse, – a generalisation of Dijkstra's weakest precondition [Dijkstra]. $L \setminus S$ is defined as the weakest specification [Hoare & He] of a program P such that $P; L$ is guaranteed to meet specification S. There is also a postspecification, similarly defined. Such inverses can be invaluable in calculating the properties of a design, even though they are not available in the eventual target programming language.

In the explanation of stepwise composition of designs, we used conjunction to represent assembly of components. Conjunction of program components is not an operator that is generally available in a programming language. The reason is that it is too easy to conjoin inconsistent component descriptions, to produce a description that is logically impossible to implement, for example,

$$(x := x + 1) \wedge (x := x + 2), \quad \text{which equals \textbf{false}}$$

So a practical programming language must concentrate on operators like sequential composition, which are carefully defined by conjunction and concealment to ensure implementability. Negation must also be avoided, because it turns **true**, which is implementable, to **false**, which is not. That is why prespecifications, which are antimonotonic in their first argument, cannot be allowed in a programming language. But there is a compensation. Any operator defined without direct or indirect appeal to negation will be monotonic, and the programmer can use for the newly defined operator the same rules for stepwise decomposition that we have described for conjunction. The whole process of software engineering may be described as the stepwise replacement of logical and mathematical operators used in specifications and designs by the implementable operators of an actual programming language. Ideally, each step should be small and its correctness should be obvious. But in many interesting and important cases, the structure of the implementation has to differ radically from the usual conjunctive structure of the specification, and the validity of the step must be checked by a more substantial proof. You do not expect to build an engine that is fast, eco-friendly, and cheap from three simpler components, each of which enjoy only one of these properties. A mismatch with implementation structure can throw into question the value of prior specification. But it should not; indeed, the value of specification to the user is greatest just when it is fundamentally and structurally simpler than its delivered implementation.

The simplest implementable operator to define is the conditional, in which the choice between components P and Q depends on the truth or falsity of a boolean expression b, which is evaluated in the initial state. So b can be interpreted as a predicate $\overleftarrow{b}$, in which all variables are replaced by their initial values.

$$\textbf{if } b \textbf{ then } P \textbf{ else } Q \quad =_{df} \quad \overleftarrow{b} \wedge P \vee (\neg \overleftarrow{b}) \wedge Q$$

All the mathematical properties of the conditional follow directly from this definition by purely propositional reasoning.

The most important feature of a programming language is that which permits the same portion of program to be executed repeatedly as many times as desired; and the most general way of specifying repetition is by recursion. Let X be the name of a parameterless procedure, and let $F(X)$ be the body of the procedure, written in the given programming language, and containing recursive calls on X itself. Since F is monotonic in the inclusion ordering of the sets of observations desribed by predicates, and since these sets can be regarded as a complete lattice, we can use Tarski's fixed point theorem to define the meaning of each call of X as the weakest possible solution of the implication $X \Rightarrow F(X)$. This definition applies also to recursively defined specifications. Incidentally, if F is expressed wholly in programming notations, it will be a continuous function, and an equivalent definition can be given as the intersection of a descending chain of iterates of F applied to **true**.

A non-terminating recursion can all too easily be specified as a procedure whose body consists of nothing but a recursive call upon itself. Our choice of the weakest fixed point says that such a program has the meaning **true**, a predicate satisfied by all observations whatsoever. The programmer's error has been punished in the most fitting way: no matter what the specification was (unless it was also trivially **true**), it will be impossible to prove that the product is correct. This interpretation of divergence does not place any obligation on an implementor of the programming language actually to exhibit the full range of allowable observations. On the contrary, the implementor may assume that the programmer never intended the divergence, and on this assumption may validly perform many useful optimisations on the program before executing it. As a result of such optimisations, the program may even terminate, for example,

$$(\textbf{while } x \leq 0 \textbf{ do } \quad x := x - 1)\,;\, x := abs(x) \quad \text{can be optimised to nothing,}$$

because the optimiser assumes that the intention of the while loop was to terminate, which only happens when x starts positive. The anomalous terminating behaviour of the optimised program for negative x is allowed by the semantics, and is entirely attributed to the fault of the programmer. Our theory of programming, whose objective is to avoid non-termination, can afford to treat all instances of non-termination as equally bad; and the whole theory can often be simplified just by regarding them as equal.

After definition of the relevant programming concepts, the next stage in the top-down exploration of the theory of programming is the formalisation and proof of the mathematical properties of programs. The simplest proprieties are those that can be expressed as algebraic laws, either equations or inequations; they are often pleasingly similar to algebraic properties proved of the familiar operators of the arithmetic of numbers, which are taught at school. For example, it is well known that disjunction (used to define non-determinism in programming) is like multiplication, in that it is associative and commutative, with **false** serving as its unit and **true** as its zero. Furthermore, conjunction distributes through disjunction, and so do most simple programming combinators, including sequential composition (Table 1). Laws are the basis for algebraic reasoning and calculation, in which professional engineers often develop considerable skill.

$$
\begin{aligned}
P \vee Q &= Q \vee P \\
P \vee (Q \vee R) &= (P \vee Q) \vee R \\
P \vee \textbf{false} &= P \\
P \vee \textbf{true} &= \textbf{true} \\
P \wedge (Q \vee R) &= (P \wedge Q) \vee (P \wedge R) \\
P; (Q \vee R) &= (P; Q) \vee (P; R) \\
(Q \vee R); P &= (Q; P) \vee (R; P)
\end{aligned}
$$

Table 1. Basic algebra of non-determinism.

The same principles of programming language definition apply to process algebras, which have the observational variable *trace* in their alphabet. One of the risks of interactive programming is deadlock; and the worst deadlock is the process that never engages in any recordable action, no matter what events the environment may offer to engage in at the same time. As a result, its trace is always empty

$$\mathbf{0} =_{df} (trace = \langle \rangle)$$

This definition is equally applicable to the process STOP in CSP.

A fundamental operation of a process algebra is external choice $P + Q$, which allows the environment to choose between its operands by appropriate selection of the first event to occur. It has an astonishingly simple definition

$$P + Q =_{df} (P \wedge Q \wedge \mathbf{0}) \vee (\overline{\mathbf{0}} \wedge (P \vee Q))$$

While the trace is empty, an event can be refused by $P + Q$ just if it can be refused by both of them. When the trace is non-empty, the subsequent behaviour is determined by either P or Q, whichever is consistent with the first event in the trace. If both are, the result is non-deterministic. As in the case of the conditional, the algebraic properties of this simple definition can be simply verified by truth tables. External choice is commutative, idempotent and associative, with unit 0; and it is mutually distributive with non-deterministic union. The corresponding operator $\Box$ in CSP has the same properties, but its definition has been made a little more complicated, to take account of the risk of divergence of one of its two operands. The top-down approach to both theories helps to elucidate exactly how two very similar theories may in some ways be subtly different.

The aim of the top-down method of system development is to deliver programs that are correct. Assurance of correctness is obtained not just by testing or debugging the code, but by the quality of the reasoning that has gone into its construction. This top-down philosophy of correctness by construction is based on the premise that every specification and every design and every program can be interpreted as a description of some subset of a mathematically defined space of observations. But the converse is certainly not true. Not every subset of the observation space is expressible as a program. For example, the empty predicate **false** represents a specification that no physical object could ever implement: if it did, the object described would be irretrievably unobservable.

The question therefore arises, what are the additional characteristics of those subsets of observations that are in fact definable in the restricted notations of a particular programming language? The answer would help us to distinguish the feasible specifications that can be implemented by program from the infeasible ones that cannot. The distinguishing characteristics of implementable specifications have been called *healthiness conditions* [Dijkstra]. They act like conservation laws or symmetry principles in physics, which enable the scientist quickly to dismiss impossible experiments and implausible theories; and similarly they can protect the engineer from many a wild-goose chase. As in the natural sciences, healthiness conditions can be justified by appeal to the real-world meaning of the variables in the alphabet. Analysis of termination gives a good example.

A characteristic feature of a program in any programming language is that if its first part fails to terminate, any fragment of program which is written to be executed afterwards will never be started, and the whole program will also fail to terminate. In our top-down theory, the non-terminating program is represented by the predicate **true**; so the relevant healthiness condition can be neatly expressed as an algebraic law, stating that **true** is a left zero for sequential composition

$$\textbf{true} \; ; \; P \; = \; \textbf{true}, \qquad \text{for all programs } P$$

This law is certainly not true for all *predicates* P; for example, when P is false, we have

$$\textbf{true} \; ; \; \textbf{false} \; = \; \textbf{false}$$

This just means that the healthiness condition is succeeding in its primary purpose of showing that unimplementable predicates like **false** can never be expressed as a program.

The majority of simple algebraic laws that are applicable to programs can be proved once-for-all as mathematical theorems about sets of observations; and they can be applied equally to designs and even to specifications. But healthiness conditions, as we have seen, are just not true for arbitrary sets: they cannot be proved and they must not be applied to specifications. Their scope is mainly confined to reasoning about programs, including program transformation and optimisation. It is therefore an obligation on a programming theorist to prove that each healthiness condition holds at least for all programs expressible in the restricted notations of the programming language, and perhaps to certain design notations as well.

The method of proof is essentially inductive on the syntax of the language. All the primitive components of a program must be proved to satisfy the healthiness condition; furthermore, all the operators of the language (including recursion) must be proved to preserve the health of their operands. Here is a proof that union and sequential composition preserve the healthiness condition that they respect non-termination

$$\textbf{true}; (P \vee Q) \qquad \{\text{rel. composition distributes through disjunction}\}$$

$$= (\textbf{true}; P) \vee (\textbf{true}; Q) \quad \{\text{by induction hypothesis, } P \text{ and } Q \text{ are healthy}\}$$

$$= \textbf{true} \vee \textbf{true} \qquad\qquad\qquad\qquad\qquad\qquad \{\vee \text{ is idempotent}\}$$

$$= \textbf{true}$$

For sequential composition

$$\textbf{true}; (P; Q) \qquad\qquad\qquad\qquad \{\text{composition is associative}\}$$

$$= (\textbf{true}; P); Q \qquad\qquad \{\text{by inductive hypothesis, } P \text{ is healthy}\}$$

$$= \textbf{true}; Q \qquad\qquad \{\text{by inductive hypothesis, } Q \text{ is healthy}\}$$

$$= \textbf{true}$$

Algebraic laws are so useful in reasoning about programs, and in transforming them for purposes of optimisation, that we want to have as many laws as possible, provided of course that they are valid. How can we know that a list of proven laws is complete in some appropriate sense? One possible sense of completeness is given by a normal form theorem, which shows that every program in the language can be reduced (or rather expanded) to a normal form (not necessarily expressible in the programming language). A normal form should be designed so that the identity of meaning of non-identical normal forms is quite easy to decide, for example, merely by rearranging their sub-terms. Furthermore, if two normal forms are unequal, it should always be possible to find an observation described by one of them but not the other. Unfortunately, there may be **no** finite set of algebraic laws that exactly characterises all true facts about the programming language. For example, even the simple relational calculus has no complete finite axiomatisation. One interpretation of the Church-Turing hypothesis states that no top-down analysis can ever exactly characterise those sets of observations that are computable by programs from those that are not. It is only by modelling computation steps of some kind of machine that we can distinguish the computable from the incomputable. Specifications are inherently incomputable. It is their negations that are recursively enumerable: and they need to be, because we want to be able to prove by counterexample that a program is *not* correct. If your chief worry is accidental description of something that is incomputable or even contradictory, top-down theory development does not immediately address this concern. Complete protection can be obtained only by starting again from the bottom and working upward.

3   Bottom-Up

A bottom-up presentation of a theory of programming starts with a definition of the notations and syntactic structure of a particular programming language. Ideally, this should be rather a small language, with a minimum provision of primitive features; the hope is that these will be sufficiently expressive to define the additional features of more complex languages. As an example language, we choose a subset of the pi-calculus at about the level of CCS. Figure 1 expresses its syntax in the traditional Backus-Naur form, and Figure 2 gives an informal specification of the meaning.

$$\begin{aligned}
\langle\text{event}\rangle \quad &:: = \langle\text{identifier}\rangle \mid \overline{\langle\text{identifier}\rangle} \\
\langle\text{process}\rangle &:: = \mathbf{0} \mid \langle\text{event}\rangle.\,\langle\text{process}\rangle \\
&\mid (\langle\text{process}\rangle \mid \langle\text{process}\rangle) \mid\,!\,\langle\text{process}\rangle \\
&\mid (\mathbf{new}\ \langle\text{identifier}\rangle)\,\langle\text{process}\rangle
\end{aligned}$$

Figure 1. Syntax

0 is the deadlock process: it does nothing.

coin.P is a process that first accepts a *coin* and then behaves like P.

$\overline{nx}.\mathbf{0}$ first emits a control signal nx and then stops.

$nx.Q$ first accepts a control signal nx and then behaves as Q.

$P \mid Q$ executes P and Q in parallel. Signals emitted by one may be accepted by the other.

$!P$ denotes parallel execution of an unbounded number of copies of P:
$P \mid P \mid P \mid \ldots$

$(\mathbf{new}\ e)\ P$ declares that e is a local event used only for interactions within its scope P.

Figure 2. Explanation

The traditional first example of a process expressed in a new process algebra is the simple vending machine VM (Figure 3). It serves an indefinite series of customers by alternately accepting a *coin* and emitting a chocolate. The expected behaviour of a single customer engaging in a single transaction is

$$\text{cust} =_{df} \overline{coin}.choc.\mathbf{0}$$

The behaviour of the whole population of customers is modelled by the unbounded set (!cust). This population can insert an indefinite number of coins; and at any time a lesser number of chocolates can be extracted. But we plan to install a simple VM that can serve only one customer at a time. To implement this sequentialisation, we need an internal control signal nx, by which the machine signals to itself its own readiness for the next customer. The complete definition of the vending machine is given in Figure 3.

$$
\begin{aligned}
\text{one} \ &=_{df} nx.coin.\overline{choc}.\overline{nx}.\mathbf{0} \\
\text{many} &=_{df} (\text{!one}) \mid (\overline{nx}.\ \mathbf{0}) \\
\text{VM} \ \ &=_{df} (\textbf{new}\ nx)\ \text{many}
\end{aligned}
$$

Figure 3. Vending Machine

The operational semantics of the programming language is presented as a collection of formulae, describing all the permitted steps that can be taken in the execution of a complete program. Each kind of step is described by a transition rule written in the form $P \rightarrow Q$, where P gives a pattern to be matched against the current state of the program, and Q describes how the program is changed after the step. For example, the rule

$$(e.P) \mid (\overline{e}.Q) \ \rightarrow \ (P \mid Q)$$

describes an execution step in which one process accepts a signal on e which is sent by the other. Emission and acceptance of the signal are synchronised, and their simultaneous occurrence is concealed; the subsequent behaviour is defined as parallel execution of the rest of the two processes involved.

The reduction shown above can be applied directly to a complete program consisting of a pair of adjacent processes written in the order shown and separated by the parallel operator |. But we also want to apply the reduction to processes written in the opposite order, to processes which are embedded in a larger network, and to pairs that are not even written adjacently in that network. Such reductions can be described by a larger collection of formulae, for example

$$
\begin{aligned}
(\overline{e}.Q) \mid (e.P) &\rightarrow Q \mid P \\
((\overline{e}.Q) \mid (e.P)) \mid R &\rightarrow (Q \mid P) \mid R \\
(e.Q \mid R) \mid (\overline{e}.P) &\rightarrow (Q \mid R) \mid P
\end{aligned}
$$

But even this is only a small subset of the number of transition rules that would be needed to achieve communication in all circumstances. A much easier way to deal with all cases is to just postulate that | is a commutative operator, that it is associative, and that it has unit **0**.

$$P \mid \mathbf{0} = P$$
$$P \mid Q = Q \mid P$$
$$P \mid (Q \mid R) = P \mid (Q \mid R) \quad [1]$$

These are called *structural* laws in a process calculus. They represent the *mobility* of process, because the implementation may use the equations for substitution in either direction, and so move a process around until it reaches a neighbour capable of an interaction with it. In a bottom-up presentation, these laws are just postulated as axioms that define a particular calculus; they can be used in the proof of other theorems, but they themselves are not susceptible of proof, because there is no semantic basis from which such a proof could be constructed.

The laws governing reduction apply only to complete programs; and they need to be extended to allow reduction steps to take place locally within a larger context. For example a local reduction can occur anywhere within a larger parallel network, as stated by the rule

$$\text{If } P \to P' \text{ then } (P \mid Q) \to (P' \mid Q)$$

A similar law applies to hiding.

$$\text{If } P \to P' \text{ then } (\mathbf{new} \text{ e}) P \to (\mathbf{new} \text{ e}) P'.$$

But there is no similar rule for $e.P$. A reduction of P is not permitted until after e has happened. It is only this omission of a rule that permits terminating programs to be distinguished from non-termination.

One of the main objectives of a theory of programming is to model the behaviour of computing systems that exist in the world today. The world-wide network of interconnected computers is obviously the largest and most important such system. Any of the connected computers can emit a communication into the network at any time. There is reasonable assurance that the message will be delivered at some later time at some destination that is willing to accept it (if any). But the exact order of delivery does not necessarily reflect the order of sending: messages in the net can overtake each other. This aspect of reality is very simply encoded in the calculus by adding a single new reduction step. This just detaches a message from its sender, and allows the message to proceed independently in its own timescale through the network to its destination.

$$\bar{e}.P \;\to\; (\bar{e}.0) \mid P$$

---

[1] These equations are more usually written with equivalence ($\equiv$) in place of equality, which is reserved for syntactic identity of two texts. They are called structural *congruences*, because they justify substitution in the same way as equality.

This means that the sender P is not delayed if the receiver is unready at the time of sending. The subsequent actions of the sender proceed in parallel with the journey undertaken by its message. A calculus with such a reduction rule is called *asynchronous*, and output prefixing is usually omitted from its syntax. That is why the algebraic laws for an asynchronous calculus are different from those of a synchronous one.

Structural laws are also used in addition to reductions to formalise the intended meaning of the constructions of the language. For example, the repetition operator $(!P)$ denotes an unbounded set of parallel instances of the same process P. The addition of a new instance of P therefore makes no difference, as stated in the unfolding law

$$!P = P \mid (!P)$$

This law can be applied any number of times

$$P \mid (!P) = P \mid P \mid (!P) = \ldots$$

If each application allows a reduction, we can generate an infinite reduction sequence leading to potential non-termination. Consider for example the process P that reduces in one step to the empty process

$$P =_{df} (e.0 \mid \bar{e}.0) \;\rightarrow\; (0 \mid 0) = 0$$

This can be put into a repetition

$$!P = (e.0 \mid \bar{e}.0) \,|!P \;\rightarrow\; 0 \,|!P = !P$$

It follows that $!P$ can be subjected to an infinite series of reductions, without ever engaging in a useful interaction with its environment. This is just what is known as divergence or livelock, and it is clearly and obviously definable on the basis of an operational semantics. A top-down presentation cannot give such an obviously appropriate *definition* of non-termination, and has to postulate that the artificial variable $\overrightarrow{ok}$ is mysteriously allowed to take the value **false** whenever there is a risk of divergence.

Another useful definition in operational semantics is that of a labelled transition, in which the transition relation $\rightarrow$ is labelled by a trace of interactions with the environment that can occur during the evolution of the process.

$$P \xrightarrow{<>} Q =_{df} P \xrightarrow{*} Q$$
$$P \xrightarrow{<e>\frown s} Q =_{df} \exists P'. P \xrightarrow{*} e.P' \wedge P' \xrightarrow{s} Q$$

where $\xrightarrow{*}$ is the reflexive transitive closure of $\rightarrow$. Now we can trace the evolution of our vending machine, using a few structural laws which seem reasonable

$$many = \quad \overline{nx}.0 \mathbin{|}! \text{ one} \qquad\qquad \{\text{expanding }!\}$$

$$= \quad \overline{nx}.0 \mathbin{|} (nx.coin.\overline{choc}.\overline{nx}.0) \mathbin{|}! \text{ one} \qquad \{\text{reduction}\}$$

$$\rightarrow \quad 0 \mathbin{|} (coin.\overline{choc}.\overline{nx}.0) \mathbin{|}! \text{ one} \qquad \{0 \text{ is unit of }!\}$$

$$= \quad coin.\overline{choc}.\overline{nx}.0 \mathbin{|}! \text{ one} \qquad \{\text{reduction, etc }\}$$

$$\rightarrow \quad coin.(\overline{choc}.\overline{nx}.0 \mathbin{|}!\text{one}) \qquad \{\text{def } \overset{coin}{\rightarrow}\}$$

$$\overset{coin}{\rightarrow} \quad \overline{choc}.\overline{nx}.0 \mathbin{|}! \text{ one} \qquad \{\text{similarly}\}$$

$$\overset{choc}{\rightarrow} \quad \overline{nx}.0 \mathbin{|}! \text{ one}$$

$$\therefore \quad many \overset{<coin,\overline{choc}>}{\longrightarrow} many \qquad \{\text{local reduction}\}$$

$$\therefore \quad VM = ((\mathbf{new}\ nx)\ many) \overset{<coin,\overline{choc}>}{\longrightarrow} VM$$

This mathematical derivation is a close simulation of the execution of the program. But does it prove that the program is correct? And what does correctness mean for a programming language that has been defined only in terms of its internal execution rather than what can be observed from outside? The usual answer to the more general question is that a program is adequately specified in the programming language itself by displaying the equations that it should satisfy. For example, perhaps what we really want to prove about the vending machine is

$$VM = coin.\ \overline{choc}.\ VM.$$

(In a more abstract language like CCS or CSP, such an equation would be permitted as a recursive definition of VM). In constructing the proof of such equations, free use may be made of all the structural laws of the calculus. But in general the structural laws are deliberately restricted to transformations on the static shape of a formula, and they do not give enough information about equality of dynamically evolving behaviour. Such reasoning would require a set of laws much larger than those postulated by the calculus. What laws should they be? And how are they justified?

The solution to this problem is of startling originality. The user of the calculus is allowed to extend its set of laws by any new equations that may be desired, provided that this does not lead to a contradiction. A contradiction is defined as the proof of an equation between processes that obviously ought to be different, like a divergent process and a non-divergent one. For example, an equation $P = Q$ leads to contradiction if you can find some program $C[P]$ containing P which does not diverge, but when P is replaced by Q, $C[Q]$ actually can diverge. Finer discriminations may be imposed by defining a function $obs(P)$, which maps a program P to some simple set of observations that may be made of it. For example, $obs(P)$ might map P onto the set of environments in which it might deadlock. In each case, one might observe the set of events offered by the environment but refused by the process. Then a contradiction is defined as a law that equates two programs with different observable refusal sets. An equation established in this way is called a *contextual equivalence*

Proving that a proposed law $P = Q$ leads to contradiction is quite a challenge, because the context $C[\,]$ that reveals it may be very large. But proving that something is *not* a contradiction can be even harder, because it involves consideration of the infinite set of all possible contexts that can be written around P and Q; such a universal hypothesis requires an inductive case analysis over all the combinators of the calculus. Sometimes, only a reduced set of contexts is sufficient; this fact is established by proof of a *context lemma*. As a result of their syntactic orientation, proofs by induction tend to be specific to a particular calculus, and care is needed in extending their results to calculi with a slightly different syntax, different reductions, or different structural laws. For this reason, each new variation of a familiar calculus is usually presented from scratch.

Heavy reliance on induction certainly provides a strong motive for keeping down the number of notations in the original syntax to an inescapable core of primitives, even if this makes the language less expressive or efficient in practical use. The pursuit of minimality tends to favour the design of a language at a relatively low level of abstraction. The power of such a language matches that of machine code, which offers enormous power, including the opportunity for each instruction to interfere with the effect of any other. In the presence of multi-threading or non-determinacy, understanding of the behaviour of an arbitrary program becomes rapidly impossible. And there are few general theorems applicable to arbitrary programs that can aid the understanding, or permit optimising transformations that preserve behavioural equivalence. The solution to this problem is to confine attention to programs that follow defined protocols and restrictive conventions to limit their mutual interaction. The meaning of conformity with the convention is defined by means of a *type system*, which is also usually presented in a bottom-up fashion. The syntax gives a notation for expressing all the types that will be needed. Then a collection of axioms and proof rules provide a means of deducing which parts of each program can be judged to belong to a particular type. In a higher level programming language the programmer may be required or allowed to provide adequate type information for variables and parameters; but most of the labour of type checking or even type inference can be delegated to a compiler. The consistency of the typing system is established by showing that pairs of programs equated by the structural laws have the same type, and that each reduction step in execution preserves the proper typing of its operand. This is called a *subject reduction* theorem. Subsequent development of the theory can then be confined to properly typed programs.

A type system based on an operational model may be designed to supply information that is highly relevant to program optimisation. For example, it can detect dead code that will never be executed, and code that will be executed at most once. Other type systems can guarantee absence of certain kinds of programming error such as deadlock. If it is known that no type can be deduced for such an erroneous program, then type consistency ensures that the error can never occur a run time. Because type systems enforce disciplined interaction, well-typed programs often obey additional laws, useful both for comprehension and for optimisation. Type systems thereby raise the level of abstraction of an operationally defined programming language; their role in the bottom-up development of a theory is complementary to that of healthiness conditions, which in a top-down development bring abstract denotational specifications closer to implementable reality.

Operational presentations of semantics are particularly appropriate for analysis of security aspects of communication in an open distributed network, where co-operation between a known group of agents is subject at any time to accidental or deliberate interference by an outsider. The main role of the language is to define and limit the capabilities of the outsider. For example, the localisation operator (**new** e) enables an agent in the system to invent an arbitrary secret code or a *nonce*, and the structural laws of the language are designed to ensure that it remains secret except to those who have received it in an explicit communication. It is then the responsibility of an implementation of the language to enforce this level of secrecy by choice of an appropriate cryptographic method. Furthermore, if the proof of security of a protocol depends on observance of type constraints, it is essential at run time to check the types of any code written by an outsider before executing it in a sensitive environment.

The purpose of a secure protocol can often be described most clearly by an equation $P = Q$, where P describes the situation before some desired interaction takes place, and Q describes the desired result afterwards. For example, we might use the equation

$$(e.P \mid \bar{e}.Q) = P \mid Q$$

to describe the intended effect of transmission of a signal e from Q to P. But this is not a valid equation in the calculus, because it is not secure against interference by an outsider R, which can intercept and divert the signal, as permitted by the reduction

$$e.P \mid \bar{e}.Q \mid e.R \rightarrow e.P \mid Q \mid R$$

This reduction will be inhibited if the name e is kept secret from the outside, so it is valid to equate

$$(\textbf{new } e)\ (e.P \mid \bar{e}.Q) = (\textbf{new } e)\,(P \mid Q)$$

Since it is assumed that the outsider is limited to the capabilities of the programming language, an arbitrary attack can be modelled by a context $C[\ ]$ placed around both sides of the equation. A standard proof of contextual equivalence would be sufficient to show that there is no such context. That is exactly what is needed to show that no outsider can detect or affect the desired outcome described by the equation. As in this example, the required protection is often achieved with the aid of the **new** operator, which prevents an outsider from detecting or communicating a signal with the new name. It is much more difficult to design a top-down theory for application to problems of security, privacy and authentication. A top-down theory has to start with a decision of exactly what an intruder could observe of another agent in the system, and what attacks are possible upon it. But this understanding is exactly what the security analysis seeks to develop; it cannot be postulated in advance.

A great deal of research effort has been expended on designing proof techniques that are simpler to apply and more efficient to mechanise than proof by non-contradiction. Many of these methods use a variation of the technique of bisimulation [Milner]. A bisimulation is a postulated equivalence between programs that is respected by the individual steps of the operational semantics of the language, i.e., if two programs belong to the same equivalence class before the step, they belong to the same equivalence class afterwards. For particular calculi and for particular kinds of bisimulation, theorists have proved that the postulation of the bisimulation as an equality will not lead to a contradiction. Then that kind of bisimulation may safely be used to prove equality of arbitrary programs in the language. For a well-explored calculus, there may be a whole range of bisimulations of varying strength, some suitable for mechanisation, and some suitable for quick disproof. They are all approximations to the truly intended notion of equality, which is defined by the more elusive concept of contextual equivalence.

As described above, much of the effort in a bottom-up theory goes into the determination of when two programs are equal. This is absolutely no problem in a top-down theory, where normal mathematical equality of sets of observations is used throughout. Conversely, much of the effort of a top-down theory goes into determination of which subsets of observations correspond to implementations. This is absolutely no problem in a bottom-up theory, where programs are always by definition computable. In each case the theorist approaches the target by a series of approximations. In the happy circumstance that they are working on the same language and the same theory, top-down and bottom-up will eventually meet in the middle.

4   Meeting in the Middle

A brief summary of the merits and deficiencies of top-down and bottom-up presentations show that they are entirely complementary.

- A top-down presentation of a theory of programming gives excellent support for top-down development of programs, with justifiable confidence that they are correct by construction. By starting with observable system properties and behaviour, it permits and encourages the advance specification of a system yet to be implemented, and the careful design of the interfaces between its major components. It provides concepts, notations and theorems that can be used throughout the design and implementation of software systems of any size and complexity. On the other hand, an abstract denotational semantics gives no help at all in the debugging of incorrect programs. It is therefore useless in the analysis of legacy systems, many of which have been written and frequently changed without regard to general design principles, clarity of structure, or correctness of code.

– A bottom-up presentation of a theory of programming gives excellent support for reasoning about the execution of programs that have already been written. By starting with a definition of the individual steps of execution, it models directly the run-time efficiency of programs. Execution traces provide the primary diagnostic information on debugging runs of incorrect programs. On the other hand, an operational semantics gives no help at all in relating a program to its intended purpose. It is therefore useless in reasoning about programs before they have been written in the notations of a particular programming language.

If programming theory is ever to make its full contribution to the practice of programming, we must offer all the benefits of both styles, and none of the deficiencies. Neither approach could be recommended by itself. It is clearly foolish to provide a conceptual framework for program design if there is no way of executing the resulting program step by step on a computer. It would be equally unsatisfactory to present an operationally defined theory if there is no way of describing what a program is intended to do.

In the natural sciences, it is a necessary condition of acceptability of a theory that it should agree with experiment. Experiments are equally important in validation of theories of programming. They test the efficiency with which a new programming concept can be implemented and the convenience with which it can be used. An experiment which requires the design, implementation and use of a completely new programming language is prohibitively time-consuming. For rapid scientific progress, it is preferable just to add a single new feature to an existing programming language, its compiler and its run time system. The first trial applications may be conducted by a group of experimental programmers, who have accepted the risk that the new feature may soon be changed or withdrawn. Even such a limited experiment is expensive; and worse, it is difficult to interpret the results, because of uncontrollable factors such as the skill and the experience of the people involved.

That is why it is advisable to restrict experimentation to test only theories that have shown the highest initial promise. The promise of a theory is not judged by its popularity or by its novelty or by its profitability in competition with rival theories. Quite the reverse: it is by its coherence and close agreement with other theories that a new theory can be most strongly recommended for test. Such agreement is much more impressive if the theories are presented in radically differing styles. From the practical point of view, it is the stylistic differences that ensure complementarity of the benefits to the user of the programming language. And the results of the experiment are much more convincing if the implementors and trial users are completely independent of the original theorists, as they usually are in more mature branches of Science.

The unification of theories is not a goal that is easy to achieve, and it often requires a succession of adjustments to the details of the theories, and in the way they are tested. The development of an abstract denotational model to match a given operational semantics is known as the problem of full abstraction. It took many years to discover fully abstract models for PCF, a simple typed functional programming language that was presented by an operational semantics. A recent model [Abramsky, Hyland] represents a type of a programming language by the rules of a two-person game, and a function by a strategy for playing the game. A large and complex collection of healthiness conditions is imposed on the games and strategies to ensure that every strategy that satisfies them can be denoted by a program expressed in the syntax of PCF. It is generally considered sufficient to prove this just for finite games, which correspond to programs that do not use recursion or any other form of unbounded iteration. That is the best that can be done, because it is impossible within an abstract model to formulate healthiness conditions that will select exactly those sets of observations that are implementable as iterative programs.

In the practical development and analysis of programs, it is quite uncommon to make a direct appeal to the definition of the programming language, whether denotational or operational. Much more useful are theorems that have been based on those definitions; many of these take the form of algebraic laws, either proven from definitions or postulated as healthiness conditions. The importance of laws is recognised both by top-downers and by bottom-uppers, who measure progress in their chosen direction by accumulation of larger collections of useful laws. When both theories have been adequately developed, I suggest that an appropriate measure of successful meeting in the middle is provided by the overlap of the two collections of laws. Adjustments can (and should) then be made to the details of both theories, until the overlap is sufficiently broad to meet all the needs of practice. If the practitioner uses just the appropriate laws in the appropriate circumstances, the merits of both approaches can be safely combined.

In a perfect meeting, the laws derived from the top-down and from the bottom-up would be exactly the same. In fact, this is not necessary. All that is needed is that the operationally defined axioms and laws should be a subset of those provable from the denotational definitions. Then all the remaining laws proveable from the denotations will be contextual equivalences. The existence of the denotational model guarantees their consistency, even without the need for an exhaustive inductive argument on contexts.

Identity of differently derived theories is not the only goal; and when applying the same derivational techniques to different programming paradigms, differences in the algebraic laws are to be expected and even welcomed. It turns out that a great many algebraic laws are common to nearly all paradigms, but it is the laws that they do not share that are even more interesting. The fundamental property that distinguishes two paradigms is often very neatly expressed by an algebraic law, free of all the clutter of detail involved in a formal definition, and unaltered when the detail changes. For example, functional programming languages are classified as lazy or non-lazy. In a non-lazy language, each function evaluates its arguments first, so if an argument aborts, so does the function call. As a consequence, functional composition (denoted by semicolon) has abortion as its left zero: **true** ; P = **true**. However, a lazy functional language does not satisfy this law. It allows a constant function K to deliver its answer without even looking at its argument: **true** ; $K = K$. However, a lazy language still satisfies a right zero law: P ; **true** = **true**. So does a non-lazy language, unless it allows an argument E to raise an exception or jump. In this case the aborting function does not get the chance to start, so: E ; **true** = E. Discussion of such laws is highly relevant to the selection and design of a programming language, as well as its implementation and optimisation. Future texts on comparative programming languages will surely exploit the power of algebra to explain the fundamental principles of the subject.

Fascination with the elegance and expressive power of laws was what inspired the development of abstract algebra as a branch of modern mathematics. Since the earliest days, mathematics has been primarily concerned with the concept of number. Its progress has been marked by the discovery of new and surprising varieties. Starting with positive integers, even the discovery of zero was a major advance. Then come negative numbers, fractions, reals, and complex numbers. In modern times, study of the foundations of mathematics has given a denotational semantics to each of these different kinds of number. Natural numbers are defined as sets, integers and fractions as pairs, and reals as sequences. Correspondingly different definitions are given for the arithmetic operations that are performed on the different kinds of number. In each case, algebraic laws are proved on the basis of the definitions. In spite of the fact that the definitions are so different, most of the laws turn out to be the same. It is the sharing of laws that justifies the use of the same arithmetic operator to denote operations with such radically different definitions. The laws have then inspired the development of other interesting mathematical structures, like quaternions and matrices, for which algebraically similar operations can be defined. Algebra, among all branches of mathematics, is the one that takes re-usability as its primary goal.

Computing Science makes progress by discovery of new patterns and paradigms of programming. These are embodied in new programming languages, and subjected to the test of trial implementation and use. The procedural paradigm was among the earliest, and still has the widest application. Now there is also a declarative paradigm, which already splits into two major branches, the logical paradigm which permits backtracking, and the functional paradigm that does not. The functional paradigm splits into lazy and non-lazy varieties. The advent of multiprocessors and networking has introduced a new paradigm of distributed computing, with even more variations. Some of them are based on sharing of global random access memory, and others on explicit communication. Communications may be ordered or unordered; they may be global or directed along channels; and they may be synchronised or buffered. In addition to notations traditionally recognised in the community as programming languages, we should consider the languages used for database queries, spreadsheets, menu generators, and other complex interfaces that are coming into wide-spread use. A significant challenge for programming theory is to bring some order into this growing range of tools, and develop an understanding to assist in the selection of an appropriate tool for each purpose, and for using them in combination when necessary. For purposes of classification, comparison, and combination, both denotational and operational semantics have far too much detail to convey the desired understanding and illumination. It is only the algebra that captures the essence of the concepts at an appropriately high level of abstraction. It is perhaps for the same reason that algebraic laws are also the most useful in practice for engineering calculation.

The primary role of algebraic laws is recognised in the most abstract of branches of algebra, namely category theory. Categories provide an excellent source of elegant laws for programming. Its objects nicely represent the types of a programming language, and its basic operation of composition of arrows is a model for the combination of actions evoked by parts of a program. Additional important operators and their types are specified entirely by the algebraic laws that they satisfy. The specification of an operator is often accompanied by a proof that there is only one operator that satisfies it – at least up to isomorphism. This gives assurance that the stated laws are complete: no more are needed, because all other categorial properties of the operator can be proved from them. Finally, a wide range of differing categories can be explored and classified simply by listing the operators which they make available and the laws which they satisfy.

These considerations suggest a third approach to the development of programming theory, one that starts with a collection of algebraic laws as a definitive presentation of the semantics of a programming language [Baeten and Weijland]. The theory then develops by working outwards in all directions. Working upwards explores the range of denotational models for languages which satisfy the laws. Working downwards explores the range of correct implementations for these languages. And working sideways explores the range of similar theories and languages that might have been chosen instead. The work of the theorist is not complete until the consequences of theory have been fully developed in all relevant directions.

Such an ambitious programme can be achieved only by collaboration and accumulation of results by members of different research traditions, each of whom shares an appreciation of the complementary contributions made by all the others.

Acknowledgements

The views put forward in this paper evolved during a long collaboration with He Jifeng on research into unifying theories of programming. They contribute towards goals pursued by the partners in the EC Basic Research Project CONCUR; and they have been subjected to test in the EC Basic Research Project PROCOS. They are more fully expounded in the reference [Hoare, He], which contains a list of 188 further references. Significant contributors to this work at Oxford include Carroll Morgan, Jeff Sanders, Oege de Moor, Mike Spivey, Jeff Sanders, Annabelle McIver, Guy McCusker, and Luke Ong. Other crucial clarifications and insights were obtained during a sabbatical visit to Cambridge in conversations with Robin Milner, Andy Pitts, Martin Hyland, Philippa Gardner, Peter Sewell, Jamey Leifer, and many others. I am also grateful to Microsoft

Research Limited for supporting my visit to Cambridge, and to researchers at Microsoft who have devoted their time to my further education, including Luca Cardelli, Andy Gordon, Cedric Fournet, Nick Benton and Simon Peyton Jones. The organisers of POPL 1999 in San Antonio invited me to present my thoughts there, and the participants gave useful encouragement and feedback. Krzysztof Apt and John Reynolds have suggested many improvements that have been made since an earlier draft of the paper, and more that could have been.

References

S. Abramsky, R. Jagadeesan and P. Malacaria. *Full abstraction for PCF*. To appear in Information and Computation.

Baeten and Weijland. *Process Algebra.* CUP 1990, ISBN 0521 400430.

E.W. Dijkstra. *A Discipline of Programming*. Prentice Hall 1976, ISBN 013 215871X.

C.A.R. Hoare and He Jifeng. *Unifying Theories of Programming*. Prentice Hall International 1998, ISBN 0-13-458761-8, available from amazon.co.uk.

J.M.E. Hyland and C.H.L. Ong. *On Full Abstraction for PCF: I, II and III*. To appear in Informatics and Computation.

A.W. Roscoe. *Theory and Practice of Concurrency*. Prentice Hall 1998, ISBN 013 674409 5.

A Triptych Software Development Paradigm: Domain, Requirements and Software

Towards a Model Development of a Decision Support System for Sustainable Development

Dines Bjørner

Department of Information Technology,
The Technical University of Denmark,
DK–2800 Lyngby, Denmark.
E–Mail: db@it.dtu.dk

Abstract. A paradigmatic three stage approach to software development is sketched in terms of a torso-like, but schematic development of informal and formal descriptions (i) of the **domain** of *sustainable development*, (ii) of **requirements** to *decision support software for developing models for and monitoring development* (claimed to be sustainable), and (iii) of rudiments of a **software architecture** for such a system.
In *"one bat we tackle three problems"*: (i) illustrating a fundamental approach to separation of concerns in software development: From domain via requirements to software descriptions; (ii) contributing towards a theory of sustainable development: Bringing some precision to many terms fraught by "political correctness"; and (iii) providing, we believe, a proper way of relating geographic information system+demographic information system systems to decision support software. Perhaps a fourth result of this paper can be claimed: (iv) Showing, as we believe it does, the structural main parts of a proper presentation of software.

1 Introduction

A paradigmatic three stage approach to software development is sketched in terms of a torso-like, but schematic development of informal and formal descriptions (i) of the **domain** of *sustainable development*, (ii) of **requirements** to *decision support software for developing models for and monitoring development* (claimed to be sustainable), and (iii) of rudiments of a **software architecture** for such a system.

In *"one bat we tackle three problems"*: (i) illustrating a fundamental approach to separation of concerns in software development: From domain via requirements to software descriptions; (ii) contributing towards a theory of sustainable development: Bringing some precision to many terms fraught by "political correctness"; and (iii) providing, we believe, a proper way of relating

E.-R. Olderog, B. Steffen (Eds.): Correct System Design, LNCS 1710, pp. 29–60, 1999.

geographic information system+demographic information system systems to decision support software. Perhaps a fourth result of this paper can be claimed: (iv) Showing, as we believe it does, the structural main parts of a proper presentation of software.

The current paper primarily presents data models. They are in the style used in denotational and in algebraic semantics domain, respectively sort definitions. But we sketch some observer functions and some axioms. The notation used is that of RSL [1], the Raise Method's [2] Specification Language.

This paper is a torso: It sketches the application of a formal specification and refinement-based software development paradigm to a field either not very well understood or covered by AI (artificial intelligence) researchers and AI programmers. AI contributions, valuable as they may be, usually, as do most contributions in software engineering, zooms in on a narrow problem, solvable (ie. expressible, programmable) in some AI–language (or other). But usually such contributions do not try to isolate the domain from possible requirements; nor the requirements from the implementation. Instead the solution "drives" the development and its presentation.

We advocate a far more comprehensive approach. First we cover, in isolation, domain problems. In the jargon of software engineering these are the "up-stream" issues based on whose precise understanding one may formulate requirements. Then we relate domains to requirements, and finally to software (more precisely software architectures). Throughout we try to make more precise such software engineering and such international aid organisation jargon as decision support system, respectively sustainable development — as well as many other terms: indicator, equity, etc.

The triptych paradigm: from domains via requirements to software (descriptions, has been covered more comprehensively in other papers, for example the recent [3–9], and is claimed to have stood its first tests of usefulness by the well-reported work of the last seven years at UNU/IIST[1]. The present paper, to be fully appreciated by readers not familiar with formal development in the styles of VDM and RAISE, must therefore be complemented by the study of for example [10] or [2], preferably both. Then a professional reader can see how to turn the sketch of this paper into full reality.

We leave it to others to compare the present approach to those of UML etc.

2   Summary Review

2.1   The Application

We *Domain analyse* (Section 4) the notions of Development as based on Resources. We then analyze the concept of Resources, their Attributes and Attribute Values and Indicators. Based on Value Indicators we define Equities. Sustainable Development is then defined in terms of Equities..

---

[1] United Nations University International Institute for Software Technology, P.O.Box 3058, Macau: http://www.unuiist.iist.unu.edu

Based on these concepts we then analyze (Section 5) the Decision Making Processes and *Capture Requirements* for a Decision Support System for Sustainable Development (DSS for SD). In this section we introduce the notion of Resource Representations.

Independently we introduce (Section 6) a *Software Architecture* model for a Federated Geographic and spatially related Demographic Information System.

This model is then related (Section 7) to the DSS for SD system: $(GaD)^2I^2S$. Section 4–7 thus relate ($\rightarrow$) as shown in figure 1:

Fig. 1. Main Paper Section Relations

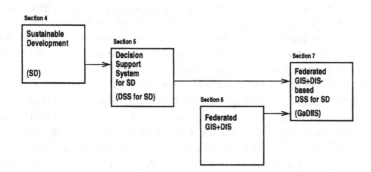

2.2   The Development Paradigm

It is here emphasized that the *Domain Analysis* of Section 4 does not refer to any software, nor to any computing or communications support. It is strictly an analysis, and a formal model, of the concept of Sustainable Development and its constituent notions. Only in Section 5 do we refer, rather implicitly, to software, computing and communications support.

It is also to be emphasized that we do not refer to any conventional notion of geographic information systems or demographic information systems. Thus Section 4, perhaps rather surprisingly to many readers, does not assume geographic information systems or demographic information systems. That "connection" is only made in the last technical section, Section 7. To prepare for that, Section 6 "speaks" solely of geographic information systems and demographic information systems — with no reference to Section 4's or 5's decision support system for sustainable development!

This decomposition of the problem is a main contribution of this paper as are the models of Sections 4–7, in decreasing order!

3 Introduction

3.1 Background, Aims and Objectives

This paper has three objectives:

A Triptych Software Paradigm: We wish to illustrate the triptych notions of:

- *domain engineering,*
- *requirements engineering* and
- *software design*

Domain engineering builds a theory of the application domain. It does so by describing it: Informally and formally. As it, the domain, is, without any reference to computing, ie. also without any reference to requirements. Normally a domain is described normatively: encompassing many actual as well as possible instantiations. And the domain need be described from the point of view of all relevant stake-holders, and at a variety of abstractions: the very basics, the domain with its support technologies, with its rules & regulations, human behaviours, etc.

Requirements engineering builds a theory of some software for the support of some activities within the domain. It does so by describing domain requirements, interface requirements and machine requirements. *Domain requirements* projects and instantiates the normative domains; and, in cases, also extends it. *Interface requirements* specify the human-computer interface (HCI): the way human users "see" the system (multi-media), dialogues between man and machine, etc. *Machine requirements* specify dependability (availability, accessibility, security, reliability, etc.), performance, and maintainability (perfective, adaptive and corrective), as well as development and execution platforms.

Finally *software design* specify the architecture of th software: How users and other software perceive or use it, its organisation: How the internal interfaces are composed. Architecture usually 'implements' domain and interface requirements. Program organisation 'implements' machine requirements.

Decision Support Systems: We attempt to combine two main streams of software technology: decision supports systems and geographic information systems in the specific context of environmentally sustainable development.

Sustainable Development: The main text of this paper will deal with this subject. The next sections will detail the points to be made.

3.2 Sustainable Development

The concept of sustainable development was brought into focus at the United Nations Conference on Environment and Development. That conference was held in Rio de Janeiro, Brasil, in June 1992.

An important document [11] submitted to that conference, and a document whose main enunciation, namely a definition of the concept of sustainable development, became a cornerstone of the result of the conference, was commonly known as the Brundtland Report.

The final document of the conference was the Agenda'21 report [12].

Definition 1 *Sustainable Development is development that meets the needs of the present without compromising the ability of future generations to meet their own needs.* [11]

It seems assumed in the above definition that it is indeed possible *to meet the needs of the present without compromising the ability of future generations to meet their own needs!*

¿From [13] we lift the quote taken from [14]:

Quotation 1 *Sustainable Development is a process of social and economic betterment that satisfies the needs and values of all interest groups, while maintaining future options and conserving natural resources and diversity.*

The above appears to have been a "first" definition of sustainable development. It also appears that it did not drew much attention. The next characterisation is due to [15]:

Characterisation 1 *Sustainable Development does not mean no development. It means improving methods for resource management in an environment of increasing demand for resource.*

It was referred to in [16]. The next quotation is due to [17]:

Characterisation 2 *Sustainability means that the evolution and development of the future should be based on continuing and renewable processes and not on the exploitation and exhaustion of the principal or the capital of living resource base.*

It was also referred to in [16]. The last characterisation is due to [18]:

Characterisation 3 *There are over 70 different definitions of sustainable development, offering a number of possible modifications of the development process and a number of different reasons for doing so.*

Also this was quoted in [16]. Finally we quote from:

Source: Paul Samson, July 1995
http://greencross.unige.ch/greencross/digiforum/concept.html

Quotation 2 *Sustainable development is currently a "catch-word"[2], and as such, is often used and abused. Therefore, before we can examine an issue of sustainable development, it is necessary to examine the concept itself. Some parameters*

---

[2] The use of double quote: "..." is Paul Samson's

for defining the concept are given here, and a number of competing visions are offered in the spirit of pluralism.

The concept of, as opposed to the term of, "sustainable development" is not new; the profound and complex problems subsumed by the term can be traced back to the earliest human civilizations and the perennial tension between population growth and economic development, on the one hand, and the use of natural resources and ecosystems on the other. *There is strong evidence suggesting that sustainable development constituted a challenge to our earliest societies, dating back to the ancient Sumerian, Mayan and Mediterranean civilizations [19]. The term "sustainable development", however, is a recent invention, coming into common usage following the publication of the Brundtland Report [11], although even the term's origins may be traced back to before the 1972 United Nations Conference on the Human Environment [20]. The Brundtland Commission is also responsible for the most frequently cited definition of sustainable development:* to meet the needs of the present without compromising the ability of future generations to meet their own needs. *As this section emphasizes, such a definition can be interpreted to have various meanings and is of little use if it is not placed within a specific context, or if the assumptions lying behind it are not clear. Indeed, as the following paragraphs will show a central point of this chapter is that the concept of sustainable development has multiple meanings, and that each is equally legitimate.*

It is noteworthy that a universally accepted definition does not exist for many basic concepts used by society, even for those which are seen to concern our well being. For example, it is often argued that the concept of security is useful precisely because its remains contested. This is why sustainable development, without a commonly accepted definition, appeals to virtually all groups who choose to participate in the environmental debate. Under such conditions, being "pro" sustainable development entails no risk or commitment to a specific set of goals or conditions since none are agreed upon [21]. Almost any group can find their own interest somewhere within the concept, and it is therefore hard to be against it in general. This allows the banner of sustainable development to be used by competing groups toward different or even contradictory ends. A number of these contradictions have been identified, and included among these are issues no less stark than "growth versus limits", "individual versus collective interests", "intergenerational versus intragenerational equity" and "adaptability versus resistance" [22]. However, these contradictions are part and parcel of human institutions and therefore, no less of Sustainability.

Further complication occurs because the concept of sustainable development can be broken into two parts. On the one hand, "Sustainability" relates to the question of the "carrying capacity" of the earth, while giving no attention to social issues, particularly those concerning equity and social justice. "Development", on the other hand, would appear to assume and even necessitate continual economic growth and ignore the question of ecological constraints or "carrying capacity". When these two concepts are put together, a very different one emerges, and the result is much more than the sum of the parts. It is therefore a multi-dimensional concept, and it must be addressed at various levels simultaneously. Sustainability may be divide into three types: social, ecological and economic. The ecological definition is perhaps the clearest and most straightforward, measuring physical and biological processes and the continued functioning of ecosystems. Economic definitions are sharply contested between those who emphasize the "limits" to growth and carrying capacity, [23] and those who see essentially no limits [24].

Similar to global environmental change, sustainable development remains first and foremost a social issue. Although the precise geo-spheric/bio-spheric "limits" of the planet are unknown, it is suggested here that the limits to the globe's Sustainability for humans are more urgently social than they are physical. In other words, we will reach the social limits of Sustainability before we reach the physical ones. Thus, our focus should be on society-based solutions for managing the multiple aspects of global change rather than on technology-based ones. It is important to emphasize the human aspect of sustainable development — for example, institutional and political constraints.

Any conclusions about the meaning of sustainable development remain dependent on considerations of context and spatial and time delimitations. At a global level, the following set of definitions serves well:

> *In the narrowest sense, global Sustainability means indefinite survival of the human species across all the regions of the world... A broader sense of the meaning specifies that virtually all humans, once born, live to adulthood and that their lives have quality beyond mere biological survival... the broadest sense of global Sustainability includes the persistence of all components of the biosphere, even those with no apparent benefit to humanity [25].*

4 Sustainable Development — A Domain Analysis

We analyze the concept of sustainable development. The analysis is decomposed into a number of parts.

4.1 Development

Development is about resources: be they natural resources, monies people, equipment, capabilities, or other. "Raw" development is (like) a function: from a set of resources to a set of resources:

type
    R
value
    D′: R* $\overset{\sim}{\to}$ R*

In "raw" development we *just develop!* — without any consideration to resources at hand, in particular: *whether sustainable or not!* Two developments with exactly, if that was ever possible, resources need not yield the same resulting resources.

The above expresses that there is an abstract type, a sort, named R, which stands for all resources, and that there is some further unspecified, ie. "grossly" underspecified function (hence partial $\xrightarrow{\sim}$), D', from sequences of resources into sequences (*) of resources.

4.2 Resources

Resources "fall" in ("main") categories (C):

Examples 1 *Land, Monies, Minerals, Crops, People, etc.*

Each category (has a name and) designates a set of resources possessing same attributes (A):

Examples 2 *Land: quality, area, location, cost, ...; Monies: kind, currency, amount, ...; ...; People: profession, quality, quantity, ...; etc.*

Each category and attribute (pair) designates a value class (VAL):

Examples 3 *(l:Land,a:Area): from one acre to maybe 20,000 acres; (p:People, a:Amount): from one to perhaps 2,000; etc.*

type
    C, A, VAL
value
    obs_RC: R → C
    obs_CRs: C → R-set
    obs_RAs: R → A-set
    obs_RAV: R × A $\xrightarrow{\sim}$ VAL
    obs_AVs: A → VAL-infset
axiom
    ∀ c:C • ∀ r,r':R •
        {r,r'} ⊆ obs_CRs(c) ⇒ obs_RAs(r) = obs_RAs(r')
        ∧ obs_RC(r) = obs_RC(r') = c ∧ ...

The above RSL notation expresses that there are further algebraic sorts: categories, attributed and values, and that there are some further unspecified observer functions.

Each resource "belongs" to one main category (obs_RC).[3] Each resource relates to a set (-set) of attributes (obs_RAs). Any given resource may or may not have a value for a given attribute (obs_RAV).

Our (domain) observer functions are not definable by us, but are defined by the domain. Observer functions are, however, characterisable by two kinds of

---

[3] We could postulate another category-observer function (obs_RCs, not shown) which to resources associated "related" categories, such that, for example two different resources of the same main category associated to not necessarily the same set of "related" categories.

axioms. Firstly general axioms that characterise the general model of sustainable development. One is shown above: It expresses that all resources of a specific category must have the same set of attributes and, of course, be of that category. We may relax the former (same set of attributes), but cannot relax the latter (be of that category). (The symbols • and ⇒ can be "pronounced" 'such that' and 'implies/imply', respectively.) Secondly instantiated, specific axioms: For a given, ie. an instantiated case of sustainable development, for example the building of a chemical plant, or fertilisation of crops, the resources, categories, attributes and values are "fixed" and a (possibly) consistent, but not necessarily complete axiom scheme "set up": one which approximates relations that are believed to hold between these specific resources, categories, attributes and values.

4.3   Indicators

An indicator is a measure of desired values of resource attributes. Sometimes an indicator is a value with, perhaps, some fuzzy membership (or probability) function. Sometimes an indicator is a pair of values (a range) (perhaps adorned with some sort of fuzziness). And, sometimes an indicator is a function, for example a simple function from time to attribute values, or a more complex function, for example a function from time and another attribute value to (perhaps fuzzy) values.

   An indicator thus expresses a desirable interval within which actual resource attribute values are to range at given times and/or in the presence of other (fuzzy) valued attributes, etc.

type
   I
   Fuzzy
value
   is_in_Rng: R × A × I $\xrightarrow{\sim}$ Fuzzy

4.4   Resources, Attributes and Indicators

In development we are interested in certain resources, and for each of these, in certain attributes, and, for each of these, in focusing on certain (intervals of) indicators. We may speak of such a "thing" as a RAIs: A resource to attribute indicator range "table":

type
   RAIs = R $\xrightarrow{m}$ (A $\xrightarrow{m}$ (I×I))

The above defines RAIs to be a space of maps from resources to maps from (their) attributes to pairs of ("lo–hi") indicators.
   An 'abstract' example could be:

Examples 4 rais:

$$\left[\begin{array}{l} r_1 \mapsto \left[\begin{array}{l} a_{1_1} \mapsto (i_{1_{1_1}}, i_{1_{1_2}}) \\ a_{1_2} \mapsto (i_{1_{2_1}}, i_{1_{2_2}}) \end{array} \right] \\ r_2 \mapsto \left[a_{2_1} \mapsto (i_{2_{1_1}}, i_{2_{1_2}}) \right] \end{array} \right]$$

The example, rais:RAIs, expresses that we are concerned with exactly two resources, and, for resource r_1 in two of its attributes. We do not, in RAIs, express resource categories nor resource attribute values: these properties are part of the resources, r_1, respectively r_2. Cf. observation functions obs_RC, respectively obs_RAV, etc.

4.5   Equities: Constraints and Objectives

Sustainable Development: Development is said to be sustainable if (i) it maintains an invariant (an equity) between resources before and after development.

Other variants of what an equity is are: if (ii) it, after development, achieves certain (indicated) resource attribute values, respectively if (iii) development is constrained, 'before and after', by indicated attribute value ranges ("within interval").

An equity, E', is therefore chosen to express a fuzzy (in general a multi-criteria, underspecified) relation.

type
   Small
   E' = (RAIs × RAIs) $\xrightarrow{\sim}$ Fuzzy
   ES' = En $\xrightarrow[m]{}$ E'
   Acceptable = Fuzzy × Small → **Bool**

We do not mandate any specific equity relation. The construction of equity relations entail oftentimes rather serious mathematical, control-theoretic, operations--analytic, knowledge-based (expert) system, or other modeling (see Section 7.3).

When applying a fuzzy equity function to pairs of resource sets combined with their attributes and the indicators of these attributes: namely a pair designating a "before–after" (development) relation, we expect to get an acceptable level (below 'small'). Thus the class 'Acceptable' denotes predicates, each of which we supply with an acceptance factor ('small').

The primed type names, for example E' and ES', designate precursors for subsequent, stepwise "refined" unprimed type names. For E see Section 5.7.

4.6   Analysis = Modeling "in the Small"

Such modeling — as was just mentioned at the end of the previous section — may stabilize only after repeated analytical experiments. That is: fixing which are the relevant indicators and which are the relevant equity functions require various kinds of mathematical modeling, i.e. analysis.

Analysis with respect to sustainable development involves:

1. identifying relevant resources (rs:RS),
2. affected attributes (a:A),
3. their indicator intervals ((li,hi):I×I),
4. specimen (analysis labeled (lbl:Lbl)) combinations of resources, attributes and indicators (rais:RAIs, and lrais:Lbl_RAIss)
5. relevant (named, En) equity functions (in ES′).

Formally, analysis amounts to:

type
    Lbl
    RS = R-**set**
    Lbl_RAIss = Lbl $\overrightarrow{m}$ RAIs
    Analysis′ = RS × Lbl_RAIss × ES′
value
    A_Result: Analysis′ $\overset{\sim}{\rightarrow}$ (En $\overrightarrow{m}$ Fuzzy)
axiom
    [proper analysis]
    ∀ (rs,lraiss,es′):Analysis′ • ∀ rais:RAIs • rais ∈ **rng** lraiss
        ⇒ **dom** rais ⊆ rs ∧ ∀ e′:E′ • e′ ∈ **rng** es′ ⇒ (rais,) ∈ **dom** e′

The result of analysis associates with each equity some fuzzy judgment as to whether a planned development, as expressed by the equity functions, achieve equity. The keywords **dom** and **rng** designate the map definition (domain), respectively the range set yielding operations.

4.7 Planning

Planning is concerned with creating descriptions of development (functions, d:D). Since these have to satisfy a variety of equities, planning also involves analysis.

type
    DS = Dn $\overrightarrow{m}$ D
    D = RAIs $\overset{\sim}{\rightarrow}$ RAIs
    Plan = Analysis′ × DS
axiom
    ∀ ((rs,nmrais,es′),ds):Plan • ∀ d:D, rais:RAIs • d ∈ **rng** ds
        ⇒ rais ∈ **dom** d ∧
            let rais′ = d(rais) **in**
            ∀ e:E • e ∈ **rng** es′ ⇒ ∃ s:Small • Acceptable(e(rais,rais′),s) **end**

4.8   Sustainable Development

Sustainable development is now the act of actually carrying out the planned development after analysis of plans has validated these according to desired equities.

type
    Development = (Plan × RS) $\overset{\sim}{\to}$ RS

Here we have taken a very simplistic view of development. A more realistic view would only add details and not further illustrate the formalisation principles we strive to adhere to.

4.9   Time Frames

Among the resources treated is time. In the RAIs arguments there will undoubtedly be various forms of time attributes and indicators: past, present and future time, time intervals, etc. Non-time attribute indicators may themselves be functions of times and intervals.

     Thus we believe, that in the above model we capture "all" conceivable needs for time parameters, time considerations, etc.

4.10   Discussion

Resources vs. Resource Representations: As always our language of communication, in the daily pursuit of our business: here sustainable development, mixes references to "real" resources with references to representations of resources. As long as we are fully aware of the dangers in possibly confusing them, OK. So far we have been referring to "real" resources, not their representation. That will be done in Section 5.1.

Function Arguments and Results: In this paper we "lump" all conceivable arguments to functions and predicates into the convenient form of one single rais:RAIs argument.

     Readers may find that when they start understanding what all these functions, like Equity "predicates", Experimental Analysis and Analysis functions, Planning and Development functions, are doing, then they may start wondering: *what happened to time considerations?; what happened to financial expenditures, what happened to the deployment of engineers, designers, construction workers, etc.?*

     The simple answer is: They are all gathered together, not as separate parameters to conventionally type functions, as in mathematics or programming, but as a rais:RAIs argument.

     Let us just show an example:

Examples 5 *A 'before'/'after' development relation:*

– *Before development:*

$$\begin{bmatrix} r_1 \mapsto [a \mapsto ii_a, t \mapsto ii_t] \\ r_2 \mapsto [a_\alpha \mapsto ii_\alpha] \end{bmatrix}$$

– *After development:*

$$\begin{bmatrix} r_1' \mapsto [a \mapsto ii_a', t \mapsto ii_t'] \\ r_2' \mapsto [a_\alpha \mapsto ii_\alpha] \\ r_3 \mapsto [a_\beta \mapsto ii_\beta] \end{bmatrix}$$

An interpretation of the above could be that in this development three resources are being changed (r_1, r_2) or created (r_3). Resource r_1 has a time attribute. Before development its value satisfied some equity indicator interval ii_t, afterwards is satisfies ii_t'. Etcetera. What we mean by 'satisfy' is again open for wide interpretation.

This example serves to show that the preparer, the analyzer and planner have very wide degree of freedom in formulating functions over almost any combination of resources and, within these, of interpretation.

5 Requirements Capture: A "DSS for SD"

By a 'DSS for SD' we mean a decision support system for sustainable development. Section 4 described what we mean by sustainable development.

In this section we will analyze the actions needed in preparing for, making plans and analyzing plans for sustainable development, and, in particular, identify the computer and communications support of these actions. That is: we capture, in this section, the requirements for a DSS for SD.

In doing so we shall repeatedly refer to subsections of section 4.

5.1 Resource Representation

In section 4 we "dealt" with "real" resources. In real reality we "deal" with representations of resources. That is: we assume that every resource (r:R) that we wish to handle can be "formally" represented, ie. modelled by some rr:RR, the class of resource representations. We therefore redefine the functions over R to also apply to RR:

type
    RR
value
    obs_RRC: RR → C
    obs_RRAs: RR → A-set
    obs_RRAV: RR × A $\xrightarrow{\sim}$ VAL
    is_in_Rng: RR × A × I $\xrightarrow{\sim}$ Fuzzy

With this follows that we redefine:

type
$\quad$ RRAIS = RR $\overrightarrow{m}$ (A $\overrightarrow{m}$ (I × I))
$\quad$ E = (RRAIS × RRAIS) $\overset{\sim}{\to}$ Fuzzy

Etcetera.

5.2   Problem Synopsis

We refer to section 4.1. The problem synopsis — in a "gross" way, to be detailed (detail-resolved) by subsequent actions — identifies (including names) the major (initially "raw") resources and development functions. **Text** stands for text that explains the pragmatics of whatever is being represented.

type
$\quad$ Q /* text */
$\quad$ Resources = Q × (Rn $\overrightarrow{m}$ (Q × RR))
$\quad$ DevtFct = (Q × (C* × C*))
$\quad$ DevtFuncts = Q × (Dn $\overrightarrow{m}$ DevtFct)
$\quad$ Synopsis = Q × Resources × DevtFuncts
$\quad$ Location
value
$\quad$ obs_RLoc: RR $\overset{\sim}{\to}$ Location

obs_RLoc is an observer function which to every resource representation associates its physical Location. Observe that only now did we actually use the notion of a resource category (c:C). When we, earlier, dealt with "real" resources there basically was no need to introduce categories of resources. Now that we work (mostly) with representations of resources, then we must introduce that type notion.

$\quad$ The overall problem synopsis is informally described (**Text**). Each resource and development function is named (Rn, Dn) and explained (**Text**), and, for the development functions, a "type"-definition of the function is given in terms of the resource categories involved. Resources themselves are, of course, not present in the decision support system for sustainable development "machinery": only representors (RR) which further locates the resources (etc.).

Requirements Capture 1 *Hence the decision support system for sustainable development must provide a repository (a data base) for 'Synopsis' as well as appropriate functions, for example for initializing PS, for inserting new, and for displaying, searching, sorting, updating, deleting existing resource representor and development function entries.*

5.3   Resource Mappings

We need establish mappings between real resources and their representors.

type

$\quad$ RRRM$'$ = RR $\underset{\widetilde{m}}{\rightarrow}$ R

$\quad$ RRRM = {| rrrm | rrrm:RRRM$'$ • **dom** rrrm = RRS |}

$\quad$ IRRRM$'$ = R $\underset{\widetilde{m}}{\rightarrow}$ RR-set

$\quad$ IRRRM = {| irrrm | irrrm:IRRRM$'$ • ∪ **rng** irrrm ⊆ RRS |}

$\quad$ RMs$'$ = RRRM × IRRRM

$\quad$ RMs = {| (rrrm,irrrm) |

$\qquad\qquad$ (rrrm,irrrm):RMs$'$ • ∀ rr:RR • rr ∈ **dom** rrrm

$\qquad\qquad$ ⇒ rrrm(rr) ∈ **dom** irrrm ∧ rrrm(rr) ∈ irrrm(rrrm(rr)) |}

The {| a | a:A • P(a) |} expression defines a sub-type of A, namely all those a of A that satisfy P(a). The prefix ∪ denotes distributed set union — since, in this case, **rng** irrrm yields a set of sets.

Requirements Capture 2 *Hence the decision support system for sustainable development must provide a repository (a data base) for these mapping as well as appropriate functions, for example for initializing RMs, for inserting new, and for displaying, searching, sorting, updating, deleting existing map entries.*

5.4   Resource Names and Resource Representations

Resources are clustered in categories and maps between representors of real resources and their (non-unique) denotations must be established:

type

$\quad$ Resource_Clusters = C $\underset{\widetilde{m}}{\rightarrow}$ Rn-set

$\quad$ RR_R_Mapping = txt:Q × RRRM

$\quad$ R_RR_Relation = txt:Q × IRRRM

$\quad$ Resource_Info = Resource_Clusters × RR_R_Mapping × R_RR_Relation

Requirements Capture 3 *Hence the decision support system for decision support must provide a repository (a data base) for Resource_Info as well as appropriate functions, for example for initializing Resource_Info, for inserting new, and for displaying, searching, sorting, updating, deleting existing category and resource representor to "actual" resource mapping entries.*

5.5   Resource Attributes, Values and Indicators

We refer to sections 5.1 and 4.4.

$\quad$ For each resource category we must identify all relevant attributes, (Cluster_Atrs) and for each specific resource (identified by its name) and attribute the (Sustainability) indicators (Resource_Inds).

type
    Cluster_Atrs = C $\xrightarrow{m}$ A-set
    Resource_Inds = Rn $\xrightarrow{m}$ (A $\xrightarrow{m}$ (I × I))
    Atrs_Inds = Cluster_Atrs × Resource_Inds

Requirements Capture 4 *Hence the decision support system for decision support must provide a repository (a data base) for Atrs_Inds as well as appropriate functions, for example for initializing Atrs_Inds, for inserting new, and for displaying, searching, sorting, updating, deleting existing category and resource representor to "actual" attribute sets, respectively attribute and indicator sets.*

5.6   Equity Identification and Definition

Preparation and analysis includes identifying equities and defining a suitable collection of equity functions: their signature (type) and their "behaviour". Some "behaviours" may be only informally defined (**Text**).

type
    Q /* text */
    Equity_Ty = C $\xrightarrow{m}$ (A $\xrightarrow{m}$ I-set)
    Equity_Df = E | Q
    Equity_Functs = En $\xrightarrow{m}$ (Equity_Ty × Equity_Df)

Requirements Capture 5 *Hence the decision support system for decision support must provide a repository (a data base) for Equity_Functs as well as appropriate functions, for example for initializing Equity_Functs, for inserting new, and for displaying, searching, sorting, updating, deleting equity function types and definitions.*

In defining equity functions modelling experiments have to be performed in order to establish appropriate models.

type
    Type
    X_Type = typ_txt:Q × ((Equity_Ty × Type) × Type)
    X_Funct = fct_txt:Q × ((RRAIs × VAL) $\xrightarrow{\sim}$ VAL)
    Nmd_Xs = Xn $\xrightarrow{m}$ (txt:Q × (X_Type × X_Funct))
    X_Res = i_txt:Q × ((RRAIs × VAL) $\xrightarrow{m}$ (r_txt:Q × VAL))
    Exec_Xs = Nmd_Xs × (Xn $\xrightarrow{m}$ X_Res)

The experiment functions (hence the use of X) form part of the model being built. They also must first be identified and defined. They finally must be executed and results recorded and annotated.

Requirements Capture 6 *Hence the decision support system for decision support must provide a repository (a data base) for Exec_Xs as well as appropriate functions, for example for initializing Exec_Xs, for inserting new, and for displaying, searching, sorting, updating, deleting experiment function types and definitions. Finally the decision support system for sustainable development must allow execution of the experiment functions.*

5.7 Analysis Function Identification and Execution

Analysis functions are defined in terms of sets, ES, of equity functions. These functions now have to be executed, results recorded and interpreted. Analysis can be viewed as a set of analyses, each named (Lbl), provided with varieties of commented (**Text**) analysis data (RAIs), and with Results also commented (interpreted) and recorded.

Each analysis function argument, besides the rais:RAIS arguments must also be provided with a resource mapping argument. So we need redefine Analysis:

type
 iARGS$'$ = RRAIs × RMs
 EARGs$'$ = iARGS$'$ × RRAIs
 EARGs = {| ((rr,rm),rr$'$) | ((rr,rm),rr$'$):EARGs$'$ • **dom** rr ∧ ... |}
 E = (Val × EARGs) $\overset{\sim}{\to}$ Fuzzy
 ES = En $\overrightarrow{m}$ E
 D = RAIs $\overset{\sim}{\to}$ RAIs
 DS = Dn $\overrightarrow{m}$ D
 Analysis = RRS × NmRRAIs × ES
 Allocation_and_Scheduling
 Plan = Analysis × DS × Allocation_and_Scheduling

Requirements Capture 7 *Hence the decision support system for decision support must provide a repository (a data base) for Plan as well as appropriate functions, for example for initializing, for inserting new, and for displaying, searching, sorting, updating, deleting analyses, including execution of functions and recording results. All insertions and updates usually require the user to provide textual comments (**Text**).*

Executing the modelling and analysis functions require naming the executions:

type
 EAn
 Exec_Res = (q:Q × (En $\overrightarrow{m}$ (q:Q × (Lbl $\overrightarrow{m}$ (q:Q × VAL))))))
 Exec_Plan = EAn $\overrightarrow{m}$ Exec_Res

Requirements Capture 8 *Hence the decision support system for decision sup-port must provide a repository (a data base) for Exec_Plan as well as appropriate functions, for example for initializing Exec_Plan, for inserting new, and for dis-playing, searching, sorting, updating, deleting analyses, including execution of functions and recording results. All insertions and updates usually require the user to provide textual comments (***Text***).*

We end our example Requirements Capture here as no new principles are being illustrated and as the rest is, from now on, trivial!

5.8   The "Grand" State Σ

Summarizing we can say that the state of a DSS for SD consists of:

type
Σ = Synopsis
   × Resource_Info
   × Atrs_Inds
   × Equity_Functs
   × Exec_Xs
   × Plan
   × Exec_Plan

Requirements Capture 9 *Hence the decision support system for sustainable development must provide a user interface to this state, to its various parts, easy selection and execution of functions: main and auxiliary, user- as well as systems defined.*

5.9   Decision Making

Throughout this and the previous section we have implied that (i) resources had to be identified, (ii) representations sought, (iii) attributes ("of interest") and (iv) indicators (likewise "of interest") had to be determined amongst alternatives, (v) equity and (vi) analysis functions defined, likewise exposing the analyzer and planner to many options. Once analysis functions were executed and (vii) results interpreted choices again arise. Finally when planning, based on analysis, commences (viii) final options present themselves (or otherwise).

All these situations must be carefully recorded; chosen paths (ie. decisions) must also be recorded and it must all be related to the various (i–iix) alternatives.

Requirements Capture 10 *Hence the decision support system for sustainable development must provide easy means for the user: preparer, analyzer and plan-ner, to record all alternatives, to mitivate choices taken, and to "play–back" paths of identification, defintions, executions and choices, also along rejected alterna-tive paths.*

5.10 "The Model"

Throughout this and the previous section we have also implied that a model of the development problem emerges. That model is, in fact, the hypertext–like woven path along alternative and chosen identifications, definitions, executions and interpretations of results and plans.

Requirements Capture 11 *Hence the decision support system for sustainable development must itself, as the user "navigates" around alternatives, selects and rejects choices, etc., build up a graph-like web of the paths taken, with nodes and edges suitably labelled with references to data and functions, explanatory, informal text that the systems elicits from the user, etc.*

We will have more to say about this in section 7.3.

6   A Federated GIS+DIS: $(GaD)^2I^2S$

By a **federated geographic information system** we understand a GIS+DIS whose main information, the spatial and (spatially related) census (and other) data and operations over these may reside across a global (i.e. worldwide) network of "ordinary", already established or future geographic information systems "plus" demographic information systems. These latter GISs+DISs may represent their information each in their own way. From a practical point of view such GISs+DISs may be managed on APIC [26], ArcInfo [27], ArcView [28], ERMapper [29], IDRISI [30], InterGraph [31], MapInfo [32], PopMap [33], Redatam [34], and other platforms.

The problem to be dealt with in this section is to properly integrate the concepts of geographic and demographic information systems (GISs, DISs) with the resource representation notions of the previous section.

Hence we need take a look at GISs and DISs. These are aggregations spatially and statistically (tabular) data. By 'federation' we mean the further aggregation of individual GISs and DISs — as they may have been created and are maintained locally, around the world, each covering "separate" but eventually, increasingly more related resources.

6.1   A First Narrative

To explain our notion of 'federation' further we first present a "picture", then some narrative, and finally a formal model.

A Picture: A *"picture is sometimes worth a thousand words"*. Later we shall claim that a formula is oftentimes worth a thousand pictures.

Yet even pictures need be explained: Squares with emanating arrows designate storage cells of type pointer. "Landscape" rectangles labelled 'text' designate unstructured, textual data (ie. text which informally describes formatted

Fig. 2. A Hierarchical GIS+DIS Federated Information System

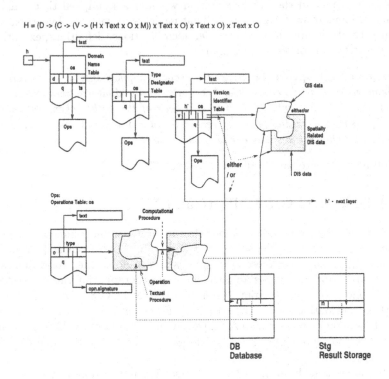

data — here, from top left to right texts may explain domain, category and version information). "Landscape" rectangles labelled 'opn.signature' designate descriptions of operation types. "Curtain" figures — of which there are two kinds — designate domain/category/version sub-directories, respectively (operation, ie. executable) code directories. The top left to right "curtain" designate sub--directories of domains, categories, and versions (DCV). Directories have fixed format entries ("rows"). Initial DCV sub-directory rows link to further DCV sub-directories. Final DCV sub-directory rows link to either formatted or un-formatted data: viz. relations, respectively images — and either directly, the upper arrow, or indirectly, via a database reference, the lower arrow. The final sub-directory rows also links, in the fashion of "recursive descent", to another, lower, layer of domain/category/version directories. The formatted or unformat-ted data is shown as grey squares or grey "clouds". Code directories link (i) to text briefly explaining the operation, (ii) to the type of the data needed as in-put to the formally or informally "executed" operation and resulting from those operations, and (iii) to either (formal, executable) code (the arrow-infixed pair of grey "clouds"), or to text (the arrow-infixed pair of grey squares) explaining how the human analyser can go about performing the analysis "by hand"! Performing an analysis function takes input from a database and delivers output to a result storage. Administrative operations, not shown, may move data from the result storage to the database.

6.2 A Second Narrative

Next we reformulate, more systematically, the above symbol explication:

Layers and Levels: Figure 2 displays one layer, with three levels, of a hierarchically structured federated and combined geographic information system and demographic information system: GIS+DIS. (Further layers are referred to implicitly.)

Each of the three large "curtains" (cascaded in the upper left corner of the figure) diagram a table like structure: Domain Name Table (the D level), Category (or rype) Designator Table (the C level), respectively Version Identifier Table (the V level).

Domain Name Tables: One accesses the (or, in general, a) Domain name table from a root, a sentinel, Hierarchy designator (h).

Each entry in the Domain name table contains a distinct domain name (d:D), a (reference to explanatory) text (q:**Text**), (a reference to) an operations table (os), and a (reference to a Category designator table (the latter only shown by an arrow).

One accesses a Category designator table "through" (or via) a Domain name table entry.

Type Designator Tables: Each Category designator table entry contains a distinct type designator (c:C), a (reference to explanatory) text (q:**Text**), (a reference to) an Operations table (os), and a (reference to a) Version identifier table.

One accesses a Version identifier table through a Category designator table entry.

Version Identifier Tables: Each Version identifier table entry contains a distinct version identifier (v:V), a (reference to explanatory) text (q:**Text**), (a reference to) an operations table (os), (a reference to) data, and a (reference to an) [sub-]hierarchy (h).

Data Access: One accesses Data through a version identifier table entry.

Traversing Hierarchy Layers: One also accesses a sub-hierarchy (the "next" layer) through the H item of a version identifier table entry.

Operations Tables: At any D, C or V level one can access an operations table. Each Operations table (O) entry contains a distinct operations name (on:On), (a reference to) explanatory text (q:**Text**), (a reference to) the type of the operation designated, and (a reference to) the operation [itself!].

Federation means that data may reside on different GIS, DIS, etc, platforms: commercial, experimental, public domain or otherwise: APIC, ArcInfo, MapInfo, IDRISI, PopMap, Redatam, winR+/GIS, etc.

6.3   A Third Narrative

Geographic, Demographic and other Data — Data: We now describe, more generally, but still informally, and from a slightly different viewpoint, the components of the proposed federated GIS+DIS. The base information unit, which usually is a highly composite entity, will be referred to as 'Data'. Examples of specific data are:

Examples 6 *A Geodetic Map of China, A Political Map of Europe, A Vegetation & Natural Crops Map of GuangDong Province (in China), A Mineral Deposits Map of France, A Spatially related Population Census of Zhuhai[4], A Cartographic and Cadestral Map of Macau, etc.*

Domain Names: By D we understand the set of domain names:

Examples 7 *China, GuangDong, Zhuhai, . . .*

Data Category Designators: By C we understand the set of composite data types:

Examples 8 *Geodetic Map, Political Map, Vegetations & Natural Crops Map, . . . , Cadestral Map, Population Consensus Data, Import/Export Statistics, . . . , Election Data.*

Version Identifiers: By V we understand the set of version designators (time stamps) of data:

Examples 9 *1982, 1996, . . . , August 12, 1999, . . .*

The Database: Data is kept in a conceptual data base (DB). The data base, as we shall see, can be interpreted as being distributed globally. Each data has a location (L).

Hierarchical Directory Structure: A (d,c,v) identification designates (geographic (GIS), demographic (DIS) and other) data in a hierarchical fashion. Assume fixed type and arbitrary version, then the domain name China could, for example, give access to some data on all of China and then to a set of properly domain-named sub-data of the same (and also other) type(s), etc. One for each (, say) Province of China. And so on, recursively, until some user-defined "smallest grain of data" — which could be a floor plan of a specific residence, a single plot of land for

---

[4] Zhuhai is a Special Economic Zone of GuangDong Province in China

agriculture, etc. This hierarchical (directory-like) recursion is modeled by the below recursion in H.

Data identified "occur" only at the V level of a 'complete' (list of one or more) (D,C,V) triples.

Use of the hierarchy (H) entails navigating "up and down" the layers of the hierarchy of (D,C,V) levels. At any one time a user has traversed a Stack of such (d,c,v)'s.

Unary and N-ary Functions — O, On: With each data version there may be some specific, named (unary) functions applicable to that specific data. Designating an operation for application shall mean that the operation is applied to the data designated by the current stack top (which will be a list of (d,c,v) triples — with the list length denoting the current depth of the traversed hierarchy wrt. the root System Hierarchy).

With each specific type we may likewise associate a set of named, unary functions. Each such function is then understood to be applicable to any version of data of that type and domain. The actual data is designated by the topmost stack element whose type matches the operation type.

With each domain we may associate a set of usually n-ary functions. Each such function is then understood to be applied to data designated by the n topmost stack elements whose types matches, in order, the designated operation type.

Some operations may not be computable. Instead text is given which directs the user to "perform" an appropriate evaluation and to enter a resulting value!

Function Result Storage — Stg: Results of operation applications must be uniquely named (by the user) and are stored in a local storage (Stg) under that name together with a historical record of the stack of the time of application, and the appropriately (D,C,V) marked operation name.

At any layer and level domain names, type names, version names, data and operations are annotated by explanatory, descriptive and other text (**Text**). Operations can be shared across domains, types and versions, as well as across layers of the recursive hierarchy.

Database Sharing and Data Filtering — F: Since also data can be shared across domains, types, versions and layers of the recursive hierarchy, a filter function (F) is provided which, for different levels and layers (etc.) may specialize, generalize or otherwise instantiate the immediately location designated data.

This potentially allows a simple information repository to be viewed, through the (D,C,V) hierarchy as a highly structured (network) of data.

6.4   A Formal (Data Structure) Model

"A small set of formulas is often worth a thousand pictures":

type
  D, C, V, Res_Typ, Res_VAL, N
  $S = H \times DB \times Stg \times Stack$
  $Stack = DCV^*$

  $H = (D \xrightarrow{\sim} (C \xrightarrow{\sim} (V \xrightarrow{\sim} (M \times H \times Q \times O)) \times Q \times O) \times Q \times O) \times Q \times O$

  $M = L \times F$
  $F = Data \xrightarrow{\sim} Data$
  $DB = L \xrightarrow{\sim} Data$
  $Stg = N \xrightarrow{\sim} (Res\_VAL \times Stack \times DCV \times On)$

  $DCV = D \mid D \times C \mid D \times C \times V$
  $OTup = ((A^* \times C^*) \times Res\_Typ)$
  $OFct = (((VAL^* \times Data^*) \mid Q) \xrightarrow{\sim} Res\_VAL)$
  $O = On \xrightarrow{\sim} OTyp \times OFct \times Q$

Yet even the formulas may have to be narrated — and that was done in the three Sections 6.1—6.3.

6.5   Data Sharing, Viewing and Gluing

The indirect reference, via M, in the database DB to the geographic information system or demographic information system Data is provided for a number of reasons:

Local Layering: For each layer descending M's (i.e. L's) may refer, in fact, to "overlapping" (probably embedded) Data. At one (say an "upper") layer an L refers to a "large" spatial area (or a large census table), whereas at a "lower" the L may refer to an "smaller" area probably properly contained in the "larger" area. The View functions F therefor serve to sub-locate the right sub-Data!
  More concretely: If a domain name at an "upper" layer is 'Europe' then through the recursive decent through some (C,V) designated H we get the domain names: 'Denmark', etc. The "upper" L designated perhaps a map of Europe, whereas the "lower" should designate a map of Denmark.
  Quite specifically: In a Cartographic & Cadestral Service the maps of a city may be in the database DB as a set of "gluable" sub-maps. These may cover areas not related to administrative or other domain nameable entities. The various layers now "zoom" in on successively "smaller", but administratively "well-rounded" areas. The purpose of the view functions are to collect from one or more sub-maps Data covering the located area and "glue" it together.

Global Distribution: The database may itself be distributed — and across the globe! Now L's (with their F's, i.e. the M's) also contain for example INTERNET information (etc.) so that the Data can be located "in somebody else's database"!

6.6 A Relational View

In the presentation of the Federated GIS+DIS given so far we may have left the reader with the impression that access to the global information is through a strict sequence of triples of domain, then type and finally version identifiers.

We now lift this seeming restriction to allow for a relational access approach. Instead of the (d,c,v)-list view so far proposed and formalized:

type
$$H = D \xrightarrow{m} (C \xrightarrow{m} (V \xrightarrow{m} (M \times H \times ...) \times ...) \times ...) \times ...$$

we instead suggest a relational view:

type
$$rH$$
$$RelH = (rH \times H)\text{-}\mathbf{set}$$
$$H = D \times C \times V \times rH \times O \times Q$$

rH is like a relation tuple identifier.

It is easy to see that any relation RelH can be mapped into either of:

type
$$H = D \xrightarrow{m} (C \xrightarrow{m} (V \xrightarrow{m} (M \times H \times ...) \times ...) \times ...) \times ...$$
$$H' = C \xrightarrow{m} (D \xrightarrow{m} (V \xrightarrow{m} (M \times H \times ...) \times ...) \times ...) \times ...$$
$$H'' = V \xrightarrow{m} (C \xrightarrow{m} (D \xrightarrow{m} (M \times H \times ...) \times ...) \times ...) \times ...$$
etc.

Given a relational representation the user can then determine, at any layer to view the information base, which ordering of the (d,c,v)'s to select — and the system can respond by presenting the tables as selected.

Initially the system "sets" the hierarchy layer (H), for example: rhr_0. Subsequently the user sets, in sequence two of either of the D, C, or V "buttons".

7   A GIS+DIS–based DSS for SD

In the decision support system for sustainable development we dealt with resources, with representations of resources, with attributes and indicators, and with functions over resources and resource representations, attributes and indicators.

7.1 Spatial Resource Maps and Filters

With respect to spatially related resources, we do not record the individual resources or their representations. Instead we typically, when it comes to for example environmental resources, record highly complex aggregations of numerous such resources in the form of for example remotely sensed images.

Fig. 3.

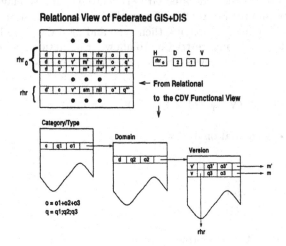

Relational View of Federated GIS+DIS

¿From these we are then, somehow, able to extract, or as we shall call it: filter, representations of resources, one-by-one. Typically, however, the (for example) remotely sensed data also contains a confusing aggregation of other data that somehow must be screened away.

type

Φ

Coordinate = **Real** × **Real** × **Real**

Area = Coordinate-**set**

SpaResMap = Area $\overrightarrow{m}$ (RR $\overrightarrow{m}$ Fuzzy)

AIs = A × I-**set**

Filter = (AIs × Data) $\xrightarrow{\sim}$ (AIs × SpaResMap)

Filters = Φ $\overrightarrow{m}$ Filter

So what we have, usually in a geographic information system are maps, or images, of complex aggregations of Data, and what we want are simple recordings, in the form of well-defined Spatial Resource Maps of resources. By a Spatial Resource Map, we understand a mapping from a an area, that is: a set of three dimensional coordinates to a map from Resource Representations to Fuzzy qualifiers. The idea is that the spatial map "cleanly" represents only those resources for which certain attribute values are present and within given indicator ranges. We choose to map from an area in order to capture averaging properties. Thus a Filter is a function from a triple of Attribute designators, Indicator ranges and (for example an image of remotely sensed) Data to a Spatial Resource Map.

Fig. 4. A Generic Spatial Resources Map and its Filters

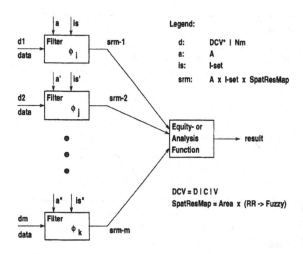

Several filter functions usually are needed to prepare input for the Equity and Analysis functions:

Requirements Capture 12 *A GIS+DIS–based DSS for DS must therefore allow the preparer, analyzer and planner to develop, record and apply filter functions (Φ).*

7.2 The "Grand" System

The Data provided to the Filter functions "come" from the $(GaD)^2I^2S$ repositories: either accessed through an appropriate DTV name list or by the name of a stored result.

This basically completes the GIS+DIS–based DSS for SD System description.

Requirements Capture 13 *A GIS+DIS–based DSS for DS must therefore allow the preparer, analyzer and planner to "link" up the DSS for SD resource concepts with the Data concepts accessible through the recursive hierarchy of domain, type and version names and through the names of results stored, with comments, after human evaluation or computed execution of Equity, Analysis and Planning functions.*

7.3 Towards "The Model"

Very briefly: the hyper-text "woven path" also includes the generation of graphs like the below:

Fig. 5. Towards a Development Model

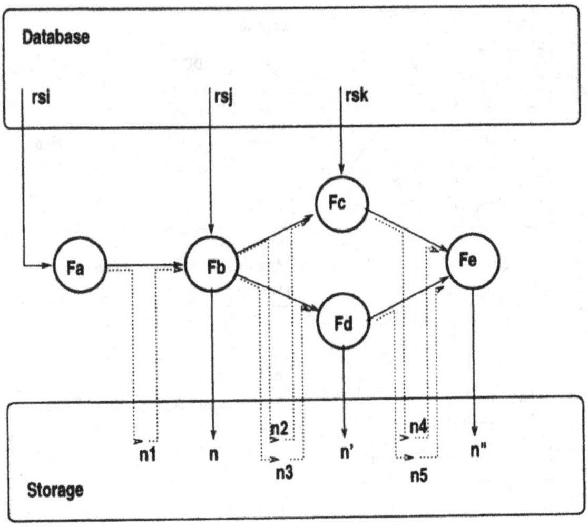

Figure 5 shows a number of Analysis functions and their interrelations with respect to input and output data. Output from some function applications serve as input to other function applications. Outputs (results) are named, and so are input arguments. The above graph (albeit conceptual and very simple) shows an overall "functionality", an overall "structure" of the problem, one that is often, in the demographic information system literature, referred as being "ill-defined" and "unstructured"! In the above picture we have simplified many aspects: simple provision of resource arguments (rather than their prior filtering through filters etc., no user provided invocation time arguments, etc.

Requirements Capture 14 *A GIS+DIS–based DSS for DS must therefore be able to draw, upon request from the preparers, analyzers, planners, developers, and decision makers, the "model" graph of all Functions invoked — whether their results were ever again applied or not — together with a complete "trace" of Data used, whether originating from the Database or from Storage (where it would reside if that Data was the result of previous Function applications).*

8   Conclusion

8.1   On DSS for SD

We have sketched a main outline of how we intend to tackle the issue of decision support system for sustainable development, for how we intend to tackle the issue of a federated geographic information system and demographic information system, and for how we intend to combine them into $(GaD)^2I^2S$: a Federated GIS+DIS DSS for SD.

We have separated two concerns: the DSS for SD from the Federated GIS+DIS. And then we have combined them.

We usually find the issue of DSS for SD "cluttered up" by the mixing of problems of for example deciphering what spatial maps contain of information and the "pure" issues of resources, their attributes, indicators and equity functions. So we have separated the two issues. To then make the whole separation work we bring the issues together.

8.2 On Software Development

We have sketched main phase and some techniques of a new approach to software development: One that is based on domain models on which requirements are then based, and on requirements models on which software development is then based.

This approach is currently under intense research, development and application [3–9].

But much work needs to be done before we can fully justify our claims: we need now carefully study relevant papers. The study will emphasize our "isolation" of the resource, attribute, indicator, equity function etc. issues in order to validate sections 4–5. The paper studies will then analyze the issues of geographic information system and demographic information system functionalities in order to validate section 6.

Meanwhile we will be "building" a "prototype" $(GaD)^2I^2S$ to make more precise the requirements Capture items mentioned in sections 5–7, and to check the conceptual elegance, consistency and comprehensiveness of the $(GaD)^2I^2S$ proposal.

8.3 Acknowledgements

I thank (i) participants in the February 1996 UNU/IIST Workshop on Software Technology for Agenda'21: Decision Support Systems of Sustainable Development [35, 36] for instigating the modelling effort of this paper and for kind remarks, (ii) my colleagues at UNU/IIST for enabling me to enjoy five stimulating years as first and founding UN director of that flourishing UN University software technology research and post-doctoral training centre in Macau, (iii) members of the IFIP WG 2.2 and IFIP WG 2.3 Working Groups for providing stimulating critique of my work, and (iv) Hans Langmaack for 20 years of close friendship.

References

1. The RAISE Language Group. *The RAISE Specification Language*. The BCS Practitioner Series. Prentice-Hall, Hemel Hampstead, England, 1995.

2. The RAISE Method Group. *The RAISE Method.* The BCS Practitioner Series. Prentice-Hall, Hemel Hampstead, England, 1992.

3. Dines Bjørner. Domains as Prerequisites for Requirements and Software &c. In M. Broy and B. Rumpe, editors, *RTSE'97: Requirements Targeted Software and Systems Engineering*, volume 1526 of *Lecture Notes in Computer Science*, pages 1–41. Springer-Verlag, Berlin Heidelberg, 1998.

4. Dines Bjørner and Jorge M. Cuellar. The Rôle of Formal Techniques in Software Engineering Education. *Annals of Software Engineering*, 1999. Editors: Norman E. Gibbs and N. Coulter.

5. Dines Bjørner. Where do Software Architectures come from ? Systematic Development from Domains and Requirements. A Re–assessment of Software Engneering ? *South African Journal of Computer Science*, 1999. Editor: Chris Brink.

6. Dines Bjørner. Pinnacles of Software Engineering: 25 Years of Formal Methods. *Annals of Software Engineering*, 1999. Editors: Dilip Patel and Wang YingYu.

7. Dines Bjørner. Domain Modelling: Resource Management Strategics, Tactics & Operations, Decision Support and Algorithmic Software. In J.C.P. Woodcock, editor, *Festschrift to Tony Hoare*. Oxford University and Microsoft, September 13–14 1999.

8. Dines Bjørner et al. Formal Models of Railway Systems: Domains. Technical report, Dept. of IT, Technical University of Denmark, Bldg. 344, DK–2800 Lyngby, Denmark, September 23 1999. Presented at the FME Rail Workshop on Formal Methods in Railway Systems, FM'99 World Congress on Formal Methods, Toulouse, France. Avaliable on CD ROM.

9. Dines Bjørner et al. Formal Models of Railway Systems: Requirements. Technical report, Dept. of IT, Technical University of Denmark, Bld.g 344, DK–2800 Lyngby, Denmark, September 23 1999. Presented at the FME Rail Workshop on Formal Methods in Railway Systems, FM'99 World Congress on Formal Methods, Toulouse, France. Avaliable on CD ROM.

10. John Fitzgerald and Peter Gorm Larsen. *Developing Software using VDM–SL.* Cambridge University Press, The Edinburgh Building, Cambridge CB2 1RU, England, 1997.

11. Gro Harlem Brundtland, editor. *Our Common Future.* World Commision on Environment and Development. Oxford University Press, WCED, UN, 1987.

12. UN. Agenda'21. United Nations, The Rio de Janeiro, Brasil, Conference on Environment, June 14 1992.

13. LI Xia and Anthony Gar-On YEH. A dss for sustainable land development in china using remote sensing and gis — a case study in dongguan. In *[35]*, 1996. Centre for Urban Planning and Environmental Management + GIS/LIST Research Centre, University of Hong Kong, Pokfulam Road, Hong Kong; hdxugoy@hkucc.hku.hk.39.

14. International Union for the Conservation of Nature. World conservation strategy. Technical report, International Union for the Conservation of Nature, Gland, Switzerland, 1980. Report highlights sustainability of natural resources.

15. A.G.Levinsohn and S.J. Brown. Gis and sustainable development in natural resource management. In M. Heit and A. Shrtreid, editors, *GIS Applications in Natural Resources*, pages 17–21. GIS World, Inc., 1991.

16. Anthony Gar-On YEH. Gis in decision support systems for sustainable development. In *[35]*, 1996. Centre for Urban Planning and Environmental Management + GIS/LIST Research Centre, University of Hong Kong, Pokfulam Road, Hong Kong; hdxugoy@hkucc.hku.hk.23.

17. U.E. Loening. Introductory comments: The challenge for the future. In A.J. Gilbert and L.C. Braat, editors, *Modelling for Population and Sustainable Development*, pages 11–17, London, England, 1991. Routeledge.
18. A. Steer and W. Wade-Grey. Sustainable development: Theory and practice for a sustainable future. *Sustainable Development*, 1(3):223–35, 1993.
19. C. Ponting. Historical perspectives on sustainable development. *Environment*, (4-9):31–33, November 1990.
20. L.K. Caldwell. Political aspects of ecologically sustainable development. *Environmental Conservation*, 11(4):299–308, 1984.
21. M.R. Redclift. *Sustainable Development: Exploring the Contradictions*. Methuen, London and New York, 1987.
22. S.R. Dovers and J.H. Handmer. Contradictions in sustainability. *Environmental Conservation*, 20(3):217–222, 1993.
23. Nicholas Georgescu-Roegen. *The Entropy Law and the Economic Process*. Harvard University Press, Cambridge, 1971.
24. Julian Simon. *The Ultimate Resource*. Princeton University Press, Princeton, N.J., 1981.
25. B.J. Brown, M.E. Hanson, D.M. Liverman, and R.W. Meredith Jr. Global sustainability: Toward definition. *Environmental Management*, 11(6):713–719, 1987.
26. Apic. Apic news: Le journal d'apic systems. Technical Report 6, Apic Systems, 25, rue de Stalingrad, F-94742 Arcueil, Cedex, France, 1995.
27. Environmental Systems Research Institute (ESRI). *Understanding GIS: The ARC/INFO Methods*. Number Version 7 for UNIX and Open VMS. GeoInformation International, 307 Cambridge Science Park, Milton Road, Cambridge, CB4 4ZD, United Kingdom, 3 edition, 1995.
28. Environmental Systems Research Institute. Introducing arcview. Manual, Environmental Systems Research Institute (ESRI), ESRI Inc. 380 New York Street, Redlands, California 92373-2853, USA, 1994.
29. Earth Resource Mapping. Er mapper 5.0 – product information. Literature with demo version, Earth Resource Mapping, Level 2, 87 Colin Street, West Perth, Western Australia, 6005, 17 January 1995.
30. J. Ronald Eastman. Idrisi for windows. User's Guide Version 1.0, Clark Labs for Cartographic Technology and Geographic Analysis, Clark University 950 Main St., Worcester, MA 01610-1477 USA, May 1995.
31. INTERGRAPH. Geographic information systems. Product info. folder, Intergraph Corporation, One Madison Industrial Park, Huntsville Albama 35807-4210, USA, 1995.
32. MapInfo. Mapinfo reference. Reference manual version 3.0, MapInfo Corporation, One Global View, Troy, New York 12180-8399, 1994.
33. UNSTAT/DESIPA. Popmap: Integrated software package for geographical information, maps and graphics databases – user's guide and reference manual. Technical Report ST/ESA/STAT/107, Department for Economic and Social Information and Policy Analysis, Statistical Division (UNSTAT), United Nations, New York, New York 10017, USA, 1994.
34. CELADE/ECLAC. Redatam-plus version 1.1. User's Manual Distr. GENERAL: LC/DEM/G.90 Series A, Nr. 201, Latin American Demographic Centre (CELADE)/United Nations Economic Commission for Latin American and Caribbean (ECLAC), Casilla 91, Santiago, Chile, December 1991.
35. Dines Bjørner, Zbigniew Mikolajuk, Mohd Rais, and Anthony Gar On Yeh, editors. *Decision Support Systems for Environmentally Sustainable Development* —

Software Technology for Agenda'21, UNU/IIST, P.O.Box 3058, Macau, February 25 — March 8 1996. IDRC (International Development Research Centre, Ottawa, Canada) and UNU/IIST (United Nations University, International Institute for Software Technology), UNU/IIST. Unpublished Workshop Hand-outs. (Workshop co-sponsored by IDRC: The Canadian Governments' Intl. Devt. Research Centre, Ottawa.)

36. P.A.V.Hall, D.Bjørner, and Z.Mikolajuk (eds.). Decision Support Systems for Sustainable Develpoment: Experience and Potential. Position Paper 80, UNU/IIST, P.O.Box 3058, Macau, August 1996. International workshop on *Decision Support Systems for Environmentally Sustainable Development — Software Technology for Agenda'21* co-sponsored by IDRC: The Canadian Governments' Intl. Devt. Research Centre, Ottawa.

Real-Time Constraints
Through the ProCoS Layers

Anders P. Ravn[1] and Hans Rischel[2]

[1] Department of Computer Science, Aalborg University, Fr. Bajers vej 7E, DK-9220 Aalborg Ø, Denmark, apr@cs.auc.dk

[2] Department of Information Technology, Technical University of Denmark, DK-2800, Lyngby, Denmark

Abstract. The Provably Correct Systems project [5, 6] developed links between layers of formal specifications for real-time systems. These layers cover requirements capture, design, programming and code generation. In this paper we trace real-time constraints through the layers in order to inspect their changing forms. They originate in constraints on continuous dynamical models of physical phenomena. However, in a digital system it is desirable to *abstract* the complexities of these models to simple clocks, and further to events in a reactive system. This paradigm is the main topic of this paper. We illustrate the different forms of timing constraints in duration calculus, a real-time interval logic.

Keywords: embedded system, hybrid system, real-time, requirements, design, formal specification.

1   Introduction

When the Provably Correct Systems (ProCoS) project was near its completion, the Lyngby team, who was responsible for case-studies and requirements, received a very long mail from Markus Müller-Olm, then in Kiel. It essentially said: "Here is your code!" and continued

```
0101000101010000100101110101010101011
1101010111111101010101011111111111100
1010100100100000100000111101010101010
. . .
```

It serves no purpose to explain details of this binary code; such interpretation is better left to digital computers. However, the main result of ProCoS was that we had some reason to believe that this particular code would have controlled suitable hardware, such that top level requirements for a gas burner [11] were satisfied.

These requirements are specified in duration calculus [14], a real-time interval logic. In order to illustrate the gap between requirements and code we give the formal requirements here, along with an informal explanation of the duration

E.-R. Olderog, B. Steffen (Eds.): Correct System Design, LNCS 1710, pp. 61–78, 1999.
© Springer-Verlag Berlin Heidelberg 1999

calculus. The logical foundations of duration calculus are treated thoroughly in [3], while other selected applications are found in [7, 9, 12, 13, 10].

The basis for duration calculus is a dynamical systems model with state functions that for each point of real time assign a value to the *states*. In the case of the gas burner

$$Heatreq, Flame, Gas, Ignition : \textbf{Bool}$$

express the physical state of the thermostat, the flame, the gas supply, and the ignition transformer. The requirements are then given by the invariance of the following formulas over arbitrary, closed intervals of time $[b, e]$ with b, e denoting non-negative real numbers, satisfying $b \leq e$.

Safe. For Safety, gas must never leak for more than 4 seconds in any period of at most 30 seconds

$$\ell \leq 30 \Rightarrow \int (Gas \wedge \neg Flame) \leq 4$$

In this formula, the interval function ℓ is the *length* of the interval $(e - b)$, and the *duration* term $\int (Gas \wedge \neg Flame)$ is the integral over the interval of the state expression $Gas \wedge \neg Flame$. It denotes exactly the (accumulated) duration of the unsafe state when gas is leaking.

Off. Heat request off shall result in the flame being off after 60 seconds

$$\lceil \neg Heatreq \rceil \Rightarrow \ell \leq 60 \ \vee \ ((\ell = 60); \lceil \neg Flame \rceil)$$

The premise in this formula asserts that the state $\neg Heatreq$ essentially holds for the full interval: $\lceil \neg Heatreq \rceil \overset{\text{def}}{=} (\int \neg Heatreq = \ell) \wedge (\ell > 0)$. In this sub-formula, the conjunct $\ell > 0$ ensures that it is a proper interval, and not a point where $b = e$. The conclusion $(\ell = 60); \lceil \neg Flame \rceil$ asserts that the interval can be "chopped" (the ';' operator) into subintervals $[b, m]$ and $[m, e]$ such that $\ell = 60$ holds for $[b, m]$ and $\lceil \neg Flame \rceil$ for $[m, e]$.

On. Heat request shall after 60 seconds result in gas burning unless an ignite or flame failure has occurred

$$\lceil Heatreq \rceil \Rightarrow \ell \leq 60 \ \vee \ ((\ell = 60); \lceil Flame \rceil) \vee \Diamond (IgniteFail \vee FlameFail)$$

The exceptional conditions are specified by $\Diamond (IgniteFail \vee FlameFail)$ which asserts that somewhere in the interval an $IgniteFail$ or an $FlameFail$ occur. For the moment we leave the formulas denoted by $IgniteFail$ and $FlameFail$ unspecified.

It is clear that the requirements **On** and **Off** are bounded progress properties; they require that a certain state is reached within a given time. Such properties are analogous to stability of a dynamical system: after some time the system remains in some bounded region. It is also intuitively clear that in programming terms they correspond to upper bounds on the time to pass through certain paths of the program. The **Safe** requirement on the other hand is analogous to a constraint of the type found in optimal control, where the objective is to minimize the unsafe state *Gas* $\wedge \neg Flame$ over the given period of 60 seconds. It is also intuitively clear that this is programmed by staying long enough in safe states before passing as quickly as possible through potentially unsafe states.

It is therefore reasonable to expect that the top level requirements are transformed into upper and lower bounds on the duration of certain program states in a design. The binary code, however, does not mention anything about upper bounds and lower bounds. The only duration that can be associated with a machine code instruction, is the number of cycles of the processor and the delays on input/output operations, including communication with (hardware) timers. The correspondence between the bounds of the design and the low level properties must be checked during compilation.

The main achievement of ProCoS was to establish semantic links and in particular corresponding syntactic transformations that allowed refinement from such top level requirements down to machine code or hardware circuits. This story has, however, been told quite a number of times, and has inspired much further work of which some is reported in other papers of this volume. The focus of this paper is on the real-time properties, and how they surface in a ProCoS design trajectory. The aim is to highlight suitable abstractions for real-time properties in a systematic development.

Activity	Documents	Language
Requirements analysis	Requirements	RL Requirements logic
System design	System specs	SL System specification language
Program design	Program source	PL Programming language

Either:

Hardware synthesis	Circuits	HL Hardware Language

Or:

Compilation	Machine code	ML Machine language

Fig. 1. ProCoS tower of development stages

Overview. The investigation follows the "ProCoS tower" shown in Figure 1. Section 2 analyzes the specification of requirements with respect to real-time properties. Section 3 introduces the architectural components: sensors, actuators and (programmed) controllers. The latter are specified by "implementable" forms which are related to timed automata. Section 4 touches briefly on transformation to programs and compilation. Finally, in the concluding Section 5 we discuss the overall development process. In particular, we enquire whether it would be useful to work from the middle out, i.e., to postulate a design in terms of timed automata and check upwards and compile downwards.

2   Requirements

In order to understand requirements for an embedded computer system one must know a little about the physical plant that it monitors or controls. Such plants are usually modelled by dynamical systems, i.e. systems with a state that evolves over time. Within the engineering disciplines, the background for the study of such systems is control theory. We outline central elements of control theory below. However, we shall use duration calculus to express top level requirements, so the next step is to make this notation precise. The final part of the section then introduces and discusses the kinds of requirements usually encountered in our case studies and gives analogies to corresponding dynamical systems properties. At the end of this section we have thus illustrated an informal link between control engineering and embedded systems requirements.

2.1   Control Theory

Typically, a model of a plant is given in terms of a vector $\mathbf{x}$ of state variables that evolve smoothly over time modelled by the reals. The characteristics of the particular plant are specified by associating a differential equation with the state:

$$\dot{\mathbf{x}}(t) = F(\mathbf{x}(t)) \quad \text{for all time points } t$$

Here, $\dot{\mathbf{x}}$ denotes the component-wise derivative of $\mathbf{x}$ with respect to time, and F is a vector function that characterizes the relationship between the different state components of the plant.

When a plant is to be controlled, the model is extended by superimposing a control input component $\mathbf{u}$ such that the model becomes

$$\dot{\mathbf{x}}(t) = F(\mathbf{x}(t), \mathbf{u}(t))$$

There are variations of this framework, e.g. with discrete time, adding disturbance to the model, or with the state as a stochastic variable. However, the main effort in control engineering is not to modify this framework, but to find a mathematically tractable model, investigate its mathematical properties, and most importantly to check that it is a good enough model of the physical plant. In formulating requirements to an embedded computer system that controls the plant, one uses explicitly or implicitly some mathematical model of the plant. The computer program is in effect observing $\mathbf{x}$ through sensors and controlling $\mathbf{u}$ through actuators, and program requirements must unavoidably be formulated in terms of these or precisely related states.

The key property that one would require of a dynamical system is *stability*, i.e. if it started in a reasonable state, then it will eventually settle in a bounded region. A stronger concept is *asymptotic stability* where the system tends to an equilibrium point as time grows beyond any bounds. However, there might be many ways of choosing a **u** term such that the system is stable. Thus one can consider additional constraints on the control input and the plant state. A general formulation is to introduce a non-negative cost function K and consider the accumulated cost

$$\int_0^T K(\mathbf{x}(t), \mathbf{u}(t))\, dt$$

where T is a fixed bound, or the amortized cost $\int_0^\infty K(\mathbf{x}(t), \mathbf{u}(t)) e^{-at}\, dt$ where a is a positive discount factor. One can then try to find an optimal control which minimizes the cost.

In summary, we would expect to find stability and some sort of optimality as the generic top level requirements also for an embedded system.

Hybrid Systems. In practical engineering, it has long been recognized that a plant might have several operating modes with different characteristics. When mode changes happen infrequently, one can analyze each mode in isolation and use the conventional theory outlined above. However, if modes change rapidly, for instance when controlled by computers, it is uncertain whether the transients can be ignored. Thus there is increasing interest in theories combining the effects of discrete transitions and continuous evolutions - theories for *hybrid systems*. However, the classical questions of stability and optimal control are still central to any extended theory. We shall not detour into hybrid systems theory, but refer the interested reader to the presentation by Branicky in [1].

2.2   Duration Calculus

The usual language for control engineering is the conventional notation of mathematical analysis, and it serves its purpose very well, when used in in traditional mathematical argumentation. However, formal reasoning is rather cumbersome when all formulas contain several quantifiers over time points, state values, etc. This was the rationale for Duration Calculus which we summarize in the following.

Syntax. The syntax of Duration Calculus distinguishes (*duration*) *terms*, each one associated with a certain type, and (*duration*) *formulas*. Terms are built from names of elementary states like **x** or *Gas*, and *rigid variables* representing time independent logical variables and are closed under arithmetic and propositional operators. Examples of terms are $\neg Gas$ and $\mathbf{x} = \mathbf{0}$ (of Boolean type) and $\dot{\mathbf{x}} - c$ (of type vector of real).

Terms of type (vector of) real are also called *state expressions* and terms of Boolean type are called *state assertions*. We use f, g for typical state expressions and P, Q for typical state assertions.

Duration terms are built from $\mathbf{b}.f$ and $\mathbf{e}.f$ denoting the *initial* and *final value* of f in a given interval, and $\int f$ denoting the *integral* of f in a given interval. For a state assertion P, the integral $\int P$ is called the *duration*, because it measures the time P holds in the given interval, when the Boolean values are encoded with 0 for *false* and 1 for *true*.

Duration formulas are built from duration terms of Boolean type and closed under propositional connectives, the chop connective, and quantification over rigid variables and variables of duration terms. We use D for a typical duration formula.

Semantics. The semantics of Duration Calculus is based on an *interpretation* $\mathcal{I}$ that assigns a fixed meaning to each state name and operator symbol of the language, and a time interval $[b, e]$. For given $\mathcal{I}$ and $[b, e]$ the semantics defines what domain values duration terms and what truth values duration formulas denote. For example, $\int f$ denotes the integral $\int_b^e f(t)\,dt$, $\mathbf{b}.f$ denotes the limit from the right in b ($f(b+)$), and $\mathbf{e}.f$ denotes the limit from the left in e ($f(e-)$).

A duration formula D *holds* in $\mathcal{I}$ and $[b, e]$, abbreviated $\mathcal{I}, [b, e] \models D$, if it denotes the truth value *true* for $\mathcal{I}$ and $[b, e]$.

The boolean connectives and quantifiers have their usual meaning. The chop operator is the only modality; given duration formulas D_1 and D_2, the formula $(D_1; D_2)$ holds on the interval $[b, e]$ just when there is a chop point m such that D_1 holds on the initial subinterval $[b, m]$ and D_2 holds on the final subinterval $[m, e]$, see Fig. 2.

D is *true* in $\mathcal{I}$, abbreviated $\mathcal{I} \models D$, if $\mathcal{I}, [0, t] \models D$ for every $t \in$ *Time*. A *model* of D is an interpretation $\mathcal{I}$ which makes D true, i.e. with $\mathcal{I} \models D$. The formula D is *satisfiable* if there exists an interpretation $\mathcal{I}$ with $\mathcal{I} \models D$.

A *behaviour* is an interpretation restricted to the names of the elementary states.

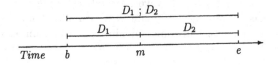

Fig. 2. Semantics of chop.

Abbreviations. The length of an interval is often used; it is the duration of the constant assertion *true* ($\int true$) which is abbreviated (ℓ), pronounced 'the length'. The property that an assertion P holds (essentially everywhere) in an interval is thus given by the atomic formula $\int P = \ell$. This holds trivially for a *point interval* of length zero, so we consider proper intervals of a positive length. The two properties are combined in the abbreviation

$$\lceil P \rceil \overset{\text{def}}{=} (\int P = \ell) \wedge (\ell > 0),$$

read as 'P holds'. We also use a variant of this notation when P holds for some time $t \geq 0$:

$$\lceil P \rceil^t \stackrel{\text{def}}{=} (\int P = \ell) \wedge (\ell = t)$$

Initialization and Invariants. Notice that when a behaviour satisfies a formula D, then D holds for every prefix $[0, t]$ of time. It means that initialization can be specified by a formula that typically has the form $\ell = 0 \vee (D_0;\ true)$, where $\ell = 0$ holds for the starting point $[0, 0]$, while D_0 gives initial constraints on the states which will hold for some arbitrarily small but positive time.

Most properties are, however, *invariants*, so we must express that they hold in any subinterval. For this purpose, the operators "somewhere" ($\diamond$) and its dual "everywhere" ($\square$) are introduced: $\diamond D \stackrel{\text{def}}{=} true;\ D;\ true$ and $\square D \stackrel{\text{def}}{=} \neg \diamond \neg D$.

Proof System. The proof system for Duration Calculus is built on four kinds of elementary laws or rules:

Math is a lifting rule that allows any result R about values or integrals which can be proven to hold for any interval using mathematical analysis (*MA*):

$$\frac{\text{MA} \vdash \forall b, e : Time \bullet b \leq e \Rightarrow R(f_1(b+), f_1(e-), \int_b^e f_1(t)\, dt, \ldots, f_n(b+), f_n(e-), \int_b^e f_n(t)\, dt)}{R(\mathbf{b}.f_1, \mathbf{e}.f_1, \int f_1, \ldots, \mathbf{b}.f_n, \mathbf{e}.f_n, \int f_n)}$$

Lifting is crucial for a smooth interface to other engineering disciplines where mathematical analysis is the standard tool.

Interval laws deal with properties of chop. This binary operator is associative and monotone w.r.t. implication:

$$\frac{D_1 \Rightarrow D_1'}{(D_1; D_2) \Rightarrow (D_1'; D_2')}$$

Monotonicity is very useful in proofs, because it allows us to drop unimportant constraints within a chopped formula.

Chop distributes over disjunction, has *false* as a zero, and a point as a unit. Chop also distributes over conjunction when the chop-points are aligned with each other: $((D_1 \wedge \ell = r); D_2) \wedge ((D_3 \wedge \ell = r); D_4) \Rightarrow ((D_1 \wedge D_3); (D_2 \wedge D_3))$. The converse follows immediately from monotonicity.

Duration-Interval laws link integrals and values over a chop. The use of integrals (durations) is really justified by the additive properties in this link.

Integral-Chop. $(\int f = v_1); (\int f = v_2) \Rightarrow \int f = v_1 + v_2$.

When the state expression f is restricted to a state assertion P with non-negative duration, the converse also holds.

Sum. $\int P = r_1 + r_2 \Leftrightarrow (\int P = r_1); (\int P = r_2)$ for non-negative r_1, r_2.

This law expresses that *Time* is dense, as also seen in the derived property: $\lceil P \rceil; \lceil P \rceil \Leftrightarrow \lceil P \rceil$.

Values. $\mathbf{b}.f = v \Leftrightarrow (\mathbf{b}.f = v)$; *true* and $\mathbf{e}.f = v \Leftrightarrow true$; $(\mathbf{e}.f = v)$.

Induction. Finite variability of state assertions is crucial for proving invariant properties. Simple induction over time is not possible, thus it is replaced by induction over discrete state changes. We do not include the general induction principle, but its most important consequence, the *P-cover* property

$$\lceil P \rceil; true \lor \lceil \neg P \rceil; true \lor \ell = 0$$

with a mirror image

$$true; \lceil P \rceil \lor true; \lceil \neg P \rceil \lor \ell = 0$$

Note that ';' binds stronger than '$\lor$' and '$\land$'.

Standard Form. In principle, constraints can be formulated using arbitrary formulas, but a standard form has turned out to be useful because it simplifies reasoning and refinement. The basis is a binary operator ($\longrightarrow$). It expresses that whenever a *pattern* given by a formula D is observed, then it is 'followed by' a *goal* state P, or stated in a negative form:

$$D \longrightarrow \lceil P \rceil \stackrel{\text{def}}{=} \Box \neg (D; \lceil \neg P \rceil)$$

This operator behaves like an implication and has a number of distributive laws. When the pattern says that an assertion holds for an interval, a *Transitive* law holds:

$$(\lceil P_1 \rceil^{t_1} \longrightarrow \lceil P_2 \rceil) \land (\lceil P_2 \rceil^{t_2} \longrightarrow \lceil P_3 \rceil) \Rightarrow (\lceil P_1 \rceil^{t_1 + t_2} \longrightarrow \lceil P_2 \land P_3 \rceil)$$

This is the law that allows a goal to be achieved through a number of intermediate states.

2.3   Requirements Analysis

Requirements are constraints on the behaviours of a system. In order to specify requirements, application specific *plant states* must be fixed. This is illustrated by the gas burner where the thermostat is modelled by the command state

Heatreq : **Bool**

while controlled states

Flame, Gas, Ignition : **Bool**

express the physical state of the flame, gas and ignition.

A particular requirement is typically a *commitment* that the design shall satisfy under certain *assumptions* about the plant. Assumptions are essentially properties which we during the design assume satisfied by the plant. In other words, they are commitments in the design of the plant as such with the role of command and controlled states reversed. Thus, we can reasonably expect that commitments and assumptions express similar properties which typically are specified by the following kinds of formulas.

Progress. The first kind specifies *progress properties*: When the command or the controlled states satisfy an assertion P, the controlled states will move to a region specified by an assertion Q within a given time t.

$$\lceil P \rceil^t \longrightarrow \lceil Q \rceil$$

These commitments are analogous to concrete stability requirements for a mode of operation that is given by P. It is easy to see that the commitments **Off** ($\lceil \neg Heatreq \rceil^{60} \longrightarrow \lceil \neg Flame \rceil$) and **On** ($\lceil Heatreq \rceil^{60} \longrightarrow \lceil Flame \rceil$) for the burner are of this form.

In fact, also the assumptions for **On** can be given this form, e.g., $\neg FlameFail$ is $\lceil Gas \wedge Flame \rceil \longrightarrow \lceil Flame \rceil$, and $\neg IgniteFail$ is $\lceil Gas \wedge Ignition \rceil^1 \longrightarrow \lceil Flame \rceil$.

A progress commitment allows a design to ignore unstable modes. If P is oscillating with a period shorter than t (An example could be the thermostat going on and off with a period shorter than 60,) the formula is trivially true, and the design may focus on other commitments. This is in contrast to the *bounded progress* property of [4] which states that occurrence of P leads to Q within t, or

$$\Box \left(\lceil P \rceil; (\ell = t) \Rightarrow \Diamond \lceil Q \rceil \right)$$

This formula requires a design to react on any occurrence of P. Any practical design must therefore at some point assume some minimal period, or alternatively weaken the commitment to express that an unstable mode is ignored: $\Box \left(\lceil P \rceil; (\ell = t) \Rightarrow \Diamond \lceil \neg P \vee Q \rceil \right)$. A formula that is equivalent to

$$\Box \left(\lceil P \rceil^t \Rightarrow \Diamond \lceil Q \rceil \right)$$

This looks like a very reasonable formulation of progress. However, it is inconvenient when the commitment says that the system should leave a mode P within time t, because taking Q to be $\neg P$ in the formula above gives a contradiction, while $\lceil P \rceil^t \longrightarrow \lceil \neg P \rceil$ expresses exactly the desired property within the progress framework.

Bounded Invariance. A progress constraint ensures that a system will move towards a goal when the current state is stable. The constraint is trivial if the current state is unstable. At the top level of requirements it is very useful to have such under-determined constraints. They absorb gracefully all questions about the behaviour of the system under unstable command inputs, because they allow any implementation. However, when components are designed or when stating assumptions, it is useful to give additional constraints that ensure orderly progress by limiting the selection of goal states.

When a progress constraint $\lceil P \rceil^t \longrightarrow \lceil Q \rceil$ is implemented by some atomic transition, it satisfies an invariant $\lceil P \rceil \longrightarrow \lceil P \vee Q \rceil$, i.e., when P is entered, it is stable until left for Q. Due to progress, it must be left at the latest after t time units. If we want to express that this invariance is time-bounded by t, we must identify the start of the P phase in the pattern:

$$(\lceil \neg P \rceil; \lceil P \rceil \wedge \ell \leq t) \longrightarrow \lceil P \vee Q \rceil$$

This formula states that a current state P for a period of t time units will either remain stable or transit to Q.

A special case of invariance keeps a current state stable. This is important in communication, because it gives other systems time to observe the current state. Unbounded invariance of P is $\lceil P \rceil \longrightarrow \lceil P \rceil$. If the system ever enters state P, then it will stay there for ever on. More useful is bounded invariance, where a system stays in P for some fixed period t:

$$(\lceil \neg P \rceil; \lceil P \rceil \wedge \ell \leq t) \longrightarrow \lceil P \rceil$$

Such an invariance ensures stability of P, as expressed in the following law,

$$(\lceil \neg P \rceil; \lceil P \rceil \wedge \ell \leq t) \longrightarrow \lceil P \rceil \Leftrightarrow \Box (\lceil \neg P \rceil; \lceil P \rceil; \lceil \neg P \rceil \Rightarrow \ell > t)$$

In order to illustrate the flavour of a proof in duration calculus, we prove the implies part by contradiction.

$\lceil \neg P \rceil; \lceil P \rceil; \lceil \neg P \rceil \wedge \ell \leq t$ $\quad \Rightarrow \{\text{Sum}\}$
$(\lceil \neg P \rceil; \lceil P \rceil; \lceil \neg P \rceil \wedge \ell \leq t); \lceil \neg P \rceil \Rightarrow \{\text{Assumption}\}$
$false$

The proof uses that the negation of $\Box (\lceil \neg P \rceil; \lceil P \rceil; \lceil \neg P \rceil \Rightarrow \ell > t)$ is the formula $\Diamond (\lceil \neg P \rceil; \lceil P \rceil; \lceil \neg P \rceil \wedge \ell \leq t)$. Using monotonicity of chop, we will have disproved this formula if we disprove the initial formula. The second step uses the Sum law to chop the last subinterval where $\neg P$ holds and to deduce that the length of subintervals is not greater than the length of the initial interval. The third step uses the assumption $(\lceil \neg P \rceil; \lceil P \rceil \wedge \ell \leq t) \longrightarrow \lceil P \rceil$ which by definition is $\Box \neg ((\lceil \neg P \rceil; \lceil P \rceil \wedge \ell \leq t); \lceil \neg P \rceil)$ which directly gives the contradiction.

Bounded invariance commitments are strong constraints that remove much non-determinism and thus design options. They should not be introduced without some consideration of the intended implementation technology. In a design, they can be refined to formulas of the same form and involving the same states, but ultimately they depend on assumption of some atomic invariance, analogous to Lipschitz conditions in a continuous model. It will thus assist a designer, if bounded invariance constraints are replaced by the weaker critical duration constraints, discussed in a following.

Bounded Critical Durations. These formulas constrain the duration of some critical controlled state. These states are typically intermediate states which are unavoidable; nevertheless they should not endure. Another interpretation of a critical duration constraint on a state P is to see it as approximate stability of the non-critical state $\neg P$.

A critical duration constraint defines the duration of a critical state P. This state shall only have a duration of c within at most t time units:

$$(\textstyle\int P > c \wedge \ell \leq t) \longrightarrow \lceil \neg P \rceil$$

For nontrivial constraints, the parameters c and t satisfy $0 \leq c \leq t$.

Another formulation is the following law.

$$((\textstyle\int P > c \wedge \ell \leq t) \longrightarrow \lceil \neg P \rceil) \Leftrightarrow \Box\,(\ell \leq t \Rightarrow \textstyle\int P \leq c)$$

Only-if is trivial. The implies is by contradiction.

$$
\begin{array}{ll}
\ell \leq t \wedge \int P > c & \Rightarrow \{\text{Sum}\} \\
\ell \leq t \wedge ((\ell \leq t \wedge \int P > c);\ \int P > 0) & \Rightarrow \{\text{Finite Variability}\} \\
\ell \leq t \wedge ((\ell \leq t \wedge \int P > c);\ \Diamond\lceil P \rceil) & \Rightarrow \{\text{Definition}\} \\
\ell \leq t \wedge ((\ell \leq t \wedge \int P > c);\ true;\ \lceil P \rceil;\ true) & \Rightarrow \{\text{Sum}\} \\
(\ell \leq t \wedge \int P > c);\ \lceil P \rceil;\ true & \Rightarrow \{\text{Assumption}\} \\
false &
\end{array}
$$

The first step applies the Sum law and a simple property of reals: If $r > c$ then there exists positive r_1, r_2 such that $r_1 > c$ and $r_1 + r_2 = r$. The second step appeals to the finite variability underlying induction: If P has a positive duration, then there is at least one subinterval where P holds. The fourth step uses the global length constraint and the Sum law to combine the first and second subinterval. The final step use that the assumption is violated on the first subintervals. The proof is completed using that $false$ is a zero for chop.

A critical duration constraint ensures that for a critical state P the proportional upper bound is c/t in the limit.

$$((\textstyle\int P > c) \wedge \ell \leq t) \longrightarrow \lceil \neg P \rceil \Rightarrow \Box\,(\textstyle\int P \leq (c/t) \cdot \ell + c)$$

The mean value of the critical duration ($\int P / \ell$) thus tends to c/t. A critical duration constraint is like an optimality constraint in dynamical systems; in a design it is refined to more concrete constraints with instability of the critical state and stability of its complement.

3   Design

Requirements are in the ProCoS approach the starting point for the design. However, another constraint on the design is a desire for a systematic decomposition of the embedded computer system. A standard paradigm is given in Figure 3

Environment

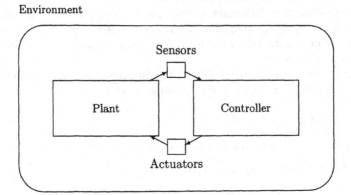

Fig. 3. Structure of an Embedded System

with sensors, actuators and the controller with its program. In the following we assume that components communicate by observing each others states. We discuss the interface provided by sensor and actuator components; but we will not cover paradigms for intelligent sensors and actuators that integrate knowledge of the plant model. Examples that illustrate such aspects are found in the design for the Steam Boiler case study [12].

3.1 Sensors

A sensor is characterized by its ability to detect that the plant is in some specific state, and it communicates this fact to the control program. We shall start with a description of a general sensor that transmits a value from the plant state to the controller state. The value of the plant state X is determined by a given formula $D(x)$ parameterized by a rigid variable x. The controller state ranges over a phase π where the sensor is enabled, and phases π_x which are entered when $D(x)$ is observed during the π phase.

Progress: When $D(x)$ holds for δ in phase π, the phase is left for the continuation phase π_x:

$$\forall x \bullet (D(x) \wedge \lceil \pi \rceil^\delta) \longrightarrow \lceil \pi_x \rceil$$

Selection: When $D(x)$ is stable, phase π moves only to π_x.

$$\lceil \neg \pi \rceil; (\lceil \pi \rceil \wedge D(x)) \longrightarrow \lceil \pi \vee \pi_x \rceil$$

The selection constraint is essential for the further use of the value of x in the continuation phase. Without this constraint a sensor might just move rapidly from π with an arbitrary value.

A common case is a guard sensor that distinguishes between a finite set of mutually exclusive plant modes $P_1, \ldots, P_n$ and ensures transition to corresponding continuation phases $\pi_1, \ldots, \pi_n$. If the set of modes do not cover the plant state, it is convenient to specify that the sensor will remain enabled until one of the modes occur. The commitments of a guard sensor in phase π are:

Progress: When P_i holds for δ in phase π, the phase is left.

$$\bigwedge_{i=1}^{n} \lceil P_i \wedge \pi \rceil^{\delta} \longrightarrow \lceil \neg \pi \rceil$$

Selection: The phase π will under P_i move to π_i only.

$$\bigwedge_{i=1}^{n} \lceil \neg \pi \rceil; \lceil \pi \wedge P_i \rceil \longrightarrow \lceil \pi \vee \pi_i \rceil$$

Stability: The default mode $P' = \bigwedge_{i=1}^{n} \neg P_i$ freezes the π phase.

$$\lceil \neg \pi \rceil; \lceil \pi \wedge P' \rceil \longrightarrow \lceil \pi \rceil$$

In general, consistency is not preserved if sensor commitments on the same phase π are combined, because one sensor may want to be stable while another may decide to progress. One shall therefore avoid introducing more than one sensor in an elementary phase. If more are needed, decomposition of the phase is generally required.

3.2   Actuators

An actuator is characterized by its ability to move the plant to a state determined by the controller. It is thus the dual of a sensor. We shall start with a description of a general actuator that transmits a value from the controller state to the plant state:

Consider controller phases π_x and a state assertion $P(x)$ over the plant state which both are dependent on a rigid variable x. An $P(x)$ actuator with reaction time δ and enabled in phases π_x is given by:

Progress: When the phase π_x has held for δ, the plant state $P(x)$ is established.

$$\forall x \bullet \lceil \pi_x \rceil^{\delta} \longrightarrow \lceil P(x) \rceil$$

Framing: If the π_x phase is reentered and $P(x)$ still holds, it continues to hold.

$$\forall x \bullet \lceil \neg \pi_x \rceil; \lceil \pi_x \wedge P(x) \rceil \longrightarrow \lceil P(x) \rceil$$

The framing property specifies that the actuator avoids unnecessary transients in the plant state. It will ultimately reduce to an assumption about time bounded stability of a plant state. The unbounded framing can be refined to bounded framing (a bounded invariance) $(\lceil \neg \pi_x \rceil; \lceil \pi_x \wedge P(x) \rceil \wedge \ell \leq \delta) \longrightarrow \lceil P(x) \rceil$ and synchronization $\lceil \pi_x \rceil^{\delta} \longrightarrow \lceil P(x) \rceil$.

Actuator commitments over the same phase combine when they control disjoint plant states.

3.3 Control Program

The design for the controller program is essentially a specification of a timed automaton, The program design is given in terms of the so called "implementables" which are formulas that reflect properties of timed automata. When $\pi, \pi_1, \ldots$ denote states or *phases* of a control program, and $\varphi, \varphi_1, \ldots$ denote combinations of sensor/actuator states or phase states, the implementable forms are:

Sequencing: $\lceil \pi \rceil \longrightarrow \lceil \pi \vee \pi_1 \vee \cdots \vee \pi_n \rceil$, where $n = 0$ means that the program is stuck in phase π, while $n > 1$ means that there is a choice of a successor phase. Sequencing constraints specify non-deterministic transitions of an untimed automaton.

Progress: $\lceil \pi \wedge \varphi \rceil^c \longrightarrow \lceil \neg \pi \rceil$, where the phase π is left at the latest when φ holds for c time units. A progress constraint specifies an upper bound on a transition. Note that c is an upper bound, the transition may be taken earlier, if selection allows it.

Progress also includes *active stability* of a state: $\lceil \pi \wedge \varphi \rceil^c \longrightarrow \lceil \pi \rceil$.

Selection: $(\lceil \neg \pi \rceil; \lceil \pi \wedge \varphi \rceil \wedge \ell \leq c) \longrightarrow \lceil \pi \vee \pi_1 \vee \ldots \vee \pi_n \rceil$, where the sequencing of state π is constrained under the condition φ for c time units (or forever, if the time-bound is omitted). If $n = 0$ the formula defines conditional, time-bounded *invariance* of the state. Note that c is a lower bound, an implementation may keep the selection open for a longer time, but not for a shorter.

Synchronization: $\lceil \pi_1 \vee \ldots \vee \pi_n \rceil^c \longrightarrow \lceil \varphi \rceil$, where the combined state $\pi_1 \vee \ldots \vee \pi_n$ will cause φ to hold after c time units. Note that c is an upper bound, an implementation is allowed to cause φ sooner but not later.

Framing: $(\lceil \neg \pi \rceil; \lceil \pi \wedge \varphi \rceil \wedge \ell \leq c) \longrightarrow \lceil \varphi \rceil$, is dual to selection. It is a commitment that the state φ will remain stable for c time units if it is present when π is entered.

These forms define a timed automaton which observes (reads) plant states or states of other automata through the φ conditions in progress and selection forms, and which changes control and plant states through synchronization and framing.

If controlled states are kept disjoint then conjunction of implementables corresponds to parallel composition of automata.

3.4 Controller Design

In ProCoS, refinement by phase splitting is pursued. We shall illustrate it by a cyclic controller.

For a finite collection of exclusive modes $P_1, \ldots, P_n$, a detection phase π and continuation phases $\pi_1, \ldots, \pi_n$, a cyclic controller with a δ delay is specified by

1. Sequencing: The selection phase π is followed by the continuation phases.

$$\lceil \pi \rceil \longrightarrow \lceil \pi \vee \bigvee_{j=1}^{n} \pi_j \rceil$$

2. Sequencing: The continuation phases return to the selection phase.

$$\bigwedge_{j=1}^{n} \lceil \pi_j \rceil \longrightarrow \lceil \pi_j \vee \pi \rceil$$

3. Progress: When P_i holds for δ in the selection phase, it is left.

$$\bigwedge_{i=1}^{n} \lceil \pi \wedge P_i \rceil^{\delta} \longrightarrow \lceil \neg \pi \rceil$$

4. Progress: When P_i holds for δ in π_j, with $j \neq i$, it is left.

$$\bigwedge_{i,j=1}^{n} (i \neq j) \Rightarrow (\lceil \pi_j \wedge P_i \rceil^{\delta} \longrightarrow \lceil \neg \pi_j \rceil)$$

5. Selection: The phase π_i is selected under P_i.

$$\bigwedge_{i=1}^{n} (\lceil \neg \pi \rceil; \lceil \pi \wedge P_i \rceil \wedge \ell \leq \delta) \longrightarrow \lceil \pi \vee \pi_i \rceil$$

6. Selection: The phase π_i will be δ-stable under P_i.

$$\bigwedge_{i=1}^{n} (\lceil \neg \pi_i \rceil; \lceil \pi_i \wedge P_i \rceil \wedge \ell \leq \delta) \longrightarrow \lceil \pi_i \rceil$$

7. Progress: The phase π_i is maintained by P_i.

$$\bigwedge_{i=1}^{n} \lceil \pi_i \wedge P_i \rceil^{\delta} \longrightarrow \lceil \pi_i \rceil$$

A cyclic controller implements the progress constraint

$$\lceil (\pi \vee \bigvee_{j=1}^{n} \pi_j) \wedge P_i \rceil^{3 \cdot \delta} \longrightarrow \lceil \pi_i \rceil$$

for an arbitrary index i. Within three delay periods control will be in the phase corresponding to a stable external state. The worst case occurs when the selection phase is left after almost a δ-period for another continuation phase (1,3). Within δ, control returns to the selection phase (2,4). The final δ-period ensures transition to the correct phase (1,5,3), where it remains (6,7).

This controller can be extended with suitable actuators enabled in the continuation phases such that the *Transitive* law ensures a correct implementation of progress commitments.

In the ProCoS case studies, designs were made more complex by a distributed framework with CSP-like channels. It required a major effort by Schenke [13] to develop systematic transformation rules from the level of implementables to this framework.

4   Implementation

At the level of programs, the timing constraints on the control program states are translated into explicit timing constructs in the programming language PL. A lower bound is translated into an delay statement of the form DELAY r, where r is a non-negative real constant. It is easily implemented by a conventional timer in the hardware, and acts functionally as a skip-statement.

An upper bound on a program segment P is specified by prefixing P with UPPERBOUND r, where r is a non-negative real constant. This is taken to be an assertion to be checked by the compiler. It must check that the code generated for P does not use more than r time units to execute. Time which is spent in an idle state during a delay is not included. It cannot in any feasible way be checked by compilation.

A check that upper bounds are satisfied by the binary code is not trivial. It requires quite an effort to prove correct compilation, but this story is better told in [8].

5   Conclusion

We have traced real-time properties from constraints on plant states through specifications for sensors, actuators and control programs to simple delay statements and upper bounds on the execution of code segments. The properties have been formulated using a few stereotypical forms. In requirements we have used bounded progress and bounded critical duration and occasionally bounded invariance which all can be expressed within the standard form for duration calculus formulas. We have outlined, how specialized forms of bounded progress and bounded invariance are used to specify constraints on timed automata that define sensor, actuator and control program properties.

In the exposition we have followed the ProCoS development process and its refinement view. We still consider the standard forms for requirements generally useful. This has been borne out by a considerable number of case studies, and is supported by the analogy to similar properties of dynamical systems. We have sometimes been asked: "why exactly these formulas?" And the honest answer is that these are the forms which we can systematically decompose and check. This is, however, not different from the situation with dynamical systems in general. It is often more efficient to model the problem reasonably well in a known framework instead of having an extremely precise model within an unexplored mathematical universe.

With respect to the design activity we are less certain that direct refinement from requirements is an effective approach. In some of the case studies there has been an amount of re-engineering taking place. The design, in the form of state machines, has been rather obvious, and the refinement has really been a way of presenting a verification. Perhaps it is more fruitful to start from the middle with a design and then check requirements, possibly even using model checking tools. Another promising approach is to work within a cyclic controller framework.

This approach is well illustrated by the work by Dierks on PLC-automata [2]. An extension to such a framework could integrate model checking with proof strategies for standard forms in a development tool.

A remaining concern is the link to the code and to a run time system. Verified compilers and compilers that check scheduling information are not common; programming language technology has been geared more towards the large market for general programming than the niche of embedded systems. Perhaps the problem will be solved by integrated development environments that translate directly from state machines to binary code, avoiding all the complications of general purpose programming languages.

ProCoS is now in the past, but it has left the challenge to develop an engineering practise for embedded systems; a practise that is based on mathematically sound techniques and linking top level requirements to the computer system at the bottom. This was the vision of the ProCoS 'fathers: Dines Bjørner, Tony Hoare and Hans Langmaack.

Acknowledgment. We thank Tony Hoare and Ernst-Rüdiger Olderog for instructive comments on previous drafts of this paper.

References

1. M. S. Branicky. Analyzing and synthesizing hybrid control systems. In G. Rozenberg and F. W. Vaandrager, editors, *Embedded Systems*, volume 1494 of *LNCS*, pages 74–113. Springer-Verlag, 1998.
2. H. Dierks. PLC-Automata: A New Class of Implementable Real-Time Automata. In M. Bertran and T. Rus, editors, *Transformation-Based Reactive Systems Development (ARTS'97)*, volume 1231 of *LNCS*, pages 111–125. Springer-Verlag, 1997.
3. M. R. Hansen and Zhou Chaochen. Duration calculus: Logical foundations. *Formal Aspects of Computing*, 9(3):283–33, 1997.
4. T. A. Henzinger, Z. Manna, and A. Pnueli. Timed transition systems. In J. W. de Bakker, C. Huizing, W.-P. de Roever, and G. Rozenberg, editors, *Real-Time: Theory in Practice, REX Workshop*, volume 600 of *LNCS*, pages 226–252. Springer-Verlag, 1992.
5. H. Langmaack. The ProCoS approach to correct systems. *Real-Time Systems*, 13:253–275, 1997.
6. H. Langmaack and A. P. Ravn. The ProCoS project: Provably correct systems. In J. Bowen, editor, *Towards Verified Systems*, volume 2 of *Real-Time Safety Critical Systems*, chapter Appendix B. Elsevier, 1994.
7. Z. Liu. Specification and verification in dc. In Mathai Joseph, editor, *Mathematics of Dependable Systems*, Intnl. Series in Computer Science, chapter 7, pages 182–228. Prentice Hall, 1996.
8. M. Müller-Olm. *Modular Compiler Verification*, volume 1283 of LNCS. Springer-Verlag, 1997.
9. E-R. Olderog, A. P. Ravn, and J. U. Skakkebæk. Refining system requirements to program specifications. In C. Heitmeyer and D. Mandrioli, editors, *Formal Methods in Real-Time Systems*, Trends in Software-Engineering, chapter 5, pages 107–134. Wiley, 1996.

10. A. P. Ravn, T. J. Eriksen, M. Holdgaard, and H. Rischel. Engineering of real-time systems with an experiment in hybrid control. In G. Rozenberg and F. W. Vaandrager, editors, *Embedded Systems*, volume 1494 of *LNCS*, pages 316–352. Springer-Verlag, 1998.
11. A.P. Ravn, H. Rischel, and K. M. Hansen. Specifying and verifying requirements of real-time systems. *IEEE Trans. Softw. Eng.*, 19(1):41–55, 1993.
12. H. Rischel, J. Cuellar, S. Mørk, A. P. Ravn, and I. Wildgruber. Development of safety-critical real-time systems. In M. Bartošek, J. Staudek, and J. Wiedermann, editors, *SOFSEM'95: Theory and Practice of Informatics*, volume 1012 of *LNCS*, pages 206–235. Springer-Verlag, 1995.
13. M. Schenke and A. P. Ravn. Refinement from a control problem to programs. In J. R. Abrial, E. Börger, and H. Langmaack, editors, *Formal Methods for Industrial Applications: Specifying and Programming the Steam Boiler Control*, volume 1165 of *LNCS*, pages 403–427. Springer-Verlag, 1996.
14. Chaochen Zhou, C. A. R. Hoare, and A. P. Ravn. A calculus of durations. *Information Proc. Letters*, 40(5), Dec. 1991.

Monotonicity in Calculational Proofs

David Gries

Computer Science, Cornell University, gries@cs.cornell.edu
Computer Science, University of Georgia, gries@cs.uga.edu

Abstract. We discuss the use of weakening and strengthening steps in calculational proofs. We present a metatheorem concerning monotonicity of positions in a formula that should have a more prominent place in the teaching of such proofs and give supporting examples.

Introduction

We are dealing with a calculational predicate logic with equality, using the notation of [3]. The universal quantification $(\forall x \mid R : P)$ is equivalent to the more standard $\forall x.R \Rightarrow P$ and the existential quantification $(\exists x \mid R : P)$ is equivalent to $\exists x.R \wedge P$. R is called the range of the quantification. Using this notation allows us to have a unified notation for expressing all sorts of quantifications, including summations and products.

A few more notational conventions: The operator $\equiv$ denotes equality on booleans; it is more traditionally represented by symbol $\Leftrightarrow$. And $f.x$ denotes the application of function f to argument x.

Now for the reason for this little paper. In making a calculational step like

$$(\forall x \mid : P \wedge R)$$
$$\Rightarrow \quad \langle \text{Weakening } P \Rightarrow P \vee Q \rangle$$
$$(\forall x \mid : (P \vee Q) \wedge R)$$

we are implicitly using the fact that the occurrence of variable P that is being replaced is in a monotonic position —weakening that position weakens the whole formula. To make the proof more precise and complete, the fact should be made explicit. We use a long-known but basically forgotten theorem for this purpose and show how it is used in several calculational proofs.

Monotonicity

A function f is *monotonic* in its argument if $x \Rightarrow y$ implies $f.x \Rightarrow f.y$ (for all x, y). It is *antimonotonic* if $x \Rightarrow y$ implies $f.x \Leftarrow f.y$ (for all x, y).

The following facts are well-known: $\vee$ and $\wedge$ are monotonic in each of their operands, negation is antimonotonic in its operand, $\Rightarrow$ is monotonic in its consequent and antimonotonic in its antecedent, $(\forall x \mid R : P)$ is monotonic in

E.-R. Olderog, B. Steffen (Eds.): Correct System Design, LNCS 1710, pp. 79–85, 1999.
© Springer-Verlag Berlin Heidelberg 1999

P but antimonotonic in R, and $(\exists x \mid R : P)$ is monotonic in both P and R. Formally, we have:

Monotonic $\lor$: $(P \Rightarrow Q) \Rightarrow (P \lor R \Rightarrow Q \lor R)$ (1)

Monotonic $\land$: $(P \Rightarrow Q) \Rightarrow (P \land R \Rightarrow Q \land R)$

Antimonotonic $\neg$: $(P \Rightarrow Q) \Rightarrow (\neg P \Leftarrow \neg Q)$ (2)

Monotonic consequent: $(P \Rightarrow Q) \Rightarrow ((R \Rightarrow P) \Rightarrow (R \Rightarrow Q))$

Antimonotonic antecedent: $(P \Rightarrow Q) \Rightarrow ((P \Rightarrow R) \Leftarrow (Q \Rightarrow R))$

Antimonotonic $\forall$**-range:** $(P \Rightarrow Q) \Rightarrow ((\forall x \mid P : R) \Leftarrow (\forall x \mid Q : R))$

Monotonic $\forall$**-body:** $(P \Rightarrow Q) \Rightarrow ((\forall x \mid R : P) \Rightarrow (\forall x \mid R : Q))$

Monotonic $\exists$**-range:** $(P \Rightarrow Q) \Rightarrow ((\exists x \mid P : R) \Rightarrow (\exists x \mid Q : R))$

Monotonic $\exists$**-body:** $(P \Rightarrow Q) \Rightarrow ((\exists x \mid R : P) \Rightarrow (\exists x \mid R : Q))$ (3)

But which of the following two formulas is valid, if either?

$$(\forall x \mid \neg P : S) \Rightarrow (\forall x \mid \neg(P \lor Q) : S)$$
$$(\forall x \mid \neg P : S) \Leftarrow (\forall x \mid \neg(P \lor Q) : S)$$

The answer is given by the following definition and theorem. Throughout, E_P^z denotes non-capture-avoiding substitution of free variable z by P in formula E. Also, $E[z := P]$ denotes capture-avoiding substitution: $E[z := P]$ is a copy of expression E in which all occurrences of variable z have been replaced by expression P, with names of dummies (bound variables) being first replaced to avoid capture.

Definition 1. *Consider an occurrence of free variable z in a formula E (but not within an operand of $\equiv$). The position of z within E is called* monotonic *if it is nested within an even number of negations, antecedents, and ranges of universal quantifications; otherwise, it is* antimonotonic.

Theorem 2. Metatheorem Monotonicity. *Suppose $P \Rightarrow Q$ is a theorem. Let expression E contain exactly one occurrence of free variable z. Then:*

    (a) Provided the position of z in E is monotonic,
       $E_P^z \Rightarrow E_Q^z$ *is a theorem.*
    (b) Provided the position of z in E is antimonotonic,
       $E_P^z \Leftarrow E_Q^z$ *is a theorem.*

[Note: Actually, E can contain more than one occurrence of z, as long as all its positions are monotonic or all its positions are antimonotonic.]

We can state (a) and (b) as inference rules:

Monotonicity: Provided z's position in E is monotonic,   (4)

$$P \Rightarrow Q \quad \longrightarrow \quad E_P^z \Rightarrow E_Q^z$$

Antimonotonicity: Provided z's position in E is antimonotonic,   (5)

$$P \Rightarrow Q \quad \longrightarrow \quad E_P^z \Leftarrow E_Q^z$$

Sketch of proof of (2). The proof is by induction on the structure of expression E. One can reduce the case analysis by first manipulating E so that one has to deal only with formulas that contain variables, constants, negations, disjunctions in which z is not in the second operand, and existential quantifications with range *true*. Thus, perform the following steps, in order:

- Replace $(\forall x \mid F1 : F2)$ by $\neg(\exists x \mid F1 : \neg F2)$.
- Replace $(\exists x \mid F1 : F2)$ by $(\exists x \mid : F1 \wedge F2)$.
- Replace $F1 \not\Leftarrow F2$ by $\neg(F1 \Leftarrow F2)$.
- Replace $F1 \Leftarrow F2$ by $F2 \Rightarrow F1$.
- Replace $F1 \not\Rightarrow F2$ by $\neg(F1 \Rightarrow F2)$.
- Replace $F1 \Rightarrow F2$ by $\neg F1 \vee F2$.
- Replace $F1 \wedge F2$ by $\neg(\neg F1 \vee \neg F2)$.
- If z is in the second operand $F2$ of $F1 \vee F2$, replace $F1 \vee F2$ by $F2 \vee F1$.

These manipulations change neither the monotonicity of the position of z nor the truth value of the formula. Now, comes a straightforward proof by induction on the structure of the more restricted expressions E, which will rely on monotonic/antimonotonic properties (1), (2), and (3).   □

Incidently, when teaching calculational logic and induction, this inductive proof is a nice exercise for students.

A Convention for Citing Monotonicity

In a weakening/strengthening step of a calculation, the hint should explain why the step is sound. Here is a simple example, where it is presumed that Weakening was proved earlier.

$$P$$
$$\Rightarrow \quad \langle \text{Weakening, } P \Rightarrow P \vee Q \rangle$$
$$P \vee Q$$

But in the following example, the hint is not precise. This is because the soundness of the step depends not only on Weakening but also on Monotonic $\wedge$.

$$P \wedge R$$
$$\Rightarrow \quad \langle \text{Weakening, } P \Rightarrow P \vee Q \rangle$$
$$(P \vee Q) \wedge R$$

We seek a uniform way of substantiating steps like the above one. Rather than rely directly on all the individual monotonicity properties (1)–(3), it is easier to rely on inference rules (4) and (5), which can be used to substantiate all such weakening/strengthening steps.

We suggest the use of "Monotonicity:" and "Antimonotonicity:" to show reliance on these inference rules, as shown below. The word "Monotonic" suggests that a monotonic position is being replaced; "Antimonotonic" suggests that an antimonotonic position is being replaced. In the examples given below, to the right we have shown how the formulas can be rewritten in terms of variable z, so that the use of the inference rules is more easily seen.

$(\forall x \mid: P \wedge R)$ $\qquad\qquad$ $(\forall x \mid: z \wedge R)_P^z$

$\Rightarrow$ $\quad$ $\langle$Monotonicity: Weakening $P \Rightarrow P \vee Q\rangle$

$(\forall x \mid: (P \vee Q) \wedge R)$ $\qquad\qquad$ $(\forall x \mid: z \wedge R)_{P \vee Q}^z$

$\neg(\forall x \mid \neg P \wedge R : S)$ $\qquad\qquad$ $\neg(\forall x \mid \neg z \wedge R : S)_P^z$

$\Leftarrow$ $\quad$ $\langle$Antimonotonicity: Weakening $P \Rightarrow P \vee Q\rangle$

$\neg(\forall x \mid \neg(P \vee Q) \wedge R : S)$ $\qquad\qquad$ $\neg(\forall x \mid \neg z \wedge R : S)_{P \vee Q}^z$

Examples of the Use of Monotonicity

When dealing with theorems of propositional logic, monotonicity is not needed at all; as [3] shows, all proofs can be done easily without weakening/strengthening steps. However, for predicate logic proofs, weakening/strengthening steps are very useful, as the following examples show. These calculational proofs, using monotonicity/antimonotonicity, are surprisingly simple, especially compared to similar proofs in other proof systems. Each step of the proof is guided by the shapes of the current formula and goal. The theorems used in these proofs are from [3].

Proving Instantiation

In [3], the One-point rule is an axiom and Instantiation is a theorem:

$\qquad$ **One-point rule:** $\;$ Provided x does not occur free in E, $\qquad\qquad$ (6)
$$(\forall x \mid x = E : P) \equiv P[x := E]$$
$\qquad$ **Instantiation:** $\;$ $(\forall x \mid: P) \Rightarrow P[x := E]$

We prove Instantiation. Let z be a variable that does not occur free in P or E. We have:

$(\forall x \mid true : P)$

$=$ $\quad$ $\langle$Dummy renaming $-z$ not free in $P\rangle$

$(\forall z \mid true : P[x := z])$

$\Rightarrow$ $\quad$ $\langle$Antimonotonicity: $true \Leftarrow z = E\rangle$

$(\forall z \mid z = E : P[x := z])$

$=$ $\quad$ $\langle$One-point rule$\rangle$

$P[x := z][z := E]$

$=$ $\quad$ $\langle$Property of textual substitution $-z$ is not free in $P\rangle$

$P[x := E]$

Mortality of Socrates

This example concerns proving English arguments sound by formalizing them and proving their formalizations. Consider the following statement.

$\qquad$ All men are mortal. Socrates is a man. Therefore, Socrates is mortal.

We introduce two predicates.

$man.m$:   person m is a man.
$mortal.m$:   person m is mortal.

We formalize the statement as follows, with S standing for Socrates, and prove the formalization. The proof relies on inference rule Modus ponens, $Q \Rightarrow P$, $Q \longrightarrow P$.

$$(\forall m \mid : man.m \Rightarrow mortal.m) \land man.S \Rightarrow mortal.S$$

$\qquad (\forall m \mid : man.m \Rightarrow mortal.m) \land man.S$
$\Rightarrow \qquad \langle \text{Monotonicity: Instantiation, with } S \text{ for } m \rangle$
$\qquad (man.S \Rightarrow mortal.S) \land man.S$
$\Rightarrow \qquad \langle \text{Modus ponens} \rangle$
$\qquad mortal.S$

Here is a second proof, which transforms the whole formula into a known theorem.

$\qquad (\forall m \mid : man.m \Rightarrow mortal.m) \land man.S \Rightarrow mortal.S$
$\Leftarrow \qquad \langle \text{Antimonotonicity: Instantiation, with } S \text{ for } m \rangle$
$\qquad (man.S \Rightarrow mortal.S) \land man.S \Rightarrow mortal.S \qquad$ —Modus ponens

Having a Heart

Now consider the English statement:

> None but those with hearts can love. Some liars are heartless. Therefore, some liars cannot love.

Using $hh.p$ for "p has a heart", $cl.p$ for "p can love", and $li.p$ for "p is a liar", we formalize this as

$$(\forall p \mid : cl.p \Rightarrow hh.p) \land (\exists p \mid : li.p \land \neg hh.p) \Rightarrow (\exists p \mid : li.p \land \neg cl.p) \quad .$$

We prove this formula.

$\qquad (\forall p \mid : cl.p \Rightarrow hh.p) \land (\exists p \mid : li.p \land \neg hh.p)$
$= \qquad \langle \text{Distributivity of } \land \text{ over } \exists \text{ —to get}$
$\qquad\qquad \text{same outer quantification as in consequent} \rangle$
$\qquad (\exists p \mid : (\forall p \mid : cl.p \Rightarrow hh.p) \land li.p \land \neg hh.p)$
$\Rightarrow \qquad \langle \text{Monotonicity: Instantiation} \rangle$
$\qquad (\exists p \mid : (cl.p \Rightarrow hh.p) \land li.p \land \neg hh.p)$
$= \qquad \langle \text{Contrapositive} \rangle$
$\qquad (\exists p \mid : (\neg hh.p \Rightarrow \neg cl.p) \land li.p \land \neg hh.p)$
$\Rightarrow \qquad \langle \text{Monotonicity: Modus ponens} \rangle$
$\qquad (\exists p \mid : \neg cl.p \land li.p)$

EA Implies AE

In [4], Carroll Morgan derives a nice proof of

$$(\exists x \mid : (\forall y \mid : P)) \;\Rightarrow\; (\forall y \mid : (\exists x \mid : P)) \quad . \tag{7}$$

Wim Feijen [2] presents convincing heuristics for the development of the proof. Here is the proof. Note that it uses Metatheorem Monotonicity, twice, although neither Morgan nor Feijen cite it.

$\qquad (\exists x \mid : (\forall y \mid : P))$
$\Rightarrow \qquad \langle$Monotonicity: $R \Rightarrow (\forall y \mid : R)$, prov. y doesn't occur free in R
$\qquad\qquad$ —introduce the necessary universal quantification over $y \rangle$
$\qquad (\forall y \mid : (\exists x \mid : (\forall y \mid : P)))$
$\Rightarrow \qquad \langle$Monotonicity: Instantiation —Eliminate universal quantification$\rangle$
$\qquad (\forall y \mid : (\exists x \mid : P))$

When we generalize (7) to allow ranges other than *true*, the proof becomes more complicated. Below, we prove:

$$\text{Provided } x \text{ not free in } Q \text{ and } y \text{ not free in } R, \tag{8}$$
$$(\exists x \mid R : (\forall y \mid Q : P)) \;\Rightarrow\; (\forall y \mid Q : (\exists x \mid R : P))$$

Since x does not occur free in the consequent, by Metatheorem Witness (9.30) of [3], (8) can be proved by proving instead

$$R \wedge (\forall y \mid Q : P) \;\Rightarrow\; (\forall y \mid Q : (\exists x \mid R : P)) \quad ,$$

which we now do:

$\qquad R \wedge (\forall y \mid Q : P)$
$\Rightarrow \qquad \langle \wedge \text{ over } \forall, \text{ since } y \text{ not free in } R \rangle$
$\qquad (\forall y \mid Q : R \wedge P)$
$\Rightarrow \qquad \langle$Monotonicity: $\exists$-Introduction$\rangle$
$\qquad (\forall y \mid Q : (\exists x \mid : R \wedge P))$
$= \qquad \langle$Trading$\rangle$
$\qquad (\forall y \mid Q : (\exists x \mid R : P))$

Discussion

Monotonicity properties (1)–(3), as well as Metatheorem Monotonicity, are well-known. They can be found, in one guise or another, in several texts on logic. But the two major books that deal with the calculational approach do a bad job of explaining how monotonicity/antimonotonicity is to be used. On page 61 of [1], Dijkstra and Scholten discuss the monotonic properties of negation and implication. But they don't state the general theorem (2) and they don't give a convention for indicating its use. On page 93 of [1], a hint explicitly states the use of monotonicity of $\wedge$ and $\exists$ in a weakening step, but on pages 73 and

77, monotonicity of ∀-body is used without mention. We think the authors just didn't anticipate the frequent use of monotonicity and the problem readers would have with it if it were not well explained.

Gries and Schneider [3] also don't treat montonicity well, and this has resulted in confusion among students about monotonicity and its use. The next edition of [3] is expected to use the approach of this note in order to eliminate the confusion.

The message of this little article is meant to be the apparent simplicity and brevity of many proofs in the calculational system when the right tools, like metatheorem Monotonicity, are available.

Acknowledgements

Thanks to an anonymous referee, who helped improve this presentation.

References

1. Edsger W. Dijkstra and Carel S. Scholten. *Predicate Calculus and Program Semantics*. Springer Verlag, New York, 1990.
2. Wim H.J. Feijen. ∃∀ ⇒ ∀∃ . WHJ189, September 1994.
3. David Gries and Fred B. Schneider. *A Logical Approach to Discrete Math*. Springer Verlag, New York 1993.
4. Carroll Morgan. Email communications in September 1995.

Part II

Programming

The Alma Project, or How First-Order Logic Can Help Us in Imperative Programming

Krzysztof R. Apt[1,2] and Andrea Schaerf[3]

[1] CWI
P.O. Box 94079, 1090 GB Amsterdam, The Netherlands
K.R.Apt@cwi.nl
[2] Dept. of Mathematics, Computer Science, Physics & Astronomy University of Amsterdam, The Netherlands
[3] Dipartimento di Ingegneria Elettrica, Gestionale e Meccanica
Università di Udine
via delle Scienze 208, I-33100 Udine, Italy
schaerf@uniud.it

Abstract. The aim of the Alma project is the design of a strongly typed constraint programming language that combines the advantages of logic and imperative programming.

The first stage of the project was the design and implementation of Alma-0, a small programming language that provides a support for declarative programming within the imperative programming framework. It is obtained by extending a subset of Modula-2 by a small number of features inspired by the logic programming paradigm.

In this paper we discuss the rationale for the design of Alma-0, the benefits of the resulting hybrid programming framework, and the current work on adding constraint processing capabilities to the language. In particular, we discuss the role of the logical and customary variables, the interaction between the constraint store and the program, and the need for lists.

1 Introduction

1.1 Background on Designing Programming Languages

The design of programming languages is one of the most hotly debated topics in computer science. Such debates are often pretty chaotic because of the lack of universally approved criteria for evaluating programming languages. In fact, the success or failure of a language proposal often does not say much about the language itself but rather about such accompanying factors as: the quality and portability of the implementation, the possibility of linking the language with the currently reigning programming language standard (for instance, C), the existing support within the industry, presence of an attractive development environment, the availability on the most popular platforms, etc.

The presence of these factors often blurs the situation because in evaluating a language proposal one often employs, usually implicitly, an argument that the

E.-R. Olderog, B. Steffen (Eds.): Correct System Design, LNCS 1710, pp. 89–113, 1999.
© Springer-Verlag Berlin Heidelberg 1999

"market" will eventually pick up the best product. Such a reasoning would be correct if the market forces in computing were driven by the desire to improve the quality of programming. But from an economic point of view such aspects as compatibility and universal availability are far more important than quality.

Having this in mind we would like to put the above factors in a proper perspective and instead concentrate on the criteria that have been used in academia and which appeal directly to one of the primary purposes for which a programming language is created, namely, to support an implementation of the algorithms. In what follows we concentrate on the subject of "general purpose" programming languages, so the ones that are supposed to be used for developing software, and for teaching programming.

Ever since Algol-60 it became clear that such programming languages should be "high-level" in that they should have a sufficiently rich repertoire of control structures. Ever since C and Pascal it became clear that such programming languages should also have a sufficiently rich repertoire of data structures.

But even these seemingly obvious opinions are not universally accepted as can be witnessed by the continuing debate between the followers of imperative programming and of declarative programming. In fact, in logic programming languages, such as Prolog, a support for just one data type, the lists, is provided and the essence of declarative programming as embodied in logic and functional programming lies in not using assignment.

Another two criteria often advanced in the academia are that the programming language should have a "simple" semantics and that the programs should be "easy" to write, read and verify. What is "simple" and what is "easy" is in the eyes of the beholder, but both criteria can be used to compare simplicity of various programming constructs and can be used for example to argue against the goto statement or pointers.

In this paper we argue that these last two criteria can be realized by basing a programming language on first-order logic. The point is that first-order logic is a simple and elegant formalism with a clear semantics. From all introduced formalisms (apart from the propositional logic that is too simplistic for programming purposes) it is the one that we understand best, both in terms of its syntax and its semantics. Consequently, its use should facilitate program development, verification and understanding.

One could argue that logic programming has realized this approach to computing as it is based on Horn clauses that are special types of first-order formulas. However, in logic programming in its original setting computing (implicitly) takes place over the domain of terms. This domain is not sufficient for programming purposes. Therefore in Prolog, the most widely used logic programming language, programs are augmented with some support for arithmetic. This leads to a framework in which the logical basis is partly lost due to the possibility of errors. For instance, Prolog's assignment statement X is t yields a run-time error if t is not a ground arithmetic expression.

This and other deficiencies of Prolog led to the rise of constraint logic programming languages that overcome some of Prolog's shortcomings. These programming languages depend in essential way on some features as the presence of constraint solvers (for example a package for linear programming) and constraint propagation. So this extension of logic programming goes beyond first-order logic.

It is also useful to reflect on other limitations of these two formalisms. Both logic programming and constraint logic programming languages rely heavily on recursion and the more elementary and easier to understand concept of iteration is not available as a primitive. Further, types are absent. They can be added to the logic programming paradigm and in fact a number of successful proposals have been made, see, e.g., [15]. But to our knowledge no successful proposal dealing with addition of types to constraint logic programs is available.

Another, admittedly debatable, issue is assignment, shunned in logic programming and constraint logic programming because its use destroys the declarative interpretation of a program as a formula. However, we find that assignment *is* a useful construct. Some uses of it, such as recording the initial value of a variable or counting the number of bounded iterations, can be replaced by conceptually simpler constructs but some other uses of it such as for counting or for recording purposes are much less natural when simulated using logic formulas.

1.2   Design Decisions

These considerations have led us to a design of a programming language Alma-0. The initial work on the design of this language was reported in [3]; the final description of the language, its implementation and semantics is presented in [2].

In a nutshell, Alma-0 has the following characteristics:

- it is an extension of a subset of Modula-2 that includes assignment, so it is a strongly typed imperative language;
- to record the initial value of a variable the equality can be used;
- it supports so-called "don't know" nondeterminism by providing a possibility of a creation of choice points and automatic backtracking;
- it provides two forms of bounded iterations.

The last two features allow us to dispense with many uses of recursion that are in our opinion difficult to understand and to reason about.

As we shall see, the resulting language proposal makes programming in an imperative style easier and it facilitates (possibly automated) program verification. Additionally, for several algorithmic problems the solutions offered by Alma-0 is substantially simpler than the one offered by the logic programming paradigm.

The following simple example can help to understand what we mean by saying that Alma-0 is based on first-order logic and that some Alma-0 programs are simpler than their imperative and logic programming counterparts.

Consider the procedure that tests whether an array a[1..n] is ordered. The customary way to write it in Modula-2 is:

```
i:= 1;
ordered := TRUE;
WHILE i < n AND ordered DO
  ordered := ordered AND (a[i] <= a[i+1]);
  i := i+1
END;
```

In Alma-0 we can just write:

```
ordered := FOR i:= 1 TO n-1 DO a[i] <= a[i+1] END
```

This is much simpler and as efficient. In fact, this use of the FOR statement corresponds to the bounded universal quantification and the above one line program equals the problem specification.

In the logic programming framework there are no arrays. But the related problem of finding whether a list L is ordered is solved by the following program which is certainly more involved than the above one line of Alma-0 code:

```
ordered([]).
ordered([X]).
ordered([X, Y | Xs]) :- X =< Y, ordered([Y| Xs]).
```

1.3   Towards an Imperative Constraint Programming Language

In Alma-0 each variable is originally *uninitialized* and needs to be initialized before being used. Otherwise a run-time error arises. The use of uninitialized variables makes it possible to use a single program for a number of purposes, such as computing a solution, completing a partial solution, and testing a candidate solution. On the other hand, it also provides a limitation on the resulting programming style as several first-order formulas, when translated to Alma-0 syntax, yield programs that terminate in a run-time error.

With the addition of constraints this complication would be overcome. The idea is that the constraints encountered during the program execution are moved to the constraint store and evaluated later, when more information is available. Then the above restriction that each variable has to be initialized before being used can be lifted, at least for the variables that are manipulated by means of constraints. Additionally, more programs can be written in a declarative way. In fact, as we shall see, an addition of constraints to Alma-0 leads to a very natural style of programming in which the constraint generation part of the program is often almost identical to the problem specification.

Constraint programming in a nutshell consists of generating constraints (requirements) and solving them by general and domain specific methods. This approach to programming was successfully realized in a number of programming languages, notably constraint logic programming languages.

Up to now, the most successful approach to imperative constraint programming is the object-oriented approach taken by ILOG Solver (see [16], [9]). In this system constraints and variables are treated as objects and are defined within a C++ class library. Thanks to the class encapsulation mechanism and the operator overloading capability of C++, the user can see constraints almost as if they were a part of the language. A similar approach was independently taken in the *NeMo+* programming environment of [18].

In our approach constraints are integrated into the imperative programming paradigm, as "first class citizens" of the language. The interaction between the constraint store and the program becomes then more transparent and conceptually simpler and the resulting constraint programs are in our opinion more natural than their counterparts written in the constraint logic programming style or in the imperative languages augmented with constraint libraries.

The reason for this in the case of constraint logic programming is that many uses of recursion and lists can be replaced by the more basic concepts of bounded iteration and arrays. In the case of the imperative languages with constraint libraries, due to the absence of non-determinism in the language, failure situations (arising due to inconsistent constraints) must be dealt with explicitly by the programmer, whereas in Alma-0 they are managed implicitly by the backtracking mechanism.

When adding constraints to a strongly typed imperative programming language one needs to resolve a number of issues. First, constraints employ variables in the mathematical sense of the word (so *unknowns*) while the imperative programming paradigm is based on the computer science concept of a variable, so a *known*, but varying entity. We wish to separate between these two uses of variables because we want to manipulate unknowns only by means of constraints imposed on them. This precludes the modelling of unknowns by means of uninitialized variables since the latter can be modified by means of an assignment.

Second, one needs to integrate the constraints in such a way that various features of the underlying language such as use of local and global declarations and of various parameter passing mechanisms retain their coherence.

Additionally, one has to maintain the strong typing discipline according to which each variable has a type associated with it in such a way that throughout the program execution only values from its type can be assigned to the variable. Finally, one needs to provide an adequate support for search, one of the main aspects of constraint programming.

So the situation is quite different than in the case of the logic programming framework. Namely, the logic programming paradigm is based on the notion of a variable in the mathematical sense (usually called in this context a *logical* variable). This greatly facilitates the addition of constraints and partly explains why the integration of constraints into logic programming such as in the case of CHIP (see [19]), Prolog III (see [4]) and CLP($\mathcal{R}$) (see [11]), to name just three examples, has been so smooth and elegant. Further, logic programming languages provide support for automatic backtracking.

However, as already mentioned, in constraint logic programming languages types are not available. Moreover, there is a very limited support for scoping and only one parameter mechanism is available.

Let us return now to Alma-0. The language already provides a support for search by means of automatic backtracking. This support is further enhanced in our proposal by providing a built-in constraint propagation. In [2] we stated that our language proposal should be viewed as "an instance of a *generic method* for extending (essentially) any imperative programming language with facilities that encourage declarative programming." That is why we think that the proposal here discussed should be viewed not only as a suggestion how to integrate constraints into Alma-0, but more generally how to integrate constraints into any strongly typed imperative language. In fact, Alma-0 can be viewed as an intermediate stage in such an integration.

The remainder of the paper is organized as follows. In Section 2 we summarize the new features of Alma-0 and in Section 3 we illustrate the resulting programming style by two examples. Then, in Section 4 we discuss the basics of our proposal for adding constraints to Alma-0 and in Section 5 we explain how constraints interact with procedures. In turn in Section 6 we discuss language extensions for expressing complex constraints and for facilitating search in presence of constraints. Finally, in Section 7 we discuss related work and in Section 8 we draw some conclusions and discuss the future work.

2   A Short Overview of Alma-0

Alma-0 is an extension of a subset of Modula-2 by nine new features inspired by the logic programming paradigm. We briefly recall most of them here and refer to [2] for a detailed presentation.

- Boolean expressions can be used as statements and vice versa. This feature of Alma-0 is illustrated by the above one line program of Subsection 1.2.
  A boolean expression that is used as a statement and evaluates to FALSE is identified with a *failure*.
- *Choice points* can be created by the non-deterministic statements ORELSE and SOME. The former is a dual of the statement composition and the latter is a dual of the FOR statement. Upon failure the control returns to the most recent choice point, possibly within a procedure body, and the computation resumes with the next branch in the state in which the previous branch was entered.
- The created choice points can be erased or iterated over by means of the COMMIT and FORALL statements. COMMIT S END removes the choice points created during the first successful execution of S. FORALL S DO T END iterates over all choice points created by S. Each time S succeeds, T is executed.
- The notion of *initialized* variable is introduced: A variable is uninitialized until the first time a value is assigned to it; from that point on, it is initialized. The KNOWN relation tests whether a variable of a simple type is initialized.
- The equality test is generalized to an assignment statement in case one side is an uninitialized variable and the other side an expression with known value.

- In Alma-0 three types of parameter mechanisms are allowed: call by value, call by variable and *call by mixed form*. The first two are those of Pascal and Modula-2; the third one is an amalgamation of the first two (see [2]). Parameters passed by mixed form can be used both for testing and for computing.

Let us summarize these features of Alma-0 by clarifying which of them are based on first-order logic.

In the logical reading of the programming language constructs the program composition S ; T is viewed as the conjunction S ∧ T. A dual of ";", the EITHER S ORELSE T END statement, corresponds then to the disjunction S ∨ T.

Further, the FOR i:= s TO t DO S END statement is viewed as the bounded universal quantification, $\forall i \in [s..t]$ S, and its dual, the SOME i:= s TO t DO S END statement is viewed as the bounded existential quantification, $\exists i \in [s..t]$ S.

In turn, the FORALL S DO T END statement can be viewed as the restricted quantification $\forall \bar{x}(S \rightarrow T)$, where $\bar{x}$ are all the variables of S.

Because the boolean expressions are identified with the statements, we can apply the negation connective, NOT, to the statements. Finally, the equality can be interpreted both as a test and as an one-time assignment, depending on whether the variable in question is initialized or not.

3   Programming in Alma-0

To illustrate the above features of Alma-0 and the resulting programming style we now consider two examples.

3.1   The Frequency Assignment Problem

The first problem we discuss is a combinatorial problem from telecommunication.

Problem 1. Frequency Assignment ([7]). Given is a set of *n cells*, $C := \{c_1, c_2, \ldots, c_n\}$ and a set of *m* frequencies (or channels) $F := \{f_1, f_2, \ldots, f_m\}$. An *assignment* is a function which associates with each cell c_i a frequency $x_i \in F$. The problem consists in finding an assignment that satisfies the following constraints.

Separations: Given *h* and *k* we call the value $d(f_h, f_k) = |h - k|$ the *distance* between two channels f_h and f_k. (The assumption is that consecutive frequencies lie one unit apart.) Given is an $n \times n$ non-negative integer symmetric matrix *S*, called a *separation matrix*, such that each s_{ij} represents the minimum distance between the frequencies assigned to the cells c_i and c_j. That is, for all $i \in [1..n]$ and $j \in [1..n]$ it holds that $d(x_i, x_j) \geq s_{ij}$.

Illegal channels: Given is an $n \times m$ boolean matrix *F* such that if $F_{ij} = true$, then the frequency f_j cannot be assigned to the cell *i*, i.e., $x_i \neq f_j$.

Separation constraints prevent interference between cells which are located geographically close and which broadcast in each other's area of service. Illegal channels account for channels reserved for external uses (e.g., for military bases).

The Alma-0 solution to this problem does not use an assignment and has a dual interpretation as a formula. We tested this program on various data. We assume here for simplicity that each c_i equals i and each f_i equals i, so $C = \{1, \ldots, n\}$ and $F = \{1, \ldots, m\}$.

```
MODULE FrequencyAssignment;
CONST N = 30;  (* number of cells *)
      M = 27;  (* number of frequencies *)

TYPE SeparationMatrix = ARRAY [1..N],[1..N] OF INTEGER;
     IllegalFrequencies = ARRAY [1..N],[1..M] OF BOOLEAN;
     Assignment = ARRAY [1..N] OF [1..M];  (* solution vector *)

VAR S: SeparationMatrix;
    F: IllegalFrequencies;
    A: Assignment;
    noSol: INTEGER;

PROCEDURE AssignFrequencies(S: SeparationMatrix; F: IllegalFrequencies;
                            VAR A: Assignment);
VAR i, j, k: INTEGER;
BEGIN
  FOR i := 1 TO N DO
    SOME j := 1 TO M DO (* j is a candidate frequency for cell i *)
      NOT F[i,j];
      FOR k := 1 TO i-1 DO
        abs(A[k] - j) >= S[k,i]
      END;
      A[i] = j
    END
  END
END AssignFrequencies;

BEGIN
  InitializeData(S,F);
  AssignFrequencies(S,F,A);
  PrintSolution(A)
END FrequencyAssignment.
```

The simple code of the procedures InitializeData and PrintSolution is omitted. The generalized equality A[i] = j serves here as an assignment and the SOME statement takes care of automatic backtracking in the search for the right frequency j.

In the second part of the paper we shall discuss an alternative solution to this problem using constraints.

3.2 Job Shop Scheduling

The second problem we discuss is a classical scheduling problem, namely the *job shop scheduling* problem. We refer to [5, page 242] for its precise description. Roughly speaking, the problem consists of scheduling over time a set of jobs, each consisting of a set of consecutive tasks, on a set of processors.

The input data is represented by an array of jobs, each element of which is a record that stores the number of the tasks and the array of tasks. In turn, each task is represented by the machine it uses and by its length. The output is delivered as an integer matrix that (like a so-called Gantt chart) for each time point k and each processor p stores the job number that p is serving at the time point k.

The constraint that each processor can perform only one job at a time is enforced by using generalized equality on the elements of the output matrix. More precisely, whenever job i requires processor j for a given time window $[d_1, d_2]$, the program attempts for some k to initialize the elements of the matrix $(j, k + d_1), (j, k + d_1 + 1), \ldots, (j, k + d_2)$ to the value i. If this initialization succeeds, the program continues with the next task. Otherwise some element in this segment is already initialized, i.e., in this segment processor j is already used by another job. In this case the execution fails and through backtracking the next value for k is chosen.

The constraint that the tasks of the same job must be executed in the provided order and cannot overlap in time is enforced by the use of the variable min_start_time which, for each job, initially equals 1 and then is set to the end time of the last considered task of the job. To perform this update we exploit the fact that when the SOME statement is exited its index variable k equals the smallest value in the considered range for which the computation does not fail (as explained in [2]).

We provide here the procedure that performs the scheduling. For the sake of brevity the rest of the program is omitted.

```
TYPE
    TaskType      = RECORD
                        machine : INTEGER;
                        length  : INTEGER;
                    END;
    JobType       = RECORD
                        tasks : INTEGER;
                        task  : ARRAY [1..MAX_TASKS] OF TaskType
                    END;
    JobVectorType = ARRAY [1..MAX_JOBS] OF JobType;
    GanttType     = ARRAY [1..MAX_MACHINES],[1..MAX_DEADLINE] OF INTEGER;

PROCEDURE JobShopScheduling(VAR job: JobVectorType; deadline:INTEGER;
                            jobs :INTEGER; VAR gantt: GanttType);
VAR
    i, j, k, h    : INTEGER;
    min_start_time : INTEGER;
```

```
BEGIN
  FOR i := 1 TO jobs DO
    min_start_time := 1;
    FOR j := 1 TO job[i].tasks DO
      SOME k := min_start_time TO deadline - job[i].task[j].length + 1
DO
        (* job i engages the processor needed for task j from time k to
           k + (length of task j) - 1.
           If the processor is already engaged, the program backtracks.
*)
        FOR h := k TO k + job[i].task[j].length - 1 DO
          gantt[job[i].task[j].processor,h] = i;
        END
      END;
      min_start_time := k + job[i].task[j].length;
        (* set the minimum start time for the next task
           to the end of the current task *)
    END;
  END
END JobShopScheduling;
```

In this program the "don't know" nondeterminism provided by the use of the SOME statement is combined with the use of assignment.

Furthermore, as already mentioned, for each value of i and j the equality gantt[job[i].task[j].processor,h] = i acts both as an assignment and as a test.

The array gantt should be uninitialized when the procedure is called. At the end of the execution the variable gantt contains the first feasible schedule it finds.

Preinitialized values can be used to enforce some preassignments of jobs to processors, or to impose a constraint that a processor is not available during some periods of time. For example, if processor 2 is not available at time 5, we just use the assignment gantt[2,5] := 0 (where 0 is a dummy value) before invoking the procedure JobShopSchedule.

As an example, suppose we have 3 jobs, 3 processors (p_1, p_2, and p_3), the deadline is 20, and the jobs are composed as follows:

		task 1		task 2		task 3		task 4	
job	tasks	proc	len	proc	len	proc	len	proc	len
1	4	p_1	5	p_2	5	p_3	5	p_2	3
2	3	p_2	6	p_1	6	p_3	4		
3	4	p_3	6	p_2	4	p_1	4	p_2	1

The first solution (out of the existing 48) for the array gantt that the program finds is the following one, where the symbol '-' means that the value is uninitialized, i.e., the processor is idle in the corresponding time point.

```
1 1 1 1 1 - 2 2 2 2 2 2 - - - 3 3 3 3 -
2 2 2 2 2 2 1 1 1 1 1 3 3 3 3 - 1 1 1 3
3 3 3 3 3 3 - - - - - - 1 1 1 1 1 2 2 2 2
```

For some applications, it is necessary to make the schedule as short as possible. To this aim, we can use the following program fragment.

```
COMMIT
  SOME deadline := 1 TO max_deadline DO
    JobShopScheduling(JobVector,deadline,jobs,Gantt)
  END
END
```

It computes the shortest schedule by *guessing*, in ascending order, the first deadline that can be met by a feasible assignment. The use of the COMMIT statement ensures that once a solution is found, the alternatives, with larger deadline values, are discarded.

4   Introducing Constraints

In what follows we discuss a proposal for adding constraints to Alma-0.

This Section is organized as follows. In Subsection 4.1 we discuss the addition of constrained types and unknowns to the language and in Subsections 4.2 and 4.3 we define the constraint store and illustrate its interaction with the program execution.

To illustrate how the proposed addition of constraints to Alma-0 provides a better support for declarative programming we illustrate in Subsection 4.4 their use by means of three example programs.

To simplify our considerations we ignore in this section the presence of procedures. In particular, we assume for a while that all declarations are at one level.

4.1   Adding Constrained Types, Unknowns and Constraints

We start by adding a new kind of variables of simple types, called unknowns. This is done by using the qualifier CONSTRAINED in declarations of *simple types*, that is INTEGER, BOOLEAN, REAL, enumeration and subrange types.

Definition 1.
 − *A type qualified with the keyword* CONSTRAINED *is called a* constrained type.
 − *A variable whose type is a constrained type is called an* unknown.

We shall see in Section 5 that this way of defining unknowns simplifies the treatment of parameter passing in presence of unknowns. From now on we distinguish between variables and unknowns. In the discussion below we assume the following declarations.

```
CONST N = 8;
TYPE Board = ARRAY [1..N] OF CONSTRAINED [1..N];
     Colour = (blue, green, red, yellow);
     Info = RECORD
```

```
     co: Colour;
     No: CONSTRAINED INTEGER;
   END;
VAR i, j: INTEGER;
   a: ARRAY [1..N] of INTEGER;
   C: CONSTRAINED [1..N];
   X, Y: Board;
   Z: Info;
```

So a, i and j are variables while C is an unknown. In turn, X and Y are arrays of unknowns and Z is a record the first component of which is a variable and the second an unknown.

Because of the syntax of Alma-0, boolean expressions can appear both in the position of a statement and inside a condition.

Definition 2. *A* constraint *is a boolean expression that involves some unknowns.*
We postulate that the unknowns can appear only within constraints or within the right hand side of an assignment.

The values of unknowns are determined only by means of constraints that are placed on them. In particular, by the just introduced syntactic restriction, one cannot use assignment to assign a value to an unknown. So in presence of the above declarations the statements X[1] := 0 and C := 1 are illegal. In contrast, the constraints X[1] = 0 and C = 1 are legal. Further, the assignments i := X[1] + X[2] and i := Y[X[2]] are also legal statements.

Initially each unknown has an *undetermined* value that belongs to the domain associated with the type. By placing constraints on an unknown its domain can *shrink*. The unknown continues to have an undetermined value until the domain gets reduced to a singleton.

If the program control reaches an occurrence of an unknown outside of a constraint, so within the right hand side of an assignment, this unknown is evaluated. If its value is at this moment undetermined, this evaluation yields a run-time error. If the value is *determined* (that is, the domain is a singleton), then it is substituted for the occurrence of the unknown. So the occurrences of an unknown outside of a constraint are treated as usual variables.

Note that during the program execution the domain of an unknown *monotonically* decreases with respect to the subset ordering. This is in stark contrast with the case of variables. Initially, the value of a variable of a simple type is not known but after the first assignment to it its value is determined though can *non-monotonically* change to any other value from its type.

Intuitively, a program is viewed as an "engine" that generates constraints. These constraints are gradually solved by means of the constraint solving process that we shall explain now.

4.2 Adding the Constraint Store

We now introduce the central notion of a *constraint store*. This is done in a similar way as in the constraint logic programming systems, though we need to take into account here the presence of variables and constants.

Definition 3. *We call a constraint C* evaluated *if each constant that occurs in it is replaced by its value and each variable (not unknown) that occurs in it is replaced by its current value. If some variable that occurs in C is uninitialized, we say that the evaluation of C yields an error. Otherwise we call the resulting boolean expression the* evaluated form *of C.*

So no variables occur in the evaluated form of a constraint. For technical reasons we also consider a *false constraint*, denoted by $\perp$, that can be generated only by a constraint solver to indicate contradiction.

Definition 4. *A constraint store, in short a* store, *is a set of evaluated forms of constraints. We say that an unknown is* present *in the store if it occurs in a constraint that belongs to the store.*

We call a store failed *if $\perp$ is present in it or if the domain of one of the unknowns present in it is empty. By a* solution *to the store we mean an assignment of values from the current domains to all unknowns present in it.*

Further, we say that a constraint is solved *if its evaluated form is satisfied by all combinations of values from the current domains of its unknowns.*

For example, in the program fragment

```
i := 1;
j := 2;
X[i] <= j;
Y[X[i+2]] <> Y[N];
```

we have two constraints, X[i] <= j and Y[X[i+2]] <> Y[N]. Here X[1] <= 2 is the evaluated form of the first one, while Y[X[3]] <> Y[8] is the evaluated form of the second one. If we deleted the assignment i := 1 the evaluations of both constraints would yield an error.

The notion of a failed store is a computationally tractable approximation of that of an inconsistent store, i.e., a store that has no solutions. Indeed, a failed store is inconsistent but an inconsistent store does not have to be failed: just consider X[1] = X[2], X[1] < X[2].

4.3 Interaction Between the Program and the Constraint Store

The program interacts with the store in the following two ways:

- By adding to it the evaluated forms of the encountered constraints. If the evaluation of such a constraint yields an error, a run-time error arises.

- By generating possible values for unknowns that are present in the store by means of some built-in primitives to be introduced in Subsection 6.2.

The store is equipped with a number of procedures called *constraint solvers*. Their form depends on the applications. One or more of them can become activated upon addition of (an evaluated form of) a constraint to the store. An activation of constraint solvers, in the sequel called *constraint solving*, can reduce the domains of the unknowns, determine the values of some unknowns by reducing the corresponding domains to singletons, delete some constraints that are solved, or discover that the store is failed, either by generating the false constraint ⊥ or by reducing the domain of an unknown to the empty set.

We assume that constraint solving is a further unspecified process that depending of application may be some form of constraint propagation or a decision procedure. We require that the result of constraint solving maintains equivalence, which means that the set of all solutions to the store does not change by applying to it constraint solvers.

The store interacts with the program as follows.

Definition 5. *Upon addition of a constraint to the store, constraint solving takes place.*

- *If as a result of the constraint solving the store remains non-failed, the control returns to the program and the execution proceeds in the usual way.*
- *Otherwise the store becomes failed and a failure arises. This means that the control returns to the last choice point created in the program. Upon backtracking all the constraints added after the last choice point are retracted and the values of the variables and the domains of the unknowns are restored to their values at the moment that the last choice point was created.*

This means that we extend the notion of failure, originally introduced in Section 2, to deal with the presence of the store.

Note that constraints are interpreted in the same way independently of the fact whether they appear as a statement or inside a condition. For example, the following program fragment

```
IF X[1] > 0 THEN S ELSE T END
```

is executed as follows: The constraint X[1] > 0 is added to the store. If the store does not fail S is executed, otherwise T is executed. So we do not check whether X[1] > 0 is *entailed* by the store and execute S or T accordingly, as one might intuitively expect. This means that constraints are always interpreted as so-called *tell* operations in the store, and never as so-called *ask* operations, which check for entailment (see Section 8 for a discussion on this point).

4.4   Examples

To illustrate use of the introduced concepts we now consider three examples. We begin with the following classical problem.

Problem 2. Eight Queens. Place 8 queens on the chess board so that they do not attack each other.

We present here a solution that uses constraints. We only write the part of the program that generates constraints. The code that actually solves the generated constraints would make use of the built-in INDOMAIN as explained in Subsection 6.2.

```
CONST N = 8;
TYPE Board = ARRAY [1..N] OF CONSTRAINED [1..N];
VAR i, j: [1..N];
    X: Board;

BEGIN
  FOR i := 1 TO N-1 DO
    FOR j := i+1 TO N DO
      X[i] <> X[j];
      X[i] <> X[j]+j-i;
      X[i] <> X[j]+i-j
    END
  END
END;
```

Each generated constraint is thus of the form X[i] <> X[j] or X[i] <> X[j] + k for some values i,j ∈ [1..N] such that i < j and k being either the value of j-i or of i-j.

Note that the above program text coincides with the problem formulation.

Next, consider the following problem that deals with the equations arising when studying the flow of heat.

Problem 3. Laplace Equations. Given is a two dimensional grid with given values for all the exterior points. The value of each interior points equals the average of the values of its four neighbours. Compute the value of all interior points.

The solution using constraints again truly coincides with the problem specification. It is conceptually much simpler than the solution based on constraint logic programming and given in [10].

```
TYPE Board = ARRAY [1..M], [1..N] OF CONSTRAINED REAL;
VAR i:[1..M];
    j:[1..N];
    X: Board;

BEGIN
  FOR i := 2 TO M-1 DO
    FOR j := 2 TO N-1 DO
      X[i,j] = (X[i+1,j] + X[i-1,j] + X[i,j+1] + X[i,j-1])/4
    END
  END
END;
```

We assume here that the constraint solver that deals with linear equations over reals is sufficiently powerful to solve the generated equations.

Finally, we present a solution to the *Frequency Assignment* problem (Problem 1) that uses constraints. Again, we only write the part of the program that generates constraints. We assume here that the variables S and F are properly initialized.

```
TYPE SeparationMatrix = ARRAY [1..N],[1..N] OF INTEGER;
     IllegalFrequencies = ARRAY [1..N],[1..M] OF BOOLEAN;
     Assignment = ARRAY [1..N] OF CONSTRAINED [1..M];
VAR S: SeparationMatrix;
    F: IllegalFrequencies;
    X: Assignment;
    i, j: INTEGER;

BEGIN
  FOR i := 1 TO N DO
    FOR j := 1 TO M DO
      IF F[i,j] THEN X[i] <> j END
    END
  END;
  FOR i := 1 TO N DO
    FOR j := 1 TO i-1 DO
      EITHER X[i] - X[j] >= S[i,j]
      ORELSE X[j] - X[i] >= S[i,j]
      END
    END
  END
END;
```

The use of the ORELSE statement creates here choice points to which the control can return if in the part of the program that deals with constraints solving a failed store is produced.

Alternatively, one could use here a disjunction and replace the ORELSE statement by

$$(X[i] - X[j] >= S[j,i]) \text{ OR } (X[j] - X[i] >= S[j,i]).$$

In this case no choice points are created but the problem of solving (disjunctive) constraints is now "relegated" to the store.

The latter solution is preferred if the constraint solver in use is able to perform some form of preprocessing on disjunctive constraints, such as the *constructive disjunction* of [8]. On the other hand, the former solution allows the programmer to retain control upon the choice generated by the system. For example, she/he can associate different actions to the two branches of the ORELSE statement.

It is important to realize that the integration of constraints to Alma-0 as outlined in this section is possible only because the unknowns are initially uninitialized.

5   Constraints and Procedures

So far we explained how the program interacts with the store in absence of procedures. In Alma-0 one level (i.e., not nested) procedures are allowed. In presence of procedures we need to explain a number of issues.

First, to keep matters simple, we disallow local unknowns. This means that the constrained types can be only introduced at the outer level. However, unknowns can be used within the procedure bodies provided the restrictions introduced in Definition 2 are respected.

Next, we need to explain how unknowns can be passed as parameters. Formal parameters of constrained types are considered as unknowns. This means that in the procedure body such formal parameters can occur only within the constraints or within the right hand side of an assignment.

We discuss first call by variable. An unknown (or a compound variable containing an unknown) passed as an actual variable parameter is handled in the same way as the customary variables, by means of the usual reference mechanism.

For example consider the following problem.

Problem 4. Given is an array which assigns to each pixel on an M × N board a colour. A *region* is a maximal set of adjacent pixels that have the same colour. Determine the number of regions.

To solve it we represent each pixel as a record, one field of which holds the colour of the pixel and the other is an unknown integer. Then we assign to each pixel a number in such a way that pixels in the same region get the same number. These assignments are performed by means of constraint solving. For instance, in the case of Figure 1 the constraint solving takes care that the value 1 is assigned to all but two pixels once it is assigned to the leftmost uppermost pixel.

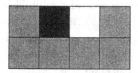

Fig. 1. Constraint Solving and Pixels

To achieve this effect in the program below we assume that the constraint solving process is able to reduce the domain of y to {a} given the constraint x = y and the fact that the domain of x equals {a}. The program uses both constraints and an assignment. In addition, the program uses the built-in KNOWN that, when used on unknowns, checks whether the domain of the argument is a singleton.

```
TYPE Colour = (blue, green, red, yellow);
     Info = RECORD
       co: Colour;
       No: CONSTRAINED INTEGER;
     END;
     Board = ARRAY [1..M],[1..N] OF Info;

PROCEDURE Region(VAR X: Board; VAR number: INTEGER);
  VAR i, j, k: INTEGER;
BEGIN
  FOR i := 1 TO M DO
    FOR j := 1 TO N DO
      IF i < M AND X[i,j].co = X[i+1,j].co
      THEN X[i,j].No = X[i+1,j].No
      END;
      IF j < N AND X[i,j].co = X[i,j+1].co
      THEN X[i,j].No = X[i,j+1].No
      END
    END
  END;
  k := 0;
  FOR i := 1 TO M DO
    FOR j := 1 TO N DO
      IF NOT KNOWN(X[i,j].No)
      THEN k := k+1; X[i,j].No = k
      END
    END
  END;
  number = k
END Region;
```

Note that for any i in [1..M] and j in [1..N], the record component X[i,j].No is of a constrained type. Here the first double FOR statement generates the constraints while the second double FOR statement solves them by assigning to the pixels that belong to the same region the same number.

Due to the call by variable mechanism, the actual parameter corresponding the formal one, X, is modified by the procedure. In particular, the second component, No, of each array element is instantiated after the procedure call.

Next, we explain the call by value mechanism in presence of unknowns. An unknown passed as an actual value parameter is treated as a customary variable: it is evaluated and its value is assigned to a local variable associated with the formal parameter. If the value of this unknown is at this moment undetermined, this evaluation yields a run-time error. This evaluation process also applies if a field or an element of a compound actual value parameter is an unknown.

6   Language Extensions

In this section we discuss some built-in procedures of the proposed language that make it easier for the user to program with constraints. In particular, in Subsection 6.1 we discuss built-ins for stating constraints, and in Subsection 6.2 we present built-ins for assigning values to unknowns.

6.1   Built-ins for Expressing Constraints

The practice of constraint programming requires inclusion in the programming language of a certain number of language built-ins that facilitate constraint formulation.

For example, if we wish to state that the unknowns of the array X must have pairwise different values, we write

```
ALL_DIFFERENT(X);
```

This call results in a constraint which is equivalent to the set of all the corresponding constraints of the form X[i] <> X[j], for i $\in$ [1..N-1] and j $\in$ [i+1..N]. [1]

Similarly, if we wish to state that at most k among the unknowns belonging to the array X can have the value v, we write

```
AT_MOST(k,X,v);
```

This sort of built-ins on arrays are present in other imperative constraint languages. We do not list all of them here, but we envision their presence in the language.

Such built-ins on arrays are the counterparts in imperative languages of the corresponding built-ins on lists provided by constraint logic programming systems such as CHIP. These languages also support symbolic manipulation of terms which makes it easy to generate arithmetic constraints. The traditional imperative programming languages lack this power and exclusive reliance on arrays can lead to artificial and inefficient solutions.

For example, suppose we are given an $n \times n$ matrix A of integer unknowns and we wish to state the constraint that the sum of the elements of the main diagonal must be equal to a given value b. A customary solution would involve resorting to an auxiliary array of unknowns in the following way:

```
VAR A: ARRAY [1..N], [1..N] OF CONSTRAINED INTEGER;
    V: ARRAY [1..N] OF CONSTRAINED INTEGER;
    b: INTEGER;

    V[1] = A[1,1];
```

---

[1] In some systems, such a constraint is kept in its original form in order to exploit constraint propagation techniques that deal specifically with constraints of this kind, see [17].

```
FOR i := 2 to N DO
   V[i] = A[i,i] + V[i-1];
END;
V[N] = b;
```

This solution, which one would write for example in ILOG Solver, has the obvious drawback of creating N new unknowns for stating one single constraint.

Therefore we propose the use of lists of unknowns (as done for example in the ICON programming language of [6] for the case of variables), identified by the keyword LIST, upon which constraints of various forms can be stated by means of built-ins. The above program fragment would then be replaced by

```
VAR A: ARRAY [1..N], [1..N] OF CONSTRAINED INTEGER;
    L: LIST OF CONSTRAINED INTEGER;
    b: INTEGER;

    Empty(L);
    FOR i := 1 to N DO
      Insert(L, A[i,i])
    END;
    Sum(L,'=',b);
```

where Sum is a built-in with the expected meaning of constraining the sum of the unknowns in L to be equal to b. Once the constraint Sum(L,'=',b) has been added to the store, the variable L can be used again for a different purpose. Note that in this solution no additional unknowns are created. In order to obtain a similar behaviour in ILOG Solver one needs either to add a similar built-in to it or to make explicit use of pointers to objects representing unknowns.

Consider now again the Frequency Assignment problem. We discuss here the formulation of an additional constraint for this problem which requires the use of lists. Suppose that we wish to state that in a particular region (i.e., a set of cells) a given frequency is used no more than a given number of times.

This type of constraint is useful in real cases. In fact, in some situations even though the pairwise interference among cells is below a given threshold and no separation is required, the simultaneous use of a given frequency in many cells can create a interference phenomenon, called *cumulative interference*.

The following procedure states the constraints for preventing cumulative interference in region R (where the type Region is an array of booleans representing a subset of the set of cells). Here max is the maximum number of cells in the region that can use the same frequency.

```
PROCEDURE RegionConstraint(R: Region; max: INTEGER; VAR X: Assignment);
VAR i, k: INTEGER;
    L: LIST OF CONSTRAINED [1..M];

BEGIN
  FOR k := 1 TO M DO
    Empty(L);
```

```
    FOR i := 1 TO N DO
      IF R[i] THEN Insert(L,X[i]) END
    END;
    AT_MOST(max,L,k)
  END
END RegionConstraint;
```

6.2 Built-ins for Assigning Values

In order to search for a solution of a set of constraints, values must be assigned to unknowns. We define the built-in procedure INDOMAIN which gets an unknown of a finite type (so BOOLEAN, enumeration or a subrange type) as a parameter, and assigns to it *one* among the elements of its domain. The procedure also creates a choice point and all other elements of the domain are successively assigned to the unknown upon backtracking.

The choice of the value to assign to the unknown is taken by the system depending on the current state of the store, based on predefined *value selection* strategies. We do not discuss the issue of which are the best value selection strategies. We only assume that all consistent values are eventually generated, and that the choice point is erased after the last value has been generated.

The procedure INDOMAIN can be also used on arrays and on lists. For example, the call INDOMAIN(A), where A is a matrix of integer unknowns, generates (upon backtracking) all possible assignments for all elements of A.

The order of instantiation of the elements of A is taken care of by the store, which applies built-in strategies to optimize the retrieval of the first instantiation of the unknowns. As in the case of value selection, we do not discuss here the issue of the *variable ordering*.

7   Related Work

We concentrate here on the related work involving addition of constraints to imperative languages. For an overview of related work pertaining to the Alma-0 language we refer the reader to [2].

As already mentioned in the introduction, the most successful imperative constraint language is the C++ library ILOG Solver [9]. The main difference between our proposal and ILOG Solver is that the latter is based on the conventional imperative language C++ and consequently it does not support automatic backtracking. Therefore the interaction with the store cannot be based on failures issued by the store constraint solvers while evaluating the statements. In ILOG Solver such an interaction is always explicit, whereas in our proposal we aim at making it transparent to the user.

We are aware of two other language proposals in which constraints are integrated into an imperative language — the commercial language CHARME of [14] and 2LP of [13]. In each language some of the issues here discussed have been addressed, but not all of them.

More specifically, in CHARME unknowns (called logical variables) and linear constraints on them are allowed. The language supports use of Prolog-like terms, arrays and sequences of logical variables and a number of features (like demons and the `element` primitive, an equivalent of INDOMAIN) adopted from the CHIP language. Also, it provides a nondeterministic `or` statement and iterations over finite domains, arrays and sequences of logical variables.

The C like syntax creates an impression that CHARME supports imperative programming. However, from the paper it is not clear whether it is actually the case. If it is, then it is not clear how the logical variables, constraints and nondeterministic statements interact with the usual features of the underlying imperative language. In particular, the use of logical variables outside of constraints, the impact of backtracking on the assignment statements and the status of choice points created within procedure bodies is not explained (probably due to space limitations). CHARME does provide bidirectional connection with C.

2LP was designed for linear programming applications. In 2LP unknowns (called *continuous* variables) are global. They vary over the real interval $[0, +\infty)$ and can be either simple ones or arrays. The only way these variables can be modified is by imposing linear constraints on them. Constraints can also appear in conditions. This leads to a conditional way of adding them to the store.

Whenever a constraint is added to the store, its feasibility w.r.t. the old constraints is tested by means of an internal simplex-based algorithm. This algorithm maintains the current feasible region, which is a polyhedron, together with a *witness point* which is a distinguished vertex.

The continuous variables can appear outside of the constraints as arguments of any procedure whose signature has a continuous variable, and as arguments to some predeclared functions like `wp` that returns the value of a witness point. In the latter case when a continuous variable is passed as a parameter, the witness point value is used.

2LP provides the nondeterministic statements analogous to the ORELSE and SOME statements of Alma-0 and a limited form for the FORALL statement. Automatic backtracking over assignment and combination of continuous and customary variables in compound variables is not supported.

8   Conclusions and Future Work

In this paper we discussed the programming language Alma-0 that integrates the imperative and logic programming paradigm and illustrated the resulting programming style by a number of examples. Alma-0 is based on first-order logic in the sense that it provides a computational interpretation for the standard connectives, so negation, disjunction and conjunction, and for various forms of quantification. In fact, many first-order formulas and their extensions by bounded quantifiers, sorts (i.e., types), and arrays, can be interpreted and executed as Alma-0 programs. The precise logical nature of this computational interpretation of first-order logic was worked out in [1].

Then we discussed a proposal how to integrate constraint programming features into the language. In this regard we believe that the use of an underlying language based on first-order logic, such as Alma-0, rather than a conventional imperative language, makes the integration of constraints more natural and conceptually simpler.

We analyzed here a number of issues related to the proposed integration, such as the use of constrained types and the unknowns, interaction between the program and the constraint store, and the parameter passing mechanisms. Finally, we presented some examples that illustrate the resulting style of programming.

In our future work we plan to extend the work carried out in [2] to the language proposal here outlined. More specifically, we envisage to

- extend the executable, operational semantics based on the ASF+SDF Meta-Environment of [12];
- extend both the Alma-0 compiler and its underlying abstract machine AAA;
- implement a set of constraint solvers or provide an interface between the language and existing constraint solvers.

The first item can be dealt with by adding to the executable semantics of Alma-0 given in [2] a few rules that formalize the interaction between the program and the store stipulated in Subsection 4.3. These rules are parameterized by the constraint solvers attached to the store.

Regarding the last item, we plan to develop a simple solver for constraints over finite domains to be used for prototyping and testing purposes. We also plan to exploit more powerful external solvers already available for subsequent releases of the system.

As already mentioned in Section 4.3, we do not allow so-called *ask* operations in the store. This is a deliberate design decision which allows us to keep the language design simple and the underlying execution model easy to implement.

Nevertheless, in future versions of the language, we plan to investigate the possibility of equipping the store with an *entailment* procedure. This procedure should check whether an evaluated form of a constraint is logically implied (or *entailed*) by the store. Upon encounter of an **ask** constraint, the entailment procedure would check whether the evaluated form is entailed by the store. If it is the case, the constraint evaluates to TRUE. Otherwise the constraint evaluates to FALSE. We would require that the entailment procedure returns correct results but would not assume that it is complete.

We did not deal here with some of the issues related to the design of the language. Specifically, we omitted discussion of

- a full set of built-ins, in particular the ones appropriate for constraint optimization,
- primitives for selecting variable and value selection strategies,
- the language support for the dynamic creation of unknowns.

These can be taken care of in a systematic way and lead to a complete and rigorous definition of an imperative constraint programming language.

Acknowledgements

We would like to thank Jan Holleman, Eric Monfroy and Vincent Partington for useful discussions on the subject of this paper. Helpful comments by Tony Hoare and other two, anonymous, referees allowed us to improve the presentation.

References

1. K. R. Apt and M. A. Bezem. Formulas as programs. In K.R. Apt, V.W. Marek, M. Truszczyński, and D.S. Warren, editors, *The Logic Programming Paradigm: A 25 Year Perspective*, pages 75–107, 1999.
2. K. R. Apt, J. Brunekreef, V. Partington, and A. Schaerf. Alma-0: An imperative language that supports declarative programming. *ACM Toplas*, 20(5):1014–1066, 1998.
3. K. R. Apt and A. Schaerf. Search and imperative programming. In *Proc. 24th Annual SIGPLAN-SIGACT Symposium on Principles of Programming Languages (POPL '97)*, pages 67–79. ACM Press, 1997.
4. A. Colmerauer. An introduction to Prolog III. *Communications of ACM*, 33(7):69–90, 1990.
5. M. R. Garey and D. S. Johnson. *Computers and Intractability—A guide to NP-completeness*. W.H. Freeman and Company, San Francisco, 1979.
6. R. E. Griswold and M. T. Griswold. *The Icon Programming Language*. Prentice-Hall, Englewood Cliffs, New Jersey, USA, 1983.
7. W. K. Hale. Frequency assignment: Theory and applications. In *Proc. of IEEE*, pages 1497–1514, 1980.
8. P. Van Hentenryck, Vijay Saraswat, and Y. Deville. Design, implementation, and evaluation of the constraint language cc(FD). In Andreas Podelski, editor, *Constraint Programming: Basics and Trends*, LNCS 910. Springer-Verlag, 1995. (Châtillon-sur-Seine Spring School, France, May 1994).
9. ILOG. ILOG optimization suite — white paper. Available via http://www.ilog.com, 1998.
10. J. Jaffar and J.-L. Lassez. Constraint Logic Programming. In *14th ACM Principles of Programming Languages Conference*, pages 111–119, Munich, F.R.G., 1987. ACM, New York.
11. Joxan Jaffar, Spiro Michaylov, Peter J. Stuckey, and Roland H. C. Yap. The CLP($\mathcal{R}$) language and system. *ACM Transactions on Programming Languages and Systems (TOPLAS)*, 14(3):339–395, July 1992.
12. P. Klint. A meta-environment for generating programming environments. *ACM Transactions on Software Engineering and Methodology*, 2(2):176–201, 1993.
13. K. McAloon and C. Tretkoff. 2LP: Linear programming and logic programming. In P. Van Hentenryck and V. Saraswat, editors, *Principles and Practice of Constraint Programming*, pages 101–116. MIT Press, 1995.
14. A. Oplobedu, J. Marcovitch, and Y. Tourbier. CHARME: Un langage industriel de programmation par contraintes, illustré par une application chez Renault. In *Ninth International Workshop on Expert Systems and their Applications: General Conference, Volume 1*, pages 55–70, Avignon, France, 1989. EC2.
15. F. Pfenning, editor. *Types in Logic Programming*. MIT Press, Cambridge, Massachusetts, 1992.

16. J.-F. Puget and M. Leconte. Beyond the glass box: Constraints as objects. In *Proc. of the 1995 International Symposium on Logic Programming*, pages 513–527, 1995.

17. J.-C. Regin. A filtering algorithm for constraints of difference in CSPs. In *AAAI-94: Proceedings of the 12th National Conference on Artificial Intelligence*, pages 362–367, 1994.

18. I. Shvetsov, V. Telerman, and D. Ushakov. *NeMo+* : Object-oriented constraint programming environment based on subdefinite models. In G. Smolka, editor, *Artificial Intelligence and Symbolic Mathematical Computations*, Lecture Notes in Computer Science, vol. 1330, pages 534–548, Berlin, 1997. Springer-Verlag.

19. P. Van Hentenryck, Helmut Simonis, and Mehmet Dincbas. Constraint satisfaction using constraint logic programming. *Artificial Intelligence*, 58:113–159, 1992.

Type and Effect Systems

Flemming Nielson and Hanne Riis Nielson

Department of Computer Science, Aarhus University, Denmark.

Abstract. The design and implementation of a correct system can benefit from employing static techniques for ensuring that the dynamic behaviour satisfies the specification. Many programming languages incorporate types for ensuring that certain operations are only applied to data of the appropriate form. A natural extension of type checking techniques is to enrich the types with annotations and effects that further describe intensional aspects of the dynamic behaviour.

Keywords. Polymorphic type systems, effect annotations, subeffecting and subtyping, semantic correctness, type inference algorithms, syntactic soundness and completeness. Analyses for control flow, binding times, side effects, region structure, and communication structure.

1   Introduction

Static analysis of programs comprises a broad collection of techniques for predicting safe and computable approximations to the set of values or behaviours arising dynamically during computation; this may be used to validate program transformations, to generate more efficient code or to increase the understanding of the software so as to demonstrate that the software satisfies its specification. We shall find it helpful to divide the techniques into the following two approaches. The *flow based* approach includes the traditional data flow analysis techniques for mainly imperative and object-oriented languages; it also includes the constraint based control flow analysis techniques developed for functional and object oriented languages; finally, it includes the use of mathematical modelling in the abstract interpretation of imperative, functional, concurrent and logic languages. The *inference based* approach includes general logical techniques touching upon program verification and model checking; it also includes type and effect systems developed for functional, imperative and concurrent languages and it is this latter group of techniques that we consider here.

We shall suppose that a typed programming language is given. In *soft typing* all programs can be typed because a "top" type can be used in the absence of meaningful "ordinary" types; this perspective is similar to that of the flow based approach and is quite useful for analysing the behaviour of programs but is less useful for enforcing the absence of dynamic errors. In this paper we focus on *strong typing* where no "top" type is around and where certain erroneous

E.-R. Olderog, B. Steffen (Eds.): Correct System Design, LNCS 1710, pp. 114–136, 1999.
© Springer-Verlag Berlin Heidelberg 1999

programs are rejected by the type system; in this way types are not only used for analysing the behaviours of programs but also for enforcing the absence of certain kinds of dynamic errors.

The overall approach of type systems is to associate types to programs; normally the types merely describe the form of the data supplied to, and produced by, programs. The association of types to programs is done by a set of inference rules that are largely syntax-directed; since subprograms may contain free variables this needs to be relative to a type environment that maps the free variables to their types. We express the typing by means of a typing judgement that is usually a ternary relation on type environments, programs and types; it is frequently written $\Gamma \vdash p : \tau$ where p is the program, τ is the type, and Γ is the type environment. The main challenges of devising type systems is *(i)* to ensure that they are semantically correct (with respect to some dynamic semantics), *(ii)* to ensure that they are decidable so that types can be checked by an algorithm, and *(iii)* to ensure that there always is a "best" type, called a principal type, so that an algorithm can produce the intended type automatically.

Type and effect systems refine the type information by annotating the types so as to express further intensional or extensional properties of the semantics of the program [18,19,20,21]. In Section 2 this takes the form of annotating the base types or the type constructors. In Section 3 we study effect systems where the annotations describe certain intensional aspects of the actions taking place during evaluation. In Section 4 we further enrich the expressivenes of effects so as to obtain causal information in the manner of process algebras. We then expose the overall methodology behind type and effect systems in Section 5 and indicate those combinations of features that challenge state-of-the-art.

Further Reading. A more thorough development of the techniques of static analysis can be found in [30] (particularly in Chapter 5 that deals with type and effect systems) as well as in the references given.

2   Annotated Type Systems

Many programming languages incorporate types as a static technique for ensuring that certain operations are only applied to data of the appropriate form; this is useful for ensuring that the dynamic behaviour satisfies the specification.

Example 1. A Typed Language.

We shall use the following simple functional language to illustrate the development; constructs for iteration, recursion and conditionals present no obstacles and have only been left out in the interest of brevity. We shall later extend the language with side effects (as in Standard ML) and communication (as in Concurrent ML) thereby suggesting that type and effect systems apply equally well to imperative and concurrent languages.

The language has expressions (or programs) e and types τ given by:

$$e ::= c \mid x \mid \mathtt{fn}_\pi \; x => e_0 \mid e_1 \; e_2 \mid \cdots$$

$$\tau ::= \mathtt{int} \mid \mathtt{bool} \mid \cdots \mid \tau_1 \rightarrow \tau_2$$

Here c denotes a family of constants (each of type τ_c), x denotes a family of variables, and π is an identification of the function abstraction to be used in the control flow analysis to be presented in Example 2.

The typing judgements of the underlying or original type system have the form $\Gamma \vdash_{\mathsf{UL}} e : \tau$ where the type environment Γ maps variables to types; the definition is as follows:

$$\Gamma \vdash_{\mathsf{UL}} c : \tau_c \qquad\qquad \frac{\Gamma[x \mapsto \tau_x] \vdash_{\mathsf{UL}} e_0 : \tau_0}{\Gamma \vdash_{\mathsf{UL}} \mathtt{fn}_\pi \; x => e_0 : \tau_x \rightarrow \tau_0}$$

$$\Gamma \vdash_{\mathsf{UL}} x : \Gamma(x) \qquad\qquad \frac{\Gamma \vdash_{\mathsf{UL}} e_1 : \tau_2 \rightarrow \tau_0 \quad \Gamma \vdash_{\mathsf{UL}} e_2 : \tau_2}{\Gamma \vdash_{\mathsf{UL}} e_1 \; e_2 : \tau_0}$$

That a function has type $\tau_1 \rightarrow \tau_2$ means that given an argument of type τ_1 it will return a value of type τ_2 in case it terminates. $\qquad\qquad\qquad\qquad$ □

Perhaps the simplest technique for extending the expressiveness of types is to add annotations to the type constructors or base types. One popular class of analyses that can be expressed using this technique consists of interprocedural control flow analyses which track the origins of where functions might have been defined [7,8,11]; this can be extended with components for tracking where functions are applied and thus has strong similarities to the classical *use-definition* and *definition-use* analyses of data flow analysis.

Example 2. Control Flow Analysis.

To obtain a control flow analysis we shall annotate the function type $\tau_1 \rightarrow \tau_2$ with information, φ, about which function it might be:

$$\varphi ::= \{\pi\} \mid \varphi_1 \cup \varphi_2 \mid \emptyset$$

$$\widehat{\tau} ::= \mathtt{int} \mid \mathtt{bool} \mid \cdots \mid \widehat{\tau_1} \xrightarrow{\varphi} \widehat{\tau_2}$$

So φ will be a *set* of function names – describing the set of function definitions that can result in a function of a given type.

The typing judgements of the control flow analysis have the form $\widehat{\Gamma} \vdash_{\mathsf{CFA}} e : \widehat{\tau}$ where the type environment $\widehat{\Gamma}$ maps variables to annotated types. The judgements are defined in Table 1; note that the clause for function abstraction annotates the arrow of the resulting function type with the information that the abstraction named π should be included in the set $\{\pi\} \cup \varphi$ of functions that could be returned. In the presence of conditionals it is essential that we use $\{\pi\} \cup \varphi$

$$\widehat{\Gamma} \vdash_{\mathsf{CFA}} c : \widehat{\tau}_c \qquad\qquad \frac{\widehat{\Gamma}[x \mapsto \widehat{\tau}_x] \vdash_{\mathsf{CFA}} e_0 : \widehat{\tau}_0}{\widehat{\Gamma} \vdash_{\mathsf{CFA}} \mathbf{fn}_\pi \; x \Rightarrow e_0 : \widehat{\tau}_x \xrightarrow{\{\pi\} \cup \varphi} \tau_0}$$

$$\widehat{\Gamma} \vdash_{\mathsf{CFA}} x : \widehat{\Gamma}(x) \qquad\qquad \frac{\widehat{\Gamma} \vdash_{\mathsf{CFA}} e_1 : \widehat{\tau}_2 \xrightarrow{\varphi} \widehat{\tau}_0 \quad \widehat{\Gamma} \vdash_{\mathsf{CFA}} e_2 : \widehat{\tau}_2}{\widehat{\Gamma} \vdash_{\mathsf{CFA}} e_1 \; e_2 : \widehat{\tau}_0}$$

Table 1. Control Flow Analysis: $\widehat{\Gamma} \vdash_{\mathsf{CFA}} e : \widehat{\tau}$ (Example 2).

rather than $\{\pi\}$ because the latter choice does not give rise to a *conservative extension* of the underlying type system: this means that there will be expressions that are typed in the underlying type system but that have no analysis in the control flow analysis; (this point is related to the issue of subeffecting to be discussed in Section 3.)

We should point out that we allow to replace $\widehat{\tau}_1 \xrightarrow{\varphi_1} \widehat{\tau}_2$ by $\widehat{\tau}_1 \xrightarrow{\varphi_2} \widehat{\tau}_2$ whenever φ_1 and φ_2 are "equal as sets". More generally we allow to replace $\widehat{\tau}_1$ by $\widehat{\tau}_2$ if they have the same underlying types and all annotations on corresponding function arrows are "equal as sets". To be utterly formal this can be axiomatised by a set of axioms and rules expressing that set union has a unit and is idempotent, commutative, and associative, together with axioms and rules ensuring that equality is an equivalence relation as well as a congruence; the abbreviation *UCAI* is often used for these properties.   □

Subtyping and Polymorphism

Another popular class of analyses that can be expressed by annotations is the binding time analyses (e.g. [13]) which distinguish data as to whether they are static (available at compile-time) or dynamic (available at run-time); these analyses form the basis of *partial evaluation* and can also be used as the basis for *security* analyses (e.g. [12]) that distinguish between secret and public information.

Example 3. Binding Time Analysis.

For binding time analysis we extend the language of Examples 1 and 2 with a let-construct:

$$e ::= \cdots \mid \mathbf{let} \; x = e_1 \; \mathbf{in} \; e_2$$

(In fact let $x = e_1$ in e_2 is semantically equivalent to (fn $x \Rightarrow e_2$) e_1.) The annotations of interest for the binding time analysis are:

$$\varphi ::= \beta \mid \mathsf{S} \mid \mathsf{D}$$
$$\widehat{\tau} ::= \mathbf{int}^\varphi \mid \mathbf{bool}^\varphi \mid \cdots \mid \widehat{\tau}_1 \xrightarrow{\varphi} \widehat{\tau}_2$$
$$\widehat{\sigma} ::= \forall(\beta_1, \cdots, \beta_n).\widehat{\tau} \mid \widehat{\tau}$$

The annotation S is used to model data that is available statically, D is used to model data that is available dynamically, and β is an annotation variable that can take its values among S and D.

A partial ordering on annotations $\varphi \sqsubseteq \varphi'$ may be defined by:

$$\varphi \sqsubseteq \varphi \qquad S \sqsubseteq D$$

Types contain annotations on the type constructors as well as on the base types; a static function operating on dynamic integers will thus have the annotated type $\mathtt{int}^D \xrightarrow{S} \mathtt{int}^D$. This type system is motivated by applications to partial evaluation and this suggests imposing a well-formedness condition on types so as to rule out types like $\mathtt{int}^S \xrightarrow{D} \mathtt{int}^S$ that are regarded as being meaningless. This is performed by the auxiliary judgement $\widehat{\tau} \triangleright \varphi$ that additionally extracts the top-level annotation φ from the annotated type $\widehat{\tau}$:

$$\mathtt{int}^\varphi \triangleright \varphi \qquad \mathtt{bool}^\varphi \triangleright \varphi$$

$$\frac{\widehat{\tau}_1 \triangleright \varphi_1 \quad \widehat{\tau}_2 \triangleright \varphi_2}{\widehat{\tau}_1 \xrightarrow{\varphi} \widehat{\tau}_2 \triangleright \varphi} \text{ if } \varphi \sqsubseteq \varphi_1 \text{ and } \varphi \sqsubseteq \varphi_2$$

In short, a static function is allowed to operate on dynamic data but not vice versa. Since we have annotation variables we can express a limited form of annotation polymorphism and we use $\widehat{\sigma}$ to denote the corresponding type schemes; for simplicity we do not incorporate type variables or type polymorphism.

The typing judgements have the form $\widehat{\Gamma} \vdash_{\mathsf{BTA}} e : \widehat{\sigma}$ where the type environment $\widehat{\Gamma}$ maps variables to type schemes (or types) and $\widehat{\sigma}$ is the type scheme (or type) for the expression e. The analysis is specified by the axioms and rules of Table 2 and is explained in the sequel. The first five axioms and rules are straightforward; note that the rule for function abstraction checks that the type is well-formed and that the rule for let makes use of type schemes.

The next rule is a subtyping rule that allows to weaken the information contained in an annotated type. The subtype ordering $\widehat{\tau} \leq \widehat{\tau}'$ is given by:

$$\mathtt{int}^\varphi \leq \mathtt{int}^{\varphi'} \text{ if } \varphi \sqsubseteq \varphi'$$

$$\mathtt{bool}^\varphi \leq \mathtt{bool}^{\varphi'} \text{ if } \varphi \sqsubseteq \varphi'$$

$$\frac{\widehat{\tau}_1' \leq \widehat{\tau}_1 \quad \widehat{\tau}_2 \leq \widehat{\tau}_2'}{\widehat{\tau}_1 \xrightarrow{\varphi} \widehat{\tau}_2 \leq \widehat{\tau}_1' \xrightarrow{\varphi'} \widehat{\tau}_2'} \text{ if } \varphi \sqsubseteq \varphi' \wedge \widehat{\tau}_1' \xrightarrow{\varphi'} \widehat{\tau}_2' \triangleright \varphi'$$

This ensures that only well-formed types are produced and that the ordering is reversed for arguments to functions; we say that $\widehat{\tau}_1 \xrightarrow{\varphi} \widehat{\tau}_2$ is *contravariant* in $\widehat{\tau}_1$ but *covariant* in φ and $\widehat{\tau}_2$. (Think of the annotated type $\widehat{\tau} \xrightarrow{\varphi'} \widehat{\tau}'$ as being analogous to the logical formula $\widehat{\tau} \Rightarrow \varphi' \wedge \widehat{\tau}'$ and use that the inference rule expresses the monotonicity of logical implication.)

The final two rules are responsible for the polymorphism. The first rule is the *generalisation rule* that is used to construct type schemes: we can quantify over

$$\widehat{\Gamma} \vdash_{\mathsf{BTA}} c : \widehat{\tau}_c \qquad \widehat{\Gamma} \vdash_{\mathsf{BTA}} x : \widehat{\Gamma}(x)$$

$$\frac{\widehat{\Gamma}[x \mapsto \widehat{\tau}_x] \vdash_{\mathsf{BTA}} e_0 : \widehat{\tau}_0}{\widehat{\Gamma} \vdash_{\mathsf{BTA}} \mathtt{fn}_\pi\ x \Rightarrow e_0 : \widehat{\tau}_x \xrightarrow{\varphi} \widehat{\tau}_0} \qquad \text{if } (\widehat{\tau}_x \xrightarrow{\varphi} \widehat{\tau}_0) \triangleright \varphi$$

$$\frac{\widehat{\Gamma} \vdash_{\mathsf{BTA}} e_1 : \widehat{\tau}_2 \xrightarrow{\varphi} \widehat{\tau}_0 \qquad \widehat{\Gamma} \vdash_{\mathsf{BTA}} e_2 : \widehat{\tau}_2}{\widehat{\Gamma} \vdash_{\mathsf{BTA}} e_1\ e_2 : \widehat{\tau}_0}$$

$$\frac{\widehat{\Gamma} \vdash_{\mathsf{BTA}} e_1 : \widehat{\sigma}_1 \quad \widehat{\Gamma}[x \mapsto \widehat{\sigma}_1] \vdash_{\mathsf{BTA}} e_2 : \widehat{\tau}_2}{\widehat{\Gamma} \vdash_{\mathsf{BTA}} \mathtt{let}\ x = e_1\ \mathtt{in}\ e_2 : \widehat{\tau}_2}$$

$$\frac{\widehat{\Gamma} \vdash_{\mathsf{BTA}} e : \widehat{\tau}}{\widehat{\Gamma} \vdash_{\mathsf{BTA}} e : \widehat{\tau}'} \qquad \text{if } \widehat{\tau} \leq \widehat{\tau}'$$

$$\frac{\widehat{\Gamma} \vdash_{\mathsf{BTA}} e : \widehat{\tau}}{\widehat{\Gamma} \vdash_{\mathsf{BTA}} e : \forall(\beta_1, \cdots, \beta_n).\widehat{\tau}} \qquad \text{if } \beta_1, \cdots, \beta_n \text{ do not occur free in } \widehat{\Gamma}$$

$$\frac{\widehat{\Gamma} \vdash_{\mathsf{BTA}} e : \forall(\beta_1, \cdots, \beta_n).\widehat{\tau}}{\widehat{\Gamma} \vdash_{\mathsf{BTA}} e : (\theta\ \widehat{\tau})} \qquad \text{if } dom(\theta) \subseteq \{\beta_1, \cdots, \beta_n\} \text{ and } \exists \varphi : (\theta\ \widehat{\tau}) \triangleright \varphi$$

Table 2. Binding Time Analysis: $\widehat{\Gamma} \vdash_{\mathsf{BTA}} e : \widehat{\tau}\ \&\ \varphi$ (Example 3).

any annotation variable that does not occur free in the type environment; this rule is usually used immediately before the rule for the let-construct. The second rule is the *instantiation rule* that can be used to turn type schemes into annotated types: we just apply a substitution in order to replace the bound annotation variables with other annotations; this rule is usually used immediately after the axiom for variables.   □

References for type systems with subtyping include [9,10,23] as well as the more advanced [16,37,38] that also deal with Hindley/Milner polymorphism (as found in Standard ML). To allow a general treatment of subtyping, these papers generally demand constraints to be an explicit part of the inference system and this is somewhat more complex than the approach taken here; such considerations are mainly motivated by the desire to obtain principal types and in order to develop syntactically sound and complete type inference algorithms as will be discussed in Section 5. Indeed, our formulation of subtyping only allows *shape conformant subtyping*, where the underlying type system does *not* make use of any form of subtyping, and is thus somewhat simpler than *atomic subtyping*, where an ordering is imposed upon base types, and *general subtyping*, where an ordering may be imposed between arbitrary types.

Strictness analyses and classical data flow analyses can also be expressed as annotated type systems but to be useful they may require the type system to be extended with conjunction or disjunction types [4,5,14,15] thereby touching upon the logical techniques. In annotated type systems, as well as in the type and effect systems considered below, the annotations are normally sets of some kind, but linking up with abstract interpretation it should be possible to allow more general annotations that are elements of a complete lattice (that is possibly of finite height as in the "monotone frameworks" of data flow analysis); however, this possibility is hardly considered in the literature except in the case of binding time analysis where the binding times (e.g. static and dynamic) are partially ordered, c.f. [13,24].

3   Type and Effect Systems

The typing judgements of type systems take the following general form: a type is associated with a program (or an expression or a statement) relative to a type environment providing the type (or type scheme) for each free variable; this also holds for the typing judgements used for the annotated type systems presented above. Effect systems can be viewed as an outgrowth of annotated type system where the typing judgements take the following more elaborate form: a type *and an effect* is associated with a program relative to a type environment. Formally, effects are nothing but the annotations already considered, but conceptually, they describe intensional information about what takes place during evaluation of the program unlike what was the case above.

Subeffecting and Subtyping

The literature has seen a great variation in the uses to which effects have been put: collecting the set of procedures or functions called [41], collecting the set of storage cells written or read during execution [40], determining what exceptions can be raised during evaluation, and collecting the regions in which evaluation takes place [44] to mention just a few. We begin by considering an analysis for collecting the set of storage cells written or read during execution.

Example 4. Adding Imperative Constructs.

To facilitate the side effect analysis we shall add imperative constructs (resembling those of Standard ML) for creating reference variables and for accessing and updating their values:

$$e ::= \cdots \mid \mathbf{new}_\pi \ x := e_1 \ \mathbf{in} \ e_2 \mid !x \mid x := e_0$$

The idea is that $\mathbf{new}_\pi \ x := e_1 \ \mathbf{in} \ e_2$ creates a new reference variable x for use in e_2 and initialises it to the value of e_1; as above we use π to identify the creation point. The value of the reference variable x can be obtained by writing $!x$ and it may be set to a new value by the assignment $x := e_0$. The type of a reference cell for values of type τ is τ **ref** and the underlying type system of Example 1 is extended with the rules:

$$\Gamma \vdash_{\mathsf{UL}} \,!x : \tau \text{ if } \Gamma(x) = \tau \text{ ref}$$

$$\frac{\Gamma \vdash_{\mathsf{UL}} e : \tau}{\Gamma \vdash_{\mathsf{UL}} x := e : \tau} \text{ if } \Gamma(x) = \tau \text{ ref}$$

$$\frac{\Gamma \vdash_{\mathsf{UL}} e_1 : \tau_1 \quad \Gamma[x \mapsto \tau_1 \text{ ref}] \vdash_{\mathsf{UL}} e_2 : \tau_2}{\Gamma \vdash_{\mathsf{UL}} \text{new}_\pi \; x := e_1 \text{ in } e_2 : \tau_2}$$

Example 5. Side Effect Analysis.

In the side effect analysis a reference variable is represented by a set ϱ of program points where it could have been created; this set is called a region and has the general form $\{\pi_1\} \cup \cdots \cup \{\pi_n\}$ which we write as the set $\{\pi_1, \cdots, \pi_n\}$. The annotations of interest are:

$$\varphi ::= \{!\pi\} \mid \{\pi := \} \mid \{\text{new}\,\pi\} \mid \varphi_1 \cup \varphi_2 \mid \emptyset$$

$$\varrho ::= \{\pi\} \mid \varrho_1 \cup \varrho_2 \mid \emptyset$$

$$\widehat{\tau} ::= \text{int} \mid \text{bool} \mid \cdots \mid \widehat{\tau}_1 \xrightarrow{\varphi} \widehat{\tau}_2 \mid \widehat{\tau} \text{ ref } \varrho$$

Here $\widehat{\tau}$ **ref** ϱ is the type of a location created at one of the program points in the region ϱ; the location is used for holding values of the annotated type $\widehat{\tau}$. The annotation $!\pi$ means that the value of a location created at π is accessed, $\pi :=$ means that a location created at π is assigned, and $\text{new}\,\pi$ that a new location has been created at π.

The typing judgements have the form $\widehat{\Gamma} \vdash_{\mathsf{SE}} e : \widehat{\tau} \,\&\, \varphi$. This means that under the type environment $\widehat{\Gamma}$, if the expression e terminates then the resulting value will have the annotated type $\widehat{\tau}$ and φ describes the side effects that might have taken place during evaluation. As before the type environment $\widehat{\Gamma}$ will map variables to annotated types; no effects are involved because the semantics is *eager* rather than *lazy*.

The analysis is specified by the axioms and rules of Table 3; these rules embody the essence of effect systems. In the clauses for constants and variables we record that there are no side effects so we use $\emptyset$ for the overall effect. The premise of the clause for function abstraction gives the effect of the function body and this effect is used to annotate the arrow of the function type whereas we use $\emptyset$ as the overall effect of the function definition itself: no side effects can be observed by simply defining the function. In the rule for function application we see how the information comes together: the overall effect is what can be observed from evaluating the argument e_1, what can be observed from evaluating the argument e_2, and what is obtained from evaluating the body of the function called.

Turning to the rules involving reference variables we make sure that we only assign a value of the appropriate type to the reference variable. Also, in each of

$$\widehat{\Gamma} \vdash_{\mathsf{SE}} c : \widehat{\tau}_c \;\&\; \emptyset \qquad\qquad \widehat{\Gamma} \vdash_{\mathsf{SE}} x : \widehat{\Gamma}(x) \;\&\; \emptyset$$

$$\frac{\widehat{\Gamma}[x \mapsto \widehat{\tau}_x] \vdash_{\mathsf{SE}} e_0 : \widehat{\tau}_0 \;\&\; \varphi_0}{\widehat{\Gamma} \vdash_{\mathsf{SE}} \mathbf{fn}_\pi \; x \Rightarrow e_0 : \widehat{\tau}_x \xrightarrow{\varphi_0} \widehat{\tau}_0 \;\&\; \emptyset}$$

$$\frac{\widehat{\Gamma} \vdash_{\mathsf{SE}} e_1 : \widehat{\tau}_2 \xrightarrow{\varphi_0} \widehat{\tau}_0 \;\&\; \varphi_1 \quad \widehat{\Gamma} \vdash_{\mathsf{SE}} e_2 : \widehat{\tau}_2 \;\&\; \varphi_2}{\widehat{\Gamma} \vdash_{\mathsf{SE}} e_1 \; e_2 : \widehat{\tau}_0 \;\&\; \varphi_1 \cup \varphi_2 \cup \varphi_0}$$

$$\widehat{\Gamma} \vdash_{\mathsf{SE}} !x : \widehat{\tau} \;\&\; \{!\pi_1, \cdots, !\pi_n\} \text{ if } \widehat{\Gamma}(x) = \widehat{\tau} \; \mathbf{ref} \; \{\pi_1, \cdots, \pi_n\}$$

$$\frac{\widehat{\Gamma} \vdash_{\mathsf{SE}} e : \widehat{\tau} \;\&\; \varphi}{\widehat{\Gamma} \vdash_{\mathsf{SE}} x := e : \widehat{\tau} \;\&\; \varphi \cup \{\pi_1 :=, \cdots, \pi_n :=\}} \text{ if } \widehat{\Gamma}(x) = \widehat{\tau} \; \mathbf{ref} \; \{\pi_1, \cdots, \pi_n\}$$

$$\frac{\widehat{\Gamma} \vdash_{\mathsf{SE}} e_1 : \widehat{\tau}_1 \;\&\; \varphi_1 \quad \widehat{\Gamma}[x \mapsto \widehat{\tau}_1 \; \mathbf{ref}(\varrho \cup \{\pi\})] \vdash_{\mathsf{SE}} e_2 : \widehat{\tau}_2 \;\&\; \varphi_2}{\widehat{\Gamma} \vdash_{\mathsf{SE}} \mathbf{new}_\pi \; x := e_1 \; \mathbf{in} \; e_2 : \widehat{\tau}_2 \;\&\; (\varphi_1 \cup \varphi_2 \cup \{\mathbf{new}\,\pi\})}$$

$$\frac{\widehat{\Gamma} \vdash_{\mathsf{SE}} e : \widehat{\tau} \;\&\; \varphi}{\widehat{\Gamma} \vdash_{\mathsf{SE}} e : \widehat{\tau} \;\&\; \varphi'} \text{ if } \varphi \subseteq \varphi'$$

Table 3. Side Effect Analysis: $\widehat{\Gamma} \vdash_{\mathsf{SE}} e : \widehat{\tau} \;\&\; \varphi$ (Examples 5, 6 and 7).

the rules we make sure to record that a location at the relevant program point might have been created, referenced or assigned.

The purpose of ϱ in the rule for new in Table 3, and the purpose of the last rule in Table 3, is to ensure that we obtain a conservative extension of the underlying type system. The last rule is called a *subeffecting* rule and is essential in the presence of conditionals. The notation $\varphi \subseteq \varphi'$ means that φ is "a subset" of φ' (modulo *UCAI*). □

Example 6. Subtyping for Side Effect Analysis.

The last rule in Table 3 can be augmented with a rule for *subtyping*:

$$\frac{\widehat{\Gamma} \vdash_{\mathsf{SE}} e : \widehat{\tau} \;\&\; \varphi}{\widehat{\Gamma} \vdash_{\mathsf{SE}} e : \widehat{\tau}' \;\&\; \varphi} \text{ if } \widehat{\tau} \leq \widehat{\tau}'$$

The ordering $\widehat{\tau} \leq \widehat{\tau}'$ on annotated types is derived from the ordering on annotations as follows:

$$\widehat{\tau} \leq \widehat{\tau} \qquad \frac{\widehat{\tau}_1' \leq \widehat{\tau}_1 \quad \widehat{\tau}_2 \leq \widehat{\tau}_2' \quad \varphi \subseteq \varphi'}{\widehat{\tau}_1 \xrightarrow{\varphi} \widehat{\tau}_2 \leq \widehat{\tau}_1' \xrightarrow{\varphi'} \widehat{\tau}_2'} \qquad \frac{\widehat{\tau} \leq \widehat{\tau}' \quad \widehat{\tau}' \leq \widehat{\tau} \quad \varrho \subseteq \varrho'}{\widehat{\tau} \; \mathbf{ref} \; \varrho \leq \widehat{\tau}' \; \mathbf{ref} \; \varrho'}$$

Here $\varphi \subseteq \varphi'$ means that φ is "a subset" of φ' (modulo *UCAI*) and similarly $\varrho \subseteq \varrho'$ means that ϱ is "a subset" of ϱ' (modulo *UCAI*); as before $\widehat{\tau}_1 \xrightarrow{\varphi} \widehat{\tau}_2$ is *contravariant* in $\hat{\tau}_1$ but *covariant* in φ and $\hat{\tau}_2$. Also $\hat{\tau}$ ref ϱ is both covariant in $\hat{\tau}$ (when the reference variable is used for accessing its value as in $!x$) and contravariant in $\hat{\tau}$ (when the reference variable is used for assignments as in $x := \cdots$) whereas it is only covariant in ϱ. This form of subtyping amounts to *shape conformant subtyping* because $\hat{\tau}_1 \le \hat{\tau}_2$ implies that the two annotated types have the same underlying types.   □

Subeffecting alone suffices for obtaining a conservative extension of the underlying type system – provided that we regard the use of ϱ in the rule for **new** as being an integral part of subeffecting; the general idea is that subeffecting allows to "enlarge" the effects at an *early* point so that they do not conflict with the demands of the type and effect system. This reduces the usefulness of the effects but by incorporating subtyping we can "enlarge" the types at a *later* point; hence more informative types and effects can be used in subprograms. Coming back to our treatment of control flow analysis in Example 2 we note that basically it is a subeffecting analysis.

Polymorphism and Polymorphic Recursion

Subtyping is one of the classical techniques for making a type more useful by allowing to adapt it to different needs. Another classical technique is Hindley/Milner polymorphism as found in Standard ML and other functional languages. Both techniques are useful for increasing the precision of the information obtainable from type and effect systems.

Example 7. Polymorphism for Side Effect Analysis.

We now once more extend the language of Examples 5 and 6 with a polymorphic let-construct:

$$e ::= \cdots \mid \text{let } x = e_1 \text{ in } e_2$$

We also allow types to contain type variables α, effects to contain annotation variables β and regions to contain region variables ρ:

$$\hat{\tau} ::= \cdots \mid \alpha \qquad \varphi ::= \cdots \mid \beta \qquad \varrho ::= \cdots \mid \rho$$

We can then define type schemes: a type scheme is a type where a (possible empty) list $\zeta_1, \cdots, \zeta_n$ of type, effect and region variables has been quantified over:

$$\hat{\sigma} ::= \forall(\zeta_1, \cdots, \zeta_n).\hat{\tau}$$

If the list is empty we simply write $\hat{\tau}$ for $\forall().\hat{\tau}$.

The typing judgements will be of the form $\widehat{\Gamma} \vdash_{\mathsf{SE}} e : \hat{\sigma} \,\&\, \varphi$ where the type environment $\widehat{\Gamma}$ now maps variables to type schemes (or types) and $\hat{\sigma}$ is a type scheme (or type). The clauses are as in Table 3 with the addition of the following rules:

$$\frac{\widehat{\Gamma} \vdash_{\mathsf{SE}} e_1 : \widehat{\sigma}_1 \ \& \ \varphi_1 \quad \widehat{\Gamma}[x \mapsto \widehat{\sigma}_1] \vdash_{\mathsf{SE}} e_2 : \widehat{\tau}_2 \ \& \ \varphi_2}{\widehat{\Gamma} \vdash_{\mathsf{SE}} \mathtt{let} \ x = e_1 \ \mathtt{in} \ e_2 : \widehat{\tau}_2 \ \& \ \varphi_1 \cup \varphi_2}$$

$$\frac{\widehat{\Gamma} \vdash_{\mathsf{SE}} e : \widehat{\tau} \ \& \ \varphi}{\widehat{\Gamma} \vdash_{\mathsf{SE}} e : \forall(\zeta_1, \cdots, \zeta_n).\widehat{\tau} \ \& \ \varphi} \qquad \text{if } \zeta_1, \cdots, \zeta_n \text{ do not occur free in } \widehat{\Gamma} \text{ and } \varphi$$

$$\frac{\widehat{\Gamma} \vdash_{\mathsf{SE}} e : \forall(\zeta_1, \cdots, \zeta_n).\widehat{\tau} \ \& \ \varphi}{\widehat{\Gamma} \vdash_{\mathsf{SE}} e : (\theta \ \widehat{\tau}) \ \& \ \varphi} \qquad \text{if } dom(\theta) \subseteq \{\zeta_1, \cdots, \zeta_n\}$$

The second and third rules are responsible for the polymorphism and are extensions of the last two rules of Table 2. The second rule is the *generalisation rule*: we can quantify over any type, annotation or region variable that does not occur free in the assumptions *or in the effect*. The third rule is the *instantiation rule*: we just apply a substitution in order to replace the bound type, annotation and region variables with other types, annotations and regions.   □

Both subtyping and polymorphism improve subeffecting by giving finer control over when to "enlarge" the types; we already explained the advantage: that more informative types and effects can be used in subprograms. Since the mechanisms used are incomparable it clearly makes sense to combine both. However, as discussed in Section 5, it may be quite challenging to develop a type and effect inference algorithm that is both syntactically sound and complete.

Example 8. Region Inference.

The `let`-construct can be used to give polymorphic types to functions. But in the Hindley/Milner approach a recursive function can only be used polymorphically outside of its own body – inside its own body it must be used monomorphically. The generalisation to allow recursive functions to be used polymorphically also inside their own bodies is known as *polymorphic recursion* but gives rise to an undecidable type system; this means that no terminating type inference algorithm can be both syntactically sound and complete. This insight is a useful illustration of the close borderline between decidability and undecidability that holds for the inference based approach to the static analysis of programs.

Even though we abstain from using polymorphic recursion for ordinary types there is still the possibility of using polymorphic recursion for the effects annotating the ordinary and possibly polymorphic types given to recursive functions. In this way, distinct uses of a recursive function inside its body can still be analysed in different ways. This approach is taken in an analysis known as region inference [44] that is used when implementing functional languages in a stack-based regime rather than a heap-based regime. More precisely, the memory model is a stack of regions of data items, and the analysis facilitates determining at compile-time in which region to allocate data and when to deallocate a region (rather than using a garbage collector at run-time).

The use of polymorphic recursion for effect and region annotations allows the inference system to deal precisely with the allocation of data inside recursive functions. Furthermore, the inference system implicitly incorporates a notion of constraint between annotation variables and their meaning (via a dot notation on function arrows); as discussed in Section 5 this is a common feature of systems based on subtyping as otherwise principal types may not be expressible. To obtain effects that are as small as possible, the inference system uses "effect masking" [21,39,40] for removing internal components of the effect: effect components that only deal with regions that are not externally visible. It is unclear whether or not this system is decidable but nonetheless it has proved quite useful in practice: a syntactically sound inference algorithm has been devised and it is sufficiently accurate that a region-based implementation of Standard ML has turned out to compete favourably with a heap-based implementation.   □

Mutually Recursive Types and Effects

So far the annotations and effects have not included any type information; as we shall see in Section 5 this is essential for being able to develop type and effect inference algorithms using a two-stage approach where first the types are determined and next the effects annotating the types. It is possible to be more permissive in allowing effects to contain type information and in allowing even the shape of types and type schemes to be influenced by the type information contained in the effects; as will be explained in Section 5 this calls for a more complex one-stage approach to type and effect inference algorithms.

Example 9. Polymorphic Typing in Standard ML.

The Hindley/Milner approach to polymorphism was originally conceived only for pure functional languages. Extending it to deal with side effects in the form of reference variables has presented quite a few obstacles. As an example consider the following program fragment in an ML-like language:

```
let x = new nil in (··· x:=cons(7,x) ··· x:=cons(true,x) ···)
```

Here x is declared as a new cell whose contents is initially the empty list nil and it might be natural to let the type of x be something like $\forall \alpha. (\alpha \ \mathtt{list}) \, \mathtt{ref}$; but then both assignments will typecheck and hence the type system will be semantically unsound as Standard ML only permits homogeneous lists where all elements have the same type.

Several systems have been developed for overcoming these problems (see e.g. [42]). One approach is to restrict the ability to generalise over "imperative" type variables: these are the type variables that may be used in an imperative manner. It is therefore natural to adapt the side effect analysis to record the imperative type variables and to prohibit the generalisation rule from generalising over imperative type variables. In this way the shape of type schemes is clearly influenced by the effect information. This idea occurred already in [39,40,48] in the form of an extended side effect analysis with polymorphism and subeffecting.   □

4   Causal Type Systems

So far the annotations and effects have had a rather simple structure in that they have mainly been sets. It is possible to be more ambitious in identifying the "causality" or temporal order among the various operations. As an example, we now consider the task of extracting *behaviours* (reminiscent of terms in a process algebra) from programs in Concurrent ML by means of a type and effect system; here effects (the behaviours) have structure, they may influence the type information (as in Example 9), and there are inference rules for subeffecting and shape conformant subtyping. These ideas first occurred in [27,29] (not involving polymorphism) and in [2,33,34] (involving polymorphism); our presentation is mainly based on [33,34] because the inference system is somewhat simpler than that of [1] (at the expense of making it harder to develop an inference algorithm); we refer to [1, Chapter 1] for an overview of some of the subtle technical details. An application to the validation of embedded systems is presented in [32] where a control program is shown not to satisfy the safety requirements.

Example 10. Adding Constructs for Communication.

To facilitate the communication analysis we shall add constructs for creating new channels, for generating new processes, and for communicating between processes over typed channels:

$$e ::= \cdots \mid \mathtt{channel}_\pi \mid \mathtt{spawn}\ e_0 \mid \mathtt{send}\ e_1\ \mathtt{on}\ e_2 \mid \mathtt{receive}\ e_0$$

Here $\mathtt{channel}_\pi$ creates a new channel identifier, $\mathtt{spawn}\ e_0$ generates a new parallel process that executes e_0, and $\mathtt{send}\ v\ \mathtt{on}\ ch$ sends the value v to another process ready to receive a value by means of $\mathtt{receive}\ ch$. We shall assume that there is a special constant () of type $\mathtt{unit}$; this is the value to be returned by the $\mathtt{spawn}$ and $\mathtt{send}$ constructs.   □

Example 11. Communication Analysis.

Turning to the communication analysis the annotations of interest are:

$$\varphi ::= \beta \mid \Lambda \mid \varphi_1; \varphi_2 \mid \varphi_1 + \varphi_2 \mid \mathtt{rec}\beta.\varphi \mid \widehat{\tau}\ \mathtt{chan}\ \varrho \mid \mathtt{spawn}\ \varphi \mid \varrho!\widehat{\tau} \mid \varrho?\widehat{\tau}$$

$$\varrho ::= \rho \mid \{\pi\} \mid \varrho_1 \cup \varrho_2 \mid \emptyset$$

$$\widehat{\tau} ::= \alpha \mid \mathtt{int} \mid \mathtt{bool} \mid \cdots \mid \mathtt{unit} \mid \widehat{\tau}_1 \xrightarrow{\varphi} \widehat{\tau}_2 \mid \widehat{\tau}\ \mathtt{chan}\ \varrho$$

$$\widehat{\sigma} ::= \forall(\zeta_1, \cdots, \zeta_n).\widehat{\tau}$$

The behaviour Λ is used for atomic actions that do not involve communication; in a sense it corresponds to the empty set in previous annotations although it

$$\widehat{\Gamma} \vdash_{\mathsf{COM}} c : \widehat{\tau}_c \ \& \ \Lambda \qquad \widehat{\Gamma} \vdash_{\mathsf{COM}} x : \widehat{\Gamma}(x) \ \& \ \Lambda$$

$$\frac{\widehat{\Gamma}[x \mapsto \widehat{\tau}_x] \vdash_{\mathsf{COM}} e_0 : \widehat{\tau}_0 \ \& \ \varphi_0}{\widehat{\Gamma} \vdash_{\mathsf{COM}} \mathbf{fn}_\pi \ x \ \texttt{=>} \ e_0 : \widehat{\tau}_x \xrightarrow{\varphi_0} \widehat{\tau}_0 \ \& \ \Lambda}$$

$$\frac{\widehat{\Gamma} \vdash_{\mathsf{COM}} e_1 : \widehat{\tau}_2 \xrightarrow{\varphi_0} \widehat{\tau}_0 \ \& \ \varphi_1 \quad \widehat{\Gamma} \vdash_{\mathsf{COM}} e_2 : \widehat{\tau}_2 \ \& \ \varphi_2}{\widehat{\Gamma} \vdash_{\mathsf{COM}} e_1 \ e_2 : \widehat{\tau}_0 \ \& \ \varphi_1 ; \varphi_2 ; \varphi_0}$$

$$\widehat{\Gamma} \vdash_{\mathsf{COM}} \mathbf{channel}_\pi : \widehat{\tau} \ \mathbf{chan} \ \{\pi\} \ \& \ \widehat{\tau} \ \mathbf{chan} \ \{\pi\}$$

$$\frac{\widehat{\Gamma} \vdash_{\mathsf{COM}} e_0 : \widehat{\tau}_0 \ \& \ \varphi_0}{\widehat{\Gamma} \vdash_{\mathsf{COM}} \mathbf{spawn} \ e_0 : \mathbf{unit} \ \& \ \mathbf{spawn} \ \varphi_0}$$

$$\frac{\widehat{\Gamma} \vdash_{\mathsf{COM}} e_1 : \widehat{\tau} \ \& \ \varphi_1 \quad \widehat{\Gamma} \vdash_{\mathsf{COM}} e_2 : \widehat{\tau} \ \mathbf{chan} \ \varrho_2 \ \& \ \varphi_2}{\widehat{\Gamma} \vdash_{\mathsf{COM}} \mathbf{send} \ e_1 \ \mathbf{on} \ e_2 : \mathbf{unit} \ \& \ \varphi_1 ; \varphi_2 ; (\varrho_2 ! \widehat{\tau})}$$

$$\frac{\widehat{\Gamma} \vdash_{\mathsf{COM}} e_0 : \widehat{\tau} \ \mathbf{chan} \ \varrho_0 \ \& \ \varphi_0}{\widehat{\Gamma} \vdash_{\mathsf{COM}} \mathbf{receive} \ e_0 : \widehat{\tau} \ \& \ \varphi_0 ; (\varrho_0 ? \widehat{\tau})}$$

$$\frac{\widehat{\Gamma} \vdash_{\mathsf{COM}} e : \widehat{\tau} \ \& \ \varphi}{\widehat{\Gamma} \vdash_{\mathsf{COM}} e : \widehat{\tau}' \ \& \ \varphi'} \quad \text{if } \widehat{\tau} \le \widehat{\tau}' \text{ and } \varphi \sqsubseteq \varphi'$$

$$\frac{\widehat{\Gamma} \vdash_{\mathsf{COM}} e : \widehat{\tau} \ \& \ \varphi}{\widehat{\Gamma} \vdash_{\mathsf{COM}} e : \forall(\zeta_1, \cdots, \zeta_n). \widehat{\tau} \ \& \ \varphi} \quad \text{if } \zeta_1, \cdots, \zeta_n \text{ do not occur free in } \widehat{\Gamma} \text{ and } \varphi$$

$$\frac{\widehat{\Gamma} \vdash_{\mathsf{COM}} e : \forall(\zeta_1, \cdots, \zeta_n). \widehat{\tau} \ \& \ \varphi}{\widehat{\Gamma} \vdash_{\mathsf{COM}} e : (\theta \ \widehat{\tau}) \ \& \ \varphi} \quad \text{if } dom(\theta) \subseteq \{\zeta_1, \cdots, \zeta_n\}$$

Table 4. Communication Analysis: $\widehat{\Gamma} \vdash_{\mathsf{COM}} e : \widehat{\tau} \ \& \ \varphi$ (Example 11).

will be more intuitive to think of it as the empty string in regular expressions or as the silent action in process calculi. The behaviour $\varphi_1 ; \varphi_2$ says that φ_1 takes place before φ_2 whereas $\varphi_1 + \varphi_2$ indicates a choice between φ_1 and φ_2; this is reminiscent of constructs in regular expressions as well as in process algebras. The construct $\mathsf{rec}\beta.\varphi$ indicates a recursive behaviour that acts as given by φ except that any occurrence of β stands for $\mathsf{rec}\beta.\varphi$ itself.

The behaviour $\widehat{\tau} \ \mathbf{chan} \ \varrho$ indicates that a new channel has been allocated for communicating entities of type $\widehat{\tau}$; the region ϱ indicates the set of program points $\{\pi_1, \cdots, \pi_n\}$ where the creation could have taken place. The behaviour $\mathbf{spawn} \ \varphi$ indicates that a new process has been generated and that it operates as described by φ. The construct $\varrho!\widehat{\tau}$ indicates that a value is sent over a channel of type $\widehat{\tau} \ \mathbf{chan} \ \varrho$, and $\varrho?\widehat{\tau}$ indicates that a value is received over a channel of that type; this is reminiscent of constructs in most process algebras (in particular CSP).

The typing judgements have the form $\widehat{\Gamma} \vdash_{\mathsf{COM}} e : \widehat{\sigma} \,\&\, \varphi$ where the type environment $\widehat{\Gamma}$ maps variables to type schemes (or types), $\widehat{\sigma}$ is the type scheme (or type) for the expression e, and φ is the behaviour that may arise during evaluation of e. The analysis is specified by the axioms and rules of Tables 4 and have many points in common with those we have seen before; we explain the differences below.

The axioms for constants and variables differ from the similar axioms in Table 3 in that Λ is used instead of $\emptyset$. A similar remark holds for the rule for function abstraction. In the rule for function application we now use sequencing to express that we first evaluate the function part, then the argument and finally the body of the function; note that the left-to-right evaluation order is explicit in the behaviour.

The axiom for channel creation makes sure to record the program point in the type as well as the behaviour, the rule for spawning a process encapsulates the behaviour of the spawned process in the behaviour of the construct itself and the rules for sending and receiving values over channels indicate the order in which the arguments are evaluated and then produce the behaviour for the action taken. The rules for generalisation and instantiation are much as before.

The rule for *subeffecting* and *subtyping* is an amalgamation of the rules in Table 3 and Example 6. Also note that there is no ϱ in the axiom for **channel** unlike in the axiom for **new** in Table 3; this is because the presence of subtyping makes it redundant. The ordering $\widehat{\tau} \leq \widehat{\tau}'$ on types is given by

$$\widehat{\tau} \leq \widehat{\tau} \qquad \frac{\widehat{\tau}_1' \leq \widehat{\tau}_1 \quad \widehat{\tau}_2 \leq \widehat{\tau}_2' \quad \varphi \sqsubseteq \varphi'}{\widehat{\tau}_1 \xrightarrow{\varphi} \widehat{\tau}_2 \leq \widehat{\tau}_1' \xrightarrow{\varphi'} \widehat{\tau}_2'} \qquad \frac{\widehat{\tau} \leq \widehat{\tau}' \quad \widehat{\tau}' \leq \widehat{\tau} \quad \varrho \subseteq \varrho'}{\widehat{\tau} \text{ chan } \varrho \leq \widehat{\tau}' \text{ chan } \varrho'}$$

and is similar to the definition in Example 6: $\widehat{\tau}_1 \xrightarrow{\varphi} \widehat{\tau}_2$ is contravariant in $\widehat{\tau}_1$ but covariant in φ and $\widehat{\tau}_2$, and $\widehat{\tau}$ chan ϱ is both covariant in $\widehat{\tau}$ (for when a value is sent) and contravariant in $\widehat{\tau}$ (for when a value is received) and it is covariant in ϱ. As before, the ordering $\varrho \subseteq \varrho'$ means that ϱ is "a subset of" of ϱ' (modulo $UCAI$). However, the ordering $\varphi \sqsubseteq \varphi'$ on behaviours is more complex than what has been the case before because of the rich structure possessed by behaviours. The definition is given in Table 5 and will be explained below. Since the syntactic categories of types and behaviours are mutually recursive also the definitions of $\widehat{\tau} \leq \widehat{\tau}'$ and $\varphi \sqsubseteq \varphi'$ need to be interpreted recursively.

The axiomatisation of $\varphi \sqsubseteq \varphi'$ ensures that we obtain a preorder that is a congruence with respect to the operations for combining behaviours. Furthermore, sequencing is an associative operation with Λ as identity and we have a distributive law with respect to choice. It follows that choice is associative and commutative. Next the axioms for recursion allow us to unfold the rec-construct. The final three rules clarify how behaviours depend upon types and regions: $\widehat{\tau}$ chan ϱ is both contravariant and covariant in $\widehat{\tau}$ and is covariant in ϱ (just as was the case for the type $\widehat{\tau}$ chan ϱ); $\varrho!\widehat{\tau}$ is covariant in both ϱ and $\widehat{\tau}$ (because a value is sent) whereas $\varrho?\widehat{\tau}$ is covariant in ϱ and contravariant in $\widehat{\tau}$ (because a value is

$$\varphi \sqsubseteq \varphi$$

$$\frac{\varphi_1 \sqsubseteq \varphi_2 \quad \varphi_2 \sqsubseteq \varphi_3}{\varphi_1 \sqsubseteq \varphi_3}$$

$$\frac{\varphi_1 \sqsubseteq \varphi_2 \quad \varphi_3 \sqsubseteq \varphi_4}{\varphi_1;\varphi_3 \sqsubseteq \varphi_2;\varphi_4}$$

$$\frac{\varphi_1 \sqsubseteq \varphi_2 \quad \varphi_3 \sqsubseteq \varphi_4}{\varphi_1 + \varphi_3 \sqsubseteq \varphi_2 + \varphi_4}$$

$$\varphi_1;(\varphi_2;\varphi_3) \sqsubseteq (\varphi_1;\varphi_2);\varphi_3$$

$$(\varphi_1;\varphi_2);\varphi_3 \sqsubseteq \varphi_1;(\varphi_2;\varphi_3)$$

$$\varphi \sqsubseteq \Lambda;\varphi \qquad \Lambda;\varphi \sqsubseteq \varphi$$

$$\varphi \sqsubseteq \varphi;\Lambda \qquad \varphi;\Lambda \sqsubseteq \varphi$$

$$(\varphi_1 + \varphi_2);\varphi_3 \sqsubseteq (\varphi_1;\varphi_3) + (\varphi_2;\varphi_3)$$

$$(\varphi_1;\varphi_3) + (\varphi_2;\varphi_3) \sqsubseteq (\varphi_1 + \varphi_2);\varphi_3$$

$$\varphi_1 \sqsubseteq \varphi_1 + \varphi_2 \qquad \varphi_2 \sqsubseteq \varphi_1 + \varphi_2$$

$$\varphi + \varphi \sqsubseteq \varphi$$

$$\frac{\varphi_1 \sqsubseteq \varphi_2}{\mathsf{spawn}\ \varphi_1 \sqsubseteq \mathsf{spawn}\ \varphi_2}$$

$$\frac{\varphi_1 \sqsubseteq \varphi_2}{\mathsf{rec}\beta.\varphi_1 \sqsubseteq \mathsf{rec}\beta.\varphi_2}$$

$$\mathsf{rec}\beta.\varphi \sqsubseteq \varphi[\beta \mapsto \mathsf{rec}\beta.\varphi]$$

$$\varphi[\beta \mapsto \mathsf{rec}\beta.\varphi] \sqsubseteq \mathsf{rec}\beta.\varphi$$

$$\frac{\varrho_1 \subseteq \varrho_2 \quad \widehat{\tau_1} \leq \widehat{\tau_2}}{\varrho_1!\widehat{\tau_1} \sqsubseteq \varrho_2!\widehat{\tau_2}}$$

$$\frac{\varrho_1 \subseteq \varrho_2 \quad \widehat{\tau_2} \leq \widehat{\tau_1}}{\varrho_1?\widehat{\tau_1} \sqsubseteq \varrho_2?\widehat{\tau_2}}$$

$$\frac{\widehat{\tau} \leq \widehat{\tau}' \quad \widehat{\tau}' \leq \widehat{\tau} \quad \varrho \subseteq \varrho'}{\widehat{\tau}\ \mathsf{chan}\ \varrho \sqsubseteq \widehat{\tau}'\ \mathsf{chan}\ \varrho'}$$

Table 5. Ordering on behaviours: $\varphi \sqsubseteq \varphi'$ (Example 11).

received). There is no explicit law for renaming bound behaviour variables as we shall regard $\mathsf{rec}\beta.\varphi$ as being equal to $\mathsf{rec}\beta'.\varphi'$ when they are α-equivalent.   □

5   The Methodology

So far we have illustrated the variety of type and effect systems that can be found in the literature. Now we turn to explaining the individual steps in the overall methodology of designing and using type and effect systems:

- devise a semantics for the programming language,
- develop a program analysis in the form of a type and effect system (this is what Sections 2, 3 and 4 have given numerous examples of),
- prove the semantic correctness of the analysis,
- develop an efficient inference algorithm,
- prove that the inference algorithm is syntactically sound and complete, and
- utilise the information for applications like program transformations or improved code generation.

Each of these phases have their own challenges and open problems that we now consider in some detail; many of these issues are rather orthogonal to the more syntactic differences used to distinguish between the formulations used in Sections 2, 3 and 4.

Semantics. Semantics is a rather well understood area. In principle both denotational and operational semantics can be used as the foundations for type and effect systems but most papers in the literature take an operational approach. This is indeed very natural when the analysis needs to express further intensional details than are normally captured by a denotational semantics. But even when taking an operational approach one frequently needs to devise it in such a manner that it captures those operational details for which the analysis is intended. The term *instrumented semantics* [17] has been coined for a class of denotational or operational semantics that are more precise about low-level machine detail (say concerning pipe-lining or the number and nature of registers) than usual. It is therefore wise to be cautious about the precise meaning of claims stating that an analysis has been proved correct with respect to "the" semantics.

The inference system. Previous sections have illustrated some of the variations possible when developing type and effect systems as well as some of the applications for which they can be used. However, it would be incorrect to surmise that the selection of components are inherently linked to the example analysis where they were first illustrated.

At the same time we illustrated a number of design considerations to be taken into account when devising a type and effect system. In our view the major design decisions are as follows:

- whether or not to incorporate
  - subeffecting,
  - subtyping,
  - polymorphism, and
  - polymorphic recursion,
- whether or not types are allowed to be influenced by effects (as was the case in Example 9 and Section 4), and
- whether or not constraints are an explicit part of the inference system (unlike what simplicity demanded us to do here).

The choices made have a strong impact on the difficulties of obtaining a syntactically sound and complete inference algorithm; indeed, for some combinations it may be beyond state-of-the-art (or even impossible) and in particular it may be hard (or impossible) to deal with subtyping without admitting constraints to the inference system. An important area of further research is how to identify those features of the annotated type and effect systems that lead to algorithmic intractability.

Often the type and effect system is developed for a typed programming language. It is then important to ensure that whenever a program can be typed in the original type system then there also exists a type in the type and effect system, and whenever there exists a type in the type and effect system then the program can also be typed in the original type system. This is established by proving that the type and effect system is a *conservative extension* of the original or underlying type system. It is also possible to investigate whether or not the type and effect system admits principal types and effects; luckily this will always be the case if a syntactically sound and complete inference algorithm can be developed.

Further studies are needed to understand the interplay between type and effect systems and the other approaches to static analysis of programs. It is interesting to note that the existence of principal types is intimately connected to the notion of Moore families used in abstract interpretation: a principal type roughly corresponds to the least solution of an equation system.

Semantic correctness. Many of the techniques needed for establishing semantic soundness (sometimes called type soundness) are rather standard. For operational semantics the statement of correctness generally take the form of a *subject reduction result*: if a program e has a type τ and if e evaluates to e' then also e' has the type τ; this approach to semantic correctness has a rather long history [24,25,49] and applies both to small-step Structural Operational Semantics and to big-step Natural Semantics [36]. It is important to stress that the correct use of covariance and contravariance (in the rules for subtyping) is essential for semantic correctness to hold.

For more complex situations the formulation of "has a type" may have to be defined coinductively [42], in which case also the proof of the subject reduction result may need to exploit coinduction (e.g. [30]), and the notions of Kripke relations and Kripke-logical relations (see e.g. [28]) may be useful when using a denotational semantics [26]. We refer to [3,39,40,45] for a number of applications of these techniques.

The inference algorithm. The development of a syntactically sound and complete inference algorithm may be based on the ideas in [20,41]. The simplest approach is a *two-stage approach* where one first determines the underlying types and next determines the (possibly polymorphic) effects on top of the explicitly typed programs. The basic idea is to ensure that the type inference algorithm operates on a *free algebra* by restricting annotations to be annotation variables only (the concept of "*simple types*") and by recording a set of constraints for the meaning of the annotation variables. This suffices for adapting the established techniques for polymorphic type inference, by means of the classical algorithm $\mathcal{W}$ developed in [6,22] for Hindley/Milner polymorphism, to the setting at hand. In this scheme one might have $\mathcal{W}(\Gamma, e) = (S, \tau, \varphi, C)$ where e is the program to be typed, τ is the form of the resulting type and φ summarises the overall effect of the program. In case e contains free variables we need preliminary information about their types and this is provided by the type environment Γ; as a result of the type inference this preliminary information may need to be modified as reported in the substitution S. Finally, C is a set of constraints that record the meaning of the annotation variables. For efficiency the algorithmic techniques often involve the generation of constraint systems in a program independent representation.

In the case of polymorphic recursion decidability becomes an issue. Indeed, polymorphic recursion over type variables makes the polymorphic type system undecidable. It is therefore wise to restrict the polymorphic recursion to annotation variables only as in [44]. There the first stage is still ordinary type inference; the second stage [43] concerns an algorithm S that generates effect and region variables and an algorithm $\mathcal{R}$ that deals with the complications due to polymorphic recursion (for effects and regions only). The inference algorithm is proved syntactically sound but is known not to be syntactically complete; indeed, obtaining an algorithm that is syntactically sound as well as complete, seems beyond state-of-the-art.

Once types and effects are allowed to be mutually recursive, the two-stage approach no longer works for obtaining an inference algorithm because the effects are used to control the shape of the underlying types (in the form of which type variables are included in a polymorphic type). This suggests a *one-stage approach* where special care needs to be taken when deciding the variables over which to generalise when constructing a polymorphic type. The main idea is that the algorithm needs to consult the constraints in order to determine a larger set of forbidden variables than those directly occurring in the type environment or the effect; this can be formulated as a *downwards closure* with respect to the constraint set [31,48] or by taking a *principal solution* of the constraints into account [39,40].

Adding subtyping to this development dramatically increases the complexity of the development. The integration of shape conformant subtyping, polymorphism and subeffecting is done in [3,31,35] that develop an inference algorithm that is proved syntactically sound; these papers aimed at integrating the techniques for polymorphism and subeffecting (but no subtyping) from effect systems [39,40,48] with the techniques for polymorphism and subtyping (but no effects) from type systems [16,37,38]. A more ambitious development where the inference system is massaged so as to facilitate developing an inference algorithm that is also syntactically complete is described in [1]; the inference system used there has explicit constraints in the inference system (as is usually the case in type systems based on subtyping).

Syntactic soundness and completeness. The syntactic soundness and completeness results to be established present a useful guide to developing the inference algorithm. Formulations of syntactic soundness are mostly rather straight-forward: the result produced by the algorithm must give rise to a valid inference in the inference system. A simple example is the following: if $\mathcal{W}(\Gamma, e) = (S, \tau, \varphi)$ then $S(\Gamma) \vdash e : \tau \,\&\, \varphi$ must hold; here it is clear that the substitution produced is intended to refine the initial information available when first calling the algorithm. A somewhat more complex example is: if $\mathcal{W}(\Gamma, e) = (S, \tau, \varphi, C)$ then $S'(S(\Gamma)) \vdash e : S'(\tau) \,\&\, S'(\varphi)$ must hold whenever S' is a solution to the constraints in C. The proofs are normally by structural induction on the syntax of programs.

The formulations of syntactic completeness are somewhat more involved. Given a program e such that $\Gamma_{\diamond} \vdash e : \tau_{\diamond} \,\&\, \varphi_{\diamond}$, the main difficulty is to show how this can be obtained from $\mathcal{W}(\Gamma, e) = (S, \tau, \varphi)$ or $\mathcal{W}(\Gamma, e) = (S, \tau, \varphi, C)$. The solution is to formally define when one "typing" is an instance of another; the notion of *lazy instance* [9] is very useful here and in more complex scenarios Kripke-logical relations (see e.g. [28]) may be needed [1]. The proofs are often challenging and often require developing extensive techniques for "normalising" deductions made in the inference system so as to control the use of non-syntax directed rules. For sufficiently complex scenarios syntactic completeness may fail or may be open (as mentioned above); luckily soundness often suffices for the inference algorithm to be of practical use.

Exploitation. Exploitation is a rather open-ended area although it would seem that the integration of program analyses and program transformations into an inference based formulation is quite promising [46]. Indeed, inference-based formulations of analyses can be seen as an abstract counterpart of the use of attribute grammars when developing analyses in compilers, and in the same way inference-based formulations of analyses and transformations can be seen as an abstract counterpart of the use of attributed transformation grammars [47].

6   Conclusion

The approach based on type and effect systems is a promising approach to the static analysis of programs because the usefulness of types has already been widely established. The main strength lies in the ability to interact with the user: clarifying what the analysis is about (and when it may fail to be of any help) and in propagating the results back to the user in an understable way (which is not always possible for flow based approaches working on intermediate representations). The main areas of further research concern the expressiveness of the inference based specifications, the complexity and decidability of the inference algorithms and the interplay with the other approaches to static analysis of programs.

Acknowledgements. We wish to thank Torben Amtoft for working with us for many years on type and effect systems; we would also like to thank the referees for their careful reading and helpful comments.

References

1. T. Amtoft, F. Nielson, and H. R. Nielson. *Type and Effect Systems: Behaviours for Concurrency.* Imperial College Press, 1999.
2. T. Amtoft, F. Nielson, and H.R. Nielson. Type and behaviour reconstruction for higher-order concurrent programs. *Journal of Functional Programming*, 7(3):321–347, 1997.
3. T. Amtoft, F. Nielson, H.R. Nielson, and J. Ammann. Polymorphic subtyping for effect analysis: The dynamic semantics. In *Analysis and Verification of Multiple-Agent Languages*, volume 1192 of *Lecture Notes in Computer Science*, pages 172–206. Springer, 1997.
4. P. N. Benton. Strictness logic and polymorphic invariance. In *Proc. Second International Symposium on Logical Foundations of Computer Science*, volume 620 of *Lecture Notes in Computer Science*, pages 33–44. Springer, 1992.
5. P. N. Benton. Strictness properties of lazy algebraic datatypes. In *Proc. WSA '93*, volume 724 of *Lecture Notes in Computer Science*, pages 206–217. Springer, 1993.
6. L. Damas and R. Milner. Principal type-schemes for functional programs. In *Proc. POPL '82*, pages 207–212. ACM Press, 1982.
7. K.-F. Faxén. Optimizing lazy functional programs using flow inference. In *Proc. SAS '95*, volume 983 of *Lecture Notes in Computer Science*, pages 136–153. Springer, 1995.
8. K.-F. Faxén. Polyvariance, polymorphism, and flow analysis. In *Proc. Analysis and Verification of Multiple-Agent Languages*, volume 1192 of *Lecture Notes in Computer Science*, pages 260–278. Springer, 1997.
9. Y.-C. Fuh and P. Mishra. Polymorphic subtype inference: Closing the theory-practice gap. In *Proc. TAPSOFT '89*, volume 352 of *Lecture Notes in Computer Science*, pages 167–183. Springer, 1989.
10. Y.-C. Fuh and P. Mishra. Type inference with subtypes. *Theoretical Computer Science*, 73:155–175, 1990.
11. N. Heintze. Control-flow analysis and type systems. In *Proc. SAS '95*, volume 983 of *Lecture Notes in Computer Science*, pages 189–206. Springer, 1995.
12. Nevin Heintze and Jon G. Riecke. The SLam calculus: Programming with Secrecy and Integrity. In *Proc. POPL '98*, pages 365–377. ACM Press, 1998.
13. F. Henglein and C. Mossin. Polymorphic binding-time analysis. In *Proc. ESOP '94*, volume 788 of *Lecture Notes in Computer Science*, pages 287–301. Springer, 1994.
14. T. P. Jensen. Strictness analysis in logical form. In *Proc. FPCA '91*, volume 523 of *Lecture Notes in Computer Science*, pages 352–366. Springer, 1991.
15. T. P. Jensen. Disjunctive strictness analysis. In *Proc. LICS '92*, pages 174–185, 1992.
16. M. P. Jones. A theory of qualified types. In *Proc. ESOP '92*, volume 582 of *Lecture Notes in Computer Science*, pages 287–306. Springer, 1992.
17. N. D. Jones and F. Nielson. Abstract Interpretation: a Semantics-Based Tool for Program Analysis. In *Handbook of Logic in Computer Science volume 4*. Oxford University Press, 1995.

18. P. Jouvelot. Semantic Parallelization: a practical exercise in abstract interpretation. In *Proc. POPL '87*, pages 39–48, 1987.

19. P. Jouvelot and D. K. Gifford. Reasoning about continuations with control effects. In *Proc. PLDI '89*, ACM SIGPLAN Notices, pages 218–226. ACM Press, 1989.

20. P. Jouvelot and D. K. Gifford. Algebraic reconstruction of types and effects. In *Proc. POPL '91*, pages 303–310. ACM Press, 1990.

21. J. M. Lucassen and D. K. Gifford. Polymorphic effect analysis. In *Proc. POPL '88*, pages 47–57. ACM Press, 1988.

22. R. Milner. A theory of type polymorphism in programming. *Journal of Computer Systems*, 17:348–375, 1978.

23. J. Mitchell. Type inference with simple subtypes. *Journal of Functional Programming*, 1(3):245–285, 1991.

24. F. Nielson. A formal type system for comparing partial evaluators. In D. Bjørner, A. P. Ershov, and N. D. Jones, editors, *Proc. Partial Evaluation and Mixed Computation*, pages 349–384. North Holland, 1988.

25. F. Nielson. The typed λ-calculus with first-class processes. In *Proc. PARLE'89*, volume 366 of *Lecture Notes in Computer Science*, pages 355–373. Springer, 1989.

26. F. Nielson and H. R. Nielson. *Two-Level Functional Languages*, volume 34 of *Cambridge Tracts in Theoretical Computer Science*. Cambridge University Press, 1992.

27. F. Nielson and H. R. Nielson. From CML to process algebras. In *Proc. CONCUR'93*, volume 715 of *Lecture Notes in Computer Science*, pages 493–508. Springer, 1993.

28. F. Nielson and H. R. Nielson. Layered predicates. In *Proc. REX'92 workshop on Semantics — foundations and applications*, volume 666 of *Lecture Notes in Computer Science*, pages 425–456. Springer, 1993.

29. F. Nielson and H. R. Nielson. From CML to its process algebra. *Theoretical Computer Science*, 155:179–219, 1996.

30. F. Nielson, H. R. Nielson, and C. L. Hankin. *Principles of Program Analysis*. Springer, 1999.

31. F. Nielson, H.R. Nielson, and T. Amtoft. Polymorphic subtyping for effect analysis: The algorithm. In *Analysis and Verification of Multiple-Agent Languages*, volume 1192 of *Lecture Notes in Computer Science*, pages 207–243. Springer, 1997.

32. H. R. Nielson, T. Amtoft, and F. Nielson. Behaviour analysis and safety conditions: a case study in CML. In *Proc. FASE '98*, number 1382 in Lecture Notes in Computer Science, pages 255–269. Springer, 1998.

33. H. R. Nielson and F. Nielson. Higher-Order Concurrent Programs with Finite Communication Topology. In *Proc. POPL '94*. Springer, 1994.

34. H. R. Nielson and F. Nielson. Communication analysis for Concurrent ML. In F. Nielson, editor, *ML with Concurrency*, Monographs in Computer Science, pages 185–235. Springer, 1997.

35. H.R. Nielson, F. Nielson, and T. Amtoft. Polymorphic subtyping for effect analysis: The static semantics. In *Analysis and Verification of Multiple-Agent Languages*, volume 1192 of *Lecture Notes in Computer Science*, pages 141–171. Springer, 1997.

36. G. D. Plotkin. A structural approach to operational semantics. Technical Report FN-19, DAIMI, Aarhus University, Denmark, 1981.

37. G. S. Smith. Polymorphic inference with overloading and subtyping. In *Proc. TAPSOFT '93*, volume 668 of *Lecture Notes in Computer Science*, pages 671–685. Springer, 1993.

38. G. S. Smith. Polymorphic type schemes for functional programs with overloading and subtyping. *Science of Computer Programming*, 23:197–226, 1994.

39. J.-P. Talpin and P. Jouvelot. The type and effect discipline. In *Proc. LICS '92*, pages 162–173, 1992.
40. J.-P. Talpin and P. Jouvelot. The type and effect discipline. *Information and Computation*, 111(2):245–296, 1994.
41. Y.-M. Tang. *Control-Flow Analysis by Effect Systems and Abstract Interpretation.* PhD thesis, Ecole des Mines de Paris, 1994.
42. M. Tofte. Type inference for polymorphic references. *Information and Computation*, 89:1–34, 1990.
43. M. Tofte and L. Birkedal. A region inference algorithm. *ACM TOPLAS*, 20(3):1–44, 1998.
44. M. Tofte and J.-P. Talpin. Implementing the call-by-value lambda-calculus using a stack of regions. In *Proc. POPL '94*, pages 188–201. ACM Press, 1994.
45. M. Tofte and J.-P. Talpin. Region-based memory management. *Information and Computation*, 132:109–176, 1997.
46. M. Wand. Specifying the correctness of binding-time analysis. In *Proc. POPL '93*, pages 137–143, 1993.
47. R. Wilhelm. Global flow analysis and optimization in the MUG2 compiler generating system. In S. S. Muchnick and N. D. Jones, editors, *Program Flow Analysis: Theory and Applications*, chapter 5. Prentice Hall International, 1981.
48. A. K. Wright. Typing references by effect inference. In *Proc. ESOP '92*, volume 582 of *Lecture Notes in Computer Science*, pages 473–491. Springer, 1992.
49. A. K. Wright and M. Felleisen. A syntactic approach to type soundness. *Information and Computation*, 115:38–94, 1994.

Part III

Automation

Proving Theorems About Java-Like Byte Code

J Strother Moore

Department of Computer Sciences
University of Texas at Austin
Austin, Texas 78712 USA
moore@cs.utexas.edu,
WWW home page: http://www.cs.utexas.edu/users/moore

Abstract. We describe a formalization of an abstract machine very similar to the Java Virtual Machine but far simpler. We develop techniques for specifying the properties of classes and methods for this machine. We develop techniques for mechanically proving theorems about classes and methods. We discuss two such proofs, that of a static method implementing the factorial function and of an instance method that destructively manipulates objects in a way that takes advantage of inheritance. We conclude with a brief discussion of the advantages and disadvantages of this approach. The formalization and proofs are done with the ACL2 theorem proving system.

1 Specification of the TJVM

The Java Virtual Machine (JVM) [10] is a stack-based, object-oriented, type-safe byte-code interpreter on which compiled Java programs are executed.

We develop a simplified JVM for the purpose of exploring verification issues related to proofs about object-oriented byte code. We refer to our machine as a "toy JVM" or "TJVM." Because we are interested in formal, mechanically checked proofs, we formalize the TJVM in a formal, mechanized logic, namely ACL2: A Computational Logic for Applicative Common Lisp. The tradition of formalizing machines in ACL2, and its predecessor, Boyer and Moore's Nqthm, is well established [1, 14, 11, 3, 5] and we follow in those well-trodden footsteps. Indeed, our TJVM is just a simplification of Rich Cohen's "defensive JVM," [6], which was formalized at Computational Logic, Inc., in the standard ACL2/Nqthm style. That style employs an operational semantics, in which the state of the machine is represented as a Lisp object. An interpreter for the machine's programming language is defined as a Lisp function. The main purpose of this paper is to illustrate how those established techniques can be applied in an object-oriented setting.

This paper provides a brief sketch of our TJVM. The details may be obtained at http://www.cs.utexas.edu/users/moore/publications/tjvm/index.html.

The state of the TJVM is a triple consisting of a *call stack* of "frames," a *heap*, and a *class table*. A *frame* contains four fields, a *program counter*, a variable binding environment called the *locals* of the frame, an operand *stack*, and the

E.-R. Olderog, B. Steffen (Eds.): Correct System Design, LNCS 1710, pp. 139–162, 1999.

byte code *program* of the method being evaluated. The *heap* is an association of integer *addresses* to "objects," which are "instances" of classes. An *instance* is a list of n tables, one for each of the n superclasses of the object. Each table enumerates the fields of a given class and specifies the contents of those fields in this particular instance. Finally, the *class table* is a list of *class declarations*, each of which specifies a class name, the names of its superclasses, the names of its fields, and the "method declarations" of the class. A *method declaration* specifies a method name, its formal parameters, and the byte coded body of the method.

Readers familiar with the JVM will recognize the TJVM as a similar machine. Here is a Java program for computing the factorial function.

```
public static int fact(int n){
  if (n>0)
    {return n*fact(n-1);}
  else return 1;
}
```

Here is an example of a TJVM method declaration corresponding to the compiled code for fact above. The comments (on the right, following the semicolons) indicate the TJVM program counter of the instruction and the JVM byte code produced by Sun's Java compiler.

Fact:
```
("fact" (n)
          (load n)                             ;  0         iload_0
          (ifle 8)                             ;  1         ifle 12
          (load n)                             ;  2         iload_0
          (load n)                             ;  3         iload_0
          (push 1)                             ;  4         iconst_1
          (sub)                                ;  5         isub
          (invokestatic "Math" "fact" 1) ;  6         invokestatic
                                               ;            <Method int fact(int)>
          (mul)                                ;  7         imul
          (xreturn)                            ;  8         ireturn
          (push 1)                             ;  9         iconst_1
          (xreturn))                           ; 10         ireturn
```

This method declaration, **Fact**, might be found in the class declaration of the "Math" class on the TJVM. The name of the method is "fact". It has one formal parameter, n, and a byte code program of eleven instructions. **Fact** is actually a Lisp constant whose first element is the string "fact", whose second element is the list containing the single symbol n, etc.

We discuss later the correspondence between TJVM byte codes and JVM byte codes, but a shallow correspondence is obvious. On the TJVM, methods refer to their local variables by name; on the JVM methods refer to their locals by position. The "8" in the TJVM ifle instruction is an instruction offset by which the program counter is incremented. The corresponding offset on the JVM counts bytes rather than instructions and some JVM instructions take more than one byte. Finally, the JVM has typed instructions, e.g., the JVM's iload loads an integer-valued variable on the stack while the TJVM's load loads any value.

When this program is invoked on the TJVM, one actual parameter, n, is popped from the operand stack of the topmost frame of the TJVM call stack; a new frame is built and pushed onto the call stack of the TJVM state. The new frame has program counter 0 and the eleven instructions above as the program. The locals of the new frame bind n to the actual n. The operand stack of the new frame is empty.

The program operates as follows. The parenthesized numbers refer to program counter values. (0) The local value, n, of n is pushed onto the operand stack. (1) The ifle instruction pops the operand stack and compares the item obtained, here n, to 0. If $n \leq 0$, the program counter is incremented by 8; otherwise it is incremented by 1. (9-10) In the former case, the program pushes a 1 on the operand stack and returns one result to the caller. The JVM uses a special, single byte instruction for pushing the constant 1, while the TJVM has one general-purpose push instruction for pushing any constant. (2) In the case that $n > 0$, the program pushes n, (3-5) pushes $n - 1$ (by (3) pushing n and (4) 1 and (5) executing a sub which pops two items off the operand stack and pushes their difference), (6) invokes this procedure recursively on one actual, in this case, the $n - 1$ on the stack, obtaining one result, here $(n - 1)!$, which is pushed on the stack in place of the actual, (7) multiplies the top two elements of the stack, and (8) returns that one result to the caller.

From the above description it should be clear how we define the semantics of the instructions illustrated above. For example, here is the function which gives semantics to the add instruction, (add).

```
(defun execute-ADD (inst s)
  (declare (ignore inst))
  (make-state
   (push (make-frame (+ 1 (pc (top-frame s)))
                     (locals (top-frame s))
                     (push (+ (top (pop (stack (top-frame s))))
                              (top (stack (top-frame s))))
                           (pop (pop (stack (top-frame s)))))
                     (program (top-frame s)))
         (pop (call-stack s)))
   (heap s)
   (class-table s)))
```

This Lisp function – which in the ACL2 setting is taken as an *axiom* defining the expression (execute-ADD *inst s*) – takes two arguments, the add instruction to be interpreted and the TJVM state *s*. Because the TJVM add instruction has no operands, execute-ADD does not actually need the instruction and so *inst* above is ignored. The function computes the state obtained from *s* by executing an add. The new state contains a modified call stack but the same heap and class table as *s*. The call stack is modified by changing only its topmost frame so that the program counter is incremented by one and the operand stack is modified by popping two items off of it and pushing their sum. The locals and program of the frame are unchanged. We call execute-ADD the *semantic function* for the TJVM add instruction.

Each instruction on the TJVM is defined by an analogous semantic function. The semantic function for the instruction (new "*class*"), which constructs a new instance of the class named "*class*", is shown below. The instruction takes as its single argument the name of a class. On our TJVM, new builds a new, uninitialized instance of that class, allocating some address in the heap for that instance and leaving that address on the top of the stack in the top frame of the call stack.

```
(defun execute-NEW (inst s)
  (let* ((class (arg1 inst))
         (table (class-table s))
         (obj (build-an-instance
                       (cons class
                             (class-decl-superclasses
                               (bound? class table)))
                       table))
         (addr (length (heap s))))
    (make-state
     (push (make-frame (+ 1 (pc (top-frame s)))
                       (locals (top-frame s))
                       (push (list 'REF addr)
                             (stack (top-frame s)))
                       (program (top-frame s)))
           (pop (call-stack s)))
     (bind addr obj (heap s))
     (class-table s))))
```

In the ACL2 definition above, *inst* is the new instruction to be executed, and *s* is the state to be "modified." The let* in the definition above just binds four variables and then evaluates the make-state expression in the "body" of the let*. The first variable, *class*, is bound to the class name in the instruction. The second variable, *table*, is bound to the class table of the state *s*. This table contains a description of all the loaded classes, their fields and their methods. The third variable, *obj*, is the uninitialized instance object constructed by new. Logically speaking, it is constructed by the ACL2 function build-an-instance from the superclass chain of *class* (starting with *class*) and the class table. The fourth variable, *addr* is the heap address at which *obj* will be placed. In the TJVM, this just the number of objects allocated so far.

The state constructed by execute-NEW above modifies the top frame of the call stack of *s* and also modifies the heap of *s*. The class table of *s* is unchanged. In the modified top frame, the program counter is incremented and a reference to *addr* is pushed onto the operand stack. (Note that the address is "tagged" with the symbol REF so that it is possible on the TJVM to distinguish integers from references to heap addresses.) In the modified heap, the new instance object, *obj*, is associated with the address *addr*.

The semantic function for the instruction (invokevirtual "*class*" "*name*" *n*) is shown below. Invokevirtual is the most complicated instruction on the TJVM. It invokes a named method, *name*, on a given number, *n*, of parameters. The *n* parameters are obtained from the operand stack. But the method invoked is determined by "method resolution," which is a function of the class of the object to which the method is applied. This object is denoted, both in Java and the TJVM, by the value of the variable symbol this. The "this" object is in essence an $n + 1^{st}$ parameter and is the deepest one on the operand stack at the time of call but it is special because of its role in method resolution.

```
(defun execute-INVOKEVIRTUAL (inst s)
  (let* ((name (arg2 inst))
         (n (arg3 inst))
         (ref (top (popn n (stack (top-frame s)))))
         (class (class-name-of-ref ref (heap s)))
         (method
          (lookup-method name
                         class
                         (class-table s)))
         (vars (cons 'this (method-formals method)))
         (prog (method-program method)))
    (make-state
     (push (make-frame 0
                       (reverse
                        (bind-formals (reverse vars)
                                      (stack (top-frame s))))
                       nil
                       prog)
           (push (make-frame (+ 1 (pc (top-frame s)))
                             (locals (top-frame s))
                             (popn (length vars)
                                   (stack (top-frame s)))
                             (program (top-frame s)))
                 (pop (call-stack s))))
     (heap s)
     (class-table s))))
```

In the ACL2 function above, *name* and *n* are the name of the method to be invoked and the number of parameters (not counting the "this" object). The instruction obtains a reference, *ref*, to the "this" object of the invocation by looking down the operand stack an appropriate distance, given *n*, the number of formals of the named method. It then obtains the class, *class*, of the referenced object and uses the given method *name* and object *class* to determine the nearest appropriate method, *method*, using the ACL2 function lookup-method, which formalizes method resolution. Let *vars* be the formal parameters of the resolved *method*, extended with one additional formal, named this, and let *prog* be the byte code program for *method*.

The instruction then modifies the existing top frame of the call stack by incrementing the program counter and popping $n + 1$ items off the operand stack.

It then pushes a new frame poised to execute the resolved method, initializing the locals in the new frame by binding *vars* to the items just popped.

Recall that our fact method used the instruction invokestatic. That instruction is similar to invokevirtual but does not involve a "this" object. Static method resolution is based on the class name used in the invokestatic instruction.

Observe that the class name argument in the invokevirtual instruction is ignored (the ACL2 function above does not use (arg1 *inst*)). Why is it provided in the first place? This is a reflection of the design of the JVM (as opposed to an oddity in the TJVM). The JVM provides a class argument in invokevirtual and the argument is irrelevant to the semantics of the instruction. But the argument is used in the implementation (via dispatch vectors) to make method resolution faster. A nice little "metatheorem" one can prove about the TJVM is that in a properly configured implementation lookup-method finds the same method identified by the dispatch vector algorithm. Such a theorem was proved by Bill Young and Rich Cohen about Cohen's dJVM.

After defining a semantic function for each TJVM instruction, we define:

```
(defun do-inst (inst s)
  (case (op-code inst)
    (PUSH           (execute-PUSH inst s))
    (POP            (execute-POP  inst s))
    (LOAD           (execute-LOAD inst s))
    (STORE          (execute-STORE inst s))
    (ADD            (execute-ADD inst s))
    (SUB            (execute-SUB inst s))
    (MUL            (execute-MUL inst s))
    (GOTO           (execute-GOTO inst s))
    (IFEQ           (execute-IFEQ inst s))
    (IFGT           (execute-IFGT inst s))
    (INVOKEVIRTUAL  (execute-INVOKEVIRTUAL inst s))
    (INVOKESTATIC   (execute-INVOKESTATIC inst s))
    (RETURN         (execute-RETURN inst s))
    (XRETURN        (execute-XRETURN inst s))
    (NEW            (execute-NEW inst s))
    (GETFIELD       (execute-GETFIELD inst s))
    (PUTFIELD       (execute-PUTFIELD inst s))
    (HALT           s)
    (otherwise s)))
```

so that (do-inst *inst* s) returns the state obtained by executing *inst* in state s. The definition enumerates the instructions supported on the TJVM and calls the appropriate semantic function.

Each of the supported instructions is modeled after one or more JVM instructions. TJVM instructions are generally simpler than their JVM counterparts. For example, we are not concerned with access attributes, types, resource limitations, or exceptions on the TJVM. The TJVM classes provide for "instance fields" but do not provide the JVM's "static fields." Unlike their counterparts on the JVM, our INVOKEVIRTUAL and INVOKESTATIC do not take "signatures." On the JVM, a method's "this" object is in local variable 0; on the TJVM it is an implicit formal parameter named this. Like its JVM counterpart, the method actually invoked by our INVOKEVIRTUAL depends on the "this" object: both invoke the nearest method of the given name found in the superclass chain of the object, but the JVM discriminates between candidate methods via their signatures and we do not. That is, the JVM supports "overloading" and the TJVM does not.

The "single stepper" for the TJVM is

```
(defun step (s)
  (do-inst (next-inst s) s))
```

where next-inst retrieves the instruction indicated by the program counter in the topmost frame of the call stack.

The TJVM is then defined as an iterated step function:

```
(defun tjvm (s n)
  (if (zp n)
      s
    (tjvm (step s) (- n 1))))
```

Thus (tjvm s n) is the result of applying step to s n times, or ($step^n$ s).

The TJVM can be viewed as a simplification of the JVM. The TJVM is in fact a simplification of Rich Cohen's "defensive JVM", [6], which includes many more JVM instructions and deals carefully with the preconditions assumed for each instruction. In principle, Cohen's specification could be used to analyze whether a given byte code verifier is sufficient to guarantee the absence of certain classes of runtime errors. Both the TJVM and the defensive JVM omit major aspects of the JVM, including floating point numbers, arrays, multiple threads, exceptions, and native methods. All but native methods could be formalized in an implementation independent way, following the basic approach.

2   Example TJVM Executions

Having defined the TJVM in Lisp, it is possible to execute it on concrete data. Consider the byte code for the "fact" program shown earlier in the constant **Fact**. Let **Math-class** denote the list constant partially displayed below.

Math-class:
("Math" ("Object") () (... Fact ...)).

This is a class declaration for a class called "Math" which is an extension of the class named "Object" (literally, the declaration says that the superclass chain of "Math" is the list containing only the class named "Object"). The "Math" class contains no fields and its methods are those listed and include **Fact**.

Consider the TJVM state

s_0:
```
(make-state
    (push (make-frame 0
                      nil
                      nil
                      '((push 5)
                        (invokestatic "Math" "fact" 1)
                        (halt)))
          nil)
    nil
    '( Math-class))
```

This state is poised to execute the three instruction program above, starting with the (push 5) at program counter 0. Note that the program pushes 5 on the stack and then invokes "fact". The class table for the state includes our **Math-class**, so "fact", here, means the byte code given in **Fact**.

The Lisp expression (top (stack (top-frame (tjvm s_0 52)))) steps s_0 52 times, and then recovers the topmost item on the operand stack of the topmost frame of the call stack. Evaluating this expression produces 120, which is indeed 5!.

How did we know to take 52 steps? The answer is: by analysis of the code in **Fact**. The following function, which we call the "clock function" for "fact", returns the number of TJVM instructions required to execute (invokestatic "Math" "fact" 1) on n. The function was written based on an inspection of the byte code in **Fact**.

```
(defun fact-clock (n)
  (if (zp n)
      5
    (++ 7
        (fact-clock (- n 1))
        2)))
```

Here, ++ is just the normal arithmetic addition function. Fact-clock has been written this way (rather than $5 + 9n$) to make it obvious how such functions are generated. To execute a call of "fact" on 5 evidently takes 50 TJVM cycles (including the call). Thus, the program in s_0 takes 52 cycles.

3   Proofs About TJVM Programs

Of more interest than mere execution is the following theorem we can prove about "fact".

> **Theorem.** "fact" is correct:
> Suppose s_0 is a TJVM state whose next instruction is (invokestatic "Math" "fact" 1), where the meaning of the name "Math" in the class table is our **Math-class**. Let n be the top of the operand stack in the

topmost frame of the call stack of s_0 and suppose n is a natural number. Then the TJVM state obtained by stepping s_0 (fact-clock n) times is state s_0 with the program counter incremented by one and the n on the operand stack replaced by $n!$. The heap is unchanged.

This informal statement can be phrased formally as follows.

Theorem. "fact" is correct:
```
(implies (and (equal (next-inst s₀)
                     '(invokestatic "Math" "fact" 1))
              (equal (assoc-equal "Math" (class-table s₀))
                     Math-class)
              (equal n (top (stack (top-frame s₀))))
              (natp n))
         (equal
          (tjvm s₀ (fact-clock n))
          (make-state
           (push (make-frame (+ 1 (pc (top-frame s₀)))
                             (locals (top-frame s₀))
                             (push (fact n)
                                   (pop (stack (top-frame s₀)))))
                             (program (top-frame s₀)))
                 (pop (call-stack s₀)))
           (heap s₀)
           (class-table s₀)))))
```

The theorem states the *total correctness* of the "fact" byte code. Weaker theorems can be stated and proved, but we here focus on theorems of this kind because they are easiest to prove.

We proved this theorem in a very straightforward manner using ACL2. The proof takes 0.33 seconds on a 200 MHz Sun Ultra 2. The theorem only looks complicated because the notation is unfamiliar!

ACL2 is an automatic theorem prover in the sense that its behavior on any given proof attempt is determined by its state immediately prior to the attempt, together with goal-specific hints provided by the user. Of great importance is the set of lemmas the system has already proved. Those lemmas determine how ACL2 simplifies expressions. To configure ACL2 to prove theorems about TJVM we followed the example described in [3]. Roughly speaking, we did the following:

- We proved half a dozen simple arithmetic lemmas; we could have loaded any of several standard ACL2 arithmetic "books."
- We proved lemmas that let ACL2 manipulate the data structures used on the TJVM, including stacks, frames, and states, as abstract data structures. One such theorem is (top (push x stack)) = x. We then "disabled" the definitions of the primitive stack, frame, and state functions so that their "implementations" in terms of conses were not visible.
- We proved the standard theorem for expanding the single step function, step, when the next-inst is explicit. We then disabled the step function. This prevents case explosion on what the next instruction is.

- We defined the standard "clock addition" function, ++, which is really just natural number addition, and disabled it. This allows us to define clock function in the structured style illustrated fact-clock and prevents the arithmetic rules from rearranging the expressions and destroying the structural "hints" implicit in the definitions. We proved the rules that allow tjvm expressions to be decomposed according to their clock expressions. For example, (tjvm s (++ i j)) is rewritten to (tjvm (tjvm s i) j). Thus, when ACL2 encounters, for example, (tjvm s_0 (++ 7 (fact-clock (- n 1)) 2)) it decomposes it into a run of length seven, followed by a run of length (fact-clock (- n 1)), followed by a run of length two, and each run must be fully simplified to a symbolic state before the next can be simplified (because of the way the step function has been limited).
- Finally we prove the standard "memory management" rules, which in the case of the TJVM tell us the algebra of association lists (used to bind variables, associate programs with method names, method names with methods, fields with their contents, etc.).

Having so configured ACL2, the theorem about "fact" above is proved by giving the theorem prover a single hint, namely to do the induction that unwinds the code in "fact".

It is important to realize that the theorem above about "fact" contributes to the further configuration of ACL2 in this capacity. The theorem causes the following future behavior of ACL2: Suppose the system encounters an expression of the form (tjvm α (fact-clock β)) to simplify. Then it first determines whether the next instruction of the state α is (invokestatic "Math" "fact" 1) where the meaning of "Math" in α is our Math-class, and whether β is on top of the operand stack of α and is a natural number. If so, it replaces (tjvm α (fact-clock β)) by the corresponding make-state expression in which the program counter has been incremented by one and β has been replaced by (fact β).

Thus, after this theorem is proved, the theorem prover no longer looks at the code for "fact". It steps over (invokestatic "Math" "fact" 1) as though it were a primitive instruction that computes the factorial of the top of the stack.

The verification of a system of methods is no harder than the combined verification of each method in the system. This remark, while trivial, has profound consequences if one clearly views the software verification problem as the specification and verification of the component pieces.

4   More Example TJVM Executions

The "fact" method does not affect the heap. That is, it does not create any new objects or modify existing objects. How does our verification strategy cope with that? We will consider a simple example of a heap modifying method. But we first illustrate such methods by simple execution. Consider the following TJVM class declaration for a class named "Point", which extends the "Object" class and has two fields, named "x" and "y". Instances of the "Point" class represent points in the Cartesian plane.

Point-class:

```
("Point" ("Object")
        ("x" "y")
        (xIncrement
         inBox))
```

Notice that the class has two methods. The first is defined by the list constant:

xIncrement:

```
("xIncrement" (dx)
              (load this)          ; 0
              (load this)          ; 1
              (getfield "Point" "x")  ; 2
              (load dx)            ; 3
              (add)                ; 4
              (putfield "Point" "x")  ; 5
              (return))            ; 6
```

We discuss this method now and will display the second constant, **inBox**, later.

The method "xIncrement" is an "instance method." It has an implicit formal parameter, this, and one explicit parameter, dx. When "xIncrement" is called with **invokevirtual**, two items are expected on the operand stack of the caller. The deeper of the two is expected to be an instance of some class and is used to select which method named "xIncrement" is actually run. That instance object is bound to the parameter this in the newly built frame and the other item on the stack is bound to the variable dx.

The byte code above increments the "x" field of this by the amount dx. Ignore for a moment the load instruction at 0. Instructions 1 and 2 push the contents of the "x" field onto the operand stack. Instruction 3 pushes dx and instruction 4 adds the two together, leaving the sum on the stack. The load instruction we ignored above, at 0, has pushed a reference to the this object onto the stack, now just under the sum. The putfield at 5 deposits the sum into the "x" field of that object, changing the heap. The return at 6 returns (no results) to the caller (i.e., this method is of return type "void"). It is convenient whenever we define a method to define the corresponding clock function for it. In the case of "xIncrement", which consists seven primitive, non-branching byte codes, the clock function is constant and returns 8. (Our convention is that the clock for a method includes the cycle for the byte code that invokes it.)

Before discussing the inBox method, we consider an extension to the "Point" class, called the "ColoredPoint" class. Here is the list constant denoting the TJVM declaration of that class.

ColoredPoint-class:

```
("ColoredPoint" ("Point" "Object")
                ("color")
                (setColor
                 setColorBox))
```

The class extends "Point" (and thus "Object") and provides the new field "color" and two methods. The first is called "setColor" and is defined below. It sets the "color" of a "ColoredPoint". The clock for this method returns 5.

setColor:
```
("setColor" (c)
            (load this)
            (load c)
            (putfield "ColoredPoint" "color")
            (return))
```

Consider the TJVM state

s_1:
```
(make-state
 (push
  (make-frame 0
              '((p . nil))
              nil
              '((new "ColoredPoint")
                (store p)
                (load p)
                (push -23)
                (invokevirtual "ColoredPoint" "xIncrement" 1)
                (load p)
                (push "Green")
                (invokevirtual "ColoredPoint" "setColor" 1)
                (load p)
                (halt)))
   nil)
 nil
 '(Point-class
   ColoredPoint-class))
```

This state is poised to execute the ten instruction program above, with one local, p, which is initially nil. The class table of the state contains both "Point" and its extension "ColoredPoint". Inspection of the code above shows that it creates a new "ColoredPoint" and stores it into p. It then invokes "xIncrement" to increment the "x" field of p by -23 and invokes "setColor" to set the "color" field of p to "Green". Of interest is the fact that the first method is in the class "Point" and the second is in the class "ColoredPoint". The "ColoredPoint" p inherits the fields and methods of its superclass, "Point".

Had the "ColoredPoint" class overridden the method "xIncrement" by including the definition of such a method, then the program above would have invoked that method rather than the one in "Point", since the method is selected by searching through the superclass chain of the this object of the invocation, which is here p, an object of class "ColoredPoint".

Consider, s'_1, the result of running the TJVM on s_1 for 21 steps,

s'_1:
```
(tjvm s1 21).
```

"21" is obtained by adding up the clocks for each instruction above.

Of interest is (deref (top (stack (top-frame s'₁))) (heap s'₁)). This expression dereferences the topmost item on the operand stack of s'₁, with respect to the heap of that state. The topmost item on the stack is, of course, the reference that is the value of the local p. That reference was created by new at the beginning of the program. Dereferencing it through the final heap produces the "logical meaning" of p at the conclusion of the program. The result is

```
(("ColoredPoint" ("color" . "Green"))
 ("Point" ("x" . -23) ("y" . 0))
 ("Object"))
```

This is an *instance* in the ACL2 semantics of the TJVM. It represents an object of class "ColoredPoint". It enumerates the fields of that class and of all its superclasses and specifies the value of each field. We see that at the conclusion of the program above the "color" of the object is set to "Green", the "x" field (in the "Point" superclass) is set to -23 as a result of our "xIncrement" and the "y" field is set to (the "uninitialized" value) 0. The "Object" class in the TJVM has no fields.

5   Proving Theorems About Objects

Our "Point" class contains a second method, called "inBox", which determines whether its this object is within a given rectangle in the plane. The rectangle is specified by two points, p1 and p2, which are the lower-left and upper-right corners of the box. Here is the definition of the method.

inBox:
```
("inBox" (p1 p2)
         (load p1)                      ;  0
         (getfield "Point" "x")         ;  1
         (load this)                    ;  2
         (getfield "Point" "x")         ;  3
         (sub)                          ;  4
         (ifgt 21)                      ;  5
         (load this)                    ;  6
         (getfield "Point" "x")         ;  7
         (load p2)                      ;  8
         (getfield "Point" "x")         ;  9
         (sub)                          ; 10
         (ifgt 15)                      ; 11
         (load p1)                      ; 12
         (getfield "Point" "y")         ; 13
         (load this)                    ; 14
         (getfield "Point" "y")         ; 15
         (sub)                          ; 16
         (ifgt 9)                       ; 17
         (load this)                    ; 18
```

```
(getfield "Point" "y")        ; 19
(load p2)                     ; 20
(getfield "Point" "y")        ; 21
(sub)                         ; 22
(ifgt 3)                      ; 23
(push 1)                      ; 24
(xreturn)                     ; 25
(push 0)                      ; 26
(xreturn))                    ; 27
```

This is a straightforward compilation (for the TJVM) of the following Java (which is written in a slightly awkward style to make the correspondence with the byte code more clear).

```
public boolean inBox(Point p1, Point p2){
if (p1.x <= this.x &
    this.x <= p2.x &
    p1.y <= this.y &
    this.y <= p2.y)
  {return true;}
else {return false;}}
```

We will specify and prove the correctness of this method in a moment. But we must develop some Lisp functions for dealing with points and in so doing illustrate our preferred style for dealing with TJVM objects in general, at the logical level.

Consider the two Lisp functions below for retrieving the x- and y-coordinates of a point.

```
(defun Point.x (ref s)
  (field-value "Point" "x" (deref ref (heap s))))

(defun Point.y (ref s)
  (field-value "Point" "y" (deref ref (heap s))))
```

Observe that they take the TJVM state, s, as arguments. That is because we apply them to *references* to Points, not to *instances*. Had we chosen the latter course, we would have defined Point.x as

```
(defun Point.x (p)
  (field-value "Point" "x" p))
```

but would have to call it by writing (Point.x (deref *ref* (heap s))). We belabor this point for a reason: when defining the Lisp concepts necessary to speak formally about TJVM objects should we focus on references or on instances? If we focus on references, we must also have available the state, or at least the heap, with respect to which those references are to be dereferenced. This is the choice we have made and yet it seems complicated.

The problem with focusing on instances is that instances may contain references. Thus, even if we focus on instances the heap is still relevant. This does not arise with "Point" instances because their fields do not contain references. But consider the class "LinkedList", with two fields, "head" and "next". Suppose the "next" field generally contains a (reference to a) "LinkedList" instance. Then a typical instance of "LinkedList" might be:

```
(("LinkedList" ("head" . 1) ("next" . (REF 45)))
 ("Object")).
```

Since the object itself might be "circular" we cannot, in general, replace (REF 45) by the instance to which it dereferences. Thus, we see that while instances may be more convenient than references for simple classes like "Point", they are no more convenient than references in general.

We therefore chose references because it tends to induce a uniform style in the definition of the logical functions for manipulating objects, that style being to dereference the reference with respect to the state, use the resulting instance and then recursively deal with the interior references. This means that the Lisp formalization of the semantics of a TJVM method may very closely resemble the algorithm implemented by the byte code. This is convenient because the verification of a method generally takes place in two steps. *In the first step we prove that the interpretation of the byte code produces the same TJVM state transformation as described at a higher level by the Lisp function. In the second step we prove that the Lisp function enjoys some desirable properties.* The first step is complicated by the semantics of the byte code interpreter and so it is convenient for the Lisp to be "close" to the byte code. Once we have gotten away from the byte code to the simpler applicative Lisp world, we deal with the complexity of proving that the Lisp "does the right thing."

In this paper we do not further consider instances that reference other instances.

We next consider the "inBox" method and focus on its "clock function." How many TJVM cycles are required to execute an invocation of that method? We can express the clock function for "inBox" with:

```
(defun inBox-clock (this p₁ p₂ s)
  (cond ((> (Point.x p₁ s)
            (Point.x this s))
         9)
        ((> (Point.x this s)
            (Point.x p₂ s))
         15)
        ((> (Point.y p₁ s)
            (Point.y this s))
         21)
        (t 27)))
```

Despite the apparent simplicity of the "inBox" method, the time it takes depends not only on the inputs *this*, p_1, and p_2, but on the state in which it is called. This is unavoidable since the very meaning of references to objects change as the heap changes.

What theorem might we wish to prove about "inBox"? The obvious theorem is that it returns 1 or 0 (the TJVM and JVM "booleans") according to whether the **this** object is within the box defined by p1 and p2. We define the Lisp function inBox as follows:

```
(defun inBox (this p₁ p₂ s)
  (and (<= (Point.x p₁ s)
           (Point.x this s))
       (<= (Point.x this s)
           (Point.x p₂ s))
       (<= (Point.y p₁ s)
           (Point.y this s))
       (<= (Point.y this s)
           (Point.y p₂ s))))
```

Observe that the Lisp inBox predicate is dependent upon the TJVM state with respect to which the TJVM objects are dereferenced. Again, this is unavoidable. Even though the references to the three points in question are constants, the x-y locations of the denoted points may change over time and whether a point is in a given box is, quite literally, a function of the TJVM state. (Indeed, the locations may be changed even by methods that are not directly passed these three references because other objects in the heap may contain these references.)

Before we state the correctness of the "inBox" method formally we do so informally. Our first statement, below, is just an approximation, modeled on the theorem we proved about "fact".

> **First Approximation** Suppose s_0 is a TJVM state whose next instruction is (invokevirtual "Point" "inBox" 2), where the meaning of the name "Point" in the class table is our **Point-class**. Let *this* be the third item on the operand stack, let p_1 be the second item, and let p_2 be the topmost item. Then the TJVM state obtained by stepping s_0 (inBox-clock *this* p_1 p_2 s_0) times is state just s_0 with the program counter incremented by one and the three items removed from the operand stack and replaced by 1 or 0 according to whether (inBox *this* p_1 p_2 s_0). The heap is unchanged.

This approximation is inadequate in two respects. First, we are not concerned with the just the instruction (invokevirtual "Point" "inBox" 2) but in any instruction of the form (invokevirtual *class* "inBox" 2). A careful reading of the semantic function for invokevirtual reveals that the semantics is independent of the first operand of the instruction! The actual method invoked is the one named "inBox" in the superclass chain of the "this" object, not the method named "inBox" in the class named in the invokevirtual instruction.[1] Therefore, rather than require that (next-inst s_0) be (invokevirtual

---

[1] This is also true of the JVM invokevirtual instruction. The reason invokevirtual has that operand is so that in a JVM implementation the given class name can be used to find a "dispatch vector" associated with the named class to shortcut the search up the superclass chain.

"Point" "inBox" 2) we require that it be a list whose first, third and fourth elements are invokevirtual, "inBox" and 2, respectively.

The second change to this approximation is that we must insist that the method found by looking up the superclass chain of *this* be **inBox**. In particular, just because we invoke "inBox" in a TJVM state in which "Point" is defined as above, do we know that the resolved method will be **inBox**? No! The superclass chain of *this* might include a class that overrides "inBox" and defines it a different way. If we add the hypothesis that the resolved method is **inBox** then we may delete the hypothesis, in our approximation above, requiring that "Point" be as defined here: it does not matter how "Point" is defined as long as the resolved method is our **inBox**.

> **Theorem.** "inBox" is correct: Suppose s_0 is a TJVM state whose next instruction is of the form (invokevirtual *class* "inBox" 2). Let *this* be the third item on the operand stack, let p_1 be the second item, and let p_2 be the topmost item. Suppose the nearest method named "inBox" in the superclass chain of *this* is **inBox**. Then the TJVM state obtained by stepping s_0 (inBox-clock *this* p_1 p_2 s_0) times is state s_0 with the program counter incremented by one and the three items removed from the operand stack and replaced by 1 or 0 according to whether (inBox *this* p_1 p_2 s_0). The heap is unchanged.

Here is the formal rendering of the theorem:

Theorem. "inBox" is correct:
```
(implies (and (consp (next-inst s0))
              (equal (car (next-inst s0)) 'invokevirtual)
              (equal (caddr (next-inst s0)) "inBox")
              (equal (cadddr (next-inst s0)) 2)

              (equal this (top (pop (pop (stack (top-frame s0))))))
              (equal p1  (top (pop (stack (top-frame s0)))))
              (equal p2  (top (stack (top-frame s0))))

              (equal (lookup-method "inBox"
                                    (class-name-of-ref this (heap s0))
                                    (class-table s0))
                     inBox))
         (equal
          (tjvm s0 (inBox-clock this p1 p2 s0))
          (make-state
           (push (make-frame (+ 1 (pc (top-frame s0)))
                             (locals (top-frame s0))
                             (push (if (inBox this p1 p2 s0) 1 0)
                                   (popn 3 (stack (top-frame s0))))
                             (program (top-frame s0)))
                 (pop (call-stack s0)))
           (heap s0)
           (class-table s0))))
```

This theorem is proved by straightforward symbolic evaluation, i.e., the repeated unfolding of the definition of tjvm, together with Boolean and arithmetic simplification.

Once proved, how is this theorem used? Suppose the ACL2 rewriter encounters a call of tjvm in which the second argument is an inBox-clock expression. (Previously proved rules about tjvm will insure that arithmetic combinations of such expressions are decomposed into appropriate nests of tjvm expressions applied to these clock functions.) Then the rewriter tries to establish that the next-inst of the TJVM state is an invokevirtual of "inBox" and the resolved method named "inBox" in the superclass chain of the *this* object is inBox. These actions are caused by backchaining. The three hypotheses equating *this*, p_1, and p_2 to stack expressions are not restrictive: they are established by binding *this*, p_1, and p_2 to the corresponding expressions. Provided the hypotheses are established, the rewriter then replaces the target call of tjvm by a new state expression in which the program counter is advanced by one, the three actuals of "inBox" are removed from the stack and the appropriate value is pushed. Thus, as with our earlier theorem about "fact", this theorem configures ACL2 to simplify a call of "inBox" almost as though it were a built-in TJVM instruction whose semantics is given in terms of the Lisp function inBox.

Before proceeding with our presentation we take a slight detour to illustrate an important but obscure aspect of using ACL2. Readers uninterested in such details can skip this paragraph. The aspect in question is the fact that ACL2 uses a pattern matcher and backchaining to determine when an equality theorem is applicable as a rewrite rule. The pattern match is based on the left-hand side of the concluding equality: when a potential "target term" matching that term is seen by the rewriter, and the hypotheses can be relieved, the target term is replaced by the corresponding instance of the right-hand side. So consider the left-hand side of the conclusion above. Note that 's_0' occurs twice, once as the first argument to tjvm and then again inside the inBox-clock expression. In actual applications, the expressions in the target term corresponding to these two occurrences of 's_0' may not be syntactically identical. The first state is that in which inBox is being invoked; the second is the state used to compute how many steps to take. The two states could be syntactically different; indeed, they could be semantically different (i.e., not equal). This would prevent a pattern match and thus prevent the application of the theorem. A logically equivalent rephrasing of the theorem has the left-hand side (tjvm s_0 k) and the additional hypothesis that k is equal to (inBox-clock *this* p_1 p_2 s_0). That is, we do not need to insist that the clock expression be '(inBox-clock *this* p_1 p_2 s_0)', only that it be an expression with the same value. We follow this line of thinking just one more step before returning to the main flow of our presentation. If we rephrase the left-hand side as (tjvm s_0 k) ACL2 performs slowly because the pattern now matches every possible call of tjvm and the applicability of the theorem is entirely dependent on whether the hypotheses can be relieved. In general, pattern matching is faster than backchaining, so it is wise to put some syntactic "hint" in the pattern that the theorem applies to an invocation of inBox rather than, say, **fact**. We can recover most of the former efficiency while preserving the wide applicability of the theorem by using the left-hand side (**tjvm** s_0 (inBox-clock *this* p_1 p_2 s_1)) and adding the additional hypothesis that (inBox-clock *this* p_1 p_2 s_1) is equal to (inBox-clock *this* p_1 p_2 s_0). That is, we can give the two original occurrences of s_0 different names and merely insist that inBox-clock return the same thing on both of them. This is our preferred phrasing. We now return to the main flow of our presentation.

We finally turn to a theorem about a method that modifies an object, i.e., that modifies the heap. This is the second method of the "ColoredPoint" class:

setColorBox:
```
("setColorBox" (p1 p2 color)
               (load this)
               (load p1)
               (load p2)
               (invokevirtual "ColoredPoint" "inBox" 2)
               (ifeq 4)
               (load this)
               (load color)
               (putfield "ColoredPoint" "color")
               (return))
```

This void instance method takes three arguments, two points and a color. If the "this" object is in the box specified by the two points, the method sets the color of the "this" object to the specified color. The clock function for "setColorBox" is

```
(defun setColorBox-clock (this p1 p2 c s)
  (declare (ignore c))
  (++ 4
      (inBox-clock this p1 p2 s)
      (if (inBox this p1 p2 s)
          5
        2)))
```

The primary effect of invoking "setColorBox" is to produce a new heap. That heap is described by

```
(defun setColorBox-heap (this p1 p2 c s)
  (if (inBox this p1 p2 s)
      (let ((instance (deref this (heap s)))
            (address (cadr this)))
        (bind
         address
         (set-instance-field "ColoredPoint" "color" c instance)
         (heap s)))
    (heap s)))
```

The theorem stating the correctness of "setColorBox" is

Theorem. "setColorBox" is correct:
```
(implies (and (consp (next-inst s0))
              (equal (car (next-inst s0)) 'invokevirtual)
              (equal (caddr (next-inst s0)) "setColorBox")
              (equal (cadddr (next-inst s0)) 3)

              (equal this (top (pop (pop (pop (stack (top-frame s0)))))))
              (equal p1  (top (pop (pop (stack (top-frame s0))))))
              (equal p2  (top (pop (stack (top-frame s0)))))
              (equal color (top (stack (top-frame s0))))

              (equal (lookup-method "inBox"
                                    (class-name-of-ref this (heap s0))
                                    (class-table s0))
                     inBox)
              (equal (lookup-method "setColorBox"
                                    (class-name-of-ref this (heap s0))
                                    (class-table s0))
                     setColorBox))
         (equal
          (tjvm s0 (setColorBox-clock this p1 p2 color s0))
          (make-state
           (push (make-frame (+ 1 (pc (top-frame s0)))
                             (locals (top-frame s0))
                             (popn 4 (stack (top-frame s0)))
                             (program (top-frame s0)))
                 (pop (call-stack s0)))
           (setColorBox-heap this p1 p2 color s0)
           (class-table s0))))
```

This theorem is exactly analogous to the one about "inBox". The effect of the theorem is to configure ACL2 so that when it sees a tjvm expression with the setColorBox-clock it increments the program counter by one, pops four things off the operand stack, and sets the heap to that described by setColorBox-heap.

Such a move is interesting by virtue of the following easy-to-prove theorem about that heap:

Theorem.
```
(implies (and (refp ref)
              (refp this))
         (equal (deref ref
                       (setColorBox-heap this p1 p2 color s))
                (if (and (equal ref this)
                         (inBox this p1 p2 s))
                    (set-instance-field "ColoredPoint" "color" color
                                        (deref this (heap s)))
                    (deref ref (heap s)))))
```

This theorem specifies the key property of the new heap. It defines how to dereference an arbitrary reference, *ref*, with respect to the new heap. If *ref* is the *this* object of the "setColorBox" invocation, and that object is within the specified box, then the dereferenced object is the result of setting the "color" of the same object in the old heap. Otherwise, dereferencing with respect to the new heap produces the same result as dereferencing with respect to the old heap. Thus, setColorBox-heap is just a succinct symbolic representation of the heap produced by "setColorBox" and whenever references arise with respect to it, they are eliminated and replaced by modified instances obtained through the old heap.

While we have not illustrated classes that chain instances together or instance methods that are recursive or iterative, these aspects of the TJVM should raise no problems not predicted by our handling of the recursive factorial and the simple instance methods shown. That is not to say that such proofs are trivial, only that their nature is entirely predictable from what has been shown here. The expectation is that the ACL2 user able to do the proofs shown would be able to develop the techniques necessary to do proofs of this more involved nature.

6   Conclusion

We have shown how a simple version of the Java Virtual Machine can be formalized in the applicative Common Lisp supported by the ACL2 theorem prover. We have discussed how ACL2 can be configured to make it straightforward to reason about static and instance methods, including recursive methods and methods which modify objects in the heap.

A common criticism of this approach is our use of "clocks." Basically, clocks arise for a deep logical reason: the function tjvm is inadmissible otherwise because it is not total. We make tjvm total by limiting the number of instructions. There are other means, e.g., limiting the stack depth (i.e., method invocation depth) and imposing some bound or measure on back jumps, or, equipping every state with a measure establishing termination. These means free the user from counting instructions, at the expense of counting some other unit of computation. We personally find instruction-level clocks conceptually simplest.

Instruction-level clocking provides "little step" operational semantics but allows the proof of lemmas, like those shown here, that provide "big step" semantics for subroutine call. Furthermore, we have shown how the two are naturally mixed.

Whether one uses instruction-level clocking or some other form of counting, clock expressions allow the user to structure proofs. Every addend in a ++-nest gives rise to a single call of tjvm which must be simplified. Thus, by choice of an appropriate clock expression one can decompose proofs into the segments about which one is prepared to reason by specially-tailored lemmas. To the extent that one can decompose a computation mechanically into such regions, one can mechanically generate clock expressions to control the proof decomposition. Clock expressions compose in the obvious way with invokevirtual and invokestatic. Iterative computations are handled similarly.

While both clock expressions and the Lisp functions describing the semantics of TJVM methods might appear complicated, it is crucial to remember the compositional nature of specifications and proofs. Once the clock expression for a method has been written and the corresponding specification has been proved, it is not necessary to think about or reveal the details. For example, one need not know that (fact-clock 5) is 50, only that (fact-clock n) is cost of running fact on n.

The use of clocks encourages a focus on terminating computations but does not preclude consideration of non-terminating computations. By adding a flag to the TJVM state indicating whether the computation halted normally or "ran out of time" it is possible to phrase partial correctness results in this framework. In this setting, typical partial-correctness theorems have the additional hypothesis "provided n is sufficient to guarantee termination." Furthermore, one can use explicit clocks, as we do, but address oneself to non-terminating computations and still characterize the state produced at certain points in the infinite computation.

Our toy JVM ignores many aspects of the JVM, as noted earlier, including the omission of many byte code instructions, the finiteness of resources, error handling, exceptions, and multiple threads. Many of these aspects could be incorporated into a formal model. Some, such as the inclusion of additional byte codes, would not affect the complexity of proofs at all. The others would preserve the basic character of the theorems and proofs described here but, in some cases, would require the explicit statement of additional hypotheses to insure the sufficiency of available resources and the absence of errors. New proof machinery would have to be created (via the proofs of suitable lemmas) to enable ACL2 to reason about TJVM computations in which exceptions are thrown or multiple threads are used.

Our experience, notably that reported in Young's dissertation, [13] and in the author's work on Piton [11], is that when dealing with resource limitations and exceptions it is best to produce several layers of abstraction, each formally related to the next by lemmas, one of which is free of those concepts and corresponds to our tjvm. That is, we see a model like our TJVM as being a component of a stack of abstract machines that enables formal discussion of programming language concepts not included in tjvm.

Cohen's defensive JVM, dJVM, [6] is an example of a machine in such a hierarchy. Since Cohen's dJVM deals realistically with a significant fragment of the actual JVM, we cannot relate it to our TJVM. But we can explain the basic concept of a "defensive machine" by imagining a "defensive TJVM."

Consider the behavior of our TJVM on the add instruction: the top two items on the operand stack are added together. What if they are non-numeric? Our TJVM model answers this question by appealing simply to the untyped ACL2 logic: add uses the total ACL2 function + to combine the two items. This is simple and allows proofs of byte code program properties. But we probably do not intend to implement the TJVM fully, i.e., we probably do not intend to mimic the model's behavior on non-numeric input. To address this we define another function, dtjvm, which is like tjvm. But we modify every semantic function so that before an instruction is executed we check that the state is acceptable. If it is not, we set some "non-normal termination" flag in the state and halt. By defining these defensive semantic functions explicitly in terms of the TJVM's semantic functions — i.e., the defensive add performs the TJVM's execute-ADD unless the check fails — it is easy to prove that dtjvm and tjvm return the "same" results when the dtjvm's non-normal termination flag is off.

Now suppose someone presents us with a "byte-code verifier." We are in a position to say what property it must have: when verified code is executed by the dTJVM, the non-normal termination flag remains off. If that property is proved of the verifier and the verifier, in turn, approves of a given byte-coded method, then we can prove the correctness of the method using the full (and simple) TJVM semantics, instead of having to reason about the dTJVM semantics and all of its error conditions.

The most problematic aspect of our TJVM may appear to be the fact that TJVM objects cannot be represented by (the non-circular) objects of applicative Common Lisp, necessitating the "reference versus instance" debate summarized here and the explicit provision of the heap in our specification functions. It cannot be denied that this is a complication. Similar problems have been dealt with in Flatau's dissertation [7], where pure Lisp is implemented on a von Neumann machine in a way that is mechanically proved correct. However, we do not think this can be avoided simply because it reflects the underlying reality of object oriented programming, in which objects contain a von Neumann sense of state.

7   Acknowledgments

I am especially grateful to Rich Cohen, who patiently explained his ACL2 model of his "defensive" Java Virtual Machine, upon which my TJVM is modeled. I am also very grateful to the undergraduates at UT to whom I have taught the TJVM, as well as my teaching assistant for that course last year, Pete Manolios.

References

1. W. R. Bevier, W. A. Hunt, J S. Moore, and W. D. Young. Special Issue on System Verification. *Journal of Automated Reasoning*, 5(4):409–530, December, 1989.
2. R. S. Boyer and J S. Moore. *A Computational Logic*. Academic Press: New York, 1979.
3. R. S. Boyer and J S. Moore. Mechanized Formal Reasoning about Programs and Computing Machines. In R. Veroff (ed.), *Automated Reasoning and Its Applications: Essays in Honor of Larry Wos*, MIT Press, 1996.
4. R. S. Boyer and J S. Moore. *A Computational Logic Handbook, Second Edition*, Academic Press: London, 1997.
5. B. Brock, M. Kaufmann and J S. Moore, "ACL2 Theorems about Commercial Microprocessors," in M. Srivas and A. Camilleri (eds.) *Proceedings of Formal Methods in Computer-Aided Design (FMCAD'96)*, Springer-Verlag, pp. 275–293, 1996.

6. R. M. Cohen, *The Defensive Java Virtual Machine Specification, Version 0.53*, Electronic Data Systems, Corp, Austin Technical Services Center, 98 San Jacinto Blvd, Suite 500, Austin, TX 78701 (email: cohen@aus.edsr.eds.com).

7. A. D. Flatau, *A verified implementation of an applicative language with dynamic storage allocation*, PhD Thesis, University of Texas at Austin, 1992.

8. M. Kaufmann and J Strother Moore "An Industrial Strength Theorem Prover for a Logic Based on Common Lisp," *IEEE Transactions on Software Engineering*, **23**(4), pp. 203–213, April, 1997

9. M. Kaufmann and J Strother Moore "A Precise Description of the ACL2 Logic," http://www.cs.utexas.edu/users/moore/publications/-km97a.ps.Z, April, 1998.

10. T. Lindholm and F. Yellin *The Java Virtual Machine Specification*, Addison-Wesley, 1996.

11. J S. Moore. *Piton: A Mechanically Verified Assembly-Level Language*. Automated Reasoning Series, Kluwer Academic Publishers, 1996.

12. G. L. Steele, Jr. *Common Lisp The Language, Second Edition*. Digital Press, 30 North Avenue, Burlington, MA 01803, 1990.

13. W. D. Young, *A Verified Code-Generator for a Subset of Gypsy*, PhD Thesis, University of Texas at Austin" 1988.

14. Y. Yu. *Automated Proofs of Object Code For a Widely Used Microprocessor*. PhD thesis, University of Texas at Austin, 1992. Lecture Notes in Computer Science, Springer-Verlag (to appear). ftp://ftp.cs.utexas.edu/pub/techreports/tr93-09.ps.Z.

Multiple State and Single State Tableaux for Combining Local and Global Model Checking *

Armin Biere[1], Edmund M. Clarke[1,2], and Yunshan Zhu[1]

[1] Verysys Design Automation, Inc, 42707 Lawrence Place, Fremont, CA 94538
armin@verysys.com, yunshan@verysys.com
[2] Computer Science Department, Carnegie Mellon University
5000 Forbes Avenue, Pittsburgh, PA 15213, U.S.A
Edmund.Clarke@cs.cmu.edu

Abstract. The verification process of reactive systems in *local model checking* [2, 9, 28] and in *explicit state model checking* [14, 16] is *on-the-fly*. Therefore only those states of a system have to be traversed that are necessary to prove a property. In addition, if the property does not hold, than often only a small subset of the state space has to be traversed to produce a counterexample. *Global model checking* [8, 24] and, in particular, *symbolic model checking* [6, 23] can utilize compact representations of the state space, e.g. BDDs [5], to handle much larger designs than what is possible with local and explicit model checking. We present a new model checking algorithm for LTL that combines both approaches. In essence, it is a generalization of the tableau construction of [2] that enables the use of BDDs but still is on-the-fly.

1 Introduction

Model Checking [8, 24] is a powerful technique for the verification of reactive systems. With the invention of symbolic model checking [6, 23] very large systems, with more than 10^{20} states, could be verified. However, it is often observed, that explicit state model checkers [11] outperform symbolic model checkers, especially in the application domain of asynchronous systems and communication protocols [12]. We believe that the main reasons are the following: First, symbolic model checkers traditionally use binary decision diagrams (BDDs) [5] as an underlying data structure. BDDs trade space for time and often their sheer size explodes. Second, depth first search (DFS) is used in explicit state model checking, while symbolic model checking usually traverses the state space in breadth first search (BFS). DFS helps to reduce the space requirements and is able to find counterexamples much faster. Finally, global model checking traverses the state space backwards, and can, in general, not avoid visiting non reachable states without a prior reachability analysis.

---

* This research is sponsored by the Semiconductor Research Corporation (SRC) under Contract No. 98-DJ-294, and the National Science Foundation (NSF) under Grant No. CCR-9505472. Any opinions, findings and conclusions or recommendations expressed in this material are those of the authors and do not necessarily reflect the views of SRC, NSF, or the United States Government.

E.-R. Olderog, B. Steffen (Eds.): Correct System Design, LNCS 1710, pp. 163–179, 1999.
© Springer-Verlag Berlin Heidelberg 1999

In [3] a solution to the first problem, and partially to the second problem, was presented, by replacing BDDs by SAT (propositional satisfiability checking procedures). In this paper we propose a solution to the second and third problems of symbolic model checking. Our main contribution is a new model checking algorithm that generalizes the tableau construction [2] of local model checking for LTL and enables the use of BDDs. It is based on a mixed DFS and BFS strategy and traverses the state space in a forward oriented manner.

Our research is motivated by the success of forward model checking [17, 18]. Forward model checking is a variant of symbolic model checking in which only forward image computations are used. Thus it mimics the *on-the-fly* nature of explicit and local model checking in visiting only reachable states. Note that [18] presented a technique for the combination of the BFS, used in BDD based approaches, with the DFS of explicit state model checkers. It was shown that especially this feature enables forward model checking to find counterexamples much faster. However, only a restricted class of properties, i.e. path expressions, can be handled by the algorithms of [17, 18].

Henzinger et. al. in [15] partially filled this gap by proving that all properties specified by Büchi Automata, or equivalently all ω-regular properties, can be processed by forward model checking. In particular, they define a forward oriented version of the modal μ-calculus [20], called *post-μ*, and translate the model checking problem of a ω-regular property into a *post-μ* model checking problem. Because LTL (linear temporal logic) properties can be formulated as ω-regular properties [29], their result implies that all LTL properties can be checked by forward model checking.

The fact, that LTL can be checked by forward model checking, can also be derived by applying the techniques of [17] to the tableau construction of [7]. However, this construction and also [15] do not allow the mixture of DFS and BFS, as in the layered approach of [18]. In addition, DFS was identified as a major reason that explicit state model checking is able to outperform symbolic model checking on certain examples.

The contribution of our paper is the following. First we present a new model checking algorithm that operates directly on LTL formulae. For example [15] requires two translations, from LTL to Büchi Automata and then to *post-μ*. A similar argument applies to [7, 10]. Second it connects the local model checking paradigm of [2] with symbolic model checking in a natural way, thus combining BDD based with on-the-fly model checking. For the modal μ-calculus this connection has already been made in [4]. However, a direct application of [4] to the tableau construction of [2], our multiple state tableau construction, results in a tableau that is exponential in the size of the model. Only the introduction of a split rule in combination with efficient splitting heuristics allows us to keep the tableau linear in the size of the model. Finally our approach shows, that the idea of mixing DFS with BFS can be lifted from path expressions [18] to LTL.

Our paper is organized as follows. In the next section our notation is introduced. Section 3 presents a variation of the single state tableau construction of [2], on which our multiple state tableau construction, introduced in Section 4, is based. The following section discusses implementation details of the algorithm. In Section 6 we investigate heuristics to generate small tableau. An important optimization is presented in Section 7. The technical part ends with a discussion of the complexity and comparison with related work in Section 8. Finally we address open issues.

2   Preliminaries

A *Kripke structure* is a tuple $K = (\Sigma, \Sigma_0, \delta, \ell)$ with Σ a finite set of states, $\Sigma_0 \subseteq \Sigma$ the set of initial states, $\delta \subseteq \Sigma \times \Sigma$ the transition relation between states, and $\ell: \Sigma \to \mathbb{P}(\mathcal{A})$ the labeling of the states with *atomic propositions* $\mathcal{A} = \{p, \ldots\}$. For technical reasons we assume that every state has at least one successor state. A *path* $\pi = (s_0, s_1, \ldots)$ is an infinite sequence of states $s_i \in \Sigma$. Define $\pi(i) = s_i$ as the i-th state in π. We also use the notation $\pi^i = (\pi(i), \pi(i+1), \ldots)$ for the suffix of π starting at $\pi(i)$. The image operation on a set of states $S \subseteq \Sigma$ is defined as $\mathrm{Img}(S) := \{t \in \Sigma \mid \exists s \in S. (s,t) \in \delta\}$.

As temporal operators we consider, the *next time* operator $\mathbf{X}$, the *finally* operator $\mathbf{F}$, the *globally* operator $\mathbf{G}$, the *until* operator $\mathbf{U}$, and its dual, the *release* operator $\mathbf{R}$. An LTL formula f is called an *eventuality* iff $f = \mathbf{F}h$ or $f = (g \mathbf{U} h)$. In this case h is called the *body* of f. We assume the formulae to be in negation normal form, as in [2, 9, 10]. Thus negations only occur in front of atomic propositions. This restriction does not lead to an exponential blow up because we have included the $\mathbf{R}$ operator that fulfills the property $\neg(f \mathbf{U} g) \equiv \neg f \mathbf{R} \neg g$.

An LTL formulae f holds on a path π, written $\pi \models f$, according to the following definitions:

$$\pi \models p \quad \textit{iff} \quad p \in \ell(\pi(0)) \qquad\qquad \pi \models \neg p \quad \textit{iff} \quad p \notin \ell(\pi(0))$$

$$\pi \models g \wedge h \quad \textit{iff} \quad \pi \models g \text{ and } \pi \models h \qquad \pi \models g \vee h \quad \textit{iff} \quad \pi \models g \text{ or } \pi \models h$$

$$\pi \models \mathbf{G}g \quad \textit{iff} \quad \forall i. \pi^i \models g \qquad\qquad \pi \models \mathbf{F}h \quad \textit{iff} \quad \exists i. \pi^i \models h$$

$$\pi \models \mathbf{X}g \quad \textit{iff} \quad \pi^1 \models g$$

$$\pi \models g \mathbf{U} h \quad \textit{iff} \quad \exists i. \pi^i \models h \text{ and } \forall j < i. \pi^j \models g$$

$$\pi \models g \mathbf{R} h \quad \textit{iff} \quad \forall i. \pi^i \models h \text{ or } \exists j < i. \pi^j \models g$$

Since we are only concerned with finding witnesses for LTL formulae, we define an LTL formula f to hold at state $s \in \Sigma$ (written $s \models f$) iff there exists a path π in Σ^{ω} starting at $\pi(0) = s$ with $\pi \models f$. In addition we define f to hold in a set of states $S \subseteq \Sigma$ (written $S \models f$) iff there exists $s \in S$ with $s \models f$.

3   Single State Tableaux

In this section we present a variation on a tableau construction for explicit state model checking of LTL properties based on [2, 19]. The nodes in these *hybrid* tableaux also contain states of the model under investigation and not just temporal formulae. The main contribution of our paper is a symbolic extension to this tableau construction and is introduced Section 4.

The LTL model checking algorithm of [19] is the dual to the tableau construction of [2]. In [2] universal path quantifiers are considered, whereas [19] and our approach solve the dual model checking problem for existential path quantifiers. A tableau in the sense of [19] can be transformed into a tableau of [2] by replacing every literal by its negation, every temporal operator by its dual, e.g. every occurrence of $\mathbf{F}$ by $\mathbf{G}$, every $\mathbf{E}$ by $\mathbf{A}$, and every boolean operator by its dual as well, e.g. $\wedge$ by $\vee$. In essence this transformation is just a negation of every formula in the tableau. The terminology of a successful tableau has also to be revised, which can be found further down.

We call the type of tableau of [19] a *single state tableau* (S-Tableau), since every node in the tableau only contains a single state. Our tableau construction, introduced in section 4, allows a set of states at each tableau node. These tableaux are called *multiple state tableaux* (M-Tableau). In the rest of this section we will present a slight modification of the S-Tableau construction of [19] and note some facts that can be derived from [2, 19].

$$R_{\mathcal{A}^+}: \frac{s \vdash \mathbf{E}(\Phi, p)}{s \vdash \mathbf{E}(\Phi)} \quad p \in \ell(s), \quad p \in \mathcal{A} \qquad\qquad R_{\mathcal{A}^-}: \frac{s \vdash \mathbf{E}(\Phi, \neg p)}{s \vdash \mathbf{E}(\Phi)} \quad p \notin \ell(s), \quad p \in \mathcal{A}$$

$$R_{\mathbf{U}}: \frac{s \vdash \mathbf{E}(\Phi, f\,\mathbf{U}\,g)}{s \vdash \mathbf{E}(\Phi, g) \qquad s \vdash \mathbf{E}(\Phi, f, \mathbf{X} f\,\mathbf{U}\,g)} \qquad\qquad R_{\wedge}: \frac{s \vdash \mathbf{E}(\Phi, f \wedge g)}{s \vdash \mathbf{E}(\Phi, f, g)}$$

$$R_{\mathbf{R}}: \frac{s \vdash \mathbf{E}(\Phi, f\,\mathbf{R}\,g)}{s \vdash \mathbf{E}(\Phi, f, g) \qquad s \vdash \mathbf{E}(\Phi, g, \mathbf{X} f\,\mathbf{R}\,g)} \qquad\qquad R_{\vee}: \frac{s \vdash \mathbf{E}(\Phi, f \vee g)}{s \vdash \mathbf{E}(\Phi, f) \qquad s \vdash \mathbf{E}(\Phi, g)}$$

$$R_{\mathbf{F}}: \frac{s \vdash \mathbf{E}(\Phi, \mathbf{F} f)}{s \vdash \mathbf{E}(\Phi, f) \qquad s \vdash \mathbf{E}(\Phi, \mathbf{X} \mathbf{F} f)} \qquad\qquad R_{\mathbf{G}}: \frac{s \vdash \mathbf{E}(\Phi, \mathbf{G} f)}{s \vdash \mathbf{E}(\Phi, f, \mathbf{X} \mathbf{G} f)}$$

$$R_{\mathbf{X}}: \frac{s \vdash \mathbf{E}(\mathbf{X}\Phi_1, \ldots, \mathbf{X}\Phi_n)}{s_1 \vdash \mathbf{E}(\Phi_1, \ldots, \Phi_n) \quad \ldots \quad s_m \vdash \mathbf{E}(\Phi_1, \ldots, \Phi_n)} \quad \{s_1, \ldots, s_m\} = \mathrm{Img}(\{s\})$$

$$R_{\mathrm{split}}: \frac{s \vdash \mathbf{E}(\Phi)}{s \vdash \mathbf{E}(\Phi)}$$

Fig. 1. S-Rules: Single state tableau rules.

A *single state sequent* (S-Sequent) consists of a single state s and a list of LTL formulae $\Phi = (\Phi_1, \ldots, \Phi_n)$, written $s \vdash \mathbf{E}(\Phi)$. The order of the formulae in the list is not important. An S-Sequent $s \vdash E(\Phi)$ holds in a Kripke structure K iff $s \models \Phi_1 \wedge \cdots \wedge \Phi_n$ in K. An S-Tableau is a finite directed graph of nodes labeled with S-Sequents that are connected via the rules shown in figure 1. The application of a rule results in edges between the premise and each conclusion. If not otherwise stated, we assume that a tableau is fully expanded, i.e. no rule can generate new sequents or edges. For technical reasons a sequent may occur several times in a tableau. In particular, we assume that two nodes labeled with the same sequent are connected with an edge generated by application of the split rule R_{split}. This assumption allows us to extract an S-Tableau from an M-Tableau without shortening paths in the tableau. Refer to Lemma 6 for more details. We further assume that the split rule is only applied finitely often which keeps the tableau finite, since the number of different sequents is finite and nodes labeled with identical sequents can only be introduced by the split rule.

An S-Path x is defined as the sequence of labels (sequents) of the nodes on a path through an S-Tableau. Since a path through a tableau can be both, finite or infinite, the same applies to an S-path. A finite S-Path x is *successful* iff it ends with a sequent $s \vdash \mathbf{E}()$, where the list of formulae is empty. An S-Tableau is *partially successful* iff the tableau contains a finite successful S-Path. It is *partially unsuccessful* iff no finite S-Path is successful.

An eventuality f, contained in the list of formulae of $x(i)$, is called *fulfilled* iff there exists j with $i \leq j < |x|$ and the body of f is contained in $x(j)$. This definition also applies to infinite paths. An infinite S-Path x is called *successful* iff every eventuality in x is fulfilled. Finally a tableau is *successful* iff it is partially successful or it contains an infinite successful S-Path. With these definitions we can derive the following theorem from [2, 19]:

Theorem 1. *An S-Tableau with root $s \vdash \mathbf{E}(f)$ is successful iff $s \models f$.*

This theorem implies that $s \models f$ iff *every* S-Tableau with root $s \vdash \mathbf{E}(f)$ is successful. Therefore completeness and correctness is independent of the order in which the rules are applied. In the construction of the tableau no backtracking is required. The freedom to choose a rule, if several are applicable, can be used to minimize the size of the tableau, and thus the running time of the model checking algorithm (see Section 6 and Section 7).

Finding successful paths seems to be an algorithmically complex problem. However, we will show that this problem can be reduced to the search for a successful strongly connected component. A strongly connected component (SCC) of a directed graph is a maximal subgraph in which every node can be reached from every other node in the subgraph. Note that in our notation a single node, not contained in any cycle, is not an SCC. We call an SCC of an S-Tableau successful iff every eventuality occurring in the SCC is fulfilled in the SCC, i.e. with every eventuality the SCC also contains its body. For an efficient implementation the following theorem is very important. As a result the search for a successful infinite path can be replaced by the search for a successful SCC, which is algorithmically much simpler.

Theorem 2. *A partially unsuccessful S-Tableau is successful iff it contains a successful SCC.*

This theorem is an easy consequence of the following Lemma, which can be used for the generation of an infinite witness, respectively counterexample, as explained below.

Lemma 3. *An S-Tableau contains an infinite successful S-Path iff it contains a successful SCC.*

Proof. For the proof from left to right let x be an infinite successful S-Path. First note that there has to be an SCC C in which a suffix of x is fully contained, since the S-Tableau is finite. Further let σ be a sequent in C with an eventuality f on the right hand side (RHS). We need to show that f is fulfilled in C. Since C is an SCC, there exists a path segment connecting σ to the start of the suffix of x in C. If the body of f occurs on this path segment then we are done. Otherwise, by the structure of the rules for eventualities, the first sequent of the suffix of x in C reached by this segment still contains f or $\mathbf{X}f$. Since x is successful the body of f has to occur in the suffix of x which is part of C.

The other direction is proven by constructing a successful S-Path from a successful SCC. This is easily done by generating a cyclic path segment through the SCC containing every sequent in the SCC. From the start of the cycle we can find another path segment back to the root of the tableau. Combining these two segments, repeating the cyclic segment infinitely often, results in an infinite successful S-path.   □

If the tableau is unsuccessful then the root sequent can not hold. If the tableau is successful then it contains a finite successful path or a successful SCC. In the first case we can extract a finite witness for the root sequent by extracting a list of states from the finite successful path. In the second case we extract the witness from the S-Path generated in the second part of the proof for Lemma 3.

If we apply our approach to a universal model checking problem by using the negation of the universal property to be checked in the root of the tableau, then the procedure described in the previous paragraph serves as an algorithm for generating counterexamples.

To find the successful SCCs of an S-Tableau in linear time, a variation of the standard algorithm of Tarjan for the decomposition of a directed graph into its strongly connected components can be used. In particular, whenever a new SCC in Tarjan's algorithm is found, we check on-the-fly if it is successful. Thus the model checking problem can be solved in linear time in the size of the tableau as well. The size of the tableau is bounded by the number of different S-Sequents. Note that the split rule is never applied in this context. The number of different S-Sequents in a tableau with root $s \vdash \mathbf{E}(f)$ is in $\mathbf{O}(|\Sigma| \cdot 2^{|f|})$, since the RHS of a sequent may contain an arbitrary subset of subformulae of f. This gives an explicit state model checking algorithm with worst case complexity linear in the size of the Kripke structure and exponential in the size of the formula. For more details compare with [2].

A *cyclic path* is an infinite path of the form $A \cdot B^{\omega}$, that starts with a finite prefix A and continues with a path segment B repeated infinitely often. Not all infinite paths through a tableau are *cyclic paths*. However, the proof of Lemma 3 shows that it is enough to consider cyclic paths only, when looking for successful paths to determine whether a tableau is successful.

4   Multiple State Tableaux

In this section we extend the tableau construction of the last section to handle multiple states in one sequent. In combination with a symbolic representation, such as BDDs, this extension potentially leads to an exponential reduction in tableau size. The idea of handling set of states on the left hand side (LHS) of sequents already occurred in [4] as an extension of local model checking for the modal μ-calculus [28]. The tableau construction in this section extends the LTL model checking algorithm of [2] in a similar way.

A *multiple state sequent* (M-Sequent) consists of a set of states S and a list of LTL formulae $\Phi = (\Phi_1, \ldots, \Phi_n)$, written $S \vdash \mathbf{E}(\Phi)$. We use the same symbol '$\vdash$' to separate left and right hand side of S-Sequents and M-Sequents, but capital letters, e.g. S, for set of states on the LHS of M-Sequents and lower case letters, e.g. s, for S-Sequents. An

$$R_{\mathcal{A}^+}: \frac{S \vdash \mathbf{E}(\Phi, p)}{S_p^+ \vdash \mathbf{E}(\Phi)} \qquad\qquad R_{\mathcal{A}^-}: \frac{S \vdash \mathbf{E}(\Phi, \neg p)}{S_p^- \vdash \mathbf{E}(\Phi)}$$

$$R_{\mathbf{U}}: \frac{S \vdash \mathbf{E}(\Phi, f\,\mathbf{U}\,g)}{S \vdash \mathbf{E}(\Phi, g) \qquad S \vdash \mathbf{E}(\Phi, f, \mathbf{X} f\,\mathbf{U}\,g)} \qquad R_{\wedge}: \frac{S \vdash \mathbf{E}(\Phi, f \wedge g)}{S \vdash \mathbf{E}(\Phi, f, g)}$$

$$R_{\mathbf{R}}: \frac{S \vdash \mathbf{E}(\Phi, f\,\mathbf{R}\,g)}{S \vdash \mathbf{E}(\Phi, f, g) \qquad S \vdash \mathbf{E}(\Phi, g, \mathbf{X} f\,\mathbf{R}\,g)} \qquad R_{\vee}: \frac{S \vdash \mathbf{E}(\Phi, f \vee g)}{S \vdash \mathbf{E}(\Phi, f) \qquad S \vdash \mathbf{E}(\Phi, g)}$$

$$R_{\mathbf{F}}: \frac{S \vdash \mathbf{E}(\Phi, \mathbf{F} f)}{S \vdash \mathbf{E}(\Phi, f) \qquad S \vdash \mathbf{E}(\Phi, \mathbf{X} \mathbf{F} f)} \qquad R_{\mathbf{G}}: \frac{S \vdash \mathbf{E}(\Phi, \mathbf{G} f)}{S \vdash \mathbf{E}(\Phi, f, \mathbf{X} \mathbf{G} f)}$$

$$R_{\text{split}}: \frac{S \vdash \mathbf{E}(\Phi)}{S_1 \vdash \mathbf{E}(\Phi) \quad \cdots \quad S_k \vdash \mathbf{E}(\Phi)} \quad S = S_1 \cup \cdots \cup S_k, \quad S_i \neq \{\}, \text{ for } i = 1 \ldots k$$

$$R_{\mathbf{X}}: \frac{S \vdash \mathbf{E}(\mathbf{X}\Phi_1, \ldots, \mathbf{X}\Phi_n)}{T \vdash \mathbf{E}(\Phi_1, \ldots, \Phi_n)} \quad T = \text{Img}(S)$$

Fig. 2. M-Rules: Multiple state tableau rules ('S_p^+' and 'S_p^-' are defined in the text).

M-Sequent *holds* in a Kripke structure K iff $S \models \Phi_1 \wedge \cdots \wedge \Phi_n$, i.e. there exists a path π in K with $\pi(0) \in S$ and $\pi \models \Phi_1 \wedge \cdots \wedge \Phi_n$. An M-Tableau is a rooted finite directed graph of nodes labeled with M-Sequents that are connected via the rules shown in figure 2, where we define the following short hand for $p \in \mathcal{A}$:

$$S_p^+ := \{s \in S \mid p \in \ell(s)\}, \qquad S_p^- := \{s \in S \mid p \notin \ell(s)\}$$

In the split rule R_{split} the set of states S on the LHS is partitioned into a nonempty pairwise disjunctive list of sets $S_1, \ldots, S_k$ that cover S. For M-Tableaux we require every node to be labeled with a unique M-Sequent. M-Paths, successful M-Path, and SCC are defined exactly as in the single state case of the last section. The only exception is a finite M-Path ending with an M-Sequent $\{\} \vdash E(\Phi)$, with an empty set of states on the left side. By definition, such an M-Path is always unsuccessful even if the list of formulae Φ is empty.

To lift Theorem 1, Theorem 2, and in particular Lemma 3 to M-Tableaux we first note that the definitions of successful paths, SCCs, and successful tableau do only depend on the RHS of the sequents, in both cases, for S-Tableaux and M-Tableaux. As an immediate consequence we have:

Theorem 4. *A partially unsuccessful M-Tableau is successful iff it contains a successful SCC.*

Lemma 5. *An M-Tableau contains an infinite successful M-Path iff it contains a successful SCC.*

The second step is to map an M-Tableau to a *set* of S-Tableau, where the M-Tableau is successful iff one S-Tableau is successful. The mapping Ψ_0 is defined along the graph structure of the M-Tableau. If $\sigma = (\{r_1,\ldots,r_n\} \vdash \mathbf{E}(\Phi))$ is the root sequent of the M-Tableau, the result of the mapping will be n S-Tableaux with roots $\sigma_i = (r_i \vdash \mathbf{E}(\Phi))$ for $i = 1\ldots n$. Now we apply the rule that has been applied to the root M-sequent to each individual root S-sequent as well, obtaining valid successor sequents in the S-Tableau. Then the newly generated nodes are extended by applying the same rule as in the M-Tableau. This process is repeated until the constructed tableau can not be extended anymore.

Let $\mathcal{T}$ be an M-Tableau with root σ, as above, then $\Psi_0(\mathcal{T})$ is defined as the set of S-Tableaux $\{\Psi(\mathcal{T},\sigma,\sigma_1),\ldots,\Psi(\mathcal{T},\sigma,\sigma_n)\}$, where Ψ is defined along the graph structure of $\mathcal{T}$ starting with the root sequent σ, as defined below. Note that Ψ returns a single S-Tableau while Ψ_0 returns a set of S-Tableaux.

To define Ψ we map every instance of an M-Rule in the M-Tableau to an application of the corresponding S-Rule in the S-Tableau using the fact that in an M-Tableaux every node can be identified uniquely by its label. Let $\sigma_M = (S \vdash \mathbf{E}(\Phi_M))$ be an M-Sequent of $\mathcal{T}$ and $\sigma_S = (s \vdash \mathbf{E}(\Phi_S))$ be an S-Sequent. Then $\Psi(\mathcal{T},\sigma_M,\sigma_S)$ is only defined iff $s \in S$ and $\Phi = \Phi_S = \Phi_M$. Now let R_Λ be the M-Rule that is applied in $\mathcal{T}$ to σ_M:

$$R_\Lambda: \frac{S \vdash \mathbf{E}(\Phi)}{S_1 \vdash \mathbf{E}(\Phi_1) \quad \cdots \quad S_k \vdash \mathbf{E}(\Phi_k)}$$

By definition of the rules, if $\Lambda \in \{\mathbf{U},\mathbf{R},\mathbf{F},\mathbf{G},\wedge,\vee\}$, then R_Λ is applicable to σ_S as an S-Rule and yields:

$$R_\Lambda: \frac{s \vdash \mathbf{E}(\Phi)}{s \vdash \mathbf{E}(\Phi_1) \quad \cdots \quad s \vdash \mathbf{E}(\Phi_k)}$$

In this case $s \in S = S_1 = \cdots = S_k$ and we continue our construction by expanding the S-Sequent $s \vdash \mathbf{E}(\Phi_i)$ by $\Psi(\mathcal{T},S \vdash \mathbf{E}(\Phi_i),s \vdash \mathbf{E}(\Phi_i))$ for $i = 1\ldots k$. If $\Lambda = \text{split}$, then there exists an j with $s \in S_j$, since the partition covers S. Therefore we can apply the S-Rule R_{split} on σ_S which yields a new node labeled with σ_S again. This new node is expanded by $\Psi(\mathcal{T},S_j \vdash \mathbf{E}(\Phi),\sigma_S)$.

Regarding the rules for atomic propositions we only consider the positive case $R_{\mathcal{A}+}$. The definition of Ψ for $R_{\mathcal{A}-}$ is similar. If $R_{\mathcal{A}+}$ is applicable to σ_S then we proceed as above. Otherwise the construction of the S-Tableau is terminated with an unsuccessful finite path and $\Psi(\mathcal{T},\sigma_M,\sigma_S)$ consists of a single node labeled with σ_S. Finally consider the $R_\mathbf{X}$ rule that involves the image operator. Let $T = \text{Img}(S)$, $T_s = \text{Img}(\{s\}) = \{t_1,\ldots,t_m\} \subseteq T$, $A = (\Phi_1\ldots,\Phi_l)$, and $\mathbf{XA} = (\mathbf{X}\Phi_1,\ldots,\mathbf{X}\Phi_l)$.

$$R_\mathbf{X}: \frac{S \vdash \mathbf{E}(\mathbf{XA})}{T \vdash \mathbf{E}(A)} \qquad\qquad R_\mathbf{X}: \frac{s \vdash \mathbf{E}(\mathbf{XA})}{t_1 \vdash \mathbf{E}(A) \quad \cdots \quad t_m \vdash \mathbf{E}(A)}$$

And again we expand the nodes labeled $t_i \vdash \mathbf{E}(A)$ with $\Psi(\mathcal{T},T \vdash \mathbf{E}(A),t_i \vdash \mathbf{E}(A))$. This simple recursive definition of Ψ may result in an infinite S-Tableau. We can keep the result finite if we exit the recursion by introducing a loop as soon as the same arguments to Ψ occur the second time, as in the following example for mapping an M-Tableau into its corresponding S-Tableaux.

Consider the Kripke structure K with two states 0 and 1, both initial states, and two transitions from state 0 to state 1 and from state 1 to state 0. Both states are labeled with

p, the only atomic proposition. An M-Tableau for checking $\mathbf{EG}p$ looks as follows

$$\frac{\{0,1\} \vdash \mathbf{E}(\mathbf{G}p)}{\dfrac{\{0,1\} \vdash \mathbf{E}(p,\mathbf{XG}p)}{\{0,1\} \vdash \mathbf{E}(\mathbf{XG}p)}}$$

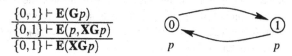

and the application of $\mathbf{R_X}$ to the leaf sequent leads back to the root sequent. The tableau represents one successful M-Path that contains only one image calculation. The given M-Tableau is mapped into the following two S-Tableaux:

$$\frac{0 \vdash \mathbf{E}(\mathbf{G}p)}{\dfrac{0 \vdash \mathbf{E}(p,\mathbf{XG}p)}{\dfrac{0 \vdash \mathbf{E}(\mathbf{XG}p)}{\dfrac{1 \vdash \mathbf{E}(\mathbf{G}p)}{\dfrac{1 \vdash \mathbf{E}(p,\mathbf{XG}p)}{1 \vdash \mathbf{E}(\mathbf{XG}p)}}}}} \qquad \frac{1 \vdash \mathbf{E}(\mathbf{G}p)}{\dfrac{1 \vdash \mathbf{E}(p,\mathbf{XG}p)}{\dfrac{1 \vdash \mathbf{E}(\mathbf{XG}p)}{\dfrac{0 \vdash \mathbf{E}(\mathbf{G}p)}{\dfrac{0 \vdash \mathbf{E}(p,\mathbf{XG}p)}{0 \vdash \mathbf{E}(\mathbf{XG}p)}}}}}$$

Again the application of $\mathbf{R_X}$ to the leaf nodes yields the root. In general, mapping an M-Tableau may produce larger tableaux.

For each generated S-Tableau it is easy to construct a graph homomorphism λ that maps nodes and edges of the S-Tableau to the nodes, respectively edges, of the M-Tableau, with the following property: If $\lambda(n_S) = n_M$, where n_S is a node of the S-Tableau, labeled with the S-Sequent $s \vdash \mathbf{E}(\Phi_S)$, and n_M is a node in the M-Tableau, labeled with an M-Sequent $S \vdash \mathbf{E}(\Phi_M)$, then $s \in S$ and $\Phi_M = \Phi_S$. Further every edge, that was generated by the application of an S-Rule R_Λ is mapped into an edge of the M-Tableau that was generated by the M-Rule R_Λ.

Let $\mathcal{T}_M$ be an M-Tableau and $\mathcal{T}_S$ be an S-Tableau with $\mathcal{T}_S \in \Psi_0(\mathcal{T}_M)$. Then we say that $\mathcal{T}_S$ *matches* $\mathcal{T}_M$. We call an S-Path x a *matching path* to an M-Path X iff the S-Tableau in which x occurs matches the M-Tableau of X and $\lambda(x) = X$ for the corresponding graph homomorphism λ.

Lemma 6. *Let X be a successful finite or cyclic M-Path in an M-Tableau $\mathcal{T}_M$. Then there exists an S-Tableau $\mathcal{T}_S$ that matches $\mathcal{T}_M$ and contains an successful S-Path x matching X.*

Proof. First let X be a finite successful path. Then X ends with a sequent $S \vdash \mathbf{E}()$ with $S \neq \{\}$. We pick an arbitrary state $s \in S$ and traverse X backward until the root is reached. At $X(i)$ we generate the S-Sequent $x(i)$ starting with $s \vdash \mathbf{E}()$.

Let $X(i) = (S_i \vdash \mathbf{E}(\Phi_i))$, then we generate $x(i) = (s_i \vdash \mathbf{E}(\Phi_i))$ with $s_i \in S_i$ and the following restriction. As long as no $R_\mathbf{X}$ rule is applied to $X(i)$ we define the LHS of $x(i)$ to be the state on the LHS of $x(i+1)$. If $R_\mathbf{X}$ is applied to $X(i)$ then we define s_i as an arbitrary predecessor of s_{i+1} in S_i.

Second let $X = Y \cdot Z^\omega$ be a cyclic successful path. The generated x will also be of the form $x = y \cdot z^\omega$, where y matches Y and z matches Z^n for some $n > 0$. We start with an arbitrary $s \in Z(m)$ where $m = |Z| - 1$ and traverse Z backward until $Z(0)$ is reached, generating S-Sequents as in the finite case. After we have reached $Z(0)$ we continue at $Z(m)$. This process is repeated until the same S-Sequent was generated twice during the visit of $Z(0)$. Termination is guaranteed because the set of states in $Z(0)$ is finite. Then z is defined as the path segment from the last occurrence of the same S-Sequent to the first. From $z(0)$ we can find a finite prefix y to the root as in the finite case.

By construction $\mathcal{T}_S = \Psi(\mathcal{T}_M, X(0), x(0))$ is defined, matches $\mathcal{T}_M$, contains the successful S-Path x, and x matches X. □

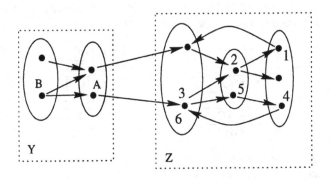

Fig. 3. Extracting an S-Path from an M-Path.

Consider the example of figure 3 where each ellipsis depicts the LHS of a sequent on which the R_X rule is applied. The small filled circles represent single states of the Kripke structure. The arrows between those circles are transitions of the Kripke structure. Thus the picture visualizes a sequence $Y \cdot Z^\omega$ of set of states with $Y(1) = \mathrm{Img}(Y(0))$ and

$$Z(0) = \mathrm{Img}(Y(1)), \quad Z(1) = \mathrm{Img}(Z(0)), \quad Z(2) = \mathrm{Img}(Z(1)), \quad Z(0) = \mathrm{Img}(Z(2))$$

Our goal is to extract a sequence of single states from $Y \cdot Z^\omega$. We start with 1, transition to 2 and pick 3 as predecessor of 2. The next transition, from 3 to 4, brings us back to the last sequent of Z but no cycle can be closed yet. We continue with 5 and reach 3 again with 6. From there we find a prefix (B, A), that leads from the initial state B to the start of the cycle at 6. The resulting witness is $(B, A) \cdot (6, 5, 4)^\omega$.

Lemma 6 allows us to derive the following completeness and correctness result for M-Tableau. Recall that $S \models f$ iff there exists $s \in S$ with $s \models f$.

Theorem 7. *An M-Tableau with root $S \vdash E(f)$ is successful iff $S \models f$.*

Proof. If an M-Tableau $\mathcal{T}_M$ is successful then it contains a successful path. Using Lemma 6 we can construct a matching successful path in a matching S-Tableau $\mathcal{T}_S$ with root sequent $s \vdash E(f)$ and $s \in S$. The correctness of the S-Tableaux construction (one part of Theorem 1) proves $s \models f$ which in turn implies $S \models f$.

Now let $\mathcal{T}_M$ be unsuccessful. Then for every $s \in S$ every matching S-Tableau $\mathcal{T}_S$ with root $s \vdash E(f)$ is unsuccessful as well. With Theorem 1 we conclude $s \not\models f$ for all $s \in S$. □

The algorithm described in the proof of Lemma 6 can be used to construct a witness for the root sequent from a successful M-Tableau, or a counterexample for the negation of the root sequent. First a matching path is constructed. Then a witness, a finite or cyclic path of states, can easily be extracted.

5   Algorithm

A more detailed description of the tableau construction follows in this section. The overall approach expands open branches in DFS manner and stops when a successful finite path has been generated, a successful SCC has been found, or finally no rule can be applied without regenerating an edge that already exists in the tableau. In the first two cases a witness for the root sequent can be generated. In the last case it is shown that the root sequent can not hold.

Finite successful paths are easy to detect. To detect and not to miss any successful SCC we use a modified version of Tarjan's algorithm for decomposing a directed graph into its strongly connected components. It is the same algorithm as used for S-Tableau in Section 3.

During the construction we have to remember the sequents that already occurred in the tableau. This can be accomplished by a partial function mapping a sequent to a node. To implement this we can sort the sequents in the tableau, use a hash table, or simply an array. In practice a hash table is the best solution.

Up to this point the algorithm is identical for both, single and multiple state tableaux. Our intention, of course, is to represent set of states with BDDs. We associate with each formula $E(\Phi)$ the list of sequents in the tableau that have $E(\Phi)$ on the RHS. To check if a sequent $\sigma \equiv (S \vdash E(\Phi))$ already occurred, we just go through the list of sequents associated with $E(\Phi)$ and check whether the BDD representing the set of states on the LHS of one of the sequents in the list is the same as the BDD representing S.

6   Heuristics

The rule R_{split} is not really necessary for the completeness but it helps to reduce the search space, i.e. the size of the generated tableau. For instance consider the construction of a tableau for the formula EFp. This formula is the negation of a simple safety property. In this case a good heuristics is to build the tableau by expanding the left successor of the rule R_F first. Only if the left branch does not yield a successful path, then the right successor is tried. If during this process a sequent $\sigma' = S' \vdash E(Ff)$ is found and a sequent $\sigma'' = S'' \vdash E(Ff)$ occurs on the path from the root to σ' and $S'' \subseteq S'$ then we can remove the set S'' from S' by applying R_{split} with $S_1 = S''$ and $S_2 = S' - S''$. The left successor immediately leads to an unsuccessful infinite path and we can continue with the right successor.

A successful path in a tableau for EFp is a counterexample for the dual safety property $AG\neg p$. Thus applying the heuristic of the last paragraph essentially implements an algorithm that computes the set of reachable states in a BFS manner while checking on-the-fly for states violating the safety property (as the *early evaluation* technique in

[1]). An example of this technique is shown in figure 4 using the Kripke structure of figure 5.

$$
\begin{array}{l}
\quad\quad\quad \longrightarrow \{1\} \vdash \mathbf{E}(\mathbf{F}p) \\
R_{\mathbf{F}} \; \overline{\quad\quad\quad\quad\quad\quad\quad\quad\quad} \\
\quad \{1\} \vdash \mathbf{E}(p) \quad\quad\quad \{1\} \vdash \mathbf{E}(\mathbf{XF}p) \\
\quad \{\} \vdash \mathbf{E}(p) \quad\quad\quad \{1,2\} \vdash \mathbf{E}(\mathbf{F}p) \\
\end{array}
$$

$$
\begin{array}{l}
\quad\quad\quad\quad\quad\quad\quad \overline{\quad\quad\quad\quad\quad\quad\quad\quad} \; R_{\mathrm{split}} \\
\longrightarrow \{1\} \vdash \mathbf{E}(\mathbf{F}p) \quad\quad \{2\} \vdash \mathbf{E}(\mathbf{F}p) \longleftarrow \\
\quad\quad\quad\quad\quad\quad\quad\quad\quad\quad\quad\quad R_{\mathbf{F}} \\
\quad\quad \{2\} \vdash \mathbf{E}(p) \quad\quad\quad \{2\} \vdash \mathbf{E}(\mathbf{XF}p) \\
\quad\quad \{\} \vdash \mathbf{E}(p) \quad\quad\quad \{2,3\} \vdash \mathbf{E}(\mathbf{F}p) \\
\end{array}
$$

$$
\begin{array}{l}
\quad\quad\quad\quad\quad\quad\quad\quad\quad \overline{\quad\quad\quad\quad\quad\quad} \; R_{\mathrm{split}} \\
\quad\quad\quad \{3\} \vdash \mathbf{E}(\mathbf{F}p) \quad\quad \{2\} \vdash \mathbf{E}(\mathbf{F}p) \\
R_{\mathbf{F}} \; \overline{\quad\quad\quad\quad\quad\quad\quad\quad\quad} \\
\quad \{3\} \vdash \mathbf{E}(p) \quad\quad\quad \{3\} \vdash \mathbf{E}(\mathbf{XF}p) \\
\quad \{\} \vdash \mathbf{E}(p) \quad\quad\quad \{1,2\} \vdash \mathbf{E}(\mathbf{F}p) \\
\end{array}
$$

$$
\begin{array}{l}
\quad\quad\quad\quad\quad\quad \overline{\quad\quad\quad\quad\quad\quad} \; R_{\mathrm{split}} \\
\{1\} \vdash \mathbf{E}(\mathbf{F}p) \quad\quad \{2\} \vdash \mathbf{E}(\mathbf{F}p)
\end{array}
$$

Fig. 4. Example tableau for on-the-fly model checking of safety properties.

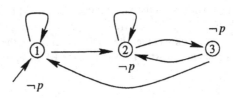

Fig. 5. Example Kripke structure for on-the-fly checking of safety properties.

Similar heuristics can be used for liveness properties. Consider the Kripke structure in figure 6 and the property $\mathbf{EG}p$. If we split a sequent as soon it LHS contains a state that already occurred in a sequent with the same RHS, then the following tableau finds a witness for $\mathbf{EG}p$ with just one image computation:

$$
\cfrac{
\cfrac{
\cfrac{
\cfrac{\{1\} \vdash \mathbf{E}(\mathbf{G}p)}{\{1\} \vdash \mathbf{E}(p, \mathbf{XG}p)} R_{\mathbf{G}}
}{\{1\} \vdash \mathbf{E}(\mathbf{XG}p)} R_{\mathcal{A}+}
}{\{1,2\} \vdash \mathbf{E}(\mathbf{G}p)} R_{\mathbf{X}}
}{\{1\} \vdash \mathbf{E}(\mathbf{G}p) \quad \{2\} \vdash \mathbf{E}(\mathbf{G}p)} R_{\mathrm{split}}
$$

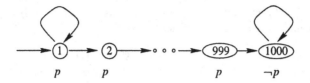

Fig. 6. Example Kripke structure for on-the-fly model checking of liveness properties.

The left sequent that results from the application of the split rule is the same as the root sequent. Thus a successful infinite path has been found and the right branch does not need to be expanded. A model checking algorithm based on standard fixpoint calculations requires 1000 image computations, i.e. traverses the whole state space, before the witness can be found.

Another heuristic is to avoid splitting the tableau as long as possible. In particular, if several rules are applicable to a sequent, then, if possible, a rule is chosen that does not result in multiple branches. For example if both R_G and R_F are applicable, then R_G is always preferred. This is one of the heuristics proposed in [27] for the construction of small tableau as an intermediate step of translating LTL into the modal μ-calculus with the algorithm of [10]. In general, these heuristics are also applicable to our approach.

7 Optimization

In an M-Tableau the number of different LHS of sequents is exponential in $|\Sigma|$, the number of states of the Kripke structure. In this section we present an optimization that reduces the maximal number of different LHS with the same RHS to $2 \cdot |\Sigma|$. In particular, with this optimization the size of an M-Tableau becomes linear in the number of states. Without this optimization the tableau construction would not be feasible at all, even in combination with BDDs.

Note that the size of the tableau may still be exponential in the size of the formula, since the RHS of a sequent is an arbitrary set of subformulae of the original property. In practice the size of the properties to be checked is usually small, but the size of the models we deal with can be arbitrary large. Thus it is much more important to have an algorithm that is linear in the size of the model.

The basic idea is to maintain the following invariant by applying the split rule: Let $S_1 \vdash \mathbf{E}(\Phi)$ and $S_2 \vdash \mathbf{E}(\Phi)$ be two M-Sequents in the M-Tableau. Then $S_1 \cap S_2 = \{\}$, $S_1 \subseteq S_2$, or $S_2 \subseteq S_1$.

Lemma 8. *Let $P \subseteq \mathbb{P}(S)$ be a set of nonempty subsets of a finite set $S \neq \{\}$. If for all $S_1, S_2 \in P$ either $S_1 \cap S_2 = \{\}$, $S_1 \subseteq S_2$ or $S_2 \subseteq S_1$ holds, then $|P| < 2 \cdot |S|$.*

Proof (Induction over $|S|$). In the base case let $|P| \leq 1$, which implies $|P| < 2 \leq 2 \cdot |S|$. In the induction step, we assume $|P| > 1$. The sets contained in P are partially ordered by set inclusion and contain at least one maximal set S_1. By defining $S_2 := S \backslash S_1$ we partition $S = S_1 \cup S_2$ into two mutually exclusive sets, S_1 and S_2. If $S_2 = \{\}$, i.e. S_1 is the *only* maximal set in P, then we define

$$P' := P \backslash \{S_1\} \quad \text{and} \quad S' := \bigcup_{T \in P'} T$$

and with $0 < |S'| < |S_1| \leq |S|$ the induction hypothesis shows

$$|P| = 1 + |P'| < 1 + 2 \cdot |S'| < 2 \cdot (|S'| + 1) \leq 2 \cdot |S_1| \leq 2 \cdot |S|$$

Now we assume $S_2 \neq \{\}$, which implies $S_1 \neq S$, and induces a partition on P with

$$P = P_1 \cup P_2 \quad \text{and} \quad P_i := \{T \in P \mid T \subseteq S_i\} \quad \text{for } i = 1, 2$$

Finally the induction hypothesis applied to S_1 and S_2 results in

$$|P| \leq |P_1| + |P_2| < 2 \cdot |S_1| + 2 \cdot |S_2| = 2 \cdot (|S_1| + |S_2|) = 2 \cdot |S|$$

$\square$

Since the LHS of a sequent can also be an empty set, Lemma 8 shows that the number of sequents with the same RHS is bounded by $2 \cdot |S|$ if the invariant is maintained. This is also the best bound that we can get, as the following example shows. Let $S_i = \{0, \ldots, 2^i - 1\}$. Then we associate a balanced binary tree of height i with each $P_i \subseteq \mathrm{IP}(S_i)$. We label each node in the tree by exactly one element of P_i, which implies $|P_i| = 2^{i+1} - 1 = 2 \cdot |S_i| - 1$. The i leaves are labeled with the singleton sets $\{0\}, \ldots, \{2^i - 1\}$. Each inner node of the binary tree is labeled with the union of the labels of its children.

Note that the image rule R_X and the atomic rules $R_{\mathcal{A}+}$ and $R_{\mathcal{A}-}$ are the only rules, except the split rule R_{split}, that actually manipulate the LHS. All other rules only generate sequents that contain the same set of states as their parents. The application of these rules can not violate the invariant. To maintain the invariant in the case of R_X, $R_{\mathcal{A}+}$ and $R_{\mathcal{A}-}$ as well we have to apply the split rule in combination with these rules: After each image calculation or application of an atomic rule the sequent is split to fulfill the invariant. For instance if the application of R_X yields:

$$R_X: \frac{\cdots}{\{1,2,3,4\} \vdash \mathbf{E}(\Phi)}$$

and the tableau already contains the two sequents:

$$\{1,2\} \vdash \mathbf{E}(\Phi) \quad \text{and} \quad \{4,5\} \vdash \mathbf{E}(\Phi)$$

Then the split rule is applied as follows. For every non empty intersection of $\{1,2,3,4\}$ with the LHS of an already existing sequent a new sequent is generated:

$$R_{\text{split}}: \frac{\{1,2,3,4\} \vdash \mathbf{E}(\Phi)}{\{1,2\} \vdash \mathbf{E}(\Phi) \quad \{3\} \vdash \mathbf{E}(\Phi) \quad \{4\} \vdash \mathbf{E}(\Phi)}$$

where the first sequent is not actually generated since it already exists in the tableau.

We have to combine the R_{split} rule with the image and atomic rules to technically avoid introducing an intermediate sequent, $\{1,2,3,4\} \vdash \mathbf{E}(\Phi)$ in the example, that might violate the invariant. The correctness and completeness results can be proven for this modification as well. Without combining these rules each application of $R_{\mathbf{X}}$, $R_{\mathcal{A}+}$ or $R_{\mathcal{A}-}$ could potentially need an additional application of R_{split}. This could potentially double the number of sequents and the number of sequents with the same RHS can only be bounded by $4 \cdot |\Sigma|$, which is still linear in the number of states.

8   Complexity and Related Work

In this section we discuss the complexity of our new algorithm based on M-Tableaux and compare it with other local and global techniques for LTL model checking.

The size of a tableau with root $\Sigma_0 \vdash \mathbf{E}(f)$, not using the optimization of the last section, is in $\mathbf{O}(2^{|\Sigma|} \cdot 2^{|f|})$. The time taken is polynomial in the size of the tableau. Thus the time complexity is (roughly) the same as the space complexity. With the optimization of the last section the size of the tableau is reduced to $\mathbf{O}(|\Sigma| \cdot 2^{|f|})$. As a consequence the time complexity of our algorithm is at most polynomial in the number of states, with a small degree polynomial, and exponential in the size of the formula. The explicit state model checking algorithms of [2, 16, 21] are linear in the number of states and the number of transitions. Note that the number of transitions may be quadratic in the number of states. If an explicit state representation is used, we conjecture that our tableau construction can be implemented with the same linear time complexity. However, with our approach we are able to use compact data structures, such as BDDs, to represent sets of states symbolically and thus can hope to achieve exponentially smaller tableaux and exponentially smaller running times for certain examples.

The method of [10] translates an LTL formula into a tableau similar to the tableaux in our approach. In [10] the nodes contain only formulae and no states. The size of the tableau can be exponential in the size of the LTL formula. The second step is a translation of the generated tableau into a μ-calculus formula that is again exponential in the size of the tableau. Additionally, the alternation depth of the μ-calculus formula can not be restricted. With [13, 22] this results in a model checking algorithm with time and space complexity that is double exponential in the size of the formula and single exponential in the size of the model K.

In [15] an ELTL formula is translated to a Büchi automata with the method of [29]. This leads to an exponential blow up in the worst case. But see [14] for an argument why this explosion might not happen in practice, which also applies to our approach. The resulting Büchi automata is translated to $\textit{post-}\mu$, a forward version of the standard modal μ-calculus, for which similar complexity results for model checking as in [13, 22] can be derived. This translation produces a μ-calculus formula of alternation depth 2 which results in an algorithm with an at least quadratic running time in $|\Sigma|$.

The LTL model checking algorithm of [15] is also forward oriented. A forward state space traversal potentially avoids searching through non reachable states, as it is usually the case with simple backward approaches. However, it is not clear how DFS can be incorporated into symbolic μ-calculus model checking.

The method of [7] translates an LTL model checking problem into a FairCTL model checking problem. With the result of [13] this leads to a model checking algorithm that is linear in the size of the model and exponential in the size of the formula. Again, these complexity results are only valid for explicit state model checking. The algorithms of [7, 15] are based on BFS and it is not clear how to implement them depth first.

The work by Iwashita [17, 18] does not handle full LTL and no complexity analysis is given. But if we restrict our algorithm to the path expressions of [17, 18], then our algorithm subsumes the algorithms of [17, 18], even for the *layered approach* of [18].

In [4] an M-Tableau construction for the modal μ-calculus was presented. The main motivation in [4] for using set of states in sequents was to be able to handle infinite state systems. Therefore no complexity results were given. In addition, the modal μ-calculus, as already discussed above, can not represent LTL properties directly without a prior translation [10, 29].

Our tableau construction is on-the-fly (see liveness example in Section 6) and only needs $O(|\Sigma|)$ image computations. Previous symbolic model checking algorithms for LTL [7, 15], based on fixpoint calculations, require $O(|\Sigma|^2)$ image computations.

9   Conclusion

Although our technique clearly extends the work of [17, 18] and bridges the gap between local and global model checking, we still need to show that it works in practice. We are currently working on proving the conjecture that our tableau construction can be implemented with linear complexity. We also want to investigate heuristics for applying the split rule. The approximation techniques of [25, 26] are a good starting point.

References

[1] I. Beer, S. Ben-David, C. Eisner, D. Geist, L. Gluhovsky, T. Heyman, A. Landver, P. Paanah, Y. Rodeh, G. Ronin, and Y. Wolfsthal. Rulebase: Model checking at IBM. In *CVA'97*, number 1254 in LNCS, pages 480–483. Springer-Verlag, 1997.

[2] G. Bhat, R. Cleaveland, and O. Grumberg. Efficient on-the-fly model checking for CTL*. In *LICS'95*. IEEE Computer Society, 1995.

[3] A. Biere, A. Cimatti, E. Clarke, and Y. Zhu. Symbolic model checking without BDDs. In *TACAS'99*, LNCS. Springer, 1999.

[4] J. Bradfield and C. Stirling. Local model checking for infinite state spaces. *Theorectical Computer Science*, 96:157–174, 1992.

[5] R. E. Bryant. Graph-based algorithms for boolean function manipulation. *IEEE Transactions on Computers*, 35(8), 1986.

[6] J. R. Burch, E. M. Clarke, and K. L. McMillan. Symbolic model checking: 10^{20} states and beyond. *Information and Computation*, 98, 1992.

[7] E. Clarke, O. Grumberg, and K. Hamaguchi. Another look at LTL model checking. *Formal Methods in System Design*, 10:47–71, 1997.

[8] E. M. Clarke and E. A. Emerson. Design and synthesis of synchronization skeletons using branching time temporal logic. In *Logic of Programs: Workshop*, LNCS. Springer, 1981.

[9] R. Cleaveland. Tableau-based model checking in the propositional mu-calculus. *Acta Informatica*, 27, 1990.

[10] M. Dam. CTL* and ECTL* as fragments of the modal mu-calculus. *Theoretical Computer Science*, 126, 1994.

[11] D. L. Dill. The MurΦ verification system. In *CAV'96*, LNCS. Springer, 1996.

[12] Y. Dong, X. Du, Y.S. Ramakrishna, C. T. Ramkrishnan, I. V. Ramakrishnan, S. A. Smolka, O. Sokolsky, E. W. Starck, and D. S. Warren. Fighting livelock in the i-protocol: A comparative study of verification tools. In *TACAS'99*, LNCS. Springer, 1999.

[13] E. A. Emerson and C.-L. Lei. Modalities for model checking: Branching time strikes back. *Science of Computer Programming*, 8, 1986.

[14] R. Gerth, D. Peled, M. Y. Vardi, and P. Wolper. Simple on-the-fly automatic verification of linear temporal logic. In *Proceedings 15th Workshop on Protocol Specification, Testing, and Verification*. North-Holland, 1995.

[15] T. A. Henzinger, O. Kupferman, and S. Qadeer. From Pre-historic to Post-modern symbolic model checking. In *CAV'98*, LNCS. Springer, 1998.

[16] G. J. Holzmann. The model checker SPIN. *IEEE Transactions on Software Engineering*, 5(23), 1997.

[17] H. Iwashita and T. Nakata. CTL model checking based on forward state traversal. In *ICCAD'96*. ACM, 1996.

[18] H. Iwashita, T. Nakata, and F. Hirose. Forward model checking techniques oriented to buggy design. In *ICCAD'97*. ACM, 1997.

[19] A. Kick. *Generierung von Gegenbeispielen und Zeugen bei der Modellprüfung*. PhD thesis, Fakultät für Informatik, Universität Karlsruhe, 1996.

[20] D. Kozen. Results on the propositional μ-calculus. *Theoretical Computer Science*, 27, 1983.

[21] O. Lichtenstein and A. Pnueli. Checking that finite state concurrent programs satisfy their linear specification. In *Symposium on Principles of Programming Languages*, New York, 1985. ACM.

[22] D. E. Long, A. Browne, E. M. Clarke, S. Jha, and W. R. Marrero. An improved algorithm for the evaluation of fixpoint expressions. In *CAV'94*, LNCS. Springer, 1994.

[23] K. L. McMillan. *Symbolic Model Checking*. Kluwer, 1993.

[24] J. P. Quielle and J. Sifakis. Specification and verification of concurrent systems in CESAR. In *Proc. 5th Int. Symp. in Programming*, 1981.

[25] K. Ravi, K. L. McMillan, T. R. Shiple, and F. Somenzi. Approximation and decomposition of binary decision diagrams. In *DAC'98*. ACM, 1998.

[26] K. Ravi and F. Somenzi. High-density reachability analysis. In *ICCAD'95*. ACM, 1995.

[27] F. Reffel. Modellprüfung von Unterlogiken von CTL*. Masterthesis, Fakultät für Informatik, Universität Karlsruhe, 1996.

[28] C. Stirling and D. Walker. Local model checking in the modal mu-calculus. *Theoretical Computer Science*, 89, 1991.

[29] M. Y. Vardi and P. Wolper. Reasoning about infinite computations. *Information and Computation*, 115(1), 1994.

On the Existence of Network Invariants for Verifying Parameterized Systems*

Parosh Aziz Abdulla and Bengt Jonsson

Dept. Computer Systems Uppsala University
P.O.Box 325, 751 05 Uppsala, Sweden
{parosh,bengt}@docs.uu.se

Abstract. Over the last decade, finite-state verification methods have been developed to an impressive tool for analysis of complex programs, such as protocols and hardware circuits. Partial-order reduction and BDD-based symbolic model checking have been instrumental in this development. Currently, much effort is devoted to advancing further the power of automated verification to cover also infinite-state systems. In this paper, we consider the class of so-called *parameterized systems*, i.e., systems with many similar processes, in which the number of processes is unbounded and their interconnection pattern may vary within the range of some constraints. We partially review the use of induction over the system structure for the verification of parameterized systems. Wolper and Lovinfosse have introduced the term *network invariant* for the induction hypothesis in such a proof by induction. They also observe that well-behaved (e.g., finite-state) network invariants do not always exist, even if the system itself satisfies the property to be verified. The main contribution of the paper is to present some sufficient conditions, under which the existence of a finite-state network invariant is guaranteed. We also relate the construction of network invariants to the search for standard inductive invariants. Two small examples of network invariants and standard invariants for parameterized systems are included.

1 Introduction

One of the advantages of producing formal models of algorithms and systems is the possibility to analyze and verify them in a rigorous way, in the best case totally automatically by computer. For nondeterministic and parallel programs, relevant verifications include absence of deadlocks, or proving that all executions of a program satisfy a desirable property expressed in temporal logic. Over the last decade, impressive tools have been developed for verification of *finite-state* systems. Partial-order reduction and BDD-based symbolic model checking have been instrumental in this development.

---

* Supported in part by the Swedish Board for Industrial and Technical Development (NUTEK) and by the Swedish Research Council for Engineering Sciences (TFR).

E.-R. Olderog, B. Steffen (Eds.): Correct System Design, LNCS 1710, pp. 180–197, 1999.

Currently, much effort is devoted to advancing further the power of automated verification to cover also infinite-state systems. Potentially practical tools for automated verification of infinite-state systems have been developed for significant special cases, such as timed automata [ACD90,BGK+96], hybrid automata [Hen95], data-independent systems [JP93,Wol86], Petri nets [JM95], pushdown processes [BS95,Sti96], and systems with unbounded communication channels [Fin94,AJ93,ABJ98].

On the border between finite-state and infinite-state systems, there is the class of *parameterized systems*. By a parameterized system, we mean a family of similar systems that depend in a regular way on a parameter. Typically, parameterized systems are built from a (small) finite set of processes, which are replicated and interconnected into networks. Examples of parameterized systems abound: a distributed algorithm can be modeled as a system of many identical processes whose interconnection topology may be arbitrary, a bus protocol consists of a linear array of identical processes where the parameter is the number of processes, etc. Also unbounded data structures, such as queues and trees, could be regarded as parameterized systems by letting each node (cell) be viewed as a process which is connected to its neighbour nodes (cells). A queue would thus be viewed as a linear array of processes of arbitrary length.

In order to make the discussion more concrete, let us consider families of systems of the form

$$P_0 \parallel P \parallel P \parallel \cdots \parallel P$$

composed of one instance of a "global" component P_0 which is common to all systems in the family, and an arbitrary number of instances of some process P. The processes are composed by some associative composition operator $\parallel$, which for the moment will be left unspecified. The verification problem for parameterized systems consists in verifying that

$$P_0 \parallel P \parallel P \parallel \cdots \parallel P \models \phi$$

for some correctness formula ϕ, for any number of copies of P. We assume that the formulation of ϕ is independent of the system size. An example of a correctness property could be "there are never two processes simultaneously in the critical section".

The most straight-forward approach to verifying a parameterized system is to verify the system for a suitable chosen number (say 5) of processes. Finite-state state-space exploration methods can be used to analyze the system efficiently. However, there is no *a priori* guarantee that the system will function correctly with 6 processes. It is therefore of interest to consider methods that verify the correctness of the system with an arbitrary number of components. It may even (as argued, e.g., by Wolper and Boigelot [WB98]) turn out that the parameterized version of the system is easier to verify, since in the best case it may concern the essential reason for correctness, and avoid the particularities of the case with 5 processes.

If we look at the problem of actually verifying correctness for any number of copies of P, we notice that the problem has an unbounded structure along two dimensions. One dimension is "time", since we must check a property of potentially unbounded execution sequences. Another dimension is "space", since the property should hold for an arbitrary system size. To verify that the system is correct, in spite of any of these unboundednesses, we may use induction. In the following two paragraphs, we describe the use of induction, first in the time dimension and then in the space dimension. Throughout the paper, we will only be concerned with safety properties.

The standard way to handle the time dimension in verification of safety properties (e.g., [MP95]) is to find an (inductive) invariant of the system, which is preserved by all computation steps of the system, and which implies ϕ. For instance, if ϕ is the correctness property "there are never two processes simultaneously in the critical section", then an inductive invariant of the system could be obtained by conjoining "at most one process has the token" (assuming that possessing the token is necessary for entering the critical section). This method of verification assumes that we can express sets of system states of arbitrary size. Finding an invariant may involve some ingenuity. However, once it is found, the rest of the verification is relatively simple and possible to automate. Computational invariants expressed in some formalism for represented sets of states of unbounded system sizes have been used e.g., in [JK95,KMM+97,EFM99,AČJYK96,AJ98,ABJN99].

A method for handling the space dimension in parameterized system verification is to find a uniform abstraction of the system which is independent of system size. Such an abstraction is a single system N whose behavior "contains" (in a sense to be made more precise later in the paper) the behavior of any system in the family. In particular, if $N \models \phi$, then $P_0 \parallel P \parallel \cdots \parallel P \models \phi$ for any system size. One sufficient criterion for checking that N is indeed an abstraction is to check that it is inductive. Letting $\leq$ denote the relation "contained in", this means that it should be checked that $P_0 \leq N$ and that $N \parallel P \leq N$ besides checking that $N \models \phi$. The term "network invariant" has been introduced by Wolper and Lovinfosse [WL89] (the method was also suggested by Kurshan and McMillan [KM89]) for an abstraction which is inductive in this sense. Again, finding a network invariant N may involve some ingenuity. However, the point is that once N is found, the correctness checks should be relatively simple and possible to automate. Network invariants have been employed in e.g., [KM89,WL89,EN95,LHR97].

For verifying a parameterized system, there are thus two basically different ways to employ induction: either using standard (computational) induction, or using induction over the structure of the parameterized system. To avoid confusion, we will use the term *computational invariant* to mean an inductive invariant in the "time-dimension".

In this paper, we will consider the question "when does there exist a computational or network invariant of a certain simple form?" If we consider the case that each component is finite-state, it is natural to try to look for "finite" computational and network invariants. In the case of computational invariants, we will take this to mean an invariant which considers an arbitrary "finite" part of the system structure. In the case of network invariants, we will take this to mean an invariant which can be expressed by a finite-state transition system. As observed by Wolper and Lovinfosse [WL89], it follows from a basic unde-cidability result by Apt and Kozen [AK86], that such invariants do not exist in general. In this paper, we will give some sufficient criteria for the existence of these invariants. We hope that this gives a better understanding in particular of the network invariant method. Mechanized search for network invariants have been considered by Lesens et al [LHR97], who employ maximal fixpoint iteration, enhanced by approximation techniques, in the verification of some examples. Ab-stractions can also be constructed without checking that it is in inductive, e.g., as in [LS97,CGJ95]. German and Sistla [GS92] have given a direct algorithm for model-checking of parameterized systems with an unordered system topology, in a slightly more restricted framework than that considered here.

The paper is organized as follows. In the next section, we introduce the ba-sic definitions of parameterized systems. The use of invariants in verification is described in Section 3. Section 4 contains criteria for the existence of compu-tational and network invariants. In Section 5, we illustrate the verification of a parameterized system in which the components are non-finite state (timed automata).

2   Basic Definitions

Parameterized Systems By a parameterized system, we mean a family of systems, each of which is a composition of form

$$M_n \equiv P_0 \parallel P[1] \parallel P[2] \parallel \cdots \parallel P[n]$$

where P_0 is an optional "global" component, common to all instances in the family, and where $P[1], \ldots, P[n]$ are identical processes. Each component $P[i]$ and P_0 is modeled as a labeled transition system. For the moment, we do not require that each component be finite-state. The labels on transitions are taken from a set of visible actions, extended by an invisible action (denoted τ). We assume that any component can always perform an idling component transition, labeled by τ, which does not change its state. We use M to denote the (infinite-state) system which is the "union" of the family $\{M_n\}_{n=0}^{\infty}$ of system instances. One could think of M as a system, which initially decides on a value of the parameter n, and then becomes M_n.

Each transition of the system M_n may involve one or more components. The pos-sible synchronizations between components are constrained by a *synchronization predicate* Φ. In the remainder of this paper, we will consider a totally unordered system topology, in which any component can communicate with any other, regardless of their positions in the syntactic description of M_n. The synchronization predicate Φ is then a set of multisets of actions. Each multiset describes a possible combination of labels on component transitions that make up a transition of the parameterized system. For instance, if the pair {send, receive} is in Φ, but neither of send nor receive is in any other set of the synchronization predicate, then each occurrence of a send must be synchronized with a matching receive. In order to be able to model broadcast and global synchronizations, we allow one of the actions in a synchronization to have the special superscript ω, meaning "all other processes". For instance, the set {send, receive$^\omega$} denotes a broadcast by one process to all other processes.

The above requirements on synchronization concern a system M_n, which is *closed* in the sense that it does not interact with its environment. Later, in Section 3.2, we will consider *open* systems which represent a part of some M_n which can synchronize with other components. Synchronizations of an open system need only contain a subset of the labels of some multiset of the synchronization predicate. Two open systems may synchronize, and the labels on transitions are formed as the union of labels of the synchronizing systems in the natural way. Continuing the above example where {send, receive} is in Φ, a transition of an open system may be labeled by send only.

We could also have considered parameterized systems with a linearly ordered topology, in which components are arranged in an order, as shown in the syntactic description of M_n. The synchronization predicate will then be a set of *strings* of labels.

Correctness Properties We will only consider linear-time safety properties of parameterized systems, which can be stated as a requirement on the executions of the controller, and a *bounded* arbitrary set of distinct components. Such properties can be transformed into invariants of the form

$$\forall i_1, \ldots, i_k. \;\; alldiff(i_1, \ldots, i_k) \implies \phi(i_1, \ldots, i_k)$$

where ϕ is a predicate on the local states of the controller and the components with indices $i_1, \ldots, i_k$, and where $alldiff(i_1, \ldots, i_k)$ states that all indices $i_1, \ldots, i_k$ are distinct. We shall call such a formula a *universal assertion*. As an example, we can specify mutual exclusion by the invariant

$$\forall i \neq j. \;\; \neg(critical[i] \wedge critical[j])$$

Examples of correctness properties that can be expressed in this form are: mutual exclusion, clock synchronization, security properties, etc.

The checking of an invariant can be equivalently reformulated as a reachability property. For instance, the above invariant means that it is not possible to reach a state which satisfies the negation $\exists i \neq j.(critical[i] \wedge critical[j])$ of the above invariant. We shall call such a formula an *existential assertion*

Example A simple example of a parameterized system is the following simple token-passing mutual exclusion algorithm. An arbitrary set of processes compete for a critical resource. Access to the resource is modeled by a process being in its critical section. In order to enter the critical section, a process must first acquire a token, which is passed in some arbitrary manner between components.

We model each process as a labeled transition system with three states: **n** (not possessing the token), **t** (possessing the token), and **c** (in the critical section), and two visible actions: **send-token** and **rec-token**. A state-transition diagram of a process is given below:

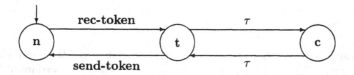

The synchronization predicate requires **send-token** and **rec-token** to occur in synchronized pairs. In a network, all process are initialized in the state **n**, except for one process, which starts in state **t**. There is no controller process. For this particular example, we could imagine both an unordered and a linearly ordered system topology (of course, any reasonable topology could be considered, but that is not in the scope of this paper).

A correctness property for this system is mutual exclusion, formulated as the invariant

$$\forall i \neq j. \; \neg(c[i] \wedge c[j])$$

3   Methods for Verification of Invariants of Parameterized Systems

In this section, we present the use of computational and of network invariants in the verification of a parameterized system.

3.1   Computational Invariants

A parametrized system can be viewed as an (infinite-state) program M (which initially decides a value of n), to which standard verification methods can be applied. A safety property in the form of an invariant can be proved in the standard way by finding a computational (inductive) invariant for M. In order to automate this method, we must find a representation of (possibly infinite) sets of states of M. For instance, if each component $P[i]$ is finite-state, then in the case of unstructured topology one might use constraints on the number of occurrences of each control state of $P[i]$. In the case of a linear network, regular expressions could serve this purpose [CGJ95,KMM$^+$97,ABJN99].

The requirements on a computational invariant I are:

1. any initial state of any M_n satisfies I,
2. each transition from a system state satisfying I leads to a system state which also satisfies I.

We say that I is *sufficiently strong* if additionally

3. I implies ϕ.

It is a standard result that the set of invariants I that satisfy these requirements form a lattice. The lattice is non-empty if and only if ϕ is an invariant of M_n for all n. There is a least computational invariant I (with respect to set-inclusion) which satisfies the first two conditions: this is the set of reachable states of M. There is also a largest I which satisfies conditions 2. and 3.

It is well-known that a sufficiently strong computational invariant always exists if ϕ is an invariant of each M_n, but there is no guarantee that it can in general be expressed in the particular chosen representation (this follows from the undecidability of parameterized system verification [AK86]). Methods for automatically searching for computational invariants include forward and backward reachability analysis, sometimes augmented by approximation techniques, using a symbolic representation of sets of states.

In what follows, we shall be particularly interested in finding computational invariants that are expressed as *universal assertions*. It turns out that backward reachability analysis suits the problem of finding universal assertions.

Example To continue the example in the previous section, we see that a sufficiently strong computational invariant of any M_n is

$$\forall i \neq j. \ \neg[(\mathbf{t}[i] \ \lor \ \mathbf{c}[i]) \ \land \ (\mathbf{t}[j] \ \lor \ \mathbf{c}[j])]$$

which is indeed a universal assertion.

Below, we describe the relation to backward reachability in more detail.

Backward Reachability Analysis The basic idea of backward reachability analysis is to start from the negation of the invariant to be checked. If the invariant is a universal assertion, then the negation is an existential assertion. We assume that we can represent sets of states of an arbitrary but bounded set of components. The idea in backward reachability analysis is to compute the set of states from which a state satisfying the negated invariant can be reached.

If we further assume that each action of the parameterized system involves a bounded number of components (i.e., the synchronization predicate does not contain any occurrence of the superscript ω), then the set of predecessors of an existential assertion can again be expressed as an existential assertion.

Having a procedure for calculating $pre(\phi)$, a formula that represents the set of predecessors of states that satisfy ϕ, we can now perform symbolic verification as follows. Assume that $final$ is the existential constraint that represent the set of undesirable states, and let $initial$ be a characterization of the initial states of a parameterized system. Typically $initial$ will contain a universal quantification over the set of all processes in the network, e.g., saying that they are in their initial states.

A simple description of an algorithm for checking whether $final$ is reachable from $initial$ is as follows [KMM+97].

Let $\phi_0 := final$
For $i = 0, 1, 2, \ldots$ **repeat**
  If $(\phi_i \wedge initial) \neq false$ **then return reachable**
  Let $\phi_{i+1} := \phi_i \vee pre(\alpha, \phi_i)$
until $\phi_{i+1} = \phi_i$
return unreachable

Note that, under the assumption that each action of the parameterized system involves a bounded number of components, each ϕ_i generated by the algorithm can be expressed as an existential assertion. This follows by induction from the observation that ϕ_{i+1} is a disjunction of the existential assertions ϕ_{i+1} and $pre(\alpha, \phi_i)$.

3.2   Network Invariants

A method, which has been proposed for the verification of infinite-state systems, is to find a finite-state abstraction of the system, which preserves the correctness properties of interest, and thereafter model-checking this finite-state abstraction [LS97,LHR97,ID99]. Adapted to our framework, this would entail the construction of an abstract process N, whose behavior "contains" the behavior of any instance M_n of the family.

Considering that we are interested in verifying invariants which are universal assertions, we define an *abstract process* to be a process in which each state n is labeled by an assertion $L(n)$ over the states of M. We define a refinement relation $\sqsubseteq$ between networks and abstract processes as follows. We say that $M_n \sqsubseteq N$, if there is a simulation relation R between the states of M_n and the states of N such that

1. Each initial state of M_n is related to some state of N,

2. whenever s R n for a state s of M_n and a state n of N, and if $s \xrightarrow{a} s'$ is a transition of M_n, then there is a transition $n \xrightarrow{a} n'$ of N with s' R n',
3. whenever s R n, then s satisfies the assertion $L(n)$.

We also define $\sqsubseteq$ to a preorder on abstract processes, by saying that $N \sqsubseteq N'$ if there is a simulation R between states of N and N' in the usual sense such that whenever n R n' for a state n of N and a state n' of N', then the assertion $L(n)$ implies the assertion $L(n')$.

A methodology, which has been proposed [KM89,WL89], is to find a process N, for which the above relation can be checked by induction, checking

1. $P_0 \sqsubseteq N$,
2. $N \parallel P \sqsubseteq N$, and
3. ϕ is implied by each assertion that labels some control state of N

The composition $N \parallel P$ between an abstract process N and a component process P is defined in the standard way. Each state of $N \parallel P$ is obtained as a composition $n \parallel t$ of a state n of N and a state t of P, which is labeled by an assertion which states that "all processes except the last one satisfy $L(n)$, and the last process is in state t". For instance, if $L(n)$ is "at most one process has the token" and t is a state where process P has the token, then $L(n \parallel t)$ could be "one or two processes have the token, and one of these is in state t".

It should be noted that each M_n and N here are considered as open systems, in the sense of Section 2. Thus in the first condition $P_0 \sqsubseteq N$, the component P_0 is regarded as an open system so that N must be able to simulate all its potential synchronizations with other components.

We define a *network* invariant to be an abstract process which satisfies the two first conditions. A network invariant is said to be *sufficiently strong* if it also satisfies the third condition. There is a least network invariant N: this is the "union" of all M_n. There is also a largest N which satisfies the two last conditions: this is the limit of the so-called quotient construction [And95,KLL$^+$97]. However, there is no guarantee that any of these be expressible by a finite-state program even if P_0 and P are finite-state. The discovery of a suitable N is therefore often performed manually (as e.g., in [WL89,KM89]), or using approximation techniques [LHR97].

Example A sufficiently strong network invariant of the system in the preceding section is the finite-state process

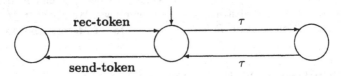

where the two left states are labeled by the assertion $\forall i.\ \neg c[i]$ and where the right state is labeled by the assertion $\forall i \neq j.\ \neg(\mathbf{c}[i] \ \wedge \ \mathbf{c}[j])$. We note that the disjunction of all $L(n)$ for states n of the network invariant need not be a computational invariant of M. It can be weaker, as long as we can check the invariant to be verified on the basis of these labels.

4   Generating Simple Invariants

In this section, we shall consider the question of finding a computational or network invariant of a particularly simple form. Recall that we only consider the verification of invariants expressed by universal assertions.

4.1   Universal Computational Invariants

We shall be concerned with finding computational invariants that are universal. For instance, in the small mutual exclusion example, it was possible to find a universal invariant. From results by Abdulla et al. [AČJYK96], the following theorem follows directly.

Theorem 1. *If P_0 and P are finite-state, and all synchronizations occur between a bounded number of components, then the largest invariant is universal. Furthermore, it (or rather its negation) can be found after a finite number of iterations of the backward reachability algorithm in Section 3.1.*

The main reason why the backward reachability algorithm terminates is that it is impossible to generate a strictly increasing and infinite sequence $\phi_0, \phi_1, \phi_2, \phi_3, \ldots$ of existential assertions. Any such sequence will converge to a largest set after a finite number of iterations. This can be seen as follows. Since we are considering an unordered system topology, a system state can be represented as a multiset of states of P_0 and P. Each existential assertion denotes an *upward closed* (wrp. to multiset inclusion) set of system states. By Dickson's lemma [Dic13], any upward closed set of multisets can be represented by a *finite* set of minimal elements (multisets). When we apply this to an infinite sequence $\phi_0, \phi_1, \phi_2, \phi_3, \ldots$ of upward closed sets of multisets, it follows that its limit is also upward closed, and that the finitely many minimal elements that characterize this limit must be included after a finite number of iterations.

These results have been extended to cover a class of finite-state systems that allow also broadcast [EFM99], and to timed automata with one clock in [AJ98]. For a slightly more restrictive framework, German and Sistla [GS92] have given an algorithm for model-checking arbitrary temporal properties of the controller.

4.2   Finite-State Network Invariants

Let us thereafter consider network invariants. A natural desideratum is that such an invariant should not be more difficult to analyze than a component process P. That is, if the processes are finite-state, then the network invariant should be finite-state. In the running example of Section 3, it was easy to find a finite-state abstraction. However, Wolper and Lovinfosse [WL89] observe that by basic undecidability results [AK86], there must be cases where a network invariant does not exist (at least if we assume that linearly structured networks are also allowed). In this section, we will present conditions under which their existence can be guaranteed.

To this end, let us employ a standard framework for describing abstractions of concurrent systems. The abstraction N will be generated by collecting states of M into equivalence classes. This can be described by an abstraction mapping h from states of the family M to states of N [Lam89]. Essentially, an abstraction mapping is a simulation relation which is also a function. The condition for N to be an abstraction is then that

1. $h(s)$ is an initial state of N whenever s is an initial state of M,
2. if $s \xrightarrow{a} s'$ is a transition of M then $h(s) \xrightarrow{a} h(s')$ is a transition of N,
3. s satisfies the assertion that labels $h(s)$.

We will now investigate conditions for when the process N is a sufficiently strong network invariant. Note that not all abstractions N are good enough. For instance, the trivial N which has only one state with self-loops for all actions will in general either not be inductive, or not strong enough. In the running example of Section 3, the single state of such a process would have to be labeled by an assertion which implies mutual exclusion (in order to be strong enough) but allows one process to be in its critical section. However, when composed in parallel with a copy of P, it would also have to be able to synchronize with a transition of P that moves from state $\mathbf{t}$ to state $\mathbf{c}$, and the resulting composed state would then not satisfy the assertion of the state of N (since it implies mutual exclusion).

Definition 1. *An abstraction mapping is* inductive *if*

1. *whenever $h(s_1) = h(s_2)$, then for any state t of P we have $h(s_1 \parallel t) = h(s_2 \parallel t)$, and*
2. *the conjunction of the assertion $L(h(s))$ and the fact that the last process is in state t implies the assertion $L(h(s \parallel t))$.*

Inductive abstraction mappings generate inductive abstractions, as shown by the following:

Theorem 2. *An abstraction N of M which is obtained from M by an inductive abstraction function, is an inductive network invariant.*

Proof. The first condition $P_0 \sqsubseteq N$ follows from the fact that N is an abstraction. To check the second condition, consider the parallel composition $N \parallel P$ of N and P. We shall prove that there exists an abstraction mapping g from states of $N \parallel P$ to N, from which the theorem follows. We first observe that an inductive abstraction mapping h from states of M to states of N induces a mapping g from states of $N \parallel P$ to states of N by letting $g(h(s) \parallel t) = h(s \parallel t)$, where s is a state of M and t is a state of P, and where $s \parallel t$ denotes the state s of M extended with one extra component in state t. The mapping g is well-defined since h is inductive. It can also be checked that g is indeed an abstraction mapping.

1. If n and t are initial, then $n = h(s)$ for some initial s, and so $g(n \parallel t) = h(s \parallel t)$ is initial.
2. If $n \parallel t \longrightarrow n' \parallel t'$ is a transition of $N \parallel P$, then there is a transition $s \longrightarrow s'$ of M with $h(s) = n$ and $h(s') = n'$. Thus $s \parallel t \longrightarrow s' \parallel t'$ is a transition of M, and hence $h(s \parallel t) \longrightarrow h(s' \parallel t') = g(n \parallel t) \longrightarrow g(n' \parallel t')$ is a transition of N.

Finally, by the second condition of Definition 1, the the conjunction of the assertion $L(h(s))$ and the fact that the last process is in state t implies the assertion $L(h(s \parallel t))$.

We will apply this theorem to obtain a result concerning the existence of finite-state abstraction mappings.

Theorem 3. *Assume that P_0 and P are finite-state, and that there is a sufficiently strong universal computational invariant which proves that M satisfies the invariant. Then there is a suffiently strong finite-state network invariant.*

Proof. Assume that that the computational invariant has k quantified variables. For each mapping from component states of P_0 and P to the set $\{0, 1, \ldots, k, \infty\}$, there is a state of N. Label each state of N by the conjunction of assertions of form "there are at most i occurrences of component state t" for each component state t which is mapped to some i different from ∞. Define an abstraction mapping h from states of M to states of N, by mapping each state s of M to the state of N which corresponds to the number of occurrences of component states of s, where ∞ means "more than k". Make N into an abstract process by inserting transitions and initial states, as required by the conditions on the abstraction function h. It can now be checked that h is inductive. Moreover, the computational invariant corresponds to a set of equivalence classes of N whose labeling imply the invariant to be verified. Hence N is also sufficiently strong.

We have thus shown that if there is a universal computational invariant, then there also exists a finite-state network invariant.

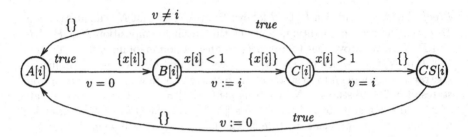

Fig. 1. Fischer's Protocol for Mutual Exclusion.

Example In the example of the mutual exclusion algorithm, the three states of the network invariant correspond to the following partitioning of the states.

left state :   0 occurrences of both **t** and **c**
middle state : 1 occurrence of **t** and 0 of **c**
right state :   0 occurrences of **t** and 1 of **c**

5 Application: Fischer's Protocol

In this section, we will illustrate the results of the preceding section by verifying a parameterized version of Fischer's protocol.

The protocol has been used as a measure of the performance of tools for verification of timed automata. The example was suggested by Fred Schneider and has been verified manually (e.g., [AL92]) and using theorem provers (e.g., [Sha93]). Several tools for verifying automata with a fixed number of clocks have been used to verify it for an increasing number of processes (e.g., [ACHH92]). Kristoffersen et al. [KLL+97] describes an experiment where the number of processes is 50.

The purpose of the protocol is to guarantee mutual exclusion in a concurrent system consisting of an arbitrary number of processes, using clocks and a shared variable. Each process has a local clock, and runs a protocol before entering the critical section. Each process has a local control state, which in our model assumes values in the set $\{A, B, C, CS\}$ where A is the initial state and CS represents the critical section. The processes also read from and write to a shared variable whose value is either $\perp$ or the index of one of the processes. A description in a graphical pseudo-code (taken from [KLL+97]) of the behavior of a process with index i is given in Figure 1.

Intuitively, the protocol behaves as follows: A process wishing to enter the critical section starts in state A. If the value of the shared variable is $\perp$, the process can proceed to state B and reset its local clock. From state B, the process can proceed to state C if the clock value is still less than 1. In other words, the clock implements a timeout which guarantees that the process either stays in state B at most one time unit, or gets stuck in B forever. When moving from B to C, the process sets the value of the shared variable to its own index i and again resets its clock. From state C, the process can proceed to the critical section if the clock is strictly more than 1 and if the value of the shared variable is still i, the index of the process. Thus, in state C the clock enforces a delay which is longer than the length of the timeout in state B. Finally, when exiting the critical section, the process resets the shared variable to $\perp$. Processes that get stuck in state C can reenter the protocol by returning to state A. Since we do not intend to model liveness properties, such as e.g., absence of starvation, we do not impose requirements that force processes to change their state[1].

A rough argument for the correctness of the protocol goes as follows. The conditions on the shared variable ensure that a process cannot reach B if any other process is in C or CS. The timing conditions on the clocks ensure that a process cannot move from C to CS if some other process is still in B. Thus, if a set of processes start the mutual exclusion protocol and all arrive in C, then the process which was the last to enter C will read its own identity in the shared variable and enter the critical section.

Verification by Backwards Reachability Analysis If we perform a backwards reachability analysis for Fischer's protocol, starting from negation of the invariant being equivalent to

$$\exists i, j. CS[i] \wedge CS[j]$$

then we end up with convergence and the following fixedpoint

$$
\begin{aligned}
&\exists i, j. \ CS[i] \ \wedge \ CS[j] \\
\vee \ &\exists i, j. \ C[i] \ \wedge \ v = i \ \wedge \ CS[j] \\
\vee \ &\exists i, j. \ B[i] \ \wedge \ x[i] < 1 \ \wedge \ CS[j] \\
\vee \ &\exists i, j. \ B[i] \ \wedge \ x[i] < 1 \ \wedge \ C[j] \ \wedge \ v = j \ \wedge \ x[i] < x[j] \\
\vee \ &\exists i, j. \ A[i] \ \wedge \ v = 0 \ \wedge \ CS[j] \\
\vee \ &\exists i, j. \ C[i] \ \wedge \ v = 0 \ \wedge \ CS[j]
\end{aligned}
$$

The negation of this assertion is a universal invariant, which can be written as follows.

$$
\begin{aligned}
&\forall i, j. \ \neg(CS[i] \ \wedge \ CS[j]) \\
\wedge \ &\forall i, j. \ (C[i] \ \wedge \ CS[j]) \implies v \neq i \\
\wedge \ &\forall i, j. \ (B[i] \ \wedge \ CS[j]) \implies x[i] \geq 1 \\
\wedge \ &\forall i, j. \ (B[i] \ \wedge \ C[j]) \implies (x[i] \geq 1 \ \vee \ v \neq j \ \vee \ x[i] \geq x[j]) \\
\wedge \ &\forall i. \ (A[i] \ \wedge \ CS[i]) \implies v \neq 0 \\
\wedge \ &\forall i. \ (C[i] \ \wedge \ CS[i]) \implies v \neq 0
\end{aligned}
$$

---

[1] In fact, our formalism cannot express such requirements, although they can be added in terms of e.g., fairness constraints.

However, a simpler to write computational invariant is the following:

$$\forall i.\ CS[i] \implies v = i$$
$$\wedge\ \forall i, j.\ (B[i] \wedge CS[j]) \implies x[i] \geq 1$$
$$\wedge\ \forall i, j.\ (B[i] \wedge C[j]) \implies (x[i] \geq 1 \vee v \neq j \vee x[i] \geq x[j])$$

Finding a Network Invariant The interface between components concerns the global variable v, the timing, and whether or not a component is in the critical section. We can therefore find a network invariant as a system with four states, shown in Figure 2. The figure shows an abstraction of a network containing

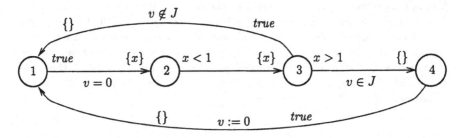

Fig. 2. Network Invariant for Fischer's Protocol. Not shown in the graph is a self-loop at state 2, which sets v to an arbitrary index in J

indices in a set J of indices. Here, the four states are abstractions of network states with the following properties. We use *idle*[i] to denote the property $A[i] \vee (B[i] \wedge x[i] \geq 1) \vee (C[i] \wedge v \neq i)$ denoting processes that are not active in competing for the critical section.

$$1: \quad \forall i.\ idle[i]$$
$$2: \quad (\forall i.\ idle[i] \vee B[i] \vee (C[i] \wedge x[i] < 1)) \wedge$$
$$\quad (\forall i, j.\ (B[i] \wedge C[j]) \implies x[i] \geq x[j])$$
$$3: \quad \forall i.\ idle[i] \vee C[i]$$
$$4: \quad \forall i.\ idle[i] \vee C[i] \vee (CS[i]) \wedge v = i)$$

Not shown in the graph is a self-loop at state 2, which sets v to an index in J.

6   Conclusion

In this paper, we have considered methods for verifying parameterized systems using induction. We have considered the use of computational induction, and of induction over the network structure. The main contribution has been to give conditions under which there are guarantees for the existence of inductive invariants of a simple form. For the case of computational induction, we have that guarantees the existence of a network invariant, provided that there is a simple computational invariant.

We should point out that our results are only partial, and we believe that they can be made stronger. As they are, they indicate that simple network invariants exists whenever simple computational invariants exist. The results also show that the construction of both simple network and computational invariants can be automated for finite-state systems with only bounded synchronization.

References

[ABJ98]   Parosh Aziz Abdulla, Ahmed Bouajjani, and Bengt Jonsson. On-the-fly analysis of systems with unbounded, lossy fifo channels. In *Proc. 10th Int. Conf. on Computer Aided Verification*, volume 1427 of *Lecture Notes in Computer Science*, pages 305–318, 1998.

[ABJN99]   Parosh Aziz Abdulla, Ahmed Bouajjani, Bengt Jonsson, and Marcus Nilsson. Handling global conditions in parameterized system verification. In *Proc. 11th Int. Conf. on Computer Aided Verification*, 1999.

[ACD90]   R. Alur, C. Courcoubetis, and D. Dill. Model-checking for real-time systems. In *Proc. 5th IEEE Int. Symp. on Logic in Computer Science*, pages 414–425, Philadelphia, 1990.

[ACHH92]   R. Alur, C. Courcoubetis, T. Henzinger, and P.-H. Ho. Hybrid automata: An algorithmic approach to the specification and verificationof hybrid systems. In Grossman, Nerode, Ravn, and Rischel, editors, *Hybrid Systems*, number 736 in Lecture Notes in Computer Science, pages 209–229, 1992.

[AČJYK96]   Parosh Aziz Abdulla, Karlis Čerāns, Bengt Jonsson, and Tsay Yih-Kuen. General decidability theorems for infinite-state systems. In *Proc. 11th IEEE Int. Symp. on Logic in Computer Science*, pages 313–321, 1996.

[AJ93]   Parosh Aziz Abdulla and Bengt Jonsson. Verifying programs with unreliable channels. In *Proc. 8th IEEE Int. Symp. on Logic in Computer Science*, pages 160–170, 1993.

[AJ98]   Parosh Aziz Abdulla and Bengt Jonsson. Verifying networks of timed processes. In Bernhard Steffen, editor, *Proc. TACAS '98, 7th Int. Conf. on Tools and Algorithms for the Construction and Analysis of Systems*, volume 1384 of *Lecture Notes in Computer Science*, pages 298–312, 1998.

[AK86]   K. Apt and D.C. Kozen. Limits for automatic verification of finite-state concurrent systems. *Information Processing Letters*, 22:307–309, 1986.

[AL92]   M. Abadi and L. Lamport. An old-fashioned recipe for real time. In de Bakker, Huizing, de Roever, and Rozenberg, editors, *Real-Time: Theory in Practice*, volume 600 of *Lecture Notes in Computer Science*, 1992.

[And95]   H.R. Andersen. Partial model checking (extended abstract). In *Proc. 10th IEEE Int. Symp. on Logic in Computer Science*, pages 398–407. IEEE Computer Society Press, 1995.

[BGK$^+$96]   J. Bengtsson, W. O. D. Griffioen, K.J. Kristoffersen, K.G. Larsen, F. Larsson, P. Pettersson, and W. Yi. Verification of an audio protocol with bus collision using UPPAAL. In R. Alur and T. Henzinger, editors, *Proc. 8th Int. Conf. on Computer Aided Verification*, volume 1102 of *Lecture Notes in Computer Science*, pages 244–256, New Brunswick, USA, 1996. Springer Verlag.

[BS95]   O. Burkart and B. Steffen. Composition, decomposition, and model check-
            ing of pushdown processes. *Nordic Journal of Computing*, 2(2):89–125,
            1995.
[CGJ95]   E. M. Clarke, O. Grumberg, and S. Jha. Verifying parameterized networks
            using abstraction and regular languages. In Lee and Smolka, editors, *Proc.
            CONCUR '95, 6th Int. Conf. on Concurrency Theory*, volume 962 of *Lec-
            ture Notes in Computer Science*, pages 395–407. Springer Verlag, 1995.
[Dic13]   L. E. Dickson. Finiteness of the odd perfect and primitive abundant num-
            bers with n distinct prime factors. *Amer. J. Math.*, 35:413–422, 1913.
[EFM99]   J. Esparza, A. Finkel, and R. Mayr. On the verification of broadcast
            protocols. In *Proc. 14th IEEE Int. Symp. on Logic in Computer Science*,
            1999.
[EN95]   E.A. Emerson and K.S. Namjoshi. Reasoning about rings. In *Proc. 22th
            ACM Symp. on Principles of Programming Languages*, 1995.
[Fin94]   A. Finkel. Decidability of the termination problem for completely specified
            protocols. *Distributed Computing*, 7(3), 1994.
[GS92]   S. M. German and A. P. Sistla. Reasoning about systems with many
            processes. *Journal of the ACM*, 39(3):675–735, 1992.
[Hen95]   T.A. Henzinger. Hybrid automata with finite bisimulations. In *Proc.
            ICALP '95*, 1995.
[ID99]   C. Norris Ip and David L. Dill. Verifying systems with replicated compo-
            nents in Murφ. *Formal Methods in System Design*, 14(3), May 1999.
[JK95]   Bengt Jonsson and Lars Kempe. Verifying safety properties of a class
            of infinite-state distributed algorithms. In *Proc. 7th Int. Conf. on Com-
            puter Aided Verification*, volume 939 of *Lecture Notes in Computer Science*,
            pages 42–53. Springer Verlag, 1995.
[JM95]   P. Jančar and F. Moller. Checking regular properties of Petri nets. In
            Proc. CONCUR '95, 6th Int. Conf. on Concurrency Theory, pages 348–
            362, 1995.
[JP93]   B. Jonsson and J. Parrow. Deciding bisimulation equivalences for a class of
            non-finite-state programs. *Information and Computation*, 107(2):272–302,
            Dec. 1993.
[KLL+97]   K.J. Kristoffersen, F. Larroussinie, K. G. Larsen, P. Pettersson, and W. Yi.
            A compositional proof of a real-time mutual exclusion protocol. In *TAP-
            SOFT '97 7th International Joint Conference on the Theory and Prac-
            tice of Software Development*, Lecture Notes in Computer Science, Lille,
            France, April 1997. Springer Verlag.
[KM89]   R.P. Kurshan and K. McMillan. A structural induction theorem for pro-
            cesses. In *Proc. 8th ACM Symp. on Principles of Distributed Computing,
            Canada*, pages 239–247, Edmonton, Alberta, 1989.
[KMM+97]   Y. Kesten, O. Maler, M. Marcus, A. Pnueli, and E. Shahar. Symbolic
            model checking with rich assertional languages. In O. Grumberg, editor,
            Proc. 9th Int. Conf. on Computer Aided Verification, volume 1254, pages
            424–435, Haifa, Israel, 1997. Springer Verlag.
[Lam89]   L. Lamport. A simple approach to specifying concurrent systems,. *Com-
            munications of the ACM*, 32(1):32–45, Jan. 1989.
[LHR97]   D. Lesens, N. Halbwachs, and P. Raymond. Automatic verification of
            parameterized linear networks of processes. In *Proc. 24th ACM Symp. on
            Principles of Programming Languages*, 1997.
[LS97]   D. Lesens and H. Saidi. Abstraction of parameterized networks. *Electronic
            Notes in Theoretical Computer Science*, 9, 1997.

[MP95]   Z. Manna and A. Pnueli. *Temporal Verification of Reactive Systems: Safety.* Springer Verlag, 1995.

[Sha93]   N. Shankar. Verification of real-time systems using PVS. In Courcoubetis, editor, *Proc. 5th Int. Conf. on Computer Aided Verification*, volume 697 of *Lecture Notes in Computer Science*, pages 280–291, 1993.

[Sti96]   C. Stirling. Decidability of bisimulation equivalence for normed pushdown processes. In *Proc. CONCUR '96, 7th Int. Conf. on Concurrency Theory*, volume 1119 of *Lecture Notes in Computer Science*, pages 217–232. Springer Verlag, 1996.

[WB98]   Pierre Wolper and Bernard Boigelot. Verifying systems with infinite but regular state spaces. In *Proc. 10th Int. Conf. on Computer Aided Verification*, volume 1427 of *Lecture Notes in Computer Science*, pages 88–97, Vancouver, July 1998. Springer Verlag.

[WL89]   P. Wolper and V. Lovinfosse. Verifying properties of large sets of processes with network invariants (extended abstract). In Sifakis, editor, *Proc. Workshop on Computer Aided Verification*, number 407 in Lecture Notes in Computer Science, pages 68–80, 1989.

[Wol86]   Pierre Wolper. Expressing interesting properties of programs in propositional temporal logic (extended abstract). In *Proc. 13th ACM Symp. on Principles of Programming Languages*, pages 184–193, Jan. 1986.

Part IV

Compilation

Verification of Compilers

Gerhard Goos and Wolf Zimmermann

Fakultät für Informatik
Universität Karlsruhe
{ggoos,zimmer}@ipd.info.uni-karlsruhe.de

Abstract. We report about a joint project of the universities at Karlsruhe, Kiel and Ulm on how to get correct compilers for realistic programming languages. Arguing about compiler correctness must start from a compiling specification describing the correspondence of source and target language in formal terms. We have chosen to use abstract state machines to formalize this correspondence. This allows us to stay with traditional compiler architectures for subdividing the compiler task. A main achievement is the use of program checking for replacing large parts of compiler verification by the much simpler task of verifying program checkers.

1 Introduction

The correctness of the code generated by compilers is at the heart of all quality problems of software: No matter what measures are taken for improving the quality of software, it does not help if the compilers finally produce erroneous executables.

A compiler C is an implementation of a mapping $f\colon SL \to TL$ from a source language SL to a target language TL, the latter usually being the machine language of a real or abstract processor. It is called correct if it preserves the semantic meaning of source programs, i.e., if a translated target program $\pi' = C(\pi)$ can be executed instead of the source program π yielding the same results as the source program. Correctness is the really interesting property of a compiler when it comes to getting high quality software.

Correctness of compilers seems to be easy to define and to understand. We will, however, see that there are several problems to be solved before we arrive at a satisfactory definition of correctness. This will be the first subject of this paper. We will then present methods for verifying correctness both on the specification and the implementation level.

This paper is based on results achieved in project Verifix, an ongoing joint project on compiler verification at the universities Karlsruhe, Kiel and Ulm. The main contributions so far are the notion of correctness, the insight that we may use traditional compiler architectures even for verified compilers, the methodology of using abstract state machines for describing operational semantics on all levels of compiling and the use of program checking for making the work feasible in practice.

E.-R. Olderog, B. Steffen (Eds.): Correct System Design, LNCS 1710, pp. 201–230, 1999.
© Springer-Verlag Berlin Heidelberg 1999

2   Correctness of Compilers

If the execution of a program may replace the execution of another one with the same results then we say that the two programs are showing the *same (semantic) behaviour*. During execution a target program $\pi' = C(\pi)$ will only show the same behaviour as its source program π if the source program and the inputs meet certain admissibility conditions. A precise definition of compiler correctness thus depends on the precise meaning of the notions *same behaviour*, *admissible program* and *admissible input data*.

2.1   Behaviour of Programs

We first discuss sequential programs. At the end of this subsection, we sketch a generalization to parallel and distributed programs. We do not consider realtime conditions.

The execution of a program can be represented by a sequence of states $q_0, q_1, \ldots$ beginning in an initial state q_0. Each state is composed of the values of variables $(v_1, \ldots, v_m)$ which together define the state space of the program execution. For a source program π in some high level language SL the state space consists of all the entities (variables, constants, objects, ...) which the program creates and refers to. For a target program π' in some machine language TL the state space consists of the registers of the processor and that part of the computer memory which is accessed during program execution. In both cases the size of the state space may vary between program executions depending on the input data and potential indeterministic behaviour.

In selected *observable states* communication with the outside world takes place: the values of certain variables are *observable* iff they contain input data fed from the outside during the foregoing state transition or they contain output values which will be made public during the next state transition. Only the communication with the outside world is observable; the remainder of the details of program execution is of little interest and may in fact greatly vary between a source program and its translated target program. We may abstract from these details and consider program execution as a sequence of observable states. The sequence of values $\bar{q}$ of the observable variables in these states q constitute the behaviour of a program execution.

A source and a target program showing the same behaviour must both run through a sequence of observable states as in Fig. 1. Between corresponding states q, q' there must hold a relation $q \, \rho \, q'$ ensuring that the observable variables in both states contain (encodings of) the same values. ρ may be difficult to define: In a source program in a high level language the observable variables are usually uniquely defined by their name x, or an access path such as $a[i]$ or $m.s.p$; in the target program, however, the corresponding variable may change its place in storage depending on the state and thus may be difficult to retrieve. In practice the observable variables are the arguments of i/o operations and thus it does not matter where we find them in storage.

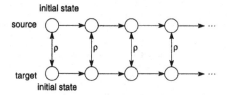

Fig. 1. Corresponding states

It is especially important that the compiled program π' produces exactly the outputs of the source program π and not more. Otherwise Trojan horses, [46], could be introduced which inform third parties about the execution of π' or show other inacceptable behaviour.

It is easy to study whether π and π' show the same behaviour if both programs implement an algorithm $\mathcal{A}$ which after a finite number of steps arrives at a final state yielding the results $\mathcal{A}(i)$ for the given inputs i. In this case only the initial and final state are observable; we must establish the relation ρ for these two states.

A sequential reactive program running through a potentially infinite sequence of observable states may be considered as a sequence of algorithmic mappings.

In both cases we must take potential indeterminism into account: If there are indeterministic choices in a source program π which upon execution may be arbitrarily decided then every possible choice leads to an *acceptable execution path* $q_0, q_1, \ldots$. The translated program $\pi' = \mathcal{C}(\pi)$ may make arbitrary choices as long as its execution path $q_0', q_1', \ldots$ shows the same behaviour as an acceptable execution path of the source program. E.g., the indeterministic program

do true $\to$ x := 1
[] **true** $\to$ x := 0
od

in DIJKSTRA's language of guarded commands assigns $x = 1$ or $x = 0$ arbitrarily as shown in Fig. 2. Especially the path which always assigns $x := 1$ is acceptable. Therefore a compiler may generate the target program from the simplified source

do true $\to$ x := 1 **od**

If on the other hand the translated program π' shows indeterministic behaviour then the indeterminism must also be present in the source program. Since we only deal with indeterminism on the level of observable states indeterminisms such as dynamic rescheduling of the order of instructions by modern processors are not relevant as long as the order of observable states and the content of observable variables is not affected.

Parallel and distributed programs generalize this situation: A state q of a program execution is composed from the states $q^{(t)}$ of all threads t currently running in parallel. The source program π defines a partial order R amongst all the observable thread states $q^{(t)}$. Synchronizations and communications between

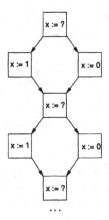

Fig. 2. State transition graph of an indeterministic program

different threads induce an order between states of different threads. A translated program π' showing thread states $q'^{(t)}$ is taking an acceptable execution path if there is a 1-to-1 mapping between the sets $\{q^{(t)}\}$ and $\{q'^{(t)}\}$ such that the induced order of the thread states $q'^{(t)}$ is a refinement of the order R for their counterparts $q^{(t)}$. The observable variables in corresponding states $q^{(t)}, q'^{(t)}$ must of course contain the same values.

Our definition of observable state constitutes the bottom line of what can be observed. We may arbitrarily extend the definition. Each such extension will, however, restrict the possible optimizations which a compiler may apply when generating the target program. E. g. when we declare the begin and (dynamic) end of all procedures observable then interprocedural optimizations will become very difficult.

2.2 Admissibility

To be admissible a program π must be well-formed according to the rules of the source language SL, i. e., it must obey the syntactic rules of SL and fulfill certain semantic consistency conditions such as providing declarations for all identifiers occurring as variables or user-definable type names. Well-formedness requires a precise formal description of the source language grammar and its associated static semantics. Thus we may trace the notion of admissibility back to the requirement of having a formal description of the source language. Even then it remains open which consistency conditions are to be checked for establishing well-formedness. Of course all such conditions must be decidable from the program text only. Today we usually consider problems of type consistency between declarations and use of declared entities in expressions as well-formedness conditions. But many programming languages can also be compiled such that typing conditions are only checked at run-time; in this case proper typing is not a well-formedness condition. Admissibility of source programs depends thus to some extent on design decisions of the compiler writer.

The termination behaviour of a program can never be a well-formedness condition: termination is undecidable in general and may also depend on input data. In the same vain a division by zero or other arithmetic exceptions do not violate well-formedness even if the compiler can predict it.

Admissibility of input data is even harder to judge: Consider a program for solving a system $\mathfrak{A}\mathfrak{x} = \mathfrak{b}$ of linear equations. For $\mathfrak{b} \neq \mathfrak{o}$ the matrix $\mathfrak{A}$ is admissible if it is non-singular. But running the program is the easiest way for checking this condition. Also, the matrix $\mathfrak{A}$ may be non-singular in the strict mathematical sense; but since computers can only deal with numbers of limited precision a target program may terminate with the error message "matrix singular" even if it was not.

Who then should be held responsible for problems arising from range and precision limitations of numbers, and from limitations of speed and storage of a computing system? Theoreticians tend to construct programs and to prove their correctness disregarding such limitations. In practice, however, it is the writer of the source program and the user feeding the input data who must take this responsibility: a compiler can neither invent a new algorithm for circumventing potentially disastrous effects of rounding errors; nor can it pay the bill for enlarging storage or increasing processor speed so that input data which are otherwise too voluminous can be processed in acceptable time. This remark also applies to the compiler itself: A correct compiler must be allowed to refuse compilation of source programs of, say, 3 trillion lines of code even if they are admissible in all other aspects.

We conclude that a compiled program may terminate with an error message for violation of resource limitations even when the source program and the input data were admissible according to ideal mathematical rules. Also a compiler may terminate with an error message for the same reasons without violating correctness conditions. All compilers are limited with respect to the size and complexity of the source programs which they can properly translate.

2.3   Correctness

We finally arrive at the following definition of compiler correctness:

A target program $\pi' = \mathcal{C}(\pi)$ is a correct translation of the admissible source program π iff for every admissible input there is an acceptable execution path $s_0, s_1, \ldots,$ of observable states for the source program and an execution path $s'_0, s'_1, \ldots$ of the target program such that $s_i \, \rho \, s'_i$ holds for $i = 0, 1, \ldots \pi'$ may terminate prematurely with an error message due to violation of resource limitations. No execution path of π' contains observable states which do not relate to possible states of π except for error states.

As before ρ is the (state dependent) relation requiring that all observable variables contain the same values.

A compiler essentially is a text manipulation tool, transforming the text of the source program into a bit sequence called the target program. The definition does not directly relate properties of source and target programs but only properties of their execution, i.e., source and target program are textual representations of execution models. The semantics of the programs which must be related are these execution models.

This insight leads to the diagram Fig. 3; ρ indicates the composite relation

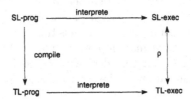

Fig. 3. Correctness diagram

between observable states from Fig. 1. The diagram must commute: Whether we go directly from SL-prog to SL-exec or via TL-prog and TL-exec we must obtain the same values of observable variables as long as the target program does not stop with an error message. [30] compares different notions of compiler correctness from the theoretical viewpoint. Our definition is specific in that we restrict ourselves to observable variables and allow for premature termination due to resource limitations.

The definition leaves it open for which source programs the compiler will emit a correct target program. For a compiler to be practically useful this class must be sufficiently large; but this requirement is not part of the correctness definition.

3   Specifications and Compiler Architecture

To prove the commutativity of the above diagram we need a formal description of the execution models, i.e., a formal semantics of the source and the target language.

When we choose a machine language as target language then its formal semantics can be stated in the form of finite state machines for every instruction describing the state changes of the processor and of memory induced by executing the instruction. On many machines combining instructions to instruction sequences is compositional: For pairs of instructions i, i'

$$\frac{\{P\}\ i\ \{Q\}}{\{Q\}\ i'\ \{R\}}{\{P\}\ i;i'\ \{R\}} \tag{1}$$

holds where P, Q, R are descriptions of the machine state. Even if the hardware may reschedule the order of instruction execution on the fly as on the Pentium II it is ensured that the order of load and store operations from and to observable registers and memory locations remains unchanged.

Also the semantics of high level programming languages is compositional: We do not list the meaning of all admissible programs but only describe language elements such as operations, expressions, assignments, conditional statements, procedures, etc. and deduce the semantic meaning of larger constructs by composing it from the elements using structural induction over the syntactic structure of the program.

Usually the semantics of high level languages is described by informally specifying an interpreter for the language. This may be augmented with certain well-formedness conditions which a compiler must take care of. For proving a compiler correct we need a formal description of the interpretation. There are several possible description methods: denotational semantics, algebraic specifications, operational semantics. Since the target machine semantics is given operationally by state machines our project has chosen to also use state machines for operationally specifying the semantics of the source language.

We are thus left with the task to prove that for all admissible source programs the state machine for the target program simulates the state machine for the source program as far as observable states are concerned. Since the target program should do not more we need the simulation also the other way around, i. e., we need a bisimulation.

Simulating state machines SM, SM' by each other can be done in several steps: We may invent state machines SM_i and then prove that in the sequence $SM = SM_0, SM_1, \ldots, SM_{n-1}, SM_n = SM'$ each machine bisimulates its successor. We arrive at the picture in Fig. 4 where the original relation

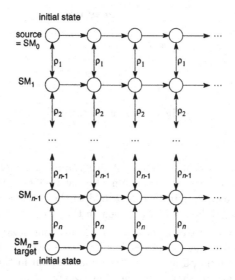

Fig. 4. Decomposed state transitions

$\rho = \rho_n \circ \rho_{n-1} \circ \cdots \circ \rho_2 \circ \rho_1$ appears decomposed.

Fig. 4 establishes the bridge to traditional compiler technology. In practical compilers we decompose the transition $SL \to TL$ into transitions $SL = IL_0 \to IL_1 \to \cdots \to IL_{n-1} \to IL_n = TL$ by creating a number of intermediate languages IL_i. If we assign semantics described by state machines SM_i to these intermediate languages IL_i then Fig. 4 indicates the proof obligations for these transitions. As is customary in many compilers we can choose the attributed syntax tree AST as an intermediate language and a low-level intermediate language LL exhibiting the control flow, data types and operations present in the semantics of the target machine. We arrive at the decomposition in Fig. 5 of the compiler.

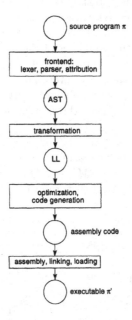

Fig. 5. Compiler structure

Due to the compositional nature of programming language semantics we cannot directly attach semantic meaning to the text of a source program π. The operational meaning is instead attached to the phrases of the context free grammar of the source language as present in the AST.

Verification of a compiler front-end is thus not concerned with the dynamic semantics of the source language but has only to show that the AST correctly represents the syntactic phrases and their composition in the source program. Additionally we have to show that the consistency conditions of the static semantics of the source language are checked as is customary in all compilers.

Similar remarks apply to the final assembly, linking and loading phase: Again the actual dynamic semantics, in this case of the target machine, is of no particular interest. Correctness depends on the question whether the compiler, linker and loader have chosen the right binary encoding for the assembly language instructions, and whether technical conditions such as proper choice of alignments, proper setting of read/write/execute permissions etc. are met.

We are left with verifying the transformation, optimization and code generation phase of the compiler. From these phases the transformation phase constitutes the core of the compiler. Its task is to relate the semantics of the source language to the semantics of the target machine. Optimization and code generation on the other hand deal with an admittedly huge selection problem amongst different alternatives of how to represent operations and (connected and disconnected) operation sequences of the intermediate language LL in assembly language but within the unifying framework of the semantics of the target language.

3.1 Summary: Verification Tasks

A *compiler specification* consists of formal descriptions of its source, intermediate and target languages, and the transformations from one language to the next. In our case the languages are specified by their operational semantics. This compiler specification must be implemented correctly. If γ is the program in a high-level programming language implementing the compiler C then γ must be compiled correctly into executable code γ' for the processor executing C, cf. Fig. 6. Thus the verification is decomposed into three tasks:

1. Verification of the compiler specification C: it must be shown that for every program π, every target π' obtained from π by C is a correct translation of π.
2. Verification of the compiler implementation γ (in a high-level programming language L'): it must be shown that the implementation is a refinement of the compiler specification.
3. Verification of the executable compiler γ': it must be shown that γ' is a correct translation of γ.

The source and target languages are initially only informally described. Therefore part of the first task, namely checking the formal specifications of these languages, can usually be achieved by experimental validation only, running validation suites against the formal specifications by hand.

4   Abstract State Machines and Compiler Specifications

The basic idea of the formalization of the language semantics is to consider the states of programs as an algebra over a given signature. The interpretation of some symbols of the signature may change on state transitions, e.g. an assignment changes the interpretation of a memory. Abstract state machines

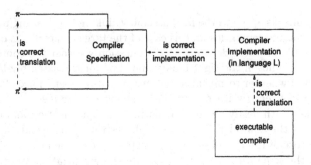

Fig. 6. Verification/construction of correct compilers

provide a formalization of this view. For proving the correctness of compilers this view allows the separation of mapping states (memory mappings) and program transformations (simulation proofs). Subsection 4.1 introduces abstract state machines. In this section we discuss the use of abstract state machines for formally describing languages (subsection 4.2) and the transformations between them (subsection 4.4).

4.1   Abstract State Machines

Abstract state machines, formerly also called dynamic or evolving algebras, are means for describing state transition systems. States are modelled as algebras $\mathfrak{A}$. Each n-ary function symbol f in the signature of $\mathfrak{A}$ defines an n-ary mapping. Transitions between states change the results $t_0 = f(t_1, \ldots, t_n)$ for selected functions f and selected arguments $(t_1, \ldots, t_n)$. Formally, an *abstract state machine* (ASM) is a tuple $\mathcal{A} = (\Sigma, \Delta, \mathfrak{A}, \mathit{Init}, \mathit{Trans})$ where

1. Σ and Δ are two (sorted) disjoint signatures (the signature of *static* and *dynamic* functions).
2. $\mathfrak{A}$ is an order-sorted Σ-algebra (the *static* algebra).
3. *Init* is a set of equations over $\mathfrak{A}$ defining the initial states of $\mathcal{A}$.
4. *Trans* is a set of *transition rules* for defining the state transitions by changing (or updating) the interpretations of functions of Δ.

A $(\Sigma \cup \Delta)$-algebra q is a *state* of $\mathcal{A}$ iff its restriction to Σ is the static algebra $\mathfrak{A}$.

   Updates of an interpretation are defined as follows: Let q be a state, $f \in \Delta$, t_i terms over $\Sigma \cup \Delta$ and x_i interpretations in q. The update

$$f(t_1, \ldots, t_n) := t_0$$

defines the new interpretation of f in the state q':

$$q' \models f(x_1, \ldots, x_n) = \begin{cases} x_0 & \text{if for all } i,\ 1 \leq i \leq n,\ q \models t_i = x_i \\ f_q(x_1, \ldots, x_n) & \text{otherwise} \end{cases}$$

A transition rule defines a set of updates which are executed in parallel. A rule has the following form:

if *Cond* **then**
    Update$_1$ ... *Update*$_n$
endif

The updates *Update*$_i$ are executed in a state q if $q \models Cond = true$.

For further details and abbreviations we refer the reader to [24].

4.2 Programming Language Semantics with ASMs

Many languages have been formally described by ASMs, cf. section 7. We illustrate the method with rules from the specifications of the languages used in Verifix:

Example 1 (High-Level Languages). The operational semantics is attached to the AST. Some AST-nodes represent dynamic tasks, e. g. the nodes of sort *WHILE* represent the decision whether to iterate the body of a while loop, and the nodes of sort *ASSIGN* represent assignments. The AST must contain some attributes, e. g. left hand sides and right hand sides of assignments (*lhs* and *rhs*), the dynamic task to be executed next (*NT*), the condition of a while loop (*cond*), and the first task of the body of a while loop (*TT*).

The operational semantics has a pointer to the task to be executed (*CT*, current task). *CT* is moving through the program during execution, i.e. *CT* is an abstract program counter. The following transition rule defines the semantics of the while loop:

if $CT \in WHILE$ **then**
    if $value(CT.cond) = true$ **then**
        $CT := CT.TT$
    else $CT := CT.NT$

An assignment assigns the value of the right hand side to the designator of the left hand side, i. e., the storage (*store*) is changed at this address. Then, the task after the assignment is executed. The transition rule is

if $CT \in ASSIGN$ **then**
    $store(addr(CT.lhs)) := value(CT.rhs)$
    $CT := CT.NT$

For high-level languages, the addresses need not be related to the addresses of target-machines. In this example, we assume abstract addresses. The storage *store* can store at each address any value. Abstract addresses do not exclude the definition of pointers: they can be represented by storing addresses.

The transition rule for a variable as designator is

if $CT \in VAR$ then
  $value(CT) := store(bind(env, CT.id))$
  $addr(CT) := bind(env, CT.id)$
  $CT := CT.NT$ □

Remark 1. Language like C define the addresses to be those of the target machine. In this case, the transition rule for the assignment statement must take into account the size of the values. For byte-oriented memory, the above transition rule provides an abstraction: the update on *store* denotes a series of updates for the memory cells required to store the value. Since pointers are generally formalized by addresses, it is straightforward to model the pointer arithmetic of C.

Example 2 (Basic Block Graphs). A basic block is a sequence of instructions. On execution all instructions are executed. The last instruction branches conditionally or unconditionally. Each basic block is named by a label. The currently executed instruction is designated by a pair consisting of such a label (*CL*: current label) and an instruction pointer *IP* ($CI \cong instr(CL, IP)$). An integer assignment instruction intassign$(a, e) \in INTASSIGN$ evaluates the source and the target (which must be an address), and assigns the value to the address. The evaluation is performed on the current state (function *eval*). Before the evaluation it is checked whether a division by zero, an arithmetic overflow, or a memory overflow would occur during this evaluation. The transition rule is:

if $CI \in INTASSIGN$ then
  if $div\_by\_zero(src(CI))$ then $exception := $ "div_by_zero"
  elsif $overflow(src(CI))$ then $exception := $ "arithmetic_overflow"
  elsif $mem\_overflow(dest(CI)) \vee mem\_overflow(src(CI))$
  then $exception := $ "memory_overflow"
  else $content(eval(dest(CI))) := eval(src(CI))$;
    $IP := IP + 1$;

The semantics of a conditional jump ifjmp$(e, L_1, L_2) \in IF$ evaluates the expression e. If the result is positive then it jumps to the first instruction of the block labeled L_1, otherwise it jumps to the first instruction of the block labeled L_2:

if $CI \in IF$ then
  if $div\_by\_zero(src(CI))$ then $exception := $ "div_by_zero"
  elsif $overflow(src(CI))$ then $exception := $ "arithmetic_overflow"
  elsif $mem\_overflow(src(CI))$ then $exception := $ "memory_overflow"
  elsif $eval(src(CI)) > 0$
  then $CL := truetarget(CI)$
    $IP := 0$;
  else $CL := falsetarget(CI)$
    $IP := 0$;

Again, it must be checked whether the evaluation performs a division by zero, raises an arithmetic overflow, or a memory overflow. □

Example 3 (DEC-Alpha Machine Language). The operational semantics of the DEC-Alpha machine language depends on the machine architecture. The state consists of the register set (*reg*), the memory (*mem*), and the program counter (*PC*). The auxiliary function *long* accesses four consecutive bytes of *mem*, the function *quad* eight bytes. A command is a machine word that can be decoded by classifying predicates, e. g. *is_load*(*c*) is true for load instructions, *is_bgt*(*c*) for a conditional jump on positive integers. There are further operations extracting the operands or operand addresses from an instruction *c*, e. g. for a load instruction *c* *reladdr*(*c*) computes the relative address to be loaded, *base*(*c*) the register containing the base address, and *dest*(*c*) the target register. For a conditional jump *c* *src*(*c*) specifies the register defining the jump condition and *target*(*c*) the jump destination (a relative address). With these abbreviations the transition rules

> **if** *is_load*(*long*(*PC*)) **then**
>   *reg*(*target*(*long*(*PC*))) := *quad*(*reg*(*base*(*long*(*PC*)) ⊕ *reladdr*(*long*(*PC*))))
>   *PC* := *PC* ⊕ 4

> **if** *is_bgt*(*long*(*PC*)) **then**
>   **if** *reg*(*src*(*long*(*PC*))) > 0
>   **then** *PC* := *PC* ⊕ *target*(*src*(*long*(*PC*)))
>   **else** *PC* := *PC* ⊕ 4

specify loading from memory and conditional jumping. □

4.3   Montages

Besides consistency checking the semantic analysis of a compiler must provide for certain attributes needed by the operational semantics of the source language. In [31] so-called *Montages* are developed as a unified framework for explicitly specifying the attribution and transition rules. Montages extend attribute grammars by transition rules for ASMs. The attribution for the control-flow and the data-flow is specified by a graph. Formally, the abstract syntax, attributes, attribution rules, and the control- and data-flow form a sub-algebra of the static algebra of the abstract state machine defined by montages.

Example 4. Fig. 7, 8 show the montages for the while-loop and the assignment.
□

Control flow edges are dashed, data flow edges (use-def) are solid. Square vertices stand for general control and data flow graphs that can be derived from a nonterminal, circular vertices stand for tasks and are not further refined. Hence, a Montage specification can be considered as a graph-rewrite system for generating the control and data flow graph.

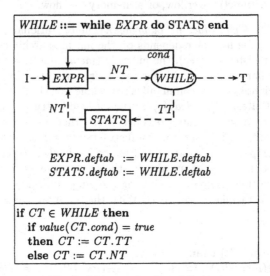

$$EXPR.deftab := WHILE.deftab$$
$$STATS.deftab := WHILE.deftab$$

if $CT \in WHILE$ then
  if $value(CT.cond) = true$
  then $CT := CT.TT$
  else $CT := CT.NT$

Fig. 7. Montage for the while loop

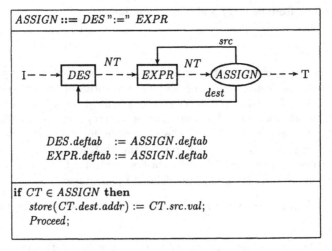

$$DES.deftab := ASSIGN.deftab$$
$$EXPR.deftab := ASSIGN.deftab$$

if $CT \in ASSIGN$ then
  $store(CT.dest.addr) := CT.src.val;$
  $Proceed;$

Fig. 8. Montage for the assignment

4.4   Transformations

A transformation from one language IL_i to the next, IL_{i+1}, maps the data and variables of IL_i to those of IL_{i+1} (*memory mapping*) and transform IL_i-programs to IL_{i+1}-programs (*program transformation*). The memory-mapping is specified by a set of data refinement rules, the program transformation by a set of program transformation rules.

In the following, cf. Fig. 4, let π be an IL_i program and π' an IL_{i+1} program obtained by memory-mapping and program transformation from IL_i to IL_{i+1}. SM_i and SM_{i+1} are the abstract state machines of π and π'. The memory mapping must

- map data types of SM_i to data types of SM_{i+1},
- map objects of π to objects of π', and
- introduce auxiliary objects in π' as required for program transformation.

For correctness, it is sufficient that every atomic object in a state of π is represented uniquely by an atomic object in the corresponding state of π'. Hence, the memory mapping defines part of the relation ρ_i. The memory mapping is usually not total; there might be states of π that cannot be mapped to a state of π' due to memory resource constraints.

Example 5. (Memory Mapping) The states of programs of a language *IS* with recursive procedures, static scoping, and anonymous objects consist of two parts: an environment, defining the current bindings of variables to objects, and a memory, holding the values of the objects. An environment is a stack of activation records for procedures containing the bindings of the local variables, the return address and a pointer to the static predecessor. Suppose that IL_{i+1} is an intermediate basic block language *MIS* with a flat, finite byte-oriented memory. Suppose further that *MIS* has no Boolean types. The memory mapping of *IS* to *MIS* consists of

(i)   a mapping from atomic data types of *MIS* to sequences of bytes
  - including the size of objects *size* and alignment conditions *align*, and
  - including a mapping from Booleans to integers, e. g. *false* $\cong$ 0, *true* $\cong$ 1;

(ii)   a refinement of the composite data types of *IS* to atomic data types of *MIS*;

(iii) a mapping from the environment to the memory of *MIS* which does
  - compute relative addresses of local variables of procedures,
  - fix a relative address for the return address and the pointer to static predecessor,
  - introduce a new variable and its relative address holding a pointer to the dynamic predecessor,
  - compute size and alignment of the activation record,
  - use the *MIS*-variable *local* for the base address of the activation record on the top of the stack;

(iv) a mapping from *IS*-addresses to *MIS*-addresses:

  – (ii) and (iii) define the mapping for local variables of procedures,
  – anonymous composite objects are decomposed according to (ii) and mapped onto addresses outside of the stack (the heap),
  – there is a heap pointer *topofheap* to maintain the heap.

It must be proven that (iii) introduces stack behavior, that the heap and the stack do not overlap, and that live objects whose value is needed later are mapped onto disjoint memory areas. Furthermore, alignment conditions must be satisfied.

Suppose that the memory of *MIS* is already the memory of the DEC-Alpha processor. Then, the memory mapping from *MIS* to DEC-Alpha basically maps the pointers *local* and *topofheap* to registers, and assigns registers to evaluate expressions, memory locations, parameters etc. Additional memory must be allocated if the available registers are not sufficient for evaluating expressions. □

Program transformations are conditional graph rewrite rules transforming the control and data flow graph of program elements as represented by montages; term rewrite rules are a special case. For correctness it must be shown that any sequence of application of the rewrite rules leads to programs π' whose abstract state machine SM_{i+1} simulates the abstract state machine SM_i of π.

Example 6. Fig. 9 shows a graph transformation for the while loop, Fig. 10 the graph transformation for the assignment. The graphical notation is an extension of the graphical notation of montages: As in montages square vertices stand for graphs, circle vertices are atomic, solid edges are data-flow edges, and dashed edges are control-flow edges. However, the names of vertices may be terms representing trees. Upper case names (nonterminals) stand for syntax trees that can be produced by the context free grammar. The name *any* stands for any term. If the names in a graph are not unique, they are subscripted. The applicability conditions can be structural as in the transformations for the while loop, and semantical as the typing conditions for the assignment. Optimizing transformations and data-flow analysis are also graph-transformations and can be modeled in the same way. □

5 Program Checking

The biggest practical problem in constructing a correct compiler is the size of the code which must be verified. Traditional approaches to program verification are not well-suited for large programs such as compilers. The use of program checking solves this problem in some cases, in particular for compilers. The technique works for all programs that transform inputs to outputs.

The basic idea is to verify that the output meets certain conditions from which the correctness of the output with regard to the given input can be deduced. The input is refused if the checker fails to verify these conditions, cf. Fig. 11.

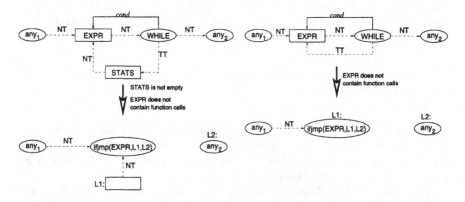

Fig. 9. Transforming while loops

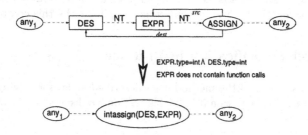

Fig. 10. Transforming assignments

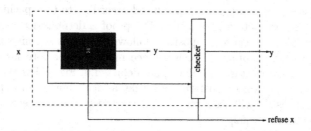

Fig. 11. Architecture of checked functions

Suppose, we have a program π implementing a function $f: I \to O$ with precondition $P(x)$ and postcondition $Q(x, \pi(x))$ on inputs x. Let $checker(x, y)$: *Bool* be a function that returns the value of $Q(x, y)$. Consider the program

function $\pi'(x : I) : O$
    $y := \pi(x)$;
    if $checker(x, \pi(x))$ **then return** y
    else abort;
end;

If *checker* is correctly implemented then $Q(x, \pi'(x))$ always holds. Under this condition if π' does not refuse the input then the output is correct. In particular, the partial correctness of π' does not depend on the partial correctness of π. Therefore we can use π without verification.

Program checking allows for verifying the results of large programs. It avoids verifying the program itself; instead only the checker and its implementation must be verified. This is particularly interesting when the checker is relatively small and easy to verify compared to the given program.

The idea carries a price, however: For compilers we do no longer verify that *every* admissible program π is correctly translated provided that resource limitations are not violated. Instead we produce a target program, check it, and if the checker accepts it then we declare π as compilable (by this compiler).

6   Compiler Verification in Practice

Project Verifix has used the methodology described so far for solving the three verification tasks from section 3.1. In this section we discuss details of this solution.

6.1   Verification of the Compiler Specification

We start from the assumption that the initial specification of the operational semantics of the source language by help of an ASM is correct. Then a compiler specification is correct iff for every source program π the abstract state machine of any target program π' produced according to the specification simulates the abstract state machine of π. The proof is decomposed vertically and horizontally. The vertical decomposition follows principles of conventional compiler architecture. In practice we introduce more intermediate languages and intermediate abstract state machines than depicted in Fig. 4. For the horizontal decomposition, for every transformation rule, a local simulation is proven correct. However, as we will see later, local correctness does not necessarily imply global correctness, cf. [52].

Vertical decomposition introduces the intermediate languages AST (attributed structure trees), basic block graphs, and machine code. Their semantics is given by abstract state machines ASM_{AST}, ASM_{BB}, and ASM_{MC}. The dynamic functions of these ASMs can be classified as instruction pointers, e.g. CT, and as memory functions, e. g. *env*, *store*, *reg*. For mapping the semantics of one language IL_i to IL_{i+1} another semantics for IL_i is defined using the memory functions of the ASM for IL_{i+1}. This semantics simulates, up to resource constraints, the original semantics, i. e., one step in the new ASM corresponds to one step in the old ASM. Then the languages IL_i and IL_{i+1} are integrated. By help of the transformation rules IL_i instructions are completely eliminated. Then a 1-1 mapping to IL_{i+1} is applied and the instruction pointers are mapped. Fig. 12 shows the steps.

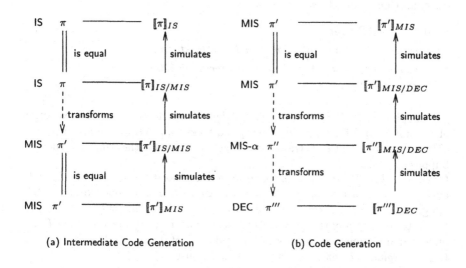

(a) Intermediate Code Generation   (b) Code Generation

Fig. 12. Vertical decomposition for verifying compiler specifications

In the first step, a semantics $[\![\cdot]\!]_{IS/MIS}$ for the source language *IS*, represented by ASTs, is constructed using the memory state space of *MIS*; i. e., the environment *env* and the storage *store* are mapped to the memory *mem* and the pointers *local* and *topofheap*. With this mapping, every transition rule of a task of *IS* can be transformed into a transition rule based on the new memory state space. The memory mapping consists of two parts: globally the environment of source programs is mapped; locally a mapping *reladdr* computes relative addresses for the local variables of a block. There are *illegal* states of IS/MIS which do not represent proper memory states of IS/MIS. For a correct memory mapping it is sufficient to prove

– all initial states of IS/MIS are legal;
– if q is a legal state, $q \to_{MIS/IS} q'$, and q' is legal then $\phi(q) \to_{IS} \phi(q')$.

Here ϕ is the mapping that recovers the original state. If a computation runs into an illegal state, then a resource constraint is violated. The following example demonstrates the proof for the while loop, the assignment, and the designator.

Example 7. The transition rule for the while loop becomes

> **if** $CT \in WHILE$ **then**
>> **if** $value(CT.cond) > 0$ **then**
>>> $CT := CT.TT$
>>
>> **else** $CT := CT.NT$

The transition rule for the assignment remains. The transition rule for a designator maps variables as follows:

> **if** $CT \in VAR$ **then**
>> $value(CT) := content(local \oplus_A reladdr(tasktoproc(CT), CT.Id));$
>> $addr(CT) := local \oplus_A reladdr(tasktoproc(CT), CT.Id))$
>> $CT := CT.NT$

Mapping a *WHILE* is proven correct by sub-casing and symbolic execution of the state transitions. For all states q and tasks t $q \models CT = t$ holds iff $\phi(q) \models CT = t$. Hence, both abstract state machines execute the same instruction. Suppose $q \models CT = t$

CASE 1: $value(CT.cond) > 0$. Then after the state transition of the IS/MIS abstract state machine, $q' \models CT = t.TT$. Since *true* is mapped to a positive integer, $q \models value(CT.cond) > 0$ iff $\phi(q) \models value(CT.cond) = true$. Hence, by the state transition of the MIS abstract state machine, $\phi(q') \models CT = t.TT$. All other dynamic functions remain unchanged, i.e., $\phi(q) \rightarrow_{IS} \phi(q')$.

CASE 2: $value(CT.cond) \leq 0$ is proven analogously.

Mapping an *ASSIGN* is straightforward to prove. The proof is based on the assumption that the addresses are mapped correctly and the values computed are the same. Mapping a *VAR* is more complicated to prove. We must distinguish between global and local variables and only consider the latter. Then the proof relies on the fact that for a local variable x $bind(b, x)$ is mapped onto $local \oplus_A reladdr(b, x)$. The simulation is correct if

$$reladdr(b, x) = reladdr(b, y) \Rightarrow x = y \qquad (2)$$

i.e., *reladdr* is injective for every procedure b. Since *reladdr* is computed by the compiler, property (2) is a good candidate for program checking.   □

The next step is to perform the transformations. After constructing the IS/MIS ASMs it is possible to execute MIS-instructions as well as IS-tasks. We also allow MIS-instructions as statements. Therefore we need not to change the state space. In particular, there is no need to distinguish optimizing transformations from the transformations for intermediate code generation. However, intermediate instructions changing control need to be changed, since CT must be updated, e.g. the rule for conditional jumps (cf. Example 2) becomes

if $CT \in IF$ **then**
    if $div\_by\_zero(src(CT))$ **then** $exception := $ "`div_by_zero`"
    elsif $overflow(src(CT))$ **then** $exception := $ "`arithmetic_overflow`"
    elsif $mem\_overflow(src(CT))$ **then** $exception := $ "`memory_overflow`"
    elsif $eval(src(CT)) > 0$
    then $CT := labeltotask(truetarget(CT))$
    else $CT := labeltotask(falsetarget(CT))$

In general, the correctness of a simulation is deduced by induction over the number of applied rules. Therefore we only need to consider single transformations and to study the local effects:

Example 8. We first consider the transformations in Fig. 9. Let q be the initial state of *EXPR*, q_1 the state executing the task *WHILE*, q_2 the state for any_2 and q_3 the initial state of *STATS*. Let q' be the state where $q' \models CT = $ ifjmp$(EXPR, L_1, L_2)$. We define the relation ρ such that $q' \; \rho \; q$ and identity otherwise

Lemma 1. *For all integers v:*
$q \models eval(EXPR) = v \;\Leftrightarrow\; q_1 \models value(CT.cond) = v.$

Lemma 2. *For all dynamic functions f except CT and all terms $t_1, \ldots, t_n, t$ which do not contain CT':*

$$q \models f(t_1, \ldots, t_n) = t \land eval(EXPR) > 0 \Rightarrow q_1 \models f(t_1, \ldots, t_n) = t$$

By help of these lemmas and sub-casing we conclude identity of states:
CASE 1: $q' \models eval(EXPR) > 0$. Then by definition of ρ, $q \models eval(EXPR) > 0$. Lemma 1 implies that $q_1 \models CT = t \in WHILE \land value(CT.cond) > 0$. By the state transitions for *WHILE* $q_3 \models CT = t.TT$. Furthermore from lemma 2 we know

$$q \models f(t_1, \ldots, t_n) = t \land eval(EXPR) > 0 \Rightarrow q_3 \models f(t_1, \ldots, t_n) = t$$

under the assumptions of the lemma. Let q'_3 be the state after q'. Then $q'_3 \models CT = tasktolab(L1) = t.TT$ holds. Furthermore, it is easy to see that

$$q' \models f(t_1, \ldots, t_n) = t \land eval(EXPR) > 0 \Rightarrow q_3 \models f(t_1, \ldots, t_n) = t$$

under the assumptions of lemma 2. By definition of ρ it holds

$$q' \models f(t_1, \ldots, t_n) = t \land eval(EXPR) > 0 \Leftrightarrow q_3 \models f(t_1, \ldots, t_n) = t.$$

Hence $q'_3 = q_3$.
CASE 2: $q' \models eval(EXPR) \le 0$ is proven analogously.

Consider now the proof for the assignment, Fig 10. Let q be the initial state of *DES*, q_1 the initial state of *EXPR*, q_2 the state for $t \in ASSIGN$, q_3 the state after t and q' the state executing the intassign-instruction. We define ρ such that $q'\ \rho\ q$ and otherwise identity on all dynamic functions except $value$ and $addr$. Let q_3' be the state after q'. We have to show that $q_3' = q_3$ except for $value$ and $addr$. We start with the following lemmas:

Lemma 3. *For all addresses* a: $q \models eval(DES) = a \Rightarrow q_1 \models addr(t) = a$ *where* t *is the last task of* DES.

Lemma 4. *For all integer values* v:

$$q \models eval(EXPR) = v \Rightarrow q_1 \models value(CT.src) = v.$$

Lemma 5. q_1 *interprets all dynamic functions as* q *except* CT *and* $addr$.

Lemma 6. q_2 *interprets all dynamic functions as* q_1 *except* CT *and* $value$.

For simplicity we omit overflows. The state transition for intassign shows that q_3' remains unchanged w.r.t. q' except that now $q_3' \models content(a) = v$ where $q' \models eval(DES) = a \wedge eval(EXPR) = v$. From the above lemmas and the state transitions for $ASSIGN$ the same follows for q_3. Hence, $q_3'\ \rho\ q_3$.   □

The graph-transformations result in a set of directed paths where exactly the first task is labeled. Each of these paths represent a basic block. Therefore, it is straightforward to map CT to the pair (CL, IP). Again, it is not hard to prove a general 1-1-simulation.

Now we consider the basic block language MIS. For constructing basic-block graphs with DEC-Alpha commands, we first map the pointers *local* and *topofheap* to registers $R0$ and $R1$ (as proposed by the DEC-Alpha-Manual). The basic approach for proving the correctness of the code generation is similar to the one for intermediate code generation. However, there are some problems with the decomposition to local correctness conditions.

Example 9. Consider the following instruction of a basic block:

intassign(addr(8), intplus(intcont(addr(8)), intcont(addr(16))))

and the term-rewrite rules:

$$intcont(addr(intconst_i)) \rightarrow X \qquad \{\text{LD } X\ i(R0)\} \qquad (3)$$

$$intplus(X, Y) \rightarrow Z \qquad \{\text{ADD } X\ Y\ Z\} \qquad (4)$$

$$intassign(addr(intconst_i), X) \rightarrow \bullet \qquad \{\text{STR } i(R0)\ x\} \qquad (5)$$

The nonterminals X, Y, Z stand for arbitrary registers. It is not hard to see that the rules are locally correct. Suppose we apply the rules in the following order with the following register assignments:

(3) on intcont(addr(8)) $X/R2$
                    yields intassign(addr(8), intplus($R2$, intcont(addr(16))))

(3) on intcont(addr(16)) $X/R2$
                         yields intassign(addr(8), intplus($R2$, $R2$))

(4) on intplus($R2$, $R2$) $X/R2\ Y/R2\ Z/R2$
                              yields intassign(addr(8), $R2$)

(5) on intassign(addr(8), $R2$) $X/R2$
Then the following code is produced:

LD $R2$ 8($R0$)
LD $R2$ 16($R0$)
ADD $R2$ $R2$ $R2$
STR 8($R0$) $R2$

This code is obviously wrong: a value is written to $R2$ although $R2$ contains a value which is still required. In [52] sufficient conditions are given for avoiding this situation. These conditions can be checked at compile-time.   □

After applying term-rewriting, the result is a basic-block graph with DEC-Alpha instructions. These instructions can already be binary encoded except jump instructions. The assembly phase stores the program into the memory and encodes jump instructions (short jumps, long jumps, or removal of jumps). The simulation proof requires that the following condition is satisfied:

> If the first instruction of a basic block starts at address a, then all preceding blocks b satisfy one of the following properties:
> - the last instruction of b is directly before a
> - the last instruction is at address a' and the command is a jump with relative address $a - a'$
> - the last instruction is at address a' and the command is a jump using a register containing a.
> Furthermore all instructions of a basic block are mapped consecutively.

Again this conditions can be checked with the approach of program checking.

6.2   Implementation of the Compiler Specification

Implementations of term-rewrite systems can be cost controlled. They use complex algorithms and heuristics, because — depending on the class of the rewrite system — problems are in NP. Additionally, for a practical compiler we need register allocators and instruction schedulers which are usually integrated into the generator that produces the code selector implementation from specifications. The back-end tool BEG, [18], generates the code selector from a set of term-rewrite rules annotated with costs and mappings to target machine code. The implementation consists of a tree pattern match phase, that finds a cost minimal cover of the program tree w.r.t. the rewrite rules. Afterwards register allocation and code emitting traversals are initiated. It is practically impossible to verify the generated C-code. We avoid this by applying program checking for verifying the results of the back-end.

The complete code selection part with register allocation and scheduling generated by the back-end can be encapsulated for checking. The correctness requirements to be checked are derived from global conditions. Figure 13 shows the architecture of the checked back-end. Input to the BEG generated part is the basic-block-graph (BBG), output is an annotated graph with rewriting attributes (ABBG).

The checker passes the concrete ABBG at runtime to the transformation phase or rejects it with an error message which finally performs the rewrite

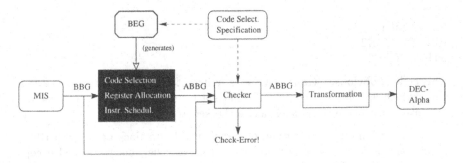

Fig. 13. Architecture checked back-end

Basic-Block-Graph

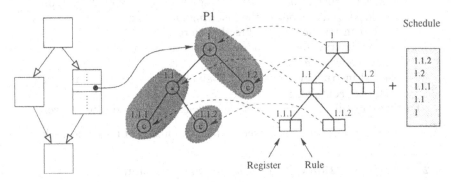

Fig. 14. Checking attributed basic-block-graphs

sequence and emits the target (DEC-Alpha) code. Attributes per ABBG node are the rule to be applied, the allocated register and an order number in the schedule in which the tree must be evaluated.

Figure 14 depicts the checking situation for the MIS expression

intadd(intmult(intconst(A),intconst(B)),intconst(C))

arising from the source language term $(A*B+C)$[1]. A typical set of code selection rules includes at least one rule for every intermediate language construct and additionally optimizing rules:

I: RULE intadd(X, Y) → Z { ADDQ X, Y, Z }
II: RULE intmult(X, Y) → Z { MULQ X, Y, Z }
III: RULE intconst[C] → X { LDA $X, \#C$(r31) }
IV: RULE intmult(intconst[C], X) → Y { MULQ $X, \#C, Y$ }
V: RULE intadd(X,intconst[C]) → Y { ADDQ $X, \#C, Y$ }

---

[1] This expression could of course be folded; we use this example for simplicity.

The parenthesized right column consists of concrete DEC-Alpha machine instructions implementing the semantics of the intermediate language pattern on the left hand side. The potential optimizations arise from the different possibilities to cover the tree, all of the possible covers are correct transformations. In our example the code selection algorithm decided to apply rules IV and V to subtrees 1.1-1.1.1 and 1-1.2 instead of applying the simpler rules I-III; In this case by this decision fewer instructions are emitted. The decision might be based on complex cost measurements that take instruction scheduling costs into account but this depends on the concrete back-end generator; proving the optimality of this process is not in the scope of our work. The checker checks whether the left hand side of a rule matches the corresponding subtree, and whether every register written does not contain a value which is read later. The latter can be checked using the register assignment and the schedule.

	Modula/Sather-K		Binary Prog.
	Lines	Byte	Byte
Generator BEG (Modula)	35.000	2 MB	1.1 MB
Generated C Code Impl. MIS Code-Selection	18.000	400 KB	500 KB
Checker (Sather-K)	500 (Parser) +300 (Checker) +400 (MIS)		200 KB
Industrial: ANDF ⇒ ST9	140.000	6.4 MB	3.5 MB

Table 1. Lines of program code to verify for example back-end

Our implementation language for the checker is Sather-K, an modern type-safe object-oriented language, [23]. The code generator generator BEG produces a C implementation with 18.000 lines of code, the generator tool is written in 35.000 lines of Modula-2 code. Table 1 compares lines of code and program sizes for our example; the relation of 1 to 15 in lines to verify shows the usefulness of program checking. [20] contains more details on a program checker for compiler back-ends.

We also applied our approach to a compiler front-end for a C subset IS, [17, 27]. For details, we refer to [26]. Table 2 shows the results.

	C/Sather-K		Binary Prog.
	Lines	Byte	Byte
Generators COCKTAIL	110.000	2.4 MB	1.2 MB
Generated C Code Impl. IS-Frontend	22.000	600 KB	300 KB
Checker (Sather-K)	500 (Parser) +100 (Compare) +700 (AST)	14 KB 3 KB 30 KB	200 KB

Table 2. Lines of program code to verify for a program-checked IS front-end

7 Related Work

Correctness of compilers was first considered in [32] but focused on the compilation of arithmetic expressions. Thereafter most people explored the potential of denotational semantics, e. g. [13, 34, 35, 39, 40, 43, 49], or of refinement calculi, e. g. [5, 7, 9, 14, 15, 28, 33, 37], structural operational semantics, e. g. [16] and algebraic models, e. g. [44]. Other approaches use abstract state machines, e. g. [6, 7, 9]. Most of these projects did not compile into machine language. Instead, they designed abstract machines, and compiled for interpreters of these abstract machines.

These semantics-based approaches lead to monolithic compilers, cf. [19, 47]. They do neither allow for reuse of traditional compiler technology nor do program reorganizations, as necessary for global optimization on the machine code level, fit into such schemes. E. g., expressions are usually refined into postfix form and then interpreted on a stack machine. The efficiency of the generated code is by magnitudes worse than that of other compilers and thus does not meet practical requirements, cf. [16, 38]. Except [33], even projects which really generated machine language, e. g. [5, 7, 36, 37], and ProCos, [28], chose the transputer, i. e., a stack machine, as their target. [33] discusses compilation of a stack-based intermediate language *Piton* into an assembly language of the register-based processor FM9001. The correctness proofs of the transformations as well as their implementation (in ACL2 logic) are checked mechanically using the ACL2 interpreter. In contrast to our work, the compilation is a macro-expansion and the source programs must be terminating regularly.

The idea of program checking was originally applied to algorithms in [1] and continued in [2, 3, 50]. [22] discusses its application to constructing correct systems. [41, 42] apply the idea to translating synchronous languages (SIGNAL, Lustre, Statecharts) to C-programs; however, their assumptions allow only for (reactive) source programs consisting of a single loop; the loop body must implement a function from inputs to outputs; only the loop body is checked.

Many languages have been described so far using abstract state machines, e. g. C [25], C++ [48], Prolog/WAM [9], Occam/Transputer [6, 7], Java [12], Java Virtual Machine [10, 11, 51], APE100 [4], ARM2 [29], DEC-Alpha [21], DLX [8].

8   Conclusions

For verifying practically useful compilers for realistic programming languages such as C, C++ or native code compilers for JAVA wie need to cope with resource limitations, the less than ideal properties of machine code and to reuse the methods of compiler technology as developed so far. Especially, the use of generators in compiler front-ends and for code selection, and the techniques for code optimization are very important in practice.

We have shown how we can deal with compiler correctness such that these techniques remain applicable. Practical experience shows that it is possible to achieve correctness for front-ends, optimizers, and code generators by help of program checking.

The verification of specifications, of the program checkers, and of the transformation from an attributed tree to some form of low-level intermediate language requires elaborate verification methods supported by tools. To this end project Verifix has developed detailed methods based on PVS which we have not discussed in this paper. Also we have not discussed how to arrive at an initially correct compiler whose source language may then be used for implementing the compiler as described here.

In summary we have shown that writing correct compilers can be mastered also for practically interesting languages although it will remain a tedious task for the foreseeable future.

Acknowledgments: We thank the anonymous referees and J. Moore for carefully reading the paper. We are grateful to Hans Langmaack, Friedrich W. von Henke, Axel Dold, Thilo Gaul, Wolfgang Goerigk, Andreas Heberle, Ulrich Hoffmann, Markus Müller-Olm, Holger Pfeifer, Harald Rueß and many students in Karlsruhe, Kiel and Ulm for their contributions to the Verifix project which made this paper possible. The Verifix project is supported by the Deutsche Forschungsgemeinschaft under contract numbers Go 323/3-2, He 2411/2-2, La 426/15-2.

References

1. M. Blum and S. Kannan. Program correctness checking ... and the design of programs that check their work. In *Proceedings 21st Symposium on Theory of Computing*, 1989.
2. M. Blum, M. Luby, and R. Rubinfeld. Self–testing/correcting with applications to numerical problems. In *Proceedings 22nd Symposium on Theory of Computing*, 1990.
3. Manuel Blum and Sampath Kannan. Designing programs that check their work. *Journal of the ACM*, 42(1):269–291, January 1995.

4. E. Börger, G. Del Castillo, P. Glavan, and D. Rosenzweig. Towards a Mathematical Specification of the APE100 Architecture: the APESE Model. In B. Pehrson and I. Simon, editors, *IFIP 13th World Computer Congress*, volume I: Technology/Foundations, pages 396–401, Elsevier, Amsterdam, the Netherlands, 1994.

5. E. Börger and I. Durdanovic. Correctness of compiling occam to transputer. *The Computer Journal*, 39(1):52–92, 1996.

6. E. Börger and I. Durdanovic. Correctness of Compiling Occam to Transputer code. *The Computer Journal*, 39:52–93, 1996.

7. E. Börger, I. Durdanovic, and D. Rosenzweig. Occam: Specification and Compiler Correctness.Part I: The Primary Model. In U. Montanari and E.-R. Olderog, editors, *Proc. Procomet'94 (IFIP TC2 Working Conference on Programming Concepts, Methods and Calculi)*. North-Holland, 1994.

8. E. Börger and S. Mazzanti. A Practical Method for Rigorously Controllable Hardware Design. In J.P. Bowen, M.B. Hinchey, and D. Till, editors, *ZUM'97: The Z Formal Specification Notation*, volume 1212 of *LNCS*, pages 151–187. Springer, 1997.

9. E. Börger and D. Rosenzweig. *The WAM-definition and Compiler Correctness.* North-Holland Series in Computer Science and Artificial Intelligence. Beierle, L.C. and Pluemer, L., 1994.

10. E. Börger and W. Schulte. A Modular Design for the Java VM architecture. In E. Börger, editor, *Architecture Design and Validation Methods*. Springer, 1998.

11. E. Börger and W. Schulte. Defining the Java Virtual Machine as Platform for Provably Correct Java Compilation. In *23rd International Symposium on Mathematical Foundations of Computer Science*, LNCS. Springer, 1998. To appear.

12. E. Börger and W. Schulte. Programmer Friendly Modular Definition of the Semantics of Java. In J. Alves-Foss, editor, *Formal Syntax and Semantics of Java*, LNCS. Springer, 1998.

13. D. F. Brown, H. Moura, and D. A. Watt. Actress: an action semantics directed compiler generator. In *Compiler Compilers 92*, volume 641 of *LNCS*, 1992.

14. B. Buth, K.-H. Buth, M. Fränzle, B. v. Karger, Y. Lakhneche, H. Langmaack, and M. Müller-Olm. Provably correct compiler development and implementation. In U. Kastens and P. Pfahler, editors, *Compiler Construction*, volume 641 of *LNCS*. Springer-Verlag, 1992.

15. B. Buth and M. Müller-Olm. Provably Correct Compiler Implementation. In *Tutorial Material – Formal Methods Europe '93*, pages 451–465, Denmark, April 1993. IFAD Odense Teknikum.

16. Stephan Diehl. *Semantics-Directed Generation of Compilers and Abstract Machines*. PhD thesis, Universität des Saarlandes, Germany, 1996.

17. A. Dold, T. Gaul, W. Goerigk, G. Goos, A. Heberle F. von Henke, U. Hoffmann, H. Langmaack, H. Pfeiffer, H. Ruess, and W. Zimmermann. The semantics of a while language IS₀. Working paper, The VERIFIX Group, July '95, 1995.

18. H. Emmelmann, F.-W. Schröer, and R. Landwehr. Beg - a generator for efficient back ends. In *ACM Proceedings of the Sigplan Conference on Programming Language Design and Implementation*, June 1989.

19. David A. Espinosa. *Semantic Lego*. PhD thesis, Columbia University, 1995.

20. T. Gaul, A. Heberle, W. Zimmermann, and W. Goerigk. Construction of Verified Software Systems with Program-Checking: An Application To Compiler Back-Ends. In *Proceedings of the Federated Logics Conference (FloC99) Workshop on Runtime Result Verification*, Trento, Italy, 1999. Electronic Proceedings, URL:http://afrodite.itc.it:1024/~leaf/rtrv/proc/proc.html.

21. T.S. Gaul. An Abstract State Machine Specification of the DEC-Alpha Processor Family. Verifix Working Paper [Verifix/UKA/4], University of Karlsruhe, 1995.
22. Wolfgang Goerigk, Thilo Gaul, and Wolf Zimmermann. Correct Programs without Proof? On Checker-Based Program Verification. In *Proceedings ATOOLS'98 Workshop on "Tool Support for System Specification, Development, and Verification"*, Advances in Computing Science, Malente, 1998. Springer Verlag. Accepted for Publication.
23. Gerhard Goos. Sather-k — the language. *Software — Concepts and Tools*, 18:91–109, 1997.
24. Y. Gurevich. Evolving Algebras: Lipari Guide. In E. Börger, editor, *Specification and Validation Methods*. Oxford University Press, 1995.
25. Y. Gurevich and J. Huggins. The Semantics of the C Programming Language. In *CSL '92*, volume 702 of *LNCS*, pages 274–308. Springer-Verlag, 1993.
26. A. Heberle, T. Gaul, W. Goerigk, G. Goos, and W. Zimmermann. Construction of Verified Compiler Front-Ends with Program-Checking. In *Proceedings of PSI '99: Andrei Ershov Third International Conference on Perspectives Of System Informatics*, pages 370–377, Novosibirsk, Russia, 1999.
27. Andreas Heberle and Dirk Heuzeroth. The formal specification of IS. Technical Report [Verifix/UKA/2 revised], IPD, Universität Karlsruhe, January 1998.
28. C.A.R. Hoare, He Jifeng, and A. Sampaio. Normal Form Approach to Compiler Design. *Acta Informatica*, 30:701–739, 1993.
29. J. Huggins and D. Van Campenhout. Specification and Verification of Pipelining in the ARM2 RISC Microprocessor. *ACM Transactions on Design Automation of Electronic Systems*, 3(4):563–580, October 1998.
30. T.M.V. Janssen. Algebraic translations, correctness and algebraic compiler construction. *Theoretical Computer Science*, 199:25–56, 1998.
31. P. W. Kutter and A. Pierantonio. Montages specifications of realisitic programming languages. *Journal of Universal Computer Science*, 3(5):416–442, 1997.
32. John McCarthy and J. Painter. Correctness of a compiler for arithmetic expressions. In Schwartz [45], pages 33–41.
33. J S. Moore. *Piton, A Mechanically Verified Assembly-Level Language*. Kluwer Academic Publishers, 1996.
34. P. D. Mosses. Abstract semantic algebras. In D. Bjørner, editor, *Formal description of programming concepts II*, pages 63–88. IFIP IC-2 Working Conference, North Holland, 1982.
35. P. D. Mosses. *Action Semantics*. Cambridge University Press, 1992.
36. Markus Müller-Olm. An Exercise in Compiler Verification. Internal report, CS Department, Universität Kiel, 1995.
37. Markus Müller-Olm. *Modular Compiler Verification*, volume 1283 of *Lecture Notes in Computer Science*. Springer-Verlag, 1996.
38. J. Palsberg. An automatically generated and provably correct compiler for a subset of ada. In *IEEE International Conference on Computer Languages*, 1992.
39. Jens Palsberg. *Provably Correct Compiler Generation*. PhD thesis, Department of Computer Science, University of Aarhus, 1992. xii+224 pages.
40. L. Paulson. *A compiler generator for semantic grammars*. PhD thesis, Stanford University, 1981.
41. A. Pnueli, M. Siegel, and E. Singermann. Translation validation. In *Tools and Algorithms for the Construction and Analysis of Systems*, volume 1384 of *Lecture Notes in Computer Science*, pages 151–166. Springer-Verlag, 1998.
42. Amir Pnueli, O. Shtrichman, and M. Siegel. The code validation tool (cvt). *Int. J. on Software Tools for Technology Transfer*, 2(2):192–201, 1998.

43. W. Polak. *Compiler Specification and Verification*, volume 124 of *LNCS*. Springer-Verlag, Berlin, Heidelberg, New York, 1981.
44. T. Rus. Algebraic processing of programming languages. *Theoretical Computer Science*, 199:105–143, 1998.
45. J. T. Schwartz, editor. *Mathematical Aspects of Computer Science*, Proc. Symp. in Appl. Math., RI, 1967. Am. Math. Soc.
46. Ken Thompson. Reflections on Trusting Trust. *Communications of the ACM*, 27(8):761–763, 1984.
47. M. Tofte. *Compiler Generators*. Springer-Verlag, 1990.
48. C. Wallace. The Semantics of the C++–Programming Language. In E. Börger, editor, *Specification and Validation Methods*. Oxford University Press, 1995.
49. M. Wand. A semantic prototyping system. *SIGPLAN Notices*, 19(6):213–221, June 1984. SIGPLAN 84 Symp. On Compiler Construction.
50. Hal Wasserman and Manuel Blum. Software reliability via run-time result-checking. *Journal of the ACM*, 44(6):826–849, November 1997.
51. W. Zimmermann and T. Gaul. An Abstract State Machine for Java Byte Code. Verifix Working Paper [Verifix/UKA/12], University of Karlsruhe, 1997.
52. W. Zimmermann and T. Gaul. On the Construction of Correct Compiler Back-Ends: An ASM Approach. *Journal of Universal Computer Science*, 3(5):504–567, 1997.

Translation Validation: From SIGNAL to C * **

A. Pnueli, O. Shtrichman, and M. Siegel

Weizmann Institute of Science, Rehovot, Israel

Abstract. *Translation validation* is an alternative to the verification of translators (compilers, code generators). Rather than proving in advance that the compiler always produces a target code which correctly implements the source code (compiler verification), each individual translation (i.e. a run of the compiler) is followed by a validation phase which verifies that the target code produced on this run correctly implements the submitted source program. In order to be a practical alternative to compiler verification, a key feature of this validation is its *full automation*.

Since the validation process attempts to "unravel" the transformation effected by the translators, its task becomes increasingly more difficult (and necessary) with the increase of sophistication and variety of the optimizations methods employed by the translator. In this paper we address the practicability of translation validation for highly optimizing, industrial code generators from SIGNAL, a widely used synchronous language, to C. We introduce new abstraction techniques as part of the automation of our approach.

1 Introduction

A significant number of embedded systems contain safety-critical aspects. There is an increasing industrial awareness of the fact that the application of formal specification languages and their corresponding verification/validation techniques may significantly reduce the risk of design errors in the development of such systems. However, if the validation efforts are focused on the specification level, the question arises how can we ensure that the quality and integrity achieved at the specification level is safely transferred to the implementation level. Today's process of the development of such systems consists of hand-coding followed by extensive unit and integration-testing.

The highly desirable alternative, both from a safety and a productivity point of view, to automatically generate code from verified/validated specifications, has failed in the past due to the lack of technology which could convincingly demonstrate to certification authorities the correctness of the generated code. Although there are many examples of compiler verification in the literature (see,

---

* This research was done as part of the ESPRIT project SACRES and was supported in part by the Minerva Foundation and an infra-structure grant from the Israeli Ministry of Science and Art

** Preliminary versions of some parts of this paper were published before in [17], [19] and [20]

E.-R. Olderog, B. Steffen (Eds.): Correct System Design, LNCS 1710, pp. 231–255, 1999.
© Springer-Verlag Berlin Heidelberg 1999

for-example, [5, 9, 10, 15, 12, 11, 14, 13]), the formal verification of industrial code generators is generally prohibitive due to their size. Another problem with compiler verification is that the formal verification freezes the design and evolution of the compiler, as each change to the code generators nullifies their previous correctness proof.

Alternately, code-validation suggests to construct a fully automatic tool which establishes the correctness of the generated code individually for each run of the code generator. In general, code-validation can be the key enabling technology to allow the usage of code generators in the development cycle of safety-critical and high-quality systems. The combination of automatic code generation and validation improves the design flow of embedded systems in both safety and productivity by eliminating the need for hand-coding of the target code (and consequently coding-errors are less probable) and by considerably reducing unit/integration test efforts.

Of course, it is not clear that every compiler and every source and target languages can be verified according to the code-validation paradigm. But the fact that the compiler we considered was highly optimized and the source and target languages had completely different structures (synchronous versus sequential code) indicates that this method has the potential of solving realistic, non-trivial cases.

The work carried out in the SACRES project proves the feasibility of code-validation for the industrial code generator used in the project, and demonstrates that industrial-size programs can be verified fully automatically in a reasonable amount of time.

1.1   Technical Introduction

In this paper we consider translation validation for the synchronous languages Signal [3]. This language is mainly used in industrial applications for the development of safety-critical, reactive systems. In particular, it is designed to be translatable into code which is as time/space efficient as handwritten code. This code is generated by sophisticated code generators which perform various analyses/calculations on the source code in order to derive highly efficient implementations in languages such as C, ADA, or JAVA.

The presented translation validation approach addresses two industrial compilers from SIGNAL to C. These compilers – which apply more than 100 optimization rules during code generation [16] – were developed in the ESPRIT project SACRES by the French company TNI and by Inria (Rennes) and are used by Siemens, SNECMA and British Aerospace. Their formal verification is prohibitive due to their size (more than 20,000 lines of code each) and the fact that they are constantly improved/extended.

While developed in the context of code generators for synchronous languages, the proposed method has wider applicability. The main feature which enables us to perform the validation task algorithmically is that the source language has a restricted explicit control structure. This is also represented by the fact that the resulting C-code consists of a single main loop whose body is a loop-free program. Source languages with these features can benefit from the method proposed in this paper. For example, the language UNITY [6] which comes from the world of asynchronous distributed systems is another possible client of the proposed method.

We present a common semantic model for SIGNAL and C, introduce the applied notion of *being a correct implementation*, formulate the correctness of the generated C code as proof obligations in first order logic, and present efficient decision procedures to check the correctness of the generated proof obligations. All translations and constructions which are presented in the course of the paper have been implemented in a tool called CVT (Code Validation Tool) [19]. CVT has been used to validate the code generated from a 6000 lines SIGNAL program with more than 1000 variables. This program is a turbine-control system which was developed as an industrial case study by SNECMA in the SACRES project.

A major advantage of a carefully designed translation validation tool is that it can replace the need for correctness proofs for *various* compilers if these compilers are based on the same definition of "correct code generation". This is the case for the TNI and the Inria compiler and, indeed, CVT is used to validate code originating from either of these two compilers.

1.2   Run Time Result Verification

There is a growing interest in the concept of verifying run-time results, rather than programs or models. A recently held workshop entitled "run-time result verification" presented various applications of run-time verification techniques. These applications, in most cases, had similar characteristics to compiler verification, although they come from a variety of domains: it is very hard, or even impossible to formally verify them in the 'traditional', single-time proof on the one hand, and on the other hand, their design often changes while the system is developed. Another motivation for this approach is that in some cases the program itself is not available for inspection due to commercial and intellectual property factors[1]. A good example of such a domain is the formal verification of decision procedures. Implementations of Decision procedures are often experimental and not very robust. They are typically complex and keep evolving over time. Being generic tools for verifying safety-critical systems, the correctness of the tools is at least as important as that of the applications they help to verify. In [21], the decision procedure generates proofs during run-time, in order to validate the decision process. An axiomatization of the proof system is presented in another formal system, which is referred to as the 'logical framework' in which the proof is carried out. The logical framework tool includes a proof checker of its own, that can check proofs of any system that is axiomatized in the framework. This enables automatic validation of every run of the decision procedure

---

[1] this is also a common argument in the domain of testing, where often 'black-box' testing is used rather than 'white-box' testing simply because the code is not available for inspection

by producing a proof script for the run and applying to it the framework's proof checker.

The concept of validating translators/compilers by proving semantical equivalence between source and target code has been applied in various other projects. In [22] and [8] the verification of the translator from a high level description language to executable code is carried out in two distinct stages: in the 'on-line' stage, each run of the translator is verified by proving several simple conditions on the syntactical structure of the results, in comparison to the source code. This stage is fully automatic and implemented by a simple 'checker'. The reduction from full translation verification to these simple rules is carried out manually in a one-time effort (the 'off-line' stage) by an expert. This approach was applicable in their case due to the relatively structured translation scheme of the source code. A declaration in the source code is translated into code which performs RNS transformations (it reduces arithmetical operations to a set of independent arithmetic operations on integers of limited size). Thus, the main task of the validation process is to verify that these transformations are correct. After computing a mapping between the input and output variables of the source and target programs, they prove that the correspondence between the 'semantic' states of the two programs is preserved by the execution steps. In this sense there model is similar to the model we will present in this paper. In [7], translation validation is done on a purely syntactic level. Their method is based on finding a bijection between abstract and concrete instruction sets (resp. variables) because they are considering a *structural* translation of one sequential program into another sequential program. Since we are dealing with optimizing compilers we have to employ a far more involved *semantic* approach.

The rest of the paper is organized as follows. In Section 2 we give a brief introduction to SIGNAL and present a running example. After introducing *synchronous transition systems* as our model of computation in Section 3 we address the formal semantics of SIGNAL. Section 4 presents the concepts which underly the generation of the proof obligations. In Section 5 we present the decision procedure to check the validity of these proof obligations. Finally, Section 7 contains some conclusions and future perspectives.

2   An Illustrative Example

In this section we first illustrate details of the compilation process by means of an example and then explain the principles which underly the translation validation process.

A SIGNAL program describes a reactive system whose behavior along time is an infinite sequence of *instants* which represent reactions, triggered by external or internal events. The main objects manipulated by a SIGNAL program are *flows*, which are sequences of values synchronized with a *clock*. A flow is a typed object which holds a value at each instant of its clock. The fact that a flow is currently absent is represented by the bottom symbol $\perp$ (cf. [3]). Clocks are unary flows, assuming the values $\{T, \perp\}$. A clock has the value T if and only if the flow associated with the clock holds a value at the present instant of time. Actually, any expression *exp* in the language has its corresponding clock *clk(exp)* which indicates whether the value of the expression at the current instant is different from $\bot$.

Besides *external* flows (input/output flows), which determine the interface of the SIGNAL program with its environment, also *internal* flows are used and manipulated by the program. Consider the following SIGNAL program DEC:

```
process DEC=
    ( ? integer FB
      ! integer N
    )
      (| N:= FB default (ZN-1)
       | ZN:= N $ init 1
       | FB^=when (ZN<=1)
       |)
    where
        integer ZN init 1 ;
end
```

Program DEC (standing for "decrement") has an input FB and an output N, both declared as integer variables. Now and then, the environment provides a new input via variable FB. Receiving a new positive input, the program starts an internal process which outputs the sequence of values FB, FB-1, ..., 2, 1 via output variable N. After outputting 1, the program is ready for the next input. This program illustrates the capability of a multi-clock synchronous language to generate a new clock (the clock of the output N) which over-samples the input clock associated with FB. The program uses the local variable ZN to record the previous value of N.

The body of DEC is composed of three statements which are executed concurrently as follows. An input FB is read and copied to N. If N is greater than 1 it is successively decremented by referring to ZN, which holds the previous value of N (using $ to denote the "previous value" operator). No new input value for FB is accepted until ZN becomes (or is, in case of a previous non-positive input value for FB) less than or equal to 1. This is achieved by the statement

```
FB^=when (ZN<=1),
```

which is read "the *clock* of FB is on when ZN $\leq$ 1", and allows FB to be present only when ZN $\leq$ 1. When the clock of FB is off, the `default` action of assigning N the value of ZN-1 is activated. A possible computation of this program is:

$$\begin{pmatrix} FB : \bot \\ N : \bot \\ ZN : 1 \end{pmatrix} \rightarrow \begin{pmatrix} FB : 3 \\ N : 3 \\ ZN : 1 \end{pmatrix} \rightarrow \begin{pmatrix} FB : \bot \\ N : 2 \\ ZN : 3 \end{pmatrix} \rightarrow \begin{pmatrix} FB : \bot \\ N : 1 \\ ZN : 2 \end{pmatrix} \rightarrow \begin{pmatrix} FB : 5 \\ N : 5 \\ ZN : 1 \end{pmatrix} \rightarrow \begin{pmatrix} FB : \bot \\ N : 4 \\ ZN : 5 \end{pmatrix} \rightarrow \ldots$$

Where $\bot$ denotes the absence of a signal. Note, that SIGNAL programs are not expected to terminate.

2.1   Compilation of Multi-clocked Synchronous Languages

The compilation scheme for SIGNAL to an imperative, sequential languages (s.a. C, ADA) proceeds as follows. The statements of a SIGNAL program P form a *Set of Logical Equations* (SLE) on the flows of P and their associated clocks. Solutions of SLE for a given set of input/register values determine the next state of the system. The compiler derives from P an imperative program C which consists of one main loop whose task is to repeatedly compute such solutions of the SLE. In order to do so, the compiler computes from SLE a *conditional* dependency graph on flows and another linear equation system – the, so called, *clock calculus* [3] – which records the dependencies amongst clocks. The produced code contains statements originating from the clock calculus and assignments to variables (representing the flows of P) whose order must be consistent with the dependency graph. These assignments are performed if the corresponding flow is currently present in the source program, i.e. the clocks of flows determine the control structure of the generated program.

The C program which is generated by the compiler from the DEC program consists of a main program containing two functions:

- An *initialization* function, which is called once to provide initial values to the program variables.
- An *iteration* function which is called repeatedly in an infinite loop. This function, whose body calculates the effect of one synchronous "step" of the abstract program, is the essential part of the concrete code.

The iteration function obtained by compiling DEC is given by:

```
logical DEC_iterate()
```

```
{
10:    h1_c = TRUE;
11:    h2_c = ZN_c <= 1;
12:    if (h2_c)
12.1:      read(FB_c);
13:    if (h2_c)
13.1:      N_c = FB_c;
       else
13.2:      N_c = ZN_c - 1;
14:    write(N_c);
15:    ZN_c = N_c;
       return TRUE;
}
```

The labels in function DEC_iterate() are not generated by the compiler but have been added for reference. We added 'c' as subscript for the program variables, to distinguish them from the SIGNAL variables.

The C-code introduces explicit boolean variables to represent the clocks of SIGNAL variables. Variable $h1_c$ is the clock of N_c and ZN_c, and $h2_c$ is the clock of FB_c.

The C program works as follows. If $h2_c$, the clock of FB_c, has the value T, a new value for FB is read and assigned to the variable N_c. If $h2_c$ is F, N_c gets the value $ZN_c - 1$. In both cases the updated value of N is output (at l_4) and also copied into ZN_c, for reference in the next step .

A computation of this program is given below. We skip intermediate states and consider complete iterations of the while loop. The notation $X : *$ is used to denote that variable X has an arbitrary value.

$$
\begin{pmatrix} FB : * \\ N : * \\ ZN : 1 \\ h1 : * \\ h2 : * \\ \pi : l_0 \end{pmatrix} \xrightarrow{*}
\begin{pmatrix} FB : 3 \\ N : 3 \\ ZN : 3 \\ h1 : T \\ h2 : T \\ \pi : l_0 \end{pmatrix} \xrightarrow{*}
\begin{pmatrix} FB : 3 \\ N : 2 \\ ZN : 2 \\ h1 : T \\ h2 : F \\ \pi : l_0 \end{pmatrix} \xrightarrow{*}
\begin{pmatrix} FB : 3 \\ N : 1 \\ ZN : 1 \\ h1 : T \\ h2 : F \\ \pi : l_0 \end{pmatrix} \xrightarrow{*}
\begin{pmatrix} FB : 5 \\ N : 5 \\ ZN : 5 \\ h1 : T \\ h2 : T \\ \pi : l_0 \end{pmatrix} \xrightarrow{*}
\begin{pmatrix} FB : 5 \\ N : 4 \\ ZN : 4 \\ h1 : T \\ h2 : F \\ \pi : l_0 \end{pmatrix} \xrightarrow{*} \cdots
$$

Taking into account that $h1_c$ is the clock of N_c and that $h2_c$ is the clock of FB_c, we have an accurate state correspondence between the computation of the SIGNAL program and the computation of the C-code, when we restrict our observations to subsequent visits at location l_0.

This state correspondence is a general pattern for programs generated by the SACRES compiler. Intuitively, the generated C-code correctly implements the original SIGNAL program if the sequence of states obtained at the designated control location l_0 corresponds to a possible sequence of states in the abstract system.

In the rest of the paper, we show how this approach can be formalized and yield a fully automatic translation validation process.

3   Computational Model and Semantics of SIGNAL

In order to present the formal semantics of SIGNAL we introduce a variant of *synchronous transition systems* (STS) [20]. STS is the computational model of our translation validation approach.

Let V be a set of typed variables. A *state* s over V is a type-consistent interpretation of the variables in V. Let Σ_V denote the set of all states over V. A *synchronous transition system* $A = (V, \Theta, \rho)$ consists of a finite set V of typed variables, a satisfiable assertion Θ characterizing the initial states of system A, and a transition relation ρ. This is an assertion $\rho(V, V')$, which relates a state $s \in \Sigma_V$ to its possible successors $s' \in \Sigma_V$ by referring to both unprimed and primed versions of variables in V. Unprimed variables are interpreted according to s, primed variables according to s'. To the state space of an STS A we refer as Σ_A. We will also use the term "system" to abbreviate "synchronous transition system". Some of the variables in V are identified as *volatile* while the others are identified as *persistent*. Volatile variables represent flows of SIGNAL programs, thus their domains contain the designated element $\perp$ to indicate absence of the respective flow.

For a variable $v \in V$ we write $clk(v)$ and $clk(v')$ to denote the inequalities $v \neq \bot$ and $v' \neq \bot$, implying that the signal v or v' is present.

A *computation* of $A = (V, \Theta, \rho)$ is an infinite sequence $\sigma = \langle s_0, s_1, s_2, \ldots \rangle$, with $s_i \in \Sigma_v$ for each $i \in \mathbf{N}$, which satisfies $s_0 \models \Theta$ and $\forall i \in \mathbf{N}.\ (s_i, s_{i+1}) \models \rho$. Denote by $\|A\|$ the set of computations of the STS A.

Before we describe how to construct an STS Φ_P corresponding to a given SIGNAL program P, let us first describe the primitives of a SIGNAL program.

3.1   A Sketch of SIGNAL Primitives

SIGNAL supports the following primitives.

1.	$v := f(u_1, \ldots, u_n)$	function extended to sequences
2.	$w := v \, \$ \, \mathbf{init}\ w_0$	shift register
3.	$v := u \ \mathbf{when}\ b$	data dependent down-sampling
4.	$w := u \ \mathbf{default}\ v$	merging with priority
5.	$P|Q$	program composition

In these primitives, u, v, w, b denote typed *signals*, i.e., sequences of values of the considered type extended with the special symbol $\bot$. In the **when** expression, the b signal is assumed boolean. In the last instruction, both P and Q denote SIGNAL programs.

The assignment $v := f(u_1, \ldots, u_n)$ can only be applied to signals $u_1, \ldots, u_n$ which share the same clock. It defines a new signal v with the same clock such that, for every $i = 1, 2, \ldots, v[i] = f(u_1[i], \ldots, u_n[i])$.

The assignment $w := v \, \$ \, \mathbf{init}\ w_0$ defined a signal w with the same clock as v and such that $w[1] = w_0$ and, for every $i > 1$, $w[i] = v[i-1]$.

The assignment $v := u \ \mathbf{when}\ b$ defines a signal whose values equal the value of u at all instances in which u and b are both defined and $b = \mathit{true}$.

The assignment $w := u \ \mathbf{default}\ v$ defines a signal w which equals u whenever u is defined and equals v at all instance in which v is defined while u is absent.

Finally, $P|Q$ is the composition of the programs (set of statements) P and Q.

3.2   System Variables

The system variables of Φ are given by $V = U \cup X$, where U are the SIGNAL *signals* explicitly declared and manipulated in P, and X is a set of auxiliary *memorization variables*, whose role is explained below.

3.3   Initial Condition

The initial condition for Φ is given by

$$\Theta: \quad \bigwedge_{u \in U} u = \bot$$

By convention, the initial value of all declared signal variables is $\bot$. The initialization of memorization variables is explained in the following subsection.

3.4   The Transition Relation and Its Properties

The composition $|$ of SIGNAL programs corresponds to logical conjunction. Thus, the transition relation ρ will be a conjunction of assertions where each SIGNAL statement gives rise to a conjunct in ρ. Below, we list the statements of SIGNAL and present for each of them the conjunct it contributes to the transition relation.

- Consider the SIGNAL statement $v := f(u_1, \ldots, u_n)$, where f is a state-function. This statement contributes to ρ the following conjunct:

$$clk(u_1') \equiv \ldots \equiv clk(u_n')$$
$$\wedge \quad v' = \text{if } clk(u_1') \text{ then } f(u_1', \ldots, u_n') \text{ else } \bot$$

This formula requires that the signals $v, u_1, \ldots, u_n$ are present at precisely the same time instants, and that at these instants $v = f(u_1, \ldots, u_n)$.

- The statement

$$r := v \, \$ \, \text{init } w_0$$

contributes to ρ the conjunct:

$$m.r' = \text{ if } clk(v') \text{ then } v' \text{ else } m.r$$
$$\wedge \quad r' = \text{ if } clk(v') \text{ then } m.r \text{ else } \bot$$

This definition introduces a memorization variable $m.r$ which stores the last (including the present) non-bottom value of v. Variable $m.r$ is initialized in the initial condition Θ to w_0. From now on we refer to flows r that are defined by this type of statement as *register flows*. Variables in an STS which represent register flows will typically be denoted by r, and the corresponding memorization variables by $m.r$. Note that unlike the other system variables in the constructed STS, memorization variables are *persistent*.

- The statement

$$v := u \text{ when } b$$

contributes to ρ the conjunct:

$$v' = \text{ if } b' = \text{T then } u' \text{ else } \bot.$$

- The statement

$$w := u \text{ default } v$$

contributes to ρ the conjunct:

$$w' = \text{ if } clk(u') \text{ then } u' \text{ else } v'.$$

According to the above explanations, the SIGNAL program DEC is represented by the following STS $A = (V_a, \Theta_a, \rho_a)$.

$V = \{\text{FB, N, ZN, m.ZN}\}$

$\Theta = (\text{FB} = \bot \ \wedge\ \text{N} = \bot \ \wedge\ \text{ZN} = \bot \ \wedge\ \text{m.ZN} = 1)$

$$\rho_a = \left\{ \begin{array}{rll} \text{N}' & = \text{if } \text{FB}' \neq \bot \text{ then } \text{FB}' & \text{else } \text{ZN}' - 1 \\[2mm] \wedge \quad \text{m.ZN}' & = \text{if } \text{N}' \neq \bot \text{ then } \text{N}' & \text{else } \text{m.ZN} \\[2mm] \wedge \quad \text{ZN}' & = \text{if } \text{N}' \neq \bot \text{ then } \text{m.ZN} & \text{else } \bot \\[2mm] \wedge \quad \text{ZN}' \leq 1 & \Leftrightarrow \quad \text{FB}' \neq \bot & \end{array} \right\}$$

In the following sections, we assume that the type definitions for variables also specify the "SIGNAL type" of variables, i.e. whether they are input, output, register, memorization or local variables. The respective sets of variables are denoted by I, O, R, M, L. Combinations of these letters stand for the union of the respective sets; e.g. IOR stands for the set of input/output/register variables of some system. Note that the M variables are not originally present in the SIGNAL program, but are introduced by its translation into the STS notation.

For the translation validation process, the generated C programs is also translated into the STS formalism. Below, we present the STS representation of the DEC_iterate() generated code, where the predicate $pres\text{-}but(U)$ indicates that all variables in the set $V \setminus U$ preserve their values during the respective transition. Thus, the values of all variables except, possibly, those in U are preserved.

$C = (V_c, \Theta_c, \rho_c)$ where

$V = \{\text{FB}_c, \text{N}_c, \text{ZN}_c, \text{h1}_c, \text{h2}_c\}$

$\Theta = (\text{ZN}_c = 1 \ \wedge\ pc = l_0)$

$$\rho_c = \left\{ \begin{array}{llll} & (pc = l_0 \ \wedge & \text{h1}'_c = \text{T} & \wedge \ pc' = l_1 \ \wedge \ pres\text{-}but(pc, \text{h1}_c)) \\ \vee & (pc = l_1 \ \wedge & \text{h2}'_c = (\text{ZN}_c \leq 1) & \wedge \ pc' = l_2 \ \wedge \ pres\text{-}but(pc, \text{h2}_c)) \\ \vee & (pc = l_2 \ \wedge \ \text{h2}_c & & \wedge \ pc' = l_{2.1} \ \wedge \ pres\text{-}but(pc)) \\ \vee & (pc = l_2 \ \wedge \neg \text{h2}_c & & \wedge \ pc' = l_3 \ \wedge \ pres\text{-}but(pc)) \\ \vee & (pc = l_{2.1} \ \wedge & & pc' = l_3 \ \wedge \ pres\text{-}but(pc, \text{FB}_c)) \\ \vee & (pc = l_3 \ \wedge \ \text{h2}_c & & \wedge \ pc' = l_{3.1} \ \wedge \ pres\text{-}but(pc)) \\ \vee & (pc = l_3 \ \wedge \neg \text{h2}_c & & \wedge \ pc' = l_{3.2} \ \wedge \ pres\text{-}but(pc)) \\ \vee & (pc = l_{3.1} \ \wedge & \text{N}'_c = \text{FB}_c & \wedge \ pc' = l_4 \ \wedge \ pres\text{-}but(pc, \text{N}_c)) \\ \vee & (pc = l_{3.2} \ \wedge & \text{N}'_c = \text{ZN}_c - 1 & \wedge \ pc' = l_4 \ \wedge \ pres\text{-}but(pc, \text{N}_c)) \\ \vee & (pc = l_4 \ \wedge & & pc' = l_5 \ \wedge \ pres\text{-}but(pc)) \\ \vee & (pc = l_5 \ \wedge & \text{ZN}'_c = \text{N}_c & \wedge \ pc' = l_0 \ \wedge \ pres\text{-}but(pc, \text{ZN}_c)) \end{array} \right\}$$

Note, that the C programs use *persistent* variables (i.e. variables which are never absent) to implement SIGNAL programs which use volatile variables. This has to be taken into account when defining the notion of "correct implementation" in the next section.

4   The "Correct Implementation" Relation

The notion of *correct implementation* used in this work is based on the general concept of refinement between synchronous transition systems.

Let $A = (V_A, \Theta_A, \rho_A, \mathcal{O}^A)$ and $C = (V_C, \Theta_C, \rho_C, \mathcal{O}^C)$ be an abstract and concrete STS's, where $\mathcal{O}^A$ and $\mathcal{O}^C$ are *observation functions*, respectively mapping the abstract and concrete states into a common data domain $\mathcal{D}$.

An *observation* of STS is any infinite sequence of $\mathcal{D}$-elements which can be obtained by applying the observation function $\mathcal{O}^A$ to each of the states in a computation of A. That is, a sequence which has the form $\mathcal{O}^A(s_0), \mathcal{O}^A(s_1), \ldots$, for some $\sigma : s_0, s_1, \ldots$, a computation of A. We denote by $Obs(A)$ the set of observations of system A. In a similar way, we define $Obs(C)$ the set of observations of STS C.

We say that system C *refines* system A, denoted

$$C \sqsubseteq A,$$

if $Obs(C) \subseteq Obs(A)$. That is, if every observation of system C is also an observation of A.

4.1   Adaptation to SIGNAL Compilation

To adapt this general definition to the case at hand, there are several factors that need to be considered.

A first observation is that whatever the SIGNAL program can accomplish in a single step takes the corresponding C program several steps of execution. In fact, it takes a single full execution of the loop's body in the C program to perform a single abstract step. Consequently, we take for the STS representation of the compared C program a system obtained by *composing* the transition relations of the individual statements inside the loop's body. Since the body does not contain any nested loops, the computation of the overall transition relation is straightforward and can be achieved by successive substitutions. We refer to the resulting STS as the *composite* STS corresponding to the C program.

A second consideration is the choice of the abstract and concrete observation functions. For the abstract SIGNAL program, the natural observation is the snapshot of the values of the input and output variables. Thus, the abstract observation will be the tuple of values for the IO variables. For example, for the DEC SIGNAL program, the observation function is given by $\mathcal{O}^A = (\text{FB}, \text{N})$.

A major feature of all the SIGNAL compilers we are treating is that all variables in the IOR set are preserved in the translation and are represented by identically named C variables. Therefore, the natural candidate for the concrete observation is the tuple of values of the IO C variables.

Unfortunately, there is a difference in the types of an IO SIGNAL variable and its corresponding C variable. While any IO signal $v \in IO$ may also assume the value $\perp$, signifying that the signal v is absent in the current step, all C variables are persistent and can never assume the value $\perp$. This implies that we have to identify for every concrete step and every IO-variable v whether the abstract version of v is present or absent in the current step.

Our decision was that an input variable v should be considered present in the current step iff a new value for v has been read during the current execution of the loop's body. Similarly, an output variable v is considered present iff the variable v was written during the current step.

To detect these events, we have instrumented the given C program by adding a boolean variable $rd.v$ for each input variable v, and a boolean variable $wr.v$ for each output variable[2]. All these auxiliary variables are set to 0 (*false*) at the beginning of the loop's body. After every **read**(v) operation, we add the assignment $rd.v := 1$, and after every **write**(v) operation, we add the assignment $wr.v := 1$.

In Fig. 1, we present the instrumented version of function DEC_iterate().

```
logical DEC_iterate()
{
        rd.FBc = F;  wr.Nc = F;
10:     h1c = TRUE;
11:     h2c = ZNc <= 1;
12:     if (h2c)
12.1:       {read(FBc); rd.FBc = T;};
13:     if (h2c)
13.1:       Nc = FBc;
        else
13.2:       Nc = ZNc - 1;
14:     {write(Nc); wr.Nc = T;};
15:     ZNc = Nc;
        return TRUE;
}
```

Fig. 1. Instrumented version of function DEC_iterate().

In Fig. 2, we present the composite STS corresponding to the instrumented C program. This presentation of the composite STS identifies the concrete observation function as $\mathcal{O}^C = (\mathcal{O}^C_{FB}, \mathcal{O}^C_N)$, where $\mathcal{O}^C_{FB}$ and $\mathcal{O}^C_N$ are defined in Fig. 2.

As can be seen in Fig. 2, the instrumented variables $rd.FB_c$ and $wr.N_c$ are defined within ρ_c and then used in the definition of the observation function $\mathcal{O}^C$. Therefore, it is possible to simplify the composite STS by substituting the

---

[2] Our final implementation does not really add these auxiliary variables but performs an equivalent derivation. Introducing these variables simplifies the explanation.

$$V_C \quad : \{FB_c, N_c, ZN_c, h1_c, h2_c, rd.FB_c, wr.N_c\}$$

$$\Theta_C \quad : ZN_c = 1 \wedge pc = l_0$$

$$\rho_C \quad : \begin{pmatrix} (h1'_c = T) \\ \wedge \ (h2'_c = (ZN_c \le 1)) \\ \wedge \ (h2'_c \Rightarrow (N'_c = FB'_c)) \\ \wedge \ (\neg h2'_c \Rightarrow (FB'_c = FB_c \wedge N'_c = ZN_c - 1)) \\ \wedge \ (ZN'_c = N'_c) \\ \wedge \ (rd.FB'_c = h2'_c) \\ \wedge \ (wr.N'_c = T) \end{pmatrix}$$

$$\mathcal{O}^C_{FB} \quad : \text{if } rd.FB_c \text{ then } FB_c \text{ else } \bot$$

$$\mathcal{O}^C_N \quad : \text{if } wr.N_c \text{ then } N_c \text{ else } \bot$$

Fig. 2. Composite STS corresponding to the instrumented C program.

definition of the instrumented variables into $\mathcal{O}^C$ and removing their definition from ρ_C. The actual implementation of the presented techniques within the code validation tool CVT never explicitly generate the instrumented version of the program but computes directly the simplified version as presented in Fig. 3.

$$V_C \quad : \{FB_c, N_c, ZN_c, h1_c, h2_c\}$$

$$\Theta_C \quad : ZN_c = 1 \wedge pc = l_0$$

$$\rho_C \quad : \begin{pmatrix} (h1'_c = T) \\ \wedge \ (h2'_c = (ZN_c \le 1)) \\ \wedge \ (h2'_c \Rightarrow (N'_c = FB'_c)) \\ \wedge \ (\neg h2'_c \Rightarrow (FB'_c = FB_c \wedge N'_c = ZN_c - 1)) \\ \wedge \ (ZN'_c = N'_c) \end{pmatrix}$$

$$\mathcal{O}^C_{FB} \quad : \text{if } h2_c \text{ then } FB_c \text{ else } \bot$$

$$\mathcal{O}^C_N \quad : N_c$$

Fig. 3. The actual (simplified) STS$_{DEC}$ as generated by the CVT tool.

Before computing the composite STS corresponding to a given C program, the CVT tool performs some syntactic checks. For example, it checks that all references to an input variable $i \in I$ syntactically succeed the statement which reads the external input into i. Symmetrically, the tool checks that all assignments to an output variable $o \in O$ syntactically precede the statement which externally writes o. Failure in any of these checks will cause the tool to declare the translation as invalid.

In summary, we expect the abstract and concrete systems to be related as depicted below:

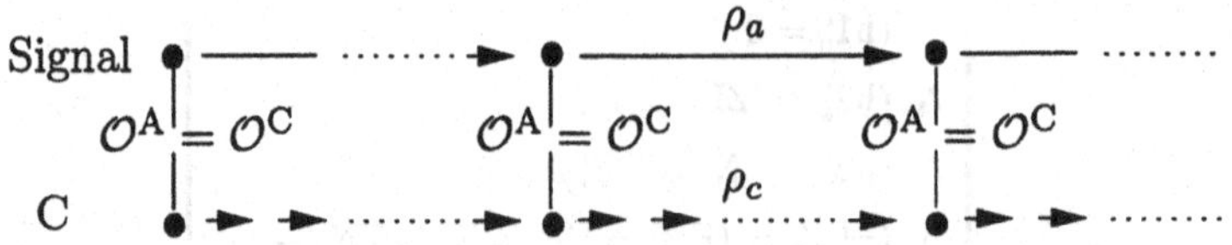

4.2   Proving Refinement by Simulation plus Abstraction Mapping

Let $A = (V_A, \Theta_A, \rho_A, \mathcal{O}^A)$ and $C = (V_C, \Theta_C, \rho_C, \mathcal{O}^C)$ be a given abstract and concrete systems. The standard way of proving that C refines A (cf. [1]) is based on the identification of an *abstraction mapping* $V_A = \alpha(V_C)$ mapping concrete states to abstract states, and establishing the premises of rule REF presented in Fig. 4. In many places, the mapping α is referred to as *refinement mapping*. Premise R1 of the rule ensures that the mapping α maps every initial concrete

---

For an abstraction mapping $V_A = \alpha(V_C)$,

R1. $\Theta_C \wedge V_A = \alpha(V_C) \qquad\qquad\qquad \rightarrow \quad \Theta_A \quad$ Initiation

R2. $V_A = \alpha(V_C) \wedge \rho_C \wedge V'_A = \alpha(V'_C) \quad \rightarrow \quad \rho_A \quad$ Propagation

R3. $V_A = \alpha(V_C) \quad \rightarrow \quad \mathcal{O}^A = \mathcal{O}^C \qquad$ Compatibility with observations

$$C \sqsubseteq A$$

Fig. 4. Rule REF.

---

state into an initial abstract state. Premise R2 requires that if the abstract state s_A and the concrete state s_C are α-related, and s'_C is a ρ_C-successor of s_C, then the abstract state $s'_A = \alpha(s'_C)$ is a ρ_A-successor of s_A. Together, R1 and R2 establish by induction that, for every concrete computation $\sigma_C : s^0_C, s^1_C, \ldots$, there exists a corresponding abstract computation $\sigma_A : s^0_A, s^1_A, \ldots$, such that $s^j_A = \alpha(s^j_C)$ for every $j = 0, 1, \ldots$. Applying premise R3, we obtain that the observations obtained from σ_A and σ_C are equal. This shows that rule REF is sound.

Rule REF , in the form presented in Fig. 4, is often not complete. In many cases we need to add an auxiliary invariant to the premises. However, in the case at hand, the relation $V_A = \alpha(V_C)$ is the only invariant we need.

4.3   Construction of the Mapping α

To complete the description of our verification methodology, it only remains to describe how we can construct automatically the abstraction mapping α.

The range of the mapping α is a tuple of values over the domains of the abstract variables V_A. In fact, for every abstract variable $v \in V_A$, the mapping α

contains a component $\alpha_v(V_c)$ which defines the value of v in the abstract state α-related to the concrete state represented by V_c.

For the abstract observable variables $v \in IO$, premise R3 already constrains us to choose $\alpha_v(V_c) = \mathcal{O}_v^C(V_c)$. It therefore remains to describe the mappings α_v for $v \in V_c - IO = MRL$.

Recall that every variable $v \in R$ gives rise to an abstract register variable v, an abstract memorization variable $m.v$ introduced into the STS corresponding to A, and a corresponding concrete variable v_c. For example, the register flow ZN in the SIGNAL program DEC, gave rise to a similarly named variable and to the memorization variable m.ZN in the STS DEC and to the concrete variable ZN_c in function DEC_iterate().

Therefore, we define for each register flow r the following two instances of the α mapping:

$$\alpha_{m.r} = r_c \qquad \alpha'_{m.r} = r'_c.$$

For example, the mapping into the abstract variable m.ZN will be given by the equation m.ZN $= ZN_c$.

It only remains to define α_v for $v \in RL$. Since variables in L do not necessarily have counterparts in the C program, it may not be so easy to find an expression over V_c which will capture their values.

Here we are helped by the fact that every compilable SIGNAL program A is *determinate* in the new values of I (the inputs) and R (the register flows). Equivalently, the corresponding STS_A is determinate in the values of I' (new inputs) and M (old memorization values). Determinateness means that a set of values for these variables uniquely define the new values of all other variables (all variables in $IORML$). Determinateness is the necessary condition for being able to compile the program into a deterministic running program. Input SIGNAL programs which are not determinate are rejected by all the SIGNAL compilers we worked with.

We use the fact that every abstract variable $v \in RL$ has a unique equation of the form $v' = eq_v$ within STS_A. In principle, determinateness implies that we could chase these equations applying successive substitutions until we find for v a defining expression all in terms of the concrete variables V_c. However, this is not actually necessary. Instead, we transform premises R1–R3 into the following two verification conditions:

W1. $\Theta_c \;\wedge\; \bigwedge_{r \in R}(m.r = r_c) \;\wedge\; \bigwedge_{v \in IORL}(v = \bot) \qquad\qquad\qquad \to \quad \Theta_A$

W2. $\bigwedge_{r \in R}\left(\begin{array}{c} m.r = r_c \\ \wedge\, m.r' = r'_c \end{array} \right) \;\wedge\; \rho_c \;\wedge\; \bigwedge_{v \in IO}(v' = (\mathcal{O}_v^C)') \;\wedge\; \bigwedge_{v \in RL}(v' = eq_v)$

$$\to \quad \rho_A$$

Obviously, we can dispense with premise R3 since $\mathcal{O}^A = \mathcal{O}^C$ is automatically guaranteed by taking $\alpha_v = \mathcal{O}_v^C$ for each $v \in IO$. In verification condition W1, we simplified the mapping α having the prior information that only the $m.r \in M$

variables have non-bottom values and they are mapped by α into their concrete counterparts r_c.

In verification condition W2 we used the fact that the only unprimed variables to which ρ_A refers are the memorization variables $m.r$. Therefore, it is sufficient to map them in the unprimed version of $V_A = \alpha(V_C)$. For the primed version of α, we used $\mathcal{O}_v^C$ for all $v \in IO$, $m.r' = r_c'$ for all $r \in R$ ($m.r \in M$). and the original STS_A equations for each $v \in RL$.

Theorem 1. *With the notation introduced above, if verification conditions W1 and W2 are valid, then $C \sqsubseteq A$.*

4.4   Illustrate on the Example

Applying these methods to the case of the SIGNAL program DEC and its translated C-program DEC_iterate(), we obtain the following two verification conditions:

$$\textbf{U1. } ZN_c = 1 \ \wedge \ m.ZN = ZN_c \ \wedge \ \begin{pmatrix} FB = \bot \\ \wedge \quad N = \bot \\ \wedge \ ZN = \bot \end{pmatrix} \ \rightarrow \ \begin{pmatrix} FB = \bot \\ \wedge \quad N = \bot \\ \wedge \quad ZN = \bot \\ \wedge \ m.ZN = 1 \end{pmatrix}$$

$$\textbf{U2. } \rho_C \ \wedge \ \begin{pmatrix} m.ZN = ZN_c \\ \wedge \quad FB' = \text{if } h2_c' \text{ then } FB_c' \text{ else } \bot \\ \wedge \quad N' = N_c' \\ \wedge \ m.ZN' = ZN_c' \\ \wedge \quad ZN' = \text{if } N' \neq \bot \text{ then } m.ZN \text{ else } \bot \end{pmatrix} \ \rightarrow \ \rho_A$$

Note that the α-mapping for the IO variables FB' and N', and for the M variable $m.ZN$ is given directly in terms of the concrete variables, while the α-mapping of ZN' is given in terms of the abstract variables N' and $m.ZN$. In principle, it is possible to substitute the definitions of N' and $m.ZN$ in the right-hand side of the definitions for ZN' and obtain a mapping which expresses all the relevant abstract variables in terms of the concrete variables. Performing the substitution and some simplifications concerning comparison to $\bot$, we obtain the following version of U2:

$$\textbf{U2a. } \quad \rho_C \ \wedge \ \begin{pmatrix} m.ZN \ = \ ZN_c \\ \wedge \quad FB' \ = \ \text{if } h2_c' \text{ then } FB_c' \text{ else } \bot \\ \wedge \quad N' \ = \ N_c' \\ \wedge \ m.ZN' \ = \ ZN_c' \\ \wedge \quad ZN' \ = \ ZN_c \end{pmatrix} \ \rightarrow \ \rho_A$$

The presented approach is immune against the optimizations performed by the industrial code generators that we considered. The proof technique exploits, in contrast to our previous work [20], only minimal knowledge about the code generation process. We only assume that IOM variables are reconstructible which is the minimal requirement for the C-code to be a correct implementation of the SIGNAL source [16].

5   Checking the Proof Obligations

As shown in the previous section, the generated proof obligations are quantifier-free implications referring to potentially infinite data domains such as the integers. Direct submission of these implications to a theorem prover such as PVS and invoking various proof procedures turned out to be far too slow.

In this section we explain the theoretical basis for an efficient BDD-based evaluation of the proof obligations on the basis of *uninterpreted functions*.

Typically, the verification conditions involve various arithmetical functions and predicates, tests for equality, boolean operations, and conditional (if-then-else) expressions. It has been our experience that the compiler performs very few arithmetical optimizations and leaves most of the arithmetical expressions intact. This suggests that most of the implications will hold independently of the special features of the operations and will be valid even if we replace the operations by *uninterpreted functions*.

5.1   The Uninterpreted Functions Encoding Scheme

Under the uninterpreted functions abstraction, we follow the encoding procedure of [2]. For every operation f occurring in a formula φ, which is not an equality test or a boolean operator, we perform the following:

- Replace each occurrence of a term $f(t_1, \ldots, t_k)$ in φ by a new variable v_f^i of a type equal to that of the value returned by f. Occurrences $f(t_1, \ldots, t_k)$ and $f(u_1, \ldots, u_k)$ are replaced by the same v_f^i iff t_j is identical to u_j for every $j = 1, \ldots, k$.
- Let $\hat{t}$ denote the result of replacing all outer-most occurrences of the form $f(t_1, \ldots, t_k)$ by the corresponding new variable v_f^i in a sub-term t of φ. For every pair of newly added variables v_f^i and v_f^j, $i \neq j$, corresponding to the non-identical occurrences $f(t_1, \ldots, t_k)$ and $f(u_1, \ldots, u_k)$, add the implication $(\hat{t_1} = \hat{u_1} \wedge \cdots \wedge \hat{t_k} = \hat{u_k}) \Rightarrow v_f^i = v_f^j$ as antecedent to the transformed formula.

Example 1. Following are ρ_c and ρ_a of program DEC, after performing the uninterpreted functions abstraction. Note how the '-' function and the '$\leq$' predicate were replaced by the new symbols v_-^i and $v_\leq^i$ respectively, where i is a running index:

$$
\rho_c = \left\{
\begin{array}{l}
(h1'_c = T) \\
\wedge\ (h2'_c = (v_\leq^1)) \\
\wedge\ (h2'_c \Rightarrow N'_c = FB'_c) \\
\wedge\ (\neg h2'_c \Rightarrow (FB'_c = FB_c \wedge N'_c = v_-^1)) \\
\wedge\ (ZN'_c = N'_c)
\end{array}
\right\}
$$

$$\rho_a = \begin{pmatrix} \mathrm{N}' = \text{ if } \mathrm{FB}' \neq \bot \text{ then } \mathrm{FB}' \text{ else } v_-^2 \\[2mm] \wedge\ \mathrm{m.ZN}' = \text{ if } \mathrm{N}' \neq \bot \text{ then } \mathrm{N}' \text{ else } \mathrm{m.ZN} \\[2mm] \wedge\ \mathrm{ZN}' = \text{ if } \mathrm{N}' \neq \bot \text{ then } \mathrm{m.ZN} \text{ else } \bot \\[2mm] \wedge\ v_\leq^2 \Leftrightarrow \mathrm{FB}' \neq \bot \end{pmatrix}$$

After adding the functionality constraints, we obtain:

$$\varphi : \ (\tilde{\alpha} \ \wedge \ (\mathrm{ZN}_c = \mathrm{ZN}' \ \wedge \ 1 = 1 \rightarrow (v_\leq^1 = v_\leq^2 \ \wedge \ v_-^1 = v_-^2)) \rightarrow (\rho_c \rightarrow \rho_a))$$

where $\tilde{\alpha}$ stands for the conjunction

$$\begin{pmatrix} \mathrm{m.ZN} = \mathrm{ZN}_c \\ \wedge\quad \mathrm{FB}' = \text{ if } \mathrm{h2}'_c \text{ then } \mathrm{FB}'_c \text{ else } \bot \\ \wedge\quad \mathrm{N}' = \mathrm{N}'_c \\ \wedge\ \mathrm{m.ZN}' = \mathrm{ZN}'_c \\ \wedge\quad \mathrm{ZN}' = \mathrm{ZN}_c \end{pmatrix}$$

as presented in the verification condition U2a. We can use the substitution $\tilde{\alpha}$ to replace all occurrences of abstract variables in φ by their corresponding concrete expressions. After some simplifications, this yields the following implication referring only to the concrete variables and the newly added v's:

$$\tilde{\varphi} : \ \begin{pmatrix} v_\leq^1 = v_\leq^2 \\ \wedge\ v_-^1 = v_-^2 \end{pmatrix} \ \wedge \ \begin{pmatrix} (\mathrm{h1}'_c = \mathrm{T}) \\ \wedge\ (\mathrm{h2}'_c = (v_\leq^1)) \\ \wedge\ (\mathrm{h2}'_c \Rightarrow \mathrm{N}'_c = \mathrm{FB}'_c) \\ \wedge\ (\neg \mathrm{h2}'_c \Rightarrow (\mathrm{FB}'_c = \mathrm{FB}_c \wedge \mathrm{N}'_c = v_-^1)) \\ \wedge\ (\mathrm{ZN}'_c = \mathrm{N}'_c) \end{pmatrix} \ \rightarrow$$

$$\mathrm{N}'_c = \text{ if } \mathrm{h2}'_c \text{ then } \mathrm{FB}'_c \text{ else } v_-^2 \quad \wedge \quad \mathrm{ZN}'_c = \mathrm{N}'_c \quad \wedge \quad v_\leq^2 \Leftrightarrow \mathrm{h2}'_c$$

Note that the third conjunct of ρ_A, the one related to ZN', has been simplified away. The reason is that this conjunct was used to define the α mapping for ZN', so it would be trivially satified after the substituition.

The resulting equality formula belongs to a fragment of first order logic which has a *small model* property [4]. This means that the validity of these formulas can be established by solely inspecting models up to a certain finite cardinality. In order to make these finite domains as small as possible we apply another technique called *range allocation*.

   The domain that can always be taken when using these kind of abstractions is simply a finite set of integers whose size is the number of (originally) integer/float variables (e.g. if there are n integer/float variables, then each of these variables ranges over $[1..n]$). It is not difficult to see that this range is sufficient for proving the invalidity of a formula if it was originally not valid. The invalidity of the formula implies that there is at least one assignment that makes the formula false. Any assignment that preserves the partitioning of the variables in this falsifying assignment will also falsify the formula (the absolute values are of no importance). This is why the $[1..n]$ range, which allows all possible partitions, is sufficient regardless of the formula's structure.

5.2   Range Allocation

The size of the state-space imposed by the $[1..n]$ range as suggested in the previous section is n^n. For most industrial-size programs this state-space is far too big to handle. But apparently there is a lot of redundancy in this range that can be avoided. The $[1..n]$ range is given without any analysis of the formula's structure. Note that our informal justification of the soundness of this method is independent of the structure of the formula we try to validate, and thus the range is sufficient for all formulas with n variables. This is probably the best we can do when the only information we have about the formula is that it has n variables. However, a more detailed analysis of the structure of the formula we wish to validate makes it possible to significantly decrease the ranges, and consequently the state space can be drastically reduced. This analysis is performed by the 'Range Allocation' module, using the *range allocation algorithm*, which significantly reduces the range of each of these (now enumerated type) variables, and enables the handling of larger programs. By applying the range-allocation technique, CVT decreases the state space of the verified formulas typically by orders of magnitude. We have many examples of formulas containing 150 integer variables or more (which result in a state-space of 150^{150} if the $[1..n]$ range is taken) which. after performing the range allocation algorithm, can be proved with a state-space of less than 100, in less than a second.

The range allocation algorithm is somewhat complex and its full description is beyond the scope of this paper. We refer the reader to [17] for more details, and describe here only the general idea.

The algorithm attempts to solve a satisfiability (validity) problem efficiently, by determining a *range allocation* $R : Vars(\varphi) \mapsto 2^{\mathbb{N}}$, mapping each integer variable $x_i \in \varphi$ into a small finite set of integers, such that φ is satisfiable (valid) iff it is satisfiable (respectively, valid) over some R-interpretation. After each variable x_i is encoded as an enumerated type over its finite domain $R(x_i)$, we use a standard BDD package, such as the one in TLV (see Section 5.5), to construct a BDD B_φ. Formula φ is satisfiable iff B_φ is not identical to 0.

Obviously, the success of our method depends on our ability to find range allocations with a small state-space.

In theory, there always exists a *singleton* range allocation R^*, satisfying the above requirements, such that R^* allocates each variable a domain consisting of a single integer, i.e., $|R^*| = 1$. This is supported by the following trivial argument:

If φ is satisfiable, then there exists an assignment $(x_1, \ldots, x_n) = (z_1, \ldots, z_n)$ satisfying φ. It is sufficient to take $R^* : x_1 \mapsto \{z_1\}, \ldots, x_n \mapsto \{z_n\}$ as the singleton allocation. If φ is unsatisfiable, it is sufficient to take $R^* : x_1, \ldots, x_n \mapsto \{0\}$.

However, finding the singleton allocation R^* amounts to a head-on attack on the primary NP-complete problem. Instead, we generalize the problem and attempt to find a small range allocation which is adequate for a *set* of formulas Φ which are "structurally similar" to the formula φ, and includes φ itself.

Consequently, we say that the range allocation R is *adequate* for the formula set Φ if, for every equality formula in the set $\varphi \in \Phi$, φ is satisfiable iff φ is satisfiable over R.

5.3 An Approach Based on the Set of Atomic Formulas

We assume that φ has no constants or boolean variables, and is given in a positive form, i.e. negations are only allowed within atomic formulas of the form $x_i \neq x_j$. Any equality formula can be brought into such positive form, by expressing all boolean operations such as $\rightarrow$, $\leq$ and the *if-then-else* construct in terms of the basic boolean operations $\neg$, $\vee$, and $\wedge$, and pushing all negations inside.

Let $At(\varphi)$ be the set of all atomic formulas of the form $x_i = x_j$ or $x_i \neq x_j$ appearing in φ, and let $\Phi(\varphi)$ be the family of all equality formulas which have the same set of atomic formulas as φ. Obviously $\varphi \in \Phi(\varphi)$. Note that the family defined by the atomic formula set $\{x_1 = x_2, x_1 \neq x_2\}$ includes both the satisfiable formula $x_1 = x_2 \vee x_1 \neq x_2$ and the unsatisfiable formula $x_1 = x_2 \wedge x_1 \neq x_2$.

For a set of atomic formulas A, we say that the subset $B = \{\psi_1, \ldots, \psi_k\} \subseteq A$ is *consistent* if the conjunction $\psi_1 \wedge \cdots \wedge \psi_k$ is satisfiable. Note that a set B is consistent iff it does not contain a chain of the form $x_1 = x_2$, $x_2 = x_3$, $\ldots$, $x_{r-1} = x_r$ together with the formula $x_1 \neq x_r$.

Given a set of atomic formulas A, a range allocation R is defined to be *satisfactory* for A if every consistent subset $B \subseteq A$ is R-satisfiable.

For example, the range allocation $R : x_1, x_2, x_3 \mapsto \{0\}$ is satisfactory for the atomic formula set $\{x_1 = x_2, x_2 = x_3\}$, while the allocation $R : x_1 \mapsto \{1\}$, $x_2 \mapsto \{2\}$, $x_3 \mapsto \{3\}$ is satisfactory for the formula set $\{x_1 \neq x_2, x_2 \neq x_3\}$. On the other hand, no singleton allocation is satisfactory for the set $\{x_1 = x_2, x_1 \neq x_2\}$. A minimal satisfactory allocation for this set can be given by $R : x_1 \mapsto \{1\}$, $x_2 \mapsto \{1, 2\}$.

Claim. The range allocation R is satisfactory for the atomic formula set A iff R is adequate for $\Phi(A)$, the set of formulas φ such that $At(\varphi) = A$.

Thus, we concentrate our efforts on finding a small range allocation which is satisfactory for $A = At(\varphi)$ for a given equality formula φ. In view of the claim, we will continue to use the terms satisfactory and adequate synonymously.

We partition the set A into the two sets $A = A_= \cup A_{\neq}$, where $A_=$ contains all the equality formulas in A, while $A_{\neq}$ contains the inequalities.

Note that the sets $A_=(\varphi)$ and $A_{\neq}(\varphi)$ for a given formula φ can be computed without actually carrying out the transformation to positive form. All that is required is to check whether a given atomic formula has a positive or negative *polarity* within φ, where the polarity of a sub-formula p is determined according to whether the number of negations enclosing p is even (positive polarity) or odd (negative polarity). Additional considerations apply to sub-formulas involving the *if-then-else* construct.

Example 2. Let us illustrate these concepts on program DEC whose validity we wish to check.

Since our main algorithm checks for satisfiability, we proceed by calculating the polarity of each comparison in $\neg\tilde{\varphi}$:

$$A_= = \{(\text{FB}'_c = \text{FB}_c),\ (\text{N}'_c = \text{FB}'_c),\ (\text{N}'_c = v^1_-),\ (\text{ZN}'_c = \text{N}'_c),$$
$$(v^1_- = v^2_-)\}$$
$$A_{\neq} = \{(\text{N}'_c \neq \text{FB}'_c),\ (\text{N}'_c \neq v^2_-),\ (\text{ZN}'_c \neq \text{N}'_c\}$$

For example, the comparison $(\text{N}'_c = v^1_-)$ in φ is contained within one negation (implied by appearing on the left hand side of the implication). Since we are considering $\neg\varphi$, this amounts to 2 negations, and since 2 is even, we add $(\text{N}'_c = v^1_-)$ to $A_=$.

This example would require a state-space in the order of 10^5 if we used the full $[1..n]$ range. The range allocation algorithm of [17] will find ranges adequate for this formula, with a state space of 32.

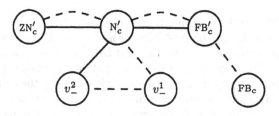

Fig. 5. The Graph $G : G_{\neq} \cup G_=$ representing $\neg\varphi$

5.4   A Graph-Theoretic Representation

The sets $A_{\neq}$ and $A_=$ can be represented by two graphs, $G_=$ and $G_{\neq}$ defined as follows:

(x_i, x_j) is an edge on $G_=$, the *equalities graph*, iff $(x_i = x_j) \in A_=$.
(x_i, x_j) is an edge on $G_{\neq}$, the *inequalities graph*, iff $(x_i \neq x_j) \in A_{\neq}$.
We refer to the joint graph as G.

An inconsistent subset $B \subseteq A$ will appear, graphically, as a cycle consisting of a single $G_{\neq}$-edge and any positive number of $G_=$-edges. We refer to these cycle as *contradictory cycles*.

In Fig. 5, we present the graph corresponding to the formula $\neg\varphi$, where $G_=$-edges are represented by dashed lines and $G_{\neq}$-edges are represented by solid lines.

The range allocation algorithm has several stages of traversing the graph, analyzing reachability, removing vertices etc. Without going into the details of the algorithm, we will present the ranges adequate for this graph, as computed by the algorithm: $R : \mathrm{ZN}'_c \mapsto \{1,2\}$, $\mathrm{N}'_c \mapsto \{1\}$, $\mathrm{FB}'_c \mapsto \{1,3\}$, $\mathrm{FB}_c \mapsto \{1,3\}$, $v^1_- \mapsto \{1,4\}$, and $v^2_- \mapsto \{1,4\}$.

Indeed, every consistent subset of the edges in the graph can be satisfied with these ranges. For example, for the subset made of the dashed edges $\{(\mathrm{FB}_c, \mathrm{FB}'_c), (\mathrm{FB}'_c, \mathrm{N}'_c), (v^2_-, v^1_-)$ and the solid edge $\{(v^2_-, \mathrm{N}'_c)\}$ we can assign $\mathrm{FB}_c = \mathrm{FB}'_c = \mathrm{N}'_c = 1$, and $v^1_- = v^2_- = 4$. Clearly this assignment satisfies the constraints that are represented by these edges.

In this case we reduced the state space from 6^6 to 32. In many cases the graphs are not as connected as this one, and therefore the reduction in the state space is much more significant. Often, 60 - 70% of the variables become constants, in the same way that N'_c became a constant in the example given above. We once more refer the reader to [17] for further details.

5.5   The Verifier Module (TLV)

The validity of the verification conditions is checked by TLV [18], an SMV-based tool which provides the capability of BDD-programming and has been developed mainly for finite-state deductive proofs (and is thus convenient in our case for expressing the refinement rule). In the case that the equivalence proof fails, a counter example is displayed. Since it is possible to isolate the conjunct(s) that failed the proof, this information can be used by the compiler developer to check what went wrong. A proof log is generated as part of this process, indicating what was proved, at what level of abstraction and when.

6   A Case Study

We used CVT to validate an industrial size program, a code generated for the case study of a turbine developed by SNECMA, which is one of the industrial case studies in the SACRES project. The program was partitioned manually (by SNECMA) into 5 units which were separately compiled. Altogether the SIGNAL specification is a few thousand lines long and contains more than 1000 variables. After the abstraction we had about 2000 variables (as explained in Section 5, the abstraction module replaces function symbols with new variables). Following is a summary of the results achieved by CVT:

Module	Conjuncts	Time (min.)
M1	530	1:54
M2	533	1:30
M3	124	0:27
M4	308	2:22
M5	860	5:55
Total :	2355	12:08

Although it is hard to assess at this stage how strongly this particular example indicates the feasibility of the Translation Validation approach, the case study undoubtedly shows that a compilation process (of the type we considered) of an industrial size program can be automatically verified in a reasonable amount of time.

7   Conclusions

We have presented the theory which underlies our translation validation approach for optimizing industrial compilers from SIGNAL to C. We described the translation of SIGNAL and C programs to STS, the generation of the substitution α and the final assembling of the proof obligations according to Rule REF as they are implemented in CVT (the Code Validation Tool). In addition, the decision procedure, including the abstraction, the Range Allocation algorithm and various other optimizations that were not presented in this paper, are also implemented in CVT. We believe that the case study that was presented in the paper is a strong indication that translation validation is a viable alternative to full compiler verification.

Dedication This paper is dedicated with friendship and appreciation to Hans Langmaack, a pioneer in the area of compiler verification, whose work proved the great value and feasibility of a seamless and fully verified development path from specification to implementation.

Acknowledgment We wish to express our gratitude to Markus Müller-Olm who reviewed an earlier version of this article in record-time and yet managed to provide us with several significant and insightful comments which led to a meaningful improvement in the quality and validity of this paper.

References

[1] M. Abadi and L. Lamport. The existence of refinement mappings. *Theoretical Computer Science*, 82(2):253–284, May 1991.

[2] W. Ackerman. *Solvable cases of the Decision Problem*. Studies in Logic and the Foundations of Mathematics. North-Holland, Amsterdam, 1954.

[3] A. Benveniste, P. Le Guernic, and C. Jacquemot. Synchronous programming with events and relations: the SIGNAL languages and its semantics. *Science of Computer Programming*, 16:103–149, 1991.

[4] E. Börger, E. Grädel, and Y. Gurevich. *The Classical Decision Problem*. Springer-Verlag, 1996.

[5] B. Buth, K.-H. Buth, M. Fränzle, B. von Karger, Y. Lakhneche, H. Langmaack, and M. Müller-Olm. Provably correct compiler development and implementation. In U. Kastens and P. Pfahler, editors, *Compiler Construction'92, 4th International Conference Paderborn, Germany*, volume 641 of *Lect. Notes in Comp. Sci.*, pages 141–155. Springer-Verlag, 1992.

[6] K.M. Chandy and J. Misra. *Parallel Program Design: a Foundation*. Addison-Wesley, 1988.

[7] A. Cimatti, F. Giunchiglia, P. Pecchiari, B. Pietra, J. Profeta, D. Romano, P. Traverso, and B. Yu. A provably correct embedded verifier for the certification of safety critical software. In O. Grumberg, editor, *Proc. 9th Intl. Conference on Computer Aided Verification (CAV'97)*, volume 1254 of *Lect. Notes in Comp. Sci.*, pages 202–213. Springer-Verlag, 1997.

[8] A. Cimatti, F. Giunchiglia, P. Traverso, and A. Villafiorita. Run-time result formal verification of safety critical software: an industrial case study. In *Run-Time Result Verification. The 1999 Federated Logic Conference*, 1999.

[9] D.L. Clutterbuck and B.A. Carre. The verification of low-level code. *Software Engineering Journal*, pages 97–111, 1998.

[10] P. Curzon. A verified compiler for a structured assembly language. In *international workshop on the HOL theorem Proving System and its applications*. IEEE Computer Society Press, 1991.

[11] J.D. Guttman, J.D. Ramsdell, and V. Swarup. The VLISP verified Scheme system. *Lisp and Symbolic Computation*, 8:33–100, 1995.

[12] J.D. Guttman, J.D. Ramsdell, and M. Wand. VLISP: A verified implementation of Scheme. *Lisp and Symbolic Computation*, 8:5–32, 1995.

[13] M. Müller-Olm. *Modular Compiler Verification: A Refinement-Algebraic Approach Advocating Stepwise Abstraction*, volume 1283 of *Lect. Notes in Comp. Sci.* Springer-Verlag, 1997.

[14] D.P. Oliva, J.D. Ramsdell, and M. Wand. The VLISP verified PreScheme compiler. *Lisp and Symbolic Computation*, 8:111–182, 1995.

[15] I.M. O'Neill, D.L. Clutterbuck, and P.F. Farrow. The formal verification of safety-critical assembly code. In *IFAC Symposium on safety of computer control systems*, 1988.

[16] Private communications with TNI (BREST), Siemens (Munich) and Inria (Rennes).

[17] A. Pnueli, Y. Rodeh, O. Shtrichman, and M. Siegel. Deciding equality formulas by small-domains instantiations. In N. Halbwachs and D. Peled, editors, *Proc. 11st Intl. Conference on Computer Aided Verification (CAV'99)*, Lect. Notes in Comp. Sci. Springer-Verlag, 1999. to appear.

[18] A. Pnueli and E. Shahar. A platform for combining deductive with algorithmic verification. In R. Alur and T. Henzinger, editors, *Proc. 8th Intl. Conference on Computer Aided Verification (CAV'96)*, Lect. Notes in Comp. Sci., pages 184–195. Springer-Verlag, 1996.

[19] A. Pnueli, M. Siegel, and O. Shtrichman. The code validation tool (CVT)- automatic verification of a compilation process. *Software Tools for Technology Transfer*, 2, 1999.

[20] A. Pnueli, M. Siegel, and E. Singerman. Translation validation. In B. Steffen, editor, *4th Intl. Conf. TACAS'98*, volume 1384 of *Lect. Notes in Comp. Sci.*, pages 151–166. Springer-Verlag, 1998.

[21] A. Stump and D. Dill. Generating proofs from a decision procedure. In *Run-Time Result Verification*. The 1999 Federated Logic Conference, 1999.

[22] P. Traverso and P. Bertoli. Mechanized result verification: an industrial application. In *Run-Time Result Verification*. The 1999 Federated Logic Conference, 1999.

Compilation and Synthesis for Real-Time Embedded Controllers

Martin Fränzle[1] and Markus Müller-Olm[2]

[1] Carl v. Ossietzky Universität, Department of Computer Science,
26111 Oldenburg, Germany
Martin.Fraenzle@Informatik.Uni-Oldenburg.DE
[2] University of Dortmund, Department of Computer Science, FB 4, LS 5,
44221 Dortmund, Germany
Markus.Mueller-Olm@cs.uni-dortmund.de

Abstract. This article provides an overview over two constructive approaches to provably correct hard real-time code generation where hard real-time code is *generated* from abstract requirements rather than *verified* against the timing requirements *a posteriori*. The first, more pragmatic approach is concerned with translation of imperative programs, extended by hard real-time commands which allow one to specify upper bounds for the execution time of basic blocks. In the second approach, Duration Calculus, a metric-time temporal logic, is used as the source language. Duration Calculus allows one to specify real-time systems at a very high level of abstraction.

1 Introduction

Due to rapidly dropping costs and the increasing power and flexibility of embedded digital hardware, digital control is becoming ubiquitous in technical systems encountered in everyday life. Modern means of transport rely on digital hardware even in vital sub-systems like anti-locking brakes, fly-by-wire systems, or signaling hardware. Medical equipment gains such a boost in functionality from exploiting the flexibility of computer control that more classical technology is replaced by digital control even in such critical applications as life-support systems or radiation treatment. Correct behavior of digital systems has thus become crucial to the safety of human life.

Formal methods are mathematical techniques developed to aid in the design of software systems. These techniques can provide correctness guarantees that are not otherwise available. Formal methods thus complement more traditional approaches for ensuring quality of software, like testing and certification by code inspection. Classical program verification is concerned with functional input/output specifications of stand-alone programs. In the application scenarios sketched above, however, correctness typically does not only depend on functional requirements but also on the time at which inputs are read and outputs are provided. Moreover, the digital system typically controls an environment of

E.-R. Olderog, B. Steffen (Eds.): Correct System Design, LNCS 1710, pp. 256–287, 1999.
© Springer-Verlag Berlin Heidelberg 1999

non-digital nature, i.e. these systems belong to the class of *real-time embedded controllers*.

The omnipresence of hard real-time systems in the realm of embedded systems urgently calls for techniques that support analysis, design, and reliable implementation with respect to both facets of their functionality, which are *logical correctness* and *timeliness* of service. As these aspects are not independent, techniques that can deal with both aspects simultaneously are particularly desirable. For early design phases like requirements capture and functional specification, this has led to the development of prototypical formalisms that tightly integrate algorithmic descriptions and timing. Prominent examples are timed automata [1] on the more operational side and metric-time temporal logics [46, 49] on the declarative side.

For later design phases, in particular code generation, it is, however, still state of the art to keep algorithmic aspects and timing separate. While compilers are generally used for generating code that is logically correct, timing behaviour is mostly analysed *a posteriori*, using profiling tools or even machine-code inspection. We suggest that the chain of formalisms and tools that support an integrated approach to functionality and timing may be extended down to the implementation level. As functionality is nowadays generally dealt with constructively by compilers or synthesis procedures, rather than through *a posteriori* analysis, this necessitates an incorporation of constructive methods for implementing hard real-time constraints into compilers or synthesizers, as well as suitably expressive source languages for these procedures.

In this article, we survey research in this direction that has been pursued by the authors in the scope of the ProCoS project [8]. On the more practical side, this was translation of a hard real-time imperative programming language which has a semantic model that — for the sake of nice algebraic properties — fully abstracts from the runtime of non-communicating statements. Here, compilation exploits invisibility of internal state changes for implementing such instantaneous statements through non-instantaneous sequential code. This consideration is part of more comprehensive work on rigorous verification of compilers which is surveyed in Sect. 2. On the more theoretical side, we have studied automatic synthesis of embedded controllers from rich subsets of Duration Calculus, an interval-based metric-time temporal logic introduced in [49]. Again, observational constraints of the environment are crucial as synthesis exploits band-limitedness or, for still richer subsets of Duration Calculus, even synchronicity properties of the environment for overcoming undecidability of Duration Calculus. This line of work is summarized in Sect. 3.

2   Compiler Verification

Although the idea of mathematically verified compilers dates back at least to the sixties [28] the complete verification of realistic compilers is still a challenge. Most documented work on compiler verification heads for a mathematical understanding of typical or semantically intricate implementation mechanisms illustrated by toy source and target languages [33, 43, 24, 38]. Target code for commercially available processors is only seldomly formally investigated. The work at CLI (Computational Logic Inc.) on the 'small stack' [7], a hierarchy of languages with mechanically proved translations between them, particularly Moore's work on the verified translation of the PITON assembly language to the binary machine code of the FM 9001 chip [31], is one of the rare exceptions. Even the impressive work on VLisp, a verified translator for Scheme, [17] ends at the level of an abstract machine that, given the abstractness of the source language Scheme, is rather close to actual hardware but is still more abstract than commercially available processors.

Apart from mathematical insight there is, however, a more practical motivation for an interest in compiler verification that certainly calls for an investigation of actual machine code: the justification of compiler-generated code from the correctness of the source code. In particular in the area of safety-critical systems, trusted verifed compilers would allow to certify control software on the source code level which would be less time-consuming and thus less costly than the current practice of inspecting machine code [39]. Moreover it would encourage a good documentation or even formal verification of the source code.

In this section we highlight an approach to verifying translations to machine code of actual processors. As a major case study we investigated the Transputer manufactured by the British company INMOS (now part of SGS-THOMSON Microelectronics Ltd) as target architecture. The source language is a prototypical hard real-time language, which allows the programmer to explicitly state upper bound requirements for the execution time of basic blocks. Such a code generator correctness proof may easily become monolithic, aimed at a narrow source language with a specific code generator for the given target processor. A proof of this kind would have little interest beyond the particular application, and might still require a large effort. We have pursued a more modular approach that should adapt to both extensions of the source and modifications to the target which justifies the effort. Like most literature on compiler verification we concentrate on the correctness proof for code generators here because construction of scanners and parsers is well-understood.

2.1 Prologue

It is natural to think of instructions of von Neumann machines as denoting assignments to machine components like accumulators and store. Hence, the effect of machine instructions can conveniently be described by imperative programs. The Transputer instruction $\mathtt{ldc}(1)$, for instance, which loads the constant value 1 to the accumulator called A, and moves A's contents to accumulator B, as well as B's contents to accumulator C (in the Transputer the registers A, B and C are used in a stack-like manner), can be represented by the multiple assignment

$$E(\mathtt{ldc}(1)) \stackrel{\text{def}}{=} \mathsf{A}, \mathsf{B}, \mathsf{C} := 1, \mathsf{A}, \mathsf{B} \ .$$

Similarly, the effect of $\mathtt{stl}(x)$, writing A's contents to variable x, moving B's value to A, C's value to B, and an unspecified value to C, can be described by

$$E(\mathtt{stl}(x)) \overset{\text{def}}{=} x, \mathtt{A}, \mathtt{B} := \mathtt{A}, \mathtt{B}, \mathtt{C} \; ; \; \mathtt{C} := ? \; ,$$

where $\mathtt{C} := ?$ denotes the nondeterministic choice between all possible assignments to C. To specify a machine by a high level program is of course not a new idea; it already underlies the concept of micro-programming [47], for instance. Such descriptions can also be used as starting point for hardware design [27, 10, 19] and thus provide a good interface to lower levels of abstraction.

If semantics of machine instructions is captured by imperative program fragments, refinement algebra [21], which provides semantics-preserving or refining program transformation rules, can be used to show that certain machine instruction sequences implement certain source programs. The following calculation proves, for example, that the code sequence $\langle \mathtt{ldc}(1), \mathtt{stl}(x) \rangle$, assumed to have the same meaning as the sequential composition of the effects $E(\mathtt{ldc}(1))$ and $E(\mathtt{stl}(x))$, is correct target code for the assignment $x := 1$; for the moment the additional effect on the accumulator C is taken to be irrelevant:

$$E(\mathtt{ldc}(1)) \; ; \; E(\mathtt{stl}(x))$$

$=$ [Definitions above]
$$\mathtt{A}, \mathtt{B}, \mathtt{C} := 1, \mathtt{A}, \mathtt{B} \; ; \; x, \mathtt{A}, \mathtt{B} := \mathtt{A}, \mathtt{B}, \mathtt{C} \; ; \; \mathtt{C} := ?$$

$=$ [(Combine-assign), (Identity-assign)]
$$x, \mathtt{A}, \mathtt{B}, \mathtt{C} := 1, \mathtt{A}, \mathtt{B}, \mathtt{B} \; ; \; \mathtt{C} := ?$$

$=$ [(Cancel-assign), (Identity-assign)]
$$x := 1 \; ; \; \mathtt{C} := ? \; .$$

In this proof we have used the following three assignment laws where x and y stand for disjoint lists of variables, e and f for lists of expressions of corresponding type, and $f[e/x]$ denotes substitution of e for x in expression f.

(Identity-assign)	$(x := e) = (x, y := e, y)$
(Combine-assign)	$(x := e \; ; \; x := f) = (x := f[e/x])$
(Cancel-assign)	$(x, y := e, f \; ; \; y := ?) = (x := e \; ; \; y := ?)$

The above calculation illustrates a basic idea of our approach to compiler verification: to use an imperative meta-language and refinement laws as proposed by Hoare [20, 22]. We write $\geq$ for the refinement relation; intuitively $P \geq Q$ means that P is better than Q in serving every purpose served by Q in every context.[1]

---

[1] Due to lack of space we cannot present a formal definition of the meta-language in this article. For the purpose of this overview an informal understanding is sufficient. Let us just mention that the imperative meta-language is interpreted by predicate transformers in the tradition of Dijkstra's wp-calculus [12] and the refinement calculus [34, 5, 32] but extended to communicating programs. For performing the abstractions we use a variant of the data refinement theory of Back [4], Gardiner & Morgan [16], and Morris [35]. Details can be found in the monograph [37].

The exposition up to now is of course oversimplified. Firstly, the model of the instruction's effect is too abstract. For example, the Transputer instructions reference memory locations basically, not variable identifiers as we assumed in the description of stl(x), and a machine program basically is not a separate entity but the executed instructions are taken from the memory. Secondly, a number of unformalized assumptions have been made in the surrounding text.

An idealized abstract model of the target processor simplifies the compiler verification. But if considerations are based on such a model alone there is a severe danger of unsoundness because the postulated model might fail to provide a safe abstraction of the processor's actual behavior. To ban this danger we interface directly to the Transputer's documentation by starting from a semi-formal model of its execution cycle provided by INMOS, the manufacturer of the Transputer, in [23]. A direct employment of this model in a compiler proof, however, would result in very long and tedious calculations which would seriously affect credibility of the proofs. How can we combine simplicity and conciseness of proofs with realistic modeling of the processor?

The idea is to derive a hierarchy of mutually consistent, increasingly abstract views to the Transputer's behavior, starting from bit-code level up to assembly levels with symbolic addressing. In each of the abstraction steps one particular phenomenon can be tackled in isolation. Afterwards we can choose for each proof task the model that allows the simplest proof or even mix reasoning at different abstraction levels without risking inconsistencies or unsoundness.

In the remaining parts of this section we describe the Transputer base model, the derived more abstract models, and the technique by which the abstraction is performed. Then we show how this hierarchy can advantageously be employed in the translation correctness proof for an imperative (un-timed) source language. Afterwards we indicate the generalization to a timed language. Due to lack of space we cannot present all formal details but invite the reader to enjoy the presentation with an informal understanding. A complete treatment can be found in the monograph [37].

2.2   Transputer Base Model

Appendix F of the Transputer Instruction Manual [23] contains a semi-formal model of the Transputer's behavior. Essentially it describes the Transputer as a state machine that communicates via four bi-directional synchronous channels called *links*, and works on a state consisting of three accumulators A, B and C (used as a small stack by most instructions), an operand register Oreg, a workspace pointer Wptr, an error flag EFlag, an instruction pointer IP, and an addressable memory Mem. We reformulate this model using the notation of the imperative meta-language mentioned above. The state components are represented by likewise named variables of appropriate type and the links by four input channels $In_0, \ldots, In_3$ and four output channels $Out_0, \ldots, Out_3$.

We introduce a process *Run* that is constrained by axioms in the form of refinement formulas. *Run* models the complete behavior of the running phase which is entered by the Transputer after the initialization phase that follows a reset. (The initialization phase need not be formally captured for the purpose of compiler verification.) In order to describe *Run* in a modular fashion we introduce auxiliary processes *Step* and *Fetch* and for each Transputer instruction *instr* a process $E_0(instr)$. *Step* models the behavior of a complete execution cycle, *Fetch* the instruction fetch phase and $E_0(instr)$ the instruction specific part of the execution cycle.

The basic property of *Run* is that it cyclically executes steps. This is captured by the axiom

$$Run \ = \ Step \ ; \ Run \ . \tag{1}$$

Step is characterized by the family of axioms (one for each Transputer instruction *instr*)

$$Step \ \geq \ \{ CurFct(instr) \} \ ; \ Fetch \ ; \ E_0(instr) \ ,^2 \tag{2}$$

where $CurFct(instr) \stackrel{\text{def}}{=} (\text{Byte}(\text{Mem}, \text{IP}) \text{ bitand } \$F0) = \text{InstrCode}(instr)$. Intuitively, $CurFct(instr)$ is a predicate that holds true if and only if the memory location pointed to by the instruction pointer IP contains just the instruction code of the instruction *instr*. The above property of *Step* means that *Step* behaves like the sequential composition of the *Fetch* phase and the process $E_0(instr)$ if activated in a state where $CurFct(instr)$ holds. *Fetch* is completely described by the axiom

$$Fetch \ = \ \text{Oreg}, \text{IP} := \text{Oreg bitor} (\text{Byte}(\text{Mem}, \text{IP}) \text{ bitand } \$0F), \text{IP} + 1 \ .$$

The effect of the single instructions is described by Z-like schemata in appendix F.3 of [23]. (The fetch phase too is described by a schema called 'InstrDecode'.) The schema for the load constant instruction ldc, for example, which loads the contents of the operand register Oreg to the evaluation stack, looks as follows [23, Page 132]:

ldc #4_	load constant
$\text{Areg}' = \text{Oreg}^0$	
$\text{Breg}' = \text{Areg}$	
$\text{Creg}' = \text{Breg}$	
$\text{Oreg}' = 0$	
$\text{Iptr}' = \text{NextInst}$	

Primed names represent the values of the corresponding register after execution and unprimed names the values before. Oreg^0 stands for the operand register's contents after the fetch phase. In our framework the effect of ldc is captured by a refinement axiom about $E_0(\text{ldc})$. As we are using an imperative programming notation we need not use primed and superscripted variables for distinguishing

---

[2] For a predicate ϕ, the *assertion* $\{\phi\}$ is a process that terminates immediately without state change if ϕ holds, and behaves chaotically, i.e. is completely unconstrained otherwise. (Formally, $\{\phi\}$ is the predicate transformer defined by $\{\phi\}(\psi) = \phi \land \psi$.) As a consequence, (2) constrains – for a given instruction *instr* – the behavior of *Step* only for initial states in which $CurFct(instr)$ holds.

register values at different stages of execution; we differentiate between them implicitly by the places at which they appear in the formulas. The register updates caused by ldc can be represented simply by a multiple assignment statement:

$$E_0(\text{ldc}) \; \geq \; \text{A}, \text{B}, \text{C}, \text{Oreg} := \text{Oreg}, \text{A}, \text{B}, 0 \; . \tag{3}$$

This refinement formula can be interpreted as an axiom on ldc's behavior. Comparing it with the Z-like schema above, the careful reader will notice that incrementation of the instruction pointer is missing. We have decided to move it consistently for all instructions to the fetch phase as this is slightly more convenient for the following exposition.

The behavior of the other instructions can be captured by similar axioms. This keeps the modularity of the description in [23]. Each instruction is described separately by one (or more) formula, which leads in the abstractions to short proofs for single instructions instead of one monolithic proof for the entire instruction set. In addition, it allows to reason formally with only a partial formalization of the instruction set; only the instructions actually used in the compiler need be considered.

The axioms on $E_0(instr)$ claim refinement, not equality. This has a particular benefit: it allows to approximate the actual effect safely if it is not completely known. As an example, let us consider the following axiom for the instruction stl (store-local). Intuitively, stl stores the top value of the register mini-stack to a certain location in the memory.

$$E_0(\text{stl}) \; \geq \; \{\text{Index}(\text{Wptr}, \text{Oreg}) \in \text{Addr}\} \; ; \\ \text{Mem}[\text{Index}(\text{Wptr}, \text{Oreg})], \text{A}, \text{B}, \text{Oreg} := \text{A}, \text{B}, \text{C}, 0 \; ; \; \text{C} := ? \; .$$

Addr denotes the set of valid word addresses and contains only those addresses for which memory is actually available. The assertion $\{\text{Index}(\text{Wptr}, \text{Oreg}) \in \text{Addr}\}$ ensures that the inequality is trivial if the referenced memory address $\text{Index}(\text{Wptr}, \text{Oreg})$ is invalid. This means that the axiom doesn't tell how stl behaves in this situation. The nice effect is that we must ensure, when reasoning about correctness of code, that stl is not used under such circumstances as we cannot otherwise show correctness.

The non-deterministic assignment $\text{C} := ?$ captures that the contents of register C after a stl location is left unspecified by the Transputer designers. Clearly, the C register will contain a certain value but our axiom does not say which. So any reasoning based on this axiom cannot rely on any specific assumption about the final value of C. Without the use of non-determinism and refinement we would be forced either to describe the effect of stl on the register C and stl's behavior when it accesses invalid addresses completely, or to work with an idealized model. The first solution is impractical as such information is not available; the second solution might lead to unsafe reasoning.

2.3 A Hierarchy of Views

The base model of the Transputer is on a rather low level of abstraction. It has not even an explicit notion of an executed machine program but instructions are taken from the memory. In principle it is possible to use this model directly in a correctness predicate relating machine code with source programs but this leads to a complicated definition and to complicated proofs. Therefore, we stepwise derive more abstract views to the Transputer's behavior. These views are successively concerned with the following topics, which in this way can be treated in isolation:

- symbolic representation of the control point, which results in a treatment of the executed machine program as a separate entity;
- word-size operands for direct functions;
- convenient access to the workspace;
- symbolic variables instead of workspace addresses; the mapping of these variables to the workspace is described by a *dictionary* δ;
- hiding of registers.

Each abstraction level comprises a collection of processes. The abstractions are performed by defining the collection of processes for the more abstract view in terms of the collection for the more concrete one. Afterwards sufficiently strong theorems are established that allow one to reason with the abstract family of processes alone, without referring to the concrete family. This is essential for meeting the objective of abstraction, viz. to increase tractability.

Table 1 shows the drastic reduction of the complexity of the terms describing the instruction ldl (load local) at the various abstraction levels. As mentioned, the assertion $\{\mathsf{Index}(\mathtt{Wptr}, \mathtt{Oreg}) \in \mathsf{Addr}\}$ present at the lower abstraction levels make the inequalities applicable only if the referenced address is valid. From Level 3 onwards this is ensured by a global assumption about the storage allocated for the workspace. The models in the hierarchy are consistent by construction, i.e. by definition and calculation.

In the following we discuss the first two abstractions in more detail and sketch the other abstractions.

Symbolic Representation of Programs. It is quite natural to think of a machine program as a separate entity consisting of a sequence of instructions. The point of execution, that is represented on the machine by the instruction pointer's contents, can be modeled by a distinguished position in that instruction sequence. More elegantly we can use a pair of instruction sequences (a, b), where a stands for the part of the machine program before the distinguished position and b for the part thereafter, i.e. the complete machine program is $a \cdot b$ and the next instruction to be executed is the first instruction of b. Progress of execution can be elegantly expressed by partitioning the sequence $a \cdot b$ differently.

Formalizing this idea we define, based on Run, a family of processes $I_1(a, b)$ (parameterized by the pair of instruction sequences a, b). $I_1(a, b)$ describes the

Table 1. Illustration of abstraction levels

The letters v and w range over words; v additionally satisfies $1 \leq v \leq l_W$, i.e., it is a valid workspace address. x is a variable of type word; it is assumed to be in the domain of δ. adr_x is the address of the memory cell allocated for x.

$$E_5^\delta(\text{ldl}, adr_x) \;\geq\; \text{SKIP}$$
$$E_4^\delta(\text{ldl}, adr_x) \;\geq\; \text{A}, \text{B}, \text{C} := x, \text{A}, \text{B}$$
$$E_3(\text{ldl}, v) \;\geq\; \text{A}, \text{B}, \text{C} := \text{Wsp}(v), \text{A}, \text{B}$$
$$E_2(\text{ldl}, w) \;\geq\; \{\text{Index}(\text{Wptr}, w) \in \text{Addr}\} \;;$$
$$\text{A}, \text{B}, \text{C} := \text{Mem}(\text{Index}(\text{Wptr}, w)), \text{A}, \text{B}$$
$$E_1(\text{ldl}) \;\geq\; \{\text{Index}(\text{Wptr}, \text{Oreg}) \in \text{Addr}\} \;;$$
$$\text{A}, \text{B}, \text{C}, \text{Oreg} := \text{Mem}(\text{Index}(\text{Wptr}, \text{Oreg})), \text{A}, \text{B}, 0$$
$$E_0(\text{ldl}) \;\geq\; \{\text{Index}(\text{Wptr}, \text{Oreg}) \in \text{Addr}\} \;;$$
$$\text{A}, \text{B}, \text{C}, \text{Oreg} := \text{Mem}(\text{Index}(\text{Wptr}, \text{Oreg})), \text{A}, \text{B}, 0$$

total behavior resulting from starting $a \cdot b$ with the first instruction of b:

$$I_1(a, b) \;\stackrel{\text{def}}{=}\; \text{var IP} ; [Loaded(a \cdot b) \wedge IPAfter(a)] ; Run ; \text{end IP} .$$

The outer block $\text{var IP} \ldots \text{end IP}$ hides the instruction pointer IP that is no longer needed because the point of execution is symbolically represented from now on. The assumption[3] $[Loaded(a \cdot b) \wedge IPAfter(a)]$ ensures that Run is started in a state where $a \cdot b$ is loaded and the instruction pointer IP points just after a. The predicates $Loaded(u)$ and $IPAfter(v)$ are defined by

$$Loaded(u) \;\stackrel{\text{def}}{=}\; |u| \leq l_P \wedge$$
$$\langle \text{Byte}(\text{Mem}, s_P), \ldots, \text{Byte}(\text{Mem}, s_P + |u| - 1) \rangle = \text{Code}(u)$$
$$IPAfter(v) \;\stackrel{\text{def}}{=}\; \text{IP} = s_P + |v| ,$$

where s_P and l_P are the start address and the length of the *program memory*, i.e. that region of memory allocated to hold the program.

We also define abstractions of the effect processes $E_0(instr)$. These ensure by a final assertion and by taking the greatest lower bound over all possible instruction sequences a, b that neither the loaded program (whatever it might be) nor the position of execution is changed or, more precisely, that changes lead to chaotic behavior:

$$E_1(instr) \;\stackrel{\text{def}}{=}\; \bigwedge_{a,b} \text{var IP} ; [Loaded(a \cdot b) \wedge IPAfter(a)] ; E_0(instr) ;$$
$$\{Loaded(a \cdot b) \wedge IPAfter(a)\} ; \text{end IP} .$$

---

[3] For a predicate ϕ, the *assumption* $[\phi]$ is a process that — like the assertion $\{\phi\}$ — terminates immediately without state change if ϕ holds but leads to miraculous success otherwise. Formally, $[\phi]$ is the predicate transformer $[\phi](\psi) = (\phi \Rightarrow \psi)$.

From these definitions and the axioms of the base model we can prove the following theorem:

Theorem 1 (I1-instruction theorem).
$I_1(a, instr(n) \cdot b) \geq \texttt{Oreg} := \texttt{Oreg bitor } n \text{ ; } E_1(instr) \text{ ; } I_1(a \cdot instr(n), b) .$

Here we write $instr(n)$ for the code sequence consisting of the single instruction $instr$ with four-bit operand n, $0 \leq n < 16$. This theorem formally reflects that a machine program that is loaded and started at some instruction $instr$ with four-bit operand n behaves as follows: n is bitwisely or-ed with the value in the operand register (this loads n to the least four bits of the operand register since every previous instruction leaves these bits cleared), and then the (abstracted) effect of $instr$ is executed. Afterwards it behaves as if the same program is executed starting at the next instruction.

Moreover, we prove for each instruction $instr$ approximations for $E_1(instr)$ that do not refer to E_0. An example for the ldl instruction can be found in Table 1.

Large Operands for Instructions. The purpose of the Transputer's operand register Oreg is to provide word-size operands for the instructions. The idea is that the operand register is filled with the operand in portions of four bits by a sequence of pfix and nfix instructions preceding the instruction for the actual function, the operand part of which provides the least significant four bits only. This special purpose and use of the operand register, however, is not directly reflected in the behavioral description of the Transputer we have available up-to-now, where Oreg is treated like any other register. The second abstraction, therefore, provides an understanding of leading pfix and nfix sequences together with a trailing non-pfix and non-nfix instruction as a multi-byte instruction.

We define a new view $I_2(a, b)$ based on $I_1(a, b)$ and an abstraction $E_2(instr, w)$ of an instruction $instr$'s effect together with a *word operand* w.[4] We then can prove a new version of the instruction theorem:

Theorem 2 (I2-instruction theorem).
$I_2(a, instr(w) \cdot b) \geq E_2(instr, w) \text{ ; } I_2(a \cdot instr(w), b) .$

Now $instr(w)$ stands for the *instruction sequence* resulting from the standard scheme for generating pfix and nfix instructions described in [23, Chapter 4]. Furthermore we prove approximations for E_2 as shown for the ldl-instruction in Table 1. Note that the I2-instruction theorem is easier to apply than the old I1-instruction theorem as it requires no explicit calculations with the operand register.

---

[4] The range of word operands differs for the different processors from the Transputer family. A typically value is $-2^{31} \leq w < 2^{31}$ for 32-bit Transputers but there are also 16-bit Transputers for which the range is $-2^{15} \leq w < 2^{15}$.

Further Abstractions. Due to lack of space we can only briefly sketch the remaining abstraction levels:

- The third level I_3 replaces the memory variable Mem by an array Wsp (the 'workspace') of a fixed length l_W. A fixed value s_W of the workspace pointer is assumed and the workspace is mapped to the sequence of memory locations just above s_W. The abstraction is based on a global assumption that this memory region is disjoint from the program storage and contains only valid addresses. It allows us to reason more easily about Transputer code that accesses the memory via the usual workspace mechanism because reasoning on this level need not reflect the mechanism by which the workspace is mapped to memory. This is done only once while performing the abstraction.
- The next level I_4^δ replaces the workspace by a list of symbolic variables. The set of introduced variables as well as their representation is described by a dictionary δ.
- The final level I_5^δ hides the remaining registers A, B, C and EFlag and provides a view in which only the communications via the links and the symbolic variables are visible.

The choice of the abstraction levels is not accidental. They correspond very well to the intuitive concepts used in informal reasoning about Transputer code and can be interpreted as semantical analogues to increasingly abstract assembler languages. A formally justified counterpart to the intuitive understanding of each abstraction level is provided by an instruction theorem like Theorem 1, special theorems for jumps and conditional jumps, and theorems about the single instructions.

2.4   Incremental Specification of Code

We benefit from the hierarchy of views to the Transputer's behavior when defining the correctness relation between source and target programs. Consider as an example a simple imperative programming language with syntactic categories of programs, statements and expressions and assume that we are globally only interested in the communication behavior of complete programs. Then it is sensible to call a Transputer instruction sequence m correct code for a program *prog* iff

$$I_5^\emptyset(\varepsilon, m) \geq \mathsf{MP}(prog) ,$$

where $\mathsf{MP}(prog)$ is the meaning of *prog* interpreted in the space of processes, ε stands for the empty code sequence, and $\emptyset$ represents the empty dictionary.

Translation of statements, however, has to take representation of variables into account. Therefore, a reasonable correctness condition relating a statement *stat* to code m must employ a non-trivial dictionary δ for the variables appearing in *stat*. When comparing m with *stat* we cannot simply use the predicate given by

$$I_5^\delta(\varepsilon, m) \geq \mathsf{MS}(stat) ,$$

since — inherited from Run — $I_5^\delta(\varepsilon, m)$ does not terminate. (For complete programs this problem does not arise: we assume that programs stop on termination which can be achieved by a stopp instruction in m). The main purpose of termination of $stat$ is to transfer control to its sequential successor. Therefore, we do not expect that the machine stops after execution of m but rather that control is transferred to the code just following m. Formalizing this idea we use the following predicate as notion of correct implementation of statements: m implements $stat$ w.r.t. dictionary δ, $CS(m, stat, \delta)$ for short, iff

$$I_5^\delta(a, m \cdot b) \geq MS(stat) ; I_5^\delta(a \cdot m, b) ,$$

for all code sequences a, b. A correctness predicate for expression translation must refer to the more concrete view I_4^δ because correct expression code is expected to leave the expression's value in register A that is not visible on Level 5.

Having defined correctness predicates, we establish for each source language constructor a theorem that shows how correct code for the composed construct can be obtained from correct code of the components. From a comprehensive set of such theorems a code generator program can be implemented without further semantic consideration. As a first example we present the theorem for sequential composition here; further examples can be found in Sect. 2.6.

Not surprisingly, the sequential composition $\mathbf{seq}(stat_1, stat_2)$ of two statements $stat_1$ and $stat_2$ can simply be implemented by concatenating machine code implementing $stat_1$ and $stat_2$.

Theorem 3 (Sequential composition translation). *Suppose* $CS(m_1, stat_1, \delta)$ *and* $CS(m_2, stat_2, \delta)$ *hold. Then* $CS(m_1 \cdot m_2, \mathbf{seq}(stat_1, stat_2), \delta)$.

The proof is by a little calculation that applies to arbitrary code sequences a and b; of course, sequential composition in the source language corresponds to the sequential composition operator ; of the meta-language:

$$
\begin{aligned}
& I_5^\delta(a, m_1 \cdot m_2 \cdot b) \\
\geq \quad & [CS(m_1, stat_1, \delta)] \\
& MS(stat_1) ; I_5^\delta(a \cdot m_1, m_2 \cdot b) \\
\geq \quad & [CS(m_2, stat_2, \delta)] \\
& MS(stat_1) ; MS(stat_2) ; I_5^\delta(a \cdot m_1 \cdot m_2, b) \\
= \quad & [\text{Definition of semantics of } \mathbf{seq}] \\
& MS(\mathbf{seq}(stat_1, stat_2)) ; I_5^\delta(a \cdot m_1 \cdot m_2, b) .
\end{aligned}
$$

The simplicity of this proof, which looks almost too straightforward to be of interest, stems from the use of the adequate abstraction level. If we had defined CS with direct reference to the Transputer base model (which is easily done by unfolding the definition of I_5^δ) the proof would be far more complex as all invariants that are kept by the code had to be explicitly treated. Now they are treated incrementally during the derivation of the abstraction levels. Moreover, we would not have such a clear way of speaking about the control point but had to refer to its coding in the instruction pointer.

2.5   Real-Time Programs

The ideas described up to now have been applied to a prototypic real-time language. We considered the language of while-programs extended by (synchronous) input/output statements and timing constructs. The timing constructs separate two fundamentally different aspects of timing of computer programs. On the one hand, means for explicitly specifying that certain actions happen at certain time instants are needed. On the other hand, the delay caused by the execution of statements must be controlled to stay in safe limits.

Time instants may be specified either relative or absolut. In a controller for an elevator, for example, we might want to specify that the elevator door opens one second after the chosen floor has been reached, which is a *relative* specification. *Absolute* time instants are needed, for example, to express the requirement that the elevator is to be shut off after closing-time, 6 o'clock p.m. (Of course this requirement needs careful refinement in order to prohibit starvation of people entering the elevator at 5:59...) To perform tasks at absolute time instants is typically delegated to the operating system (consider, for example, the UNIX at daemon); thus absolute timing constructs are not crucial for a real-time language. Relative timing, however, is indispensable in control programs. Common means for specifying relative timing are WAIT statements and time-out clauses. For implementing these constructs, a compiler typically exploits specific features of the implementing hardware, like timers, or applies some service provided by the operating system. Therefore, they don't provide a particular challenge for a compiler. Our work focussed thus on mastering the execution delay.

From the specification point of view the delay caused by statement execution is an undesirable inconvenience but it is an inevitable companion of computation. As it is typically orders of magnitude smaller than the timing requirements of the application, it is often not explicitly adressed in real-time formalisms, e.g., in synchronous languages [18, 6]. If computation load is high, however, the implementing code must be analysed in order to guarantee the timing requirements of the application. We are heading for an approach that avoids such an *a posteriori* analysis but remains as convenient as possible for the programmer.

The idea is to allow the programmer to specify upper bounds for the tolerated execution time of basic blocks in the source language. It is the obligation of the compiler to check whether these upper bounds are met by the generated code. There is no point in specifying lower bounds on execution delay: faster execution should always be an improvement. Note that faster execution does not affect explicit delays as in WAIT statements, as these are implemented by primitives that are not influenced by processor speed. To specify only upper bounds has the benefits that the compiler has to perform just a worst-case timing analysis and that migration to faster processors without recompilation is possible. It would, however, be rather inconvenient for the programmer, if any statement must be guarded by an upper-bound. We offer the idealization that internal computation, like assignments and evaluation of guards of loops and conditionals, proceeds in zero time. Thus only input/output statements must be guarded and smooth program transformation laws are valid. Assignments, for example, can be moved in and out of time bounds, and logically redundant assignments can freely be introduced or eliminated without affecting the timing behavior of programs. This idealization, which is akin to that found in synchronous languages, can be justified by exploiting that internal computation is not directly observable. We describe in Sect. 2.6 how this challenge was met in a semantic compiler proof.

Let us illustrate both aspects of timing by means of a small program fragment taken from a control program for the ProCoS gas burner (cf. Sect. 3.6):

```
. . .
heatreq := false
WHILE not(heatreq) DO
  SEQ
    WAIT 1/2
    UPPERBOUND 1/8
      input(hr, heatreq)
. . .
```

We use an OCCAM-like concrete syntax of programs, where indentation indicates block structure; SEQ is the sequential composition operator, the other constructors are self-explaining.

The statement input(hr, heatreq) reads the current state of a thermostat, which is connected to the program via channel hr, and stores it to the variable heatreq. The purpose of the above program fragment is to poll the thermostat until it reports that heat is requested. Each iteration of the loop first waits half a second and then questions channel hr for the current status of the thermostat. The input statement is guarded by the UPPERBOUND 1/8 clause, which ensures that it takes at most 1/8 seconds to read in the current state of the thermostat.[5] The programmer can safely assume that all other activity is instantaneous, the initial assignment to variable heatreq as well as the evaluation and checking of the loop's guard not(heatreq). He can also assume that WAIT 1/2 waits precisely half a second. The actual execution time of the code implementing these statements, as well as the deviation of the implementation of the WAIT statement from the ideal timing is shifted by the compiler to the input statement and then settled with the upperbound; thus the total overhead of each iteration is bounded by 1/8 seconds. Consequently, the polling loop ensures that a change to the heat request state of the thermostat is detected after at most 5/8 seconds.

The idealized timing properties supported by the compiler allow one to specify such a reactivity requirement in a simple way. Otherwise, all statement would have to be bounded but it would be quite difficult to guess adequate bounds because the generated code is not known in advance.

---

[5] Communication is synchronous; hence both input and output statements stall until the corresponding communication partner becomes ready. The duration of this stalling cannot be bounded by the compiler; it is totally dependent on the environment. By convention, it is not included into the time bounded by UPPERBOUND; the UPPERBOUND only refers to the time used for preparation of the communication. In the example program fragment, we assume that the thermostat is always ready to output its current state on channel hr such that there is no stalling.

2.6 Time Shifts

In this section we discuss the additional ingredients of the compiler correctness proof for the timed language.

First of all, the imperative meta-language is provided with a timed interpretation and extended by delays $\Delta\, d$ and time bounds $\lceil P \rceil \preceq d$, where $d \in \mathbb{R}_{\geq 0} \cup \{\infty\}$. This is done in such a way that all constructs except delays execute in zero time. The bound operator constrains the time consumed by the enclosed process P (not counting the time that P stalls waiting for communication partners to become ready); $\Delta\, d$ executes in at most d time units without state change. For simplicity, we use the duration of one execution cycle of the target processor as the unit of time in this section.

We add delays to the axioms describing the effect of instructions. For example, the timed version of Axiom (3) looks as follows:

$$E_0(\mathtt{ldc}) \;\geq\; \Delta\, 1 \;;\; \mathtt{A,B,C,IP,Oreg} := \mathtt{Oreg,A,B,IP}+1,0 \;.$$

This expresses that $\mathtt{ldc}$ uses at most one execution cycle for execution. The timing information is taken from the tables in [23, Appendix D].

A particularly interesting aspect of the code generator proof is that it justifies the idealization of instantaneous execution for all internal constructs of the timed source language, i.e. all constructs except input/output statements. Of course, the code implementing, say, an assignment needs time to execute. The idea is to shift such excess time of code implementing internal activity to a sequentially successive process that is compiled to a machine program needing less time for execution than allowed by the source [15]. This can be accomplished by adding two parameters L and R to the correctness predicate for statements, where L states the excess time of the sequential predecessor that is absorbed and R states the excess time that is handed over to the sequential successor for absorption. A third new parameter E is introduced that asserts a time bound for the source statement. This leads to the following definition: a machine program m implements source statement $stat$, absorbing excess time L from its sequential predecessor, exporting excess time R to its sequential successor, under time bound E, iff for all instruction sequences a and b

$$\Delta\, L \;;\; I_5^\delta(a, m \cdot b) \;\geq\; \lceil \mathsf{MS}(stat) \rceil \preceq E \;;\; \Delta\, R \;;\; I_5^\delta(a \cdot m, b) \;.$$

For brevity, we denote this implementation property by $\mathsf{CS}'(m, stat, \delta, L, R, E)$. Let us now have a look at some example translation theorems.

The theorem that allows to translate time bounds in the source program looks as follows:

Theorem 4 (Translation of time bounds). *Suppose* $\mathsf{CS}'(m, stat, \delta, L, R, E)$. *If* $E \leq t$ *then* $\mathsf{CS}'(m, \mathbf{upperbound}(P, t), \delta, L, R, E)$.

Thus, a compiler encountering an upper bound operator in the source statement needs only check whether the required time bound is more liberal than the one asserted upon the code generated for the enclosed statement. If it is, then no further action is necessary, as the real-time requirement expressed by the bound is met. If it is less liberal, on the other hand, the source statement cannot be adequately compiled for the given target hardware with the given code generation strategy, and should be rejected (or perhaps another code generator should be activated). The proof of Theorem 4 is quite simple, given the following law.

$$\text{(Multiple-bound)} \qquad (||\,P\,| \preceq t_1 | \preceq t_2) = (|\,P\,| \preceq \min(t_1, t_2))$$

Let us now have a look at the theorem for the translation of an assignment statement $\mathbf{assign}(x, e)$. In the theorem below, CE is the correctness condition for expression translation. Intuitively, $\mathsf{CE}(e, m_{,1}, \delta, E_1)$ holds, if m_1 is a piece of code that evaluates e assuming that variables are represented according to the dictionary δ. $\mathsf{CE}(e, m_{,1}, \delta, E_1)$ also asserts that m_1 executes in at most E_1 time units.

Theorem 5 (Assignment translation).
Suppose $\mathsf{CE}(e, m_1, \delta, E_1)$, $m = m_1 \cdot \mathtt{stl}(adr_x)$, *and* $R \geq L + E_1 + ldt(adr_x) + 1$. *Then* $\mathsf{CS}'(\mathbf{assign}(x, e), m, \delta, L, R, E)$.

The proposed code m is composed from evaluation code for the expression e and a $\mathtt{stl}$-instruction that stores the result value to the location allocated for x. Its execution time is the sum of the time E_1 needed for evaluating the expression e, the time $ldt(adr_x)$ needed for loading the operand of the final $\mathtt{stl}$ instruction, i.e. the address of x, and one additional time unit for the execution of the $\mathtt{stl}$ instruction itself. Note that the entire execution delay $E_1 + ldt(adr_x) + 1$ of m is handed over via the parameter R to the sequential successor for absorption together with the time L to be absorbed. Note also that there is no condition on E. Hence, any time bound can be asserted for an assignment. This justifies the idealization of immediate execution.

For communication statements, on the other hand, immediate execution cannot be assumed as their effect is visible to the environment. Also the time absorbed from predecessor code becomes visible here. Let us have a look at the theorem concerned with translation of an output statment $\mathbf{output}(\mathsf{Out}_i, expr)$, which, intuitively, outputs the value of expression $expr$ on link i $(i = 0, \ldots, 3)$.

Theorem 6 (Output translation).
Suppose $\mathsf{CE}(expr, m_1, \delta, E_1)$, $m = m_1 \cdot \mathtt{mint} \cdot \mathtt{ldc}(i) \cdot \mathtt{bcnt} \cdot \mathtt{add} \cdot \mathtt{rev} \cdot \mathtt{outword}$, $R \geq outdelay_2$, *and* $E \geq L + E_1 + outdelay_1 + 8$. *Then* $\mathsf{CS}'(\mathbf{output}(\mathsf{Out}_i, expr), m, \delta, L, R, E)$.

The code is composed from expression evaluation code m_1, a piece of code $\mathtt{mint} \cdot \mathtt{ldc}(i) \cdot \mathtt{bcnt} \cdot \mathtt{add} \cdot \mathtt{rev}$ (executing in 8 cycles) that fills the Transputer registers with adequate parameters, and a final $\mathtt{outword}$ instruction which initiates the actual output. The execution of $\mathtt{outword}$ consists of three phases. After the first phase, which executes in (at most) $outdelay_1$ time units, the commuicated value is available on the link i. In the second phase the Transputer waits for its communication partner to become ready (recall that communication is synchronous) and exchanges the actual value. The time spent during this phase cannot be controlled by a process but depends solely on the environment; it is ignored in the semantic model used. The third phase, which executes in (at most) $outdelay_2$ time units, is concerned with some operation after the communication commenced.

The time $E_1 + outdelay_1 + 8$ spent by the code before the communicated value becomes available to the environment cannot be handed over to the successor as the communication is visible to the environment. Together with the time L to be absorbed from the predecessor it poses a constraint on time bounds that can be guaranteed for the output statement. This is expressed by the condition on E. The time $outdelay_2$ spent after the communication takes place, on the other hand, is handed over to the sequential successor for absorption via parameter R.

Let us finally have a look at the timed version of Theorem 3.

Theorem 7 (Sequential composition translation).
Suppose $\mathsf{CS}'(stat_1, m_1, \delta, L_1, R_1, E_1)$, $\mathsf{CS}'(stat_2, m_2, \delta, L_2, R_2, E_2)$, *and* $R_1 \leq L_2$. *Then* $\mathsf{CS}'(\mathsf{seq}(stat_1, stat_2), m_1 \cdot m_2, \delta, L_1, R_2, E_1 + E_2)$.

Here, the premise $R_1 \leq L_2$ expresses that the code m_2 for the second component $stat_2$ must be able to absorb at least the excess time R_1 handed over from the first component. Note that we can assert for a sequential composition the sum of time bounds for its components.

From a collection of such theorems that describe construction of correct code for each operator of the source language we have developed a code generator written in the functional language Standard ML [30]. By adding a frontend, we have constructed a prototypical compiler [36].

This concludes this overview on the modular verified design of code generators. The modularity of the approach facilitates the construction of code generators and assists rigorous control procedures because it allows to split both tasks into relatively small, independent sub-tasks. Moreover, it enables reuse. The derived views to the Transputer, e.g., can be exploited for different source languages or even used when verifying boot programs or operating systems. To use some form of refinement as underlying notion of correctness instead of semantic equivalence allows a proper treatment of under-specification in the target and the source language, which allows, e.g., to give a proper meaning to uninitialized variables. Moreover it accommodates modularization. Like the work at CLI (Computational Logic Inc.) on the 'small stack' [7] we have put emphasis on consistent interfaces to higher and lower levels of abstraction.

3 Synthesis of Embedded Real-Time Controllers

We will now turn to the problem of directly synthesizing real-time embedded controllers from metric-time temporal logic specifications. In comparison to imperative programming languages, such logics provide a very abstract means of specifying what the system should do rather than saying how to achieve this. Thus, using such logics as source languages for compilation or synthesis methods for embedded controllers would be desirable. This is particularly true for those logics that provide a very high level of abstraction from operational detail, like e.g. the monadic second order logic of temporal distance [46] or the Duration Calculus [49].

Unfortunately, in the realm of dense metric time, logics featuring rich metric-time vocabulary and full negation tend to become undecidable (e.g., above two are), which has direct impact on the feasibility of sound and complete automatic synthesis procedures. However, the argument which makes decidability a necessary condition for feasibility of synthesis (to be reviewed in Sect. 3.4) relies on an essentially unconstrained environment dynamics. We argue that through exploitation of general constraints on environment dynamics, synthesis methods can be exposed even for some undecidable metric real-time logics, and exemplify this on synthesis procedures for timed controllers from dense-time Duration Calculus in Sect. 3.5.

3.1   Duration Calculus

Duration Calculus (abbreviated DC in the remainder) is a real-time logic that is specially tailored towards reasoning about durational constraints on time-dependent Boolean-valued states. The syntax of the subsets of DC formulae that we will study is

$$\langle formula \rangle ::= \langle atomicform \rangle \mid \neg \langle formula \rangle \mid$$
$$(\langle formula \rangle \wedge \langle formula \rangle) \mid (\langle formula \rangle ; \langle formula \rangle)$$
$$k ::\in \mathbb{N}$$
$$\langle state \rangle ::= \langle variable \rangle \mid \neg \langle state \rangle \mid (\langle state \rangle \wedge \langle state \rangle)$$
$$\langle variable \rangle ::\in Varname$$

Concerning the available atomic formulae, we distinguish two different subsets of DC. In the first subset, often called the $\{\lceil P \rceil, \ell = k\}$ fragment, atomic formulae take the form

$$\langle atomicform \rangle ::= \lceil \langle state \rangle \rceil \mid \ell = k \ ,$$

while in the so-called $\{\int P = k\}$ fragment,

$$\langle atomicform \rangle ::= \int \langle state \rangle = k \ .$$

Duration Calculus is interpreted over trajectories

$$tr \in Traj \stackrel{\text{def}}{=} \{tr : Time \rightarrow Varname \rightarrow \mathbb{B} \mid Time = \mathbb{R}_{\geq 0}, tr \text{ finitely variable}\}$$

that provide a finitely variable, time-dependent, Boolean-valued valuation of variables. Finite variability — sometimes also called non-Zenoness — means that only finitely many state changes may occur within any finite time interval. The definition of satisfaction of a formula ϕ by a trajectory tr, denoted $tr \models \phi$ is given in Table 2. The set of models of ϕ, i.e. trajectories satisfying ϕ, is denoted $\mathcal{M}[\![\phi]\!]$.

As usual, we say that ϕ *is valid* iff $\mathcal{M}[\![\phi]\!] = Traj$. According to [48], validity is undecidable for the fragment $\{\lceil P \rceil, \ell = k\}$. Consequently, the same applies for the fragment $\{\int P = k\}$, as $\lceil P \rceil$ can be encoded as $\int \neg P = 0 \wedge \neg (\int \text{true} = 0)$ and $\ell = k$ as $\int \text{true} = k$, resp.

Table 2. Semantics of Duration Calculus

$tr, [a, b] \models \phi$ denotes that trajectory tr satisfies a formula ϕ within a time interval $[a, b] \subset \mathbb{R}_{\geq 0}$. It is defined by

$$
\begin{array}{lll}
tr, [a, b] \models \int P = k & \text{iff} & \int_a^b \chi_{P,tr}(t)\, dt = k \ , \\
tr, [a, b] \models \lceil P \rceil & \text{iff} & b > a \wedge \int_a^b \chi_{P,tr}(t)\, dt = b - a \ , \\
tr, [a, b] \models \ell = k & \text{iff} & b - a = k \ , \\
tr, [a, b] \models \neg\phi & \text{iff} & tr, [a, b] \not\models \phi \ , \\
tr, [a, b] \models (\phi \wedge \psi) & \text{iff} & tr, [a, b] \models \phi \ \text{ and } \ tr, [a, b] \models \psi \ , \\
tr, [a, b] \models (\phi ; \psi) & \text{iff} & \exists m \in [a, b] . \begin{pmatrix} tr, [a, m] \models \phi \ \text{ and} \\ tr, [m, b] \models \psi \end{pmatrix} ,
\end{array}
$$

where $\chi_{P,tr}(t) = 1$ iff the state formula P evaluates to true in time instant t over trajectory tr, and $\chi_{P,tr}(t) = 0$ otherwise.

A trajectory tr *satisfies a formula* ϕ, denoted $tr \models \phi$, iff all finite prefixes of tr satisfy ϕ — formally, $tr \models \phi$ iff $tr, [0, t] \models \phi$ for each $t \in \mathbb{R}_{\geq 0}$. Accordingly, a trajectory is a counterexample of ϕ, i.e. does not satisfy ϕ, iff some of its finite prefixes satisfies $\neg\phi$.

3.2 Timed Controllers

We do now turn to the implementation "technology" we are aiming at. For the purpose of this overview, it is timed transition tables in the sense of Alur and Dill [1] extended by a notion of environment input and transition-table output. Thus, it is basically an untimed, Mealy-type transition table (Σ, σ_0, T), where

- Σ is a finite, nonempty set of states,
- $\sigma_0 \in \Sigma$ is the initial state,
- $T \subseteq \Sigma \times \alpha \times \Sigma$ is the transition relation, where the alphabet α is of the form $(I \uplus O) \to \mathbb{B}$ with I being the finite set of (Boolean-valued) input ports and O being the finite set of (Boolean-valued) output ports (i.e. α assigns binary values to input and output ports),
- T is *input-open*, which means that from any state $\sigma \in \Sigma$ there is a transition for each input $i \in I \to \mathbb{B}$.

However, in timed transition tables these basic untimed transition tables are extended with a finite number of real-valued clocks that can be reset upon transitions and can be compared against constants in transition guards. Thus, transitions are of the extended form $(\sigma, a, \sigma', guard, reset)$, with $a \in \alpha$, $\sigma, \sigma' \in \Sigma$, $guard$ an integer-bounded interval constraint on the clocks Cl, and $reset \subseteq Cl$.

Intuitively, a timed transition table may take transition $(\sigma, a, \sigma', guard, reset)$ when it is in internal state σ, the (internal) clock reading satisfies $guard$, and the current input is $a|_I$. It then produces output valuation $a|_O$ at its output ports, which persists until the next transition, moves to internal state σ', and synchronously resets the clocks in $reset$ to 0. The timed transition table thus produces a time-dependent valuation of its input and output ports, i.e. a trajectory. For any timed transition table C, the set of its trajectories is denoted $\mathcal{C}[C]$.

Finally, if timed transition tables are to be used as embedded controllers, we must require that they be input open. Due to the clock-dependent behaviour, this involves a slight extension to above notion of being input-open: a timed transition table is *input-open* iff from any state σ under any possible clock valuation there is a transition for each $i \in I \rightarrow \mathbb{B}$. A timed transition table with that property is called *timed controller (with input I and outputs O)* in the remainder.

Based on the definition of trajectories of timed controllers, it is straightforward to define when a timed controller satisfies a DC formula. The criterion is trajectory inclusion.

Definition 8 (Satisfaction). *Let C be a timed controller and ϕ a Duration Calculus formula. We say that C satisfies ϕ iff $C[\![C]\!] \subseteq \mathcal{M}[\![\phi]\!]$.*

3.3 Control Problems and Controller Synthesis

Duration Calculus was designed for bridging the gap between requirements capture and controller implementation in an embedded-controller design activity. Consequently, we are interested in the satisfaction problem between controllers from the design space and *control problems* expressed in Duration Calculus.

Definition 9 (Control problem). *A control problem is a pair (Req, I), where Req is a formula of Duration Calculus specifying the admissible controller behaviours and $I \subseteq Varname$ is a set of variable names specifying the inputs to the controller, i.e. those variables that the controller cannot control and hence is not allowed to constrain in their evolution over time. We say that a control problem (Req, I) is a $\{\lceil P \rceil, \ell = k\}$ control problem (or a $\{\int P = k\}$ control problem) iff Req is a $\{\lceil P \rceil, \ell = k\}$ formula (a $\{\int P = k\}$ formula, resp.).*

A controller C is said to solve the control problem (Req, I) iff C has inputs I and satisfies Req.

Aiming at solutions to control problems we are interested in synthesis methods that derive controllers from control problems. Such a synthesis method can be understood as a partial mapping *synt* from control problems to controllers. Let *synt* be a (for the moment not necessarily effective) partial function from the set of control problems to controllers. We will now define when *synt* provides a sound and complete synthesis method for control problems.

Definition 10 (Soundness and completeness of a synthesis procedure). *We say*

1. *that synt is sound iff it maps control problems to solutions thereof, and*
2. *that synt is $\{\lceil P \rceil, \ell = k\}$-complete (or $\{\int P = k\}$-complete) iff its domain contains all $\{\lceil P \rceil, \ell = k\}$ control problems ($\{\int P = k\}$ control problems, resp.) that are solvable by timed controllers.*

The interesting question is whether there is a sound and complete *mechanic* synthesis method for timed controllers from DC-based control problems. Unfortunately, the answer is negative, as is shown in the next section.

276 M. Fränzle and M. Müller-Olm

3.4 Synthesis Under Unconstrained Environment Dynamics

We start with analyzing the synthesis problem with respect to unconstrained environment dynamics. I.e., inputs may change arbitrarily — but of course finitely variable — over time. Then, a controller cannot contribute to requirements that are in terms of inputs only:

Lemma 11. *Let ϕ be a duration formula and let C be an arbitrary controller with inputs $I \supseteq free(\phi)$. Then C satisfies ϕ iff ϕ is valid.*

Proof. It is obvious that validity of ϕ implies that C satisfies ϕ, as the trajectories of C are necessarily a subset of the universe *Traj* of trajectories. For the converse implication observe that satisfaction of ϕ by a trajectory tr does only depend on the valuation that tr assigns to variables in $free(\phi)$. Assume that ϕ is invalid and let $tr \not\models \phi$. As C has inputs I, C has a trajectory tr' that coincides with tr on all variables in $I \supseteq free(\phi)$. As satisfaction of ϕ depends only on the valuation of its free variables, $tr' \not\models \phi$ follows. I.e., C does not satisfy ϕ. $\square$

This lemma has direct consequences for the feasibility of automatic synthesis.

Theorem 12. *Any synthesis procedure is necessarily unsound or $\{\lceil P \rceil, \ell = k\}$-incomplete (and hence also $\{\int P\}$-incomplete) or ineffective. I.e., there is no effective procedure that generates solutions for any solvable $\{\lceil P \rceil, \ell = k\}$ control problem.*

Proof. Let *synt* be a sound and complete mapping from $\{\lceil P \rceil, \ell = k\}$ control problems to timed controllers. Let ϕ be a $\{\lceil P \rceil, \ell = k\}$ formula.

According to Lemma 11, the control problem $(\phi, free(\phi))$ has a solution iff ϕ is valid. As *synt* is sound and complete it follows that $(\phi, free(\phi)) \in dom\,(synt)$ iff ϕ is valid. Thus, an effective mapping *synt* would provide a decision procedure for $\{\lceil P \rceil, \ell = k\}$ formulae, in contrast to the undecidability result of [48]. This implies that *synt* cannot be effective. $\square$

Thus, automatic synthesis of controllers is impossible even for the restricted class of $\{\lceil P \rceil, \ell = k\}$ control problems, unless one is willing to sacrifice completeness.

However, it is enlightening to observe that the reduction of the decision problem to the synthesis problem performed in above proof is based on the reduction of the validity problem to a satisfaction problem in Lemma 11, which in turn crucially relies on the unconstrained input dynamics of timed controllers. The latter allows inputs to exhibit arbitrary finitely variable dynamics, which permits above reductions. However, embedded real-time controllers are embedded into an environment which may not be able to provide arbitrary finitely variable stimuli. Hence, it is questionable whether the full range of finitely variable trajectories should be regarded as crucial to the satisfaction problem between controllers and control problems. In most (if not all) application domains, more restrictive constraints on the temporal evolution of trajectories can be justified from physical properties of the systems. Therefore, it makes sense to investigate the synthesis problem for Duration Calculus under suitable restrictions of the possible input and output behaviour.

3.5 Constrained Environment Dynamics

In the remainder, we will investigate the synthesis problem under some reasonable constraints on the possible input and output dynamics. Therefore, we say that $Traj_I \subseteq Traj$ is a *constraint on input behaviour* for the inputs $I \subset Varname$ iff $tr \in Traj_I$ implies $tr' \in Traj_I$ for any $tr' \in Traj$ that differs from tr only on non-input variables (i.e., any tr' that satisfies $tr(t)(x) \neq tr'(t)(x) \Rightarrow x \notin I$). Similarly, $Traj_O \subseteq Traj$ is a *constraint on output behaviour* iff $tr \in Traj_O$ implies $tr' \in Traj_O$ for any $tr' \in Traj$ that differs from tr only on non-output variables.

Definition 13 (Satisfaction under behavioural constraints). *We say that a controller C satisfies Req under input constraint $Traj_I$ and output constraint $Traj_O$ iff $Traj_I \cap C[\![C]\!] \subseteq \mathcal{M}[\![Req]\!] \cap Traj_O$. I.e., if C is used in a context where the environment guarantees the constraint on input behaviour then C guarantees both Req and the constraint on output behaviour.*

Now, it is straightforward to define when a controller solves a control problem under input and output constraints and when synthesis is sound and complete with respect to given input and output behavioural constraints.

With this machinery, we are now prepared for investigating the synthesis problem under behavioural constraints.

Bounded Variability of Input and Output Behaviour. Considering the fact that any physically realizable reactive system is subject to band-limitedness, an easily justifiable assumption on *realistic* device models is that state changes can only come arbitrarily close in time if they originate from different subsystems. As the number of subsystems in a given technical system is finite this implies that the number of state changes observable at the controller's interface within a time unit is bounded by a system-dependent natural number. An appropriate behavioural model is that of *n-bounded trajectories*, which are those trajectories that exhibit at most n state changes over any unit-length interval of time, where $n \in \mathbb{N}$ is a system-dependent parameter. The set of n-bounded trajectories is denoted $Traj_n$. Given inputs I and outputs O, we furthermore denote by $Traj_{I,n}$ ($Traj_{O,m}$) the sets of trajectories which after projection to the inputs I (outputs O, resp.) are n-bounded (m-bounded, resp.).

$Traj_{I,n}$ and $Traj_{O,m}$ represent constraints on input and output behaviour. With respect to synthesis it is interesting to see that these easily justifiable constraints suffice to facilitate synthesizing timed controllers from $\{\lceil P \rceil, \ell = k\}$ control problems:

Theorem 14. *There is an effective, sound, and $\{\lceil P \rceil, \ell = k\}$-complete synthesis procedure for timed controllers when input dynamics is constrained to be n-bounded and output dynamics is constrained to be m-bounded for given $n, m \in \mathbb{N}$.*

Proof. Using standard techniques, an effective mapping of $\{\lceil P \rceil, \ell = k\}$ formulae that do contain *exactly one, outermost, negation* to timed automata that recognize their counterexamples of *finite* variability can be defined. Using the timed regular expression notation proposed by Asarin, Caspi, and Maler in [2], such an automata-theoretic representation of the counterexamples can be achieved through the mapping

$$Counterexamples(\neg\phi) \stackrel{\text{def}}{=} FiniteModels(\phi) \cdot \alpha^\omega$$

of $\{\lceil P \rceil, \ell = k\}$-formulae to timed regular expressions, where α is the set of min-terms over the free state variables of ϕ and

$$FiniteModels(\lceil P \rceil) \stackrel{\text{def}}{=} \left(\left(\bigvee_{a \in \alpha, a \models P} a \right)^* \right)_{(0,\infty)} \;,$$

$$FiniteModels(\ell = k) \stackrel{\text{def}}{=} (\alpha^*)_{[k,k]} \;,$$

$$FiniteModels(\phi \wedge \psi) \stackrel{\text{def}}{=} FiniteModels(\phi) \wedge FiniteModels(\psi) \;,$$

$$FiniteModels(\phi \,;\, \psi) \stackrel{\text{def}}{=} FiniteModels(\phi) \cdot FiniteModels(\psi) \;.$$

As the timed regular languages of variability $n + m$ are furthermore effectively closed under complementation (relative to the set of $(n + m)$-bounded trajectories) [45], this procedure can be extended to deal with inner negation also if only the $(n + m)$-bounded counterexamples are of interest. Therefore, any formula ϕ of the $\{\lceil P \rceil, \ell = k\}$ fragment of DC can be effectively assigned a timed automaton $A_{Traj_{n+m} \backslash \phi}$ recognizing its $(n + m)$-bounded counterexamples. While the deterministically recognizable timed regular languages are in general a proper subclass of the non-deterministically recognizable ones, these two classes coincide for the timed regular languages of variability $n + m$. In particular, $A_{Traj_{n+m} \backslash \phi}$ can be made deterministic.

Now, $A_{Traj_{n+m} \backslash \phi}$ can be easily extended to an (again deterministic) timed automaton $A_{Traj_{n+m} \backslash (\phi \cup Traj_{O,m}) \cap Traj_{I,n}}$ that, besides recognizing any $(n + m)$-bounded counterexample of ϕ, also recognizes all trajectories violating the m-boundedness constraints on outputs, yet excludes trajectories violating the n-boundedness constraint on inputs. This effectively reduces the controller synthesis problem to a strategy construction problem in a timed regular game, where $A_{Traj_{n+m} \backslash (\phi \cup Traj_{O,m}) \cap Traj_{I,n}}$ is the game graph. As effective synthesis procedures for timed regular games are known from the literature (cf. [3, 26]), this solves the controller synthesis problem.   □

Unfortunately, Theorem 14 does not generalize to $\{\int P = k\}$ control problems, as their requirements formulae feature accumulated durations and thus are considerably more expressive than the $\{\lceil P \rceil, \ell = k\}$ control problems: As was shown in [14], page 35ff., by means of a real-time pumping lemma, it is in general undecidable whether $Traj_n \subseteq \mathcal{M}[\![\phi]\!]$ for $\{\int P = k\}$ formulae ϕ. Thus, by an argument akin to that used in the proof of Theorem 12, it follows that there is no effective, sound, and $\{\int P = k\}$-complete synthesis procedure even when interface dynamics is restricted to n-bounded inputs and m-bounded outputs.

Time-Wise Discrete Input and Output Behaviour. In order to obtain automatic synthesis procedures for $\{\int P = k\}$ control problems, we may try to reduce the model class that is regarded crucial to satisfaction still further. If the devices to be designed are embedded into a synchronously clocked environment it makes sense to consider trajectories that are changing state only at evenly spaced time instants. This is captured by studying *time-wise discrete trajectories*, where a trajectory $tr \in Traj$ is called time-wise discrete iff it has discontinuities only in time instants which are multiples of the time unit. The set of time-wise discrete trajectories is denoted $DTraj$. Accordingly, the input constraint that restricts inputs to change only in time instants which are multiples of the time unit is denoted $DTraj_I$, while the corresponding behavioural output constraint is denoted $DTraj_O$.

The restriction to such time-wise discrete interface behaviour allows automatic synthesis even for $\{\int P = k\}$ control problems:

Theorem 15. *There is an effective, sound, and $\{\int P = k\}$-complete (and thus also $\{\lceil P \rceil, \ell = k\}$-complete) synthesis procedure for timed controllers when input and output behaviour is constrained to be time-wise discrete.*

Proof. It is a tedious, yet mostly straightforward exercise to show that for any formula ϕ of the $\{\int P = k\}$ fragment, $\mathcal{M}[\![\phi]\!] \cap DTraj$ is an unrolling of an ω-regular language to real-time based on the convention that one letter per time unit is traversed. A corresponding ω-automaton Aut_ϕ^{twd} can be effectively constructed (the construction is fully pursued in [14, chapter 6.3]).

Now, a similar construction as in the proof of the previous theorem can be applied to Aut_ϕ^{twd} to obtain an appropriate game graph representing the behaviorally constrained synthesis problem. However, this time the game graph obtained is ω-regular as Aut_ϕ^{twd} is an untimed finite automaton and the behavioural constraints can also be formalised with untimed automata using the convention that one letter per time unit is traversed. This effectively reduces the synthesis problem to strategy construction in ω-regular games. As algorithms for the latter are well-known (cf. e.g. [44]), this yields the desired synthesis method. Details of the construction can be found in [13, 14]. □

As, for example, the ProCoS gas-burner requirements specification [41] can be expressed in the $\{\int P = k\}$ subset of DC, this allows automatic synthesis of a timed controller directly from the requirements specification of the gas-burner, which is shown in the next section.

3.6 A Case Study: Synthesizing a Synchronous Controller for the ProCoS Gas-Burner

The ProCoS gas-burner [41, 42] is a simple model of a computer-controlled gas-burner, depicted in Fig. 1. Its embedded controller has just three binary control lines connected to the environment: *hr* signals heat requests from a thermostat, *fl* signals whether the flame is burning, and *gas* controls the gas valve. The gas valve is the only actuator in the system, and gas is expected to usually ignite spontaneously once the gas valve is opened.[6] However, gas may sometimes fail to ignite, leading to an increasing concentration of flammable gas in the environment, which is an obvious risk. The task of the controller is to prevent unsafe gas concentration in the environment through detection of ignition failures and appropriate actions, and to deliver service as required by *hr* if ignition works as expected.

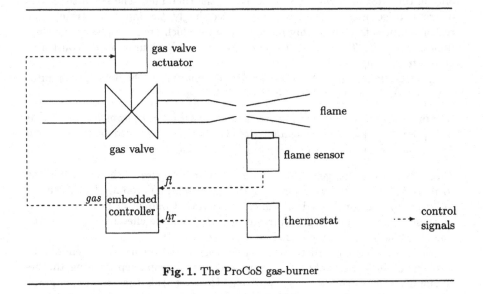

Fig. 1. The ProCoS gas-burner

The corresponding requirements can be easily formalized using $\{\int P = k\}$ formulae. Indeed, the patterns occurring have been the key motivation for development of the Duration Calculus. In the following, we stick to the original requirements given in [41, 9], but sometimes reduce time constants.

The foremost requirement the controller has to ensure is that the gas concentration in the environment is kept below flammable level. As sensors for directly detecting the gas concentration are expensive, the gas concentration has to be safely estimated from the length and temporal distance of periods of leakage of unignited gas to the environment. We assume that safety engineers have shown that the system is safe if unignited gas may not leak from the burner for more than 3 seconds within any 6 seconds of operation.[7] Using DC, this can be for-

---

[6] The reader reluctant to the idea of spontaneous ignition may equally well think of an ignition device being coupled to the gas valve such that both can be simultaneously controlled by the single control signal *gas*.

[7] In the original formulation of the problem, the corresponding figures where a maximum of 4 seconds leak time within 30 seconds, but these have been reduced in order to make the synthesized controller fit on a page.

malized as

$$safe \stackrel{\text{def}}{=} \Box \left(\ell < 6 \Rightarrow \int leak < 3 \right) ,$$

where $\Box\phi \stackrel{\text{def}}{=} \neg(\textbf{true};(\neg\phi);\textbf{true})$ and $\int P < k \stackrel{\text{def}}{=} \neg(\int P = k\,;\textbf{true})$. Using the available sensors, leakage — or indeed a sufficient approximation of leakage — is detected through observing the flame sensor when the gas valve is open: gas is deemed to be leaking iff the flame sensor senses that the flame is not burning while the gas valve is open.

$$leak \stackrel{\text{def}}{=} gas \wedge \neg fl .$$

Requirement *safe* alone is easily satisfied: as leaks can only occur when the gas valve is open, a controller permanently setting control line *gas* to false and thus keeping the gas valve closed will satisfy *safe*. However, a customer will not be satisfied with a gas-burner never delivering service. Therefore, some requirements concerning controllability of the system through *hr* are added. First, we require that $\neg hr$ will shut the gas supply within one second:

$$stop \stackrel{\text{def}}{=} (\lceil \neg hr \rceil \wedge \ell = 1) \leadsto \lceil \neg gas \rceil ,$$

where $\phi \leadsto \lceil P \rceil \stackrel{\text{def}}{=} \neg(\textbf{true};\phi;\lceil \neg P \rceil;\textbf{true})$. Furthermore, we would like to require that *hr* leads to heat supply within a reasonable time span. However, this demand can only be realized if gas does not fail to ignite after opening the valve. Therefore, the startup requirement is relative to an environment assumption which formalizes the normal ignition behaviour. The normal ignition behaviour is that gas ignites soon after opening the valve such that the flame sensor reports a burning flame within 2 seconds. Whenever this is the case, heat should be supplied after at most 8 seconds of continuous heat request:

$$start \stackrel{\text{def}}{=} flame\ ok \Rightarrow ((\lceil hr \rceil \wedge \ell = 8) \leadsto \lceil fl \rceil) ,$$

$$flame\ ok \stackrel{\text{def}}{=} (\lceil gas \rceil \wedge \ell = 2) \leadsto \lceil fl \rceil .$$

The requirement to be guaranteed by the embedded controller is the conjunction of above three requirements:

$$GBReq = safe \wedge stop \wedge start .$$

Furthermore, the design has to respect the signature imposed by the application, namely that *hr* and *fl* are inputs to the controller and that *gas* is an output. The control problem to be solved thus is $(GBReq, \{hr, fl\})$.

The synthesis procedure outlined in Theorem 15 has successfully been applied to this control problem. As the control problem is underconstrained (sometimes it allows free choice between switching *gas* on or off in a certain time instant), this yields a non-deterministic control strategy with respect to the controlled output *gas*. Adding a simple heuristics for resolving this nondeterminism, namely

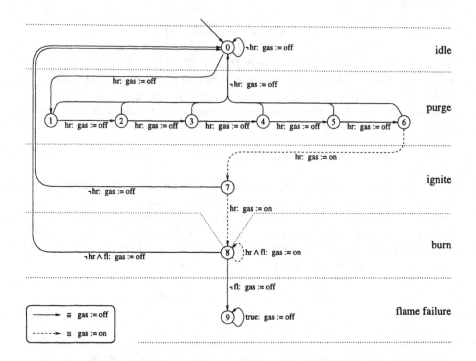

The automatically synthesized timed transition table for the gas burner control problem. As the timed transition table takes one transition every time unit, the clock constraints and resets have been omitted from the transition diagram. For completeness, a single clock c has to be added, and each transition has to be decorated with guarding condition $c = 1$ and reset function $c := 0$.

Incidentally, the synthesized controller resembles the phase design of the manually developed gas burners of [41, 9]. The corresponding phase names used in those designs are indicated on the right.

Fig. 2. The synthesized gas-burner controller

switching *gas* off whenever possible, and finally applying automaton minimization, we obtained a control automaton with only 10 states, which is depicted in Fig. 2.

We were surprised to see that the resulting controller, although generated by a fully effective procedure, even resembles the phase structure of the manually developed controllers of A. P. Ravn, H. Rischel, and K. M. Hansen [41]. Ravn, Rischel, and Hansen developed their control skeleton around the idea of an *idle phase*, where the controller waits for the next heat request, a *purge phase*, where the gas concentration in the environment is reduced through keeping gas shut off for a while before doing an ignition attempt, an *ignite phase* opening the valve long enough to get the flame burning if *flame ok* holds, and a *burn phase* being entered once the flame is stably burning and being left if it either extinguishes or heat request *hr* is withdrawn. See Fig. 2 for more details of the phase design of [41] and how these phases can be identified in the automatically generated gas-burner controller.

3.7 Complexity of Synthesis

While the gas burner case study shows that engineering-quality controllers can in principle be obtained from DC-based automatic synthesis, it is the complexity of the automata-theoretic constructions involved that impairs practicality of Duration Calculus as a source language for embedded systems synthesis. Even for the simplest subsets of DC that feature chop and negation — not even metric time is necessary — the worst case complexity of the synthesis problem is non-elementary in the size of the specification, irrespective of the particular trajectory class used. The reason is that chop and negation are akin to concatenation and complement of languages s.t. the non-elementary emptiness problem of extended regular languages can be linearly encoded in DC (see [14, Lemma 6.25] for the details of such an encoding). Thus, for practical applications it may be better to seriously restrict the use of chop and/or negation, as is done in the work of H. Dierks [11], where synthesis from a subset of the so-called DC implementables [40] is explored. DC implementables contain exactly one, outermost negation and are restricted to certain patterns of using chop. Beyond circumventing the non-elementariness problem by essentially forbidding negation, the gains of the extra restrictions adopted by Dierks are that timing constants can be dealt with essentially syntactically.

However, our focus has less been on exhibiting practical controller synthesis procedures than on demonstrating the fundamental impact that observational constraints of the environment have on the synthesis process. To this end, we have been able to show that by suitable restriction of the model class used in behavioural descriptions of system dynamics, automatic synthesis for large and even undecidable subsets of Duration Calculus becomes theoretically possible. Thereby, the particular behavioural restrictions adopted are motivated by physical properties of practical control problems, namely band-limitedness of reactive systems and synchronicity of clocked systems.

4   Conclusion

We have summarized two approaches to the provably correct and automatic implementation of abstractly described hard real-time controllers. The more conservative of the two is an extension of an imperative programming language by hard real-time commands that allows one to specify upper bounds for the execution time of basic blocks. This extension allows one to specify absolute timing requirements in the imperative source code, thereby obliging the compiler to generate corresponding machine code. The other source language investigated is

Duration Calculus, a metric-time temporal logic designed for reasoning about real-time systems at a high level of abstraction.

Both approaches exploit in an essential way that the observational power of the environment is limited: Firstly, the majority of the state-space of the embedded controller is hidden from it due to the clear-cut interface between the two. Secondly, protocol restrictions or even physical limitations, like band-limitedness, apply to this interface. These observational limitations can be exploited for gaining implementation freedom, thus facilitating correct implementation of idealized behavioral models. While in the compilation approach this is used to justify the idealization of immediate execution for internal statements it is exploited in the synthesis approach for overcoming undecidability of the synthesis problem.

A key difference between the approaches is the complexity of the resulting procedures. In the case of synthesis from Duration Calculus it is in general non-elementary (ways of improving on this have been discussed at the end of Sect. 3). The complexity of the compilation procedure on the other hand is linear. The other side of the coin is of course the power of the formalisms. The compilation work uses an imperative programming language. It requires one to specify exactly how the desirable behavior is achieved and timing requirements have to be specified rather locally, although this is defused a bit by the immediate execution idealization together with time bounds. In contrast, Duration Calculus supports, by being a full-fledged metric-time temporal logic, extremely advanced programming techniques when used as a source language for automatic code generation. A prominent example, which builds upon the availability of logical negation, is the paradigm of *programming by counterexample*, i.e. specifying what should never happen rather than saying how exactly to achieve this. Furthermore, global timing requirements may be easily specified.

Acknowledgements. The research reported in this article has mainly been performed while the authors were with the Computer Science Department of the Christian-Albrechts-Universität Kiel, Germany, working in the ProCoS project and related projects under the supervision of Hans Langmaack. Over many years he strongly influenced the direction of our research through constant encouragement, insistence, and support. It is a great pleasure to present a summary of the results in a volume dedicated to him on the occasion of his retirement.

We thank the members of the ProCoS project for many fruitful discussions as well as J Moore and Bernhard Steffen for many valuable comments on a draft version of this article. We acknowledge the support of the European Union under grants ESPRIT BRA 3104 and 7071 and of the German Research Council DFG under contract DFG La 426/13-1,2.

References

1. R. Alur and D. L. Dill. A theory of timed automata. *Theoretical Computer Science*, 126:183–235, 1994.
2. E. Asarin, P. Caspi, and O. Maler. A Kleene theorem for timed automata. In G. Winskel, editor, *12th Annual IEEE Symposium on Logic in Computer Science (LICS'97)*. IEEE Computer Society Press, 1997.
3. E. Asarin, O. Maler, and A. Pnueli. Symbolic controller synthesis for discrete and timed systems. In P. Antsaklis, W. Kohn, A. Nerode, and S. Sastry, editors, *Hybrid Systems II*, LNCS 999, Springer-Verlag, 1995.
4. R. J. R. Back and J. von Wright. Refinement calculus, Part I: Sequential nondeterministic programs. In J.W. de Bakker, W.-P. de Roever, and G. Rozenberg, editors, *Stepwise Refinement of Distributed Systems — Models, Formalisms, Correctness. REX Workshop*, LNCS 430, pages 42–66, Springer-Verlag, 1989.
5. R. J. R. Back and J. von Wright. Duality in specification languages: A lattice theoretic approach. *Acta Informatica*, 27(7):583–625, 1990.
6. G. Berry. The foundations of Esterel. In G. Plotkin, C. Stirling, and M. Tofte, editors, *Proof, Language, and Interaction: Essays in Honour of Robin Milner*. MIT-Press, to appear.
7. W. R. Bevier, W. A. Hunt, J S. Moore, and W. D. Young. Special issue on system verification. *Journal of Automated Reasoning*, 5(4), 1989.
8. J. P. Bowen, C. A. R. Hoare, H. Langmaack, E.-R. Olderog, and A. P. Ravn. A ProCoS II project final report: ESPRIT Basic Research project 7071. *Bulletin of the European Association for Theoretical Computer Science (EATCS)*, 59, 1996.
9. J. P. Bowen, M. Fränzle, E.-R. Olderog, and A. P. Ravn. Developing correct systems. In *Proc. 5th Euromicro Workshop on Real-Time Systems, Oulu, Finland*, pages 176–189. IEEE Computer Society Press, 1993.
10. G. M. Brown. Towards truly delay-insensitive circuit realizations of process algebras. In G. Jones and M. Sheeran, editors, *Designing Correct Circuits*, Workshops in Computing, pages 120–131. Springer-Verlag, 1991.
11. H. Dierks. Synthesizing controllers from real-time specifications. In *Tenth International Symposium on System Synthesis (ISSS '97)*, pages 126–133. IEEE Computer Society Press, 1997.
12. E. W. Dijkstra. *A Discipline of Programming*. Prentice Hall, 1976.
13. M. Fränzle. Synthesizing controllers from duration calculus. In B. Jonsson and J. Parrow, editors, *Formal Techniques in Real-Time and Fault-Tolerant Systems (FTRTFT '96)*, LNCS 1135, pages 168–187, Springer-Verlag, 1996.
14. M. Fränzle. *Controller Design from Temporal Logic: Undecidability need not matter*. Dissertation, Technische Fakultät der Christian-Albrechts-Universität Kiel, Germany, 1997. Available as Bericht Nr. 9710, Institut für Informatik und Prakt. Mathematik der Christian-Albrechts-Universität Kiel, Germany, and via WWW under URL http://ca.informatik.uni-oldenburg.de/~fraenzle/diss.html.
15. M. Fränzle and M. Müller-Olm. Towards provably correct code generation for a hard real-time programming language. In P. A. Fritzson, editor, *Compiler Construction '94, 5th International Conference Edinburgh U.K.*, LNCS 786, pages 294–308, Springer-Verlag, 1994.
16. P. H. B. Gardiner and C. C. Morgan. Data refinement of predicate transformers. *Theoretical Computer Science*, 87, 1991. Also in [32].
17. J. D. Guttman, J. D. Ramsdell, and M. Wand. VLISP: A verified implementation of Scheme. *Lisp and Symbolic Computation*, 8:5–32, 1995.

18. N. Halbwachs. *Synchronous Programming of Reactive Systems.* Kluwer, 1993.
19. He Jifeng, I. Page, and J. P. Bowen. Towards a provably correct hardware implementation of Occam. In G. J. Milne and L. Pierre, editors, *Correct Hardware Design and Verification Methods*, LNCS 683, pages 214–225. Springer-Verlag, 1993.
20. C. A. R. Hoare. Refinement algebra proves correctness of compiling specifications. In C. C. Morgan and J. C. P. Woodcock, editors, *3rd Refinement Workshop*, Workshops in Computer Science, pages 33–48. Springer-Verlag, 1991.
21. C. A. R. Hoare, I. J. Hayes, He Jifeng, C. C. Morgan, A. W. Roscoe, J. W. Sanders, I. H. Sorenson, J. M. Spivey, and B. A. Sufrin. Laws of programming. *Communications of the ACM*, 30(8):672–687, 1987.
22. C. A. R. Hoare, He Jifeng, and A. Sampaio. Normal form approach to compiler design. *Acta Informatica*, 30:701–739, 1993.
23. inmos limited. *Transputer Instruction Set – A Compiler Writer's Guide.* Prentice Hall International, first edition, 1988.
24. J. J. Joyce. Totally verified systems: Linking verified software to verified hardware. In Leeser and Brown [25], pages 177–201.
25. M. Leeser and G. Brown, editors. *Hardware Specification, Verification and Synthesis: Mathematical Aspects*, LNCS 408, Springer-Verlag, 1990.
26. O. Maler, A. Pnueli, and J. Sifakis. On the synthesis of discrete controllers for timed systems. In Meyer and Puech [29], pages 229–242.
27. A. J. Martin. The design of a delay-insensitive microprocessor: An example of circuit synthesis by program transformation. In Leeser and Brown [25], pages 244–259.
28. J. McCarthy and J. Painter. Correctness of a compiler for arithmetic expressions. In J. Schwarz, editor, *Proc. Symp. Applied Mathematics*, pages 33–41. American Mathematical Society, 1967.
29. E. W. Meyer and C. Puech, editors. *Symposium on Theoretical Aspects of Computer Science (STACS 95)*, LNCS 900, Springer-Verlag, 1995.
30. R. Milner, M. Tofte, and R. Harper. *The Definition of Standard ML.* The MIT Press, 1990.
31. J S. Moore. *Piton, A Mechanically Verified Assembly-Level Language.* Kluwer Academic Publishers, 1996.
32. C. Morgan and T. Vickers (Eds.). *On the Refinement Calculus.* Springer-Verlag, 1994.
33. F. L. Morris. Advice on structuring compilers and proving them correct. In *Proceedings ACM Symposium on Principles of Programming Languages (PoPL'93)*, pages 144–152, 1973.
34. J. M. Morris. A theoretical basis for stepwise refinement and the programming calculus. *Science of Computer Programming*, 9:287–306, 1987.
35. J. M. Morris. Laws of data refinement. *Acta Informatica*, 26:287–308, 1989.
36. M. Müller-Olm. A short description of the prototype compiler. ProCoS Technical Report Kiel MMO 14/1, Christian-Albrechts-Universität Kiel, Germany, August 1995.
37. M. Müller-Olm. *Modular Compiler Verification: A Process-Algebraic Approach Advocating Stepwise Abstraction*, LNCS 1283, Springer-Verlag, 1997.
38. T. S. Norvell. Machine code programs are predicates too. In D. Till, editor, *6th Refinement Workshop*, Workshops in Computing. Springer-Verlag and British Computer Society, 1994.
39. D. J. Pavey and L. A. Winsborrow. Demonstrating equivalence of source code and PROM contents. *The Computer Journal*, 36(7):654–667, 1993.

40. A. P. Ravn. *Design of Embedded Real-Time Computing Systems*. Doctoral dissertation, Department of Computer Science, Danish Technical University, Lyngby, DK, 1995. Available as technical report ID-TR: 1995-170.

41. A. P. Ravn, H. Rischel, and K. M. Hansen. Specifying and verifying requirements of real-time systems. *IEEE Transactions on Software Engineering*, 19(1):41–55, 1993.

42. A. P. Ravn and H. Rischel. Real-time constraints in the ProCoS layers. In E. R. Olderog and B. Steffen, editors, *Correct System Design*, this volume.

43. J. W. Thatcher, E. G. Wagner, and J. B. Wright. More on advice on structuring compilers and proving them correct. *Theoretical Computer Science*, 15:223–249, 1981.

44. W. Thomas. On the synthesis of strategies in infinite games. In Meyer and Puech [29], pages 1–13.

45. T. Wilke. *Automaten und Logiken zur Beschreibung zeitabhängiger Systeme*. Dissertation, Technische Fakultät der Christian-Albrechts-Universität Kiel, Germany, 1994.

46. T. Wilke. Specifying timed state sequences in powerful decidable logics and timed automata. In H. Langmaack, W.-P. de Roever, and J. Vytopil, editors, *Formal Techniques in Real-Time and Fault-Tolerant Systems (FTRTFT '94)*, LNCS 863, pages 694–715, Springer-Verlag, 1994.

47. M. W. Wilkes and J. B. Stringer. Micro-programming and the design of the control circuits in an electronic digital computer. *Proc. Cambridge Phil. Soc.*, 49:230–238, 1953. also *Annals of Hist. Comp.* 8, 2 (1986) 121–126.

48. Zhou Chaochen, M. R. Hansen, and P. Sestoft. Decidability and undecidability results for duration calculus. In P. Enjalbert, A. Finkel, and K. W. Wagner, editors, *Symposium on Theoretical Aspects of Computer Science (STACS 93)*, LNCS 665, pages 58–68, Springer-Verlag, 1993.

49. Zhou Chaochen, C. A. R. Hoare, and A. P. Ravn. A calculus of durations. *Information Processing Letters*, 40(5):269–276, 1991.

Optimization Under the Perspective of Soundness, Completeness, and Reusability

Jens Knoop and Oliver Rüthing

Universität Dortmund, Baroper Str. 301, D-44221 Dortmund, Germany
{knoop,ruething}@ls5.cs.uni-dortmund.de
http://sunshine.cs.uni-dortmund.de/

Abstract. While *soundness* and *completeness* are unchallengedly the surveyor's rod for evaluating the worthiness of proof calculi in program verification, it is not common to refer to these terms for rating the worthiness of performance improving transformations in program optimization. In this article we reconsider optimization under the perspective of soundness, completeness, and, additionally, reusability. Soundness can here be interpreted as semantics preservation, completeness as *optimality* in a specific, well-defined sense, and reusability as paradigm-transcending *robustness* of the rationale guaranteeing soundness and completeness of an optimization for a specific setting. Using *partial redundancy elimination* (*PRE*) for illustration, we demonstrate that these rationales are usually quite sensitive to paradigm changes. Neither completeness nor soundness are generally preserved. Hence, the reuse of optimization strategies in new paradigms requires usually paradigm-specific adaptations in order to accommodate their specifics. We exemplify this for PRE, and demonstrate that it is generally worth the effort, and an effective means for mastering the complexity of compiler construction in the specific field of code optimization.

Keywords: Programming paradigms (imperative, explicitly parallel, object-oriented), program optimization, data-flow analysis, safety and coincidence theorems, optimizer generators, code motion, soundness, completeness, reusability, admissibility, optimality.

1 Motivation

Partial redundancy elimination (*PRE*) (cf. [32]), often also referred to as *code motion* (*CM*), is a powerful classical optimization which is widely used in practice.[1] Intuitively, it improves the performance of a program by avoiding un-

---

[1] An early example is the PL.8 compiler [1]. It performs code motion based on an extension of Morel and Renvoise's pioneering algorithm of [32] for partial redundancy elimination. A current example is the Sun SPARCompiler language systems (SPARCompiler is a registered trademark of SPARC International, Inc., licensed exclusively to Sun Microsystems, Inc.). It performs partial redundancy elimination based on the algorithm for *lazy code motion* of [20, 21]. A variant of this algorithm has been developed at Siemens-Nixdorf [7]. Throughout this article we consider its basic version for *busy code motion* as running example.

E.-R. Olderog, B. Steffen (Eds.): Correct System Design, LNCS 1710, pp. 288–315, 1999.
© Springer-Verlag Berlin Heidelberg 1999

necessary recomputations of values at run-time. This is achieved by replacing the original computations of a program by temporaries which are initialized at suitable program points as illustrated in Figure 1(a) and Figure 1(b).

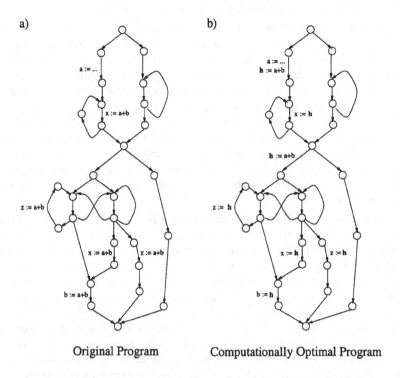

a)   b)

Original Program   Computationally Optimal Program

Fig. 1. Illustrating the essence of partial redundancy elimination.

Obviously, an optimization must obey some minimum requirements in order to be reasonable. It must not affect the semantics or decrease the performance of a program. Under these constraints, it should produce a program which is *better* than any other program resulting from an optimization of the same transformation class. In optimization these requirements are usually called *admissibility* and *optimality* of an optimization.

Though it is not common in program optimization to rephrase admissibility and optimality in terms of program verification, they can be rephrased as soundness and completeness. Considering partial redundancy elimination for illustration, a PRE-transformation is *sound* (i.e., admissible), if (1) inserted statements do not introduce the computation of a new value on any path, and if (2) temporaries replacing original computations always represent the same value as the computations they replace. It is *complete* (i.e., optimal), if the program it produces requires on every path at most as many computations as any other program resulting from a sound PRE-transformation.

For convenience, we call a program resulting from a sound and complete PRE-transformation *optimal*, too. According to this convention, the program of Figure 1(b) is optimal with respect to the program of Figure 1(a). In optimization, this notion of optimality, which refers to the number of computations performed at run-time, is usually called *computational optimality* [20, 21].

The rationale underlying the transformation of Figure 1(b) is to place computations *as early as possible* in a program, i.e., at the *earliest safe* program points. Intuitively, a program point n is *safe* for a computation t if on every path from the program's entry to its exit passing n, t is computed without that any of its operands is modified before reaching n, or before any of its operands is modified after leaving n. A safe program point is *earliest*, if a computation of t at an earlier point would either be not safe, or would yield a different value because of a modification of an operand of t. In the *intraprocedural* setting, the PRE-transformation realizing the as-early-as-possible placing strategy is sound and complete, i.e., it is admissible and yields computationally optimal programs [20, 21]. Throughout this article we will denote this transformation as SE-transformation.[2]

The example of the SE-transformation shows that optimization is a two-level approach. The *transformation* phase is preceded by an *analysis* phase computing information about the program the transformation relies on. Considering the SE-transformation as example, the insertion and replacements of computations constituting the transformation is preceded by an analysis computing the earliest safe program points. Hence, in optimization the issues of soundness and completeness do not only arise on the *transformation* level but also on the *analysis* level. On the analysis level, *soundness* means that a program analysis properly approximates a property of interest, while *completeness* means that it decides this property. This means that it precisely computes the set of program points enjoying the property under consideration. Considering safety as example, a complete program analysis computes exactly the set of program points, which are safe in the sense informally defined above. In contrast, a sound analysis for safety is only required to compute a subset of these points, i.e., it is allowed to classify program points too often as unsafe, however, not vice versa.

Soundness and completeness of an optimization for a specific setting raise another important issue, the one of *reusability*. Considering PRE as example, the success of the as-early-as-possible placing strategy in the intraprocedural setting suggests to reuse it for the construction of PRE-algorithms and the elimination of partially redundant computations in advanced settings and paradigms. More generally, this raises the question of the robustness of the rationale guaranteeing the soundness and completeness of an optimization for a specific setting with respect to paradigm changes. In terms of program verification, robustness, the paradigm-transcending validity of a rationale, can be considered a specific kind of *invariance* property. Of course, in addition to this invariance property the successful reuse of a strategy relies on the successful enhancement of the analyses

---

[2] In [21] it is called *busy code motion*.

computing the program properties involved to the new settings and paradigms of interest.

In this article we will reconsider optimization under the perspective of soundness, completeness, and reusability on both the transformation and the analysis level. We will illustrate this approach considering PRE as running example. By means of the placing strategy underlying the SE-transformation we will particularly demonstrate that the rationale guaranteeing the soundness and completeness of an optimization for a specific setting is usually quite sensitive to paradigm changes. Neither completeness nor even soundness are generally preserved. This shows that the reuse of optimization strategies in advanced settings and paradigms requires typically paradigm-specific adaptations. In particular, it demonstrates that the successful extension of the analyses computing the program properties involved in a transformation like safety and earliestness for the example of the SE-transformation is necessary to reuse an optimization strategy, but generally not sufficient. We will exemplify this for PRE, and demonstrate that paradigm-specific adaptations are generally worth the effort. They yield an effective contribution to the challenge of mastering the complexity of compiler construction in the specific field of code optimization.

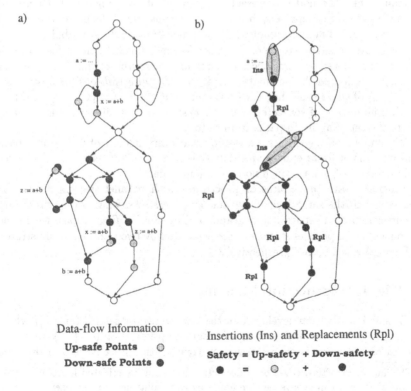

Fig. 2. Illustrating the essence of computationally optimal code motion.

Structure of the Article. After introducing our preliminaries in Section 2, we recall in Section 3 the essence of intraprocedural PRE under the perspective of soundness and completeness. Central are then Section 4, 5, and 6, where we consider PRE in the interprocedural, explicitly parallel and the object-oriented setting under the perspective of soundness and completeness, and particularly, under the one of reusability. We will demonstrate that the rationale underlying the SE-transformation leading to sound and complete PRE in the intraprocedural setting is generally not robust with respect to paradigm changes. In Section 7 we discuss in terms of safety properties the inherent reasons causing the missing robustness of this rationale, and how to cope with it on the analysis and transformation level. In Section 8, finally, we present our conclusions.

2   Preliminaries

In optimization programs are commonly represented by directed *flow graphs* $G = (N, E, s, e)$ with node set N, edge set E, and a unique *start node* s and *end node* e, which are assumed to have no incoming and outgoing edges, respectively (cf. [8, 34–36]). Following [17] we here consider *edge-labeled* flow graphs G, i.e., the edges of G represent the elementary statements like assignments of the underlying program, while the nodes represent program points (cf. Figure 1). Unlabeled edges are assumed to represent the empty statement "skip." As usual, the control flow is interpreted nondeterministically in order to avoid undecidabilities.

For a node n and an edge e of G, let $pred(n)$ and $succ(n)$ denote the set of all immediate predecessors and successors of n, and let $source(e)$ and $dest(e)$ denote the source node and the destination node of e. A *finite path* in G is a sequence $(e_1, \ldots, e_q)$ of edges such that $dest(e_j) = source(e_{j+1})$ for $j \in \{1, \ldots, q-1\}$. It is a path from m to n, if $source(e_1) = m$ and $dest(e_q) = n$. Additionally, let $\mathbf{P}[m, n]$ denote the set of all finite paths from m to n.

Without loss of generality we assume that every node n of G lies on a path from its entry s to its exit e, and that G is free of *critical edges*, i.e., of edges leading directly from a branch node to a join node.[3]

Programs with procedures or procedures with parallel statements can be represented in the same fashion by *flow graph systems*, where every procedure is represented by a separate flow graph, and by *parallel flow graphs*, where the components of a parallel statement are separated by two parallels as illustrated by Figure 4 and Figure 7, respectively.

3   The Intraprocedural Setting

PRE has originally been developed for the *intraprocedural* setting (cf. [32]), which can be considered the basic setting of program optimization (cf. [35]). Intraprocedural optimization is characterized by treating the procedures of a program

---

[3] The impact of critical edges on code motion has been investigated in detail in [40]. Note that they can always be eliminated by edge splitting, i.e., by inserting a new node on them.

separatly and independently of each other. In this section, we recall the essence of PRE for this setting under the perspective of soundness and completeness on both the transformation and the analysis level.

3.1 Transformation Level

As recalled in Section 1, the essence of PRE is to insert at some program points initializations of a specific temporary with the computation under consideration, and to replace some of the original occurrences of this computation by the respective temporary. Computations of different patterns, i.e., of lexically different computations, are treated separately by this approach.[4] As usual, we will thus develop the background of PRE for an arbitrary, but fixed computation pattern t. As a side-effect, this allows us to use a simple, unparameterized notation.

Sound PRE. Intuitively, a PRE-transformation is *sound*, if it does not affect the program semantics. This requires that insertions and replacements are admissible. For insertions, this means that they are only made at safe program points. This guarantees that there is no program path on which the computation of a new value is introduced. In particular, no path may suffer from a new run-time error. For replacements, admissibility means that every program path reaching a program point where an original computation has been replaced by a temporary has passed an insertion point, which is not followed by a modification of an operand of the computation under consideration. This guarantees that wherever a computation has been replaced by a temporary, the value of this temporary coincides with the value produced by an evaluation of the computation.

Note that soundness as defined here is slightly more liberal as its informally introduced counterpart of Section 1. It does not require performance preservation, i.e., it does not require that PRE-transformations must not decrease the performance of programs. We make this distinction explicit by speaking of *weak* and *strong* admissibility, respectively. This will be important in Section 4 and Section 5. As usual for PRE, the performance aspect addressed by strong admissibility is taken into account by the issue of completeness.

Complete PRE. While soundness of PRE in its weak sense focuses on *semantics* preservation, completeness focuses on *performance* preservation and improvement. For PRE, it is common to measure performance in terms of the number of computations which are executed on a program path. Formally, this leads us to the notion of *computationally optimal* PRE-transformations, which are the "greatest" elements of a pre-order "computationally better" on the set of sound PRE-transformations.

A PRE-transformation T is *computationally better* than a PRE-transformation T' if for every program the program produced by T requires on every path from its entry to its exit at most as many computations as the program produced by

---

[4] For clarity, this is sometimes called *syntactic* PRE in contrast to the more ambitious *semantic* PRE, which aims at eliminating partially redundant computations also among lexically different, but semantically equivalent computations (cf. [25]).

T' on the corresponding path. A sound PRE-transformation T is *computationally optimal*, if and only if it is computationally better than any other sound PRE-transformation. In this article we define completeness of PRE in the sense of computational optimality, i.e., a sound PRE-transformation is called *complete*, if and only if it is computationally optimal.[5]

The SE-Transformation. As recalled in Section 1, the SE-transformation inserts computations at their earliest safe computation points. Intuitively, this as-early-as-possible placing strategy maximizes the potential for redundancy elimination in a program. Formally, it is defined by specifying the set of edges where computations have to be inserted and replaced. Note that **h** is a fresh variable introduced for the computation pattern t under consideration.

- *Insertions*: Insert on every edge ending in an earliest safe node an assignment of the form $\mathbf{h} := t$. If such an edge is already labeled by a statement, the new one is inserted behind the already present one.[6]
- *Replacements*: Replace every original computation of t by **h**.

We have (cf. [20, 21]):

Theorem 1 (Soundness and Completeness).
The SE-transformation is sound and complete, i.e., it is admissible and computationally optimal.

Obviously, an implementation of the SE-transformation requires to compute its insertion points, which, in turn, requires to compute the set of program points n being safe, in symbols $\mathtt{Safe}(n)$. The key to the algorithmic solution of this problem lies in the decomposition of safety into the properties of *up-safety* and *down-safety*, which are dual to each other.[7] A program point n is *up-safe* for a computation t, in symbols $\mathtt{Up\text{-}Safe}(n)$, if on every path from the program's entry to n, t is computed without a subsequent modification of any of its operands. Dually, n is *down-safe* for t, in symbols $\mathtt{Dn\text{-}Safe}(n)$, if t is computed on every path originating in n and reaching the program's exit before any of its operands is modified.

The notions of down-safety and up-safety lead to an equivalent characterization of the insertion points of the SE-transformation: a program point is earliest safe if and only if it is down-safe but not up-safe and it is either the start node **s**, or it has a predecessor m such that (m, n) is not transparent or m violates

---

[5] Advanced PRE-techniques like *lazy code motion* or *sparse code motion* take additional quality criteria into account like the lifetimes of temporaries introduced by PRE (cf. [20, 21]), the lifetimes of all program variables (cf. [41, 42]), or the code size (cf. [43]). For the purposes of this article it suffices to consider the number of computations performed, whose minimization is in fact the primary goal of PRE.

[6] We assume that the start node **s** is reached by a "virtual" edge, where in case of need the required insertions are made.

[7] Up-safety and down-safety are also known as *availability* and *very busyness* or *anticipability*, respectively (cf. [8, 35]).

the safety property. Following [21] we will think of the as-early-possible placing strategy and the SE-transformation realizing it throughout this article in terms of this characterization of insertion points. The equivalence proof of the two characterizations relies on the Safety Lemma 1. It states that in the intraprocedural setting safety can equivalently be expressed as the disjunction of up-safety and down-safety.

Lemma 1 (Safety). $\forall n \in N.\ \texttt{Safe}(n) \Longleftrightarrow \texttt{Up-Safe}(n) \vee \texttt{Dn-Safe}(n)$.

This lemma plays actually a major role in the soundness and completeness proof of the SE-transformation (cf. [21]), but usually fails in more advanced settings as we we are going to demonstrate in Section 7. Crucial in the proof of this lemma is only the proof of the forward implication. The validity of the converse implication is indeed obvious from the definitions. The forward implication is essentially a consequence of considering branching nondeterministically. This allows us to complete every path leading to a node by every path starting at that node. In particular, this allows us to link every path violating the up-safety condition at a node n with every path violating the down-safety condition at n. Every path resulting from this violates the safety condition at n, which proves the contrapositive of the forward implication.

Technically, the sets of program points which are up-safe and down-safe for a computation t evolve as the greatest solutions of the Equation Systems 1 and 2, respectively, where *Comp* and *Transp* denote two predicates of edges. They are true for an edge e, if it contains an occurrence of t, and if it does not modify an operand of t, respectively.

Equation System 1 (Up-safety).

$$\mathbf{us}(n) = \begin{cases} \textit{false} & \textit{if } n = \mathbf{s} \\ \bigwedge_{m \in pred(n)} (Comp_{(m,n)} \vee \mathbf{us}(m)) \wedge Transp_{(m,n)} & \textit{otherwise} \end{cases}$$

Equation System 2 (Down-safety).

$$\mathbf{ds}(n) = \begin{cases} \textit{false} & \textit{if } n = \mathbf{e} \\ \bigwedge_{m \in succ(n)} Comp_{(n,m)} \vee (\mathbf{ds}(m) \wedge Transp_{(n,m)}) & \textit{otherwise} \end{cases}$$

In the following section we reconsider the theoretical background of program analysis providing the formal foundation for proving these claims.

3.2   Analysis Level

In the context of optimizing compilers program analysis is usually called *dataflow analysis (DFA)*. Its essence is to compute run-time properties of a program without actually executing them. Theoretically well-founded are DFAs based on the theory of *abstract interpretation* (cf. [3–6, 31, 37]). The point of this approach is to replace the "full" semantics of a program by a simpler more abstract version, which is tailored for a specific problem. Basically, an abstract semantics is characterized by two objects: *data-flow facts*, and *data-flow functions*. Typically, the data-flow facts are given by the elements of a complete (not necessarily finite) lattice C of finite height, and the data-flow functions by transformations $[\![\,.\,]\!]$ on these lattices. In practice, these functions are *monotonic* or even *distributive*.[8] They define the abstract semantics of elementary statements.

DFA then computes for every program point n a data-flow fact representing valid data-flow information at n with respect to some *start assertion*. This is a data-flow fact $c_0 \in C$, which is assured to be valid on calling the program under consideration. Formally, this is characterized by the so-called *maximal-fixed-point* (*MFP*) approach. It relies on a system of equations, which specify consistency constraints which have to be obeyed by any reasonable annotation of a flow graph with data-flow facts $c \in C$.

Equation System 3 (*MFP*-**Equation System**).

$$\mathbf{info}(n) = \begin{cases} c_0 & \text{if } n = \mathbf{s} \\ \sqcap \{\, [\![(m,n)]\!](\mathbf{info}(m)) \mid m \in pred(n) \,\} & \text{otherwise} \end{cases}$$

The *MFP*-approach is practically relevant, since Equation System 3 induces an iterative computation procedure approximating its greatest solution denoted by $\mathbf{info}^*_{c_0}$. It defines the solution of the *MFP*-approach with respect to the start assertion $c_0 \in C$:

The *MFP*-Solution: $\forall c_0 \in C\ \forall n \in N.\ MFP(n)(c_0) = \mathbf{info}^*_{c_0}(n)$

The *MFP*-solution can effectively be computed, if the local semantic functions are monotonic and the lattice is of finite height. This gives rise to consider it the *algorithmic* solution of a DFA problem. Of course, this directly raises the questions of its soundness and completeness.

Sound and Complete Analyses. Soundness and completeness of the *MFP*-approach are defined with respect to a second globalization of the abstract semantics underlying the *MFP*-approach. Formally, it is given by the so-called *meet-over-all-paths* (*MOP*) approach. It has an operational flavour. Intuitively, for every program point n it "meets" (intersects) all informations contributed by some path p reaching n. Thus, the *MOP*-approach mimics the effect of possible program paths, which intuitively reflects one's desires. Formally, the *MOP*-solution is defined as follows, where $[\![p]\!]$ denotes the sequential composition of the data-flow functions associated with the edges of p. Note, if p is the empty path, $[\![p]\!]$ equals the identity on C.

The *MOP*-Solution: $\forall c_0 \in C\ \forall n \in N.\ MOP(n)(c_0) = \sqcap \{\, [\![p]\!](c_0) \mid p \in \mathbf{P}[\mathbf{s},n] \,\}$

---

[8] A function $f : C \to C$ is called *monotonic* iff $\forall c, c' \in C.\ c \sqsubseteq c' \Rightarrow f(c) \sqsubseteq f(c')$. It is called *distributive* iff $\forall C' \subseteq C.\ f(\sqcap C') = \sqcap \{f(c) \mid c \in C'\}$. Monotonicity can equivalently be characterized as follows: $\forall C' \subseteq C.\ f(\sqcap C') \sqsubseteq \sqcap \{f(c) \mid c \in C'\}$. We prefer this characterization of monotonicity here because it directly pin-points the difference between monotonicity and distributivity.

In terms of program verification, the *MOP*-solution at a program point n can be considered the *strongest post-condition* at n with respect to the pre-condition c_0 at the program's entry s. This gives rise to consider the *MOP*-solution the *specifying* solution of a DFA problem.[9] Consequently, we define: the algorithmic *MFP*-solution of a DFA problem is *sound*, if it is a lower bound of the *MOP*-solution. It is *complete*, if it coincides with the *MOP*-solution. In DFA these two properties are usually called safety and coincidence of the *MFP*-solution with respect to the *MOP*-solution (cf. [9,10]).

The following two theorems proposed by Kildall [10], and Kam and Ullman [9], which are known as Safety Theorem (Theorem 2) and Coincidence Theorem (Theorem 3), give sufficient conditions for the soundness and completeness of the *MFP*-solution with respect to the *MOP*-solution. These theorems are used in practice for proving the soundness and completeness of a DFA. Note that they do not rely on the finite height condition of the lattice under consideration. This constraint is only required to guarantee the effectivity of the fixed point process computing the *MFP*-solution.

Theorem 2 (Soundness).
The MFP-solution is sound for the MOP-solution, i.e., it is a safe approximation of the MOP-solution, in symbols $\forall n \in N.\ MFP(n) \sqsubseteq MOP(n)$, if the semantic functions $[\![e]\!]$, $e \in E$, are all monotonic.

Theorem 3 (Completeness).
The MFP-solution is complete for the MOP-solution, i.e., it coincides with the MOP-solution, in symbols $\forall n \in N.\ MFP(n) = MOP(n)$, if the semantic functions $[\![e]\!]$, $e \in E$, are all distributive.

Note that distributivity implies monotonicity. Thus, on the analysis level of optimization completeness implies soundness. The analogy of soundness and completeness in program verification and program analysis is thus not really one-to-one.

From the perspective of reuse, and hence, for the construction of optimizing compilers, it is most important that the procedure computing the *MFP*-solution can be generically organized. Hence, it can be reused. Feeding the generic *MFP*-algorithm with instances of data-flow facts and data-flow functions yields automatically the incidental concrete DFA algorithm. This is illustrated in Figure 3. The principle showing up in this figure is the basis of the intraprocedural version of the DFA&OPT-METAFrame tool kit, a DFA generator (cf. [11,24]).

Following the pattern of Figure 3 the solution of the DFA problems for up-safety and down-safety, which have informally been defined in Section 3.1, reduce to providing the intraprocedural DFA generator with the appropriate specifications of these two properties.

---

[9] Unfortunately, its definition does generally not induce an effective computation procedure. Think e.g. of loops in a program, which cause the existence of an infinite number of paths reaching a specific program point.

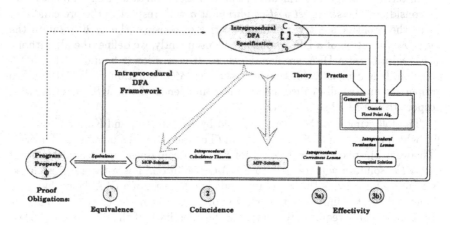

Fig. 3. The intraprocedural DFA generator.

Computing Up-safety and Down-safety. Let $\mathcal{B}$ denote the set of Boolean truth values *true* and *false*, and let Cst_{true}, Cst_{false}, and $Id_\mathcal{B}$ denote the constant functions and the identity on $\mathcal{B}$. Then, the specifications for the up-safety and down-safety problem for t are as follows.

1. **Up-safety**:
   (a) *Data-flow facts*: $(\mathcal{C}, \sqcap, \sqsubseteq, \perp, \top) =_{df} (\mathcal{B}, \wedge, \leq, false, true)$
   (b) *Data-flow functions*: $[\![\ ]\!]_{us} : E \rightarrow (\mathcal{B} \rightarrow \mathcal{B})$ defined by

$$\forall e \in E . [\![e]\!]_{us} =_{df} \begin{cases} Cst_{true} & \text{if } Comp_e \wedge Transp_e \\ Id_\mathcal{B} & \text{if } \neg Comp_e \wedge Transp_e \\ Cst_{false} & \text{otherwise} \end{cases}$$

   (c) *Start assertion*: $false \in \mathcal{B}$

2. **Down-safety**:
   (a) *Data-flow facts*: $(\mathcal{C}, \sqcap, \sqsubseteq, \perp, \top) =_{df} (\mathcal{B}, \wedge, \leq, false, true)$
   (b) *Data-flow functions*: $[\![\ ]\!]_{ds} : E \rightarrow (\mathcal{B} \rightarrow \mathcal{B})$ defined by

$$\forall e \in E . [\![e]\!]_{ds} =_{df} \begin{cases} Cst_{true} & \text{if } Comp_e \\ Id_\mathcal{B} & \text{if } \neg Comp_e \wedge Transp_e \\ Cst_{false} & \text{otherwise} \end{cases}$$

   (c) *Start assertion*: $false \in \mathcal{B}$

Obviously, the lattice $\mathcal{B}$ of Boolean truth values is of finite height, and the data-flow functions Cst_{true}, Cst_{false}, and $Id_\mathcal{B}$ are distributive. Hence, for both problems the automatically generated fixed point algorithm terminates with the

MFP-solution. Moreover, according to Theorem 3, it coincides as desired with the corresponding *MOP*-solution. Hence, the instantiated *MFP*-algorithms are sound and complete.

It is worth noting here that Equation System 1 and Equation System 2 are direct specializations of Equation System 3. This is obvious for up-safety. For down-safety, which requires a backward analysis of the program under consideration, it gets obvious, when reversing the flow of control. This is the usual trick in DFA to handle forward and backward problems in a uniform setting.

The main result of this section now is that the DFAs for up-safety and down-safety induced by the appropriately instantiated generic *MFP*-algorithm are sound and complete. We have:

Theorem 4 (Soundness and Completeness).
The DFAs for up-safety and down-safety are sound and complete.

In the following sections we reconsider optimization in advanced settings under the perspective of soundness and completeness. In particular, we focus on the robustness of the placing strategy underlying the SE-transformation with respect to setting and paradigm changes, and hence on the issue of reusability. We start with re-considering the so-called interprocedural setting of optimization.

4 The Interprocedural Setting

Like intraprocedural optimization, also interprocedural one has its roots in the imperative programming paradigm. In contrast to intraprocedual optimization, however, it aims at capturing a program as a whole instead of treating its procedures separately. Most importantly, this requires to take the effects of procedure calls into account instead of making worst-case assumptions about them as intraprocedurally. Interprocedural optimization is thus much more ambitious than intraprocedural one, however, generally also much more powerful.

In this section, we consider a setting where programs are composed of a finite number of possibly mutually recursive procedures, which may have local variables and value parameters. We assume that there is a unique procedure, the *main program*, which cannot be called by other procedures. Local variables of the main program are global variables of the remaining procedures of a program. Moreover, we assume that procedures are not statically nested. This setting is already complex enough for the purpose of this article.

Intuitively, reusing the placing strategy of the SE-transformation in the interprocedural setting means that the interprocedural counterpart of the SE-transformation, the ISE-transformation, inserts computations *interprocedurally* as early as possible, i.e., at the *interprocedurally earliest safe* program points. Figure 4(b) shows the effect of this transformation for the program of Figure 4(a). It is computationally optimal. At first sight this suggests that the ISE-transformation is *interprocedurally* sound and complete, i.e., admissible and *interprocedurally* computationally optimal. In the following we will investigate the validity of this conjecture in more detail. We will start our considerations on

safety and completeness of interprocedural optimization on the analysis level
because the successful extension of the program analyses computing the properties involved in a transformation is a prerequisite for the successful reuse of an
optimization strategy. Concerning our running example, this means reuse of the
as-early-as-possible placing strategy in the interprocedural setting.

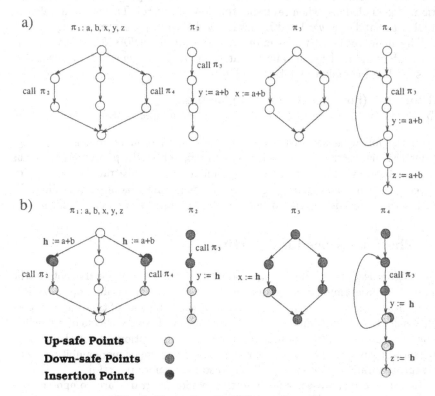

Fig. 4. Illustrating the ISE-transformation.

4.1   Analysis Level

Conceptually, the most important difference between the intraprocedural and
interprocedural setting is due to local variables and parameters of (mutually) recursive procedures. At run-time there can exist an unbounded number of copies
of local variables and parameters belonging to dynamically nested invocations
of recursive procedures which have been called but not yet finished. The proper
treatment of this phenomenon requires to implicitly mimic the run-time stack on
the analysis side. In [28] this was first achieved by introducing a so-called DFA
stack on the analysis side. Intuitively, its entries mimic the activation records of
the corresponding run-time stack. In addition to data-flow facts and data-flow

functions defining an intraprocedural DFA problem, the specification of an interprocedural DFA problem requires a third component, so-called *return functions*
for handling the return from (recursive) procedure calls. Intuitively, the effect of
a (recursive) procedure call on global variables must be maintained, while the
one on local variables must be reset to the state valid immediately before the
call. Return functions realize this by conflating the two top-most entries of the
DFA stack storing the data-flow facts valid when calling the procedure under
consideration, and the data-flow fact valid immediately before leaving it to the
data-flow fact representing the valid data-flow information after finishing the
call.

Based on this extension, the interprocedural variant of the *MFP*-approach,
the *IMFP*-approach, proceeds almost as in the intraprocedural case. In addition
to the intraprocedural setting, however, it relies on a preprocess for computing
the global abstract semantics of procedures. This is a second-order approach
operating on data-flow fact transformers representing the global semantics of
procedures instead of single data-flow facts. The transformers computed by the
preprocess can then be used to compute the algorithmic solution of the problem
under consideration almost as in the intraprocedural setting. The details of the
complete process, which defines the interprocedural version of the *MFP*-solution,
the *IMFP*-solution, have originally been given in [28], and for a more general
setting in [14]. Similar to its intraprocedural counterpart, the *IMFP*-solution
defines the *algorithmic* solution of an interprocedural DFA problem. It can effectively be computed, whenever the function lattice of the lattice of data-flow
facts is of finite height, and the data-flow functions and return functions defining
the abstract semantics of elementary statements are monotonic.

Sound and Complete Interprocedural Analyses. Similar to its intraprocedural counterpart, soundness and completeness of the *IMFP*-approach are
defined with respect to an operational globalization of the abstract semantics
underlying it. For the purposes of this article, it is sufficient to note the sim-
ilarity of the definition of the interprocedural *MOP*-solution, in symbols the
IMOP-solution, and its intraprocedural counterpart. The details are indeed not
necessary. Thus, we only remark that *newstack* is a function, which yields a
DFA stack containing its argument as single entry, and that $\mathbf{IP}[m, n]$ denotes
the set of so-called *interprocedurally valid* paths connecting two nodes m and
n. Intuitively, interprocedurally valid paths respect the call/return-behaviour of
procedure calls (cf. [44]). The meet-operation, finally, occurring in the definition
of the *IMOP*-solution is the ordinary meet on the lattice under consideration
applied to the top-components of the argument stacks.

The *IMOP*-Solution:

$$\forall c_0 \in \mathcal{C} \ \forall n \in N. \ IMOP(n)(c_0) = \bigsqcap \{ \ [\![p]\!] (newstack(c_0)) \mid p \in \mathbf{IP}[\mathbf{s}, n] \}$$

Now, we define: the algorithmic *IMFP*-solution of an interprocedural DFA
problem is *sound*, if it is a lower bound of the *IMOP*-solution. It is *complete*,
if it coincides with the *IMOP*-solution. The Interprocedural Safety Theorem 5

and the Interprocedural Coincidence Theorem 6 give sufficient conditions for the soundness and completeness of the *IMFP*-solution [28]. Note that the finiteness condition on the height of the function lattice of the data-flow fact lattice $\mathcal{C}$ is only required to guarantee the effectivity of the fixed point process computing the *IMFP*-solution.

Theorem 5 (Interprocedural Soundness).
The IMFP-solution is sound for the IMOP-solution, i.e., it is a safe approximation of the IMOP-solution, in symbols $\forall n \in N.\ IMFP(n) \sqsubseteq IMOP(n)$, if the semantic functions $[\![e]\!]$, $e \in E$, and the return functions are all monotonic.

Theorem 6 (Interprocedural Completeness).
The IMFP-solution is complete for the IMOP-solution, i.e., it coincides with the IMOP-solution, in symbols $\forall n \in N.\ IMFP(n) = IMOP(n)$, if the semantic functions $[\![e]\!]$, $e \in E$, and the return functions are all distributive.

After these preliminaries we can now apply the framework introduced above to the computation of the program properties involved in the ISE-transformation. In fact, the definitions of *interprocedurally earliest safe* program points as well as those of *interprocedurally down-safe* and *interprocedurally up-safe* program points can straightforwardly be derived from their intraprocedural counterparts. The specifications of the corresponding DFAs for interprocedural up-safety and down-safety have been given in detail in [24], and we thus omit recalling them here. The specifications of these DFAs satisfy both the effectivity requirements of the *IMFP*-approach, and the completeness requirements imposed by the Completeness Theorem 6.

Hence, the analyses for up-safety and down-safety can successfully be enhanced to the interprocedural setting. As mentioned before, this is necessary for the successful reuse of the placing strategy underlying the SE-transformation in the interprocedural setting. In the following section we will investigate whether it is sufficient, too.[10]

4.2   Transformation Level

In analogy to intraprocedural PRE, we define soundness and completeness of *interprocedural PRE (IPRE)* as semantics preservation and computational optimality. This is rather straightforward, but it directly allows us to expose a most important difference between PRE in the intraprocedural and interprocedural setting. In contrast to the intraprocedural setting, it turns out that in the interprocedural one computationally optimal results in general do not exist. For illustration, consider the example of Figure 5. Obviously, the IPRE-transformations

---

[10] In [14] the soundness and completeness theorems have been given for a more general setting including also formal procedure parameters and formal reference parameters. Even for this more general setting the interprocedural versions of the DFAs for up-safety and down-safety satisfy the effectivity and completeness requirements of the *IMFP*-approach.

producing the programs of Figure 5(b) and Figure 5(c) are sound, and improve
on the performance of the program of Figure 5(a). However, both transformations are incomparable with respect to the relation "computationally better,"
and it is easy to check that there is no program, and hence no transformation
either, which uniformly improves on both the programs of Figure 5(b) and (c).

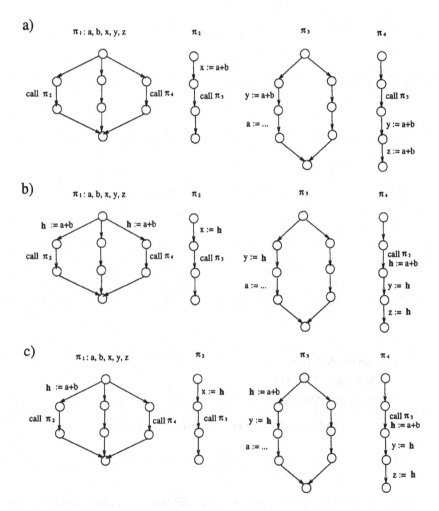

Fig. 5. Incomparable computationally minimal programs.

This excludes the existence of computationally optimal IPRE-transformations
in general. Hence, we are left with the soundness of the ISE-transformation,
which we investigate both in the weak and in the strong sense. The first result
is negative. The ISE-transformation relying on the as-early-as-possible placing

strategy fails soundness in the strong variant, i.e., it is generally not performance preserving. This is demonstrated by the example of Figure 6(b). It shows the result of the ISE-transformation applied to the program of Figure 6(a). In this example the ISE-transformation moves a computation from an acyclic program part to a cyclic one.

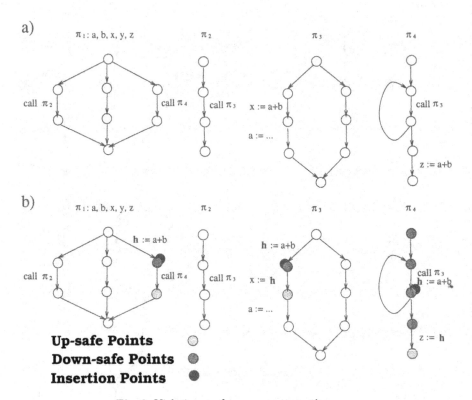

Fig. 6. Violating performance preservation.

While as any IPRE-transformation the ISE-transformation cannot be expected to be interprocedurally computationally optimal, it may be surprising that it meets soundness only in the weak sense of semantics preservation. This, however, shows the sensitivity of the rationale underlying the soundness and completeness of the SE-transformation, when switching from the intraprocedural to the interprocedural setting. In Section 7 we will discuss the inherent reasons for this failure and some general means of how to cope and overcome the sometimes pathological behaviour of the ISE-transformation.

5   The Explicitly Parallel Setting

In this section we switch to a setting with *explicitly parallel* programs with *interleaving semantics* and *shared memory*, which has been defined in detail in [29] and [30]. We assume that parallelism is syntactically expressed by means of a par statement, whose components are executed concurrently. As usual, we assume that there are neither jumps into a component of a parallel statement from outside nor vice versa.

In the remainder of this section we investigate the reasonability of reusing the placing strategy underlying the SE-transformation for eliminating partially redundant computations when switching to this setting. Following the structure of the previous section we will first deal with soundness and completeness on the analysis level, and subsequently on the transformation level.

5.1   Analysis Level

Conceptually, the most important differences between the sequential and the parallel setting are due to the phenomena of *interference* and *synchronization* of components of parallel statements. They are responsible for the combinatorial explosion of the size of an state-oriented system representation. In the context of model-checking based verification this is known as *state explosion* problem, which turned out of being a major obstacle of successfully analysing such systems. Also DFA of explicitly parallel programs has to cope with this problem, which may be the reason that the transfer of sequential optimizations to the parallel setting has only been tackled in a few recent approaches as the extension of the analyses to the parallel setting is a prerequisite of any such transfer. In [29, 30] it could be shown that for unidirectional *bitvector* problems the state explosion problem can be completely avoided. Based on a two-step approach resembling the interprocedural *MFP*-approach, the intraprocedural *MFP*-approach could successfully be enhanced to the parallel setting. For unidirectional bitvector problems, this led to the parallel version of the *MFP*-solution of a DFA problem, in symbols the *PMFP*-solution. It can be computed within the same worst-case time complexity as its counterpart of the sequential setting. In practice, this is quite important because numerous optimizations, which are widely used in sequential optimizers, rely on DFAs of this type only. This applies also to the SE-transformation for eliminating partially redundant computations.

Hence, successfully extending the analyses for up-safety and down-safety to the parallel setting establishes the precondition for reusing the placing strategy of the SE-transformation in this setting. As a minimum this requires that the *PMFP*-solution of a unidirectional bitvector problem like up-safety or down-safety coincides with its operational counterpart, the parallel version of the *MOP*-solution, in symbols the *PMOP*-solution. Denoting by $\mathbf{PP}[m, n]$ the set of *interleaving sequences* connecting two nodes m and n, it is defined as follows.

The *PMOP*-Solution:

$$\forall\, c_0 \in \mathcal{C} \ \forall\, n \in N.\ PMOP(n)(c_0) = \bigsqcap \{\, [\![\, p \,]\!](c_0) \mid p \in \mathbf{PP}[\mathbf{s}, n] \,\}$$

Analogously to the previous sections, we define: the algorithmic *PMFP*-solution of a parallel DFA problem is *sound*, if it is a lower bound of the *PMOP*-solution. It is *complete*, if it coincides with the *PMOP*-solution. We have [29, 30]:

Theorem 7 (Parallel Completeness).

For unidirectional bitvector problems, the PMFP-solution is sound and complete for the PMOP-solution, i.e., it coincides with the PMOP-solution, in symbols $\forall\, n \in N.\ PMFP(n) = PMOP(n).$

It is worth noting that we do not have a separate soundness theorem here. This is because the semantic functions of unidirectional bitvector problems are always distributive. For every bit representing the data-flow fact for a program entity like a variable or a term, the semantic functions are one of the constant functions Cst_{true} and Cst_{false} or the identity $Id_{\mathcal{B}}$ on the set $\mathcal{B}$ of Boolean truth values. Hence, they satisfy the stronger pre-condition of the completeness theorem. For the same reason, there is apparently no side-condition for the coincidence of the *PMFP*-solution and the *PMOP*-solution. It is implicitly contained in the restriction of the theorem to unidirectional bitvector problems.

Similar to the sequential setting, the algorithm computing the *PMFP*-solution of uni-directional bitvector problems can be generically organized (cf. [30]). It can directly be fed with the specifications for up-safety and down-safety given in Section 3. As a corollary of Theorem 7 we obtain that the parallel versions of the DFA problems for up-safety and down-safety are complete, i.e., they coincide with the property of interest. In fact, the specification of these problems is the very same as in the sequential setting. The treatment of interference and synchronization is completely hidden inside the generic algorithm computing the *PMFP*-solution (cf. [29, 30]).

Hence, as for the interprocedural setting, the analyses for up-safety and down-safety can successfully be enhanced to the parallel setting, too. The pre-condition for the successful reuse of the placing strategy of the SE-transformation in the parallel setting is thus established.

5.2   Transformation Level

Analogously to the previous sections, we define soundness and completeness of *parallel PRE (PPRE)* as semantics preservation and computational optimality. Considering now the reuse of the as-early-as-possible placing strategy underlying the SE-transformation for eliminating partially redundant computations, it turns out that in the parallel setting this strategy fails soundness even in the weak sense (cf. Section 3). This means that the parallel version of the SE-transformation, in symbols the PSE-transformation, generally fails the indispensable requirement of semantics preservation. This is demonstrated by the example of Figure 7(b). It shows the result of the PSE-transformation applied to the program of Figure 7(a).

The point of this example is that the properties of up-safety and down-safety appear and disappear quasi "magically" because of the effects of synchronization

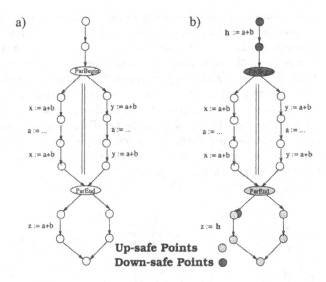

Fig. 7. Violation of soundness by the as-early-as-possible placing strategy.

and interference. Intuitively, this is because up-safety and down-safety reflect properties of interleaving sequences, which cannot adequately be made use of in a parallel program, which can be considered a "compact" finite representation of all interleaving sequences. As a consequence, the insertion at the program's entry can never be used, though it is down-safe. On the other hand, a computation of $a + b$ at the use site of the temporary **h** will (usually) yield a different value than the one which is stored in this temporary because of the assignments to **h** executed in the parallel statement. A reinitialization, however, is suppressed, since $a + b$ is up-safe, i.e., available, after leaving the parallel statement. In the sequential setting, this guarantees that the temporary stores the desired value, and hence, suppressing the reinitialization is correct. In the parallel setting, this does not hold (cf. [27]). We will discuss the reason of this failure in more detail in Section 7.

Besides the loss of soundness of the PSE-transformation, a second new phenomenon shows up in the parallel setting. Defining completeness of a PRE-transformation in terms of computational optimality is by no means adequate at all. This is demonstrated in the example of Figure 8. For this example, the PSE-transformation is sound, i.e., it preserves the semantics of the original program. Figure 8(b) shows the result of the PSE-transformation for the program of Figure 8(a). Note that both programs are computationally optimal, however, the performance of the program of Figure 8(b) will be worse than that of the program of Figure 8(c). The point here is that the relation "computationally better" is based on a simple count of the occurrences of computations on (sequentialized) program paths, i.e., on a pure interleaving view. It does not distinguish between computations in sequential and parallel program parts. The execution time of a parallel program, however, is extremely sensitive to this distinction: e.g., computations in a parallel component can be for "free." The execution time of the considered execution is determined by the computations of the *bottleneck* component, i.e., the component which requires most activity. Thus, the as-early-as-possible placement strategy, which in the sequential setting leads to computationally (and executionally) optimal results, is inappropriate for the parallel setting because here computational optimality it is aiming at does not induce the desired *executional optimality*. In the parallel setting reasonable PRE-transformations must take the difference between computational and executional optimality, which does not show up in the sequential setting, into account. In Section 7 we discuss means for achieving this.

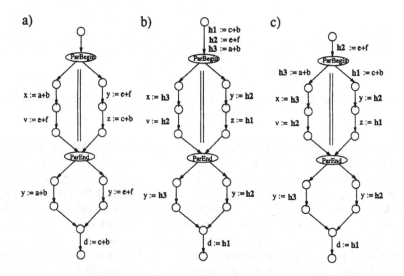

Fig. 8. Computational optimality vs. executional optimality.

6   The Object-Oriented Setting

In this section we switch to the object-oriented programming paradigm. The spectrum of languages belonging to this paradigm is quite large. It ranges from untyped languages like Smalltalk over hybrid ones like C++ to strongly typed languages like Oberon-2. However, there is an important feature common to all of them. Late procedure binding, dynamic function dispatch, or dynamic method binding. These are all different language dependent jargons for essentially the same facts. The procedure called at a specific call site is usually not compile-time but run-time determined. Replacing late procedure binding by the more efficient early binding, where possible, is one of the most common and important optimizations of object-oriented programs [38, 39]. Essentially, this amounts to determining the receiver of a method call as precisely as possible.

The class of program analyses computing this information are commonly known as *type analysis*. This is particularly challenging in the presence of additional features like inheritance and polymorphism. While this is often considered to reflect a flavour quite specific for object-oriented languages, it is worth noting that procedure variables and formal procedures introduce similar phenomena in programs of classical imperative languages (cf. [13]). In fact, concerning PRE, one encounters essentially the same problems as in the interprocedural setting. The reusability of the as-early-as-possible placing strategy in the object-oriented setting is liable to the same limitations than in the interprocedural one. We thus do not discuss this in more detail here, but refer to [16] and [26], where this has been sketched for a Smalltalk and an Oberon-like language, respectively, based on specific versions of soundness and completeness theorems applying to the respective settings considered there.

7   Discussion: Failures, Remedies, and Reuse

Reasons of Failure. Intuitively, an important reason for the missing robustness of the as-early-as-possible placing strategy with respect to paradigm changes is the failure of the Safety Lemma 1. In fact, this lemma does generally not carry over to more advanced settings and paradigms. In Figure 9 this is demonstrated for the interprocedural and the explicitly parallel setting. Each of the nodes of procedure π_2 in Figure 9(a) is safe, however, none of them is up-safe or down-safe. Analogously, this holds for the marked node of the right component of the explicitly parallel program shown in Figure 9(b).

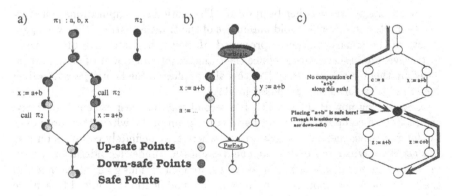

Fig. 9. Failure of Safety Lemma 1 in advanced settings.

The failure of the Safety Lemma 1 in advanced settings is in fact quite typical. As demonstrated e.g. in [25], it also fails in the intraprocedural setting when switching from syntactic to semantic PRE. In the example of Figure 9(c) the blackened node is safe without being up-safe or down-safe.

The impact on the reusability of the as-early-as-possible placing strategy, however, is setting-dependent. While for semantic PRE only completeness is affected,[11] in the interprocedural and explicitly parallel setting even soundness is affected for the less ambitious syntactic PRE. Interprocedurally, in its strong, explicitly parallel, even in its weak variant. This directly shows that the successful extension of the analyses computing the properties involved in the as-early-as-possible placing strategy is a necessary, however, not a sufficient condition for its transferrability. In fact, on the transformation level setting and paradigm specific adaptations are required in order to accommodate their specifics. In the following section we will discuss this by means of the interprocedural and the explicitly parallel setting.

Remedies: Adaptations of the Placing Strategy. Essentially, there are two general ways for coping with the problems showing up with the as-early-as-possible placing strategy in advanced settings. First, dropping generality of the transformation while preserving computational optimality for a subset of programs; second, dropping computational optimality while preserving generality of the transformation. In practice both ways have been taken.

Starting with IPRE, in [14] the first way has been taken. The application of the ISE-transformation is restricted to programs where the program it produces obeys a *canonicity* constraint. Intraprocedurally, this constraint holds for every program subjected to the SE-transformation. Intuitively, it requires that insertions are used on every program continuation (note that this constraint is violated in the example of Figure 6!). Canonicity is quite a natural constraint, and can easily be checked. Moreover, it characterizes a situation met by a large class of interprocedural programs, where there is no difference to the intraprocedural setting.

In [33] the second way has been taken. The motion of computations is heuristically limited in order to avoid anomalies of the transformation. This way, generality of the transformation is preserved. However, heuristics are often overly restrictive, and unnecessarily reduce the transformational power of an algorithm based on them. As discussed in [14] this also applies to the heuristics controlling the IPRE-transformation proposed in [33].

Considering now PPRE, in [27] the second way has been taken. Intuitively, the motion of computations from parallel program parts, where they are possibly for free, to sequential program parts, where they definitely count, is limited to situations, where occurrences of the computation under consideration are removed from every component of a parallel statement.[12] This guarantees that also the "bottleneck" component is improved. The modifications required to achieve this behaviour are actually limited to the treatment of synchronization of parallel components. They can completely be hidden inside the generic algorithm computing the fixed point solution of a DFA problem (cf. [27]). The final trans-

---

[11] In particular, for semantic PRE a difference between "motion"-based and "placement"-based PRE-techniques shows up (cf. [25]).

[12] A similar modification has been used in [12] in order to avoid anomalies when extending partial dead-code elimination (cf. [22]) to the parallel setting.

formation resulting from this adaptation guarantees admissibility, i.e., soundness (in the strong sense), and executional improvement, i.e., *relative* completeness. Actually, this is the best we can hope for, since executional optimality is out of the scope of any static approach because the property of being the bottleneck component of a parallel statement is highgradely run-time dependent.

Reuse on the Analysis and Transformation Level. Reusability has a slightly different flavour on the analysis and transformation level. On the transformation level reusability amounts essentially to the robustness of a specific optimization strategy with respect to setting and paradigm changes, on the analysis level it amounts essentially to the uniformity of the specification of a DFA problem which can possibly be fed into a generic paradigm-dependent algorithm producing the concrete algorithm for solving the corresponding DFA problem.

On the analysis level, reusability in the sense of uniformity has been achieved to quite a large extent. In fact, the DFA approaches of the various settings considered can be condensed to the abstract version shown in Figure 10 (cf. [15]). Though the specifics of the various paradigms and settings are different, from the point of view of a DFA designer, the specification interfaces and proof obligations to guarantee soundness and completeness are almost the same. In particular, this allows us the construction of DFA generators in the fashion of [11] and [15]. On the analysis level of optimization, this is an important contribution to enhance *reusability* and *portability* of know-how and of techniques based thereon.

Similarly, this also holds on the transformation level of optimization even though reuse on this level, i.e., of specific optimization strategies, demands usually for setting and paradigm-dependent adaptations in order to accommodate the specifics of a new setting as we demonstrated here by means of PRE. Generally, however, this is worth the effort. In fact, often an optimization turns out to be much more powerful in a setting different from the one it was designed for. A striking example was the extension of *partial dead-code elimination* [22] and *partial redundant-assigment elimination* [23] and their combination for *distribution assignment placement (DAP)* [18, 19] in *High Performance Fortran (HPF)*, a data-parallel language. Though the completeness or optimality results applying to the individual transformations in the basic intraprocedural setting do not carry over to the data-parallel setting of HPF, DAP proved to be most powerful in practical experiments, which have been performed by means of the Vienna Fortran Compilation System [2, 45]. Often, improvements of several hundred per cent could be observed, which are rather unlikely of being ever observed for intraprocedural sequential programs. In HPF programs they are rendered possible by the specifics of distribution statements causing (costly!) communication.

8   Conclusions

In this article, we reconsidered optimization under the perspective of soundness, completeness, and, additionally, reusability. While the choice of soundness and completeness aimed at highlighting an analogy between program optimization and program verification, which are usually considered independent or at most

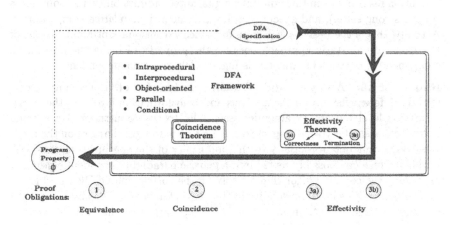

Fig. 10. The black-box view of DFA frameworks.

loosely related fields, the choice of reusability aimed at addressing a challenge which can be considered central for computer science: mastering complexity in software design. In fact, an inexpensive means for this is reuse of successful approaches in new environments. Under the perspective of reusability, we investigated the benefits and limitations of this approach for optimizing compilation. Using PRE as example we demonstrated that usually the rationale guaranteeing the soundness and completeness of an optimization in a specific setting is quite sensitive to setting and paradigm changes. In general, this requires setting and paradigm-dependent adaptations in order to accommodate their specifics. However, as demonstrated by PRE this is generally worth the effort. In fact, the example of distribution assignment placement, the combination of partially redundant assignment elimination and partially dead-code elimination, shows that optimizations are often much more powerful in a setting different from the one they were originally designed for. Further research in this direction is a major concern of future work. Progress on this issue, in particular, the intensified development of paradigm-transcending approaches can substantially contribute to bridging gaps between communities working (too) often on quite similar problems in different paradigms without utilizing synergies of their work, and hence, to solving the overall problem: mastering complexity.

Acknowledgements. We dedicate this article to Hans Langmaack. It presents a profile of our work on optimizing compilation under the perspective of soundness and completeness, a focal point of his research interests. We appreciate his constant encouragement and support, and gratefully acknowledge the inspiring and stimulating impact of his advice and attitude towards computer science on our research.

References

1. M. Auslander and M. Hopkins. An overview of the PL.8 compiler. In *Proceedings of the ACM SIGPLAN Symposium on Compiler Construction (SCC'82)* (*Boston, Massachusetts*), volume *17*, 6 of *ACM SIGPLAN Notices*, pages 22 – 31, 1982.
2. S. Benkner, S. Andel, R. Blasko, P. Brezany, A. Celic, B. M. Chapman, M. Egg, T. Fahringer, J. Hulman, E. Kelc, E. Mehofer, H. Moritsch, M. Paul, K. Sanjari, V. Sipkova, B. Velkov, B. Wender, and H. P. Zima. *Vienna Fortran Compilation System - Version 1.2 - User's Guide.* Institute for Software Technology and Parallel Systems, University of Vienna, Vienna, Austria, 1996.
3. P. Cousot. Abstract interpretation. *ACM Computing Surveys*, 28(2):324 – 328, 1996.
4. P. Cousot and R. Cousot. Abstract interpretation: A unified lattice model for static analysis of programs by construction or approximation of fixpoints. In *Conference Record of the 4th Annual Symposium on Principles of Programming Languages (POPL'77)* (*Los Angeles, California*), pages 238 – 252. ACM, New York, 1977.
5. P. Cousot and R. Cousot. Systematic design of program analysis frameworks. In *Conference Record of the 6th Annual Symposium on Principles of Programming Languages (POPL'79)* (*San Antonio, Texas*), pages 269 – 282. ACM, New York, 1979.
6. P. Cousot and R. Cousot. Abstract interpretation frameworks. *Journal of Logic and Computation*, 2(4):511 – 547, 1992.
7. K.-H. Drechsler and M. P. Stadel. A variation of Knoop, Rüthing and Steffen's LAZY CODE MOTION. *ACM SIGPLAN Notices*, 28(5):29 – 38, 1993.
8. M. S. Hecht. *Flow Analysis of Computer Programs.* Elsevier, North-Holland, 1977.
9. J. B. Kam and J. D. Ullman. Monotone data flow analysis frameworks. *Acta Informatica*, 7:305 – 317, 1977.
10. G. A. Kildall. A unified approach to global program optimization. In *Conference Record of the 1st Annual Symposium on Principles of Programming Languages (POPL'73)* (*Boston, Massachusetts*), pages 194 – 206. ACM, New York, 1973.
11. M. Klein, J. Knoop, D. Koschützki, and B. Steffen. DFA&OPT-METAFrame: A tool kit for program analysis and optimization. In *Proceedings of the 2nd International Workshop on Tools and Algorithms for the Construction and Analysis of Systems (TACAS'96)* (*Passau, Germany*), Lecture Notes in Computer Science, vol. 1055, pages 422 – 426. Springer-Verlag, Heidelberg, Germany, 1996.
12. J. Knoop. Eliminating partially dead code in explicitly parallel programs. *Theoretical Computer Science*, 196(1-2):365 – 393, 1998. (Special issue devoted to *Euro-Par'96*).
13. J. Knoop. Formal callability and its relevance and application to interprocedural data-flow analysis. In *Proceedings of the 6th IEEE Computer Society 1998 International Conference on Computer Languages (ICCL'98)* (*Chicago, Illinois*), pages 252 – 261. IEEE Computer Society, Los Alamitos, 1998.
14. J. Knoop. *Optimal Interprocedural Program Optimization: A new Framework and its Application.* PhD thesis. University of Kiel, Germany, 1993. Lecture Notes in Computer Science Tutorial, vol. 1428, Springer-Verlag, Heidelberg, Germany, 1998.
15. J. Knoop. From DFA-frameworks to DFA-generators: A unifying multiparadigm approach. In *Proceedings of the 5th International Conference on Tools and Algorithms for the Construction and Analysis of Systems (TACAS'99)* (*Amsterdam, The Netherlands*), Lecture Notes in Computer Science, vol. 1579, pages 360 – 374. Springer-Verlag, Heidelberg, Germany, 1999.

16. J. Knoop and W. Golubski. Abstract interpretation: A uniform framework for type analysis and classical optimization of object-oriented programs. In *Proceedings of the 1st International Symposium on Object-Oriented Technology "The White OO Nights" (WOON'96) (St. Petersburg, Russia)*, pages 126 – 142, 1996.

17. J. Knoop, D. Koschützki, and B. Steffen. Basic-block graphs: Living dinosaurs? In *Proceedings of the 7th International Conference on Compiler Construction (CC'98) (Lisbon, Portugal)*, Lecture Notes in Computer Science, vol. 1383, pages 65 – 79. Springer-Verlag, Heidelberg, Germany, 1998.

18. J. Knoop and E. Mehofer. Interprocedural distribution assignment placement: More than just enhancing intraprocedural placing techniques. In *Proceedings of the 5th IEEE International Conference on Parallel Architectures and Compilation Techniques (PACT'97) (San Francisco, California)*, pages 26 – 37. IEEE Computer Society, Los Alamitos, 1997.

19. J. Knoop and E. Mehofer. Optimal distribution assignment placement. In *Proceedings of the 3rd European Conference on Parallel Processing (Euro-Par'97) (Passau, Germany)*, Lecture Notes in Computer Science, vol. 1300, pages 364 – 373. Springer-Verlag, Heidelberg, Germany, 1997.

20. J. Knoop, O. Rüthing, and B. Steffen. Lazy code motion. In *Proceedings of the ACM SIGPLAN Conference on Programming Language Design and Implementation (PLDI'92) (San Francisco, California)*, volume 27,7 of *ACM SIGPLAN Notices*, pages 224 – 234, 1992.

21. J. Knoop, O. Rüthing, and B. Steffen. Optimal code motion: Theory and practice. *ACM Transactions on Programming Languages and Systems*, 16(4):1117–1155, 1994.

22. J. Knoop, O. Rüthing, and B. Steffen. Partial dead code elimination. In *Proceedings of the ACM SIGPLAN Conference on Programming Language Design and Implementation (PLDI'94) (Orlando, Florida)*, volume 29,6 of *ACM SIGPLAN Notices*, pages 147 – 158, 1994.

23. J. Knoop, O. Rüthing, and B. Steffen. The power of assignment motion. In *Proceedings of the ACM SIGPLAN Conference on Programming Language Design and Implementation (PLDI'95) (La Jolla, California)*, volume 30,6 of *ACM SIGPLAN Notices*, pages 233 – 245, 1995.

24. J. Knoop, O. Rüthing, and B. Steffen. Towards a tool kit for the automatic generation of interprocedural data flow analyses. *Journal of Programming Languages*, 4(4):211–246, 1996.

25. J. Knoop, O. Rüthing, and B. Steffen. Code motion and code placement: Just synomyms? In *Proceedings of the 7th European Symposium on Programming (ESOP'98) (Lisbon, Portugal)*, Lecture Notes in Computer Science, vol. 1381, pages 154 – 169. Springer-Verlag, Heidelberg, Germany, 1998.

26. J. Knoop and F. Schreiber. Analysing and optimizing strongly typed object-oriented languages: A generic approach and its application to Oberon-2. In *Proceedings of the 2nd International Symposium on Object-Oriented Technology "The White OO Nights" (WOON'97) (St. Petersburg, Russia)*, pages 252 – 266, 1997.

27. J. Knoop and B. Steffen. Code motion for explicitly parallel programs. In *Proceedings of the 7th ACM SIGPLAN Symposium on Principles and Practice of Parallel Programming (PPoPP'99) (Atlanta, Georgia)*, pages 13 - 14, 1999.

28. J. Knoop and B. Steffen. The interprocedural coincidence theorem. In *Proceedings of the 4th International Conference on Compiler Construction (CC'92) (Paderborn, Germany)*, Lecture Notes in Computer Science, vol. 641, pages 125 – 140. Springer-Verlag, Heidelberg, Germany, 1992.

29. J. Knoop, B. Steffen, and J. Vollmer. Parallelism for free: Bitvector analyses
    → No state explosion! In *Proceedings of the 1st International Workshop on
    Tools and Algorithms for the Construction and Analysis of Systems (TACAS'95)
    (Aarhus, Denmark)*, Lecture Notes in Computer Science, vol. 1019, pages 264 –
    289. Springer-Verlag, Heidelberg, Germany, 1995.
30. J. Knoop, B. Steffen, and J. Vollmer. Parallelism for free: Efficient and optimal
    bitvector analyses for parallel programs. *ACM Transactions on Programming Lan-
    guages and Systems*, 18(3):268 – 299, 1996.
31. K. Marriot. Frameworks for abstract interpretation. *Acta Informatica*, 30:103 –
    129, 1993.
32. E. Morel and C. Renvoise. Global optimization by suppression of partial redun-
    dancies. *Communications of the ACM*, 22(2):96 – 103, 1979.
33. E. Morel and C. Renvoise. Interprocedural elimination of partial redundancies.
    In S. S. Muchnick and N. D. Jones, editors, *Program Flow Analysis: Theory and
    Applications*, chapter 7, pages 160 – 188. Prentice Hall, Englewood Cliffs, New
    Jersey, 1981.
34. R. Morgan. *Building an Optimizing Compiler*. Digital Press, 1998.
35. S. S. Muchnick. *Advanced Compiler Design and Implementation*. Morgan Kauf-
    mann, San Francisco, California, 1997.
36. S. S. Muchnick and N. D. Jones, editors. *Program Flow Analysis: Theory and
    Applications*. Prentice Hall, Englewood Cliffs, New Jersey, 1981.
37. F. Nielson. A bibliography on abstract interpretations. *ACM SIGPLAN Notices*,
    21:31 – 38, 1986.
38. J. Palsberg and M. I. Schwartzbach. *Object-oriented Type Systems*. John Wiley &
    Sons, 1994.
39. Jens Palsberg. Type inference for objects. *ACM Computing Surveys*, 28(2):358–
    359, June 1996.
40. O. Rüthing. Bidirectional data flow analysis in code motion: Myth and reality. In
    Proceedings of the 5th Static Analysis Symposium (SAS'98) (Pisa, Italy), Lecture
    Notes in Computer Science, vol. 1503, pages 1 – 16. Springer-Verlag, Heidelberg,
    Germany, 1998.
41. O. Rüthing. *Interacting Code Motion Transformations: Their Impact and Their
    Complexity*. PhD thesis. University of Kiel, Germany, 1997. Lecture Notes in
    Computer Science, vol. 1539, Springer-Verlag, Heidelberg, Germany, 1998.
42. O. Rüthing. Optimal code motion in the presence of large expressions. In *Proceed-
    ings of the 6th IEEE Computer Society 1998 International Conference on Com-
    puter Languages (ICCL'98) (Chicago, Illinois)*, pages 216 – 225. IEEE Computer
    Society, Los Alamitos, 1998.
43. O. Rüthing, J. Knoop, and B. Steffen. Sparse code motion. Technical Report
    712/1999, Department of Computer Science, University of Dortmund, Germany,
    1999.
44. M. Sharir and A. Pnueli. Two approaches to interprocedural data flow analysis.
    In S. S. Muchnick and N. D. Jones, editors, *Program Flow Analysis: Theory and
    Applications*, chapter 7, pages 189 – 233. Prentice Hall, Englewood Cliffs, New
    Jersey, 1981.
45. VFCS/VFC Homepage. Institute for Softwaretechnology and Parallel Sys-
    tems, University of Vienna, Austria, http://www.par.univie.ac.at/research/lang-
    comp/lang-comp.html.

Part V

Application

Verification of Automotive Control Units

Tom Bienmüller[1], Jürgen Bohn[2], Henning Brinkmann[1], Udo Brockmeyer[2],
Werner Damm[1,2], Hardi Hungar[2], and Peter Jansen[3]

[1] Carl von Ossietzky Universität, Ammerländer Heerstraße 114–118, P.O. Box 2503,
26111 Oldenburg, Germany
[2] OFFIS, Escherweg 2, 26121 Oldenburg, Germany
[3] BMW AG, 80788 Munich, Germany

Abstract. This paper describes the application of model-checking based verification tools to specification models of automotive control units. It firstly discusses the current state of a tool set which copes with discrete controllers described in STATEMATE, and then reports on proposed extensions currently under development to deal with hybrid ones which involve continuous values, too. First results based on an extension of abstraction techniques to verify such units are reported.

1 Introduction

This paper advocates the use of model-checking based verification technology to cope with the challenge in designing electronic control units (ECUs) for automotive applications whose correct functioning is often safety critical. Model checking comprises an algorithm which takes a model of the system under design (SUD) and a (e.g. safety-critical) property, and checks—in a mathematically rigorous sense—that the SUD satisfies this property. From its basic algorithmic definition [CES83], model checking has matured to a state where it is on the edge of introduction into industrial design processes [Kur97]. Important milestones on this path were the introduction of symbolic representations of the SUD [McM93], and the use of abstraction techniques [BBLS92,CGL94] to focus the representation of the SUD to its relevant parts. The integration of these techniques with an industry-standard design tool like STATEMATE makes the technology usable in an industrial setting.

One particularly interesting application domain can be found in the automotive industry. Over the recent years, the number of electronic components built into cars has been increasing rapidly. They serve to improve safety, to reduce emission and fuel consumption or to improve comfort and driver information. Among these systems are such safety-critical systems like a brake control or a dynamic drive control. A high-end version of an upper-class vehicle contains systems with up to 50 embedded control units (see Figure 1). All these components are connected via several bus systems. An essential characteristic of the automotive electronic architecture is a net of multiple local control units. Not only the number of embedded control units, but also the range of usage of these systems increases. As shown in Figure 2, future ECU designs might even take

E.-R. Olderog, B. Steffen (Eds.): Correct System Design, LNCS 1710, pp. 319–341, 1999.
© Springer-Verlag Berlin Heidelberg 1999

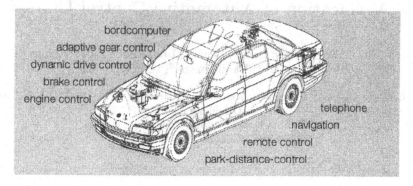

Fig. 1. View of electronic components in a car

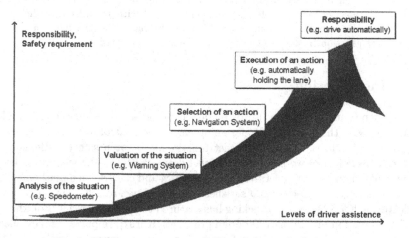

Fig. 2. The increasing responsibility of electronic features

full responsibility, e.g. driving a car automatically. Electronic components to be built into cars must satisfy strong reliability requirements. We might take the recent discussion about airbag control as an example. While it is recognized that airbags statistically enhance the protection of occupants in a car in case of an accident, there have also been cases where airbags proved to be harmful. The most prominent issue in the debate centered around fatal injuries to infants occupying the passenger seat caused by airbags which where released though they were believed to be disabled. Generally, it is considered unacceptable to use control units in serial production which have systematic errors which might endanger people under particular, even unlikely circumstances.

This obviously applies to systems like a brake control. But also for other, apparently less safety-critical systems, there are usually some safety requirements. For instance, a central-locking control must guarantee that the doors get unlocked in case of a crash.

To develop such systems of both high complexity and strong reliability requirements is one of the main challenges faced by the industry, and putting more and more functions under the control of electronic components will aggravate the problem in the future. To cope with it, traditional design methods are inadequate, and therefore, for instance at BMW (Bayerische Motorenwerke AG, Munich, Germany), heterogeneous CASE tools are in use.

Here, we will focus on the STATEMATE tool, which allows a designer to develop abstract versions of an ECU. This abstract version is analyzed extensively until it can be termed to satisfy the requirements and be used as a reference model in the further development steps which lead to the final implementation. Part of the analysis might be a test of the control unit within its environment in a car. For this, a software prototype is derived from the abstract version via the STATEMATE code-generation facilities and run on a high-end PC in the test vehicle. But before this is done, other methods as high-level simulation and virtual integration with a co-simulated environment are being used on the abstract design and, what will be the main theme of this paper, model checking.

One might ask the question how well model checking is suited for the analysis of the sort of controllers found in this domain. In its pure essence, model checking is inherently a method for the analysis of finite state systems. Hence model variables with non-finite types must be abstracted into finite types for the method to be applicable in its current maturity level. Assuming for the moment finite models, the immediate question popping up asks for a quantification. The breakthrough alluded to above [McM93] is the step from roughly a million states, i.e. 10^6 possible valuations of model inputs and variables, to, say, 10^{100} such valuations. This has been accomplished by using symbolic representations employing binary decision diagrams [Bry92] instead of explicit ones. Our experience shows that there are many systems whose size is within this order of magnitude. If a full controller exceeds this size, one option is to restrict attention to some of its central components. Moreover, there are complementary techniques—besides the already mentioned abstraction, the orthogonal approach of compositional verification [Jos93]—allowing us to handle much larger systems, as long as the part of the design relevant to the property under consideration can be reduced to this size.

However, the estimation of the system size for which model checking is possible comes with a caveat. The symbolic representation encodes the model in valuations of linearly ordered binary variables, and the size of the encoding is sensitive to the selected ordering [Bry92]. In fact one and the same model can have encodings greatly varying in size. Even worse, there are clear-cut theoretical arguments, why not all finite state machines can have succinct representations, and why finding the best encoding is in practice not feasible. While this might sound discouraging, it turns out that control-dominated, well-structured designs constitute a good match for the heuristics underlying the symbolic encodings and the employed analysis algorithms. And it is exactly this class of designs we find in safety-critical ECU designs. For such designs, it seems safe to say that models in the order of 10^{100} possible valuations can be handled.

The EMF example which is described later in the paper might be taken to illustrate this point. We experienced that an early, badly structured design could not be handled by the model checker. A redesign of the controller, which has been developed following guidelines with the objective to produce accessible and maintainable controllers were followed, had essentially the same number of states but was well within the reach of that technique.

This describes our findings about the application of model checking to finite state systems, see also [BBD+99]. However, in the automotive as well as in other areas, a large part of the ECUs deal not only with discrete but also with continuous values. In this case, the ECU can usually not be viewed as a finite state system. It would not help much to translate real values into their floating-point computer representation, because the induced complexity would be too high in most cases. Small controllers in which the continuous values play the major rôle might be handled by specialized techniques like the ones implemented in the tool HyTech [HHWT97]. These techniques are, however, unable to deal with designs featuring also the nontrivial discrete control logic common to most ECUs. With our approach, we aim for a class of systems where the discrete part is the most important, while continuous variables, though present, play a minor part.

To be able to apply symbolic model checking in the presence of continuous values, it is mandatory to use reduction techniques. In the classical framework of abstraction, one defines a mapping of (large) data spaces to (small) abstract value sets. On the abstract representation, the validity of formulas is approximated conservatively. On an abstract run, a property holds if it holds for all concrete runs mapped to it. For that to give meaningful results, the abstraction mapping has to be chosen with care. I.e., the choice of a good mapping requires considerable insight into the workings of the SUD.

A different approach called first-order model checking has been proposed in [HGD95,BDG+98]. There, only a set of data variables has to be picked on which the abstraction is to be performed. Then, an extension of the standard symbolic model-checking algorithm computes the abstraction automatically, in that it works with the relevant *properties* of the data variable valuations instead of the valuations themselves. These data properties are those mentioned in the specification, conditions in the SUD and the ones established by its assignments. Usually, as steps of the SUD are executed by the model checker, the set of relevant properties has to be extended dynamically. In the application domain of embedded control units, the set of relevant propositions often remains finite. In that case, the model checker terminates with a first-order condition on the data domain characterizing the correctness of the SUD. A version of this extended symbolic model checker is currently under development, and first tests produced promising results.

In applications where continuous values enter only in a specific, restricted form, the set of relevant properties can be computed beforehand, as well as the part of the domain theory which is needed. In that case, we can compute the abstraction on the SUD in the classical sense and use a standard model checker. This restricted version of first-order model checking is already implemented, and we will report on its successful first applications.

This paper is structured as follows. An example of an ECU developed at BMW is described in Section 2. Section 3 gives an overview of the current state of the STATEMATE verification environment and reports on its application to the example. The results are compared to the ones obtained by applying the restricted form of first-order model checking. We explain the ideas behind first-order model checking in Section 4, and present the restricted algorithm for memoryless systems in the section following it. We discuss what we have achieved and what we hope to accomplish in the future in Section 6.

2   Electronic Brake Management as an Example of an ECU

One of the ECUs developed recently at BMW is a brake management system (EMF). Of course this is a highly safety-critical application. As this is not a toy example but meant to be go into production its functions cannot be described in detail. Let us mention that one of its functions is, if the driver pushes the brake pedal and the vehicle stops, then the vehicle is held by the brake without the brake pedal being pushed. If the driver then presses the accelerator, this "hold function" will be canceled. Of this controller, a STATEMATE version has been developed and model checking has been applied in its analysis.

Figure 3 shows the top-level activity chart of the STATEMATE model. In total, this model consists of 14 charts. The statechart BRAKE_FKT_CT_EC controls the sub-functions of this model. It starts and stops the activities MOTOR_OFF_AC_EC, MOTOR_ON_1_AC_EC and MOTOR_ON_2_AC_EC. MOTOR_OFF_AC_EC controls the brake if the engine is off. MOTOR_ON_1_AC_EC takes over the control of the brake if the engine is on and the vehicle stands, and MOTOR_ON_2_AC_EC is put in charge if the car is moving. There are some information flows to and from other ECUs. E.g. some sensor values come from the DME (Digital Motor Electronics), also some lamps in the cockpit have to be controlled (information flow INDICATOR_CTRL).

There is a switch in the car to disable the hold function. One requirement for this system is: Whenever the switch is pressed and the hold function is active, it has to be deactivated within the next time unit. Figure 4 shows the formalization of this property in terms of a *symbolic timing diagram* which provides a graphical interface for temporal logic.

The variable which represents the hold function is called DECELERATION. In this diagram, the value 10.0 represents the absence of deceleration (while 0 would mean maximum deceleration).

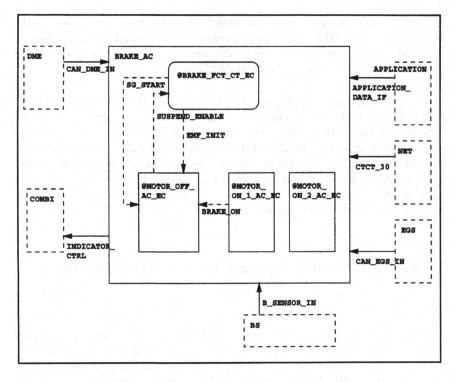

Fig. 3. Top level activity of the braking system

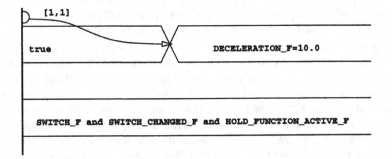

Fig. 4. Example property of the braking system

3   Model Checking of Automotive Control Units

3.1   The Verification Environment for Statemate

During the past four years a verification environment for STATEMATE designs
has been developed, allowing the formal verification of relevant system properties
for the modeled embedded controllers.

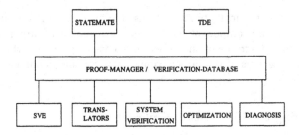

Fig. 5. The STATEMATE Verification Environment

Figure 5 shows central components of the verification environment. For a user of the tool set, the component called *proof manager* is of central importance. It supports a graphical interface from which the other components are invoked in order to hide internal technicalities from the user. Furthermore, it keeps track of all proofs already done. In particular, if a component of a system has to be changed to correct a flaw, the *proof manager* invalidates all proofs that are affected by these changes. These consistency checks are done on a *verification database*, which stores relationships between the subcomponents of a regarded system and the associated requirement specifications.

We consider STATEMATE descriptions of ECUs. Activity-charts are used to describe the functional decomposition of systems and the interfacing of the sub-components, while the behavioral descriptions are given as statecharts. Requirements capturing is performed with the timing diagram editor (TDE). TDE allows a graphical specification of the requirements by the means of *symbolic timing diagrams* [DJS95]. These can be viewed as a graphical format for temporal logic—and indeed, in the verification environment they are translated to temporal logic—which are easier accessible to the developers in industry than textual formulas would be. The verification of the desired properties with respect to a given STATEMATE model can be done with the assumption/commitment style model checker SVE[1].

To employ model checking, the gaps between the high-level specification formalisms STATEMATE and TDE and the input languages of SVE have to be bridged. This is done automatically by a set of tools in the *translators* box, which are initiated by the *proof manager*. The *optimizations* box offers several tools allowing state-of-the-art improvements, e.g. code optimizations, cone-of-influence slicing and abstraction techniques.

If the model checker falsifies a given property, counterexamples may be generated. The tools in the *diagnosis* box will visualize counter examples as a timing diagram or simulate them within the STATEMATE design, thus providing a convenient way to analyze erroneous behavior.

The *system verification* box represents a set of tools supporting compositional verification techniques. The correct interplay of communicating subcomponents

---

[1] SVE is a registered trademark of Siemens AG, Munich.

can be verified automatically by these tools. Timing diagrams specify the behavior of each single subcomponent as well as the behavior of larger components. Using the timing diagrams of the subcomponents as premises, the tools try to verify timing diagrams of the larger components by the technique of tautology checking.

3.2   Applying the Verification Environment

The verification environment has been applied to several case studies from the automotive area, from avionics and the control of chemical processes. In particular, some of them were supplied by BMW, taken from some current designs. They were parts of the control systems responsible for safety, convenience, and driving support. We analyzed the EMF example introduced above and another sample case study which is called ELV, the latter being a subsystem of the body electronic. With moderate changes—we will come back to that point—the STATEMATE designs could be translated by our tools. The timing diagram specifications were derived from textual requirements, also provided by BMW. Several relevant properties have been verified with the model checker. Also some errors have been uncovered during the verification. As an example, remember that the EMF should cancel the "hold function" as soon as the driver presses the accelerator. The model checker found an erroneous behavior of the model, such that after stopping the vehicle the "hold function" remains activated forever under some environment conditions, regardless of pressing the accelerator or not. This means, that in such a situation the driver could not set the car into motion again without restarting the engine. The design flaw could be corrected easily by modifying the guard of one statechart transition within the EMF model.

We already mentioned that the translation of the STATEMATE designs required moderate changes. The models had to undergo some manual transformations like mapping objects with infinite domain to finite ones before they could be model checked. As is the case with a majority of the ECUs found in automotive applications, continuous variables occurred in its original STATEMATE description. For instance, the EMF variable DECELERATION was of type real and had been changed to an integer ranging from 0 to 15 for the verification.

These transformations have been done manually, since presently the environment does not offer any tool support for this purpose. It was not too hard to find an adequate discrete representation of the value spaces because the reals occurred in a rather restricted way. Thresholds were tested on them, and outputs were set to values which came from continuous subsystems not represented in STATEMATE (i.e., those values were input to the STATEMATE design). But of course, such ad hoc transformations are a potential source of errors and should be replaced by a theoretically clean, and if possible even automatic method.[2]

Table 1 shows some results gained from analyzing the main controllers of the EMF case study. The translation of the EMF design took 4965 seconds of

---

[2] The abstractions currently supported in the verification environment for STATEMATE serve other abstraction aims.

Table 1. Model checking results for the EMF with manual abstractions

	EMF-1	EMF-2	EMF-3
generating FSM [sec]	4965	4965	4965
BDD nodes [#]	205480	205480	205480
FSM state bits (opt.) [#]	271 (100)	271 (95)	271 (95)
FSM input bits (opt.) [#]	140 (68)	140 (68)	140 (68)
FSM optimization [sec]	45.2	44.7	44.6
model checking [sec]	351	1320	1019
total time [sec]	5362	6330	6029

CPU time on an UltraSPARC-II with 296 Mhz. The finite state machine representation counts 140 (68 after applying optimizations) bits to encode the input variables, and 271 (95 – 100 after applying optimizations) bits for the state variables. The resulting number of necessary BDD nodes is 205480. The model checking line shows the times required to verify relevant properties for the regarded control unit. Properties EMF-1 (351 sec.) and EMF-2, the one formalized in Figure 4, (1320 sec.) represent safety requirements. The last property (1019 sec.) specifies a liveness requirement.

3.3   Desired Improvements of the Verification Environment

The results above demonstrate very clearly that the verification can be profitably applied in the design process. Nevertheless, it must be said that it is still limited in its applicability, mainly due to complexity reasons. Not only that the analyzed EMF model is rather close to the maximal complexity which can currently be handled, the STATEMATE design had to undergo some manual transformations in order to map objects with infinite domains to abstract, finite domains.

It would be of great benefit, if this error-prone and laborious task could be replaced by an automatic and flawless tool. In fact, in the first section we already presented the ideas of a new, promising technique of abstractions which could help to cope with continuous values in the examples properly. In the approach of first-order model checking, an extended model-checking algorithm computes the abstractions automatically, if the designs follow some particular patterns. The details of this technique will be explained in the following sections. For now, let us have a look at the results. A simple version of first-order model checking (see Sec. 5) has been implemented which permits a fully automatic verification if applicable. It turned out that the EMF (as well as the ELV mentioned above) satisfies the applicability conditions of first-order model checking. Table 2 lists some results for the EMF case study. It shows that due to the automatic transformation, the verification effort needed significantly less time and space compared with the results of Table 1. I.e., this technique constitutes a practically relevant improvement of the verification technology currently integrated into our tool set.

In the following sections, we will first present the idea and algorithmic formulation of first-order model checking, and then go on (Sec. 5) to explain the simplified version which has been used to obtain the results from Table 2.

Table 2. First-order model-checking results for the EMF

	EMF-1	EMF-2	EMF-3
abstraction [sec]	2.7	2.6	9.3
propositions [#]	26	26	26
invariant conjuncts [#]	4	10	10
generating FSM [sec]	2966	3514	3614
BDD nodes [#]	134369	193624	193624
FSM state bits (opt.) [#]	243 (99)	240 (95)	240 (95)
FSM input bits (opt.) [#]	136 (65)	139 (68)	139 (68)
FSM optimization [sec]	23.6	30.9	32.3
model checking [sec]	160	579	504
total time [sec]	3153	4127	4160

4 First-Order Model Checking

The possibility to perform verification via model checking automatically depends
on the restriction to systems with finite or finitely representable state spaces.
Systems like Automotive Control Units react typically on continuously changing sensor readings, monitoring the controlled system or its environment. Thus,
models of these systems contain reals. For verification purposes it is then necessary to abstract from unbounded domains to get a finite representation of
the system model that fits to the restrictions of classical decision procedures
like symbolic model checking. Generally, the idea of abstraction is to reduce the
model to those aspects that are required to answer the requested properties.
During first-order model checking a kind of abstraction is computed automatically. Roughly, this abstraction reduces aspects of unbounded data variables to a
set of data propositions. This set is not necessarily finite, but in our automotive
applications the set of properties that are relevant for the verification is not only
finite but also rather small.

Generally, we find such small sets of relevant data properties in applications
where complex control is combined with rare computations on sampled data.
Such applications have in common, that there is a clear separation between
control and *data*. This class includes embedded controllers and processors with
nontrivial data paths.

Typically, embedded controllers in automotive applications are not independent from data input, but their control reaction depends only on a small number
of certain data properties such as thresholds. Even if there are complicated computations on data, the control and the data-dependent parts of the system may
be separated into subcomponents that communicate only by control or only via
data properties. This observation is used in first-order model checking: while
the control part is represented by BDDs as in other approaches to finite system verification, the data part is reduced to properties that are represented
in terms of first-order predicate logic. The verification algorithm of first-order
model checking performs explicit substitutions on the predicate syntax during
system steps.

This kind of computation on predicates is known from Hoare logic [Hoa69]. To capture the backwards effect of an assignment

$$W := t$$

to a predicate p involving the continuous variable W, we substitute t for W in p. I.e., we apply the well-known assignment rule

$$\{p[t/W]\}\ W := t\ \{p\}\ .$$

Data input is captured logically by either universal or existential quantification over the input variable, depending on whether we are doing a universal or existential next-step computation during model checking.

Both substitution and quantification may introduce new predicates into the model-checking process. If the predicates were treated completely uninterpreted, this would lead in most cases to infinite sequences of generated data predicates and thus to non-termination of the whole verification process. But already straightforward simplifications of, for example, variable-free predicates (such as $0 < 10$ yields *true*) ensure termination in many applications (e.g. in the EMF). More sophisticated reductions of predicates and interpretations of terms—that may depend on knowledge of the application domain—enable the application to hybrid controllers not only in the automotive area.

First-order model checking extends standard symbolic model checking for CTL in two aspects: the model, a finite state machine (FSM) extended with continuous variables, may contain in the first-order case transitions that depend on *data propositions*, i.e. predicates on data variables with infinite domain, and that perform assignments to data variables. The specification that is to be verified is presented in first-order CTL (FO-CTL), which extends CTL by quantification over rigid variables.

The representation of the model is BDD-based. Each data proposition enters the BDDs as a single bit. A separate *proposition table* is used to manage the propositions and their associations to these single bits. The initial propositions are taken from data-dependent conditions in the control-unit design (e.g. STATEMATE model) and from data properties in the requirements specification. Assignments to data variables in such a design are managed in an additional *value table*. This table contains for each assignment to a data variable the condition under which this assignment is to be performed within a step. During the verification process, assignments are handled as substitutions on data propositions which may lead to new propositions that are added to the proposition table.

Ordinary model checking for CTL computes the set of states that fulfill a given CTL specification. A consequence of our first-order extension is that the descriptions of these states may depend on data propositions. Thus, our new verification algorithm incrementally computes a set of pairs consisting of a control state set and a first-order predicate, characterizing validity of the FO-CTL formula to be proven. In contrast to symbolic model checking, where the answer of the algorithm is always either *true* or *false* (depending on a comparison between the set of initial states with the valid set), we now may end up with a first-order predicate that describes conditions on data propositions that are necessary for a validation of the specification. Due to the BDD-based representation, we get propositional simplifications of verification conditions "for free".

Our verification procedure is automatic, though it will not always terminate. Termination is guaranteed e.g. for Wolper's class of data-independent systems [Wol86], where there is neither testing nor computing on data values. Either testing or computing can be permitted, but unrestricted use of both may lead to non-termination of our procedure.

Let us demonstrate our procedure on a simple example. One run through the following pseudo program describes a step of a controller that sets an alarm if a frequently read input value grows too fast:

```
REAL INPUT SENSOR;
BOOL OUTPUT ALARM := false;
REAL LOCAL NEW, OLD := 0;
BOOL LOCAL INIT := false;

ALARM := false;
NEW    := SENSOR;
CASE
    []        NEW − OLD > 2.5 → CASE
                                    []     INIT → SKIP
                                    []  not(INIT) → ALARM := true
                                ESAC
    []   not(NEW − OLD > 2.5) → SKIP
ESAC;
OLD  := NEW;
INIT := false
```

The controller repeats this step infinitely often. It compares new input from a sensor with the old input of the previous step and sets $ALARM$, if the new value is more than 2.5 units larger than the old one and if the controller is not in the first (initial) step. Therefore, the local control variable $INIT$ is initialized by true. If we assume for this example that the input is a real value then the local variables NEW and OLD have to be reals. The condition $NEW − OLD > 2.5$ defines a proposition on these data variables. At the end of a step, the value of the output variable $ALARM$—which is a boolean control variable—depends on this proposition.

To specify requirements, we use first-order computation tree logic, FO-CTL. It has the following negation-free syntax.

$$\phi ::= \mathsf{A} \mid \overline{\mathsf{A}} \mid \mathsf{b} \mid \phi \wedge \phi \mid \phi \vee \phi \mid \mathbf{q}\,\mathsf{x}.\,\phi \mid \mathbf{Q}\,\psi$$
$$\psi ::= \mathbf{X}\,\phi \mid \phi\,\mathbf{U}\,\phi \mid \phi\,\mathbf{W}\,\phi$$

where $\mathsf{A} \in \mathcal{A}$ are atomic propositions, $\mathsf{x} \in \mathsf{V}$ for the variable set V and b a boolean condition over V, $\mathbf{q} \in \{\forall, \exists\}$ and $\mathbf{Q} \in \{\mathbf{A}, \mathbf{E}\}$.

First-order quantifiers are interpreted *rigidly*, i.e. the value is fixed for the evaluation of the formula in its scope, it does not change over time. As in the following example formula ϕ, we use standard abbreviations in specifications. Expanding logical implication requires moving negation through a formula down to atoms. $\mathbf{AG}\,\phi_1$ is defined as $\mathbf{A}[\phi_1\ \mathbf{W}\ false]$ as in CTL.

$$\phi =_{df}\ \forall\, X\quad \mathbf{AG}\,(SENSOR = X \land INIT = false$$
$$\rightarrow \mathbf{AX}\,(SENSOR\text{-}X > 3 \rightarrow \mathbf{AX}\,(ALARM\text{=}true)))$$

The formula ϕ specifies a desired relation between input and output of the controller. Note that we use the first-order variable X to "store" the value of *SENSOR* through one next-step computation such that a comparison between new and old input values becomes possible. In Section 4.3 we explain how the previously introduced control program is checked against this specification. Before we do so, we present first-order model checking in more technical detail.

4.1   The Tableau of a Formula

The tableau Tab_ϕ of a formula ϕ consists of a finite set of nodes. It captures the dependencies from the validity of subformulas of ϕ, to be exploited during model checking. Each node consists of a boolean combination of subformulas of ϕ, and a set of variables indicating the free variables of the labeling formula which are quantified within ϕ. There are two sorts of connections between nodes: $\mapsto$, which indicates dependency of validity within the same state, and $\rightarrow$, which indicates a reference to the successor states. The tableau Tab_ϕ is finite for every ϕ. An example is presented in Figure 6.

4.2   The BDD-Based Verification Algorithm

The first-order model checker computes—bottom up in the tableau—annotations that represent the set of states that fulfill the (sub-)formula at this node. Our approach is based on the idea of combining BDD procedures for finite (small) data domains with first-order representations for infinite or large data domains. We assume that the variables V of the controller program and quantified variables W from the FO-CTL specification are split accordingly into two classes: *Control* variables whose valuations will be represented by BDDs, and *data* variables whose valuations will be represented by first-order predicates.

First-order data predicates enter the BDD representation of an annotation in the form of propositions, which are atomic for the BDD. I.e., the BDD refers via proposition bits to first-order formulas. Thus, one part of an annotation BDD represents sets of control valuations, as an ordinary BDD would do.

The other part describes what is left after partial evaluation w.r.t. control values: first-order formulas, which are viewed as boolean combinations of data propositions. The meaning of the proposition bits are kept in a separate *proposition table*.

Let ϕ be the specification presented above, $\phi = \forall X\, \mathbf{AG}\,(\phi_1)$, with sub-specifications

$$\phi_1 \;=_{\mathrm{df}} (\phi_{1,1} \wedge \phi_{1,2}) \rightarrow (\mathbf{AX}\,(\phi_{2,1} \rightarrow \phi_{2,2}))$$
$$\phi_{1,1} =_{\mathrm{df}} SENSOR{=}X$$
$$\phi_{1,2} =_{\mathrm{df}} INIT{=}false$$
$$\phi_{2,1} =_{\mathrm{df}} SENSOR{-}X > 3$$
$$\phi_{2,2} =_{\mathrm{df}} \mathbf{AX}\,(ALARM{=}true)$$

Then Tab_ϕ has the form as shown to the right. $\mathbf{AG}\,(\phi_1) = \mathbf{A}[\phi_1\,\mathbf{W}\,false]$ introduces a $\mathbf{W}$ cycle, which is condensed to a self loop in the picture. Furthermore, the annotation of nodes below the root by variable X is omitted. The relation $\mapsto$ is drawn as a simple line insight the figure.

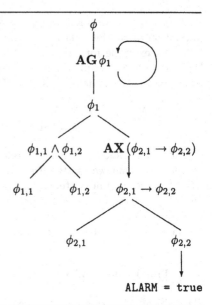

Fig. 6. Tableau example

The proposition table includes, for each proposition, a bit q_i and in the case of a basic proposition the syntactical description of the first-order formula that it represents. Boolean compositions of propositions define new propositions, that are represented via BDDs on proposition bits. Note that a proposition does not contain any control variables.

Substitution and quantification of data variables : Assignments to data variables in a step of the model are reflected during model checking by changes to the propositions. A special *value table* is created during the FSM generation. This table contains all right-hand sides of assignments to data variables and BDD-represented guards that enable or disable the assignments. The effect of taking a transition step on control variables is captured canonically using functional BDDs.

Assignments of data terms affect the annotations and hence the proposition table. Substitutions can be distributed to single propositions. They may lead to the introduction of new entries in the proposition table, if the result is not already covered by the present set. Quantifications have to be applied to whole boolean combinations, and they may enforce new propositions, too.

4.3   Application to the Example

Let us consider the running example. The only control variables are $ALARM$ and $INIT$, whereas $SENSOR$, NEW and OLD are data. The proposition table is initialized by q_1, q_2 and q_3 while the other rows in the table below are filled during a run of the algorithm. Starting the model checking bottom-up with the atomic propositions yields the annotation q_2 for node $\phi_{1,1}$ and $INIT = false$ (as BDD) for node $\phi_{1,2}$ and therefore $q_2 \wedge INIT = false$ for the parent of both nodes.

Proposition table:

name	proposition	free data variables
q_1	$SENSOR - X > 2.5$	$SENSOR, X$
q_2	$SENSOR = X$	$SENSOR, X$
q_3	$SENSOR - X > 3$	$SENSOR, X$
q_4	$SENSOR - OLD > 2.5$	$SENSOR, OLD$
q_5	$SENSOR' - SENSOR > 2.5$	$SENSOR', SENSOR$
q_6	$SENSOR' - X > 3$	$SENSOR', X$
q_7	$\forall SENSOR'. (q_6 \rightarrow q_5)$	$SENSOR, SENSOR, X$
q_8	$SENSOR'' = X$	$SENSOR'', X$
q_9	$SENSOR' - SENSOR'' > 2.5$	$SENSOR', SENSOR''$
q_{10}	$\forall SENSOR''. (q_8 \rightarrow q_9)$	X
q_{11}	$\forall X. q_{10}$	

The right side of the tableau (see Figure 6) needs some more attention. We initialize the atoms $\phi_{2,1}$ and $ALARM = true$ with q_3 and the BDD-represented state for $ALARM = true$, respectively. The precondition for $ALARM$ is q_4. The proposition q_4 annotates therefore the tableau node $\phi_{2,2}$. For the node $\phi_{2,1} \rightarrow \phi_{2,2}$ we get $q_3 \rightarrow q_4$. The computation of the annotation for the second next-step operator requires quantification of the data input $SENSOR$. Renaming $SENSOR$ in q_3 and q_4 by $SENSOR'$ and substituting $SENSOR$ for OLD introduces the new propositions q_5 and q_6 into the proposition table. The quantification performed afterwards yields q_7 as annotation for the node $(\mathbf{AX}(\phi_{2,1} \rightarrow \phi_{2,2}))$.

Starting the fixed point computation with $(q_2 \wedge INIT = false) \rightarrow q_7$ introduces another version $SENSOR''$ of the quantified variable $SENSOR$ and removes the dependency from $INIT$ after one iteration step. The second iteration step temporarily generates propositions with a new variable $SENSOR'''$, but these propositions coincide with previously generated ones modulo the quantified sensor variable. A simple matching algorithm integrated in a BDD-comparison function detects this kind of equality, and thus the fixed-point loop terminates.

The last step computes $\forall X. q_{10}$ as proof obligation for node ϕ. Slightly simplified, this obligation states

$$\forall X, SENSOR'. SENSOR' - X > 3 \rightarrow SENSOR' - X > 2.5.$$

This formula is a tautology which has to be established by a subsequent procedure. After that has been done, it is verified that the controller fulfills the required specification.

5 A Simplified Version of First-Order Model Checking

Let us summarize the main concepts of the verification algorithm of the previous section. First-order model checking replaces computing with expanded values of data variables by operating on boolean propositions which represent the relevant first-order properties of the data. The set of propositions is expanded on demand, where ordinary assignments and input statements are responsible for the introduction of new ones via substitution and quantification. All this is done by a specific, BDD-based procedure, which outputs a first-order verification condition in case of termination. In some cases, we can simplify the procedure to the point that we can map to a standard model-checking problem.

If the relevant propositions were known in advance, one could avoid having to generate propositions dynamically and checking the verification condition a posteriori. Instead, the necessary computations on propositions could be inserted directly into the system representation, and the logical dependencies between propositions could be computed beforehand to be taken into account during model checking.

Though we cannot do that in general, there are favorable cases where a sufficiently accurate approximation of that procedure can be applied. One of these cases occurs if the SUD does not store continuous values from one step to the next. We call such systems *memoryless* w.r.t. continuous values. A memoryless system may test continuous values against constants or one another, and it may use inputs to produce continuous outputs "immediately". But since there are no local continuous variables to store continuous values, the substitutions induced by data assignments will produce only a finite set of propositions. To see that, consider a data assignment $W := t$. It induces the substitution $[t/W]$ to be performed on the propositions. Since the term t contains only input variables, the substitution eliminates the output variable W from all propositions without introducing others. Thus, applying the substitutions removes, step by step, all output variables from the propositions to which they are applied. This implies that the closure of the initial set of propositions under the substitutions is finite.

In the form of ordinary boolean variables, the propositions computed in the substitution closure replace the data variables appearing in the system. Substitutions to be performed during a step in ordinary first-order model checking are modeled as boolean assignments in the system description. Quantifications are avoided by resorting to some kind of approximation which will be explained in due course.

Like the set of propositions, also a set of first-order verification conditions is computed in advance. If a potential condition evaluates to true, this fact is supplied as an invariant to the model checker. Since no quantifiers do occur, only boolean dependencies between the propositions are considered. For instance, if the set of propositions includes $W2 = X$, $W3 = Y$ and $W2 + W3 = X + Y$, then the implication $W2 = X \land W3 = Y \to W2 + W3 = X + Y$ is a tautology and will be an invariant. The model checker will consider only runs of the systems obeying the invariants.

The resulting system, together with the set of precomputed tautologies, is checked against a modified specification where all data references are replaced by the respective proposition variables. If the precomputed dependencies suffice to cover the characterizing verification condition, the result will be *"true"*. A negative answer, on the other hand, may have its cause in a correctly detected system error, or insufficient accuracy of the approximation of first-order model checking.

The main point about all this is that once we have transformed system and specification, we can use a standard (symbolic) model checker to verify a system, as all first-order operations are coded in the discrete boolean domain. The transformation has been implemented and used to produce the results of Table 2. In the following, we will present the algorithm in more detail, illustrate it via an example, and sketch the arguments proving its soundness.

5.1 Model Checking of Memoryless Controllers

The complete algorithm of *memoryless first-order verification* consists of the seven-step procedure below.

Let a system description S and a specification ϕ be given.

1. Check that S is memoryless and that ϕ contains only universal path quantifiers and that continuous variables, if quantified at all, are universally quantified at the outside of the formula.
2. Extract the atomic data conditions appearing in S and ϕ as the initial set of propositions.
3. Close the set of propositions under the substitutions induced by data assignments. I.e., if p is a proposition and $W := t$ is an assignment to a data variable W, add $p[t/W]$ to the set of propositions.
4. Transform S.
   (a) For each proposition in the closure, add a boolean variable to S. If the proposition depends on some data input, the proposition variable is declared as an input to the system. Otherwise, it is an output. For outputs, if the proposition depends on quantified variables, it is initialized to a random value, otherwise according to the initialization of the original system variables.
   (b) Replace data conditions by the corresponding proposition variables, and data assignments $W := t$ by $p_{i_1} := p_{i_1}[t/W]; \ldots ; p_{i_l} := p_{i_l}[t/W]$, where the p_{i_j} are the output proposition variables depending on W.
5. Transform ϕ, by replacing data conditions by the corresponding proposition variables and removing data quantifiers.
6. Compute dependencies between the propositions, i.e. a set of boolean formulas over the propositions which are domain tautologies.
7. Let a model checker decide truth of the transformed ϕ for the transformed S assuming the dependencies. If it returns true, the original system is verified. A negative result, on the other hand, does not imply the specification to be false.

The soundness of the procedure will be shown in Sec. 5.2.

The restriction to universal path quantifiers in ϕ (step 1) is essential for the soundness of the procedure. Permitting only the specified kind of first-order quantification was done to simplify the implementation as the examples which were to be considered all had that pattern.

Note that the precomputed substitution closure contains all propositions possibly needed in Step 4b, which translates the Hoare-rule application into the system code.

The dependency computation (Step 6) exploits mainly compositionality and transitivity of "=" and transitivity of "<", and evaluates constants. It approximates the quantifier-free theory of the real numbers.

Below, we will demonstrate the workings of the memoryless first-order procedure. Consider the following system which, depending on a threshold on input $W4$, computes the continuous output $W1$ from the two inputs $W2$ and $W3$.

$REAL\ INPUT\ W2,\ W3,\ W4;$
$REAL\ OUTPUT\ W1 := 0;$
$CASE$
    $[]$ $W4 > 2.5\ \rightarrow W1 := W2 + W3$
    $[]$ $not(W4 > 2.5) \rightarrow SKIP$
$ESAC$

This system is memoryless, i.e. it meets the applicability conditions of the algorithm. We take as specification

$$W1 = 0 \wedge \forall X, Y.\, \mathbf{AG}\,(W2 = X \wedge W3 = Y \wedge W4 > 2.5 \rightarrow \mathbf{AX}\, W1 = X + Y)\ ,$$

where the term $W1 = 0$ reflects the initial value of $W1$ while the rest specifies the expected output if the threshold is exceeded. The initial set of propositions is

$$
\begin{aligned}
&p_1\ W4 > 2.5 \\
&p_2\ W1 = 0 \\
&p_3\ W2 = X \\
&p_4\ W3 = Y \\
&p_5\ W1 = X + Y\ .
\end{aligned}
$$

The assignment $W1 := W2 + W3$ affects the propositions p_2 and p_5 and the Hoare rule for assignment tells us to add

$$
\begin{aligned}
&p_6\ W2 + W3 = 0 \\
&p_7\ W2 + W3 = X + Y
\end{aligned}
$$

to the substitution closure. Thus, in the transformed system we have seven boolean variables corresponding to the propositions. The boolean variables p_2 and p_5 get declared as outputs as they do not refer to inputs of the original system. p_2 is initialized to *true* and p_5 to a random value. This reflects the truth value of the propositions in the initial states of the original system. The others become inputs of the transformed system, because their value depends on inputs (and is thus not controlled by the system). The transformed system is

$BOOL\ INPUT\ p_1,\ p_3,\ p_4,\ p_6,\ p_7;$
$BOOL\ OUTPUT\ p_2 := true, p_5 :=?;$
$CASE$
$\quad\quad [] \quad\quad\quad p_1 \rightarrow p_2 := p_6;\ p_5 := p_7$
$\quad\quad [] \quad not(p_1) \rightarrow SKIP$
$ESAC$,

with specification

$$p_2 \wedge \mathbf{AG}\,(p_3 \wedge p_4 \wedge p_1 \rightarrow \mathbf{AX}\,p_5)\ .$$

The result is a system model with specification involving only discrete variables. We can hand it to a standard (symbolic) model checker. If we add as an invariant $p_3 \wedge p_4 \rightarrow p_7$, which represents a tautology in the original setting, it will return the answer "true". Why this allows us to conclude that the original system satisfies its specification is explained in the following.

5.2   First-Order Model Checking as Abstraction

Abstraction techniques [BBLS92,CGL94,Wol86] complement ordinary symbolic model checking [McM93] by providing means to reduce huge or even infinite state spaces to a manageable size. They are usually done in a way that the validity of a requirement regarding the original design can be concluded from the successful verification of the abstract requirement w.r.t. the abstract model. One major challenge in dealing with the application of such techniques is *accuracy*, i.e. to preserve enough information about the original design in the abstract version to be able to verify a requirement on the abstract level. The restricted version of first-order model checking yields an automatic abstraction technique for memoryless designs. References to infinite objects are substituted by boolean propositions, hence defining a mapping between a concrete and an abstract state space. In the sequel, we explain this view in more detail. First, we briefly outline the general mechanism of abstraction, following essentially [CGL94].

Let S be the concrete state space and let

$$\alpha : S \rightarrow S' = \alpha(S)$$

be a function mapping concrete states to abstract ones. This induces an interpretation of atomic properties p and a transition relation on S' by

$$s' \models p \Leftrightarrow \forall s.\, \alpha(s) = s' \Rightarrow s \models p$$
$$s_1' \rightarrow s_2' \Leftrightarrow \exists s_1, s_2.\, \alpha(s_1) = s_1' \wedge \alpha(s_2) = s_2' \wedge s_1' \rightarrow s_2'\ .$$

Then for any CTL formula ϕ without existential path quantifiers and without negation[3],

$$S' \models \phi \;\Rightarrow\; S \models \phi \;.$$

This means that the abstraction is *sound*, i.e. that one can verify (but not in general refute) properties of the original system by considering its abstraction.

It is, however, not in general feasible—or even impossible—to compute the abstract system model given some α, since this might require the construction of the complete original model. Fortunately, the abstract system may be approximated by enlarging the abstract state space (to some $S'' \supset \alpha(S)$) and the transition relation while restricting truth of atomic properties. Thereby one retains soundness, but loses some accuracy, i.e. one gets more often a negative answer to a verification problem.

We now relate the memoryless version of first-order model checking to this setting. The state space of a design is spanned by the valuations of its variables, i.e. it takes the form

$$S \;=\; D_{V_1} \times \ldots \times D_{V_n} \times D_{W_1} \times \ldots \times D_{W_m} \;,$$

where $V_1, \ldots, V_n$ are its discrete (finite) and $W_1 \ldots W_m$ its continuous (infinite) variables. The abstract state space is within

$$D_{V_1} \times \ldots \times D_{V_n} \times D_{p_1} \times \ldots \times D_{p_k} \;,$$

where $p_1, \ldots, p_k$ are the boolean variables representing the propositions. The abstraction function α maps concrete states to abstract states, with

$$\alpha(s)(X) \;=\; \begin{cases} s(X) & \text{if } X \in \{V_1, \ldots, V_n\} \\ s \models X & \text{if } X \in \{p_1, \ldots, p_k\} \end{cases}$$

Our transformation approximates the abstraction induced by this α in the following way.

Its state set S'' consists of all valuations of $V_1, \ldots, V_n, p_1, \ldots, p_k$ which satisfy the dependencies on the proposition part. Since the dependencies are tautologies in S, the set S'' includes all states of $\alpha(S)$ as required.

W.r.t. the transition relation, recall that we declare all propositions depending on some system input to be a boolean input of the abstract system. Since inputs are set to an arbitrary value in each step, this guarantees the existence of an abstract transition for each concrete one w.r.t. the valuation of these propositions. The randomization of input-dependent propositions also leads to a safe approximation of quantifications in regular first-order model checking, which, in its backward step evaluation, retains exactly the information about the combinations of data values in the following step. Now, the invariants provide the only information which is considered.

---

[3] In this sketch of the idea of abstraction, we leave out all considerations concerning first-order data quantifiers and negation of atomic properties.

Due to the restriction to memoryless systems, the remaining proprositions involve only output values and quantified variables. An output is either set during a step in an assignment or remains unchanged. Propositions which do depend only on outputs which are not changed also retain their value throughout a step, a property which is shared by the original and the transformed system. Assignments to data outputs affect the truth value of proposition exactly as described by the substitution found in the Hoare rule. So the assignments in the abstract system, which mimic Hoare rule applications, are guaranteed to produce abstract behavior conforming to the concrete one.

This shows that our system transformation yields indeed an approximation of an abstraction, as it possibly enlarges the state space and the transition relation and does not affect the interpretation of atomic properties. The transformation of the formula is rather straightforward. Of course we have to replace the atomic formulas referring to data variables by the corresponding proposition names, for instance $W1 = 0$ by p_2. Universal data quantifiers may be dropped as the nondeterminism in the abstract system subsumes the potential effects of universal quantification.[4] Either a proposition with universally quantified variables contains inputs and is set randomly at each step, so the model checker considers all possibilities conjunctively at each step, which is more than sufficient. Or it contains no input and is initialized to a random value, which again implies conjunction over all cases.

We conclude, by the informal reasoning above, that our transformation for memoryless controllers constitutes an instance of a sound abstraction method. As a consequence, we get that the validity of a specification in the universal fragment of FO-CTL for the transformed system implies its validity for the original system. Thus, we may safely apply the restricted version of first-order model checking to verify controllers involving continuous variables. The technique has the virtues of being completely automatic (it replaces all continuous variables by propositions) and of not relying on any specific model-check routine.

5.3   Results

This simplified version of first-order model checking working for memoryless systems has been implemented as a supplement to the verification environment [Bri99]. The results of its application to the EMF have already been presented at the end of Section 3. As the verification times with the automatic abstraction were even shorter than the ones after manual abstraction, these experiments demonstrate very clearly the usefulness of the approach. Not only that it avoids cumbersome, manual interaction with its potential for flaws, it does so without increasing the time needed for verification.

---

[4] Note that nondeterminism in the system forces the model checker to compute the conjunction over the results of all possible branches as the formula contains only universal path quantifiers.

6   Conclusion

We have developed a tool set supporting the formal analysis of STATEMATE designs based on symbolic model checking. It fits into the development process found in the car industry, in particular the one at BMW, where the tool set has already been introduced. There, it serves to analyze and debug designs at early stages of their development. It meets the challenge faced by the car industry to manage an increasing number of complex ECU design tasks, with high reliability requirements.

Traditional symbolic model checking can cope with control-dominated ECUs. The majority of designs, however, involves computations on continuous values, which are difficult to deal with in pure model checking. Thus, accompanying techniques are called for. We have come up with a new approach we called first-order model checking. This algorithm introduces a logical representation for data values. It is meant to be applicable to the verification of units which observe and control continuous values, but do not perform substantial computations. We found that even stronger restrictions than these are often met by real-life designs. A simplified version of first-order model checking has been implemented in the form of an automatic abstraction technique and produced convincing results. With the more general version of first-order model checking and further accompanying techniques, we intend to cover a major part of the ECUs developed in the automotive area.

The next challenge to be met is to cope with real hybrid controllers, i.e. ones that do more extensive computations on real values. These occur quite often in the automotive area. They may, for instance, have the form of a STATEMATE design responsible for the discrete signals which is coupled with a MATRIXX design doing the continuous computations. It is surely out of the scope of rigid formal methods to fully analyze such complex hybrid systems. But we do hope that suitable approximations can be treated with the help of our technique of logical representation of data properties. This, however, is something to be tried in the future.

Acknowledgments

Much of the current verification environment has been developed within the projects KORSYS(BMBF) and SACRES (Esprit), in close cooperation with the team at Siemens ZT lead by Wolfram Büttner and Klaus Winkelmann, and with i-Logix Inc., Andover, USA. The model checker underlying the STATEMATE[5] verification environment has been developed at Siemens ZT, Munich, FRG. The semantic foundation was laid jointly with Amir Pnueli, Weizmann Institute of Sciences, Rehovoth, Israel [DJHP98].

---

[5] STATEMATE is a registered trademark of i-Logix, Inc.

References

[BBD+99] Tom Bienmüller, Udo Brockmeyer, Werner Damm, Gert Döhmen, Claus Eßmann, Hans-Jürgen Holberg, Hardi Hungar, Bernhard Josko, Rainer Schlör, Gunnar Wittich, Hartmut Wittke, Geoffrey Clements, John Rowlands, and Eric Sefton. Formal Verification of an Avionics Application using Abstraction and Symbolic Model Checking. In Felix Redmill and Tom Anderson, editors, *Towards System Safety – Proceedings of the Seventh Safety-critical Systems Symposium, Huntingdon, UK*, pages 150–173. Safety-Critical Systems Club, Springer Verlag, 1999.

[BBLS92] S. Bensalem, A. Bouajjani, C. Loiseaux, and J. Sifakis. Property preserving simulations. In G.v. Bochmann and D.K. Probst, editors, *4th Int. Workshop on Computer Aided Verification*, LNCS 663, pages 260–273. Springer, 1992.

[BDG+98] J. Bohn, W. Damm, O. Grumberg, H. Hungar, and K. Laster. First-order CTL model checking. In V. Arvind and R. Ramanujam, editors, *FSTTCS 98*, LNCS 1530, pages 283–294, 1998.

[Bri99] Henning Brinkmann. Verifikation eines hybriden Steuersystems mit Hilfe erweiterter Abstraktionsmethoden. Master's thesis, Carl von Ossietzky Universität Oldenburg, February 1999.

[Bry92] Randal E. Bryant. Symbolic boolean Manipulation with ordered Binary-Decision Diagrams. *ACM Comp. Surveys*, 24:293–318, 1992.

[CES83] Edmund M. Clarke, E.A. Emerson, and A.P. Sistla. Automatic verification of finite state concurrent systems using temporal logic specifications: A practical approach. In *Procceedings of the 10th ACM Symposium on Principles of Programming Languages*, pages 117–126, 1983.

[CGL94] Edmund M. Clarke, Orna Grumberg, and David E. Long. Model checking and abstraction. In *ACM Transactions on Programming Languages and Systems*, volume 16, pages 1512–1542, September 1994.

[DJHP98] Werner Damm, Bernhard Josko, Hardi Hungar, and Amir Pnueli. A compositional real-time semantics of STATEMATE designs. In W.-P. de Roever, editor, *Proceedings, International Symposium on Compositionality – The Significant Difference*, LNCS 1536, pages 186–238. Springer-Verlag, 1998.

[DJS95] W. Damm, B. Josko, and R. Schlör. Specification and verification of VHDL-based system-level hardware designs. In E. Börger, editor, *Specification and Validation Methods*, pages 331–410. Oxford Univ. Press, 1995.

[HGD95] H. Hungar, O. Grumberg, and W. Damm. What if model checking must be truly symbolic. In P. Camurati and H. Eveking, editors, *CHARME 95*, LNCS 987, pages 1–20. Springer Verlag, 1995.

[HHWT97] T.A. Henzinger, P.-H. Ho, and H. Wong-Toi. HyTech: A model checker for hybrid systems. *Software Tools for Technology Transfer*, 1:110–122, 1997.

[Hoa69] C.A.R. Hoare. An axiomatic basis for computer programming. *Communications of the ACM*, 12:576–583, 1969.

[Jos93] Bernhard Josko. Modular Specification and Verification of Reactive Systems. Carl von Ossietzky Universität Oldenburg, 1993. Habilitationsschrift.

[Kur97] R.P. Kurshan. Formal verification in a commercial setting. In *Proc. 34th Design Automation Conference*, pages 258–262, 1997.

[McM93] Kenneth L. McMillan. *Symbolic Model Checking*. Kluwer Academic Publishers, 1993.

[Wol86] Pierre Wolper. Expressing interesting properties of programs in propositional temporal logic. In *Proceedings of the 13th Annual ACM Symposium in Principles of Programming Languages*, pages 184–193, 1986.

Correct Real-Time Software for Programmable Logic Controllers *

Ernst-Rüdiger Olderog

Fachbereich Informatik, Universität Oldenburg
Postfach 2503, D-26111 Oldenburg
Germany
E-mail: olderog@informatik.uni-oldenburg.de

Abstract. We present an approach to the design of correct real-time software for Programmable Logic Controllers (PLCs), a widespread hardware platform in the area of traffic and automation control [19, 26].

Requirements are formulated in a graphical formalism called Constraint Diagrams (CDs) [12]. A CD consists of waveforms that describe the time-wise behaviour of observables and of arrows that describe the timed interdependencies between these waveforms. Design specifications are formulated as so-called PLC-Automata [7]. These can be understood as a special class of timed automata that model in an abstract way the cyclic behaviour of PLCs. Programs are formulated in ST (Structured Text), a dedicated programming language for PLCs. PLC-Automata can be easily compiled into ST code.

The semantic link between CDs and PLC-Automata is stated in terms of the Duration Calculus [37], a logic and calculus for specifying real-time behaviour. This enables us to formally establish the correctness of designs with respect to the requirements.

The approach is illustrated by a case study defined by an industrial partner engaged in designing railway signalling systems [23]. It is supported by a tool called MOBY/PLC [11].

1 Introduction

Real-time systems are reactive systems where reactions to certain inputs have to occur within given time intervals [14, 24, 21, 22, 18]. These systems usually consist of some physical *process* for which a suitable *controller* has to be constructed such that the controlled process exhibits the desired time dependent behaviour. The interaction between process and controller proceeds via *sensors* and *actuators* as shown in Fig. 1. When constructing the controller the reaction times of all components of this system have to be taken into account.

The design of a real-time controller typically involves several levels of abstraction, in particular the levels of

---

* This work was partially funded by the German Ministry for Education and Research (BMBF), project UniForM, grant FKZ 01 IS 521 B3, and the Leibniz Programme of the German Research Council (DFG) under grant Ol 98/1-1.

E.-R. Olderog, B. Steffen (Eds.): Correct System Design, LNCS 1710, pp. 342–362, 1999.

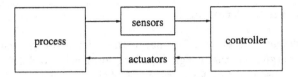

Fig. 1. Real-time system

- requirements,
- design specifications,
- programs.

Typically, each of these levels comes with its own notation. A problem is thus how to guarantee correctness across these levels, i.e. how to link these different notations in such a way that

- the design specifications *satisfy* or *correctly refine* the requirements,
- the programs *correctly implement* the design specification.

This paper is concerned with the following aspects of this problem:

- *concepts* : How to define relationships like "correctly refines" and "correctly implements" ?
- *methods* : How to establish these relationships in practical applications ?

Our answer to the conceptual aspect is the use of a logic-based approach developed in the ProCoS project [17]. Our answer to the methodological aspect is not a general one. Rather we suggest that such a method should be tailored towards particular application areas or technological constraints. In this paper we consider the area of traffic control where Programmable Logic Controllers are a widespread hardware platform.

The remainder of this paper is organised as follows. Section 2 explains the general logic-based approach which we pursue. Section 3 introduces a case study from the area of railway signalling that motivated our method to the design of real-time systems explained in this paper and that serves to illustrate the different aspects of the method. Section 4 explains Constraint Diagrams as a graphical notation for formalising real-time requirements. Section 5 introduces PLC-Automata as a graphical formalisation of the PLC concepts. Section 6 gives an idea of the progamming notation Structured Text used for PLCs. Section 7 explains details of the Duration Calculus and its role as a semantic basis for Constraint Diagrams and PLC-Automata. Section 8 sketches the tool MOBY/PLC supporting the method described so far. Finally, Section 9 draws some conclusion.

2   Logic-Based Approach

How can different notations and formal methods for real-time systems be tied together? We argue here that a logic-based approach helps to clarify the concepts involved and is useful for proving properties of the systems.

Our basic assumption is that a real-time system can be described by a set of time dependent *observables obs* which are functions

$$obs : \text{Time} \longrightarrow D_{obs}$$

where Time is a continuous *time domain*, here the nonnegative real numbers $\mathbb{R}_{\geq 0}$, and D_{obs} is the type or data domain of *obs*. For example, a gas valve might be described using a Boolean valued observable

$$gas : \text{Time} \longrightarrow \{0, 1\}$$

indicating whether gas is present or not [30], a railway track by an observable

$$track : \text{Time} \longrightarrow \{empty, appr, cross\}$$

where *appr* means a train is approaching and *cross* means that it is crossing the gate [29], and the current communication trace of a reactive system by an observable

$$tr : \text{Time} \longrightarrow Comm^*$$

where $Comm^*$ denotes the set of all finite sequences over a set $Comm$ of possible communications [34, 35]. Thus depending on the choice of observables we can describe a real-time system at various levels of abstraction.

To describe properties of observables we use *predicates* of a suitable logic. As a consequence of such a logic-based approach the semantics of different syntactic descriptions of a real-time system can be given in terms of predicates in the same logic. The advantage is that then *correctness* can be expressed simply as logic implication between predicates. For any two syntactic descriptions $term_1$ and $term_2$ we write

$$term_1 \Rightarrow term_2$$

if the semantic predicate associated with $term_1$ logically implies the semantic predicate associated with $term_2$. Conceptually, this means that $term_1$ *satisfies* or *refines* all the properties of $term_2$, i.e. is *correct* w.r.t. $term_2$.

For example, if $term_2$ is a requirement *req* and $term_1$ is a design specification *spec* then

$$spec \Rightarrow req$$

expresses that *spec* correctly refines *req*, and if $term_2$ is a specification *spec* and $term_1$ is a program *prog* then

$$prog \Rightarrow spec$$

expresses that *prog* correctly implements *spec*. By the transitivity of $\Rightarrow$ we can deduce *prog* $\Rightarrow$ *req* from the above two facts, i.e. *prog* correctly implements the requirement *req*.

This picture gets more complicated if the predicates associated with $term_1$ and $term_2$ involve different observables, say $term_1$ involves more concrete observables c and $term_2$ more abstract ones a. Then we need a *linking invariant* that relates the values of a and c. Such an invariant is known from data refinement [33]; it can also be expressed as a predicate, say $link_{a,c}$. Then correctness becomes

$$term_1 \wedge link_{a,c} \Rightarrow term_2,$$

i.e. the conjunction of $term_1$ and $link_{a,c}$ has to imply $term_2$.

At this point one may argue that working with logical formulae expressing the semantics of complex objects like requirements, specifications and programs is not practical. Here our approach is to keep the logic as much as possible in the background, i.e. to use rules and algorithms that are based on the logic in order to guarantee their correctness but to avoid exhibiting all details of the logic to the users of the method. In the following we shall instantiate this approach by particular choices for the levels of requirements, specifications and programs, and for the logic.

3 Case Study: Tram Control

In this paper we look at an application area motivated by the UniForM project that was performed jointly with the University of Bremen and the industrial partner Elpro in Berlin. The project was concerned with a tool supported combination of formal methods for the development of correct software for distributed, communicating and time-critical systems [23].

More specifically, Elpro is engaged in the application domain of railway control. As a case study the *safe control of a single track segment* for trams (SCS) was chosen (see Fig. 2). Single track segments represent possible dangerous situations that occur for example in the event of repair work.

The task of the SCS is to safely guide trams driving in opposite directions through a single track segment so that no collision can occur on this segment. To this end, suitable sensors and traffic lights are installed along the track. For each direction $i \in \{1, 2\}$ of the trams there are three sensors called *ESi* (entry sensor), *CSi* (critical sensor) and *LSi* (leave sensor) as shown in Fig. 2. From the values of these sensors the control under development has to compute the signals for the traffic lights of both directions. For each direction there are three possible signals: *Go*, *Stop* and *Ack*, an acknowledgement for the tram drivers requesting to pass the single track segment. There are several informal requirements that the SCS should satisfy.

Safety. No collision should occur on the single track segment, i.e. this critical segment should be used in *mutual exclusion*.

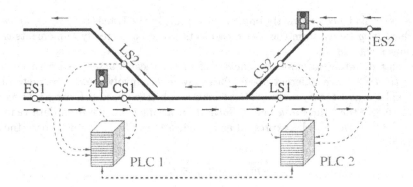

Fig. 2. Single track segment

Utility. Trams operate according to several *driving policies*. One such policy requires that first all trams from one direction are guided through the single track segment and then all trams from the other direction. Another policy gives the right of way alternatively to one tram from one direction and then one from the other direction.

Fault tolerance. In the physical devices along the track subtle faults can occur. For example, the task of the sensors *ESi*, *CSi* and *LSi* is to count how many trams are in the corresponding track segments. However, these sensors may *stutter*, i.e. issue more than one output signal when in reality only a single tram has passed the sensor. Such a sensor fault must not lead to a wrong image of the reality inside the control software.

A solution to this problem is to require that suitable filters for such faults are present. The idea is that these filters should ignore the possible stuttering of sensors for a short period of time such as 5 seconds. This requirement indicates that the whole control software is indeed a real-time software.

Target hardware. A further requirement for the control software is that it should run on *Programmable Logic Controllers* (PLCs for short). These represent a hardware platform used in the application domains of process automation and traffic control. PLCs are simple computing devices connected to sensors and actuators; they have a simple operating system that continuously performs a cycle consisting of three phases:

- inputing the current sensor values,
- computing the next state based on these values,
- outputting part of this state to the actuators.

What makes PLCs so interesting for implementing real-time systems is that they come with explicit timers that can be used in the computation of the next state. For performing real-time computations the cycle time of the PLC has to be taken into account. Thus PLCs cannot react arbitrarily fast to changes of the sensor values.

Developing a method for the design of correct real-time software for PLCs has been a challenge for the author's research group. In the following sections we describe the results achieved so far.

4 Requirements: Constraint Diagrams

When discussing and formalising the requirements of a system, application experts and computer science experts have to come to an agreement. The direct use of logic is often claimed to be an obstacle for engineers. Therefore graphic notations have been proposed for the specification of behavioural properties.

Most prominent are *Message Sequence Charts* (MSCs) developed for the area of telecommunication [20, 27]. In its original form MSCs describe only individual typical communication traces of a reactive system. Various extensions of MSCs are currently under development, e.g. to deal with real-time [2], but there is the danger that these extensions lack the intuitive appeal of the original MSCs. For the graphic description of temporal properties *Symbolic Timing Diagrams* have been developed and successfully applied in several industrial projects [36, 5].

To deal with real-time properties graphically, we use so-called *Constraint Diagrams* (abbr. CDs) [12, 9]. A CD describes the timing behaviour of one or more observables in the sense of Section 2 in an assumption-commitment style. For each observable it displays a sequence of values, possibly annotated with time intervals describing their duration. The time-wise relationship between the values of different observables is described by arrows connecting these values, again possibly annotated with time intervals. Both observation values and time intervals can be surrounded by boxes. Whereas normal values and intervals represent assumptions, boxed values and intervals represent commitments. Semantically, a CD represents a logic implication of the form

$$assumptions \;\Rightarrow\; commitments.$$

We introduce CDs by way of an example.

Example 1. A *watchdog* is a real-time system for continuously checking an input signal S. If S has been absent for more than 10 seconds an alarm A should be raised within 1 second. To model this system we consider two Boolean observables:

$$S : \text{Time} \longrightarrow \{0, 1\}$$
$$A : \text{Time} \longrightarrow \{0, 1\}.$$

The behavioural requirements for these two observables can be specified by the following CD:

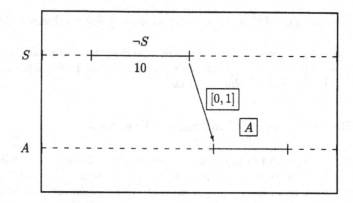

Here the two horizontal lines describe the behaviour of S and A in isolation. The arrow describes the link between S and A. Semantically the diagram represents an implication in the assumption-commitment style: If for a duration of 10 seconds $\neg S$ was observed (*assumption*) then within 1 second a period where A holds has to occur (*commitment*). The boxes around A and $[0,1]$ indicate that these are commitments whereas the remaining parts are all assumptions. The dashed parts of the lines represent arbitrary behaviour of S and A.

4.1   A Real-Time Filter

A technical problem is that sensors may stutter, i.e. issue more than one output signal when in reality only a single tram has passed the sensor. To avoid wrong data in the drive controller for the trams a suitable *filter* is needed for each sensor. We consider here a filter *FES* reading input values no_tr, tr and *Error*

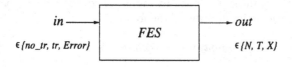

Fig. 3. Filter

from the entry sensor *ES* and transforming them into output values N (for *no tram*), T (for *tram*) and X (for *exception*). This is indicated by Fig. 3 and the corresponding observables:

$$in : \text{Time} \longrightarrow \{no\_tr, tr, Error\}$$
$$st : \text{Time} \longrightarrow \{N, T, X\}$$

The desired real-time behaviour is shown in the timing diagram in Fig. 4. When an input tr from the sensor *ES* is detected the filter *FES* should (after a reaction time of at most ε) output T (*tram detected*). In the subsequent 5 seconds the filter should ignore any further stuttering of inputs *no_tr* or *tr* from the sensor and stay with output T. We stipulate here that successive trams are at least 6 seconds apart and that after 5 seconds any stuttering of the sensor has ceased so that the input is *no_tr* and the filter (after a reaction time of at most ε) can return to output N. Afterwards any further input *tr* will be treated as signalling that a new tram approaches, thus causing again output T.

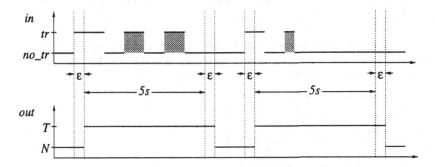

Fig. 4. Timing diagrams for the filter

There is one input though which the filter *FES* must not ignore: the input *Error* indicating an erroneous sensor value. Then the filter should proceed as fast as possible (i.e. after a reaction time of at most ε) to (state and) output X.

These informal requirements can be formalised using Constraint Diagrams. In the sequel we show CDs for the most important aspects of the desired filter behaviour.

Initial state. The commitment is that the initial output is N.

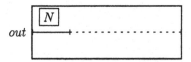

Filtering inputs for 5 seconds. Assuming that input *tr* is present for ε seconds while output is N, the filter is committed to change its output to T and keep this output for the next 5 seconds provided no *Error* (i.e. only *no_tr* or *tr*) occurs as input. Note that if the input *tr* is present for less than ε seconds, nothing is required from the filter. The assumption of *tr* being present for some duration of time anticipates that hardware cannot react arbitrarily fast.

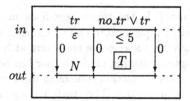

The arrows annotated with 0 represent simultaneity. Formally, 0 abbreviates here the point interval [0,0]. Also the annotation ≤ 5 is an abbreviation standing for the time interval [0,5].

Reset after 5 seconds. Assuming that after a period of 5 seconds of output T an input *no_tr* is present for ε seconds while output is still T, the filter is committed to change its output to N.

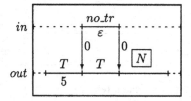

Error handling. Assuming the input *Error* is present for ε seconds, the filter is committed to output X after this time.

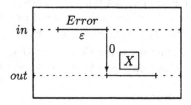

Exceptional state is kept. Assuming the filter is in X it is committed to stay in this state.

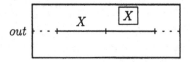

5   Design Specifications: PLC-Automata

When designing real-time controllers some details of the target architecture on which these controllers are to be implemented have to be taken into account in order to guarantee that the required real-time constraints are realizable. Our method aims at *Programmable Logic Controllers* (PLCs) because they are simple devices that are widespread in automation and traffic technology [19, 26].

A PLC interacts with sensors and actuators in a cyclic manner. Each cycle consists of three phases: an input phase where sensor values are read and stored in local variables, a state transformation phase where all local variables are updated according to the stored program, and an output phase where the values of some of the local variables are output to the actuators. Real-time constraints can be implemented on PLCs with the help of *timers* that can be set and reset during the state transformation phase. Also the *cycle time* of the PLC has to be taken into account.

Design specifications will abstract from most of the details of PLCs but keep the concepts of timers and cycle time. In order to be understandable to engineers they should also have a graphic representation. Most popular are state-transition models. Finite state machines or automata are well understood since the early days of computing and come with a graphic representation that appeals to engineers. This model has been extended in several ways: *Petri nets* allow an explicit representation of concurrency [32], *state charts* do this as well but also add a concept of hierarchy [16], *action systems* allow to overcome the limitations of a finite control state space [3], *timed automata* allow to model time by adding explicit clocks [1].

We use an automata model with states and transitions suitably extended with concepts of time and hierarchy. These automata are called *PLC-Automata* [7] and can be understood as a variant of timed automata geared towards modelling the PLC behaviour. We introduce PLC-automata by way of an example.

Example 2. Fig. 5 displays a PLC-Automaton serving as a design specification for the filter *FES*. It consists of three states and reacts to inputs tr, no_tr and *Error* by outputting N, T and X. Inputs mark the transitions and outputs appear inside the states. In the initial state (marked by an in-going arc) the automaton outputs N (no train) and stays in this state as long as the input is *no_train*. Once an input tr is detected, the automaton switches to the state where the output is T (train). In case an input *Error* is detected, the automaton switches to the state where the output is X (exception). In this state the automaton stays under all possible inputs.

As for real PLCs, the real-time behaviour of a PLC-Automaton is determined by an additional parameter, the cycle time ε_{PLC}, i.e. the upper bound for the duration of one cycle. Since the input values are read only at the beginning of each cycle, it takes up to ε_{PLC} seconds for a PLC-Automaton to detect a new input value provided this value is stable for that period of time. Glitches of input values may not be detected by a PLC-Automaton. Then it takes up to ε_{PLC} seconds for a PLC-Automaton to react to this new input. Thus in the worst case it takes up to $2 \cdot \varepsilon_{PLC}$ seconds for a PLC-Automaton to react to a new input value.

Additionally, explicit timing inscriptions can appear in the lower parts of states. In this example we see that the states with output N and X have the inscriptions $0s$ and *all*. This specifies that in these states the automaton should

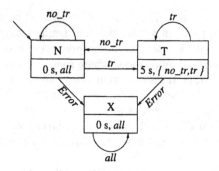

Fig. 5. PLC-Automaton for the filter *FES*

react as fast as possible to the input values. However in the state with output
T the inscriptions are $5s$ and $\{no, no\_tr\}$. This specifies that in this state the
automaton should ignore all inputs *no* and *no_tr* for 5 seconds. This realises
the filter requirement of *FES* discussed in Section 4. On the other hand, the
automaton should react to an input *Error* as fast as possible by switching to the
state with output X. As fast as possible means here within $2 \cdot \varepsilon_{PLC}$ seconds.

6   Programs: Structured Text

For PLCs several dedicated programming notations have been devised. The one
resembling most clearly other imperative programming languages is ST (*Structured Text*) [19, 26].

Fig. 6 shows an ST program PRG_FES implementing the PLC-Automaton of
Fig. 5. In ST timers are declared as variables of a special type TP. The program
PRG_FES contains a declaration of such a variable called **timer**. The statement

$$\text{timer}(\text{IN} := \text{TRUE}, \text{PT} := t\#5.0s)$$

switches the timer on and sets it to 5 seconds. This statement is executed when
entering state 1. The condition **NOT timer.Q** is true as soon as the **timer** has
expired. This condition has to be met in order to react to the input **no_tr** by
switching to state 0. The statement

$$\text{timer}(\text{IN} := \text{FALSE}, \text{PT} := t\#0.0s)$$

switches the **timer** off. It is executed when leaving state 1.

7   Semantic Link

We have now discussed three levels of abstraction for real-time systems, each
one with its own notation: requirements, design specifications, and programs.
How can these notations be linked together in a correct way? To this end, we
instantiate the logic-based approach outlined in Section 2.

```
PROGRAM PRG_FES
VAR
   state  : INT := 0; (* 0:=N, 1:=T, 2:=X *)
   timer  : TP;
ENDVAR
IF state=0 THEN
       %output:=N;
       IF %input = tr THEN
               state:=1;
               %output:=T;
       ELSIF %input = Error THEN
               state:=2;
               %output:=X;
       ENDIF
ELSIF state=1 THEN
       timer(IN:=TRUE,PT:=t#5.0s);
       IF (%input = no_tr AND NOT timer.Q) THEN
               state:=0;
               %output:=N;
               timer(IN:=FALSE,PT:=t#0.0s);
       ELSIF %input = Error THEN
               state:=2;
               %output:=X;
               timer(IN:=FALSE,PT:=t#0.0s);
       ENDIF
ENDIF
```

Fig. 6. ST program for the filter *FES*

7.1   A Real-Time Logic

We use *Duration Calculus* (abbreviated DC), a real-time interval temporal logic and calculus developed by Zhou Chaochen and others [37, 31, 15], to describe properties of real-time systems. This choice is partly motivated by our previous experience with this logic, and partly by the convenience with which the interval and continuous time aspects of DC allow us to express and reason about reaction times of components.

Syntax. Formally, the syntax of Duration Calculus distinguishes *terms*, *duration terms* and *duration formulae*. Terms τ have a certain type and are built from time dependent observables *obs* like *gas* or *track*, *rigid variables* x representing time independent variables, and are closed under typed operators *op*:

$$\tau \ ::= \ obs \mid x \mid op(\overline{\tau})$$

where $\overline{\tau}$ is a vector of terms. Terms of Boolean type are called *state assertions*. We use S for a typical state assertion.

Duration terms θ are of type real but their values depend on a given time interval. The simplest duration term is the symbol ℓ denoting the *length* of the given interval. The name Duration Calculus stems from the fact that for each state assertion S there is a duration term $\int S$ measuring the *duration* of S, i.e. the accumulated time S holds in the given interval. Formally:

$$\theta ::= \ell \mid \int S \mid op_{real}(\overline{\theta})$$

where op_{real} is an real-valued operator and $\overline{\theta}$ a vector of duration terms.

Duration formulae denote truth values depending on a given time interval. They are built from the constants *true* and *false*, relations *rel* applied to duration terms, and are closed under the *chop operator* (denoted by ;), propositional connectives op_{Boole}, and quantification $Q \in \{\forall, \exists\}$ over rigid variables x. We use F for a typical duration formula:

$$F ::= rel(\overline{\theta}) \mid F_1 ; F_2 \mid op_{Boole}(\overline{F}) \mid Q\,x.F$$

where $\overline{F}$ is a vector of duration formulae. Besides this basic syntax various abbreviations are used for duration formulae:

point interval : $\lceil\rceil \overset{\text{def}}{=} \ell = 0$
everywhere : $\lceil S \rceil \overset{\text{def}}{=} \int S = \ell \,\wedge\, \ell > 0$
somewhere : $\Diamond F \overset{\text{def}}{=} true \,;\, F \,;\, true$
always : $\Box F \overset{\text{def}}{=} \neg\Diamond\neg F$

Semantics. The semantics of Duration Calculus is based on an *interpretation* $\mathcal{I}$ that assigns a fixed meaning to each observable, rigid variable and operator symbol of the language. To an observable *obs* the interpretation $\mathcal{I}$ assigns a function

$$obs_{\mathcal{I}} : \mathsf{Time} \longrightarrow D_{obs}.$$

This induces inductively the semantics of terms and hence state assertions. For a state assertions S it is a function

$$S_{\mathcal{I}} : \mathsf{Time} \longrightarrow Bool$$

where *Bool* is identified with the set $\{0, 1\}$.

The semantics of a duration term θ is denoted by $\mathcal{I}(\theta)$ and yields a real value depending on a given time interval $[b, e] \subseteq \mathsf{Time}$. In particular, ℓ denotes the length of $[b, e]$ and $\int S$ the duration of the state assertion S in $[b, e]$ as given by the integral. Formally:

$$\mathcal{I}(\ell)[b, e] = e - b,$$
$$\mathcal{I}(\int S)[b, e] = \int_b^e S_{\mathcal{I}}(t)dt.$$

The semantics of a duration formula F denotes a truth value depending on $\mathcal{I}$ and a given time interval $[b, e]$. We write $\mathcal{I}, [b, e] \models F$ if that truth value is *true* for $\mathcal{I}$ and $[b, e]$. The definition is by induction on the structure of F. The cases of relations, propositional connectives and quantification are handled as usual. For example, $\mathcal{I}, [b, e] \models \int S \leq k$ if the duration $\int_b^e S_{\mathcal{I}}(t)dt$ is at most k. For $F_1 ; F_2$ (read as F_1 *chop* F_2) we define $\mathcal{I}, [b, e] \models F_1;F_2$ if the interval $[b, e]$ can be "chopped" into two subintervals $[b, m]$ and $[m, e]$ such that $\mathcal{I}, [b, m] \models F_1$ and $\mathcal{I}, [m, e] \models F_2$.

Since in our application to the design of real-time systems the initial values of observables are important, we especially consider time intervals starting at time 0 and define that a duration formula F *holds* in an interpretation $\mathcal{I}$ iff $\mathcal{I}, [0, t] \models F$ for all $t \in$ Time. To formalise requirements in DC one states a number of suitable duration formulae and considers all interpretations for which the conjunction of the DC formulae holds in this sense.

7.2   Semantics of Constraint Diagrams

In this section we indicate how Duration Calculus can be used to provide a formal semantics for Constraint Diagrams. In fact, we need only a small subset of Duration Calculus for this semantics. Full details can be found in [12].

Example 3. Let us consider the CDs for the filter requirements of Section 4 and use the following abbreviations:

a abbreviates $in = a$ for $a \in \{no\_tr, tr, Error\}$
A abbreviates $out = A$ for $A \in \{N, T, X\}$

The CD for the *initial state* has the following semantics in Duration Calculus:

$$\lceil\rceil \vee \lceil N\rceil ; true$$

Thus for every observation interval $[0, t]$ the following is required: either it is the empty interval or it starts with an initial segment where $out = N$ holds.

In general the semantics of a CD represents an implication of the form

$$assumptions \Rightarrow commitments.$$

Additionally, we use rigid variables x and quantification over them to formulate common durations in the assumption and commitment part of the implication. For example, the *filter requirement* has the following semantics:

$\forall x, y \in$ Time $\bullet$
$\ell = x; (\lceil tr \wedge N\rceil \wedge \ell = \varepsilon); (\lceil no\_tr \vee tr\rceil) \wedge \ell = y \wedge y \leq 5); true \Rightarrow$
$\ell = x + \varepsilon; (\lceil T\rceil \wedge \ell = y); true$

Here universal quantification over the rigid variable x represents the unknown length of the dashed initial part in the corresponding CD. Similarly, the semantics of the requirement *reset after 5 seconds* is represented by the formula

$\forall x \in$ Time $\bullet$
$\ell = x; (\lceil T\rceil \wedge \ell = 5); (\lceil no\_tr \wedge N\rceil \wedge \ell = \varepsilon); true \Rightarrow$
$\ell = x + 5 + \varepsilon; \lceil N\rceil ; true$

Simpler are the semantic formulae of the two CDs formalising the *error handling*:

$$\forall x \in \mathsf{Time} \bullet \ \ell = x; (\lceil Error \rceil \wedge \ell = \varepsilon); true \quad \Rightarrow \quad \ell = x + \varepsilon; \lceil X \rceil ; true$$

and

$$\forall x \in \mathsf{Time} \bullet \ \ell = x; \lceil X \rceil ; true \quad \Rightarrow \quad \ell = x; \lceil X \rceil$$

This example shows that CDs are easier to understand than the corresponding Duration Calculus formulae. On the other hand, such formulae allow us to argue precisely about the correctness of refinement steps and designs.

7.3   Semantics of PLC-Automata

To define a Duration Calculus semantics of PLC-Automata, we view each automaton as describing the behaviour of its input, state and output by three observables

$$in : \mathsf{Time} \longrightarrow Inputs,$$
$$st : \mathsf{Time} \longrightarrow States,$$
$$out : \mathsf{Time} \longrightarrow Outputs$$

where *Inputs*, *States* and *Outputs* are finite sets. We use the following meta variables: $b \in Inputs$ and $B \subseteq Inputs$ and $q \in States$ and $Q \subseteq States$. The output depends only on the state by some function

$$\lambda : States \longrightarrow Outputs.$$

In DC this can be expressed by the invariance formula

$$\Box(\lceil \rceil \vee \lceil out = \lambda(st) \rceil),$$

i.e. for every subinterval *out* depends on *st* as described by the function λ.

To describe the relationship of *in* and *st*, we shall use a subset of Duration Calculus called DC *implementables* and due to A.P. Ravn [31]. DC implementables make use of the following idioms where $s, t \in \mathsf{Time}$:

- *followed-by*: $F \longrightarrow \lceil S \rceil \ \stackrel{\text{def}}{=} \ \Box\neg(F; \lceil \neg S \rceil)$
- *timed up-to*: $F \stackrel{\leq s}{\longrightarrow} \lceil S \rceil \ \stackrel{\text{def}}{=} \ (F \wedge \ell \leq s) \longrightarrow \lceil S \rceil$
- *timed leads-to*: $F \stackrel{t}{\longrightarrow} \lceil S \rceil \ \stackrel{\text{def}}{=} \ (F \wedge \ell = t) \longrightarrow \lceil S \rceil$

Intuitively, $F \longrightarrow \lceil S \rceil$ expresses that whenever a pattern given by a formula F is observed, it will be "followed by" an interval where S holds. In the "up-to" form the pattern is bounded by a length "up to" s, and in the "leads-to" form this pattern is required to have a length s. Note that the "leads-to" does not simply say that whenever F holds then t time units later $\lceil S \rceil$ holds, but it rather requires a *stability* of F for t time units before we can be certain that $\lceil S \rceil$

holds. It is this kind of stability requirement that ultimately enables a PLC to implement the "leads-to".

Implementables are certain formats of formulae about the observables *in* and *st*. We illustrate these formats by providing semantics for parts of the PLC-Automaton in Fig. 5 using the following abbreviations:

b abbreviates $in = b$
B abbreviates $in \in B$
q abbreviates $st = q$
$\neg q$ abbreviates $st \neq q$
Q abbreviates $st \in Q$

The DC implementables are then of the form:

- Initialisation: $\lceil\rceil \vee \lceil q_0 \rceil ; true$
  says that the system must start in a state where q_0 holds. More precisely, each observation interval starting at time 0 is either a point interval or it has an initial (non-point) subinterval where q_0 holds everywhere.

  Example : $\lceil\rceil \vee \lceil N \rceil ; true$

- Sequencing: $\lceil q \rceil \longrightarrow \lceil q \vee Q \rceil$
  says that being in state q the system can either remain in this state or at most evolve into a state in the set Q.

  Examples :
  $\lceil N \rceil \longrightarrow \lceil N \vee T \vee X \rceil$
  $\lceil T \rceil \longrightarrow \lceil N \vee T \vee X \rceil$
  $\lceil X \rceil \longrightarrow \lceil X \rceil$

  Note that the first two sequencing constraints are trivial because N, T and X are *all* possible values of *out*.

- Unbounded Stability: $\lceil \neg q \rceil ; \lceil q \wedge B \rceil \longrightarrow \lceil q \vee Q \rceil$
  says that if the system enters state q while B holds, it is guaranteed to stay in q or to evolve to one of the states in Q.

  Examples :
  $\lceil \neg T \rceil ; \lceil T \wedge tr \rceil \longrightarrow \lceil T \rceil$
  $\lceil \neg T \rceil ; \lceil T \wedge no\_tr \rceil \longrightarrow \lceil T \vee N \rceil$

- Bounded Stability: $\lceil \neg q \rceil ; \lceil q \wedge B \rceil \xrightarrow{\leq s} \lceil q \vee Q \rceil$
  says that if the system enters state q while B holds, it is guaranteed for s time units to stay in q or to evolve to one of the states in Q.

  Example : $\lceil \neg T \rceil ; \lceil T \wedge (tr \vee no\_tr) \rceil \xrightarrow{\leq 5} \lceil T \rceil$

- Progress: $\lceil q \wedge B \rceil \xrightarrow{t} \lceil \neg q \rceil$
  is the only form of implementable requiring that the present state q must be left: being in q while B holds the system must leave q within t time units.

  Example : $\lceil T \wedge Error \rceil \xrightarrow{2 \cdot \varepsilon PLC} \lceil \neg T \rceil$

Full details of the DC semantics for PLC-Automata are more elaborate and can be found in [7].

7.4 Linking the Levels

Once two neighbouring levels of formal descriptions of real-time systems have been given a semantics in the same semantic domain, here the Duration Calculus, we can formally argue about correctness.

Consider a PLC-Automaton $\mathcal{A}$ and a collection of Constraint Diagrams $\mathcal{C}$. The semantics of $\mathcal{A}$ is given by a DC formula $[\![\mathcal{A}]\!]_{\mathrm{DC}}$ and the semantics of $\mathcal{C}$ by a DC formula $[\![\mathcal{C}]\!]_{\mathrm{DC}}$. Then

$$\mathcal{A} \text{ correctly refines } \mathcal{C} \text{ iff } [\![\mathcal{A}]\!]_{\mathrm{DC}} \Rrightarrow [\![\mathcal{C}]\!]_{\mathrm{DC}}.$$

Example 4. Let $\mathcal{C}_{FES}$ be the collection of the five Constraint Diagrams formalising the requirements for the filter *FES* in subsection 4.1 and $\mathcal{A}_{FES}$ the PLC-Automaton of Fig. 5. Then we can prove:

$$\text{If } \varepsilon_{PLC} \leq \varepsilon/2 \text{ then } [\![\mathcal{A}_{FES}]\!]_{\mathrm{DC}} \Rrightarrow [\![\mathcal{C}_{FES}]\!]_{\mathrm{DC}}.$$

Recall that ε is the required reaction time of the filter to changes of the input values and ε_{PLC} is the cycle time of the PLC-Automaton $\mathcal{A}_{FES}$. It is typical that correctness statements about PLC-Automata depend on certain constraints on their cycle time. Using the continuous time domain Time such constraints can be conveniently stated and solved.

For the programming language ST we have not worked out any formal semantics. It is clear that this is also desirable as it would enable us to prove that ST programs correctly implement PLC-Automata and more generally address the problem of compiler correctness. This is left for future work. A possible approach can be found in [17].

8 Tool Support: Moby/PLC

Once such a semantic link based on logic has been well understood, tools can be developed to support the design method. This has been done for the method described in this paper by a tool called MOBY/PLC [11]. It is implemented on the basis of a C++ class library and emphasises graphic representations of the objects. The architecture of MOBY/PLC is displayed in Fig. 7; it consists of the following components:

- a graphic editor for PLC-Automata,
- a simulator for networks of PLC-Automata,
- a compiler generating code from PLC-Automata into the target language ST for PLCs,
- an algorithm for the static analysis of reaction times [7],
- a synthesis algorithm for generating PLC-Automata from a subset of Duration Calculus that corresponds to DC implementables [8, 28],
- algorithms for translating PLC-Automata into timed automata in order to be able to use UPPAAL [4, 25] and KRONOS [6] for model checking of additional real-time properties [10].

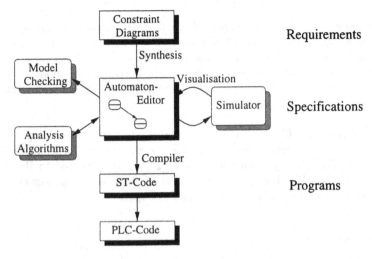

Fig. 7. Architecture of Moby/PLC

Using MOBY/PLC the case study *Single Track Control* has been tackled by H. Dierks. Starting point were the informal requirements of the customer, in this case the Berlin Traffic Company. To deal with the safety, functional and time critical parts of the requirements, an architectural plan for the control software was developed identifying a number of logical components like filters, counters, drive controller, error detection and traffic light actuators. Then for each of these components the corresponding requirements were formalised using DC implementables (corresponding to a subset of Constraint Diagrams).

From these formalised requirements corresponding PLC-Automata were synthesised for each component yielding a network of 14 PLC-Automata. Real-time properties were relevant for some of these automata, in particular for the filters for stuttering sensors as discussed in the Sections 4 and 5. Using MOBY/PLC this network could be checked by simulation. Additional correctness properties were proven, for example that it is never the case that the traffic lights of the two opposite directions show the *Go* signal at the same time. The PLC-Automata network was then compiled into an ST program with 700 lines of code for execution on a single PLC. The program was again validated using a commercially available PLC simulator.

9   Conclusion

In this paper we showed how ideas from the theory of real-time systems can be used in an application area from the industrial practice: the design of railway signalling systems based on Programmable Logic Controllers.

Our approach is in contrast to current industrial practice where software is produced directly using languages like ST or of a lower level of abstraction and then tested extensively to catch errors. Constraint Diagrams and PLC-Automata allow for a more abstract and clearer view on the controller under design and enable a formal verification of real-time properties.

Future research is concerned with the automatic verification (model checking) of real-time properties for PLC-automata or more general real-time systems with reaction times.

Acknowledgements. The work described in this paper is motivated by my participation in the projects ProCoS (*Provably Correct Systems* [17]) and UniForM (*Universal Workbench for Formal Methods* [23]). I am indepted to H. Dierks, C. Dietz, H. Fleischhack and J. Tapken for their work on various aspects of the approach to real-time design described in this paper.

References

1. R. Alur, D. Dill. A theory of timed automata. *Theoret. Comput. Sci.*, 126, 1994, 283–235.
2. R. Alur, G.J. Holzmann, D. Peled. An analyzer for message sequence charts. In: T. Margaria and B. Steffen (Eds.), *Tools and Algorithms for the Construction and Analysis of Systems*. LNCS 1055 (Springer-Verlag, 1996) 35–48.
3. R.J.R. Back. Refinement calculus, part II: parallel and reactive Programs. In J.W. de Bakker, W.P. de Roever and G. Rozenberg (Eds.), *Stepwise Refinement of Distributed Systems – Models, Formalisms, Correctness*. LNCS 430 (Springer-Verlag, 1990) 67–93.
4. J. Bengtsson, K.G. Larsen, F. Larsson, P. Pettersson, W. Yi. UPPAAL – a tool suite for automatic verification of real-time systems. In: *Proc. 4th DIMACS Workshop on Verification and Control of Hybrid Systems*. New Brunswick, New Jersey, Oct. 1995.
5. T. Bienmüller, J. Bohn, H. Brinkmann, U. Brockmeyer, W. Damm, H. Hungar, P. Jansen. Verification of Automotive Control Units. *This volume.*
6. C. Dawsa, A. Olivero, S. Tripakis, S. Yovine. The tool KRONOS. In: R. Alur, T.A. Henzinger, E.D. Sontag (Eds.), *Hybrids Systems III – Verification and Control.* LNCS 1066 (Springer-Verlag, 1996).
7. H. Dierks. PLC-automata: a new class of implementable real-time automata. In: M. Bertran and T. Rus (Eds.), *Transformation-Based Reactive Systems Development.* LNCS 1231 (Springer-Verlag, 1997) 111–125. (Revised version to appear in TCS)
8. H. Dierks. Synthesising controllers from real-time specifications. In: *Tenth International Symposium on System Synthesis* (IEEE CS Press, September 1997) 126–133.
9. H. Dierks, C. Dietz. Graphical specification and reasoning: case study "Generalized Railroad Crossing". In J. Fitzgerald, C.B. Jones, and P. Lucas, editors, *Formal Methods: Their Industrial Application and Strengthened Foundations (FME'97)*, LNCS 1313 (Springer-Verlag, 1997) 20–39.
10. H. Dierks, A. Fehnker, A. Mader, F.W. Vaandrager. Operational and logical semantics for polling real-time systems. In A.P. Ravn, H. Rischel, editors, *Formal Techniques in Real-Time and Fault-Tolerant Systems (FTRTFT'98)*, Lecture Notes in Computer Science volume 1486, pages 29–40, Springer-Verlag, 1998.

11. H. Dierks, J. Tapken. Tool-supported hierarchical design of distributed real-time systems. In: Proc. IEEE *EuroMicro'98*, Berlin, 1998.
12. C. Dietz, Graphical formalization of real-time requirements. In B. Jonsson and J. Parrow, editors, Formal Techniques in Real-Time and Fault-Tolerant Systems, LNCS 1135 (Springer-Verlag, 1996) 366–385.
13. S. Fowler, A. Wellings. Formal analysis of a real-time kernel specification. In: [21] 440–458.
14. R.L. Grossman, A. Nerode, A.P. Ravn, H. Rischel (Eds.). *Hybrid Systems*. LNCS 736 (Springer-Verlag, 1993)
15. M.R. Hansen, Zhou Chaochen, Duration Calculus: Logical Foundations. *Formal Aspects of Computing*, 9 (1997) 283-330.
16. D. Harel. Statecharts: a visual formalism for complex systems. *Science of Comp. Progr.* (1997) 231–274.
17. Jifeng He, C.A.R. Hoare, M. Fränzle, M. Müller-Olm, E.-R. Olderog, M. Schenke, M.R. Hansen, A.P. Ravn, and H. Rischel. Provably correct systems. In: [24] 288–335.
18. C. Heitmeyer and D. Mandrioli (Eds.), *Formal Methods for Real-Time Computing*. Trends in Software, Vol.5, (Wiley, 1996).
19. IEC International Standard 1131-3, Programmable Controllers, Part 3, Programming Languages, 1993
20. ITU-T, ITU-T Recommendation Z.120: Message Sequence Chart (MSC). ITU General Secretariat, Geneva, 1994.
21. B. Jonsson, J. Parrow (Eds.), *Formal Techniques in Real-Time and Fault-Tolerant Systems*. LNCS 1135 (Springer-Verlag, 1996).
22. M. Joseph (Ed.). *Real-time Systems – Specification, Verification and Analysis* Prentice Hall, 1996.
23. B. Krieg-Brückner, J. Peleska, E.-R. Olderog, D. Balzer, A. Baer. UniForM – Universal Formal Methods Workbench. In: U. Grote and G. Wolf (Eds.), *Statusseminar des BMBF Softwaretechnologie* (BMBF, Berlin, 1996) 357–377.
24. H. Langmaack, W.-P. de Roever, J. Vytopil (Eds.). *Formal Techniques in Real-Time and Fault-Tolerant Systems*. LNCS 863 (Springer-Verlag, 1994).
25. K.G. Larsen, B. Steffen, C. Weise. Countinuous modeling of real time and hybrid systems: from concepts to tools. *Software Tools for Technology Transfer (STTT)* 1, 1997, 64–85.
26. R.W. Lewis. *Programming industrial control systems using IEC 1131-3*. The Institution of Electrical Engineers, 1995.
27. S. Mauw, M.A. Reniers. An Algebraic Semantics of Basic Message Sequence Charts. *The Computer Journal* 37, No. 4 (1994) 269–277.
28. E.-R. Olderog, H. Dierks, Decomposing real-time specifications. In H. Langmaack, A. Pnueli, W.-P. de Roever, editors, *Compositionality: The Significant Difference*, LNCS (Springer-Verlag, 1998) 465–489.
29. E.-R. Olderog, A.P. Ravn, J.U. Skakkebæk. Refining system requirements to program specifications. In: [18] 107–134.
30. A.P. Ravn, H. Rischel, K.M. Hansen. Specifying and verifying requirements of real-time systems. *IEEE Transactions on Software Engineering*, vol. 19,1 (1993) 41–55.
31. A.P. Ravn. *Design of Embedded Real-Time Computing Systems*. Thesis for the Doctor of Technics. Technical Report ID-TR: 1995-170, Technical University of Denmark, 1995.
32. W. Reisig. *Petri Nets – An Introduction*. Springer-Verlag, 1985.

33. W.-P. de Roever, K. Engelhardt. *Data Refinement: Model-Oriented Proof Methods and their Comparison* (Cambridge, 1998).
34. M. Schenke, E.-R. Olderog, Transformational design of real-time systems – part I: from requirements to program specifications. *Acta Informatica 36*, 1999, 1–65.
35. M. Schenke, Transformational design of real-time systems – part II: from program specifications to programs. *Acta Informatica 36*, 1999, 67–96.
36. R. Schlör, W. Damm. Specification and verification of system level hardware designs using timing diagrams. In *Proc. European Conf. on Design Automation*, Paris, 1993.
37. Zhou Chaochen, C.A.R. Hoare, A.P. Ravn. A calculus of durations. *Information Processing Letters*, 40/5, 1991, 269–276.

Formal Methods for the International Space Station ISS

Jan Peleska[1,2] and Bettina Buth[1]

[1] TZI-BISS, University of Bremen, EMail {bb,jp}@tzi.org
[2] Verified Systems International GmbH, Bremen, EMail jp@verified.de

Abstract. This article summarises and evaluates the results and experiences obtained from a verification, simulation and test suite for a fault-tolerant computer system designed and developed by DaimlerChrysler Aerospace for the International Space Station ISS. Verification and testing focused on various aspects of system correctness which together ensure a high degree of trustworthiness for the system. The verification and test approach is based on CSP specifications, the model-checking tool FDR and the test automation tool RT-Tester. Furthermore, Generalised Stochastic Petri Nets (GSPN) have been used with the tools DSPN-Express and TimeNet to perform a statistical throughput analysis by means of simulation. The objective of this article is to present, motivate and evaluate our approach that strongly relied on the combination of different methods, techniques and tools in order to increase the overall efficiency of the verification, simulation and test suite. The isolated techniques applied are illustrated by small examples; for details, references to other publications are given.

Keywords: Fault-Tolerant Systems — Byzantine Agreement Protocol — Formal Verification — CSP — Test Automation — Model Checking — Generalised Stochastic Petri Nets — Hardware-in-the-loop Test — International Space Station

1 Introduction

Objectives. This article is intended as a summary and an evaluation of a verification, simulation and test suite performed in several steps between 1995 and 1998 for a fault-tolerant system to be integrated in the International Space Station (ISS). The system inspected during this suite is the 4-redundant *Fault-Tolerant Computer (FTC)* which is the main component of the *Data Management System (DMS-R)* developed by DaimlerChrysler Aerospace (DASA) for the Russian module of the ISS. More details about the FTC, including an overview of the FTC hardware and software architecture are given in Section 2.

The verification, simulation and test project started in 1995 when JP Software-Consulting (now Verified Systems International GmbH) in collaboration with the Bremen Institute of Safe Systems (BISS) were contracted by DASA to perform

E.-R. Olderog, B. Steffen (Eds.): Correct System Design, LNCS 1710, pp. 363–389, 1999.
© Springer-Verlag Berlin Heidelberg 1999

a sequence of various product assurance tasks for the FTC. The main objectives for this contract were:

- Maximise the confidence into the overall correctness of the FTC by performing additional verification, simulation and test tasks complementary to the activities already carried out by the DASA product assurance team and the software developers.
- Let some of the most critical product assurance activities be performed by an independent party, as is recommended by various development standards in avionics and space technology (JP Software-Consulting/Verified Systems and BISS are independent institutions without organisational links to DaimlerChrysler).
- Increase the efficiency of critical product assurance activities by using automated verification, simulation and test methods based on formal specifications.

Complexity Problems. To reach these objectives, two complexity problems had to be overcome: first the main objective "maximise the overall correctness" had to be structured into a collection of correctness requirements which could be handled in a systematic way. It should be emphasised that a system of this complexity cannot be completely specified by a set of formal specifications in a straightforward way: the diversity and number of FTC system requirements was so large that it would have taken several man years to formalise them. Moreover, the possible ambiguity of informal requirements was not a major concern, therefore the formalisation alone would not have contributed anything to the quality of the implemented system. As a consequence, the verification suite could only investigate a subset of requirements, and it had to be ensured that the correctness aspects investigated would really cover the critical features of the system. Second, the size of the system (about 24,000 lines of OCCAM programming code and related detailed design specifications had to be analysed in the formal verification activities performed during the whole suite, additional code was covered in the tests) was obviously too large to be treated formally as one chunk in formal specifications and verifications. Therefore, it was essential to find strategies how to decompose the system, verify small portions and combine the verification results to conclude whether the full system met a correctness requirement or not.

Structured Correctness Requirements. Among the wide spectrum of possible correctness requirements, the following have been identified to be the most important ones for the successful operation of the FTC in the ISS:

1. deadlock freedom of the system software responsible for FTC communication and fault management,
2. livelock freedom of the same software,
3. correct implementation of the voting algorithms used to detect corrupted data originating from a faulty FTC component,
4. correct implementation of the Byzantine protocol (see Lamport [13]) used to reach agreement among non-faulty FTC components,

5. meeting of the performance requirements defined for the FTC network interface,
6. correct FTC behaviour in presence of exceptions, that is, correct isolation of faulty components, consistent re-configuration of remaining components and consistent re-integration of repaired ones,
7. correct integration of system software on the customised computer and communication hardware which has been specifically designed for space missions.

Selection of Methods. The correctness requirements 1 — 4 are obviously independent of the underlying hardware, therefore it was decided to analyse the FTC software by means of formal verification techniques. The starting point for these verifications were the FTC detailed design document and the software code. For the performance requirements 5, not only the concrete throughput figures which could be obtained with the FTC were of interest, but also the impact of certain design decisions on the communication performance. Therefore it was decided to analyse throughput properties in two ways: (1) Simulations based on the software design and on the known performance properties of the hardware: here the main objective was to study the impact of design decisions on performance; (2) Hardware-in-the-loop tests[1] with the complete FTC hardware and software to check the quantitative performance values. Requirements 6 and 7 are related to hardware/software integration, therefore it was decided to analyse the respective FTC behaviour in hardware-in-the-loop tests.

Verification Strategy. To tackle the complexity problem presented by the system size, a verification approach was elaborated, combining the following four fundamental methods:

- *Abstraction methods* transforming program code or detailed design specifications into simplified formal specifications which could be analysed with respect to accordingly transformed requirements, such that correctness on formal specification level implied correctness on code/design level.
- *Model checking of refinement relations* to prove local properties of small sub-systems.
- *Compositional reasoning* to deduce overall system correctness from local properties of small sub-systems.
- *Generic theories* to re-use correctness results which only depend on generic characteristics of (sub-)systems; these can be applied to instance processes belonging to the same generic class.

This approach is described in more detail in Section 3.

---

[1] These tests are used to investigate the correct behaviour of integrated hardware/software (sub-) systems: Tests are driven by separate computer components stimulating the system input interfaces and evaluating the system behaviour by observing its output interfaces. This results in closed-loop test configurations consisting of the system under test and the test driver.

Methods and Tools. The time-independent verification goals deadlock freedom, livelock freedom and correct implementation of Byzantine agreement protocol were modelled with untimed CSP using various semantic models described by Hoare and Roscoe [12, 24][2]. Verification of sub-system properties was performed by model checking of refinement conditions using the FDR-tool [9]: The FDR-tool compares pairs of CSP processes (P_1, P_2) and checks whether a CSP refinement relation holds between the two. For compositional reasoning and to check the applicability of specific abstraction techniques, manual proofs were worked out and cross-checked in the project team. Code verification for the sequential voting algorithms was performed using Hoare-style reasoning with pre-/postconditions. Here, the PAMELA tool [4] could be applied, but some proof obligations had to be discharged by manual reasoning. The simulation for performance analysis was based on Generalised Stochastic Petri Nets (GSPNs) and supported by the tools DSPN-Express and TimeNet(see Schlingloff [30] for an introduction). Finally, real-time tests were specified with Timed CSP interpreted in the semantics given by Schneider [26] and executed and evaluated using the RT-Tester tool.

Overview. In Section 2, the FTC is introduced in more detail. Section 3 describes our formal verification approach, Section 4 describes the test activities and presents the basic concept of the RT-Tester tool. In the final Section 5, we give a detailed discussion of the results obtained during the whole verification, simulation and test suite and describe some trends in the field of verification and test which – according to our estimation – will become important in the future, in order to cope with increasingly complex systems and to improve the efficiency of verification and testing.

Since this article is intended as an overview and evaluation of the verification, simulation and test suite performed, we only give small examples to illustrate specific aspects of our approach. A more detailed description for the different topics can be found in Peleska [31] (detailed description of the FTC), Buth et.al. [5] (deadlock analysis), [6, 7] (livelock analysis), Peleska et.al. [27] (detailed description of abstraction methods and verification of the Byzantine agreement protocol), Schlingloff [30] (load analysis using GSPNs) and Buth et.al. [3] (efficient use of generic theories in the verification of fault-tolerant systems).

2   Engineering Background: ISS, DMS-R and the Fault-Tolerant Computer FTC

In its final construction stage, the International Space Station ISS will consist of several modules developed by different nations. For the Russian service module, DaimlerChrysler have developed hardware and system software for the central data management system, called DMS-R. The DMS-R provides an operational

---

[2] It is assumed in this article that readers are familiar with the basics of CSP notation and semantics. If this is not the case, Hoare and Roscoe [12, 24] are recommended as comprehensive descriptions of untimed CSP, and Schneider [26] gives a quick introduction into the timed aspects.

platform for software applications managing experiments performed on the ISS, and for control software used during the assembly phase of the station and for the purpose of re-boost operations. The DMS-R core component is the fault-tolerant computer FTC. The FTC overall architecture consists of three or four lanes (each lane is a separate computer sub-system) operating according to the principle of *active redundancy* (see Figure 1): the lanes perform their tasks in a synchronised way, and state information is kept consistent between lanes. Each DMS-R application implemented on the FTC runs on all four lanes in parallel; it communicates with other systems in the ISS via six independent MIL-STD 1553 busses.

Below the applications layer, each of the four lanes is structured into an application services layer (ASS), a fault management layer (FML), and the avionics interface (AVI). Applications and the ASS reside on a computer board using a customised SPARC-type CPU specifically manufactured for space applications by Matra. The VxWorks operating system is used for the scheduling of ASS tasks and applications and for resource management. Applications are programmed in C. Both FML and AVI reside on separate transputer boards. The OCCAM programming language has been used for the implementation of FML and AVI software.

The AVI interfaces to the six MIL-STD 1553 busses. This bus type supports a master (bus controller) and slave (remote terminal) concept and allows synchronised data transmission/acquisition. The AVI implements a bus controller mode for four busses and a remote terminal mode for the remaining two. Moreover, the AVI manages a time-tagged frame protocol layer on top of the MIL-STD 1553 protocol which has been specified for global use within the ISS.

The purpose of the FML is twofold:

- The FML provides the interface between the ASS and AVI of one lane, transferring messages from AVI to ASS and vice versa. For communication between ASS and FML, a VME Bus interface is used; communication between FML and AVI is performed on transputer links.
- The FML performs the data transfer between lanes, thus allowing communication between the fault management layers of all lanes. This communication is the basis for error detection, error correction, lane isolation (in the case of an unrecoverable error), and lane reintegration. For this inter-lane communication, transputer links called *cross strapping links* are used: the FML of each lane is connected to the FMLs of all other lanes.

To reach unanimous decisions among correctly operating lanes and as a means for error detection, a two round Byzantine distribution schema introduced by Lamport [13] is used, where data is communicated between FMLs and voted using various voters specialised on different types of data. The objective of the protocol is to ensure that

1. All ASS instances of non-faulty lanes get identical messages from FML,
2. All AVI instances of non-faulty lanes get identical messages from FML,

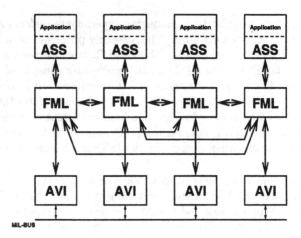

Fig. 1. FTC architecture

3. For data calculated by all lanes (congruent source messages) all non-faulty lanes get the correct(ed) message,
4. For data calculated by one lane (single source messages) all non-faulty lanes get the correct message if the originator is not faulty.

The software architecture of the FML in one lane consists of a number of processes which communicate over a set of channels and jointly use a global memory and a separate global buffer. Figure 2 presents a simplified overview of this architecture. Each of the main processes itself is built from smaller subprocesses not shown in the figure, which communicate over local channels. For the AVI, similar architectural concepts have been used.

3   Verification Techniques

As indicated in the introduction above, formal verification for the FTC became manageable by an approach combining abstraction, verification of local properties by model checking, compositional reasoning and application of generic theories. This approach will be described in more detail in this section. It focuses on the correctness properties deadlock freedom, livelock freedom and correct implementation of the Byzantine protocol. This verification could be performed by analysis of the AVI and FML software sub-system only, since the ASS had been (informally) verified with respect to deadlock/livelock freedom beforehand by the DASA team and the application layer was not under DASA responsibility. The verification of the Byzantine protocol could even focus on the FML alone, since none of the other layers contribute to its implementation.

In Section 3.1, correctness properties defined on programming language level – in case of AVI and FML verification, OCCAM program properties – are related to corresponding properties on formal specification language – in our case, CSP –

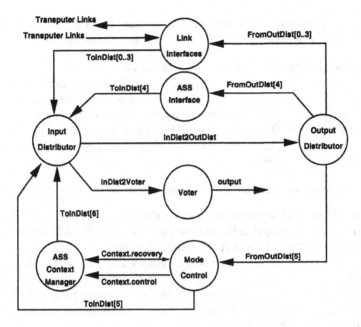

Fig. 2. FML processes allocated in each lane.

level. Section 3.2 describes abstraction methods that have been used to make the verification process feasible, and in Section 3.3 we sketch how properties verified for small software components can be composed to derive the global verification goals.

3.1 Relating OCCAM to CSP Process Properties

To motivate how properties p on OCCAM level can be related to properties $\mathcal{A}^*(p)$ on (untimed) CSP level it is important to note that the concepts of traces and refusals are defined for OCCAM processes in a straightforward way: traces are sequences of OCCAM channel events, a refusal after a trace s is a set of OCCAM channels which are blocked since either one or both communication partners are not ready to pass messages along them. Therefore the concepts of trace refinement and failures refinement may be applied on OCCAM level as well. We can even investigate trace and failures refinement relations between a CSP process Q and an OCCAM process P, if the alphabet of Q is defined by the set of OCCAM channels with identical channel alphabets (on OCCAM level you would call the channel alphabets "protocols"). Furthermore, it was ensured in the AVI and FML OCCAM code that every loop has a constant finite upper bound. As a consequence, divergence could only occur by execution of unbounded chains of channel communications over cycles of internal channels without any external interface communication interleaved. This means that the failures-divergence refinement relation is well-defined between CSP processes and FTC OCCAM processes as well. Next observe the following facts:

- Deadlock freedom is preserved under failures refinement.
- If $Q \setminus \{c_1, c_2, \ldots, c_n\}$ is free of livelocks and Q' is livelock-free and a trace refinement of Q, then $Q' \setminus \{c_1, c_2, \ldots, c_n\}$ is free of livelocks, too[3].
- If $Q = (Q_1 \| \ldots \| Q_k)$ specifies the Byzantine agreement protocol between processes Q_i and $Q' = (Q'_1 \| \ldots \| Q'_k)$ is free of deadlocks and livelocks and the Q'_i are trace refinements of the Q_i, then Q' is a correct implementation of the protocol as well[4].

These considerations motivate the following global verification strategy:

- To establish deadlock freedom, find an abstract deadlock-free CSP process system which is refined in the failures model by the OCCAM process system consisting of the FML and AVI running in parallel.
- To establish livelock freedom, find an abstract CSP process Q with the same interface channels $\{d_1, d_2, \ldots, d_\ell\}$ and internal channels $\{c_1, c_2, \ldots, c_n\}$ as the OCCAM system P consisting of the AVI running in parallel with the FML and prove that (1) $Q \setminus \{c_1, c_2, \ldots, c_n\}$ is free of livelocks and (2) Q is refined by P in the trace model.
- To prove correct implementation of the Byzantine protocol, specify the protocol as a CSP process $BYZAN$ (this is a direct transcription of the semi-formal protocol specification given in Lamport [13]), use the fact that the FML has been shown to be free of deadlocks and livelocks and prove that the FML is a trace refinement of $BYZAN$.

3.2   Abstraction Methods

Purpose and Definition of Abstractions. Abstraction methods were applied in two situations:

- To transform OCCAM code into CSP, so that formal analysis of correctness properties could be performed on the level of a formal specification language instead on programming language level,
- To transform CSP specifications into simpler ones which were still sufficiently detailed to verify the correctness property under investigation, but small enough to be analysed by model checking without running into state explosion problems.

For our purposes, the abstraction principle can be formally defined as follows:

---

[3] Livelock freedom for Q' must be stipulated in order to exclude pathological divergence cases such as $Q' = Q' \sqcap Q$.

[4] To prove this, one has to observe that the communication decisions of the protocol are deterministic for the correctly functioning communication partners, and the communications are completely determined by the number k of processes and the message contents communicated along the channels.

Definition 1. *Let P be an OCCAM or CSP process and p a property of P to be verified. Let $\mathcal{A}(P)$ denote a CSP process and $\mathcal{A}^*(p)$ a property defined on CSP level. Then the pair $(\mathcal{A}(P), \mathcal{A}^*(p))$ is called a valid abstraction for (P, p), if*

$\mathcal{A}(P)$ *satisfies* $\mathcal{A}^*(p)$ *always implies* P *satisfies* p.

□

Abstraction Through Refinement. According to the fact that CSP refinement can be extended to OCCAM and due to the observation that the three correctness properties under consideration can be expressed as refinement properties, a first set of valid abstractions can be constructed according to the following rules:

- To analyse deadlock freedom, property p is defined by an assertion of the type "P refines DF in the failures model" (formally written as $DF \sqsubseteq_F P$), where DF is a given deadlock-free process with the same alphabet as P. The abstracted property $\mathcal{A}^*(p)$ is identical to p, that is $DF \sqsubseteq_F \bullet$. Abstraction process $\mathcal{A}(P)$ must be chosen such that it is refined by the OCCAM process system P in the failures model. Then, if $DF \sqsubseteq_F \mathcal{A}(P)$ can be proven, deadlock freedom of P follows from the transitivity of refinement.
- To analyse livelock freedom, $\mathcal{A}(P)$ must be chosen such that it contains the same interface channels $\{d_1, d_2, \ldots, d_\ell\}$ and internal channels $\{c_1, c_2, \ldots, c_n\}$ as P and is refined by P in the trace model. Then, if livelock freedom of $\mathcal{A}(P) \setminus \{c_1, c_2, \ldots, c_n\}$ can be proven, the same follows for P.
- To analyse correct implementation of the Byzantine protocol (after having verified deadlock and livelock freedom), $\mathcal{A}(P)$ must be chosen such that it is refined by P in the trace model. Then, if it can be shown that $\mathcal{A}(P)$ refines the protocol specification process $BYZAN$ in the trace model, P is a correct implementation of the protocol, too.

The abstraction principle described above is called *abstraction through refinement* (see Roscoe and Peleska et.al. [24, 27] for further details on this topic): concrete (OCCAM or CSP) process and abstract CSP process operate on the same alphabet and are related by refinement. Simplification of the abstraction process in comparison with the concrete process is only possible by hiding irrelevant details and increasing nondeterminism through replacing conditions if *condition* **then** P_1 **else** P_2 by internal choice $P_1 \sqcap P_2$. This abstraction principle has the advantage that it is transitive (since refinement is) and distributes through the CSP operators (since refinement does), but it has a serious drawback: by increasing the degree of nondeterminism it is often the case that the abstraction no longer fulfils the required property, and the reason is not an implementation error but the fact that too many relevant data-dependent decisions in the implementation have been replaced by internal choice in the abstracted process.

Abstraction Through Data Independence. What is needed, is a more subtle abstraction method allowing us to reduce the channel alphabets and the data range of local process variables if these do not contribute to communication decisions and – in case of the Byzantine protocol verification – do not represent relevant protocol data.

Example 1. Suppose that channels c, d range over the natural numbers. We wish to prove that process system

$$SYSTEM = (P \parallel_{\{|c|\}} Q)$$
$$P = c!0 \to STOP \sqcap c!1 \to STOP$$
$$Q = c?x \to (\text{if } (x < 10) \text{ then } (d!0 \to STOP) \text{ else } (d!10 \to STOP))$$

always produces event $d.0$. Formally, this property p can be expressed as $(d.0 \to STOP) \sqsubseteq_T SYSTEM \setminus \{| c |\}$, $\sqsubseteq_T$ denoting the trace refinement relation. Since the condition in Q only depends on the two situations $x < 10$ and $x \geq 10$, it suffices to analyse the abstracted process system

$$SYSTEM' = (P' \parallel_{\{|c'|\}} Q')$$
$$P' = c'!0 \to STOP$$
$$Q' = c'?x \to (\text{if } (x == 0) \text{ then } (d'!0 \to STOP) \text{ else } (d'!10 \to STOP))$$

where channels c', d' are defined with the finite alphabet $\{0, 10\}$ instead of the infinite set $\mathbb{N}$. The abstracted property $\mathcal{A}^*(p)$ now differs from the original p: $\mathcal{A}^*(p)$ would be defined as $(d'.0 \to STOP) \sqsubseteq_T SYSTEM' \setminus \{| c' |\}$, referring to abstracted channels c', d'.   □

This type of abstraction is called *abstraction through data independence* and has been formally investigated by Lazic and Roscoe [16, 24]. It is much more powerful with respect to the construction of valid abstractions with considerably reduced state spaces. For our verification suite, abstraction through data independence was used to extend the verification strategy by further simplifying the CSP processes constructed before according to the abstraction through refinement principle (details can be found in Buth et.al. [5, 6] and Peleska et.al. [27]).

- For the verification of deadlock and livelock freedom, the channels c used by OCCAM processes and on the first CSP abstraction level were abstracted to single-event channels c' if the data communicated along c did not influence communication decisions. If the data communicated along c could lead to n different communication decisions, the set $\{1, \ldots, n\}$ was used for the alphabet of c'.
- For the Byzantine protocol verification, it could be shown that the range of data to be passed along the protocol channels for comparison in the voting procedure could be reduced to a set of 7 elements.

3.3   Compositional Reasoning and Use of Generic Theories

Even after the application of the abstraction methods described above, it would have been infeasible to verify the correctness properties in one step simply by model checking abstractions of the full AVI and/or FML layers against reference processes satisfying the properties. Instead, the abstraction principles were applied to smaller sub-systems – for example to each of the process sub-systems shown in Figure 1 – in order to prove a modified local verification goal. The new goals defined for the sub-systems were elaborated in such a way that the original correctness requirements could be deduced from the new goals by compositional reasoning over the parallel combination of sub-systems. To increase the efficiency of the compositional reasoning process, it was tried to identify whether sub-systems could be regarded as (refinements of) instances of generic process classes with known compositional properties.

Example 2. In the compositional reasoning process performed to prove deadlock freedom of the FML, it could be shown by model checking that each of the process sub-systems depicted in Figure 1 is a refinement of a process of type "multiplexer/concentrator" specified as *MUXCON* below. The definition of *MUXCON* is generic in the number N specifying how many outputs must be produced before the next input can be accepted and the number, names and alphabet of input channels $\{in_1, \ldots, in_n\}$ and output channels $\{out_1, \ldots, out_m\}$. Observe that an instance of *MUXCON* defined with $N = 0$ never refuses an input.

$$MUXCON[N, \{in_1, \ldots, in_n\}, \{out_1, \ldots, out_m\}] =$$
$$MC[N, \{in_1, \ldots, in_\ell\}, \{out_1, \ldots, out_m\}](0)$$

$$MC[N, \{in_1, \ldots, in_\ell\}, \{out_1, \ldots, out_m\}](n) =$$
$$\textbf{if } (n = 0)$$
$$\textbf{then } (GET[N, \{in_1, \ldots, in_\ell\}, \{out_1, \ldots, out_m\}]$$
$$\square (STOP \sqcap PUT[N, \{in_1, \ldots, in_\ell\}, \{out_1, \ldots, out_m\}](1)))$$
$$\textbf{else } PUT[N, \{in_1, \ldots, in_\ell\}, \{out_1, \ldots, out_m\}](n)$$

$$GET[N, \{in_1, \ldots, in_\ell\}, \{out_1, \ldots, out_m\}] =$$
$$(\square e : \{| in_1, \ldots, in_\ell |\} \bullet$$
$$e \rightarrow MC[N, \{in_1, \ldots, in_\ell\}, \{out_1, \ldots, out_m\}](N))$$

$$PUT[N, \{in_1, \ldots, in_\ell\}, \{out_1, \ldots, out_m\}](n) =$$
$$(\sqcap e : \{| out_1, \ldots, out_m |\} \bullet$$
$$e \rightarrow MC[N, \{in_1, \ldots, in_\ell\}, \{out_1, \ldots, out_m\}](n - 1))$$

The following generic theory is associated with the above process class:

Theorem 1. *A network of process instances $P_1, \ldots, P_q$ from class $MUXCON[N, \{in_1, \ldots, in_n\}, \{out_1, \ldots, out_m\}]$ is free of deadlocks, if every communication cycle*

$$\boxed{P_{j_1}} \xrightarrow{c_{j_1}} \boxed{P_{j_2}} \xrightarrow{c_{j_2}} \ldots \xrightarrow{c_{j_k-1}} \boxed{P_{j_k}} \xrightarrow{c_{j_k}} \boxed{P_{j_1}}$$

contains at least one process instance P_{j_ℓ} defined with $N = 0$.   □

It could be shown by model checking that for each communication cycle in the network of sub-systems shown in Figure 1, at least one sub-system is a refinement of a *MUXCON* instance defined with $N = 0$. Since deadlock freedom is preserved under refinement and refinement distributes through the parallel operator, this established deadlock freedom for the full FML layer.   □

The above example is only one type of compositional reasoning and generic theory applied in the FTC verification suite. Additional methods have been described by Buth et.al. [3, 5–7].

4   Test Automation Techniques

4.1   Test Objectives

As explained in Section 1, the objective of the test suite was to complement the verification and simulation activities. As a consequence, we did not perform unit or integration tests on software level (these had been performed by the development team in earlier stages of the projects), but designed and executed a *hardware-in-the-loop test* suite, with an FTC *engineering qualification model (EQM)* as *system under test*. An EQM consists of the original hardware as it will be used in space, with the original flight software integrated on the computers. The test objective was to investigate the correctness of hardware/software integration, and the test concept had the following characteristics:

- All relevant aspects of FTC functionality were tested in parallel, so that hidden dependencies between different functional components of the AVI, FML and ASS software layers could be detected.
- Each functional aspect was tested with respect to *normal behaviour* (all environment components act as required) and *exceptional behaviour* (some environment components provide corrupt data, show timing jitters etc.). Normal and exceptional behaviour test phases were interleaved with each other. Exceptional behaviour tests for one functional aspect could occur in parallel with normal behaviour tests for other aspects.
- Tests were executed in non-stop fashion, so that the FTC dependability could be investigated over long operational time intervals. Even the occurrence of errors should not stop the test as long as at least one FTC lane remained operational. It was a major test objective that lanes which failed due to a fault injection or due to an unexpected error should be re-integrated into the system in an automatic way.

Apart from the check of various functional features of the FTC system services, the tests had to investigate specific properties related to communication throughput:

- Keeping of the nominal and maximum data throughput under various bus load profiles[5],

---

[5] A load profile distributes a given throughput (e.g., 60KBytes/sec) in a specific way on the protocol frames which are transmitted per time unit. The FTC services time frames at a rate of 80Hz, and each frame may transport up to 408 16-Bit words.

- Robustness in overload situations.

Basically, these properties had already been investigated by the GSPN simulations. However, the criticality of the FTC throughput properties required to re-validate these aspects with dynamic testing, since simulation models are generally based on some simplifying assumptions about the behaviour of hardware components, schedulers and processes.

A specific problem had to be solved in the test configuration development: The FTC has been designed as a fault-tolerant multi-purpose system, where different application layers may be installed on top of the ASS layer. As a consequence, no specific application software was available, and a *test application software layer (TASL)* had to be developed such that successful execution of tests using the TASL implies that the FTC will also run properly with any concrete application layer.

4.2 The RT-Tester Tool

For FTC tests, the RT-Tester tool developed by JP Software-Consulting (now Verified Systems International GmbH) in cooperation with the TZI-BISS at Bremen University was used. RT-Tester has been designed to perform automated hardware-in-the-loop tests for embedded real-time systems or software tests on process and thread level. The RT-Tester functional components are shown in Figure 3.

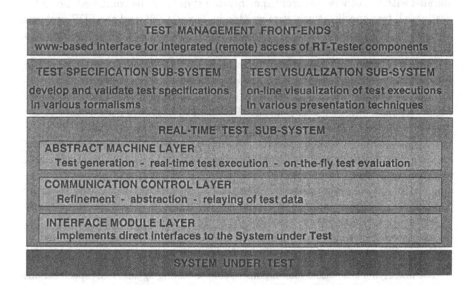

Fig. 3. RT-Tester functional components.

The *test specification sub-system* supports the development of test specifications in various formal specification styles. For each formalism, specifications are translated into binary representations as *generalised labelled transition systems (GLTS)*. These GLTS extend LTS as introduced by Milner [18] and others as follows:

- LTS nodes are annotated with acceptance sets to specify nondeterminism (this concept has also been used for model representations in the FDR tool [9]),
- Multiple clocks (in the sense of timers) may be associated with LTS states by introduction of auxiliary events to set timers and to react on elapsed timers (this extends the LTS alphabet Σ by set-/elapsed timer events from a set Σ_{Timer}, see Peleska [22]),
- Each LTS is extended by a set of additional state variables from a set $\mathcal{V}$ (this may be used to reduce the overall number of LTS nodes),
- Transition labels may be specified as
  - LTS events $e \in \Sigma$,
  - Auxiliary timer events $e \in \Sigma_{Timer}$,
  - Conditions on the values of variables $v \in \mathcal{V}$,
  - Conjunctions of LTS event occurrences and conditions.

The GLTS model is rich enough to encode different timed specification formalisms, such as Timed CSP [26], Timed Automata (at present, we use a variant of Timed Automata as introduced in [8]), Message Sequence Charts [1] and Statecharts [11]. A complete test is specified by one or more specification, each describing a different aspect of system under test functionality to be tested in parallel with the others. Different specification styles may be combined. For FTC testing, all test specifications were written in Timed CSP, and the FDR tool was used as an integrated RT-Tester component to validate CSP specifications and to transform them into GLTS representations[6].

The RT-Tester core component consists of the *real-time test sub-system*. In its *abstract machine layer (AML)*, one or more interpreters called *abstract machines* are executed during a test run, each abstract machine interpreting the GLTS representation of a test specification. Depending on the semantics of the specification language, different types of abstract machines are used for GLTS interpretation. Each abstract machine evaluates the GLTS structure in real-time to determine which inputs may be sent to the interfaces of the system under test, which outputs are to be expected from the system under test and which timing conditions are to be observed. The GLTS graph structure is used to apply various test strategies in order to achieve good test coverage. The timed traces of inputs sent to and outputs received from the system under test are recorded in execution logs which can be used for automatic test documentation and to perform offline evaluation of specific correctness aspects.

---

[6] The underlying theoretical foundations related to testing against CSP specifications have been described in more detail in [19–22]. Note that the prototype version of the product was called VVT-RT.

To facilitate the setup of new test configurations, a generic architecture is used for the real-time test sub-system: as sketched above, test specifications are executed by the AML. Communication between abstract machines and the mapping from abstract events to concrete data that may be passed to the interface of the system under test, as well as the abstraction of raw system output data to abstract events that may be consumed by the abstract machines is performed in the *communication control layer (CCL)* of the test engine. The *interface module layer (IFML)* connects to the concrete interfaces of the system under test. While AML and CCL always reside on the same computer called the *RT-Tester Engine*, the IFML may be allocated on specialised hardware, if the system under test is equipped with non-standard interfaces which cannot be directly interfaced from the test engine. In this case, test engine and interface modules (IFMs) use standard interfaces (Ethernet, parallel or serial links) to communicate with each other.

4.3   FTC Test Configuration

The instantiation of the generic RT-Tester configuration for FTC tests is shown in Figure 4. The system under test consists of an FTC EQM operating in a 4-lane configuration. The interface to the operational environment consists of 6 MIL busses (4 busses used in bus controller mode, 2 as remote terminals). Each of the 6 busses has a redundant spare wire and interfaces to a specific FTC lane. In addition, two auxiliary interfaces are used to support specific fault injections during testing. For the software layers AVI, FML and ASS, the original flight software was used. Since no concrete application software layer was available, a test application software layer (TASL) was developed and installed on top of the ASS (see Section 4.4 below).

The RT-Tester engine consists of a SUN ULTRA SPARC computer with two 300MHz CPUs, running the SOLARIS 2.6 operating system. To connect these FTC interfaces to the RT-Tester system, an IFML comprising the three interface modules MBSU, BTS, FTC-TE has been used: The *MIL Bus Simulation Unit (MBSU)* sends and receives data on the MIL busses, implementing the ISS frame protocol layer on top of the MIL-STD 1553 protocol. Frames read from the busses are relayed to the RT-Tester engine. Conversely, the test engine sends commands for test control and frames to be passed on to the corresponding MIL busses to the MBSU. The *Byzantine Traitor Simulator (BTS)* provides a fault injection interface at the cross strapping links between lanes. This is used by RT-Tester to exercise exceptional-behaviour tests on the target system in order to analyse the correctness of the Byzantine agreement protocol and the voting mechanisms implemented in the FTC lanes. The *FTC Test Equipment (FTC-TE)* provides an interface to stimulate VME interrupt errors, clock errors and to reset a lane completely.

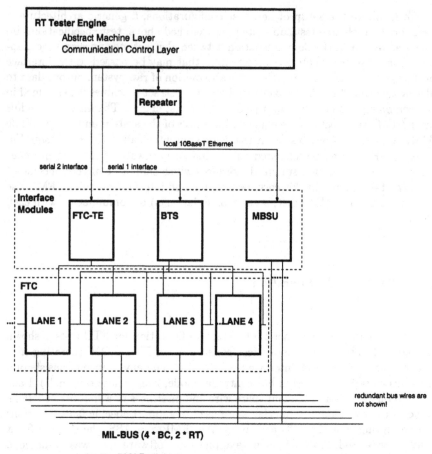

Fig. 4. FTC hardware-in-the-loop test configuration.

4.4   Dealing with Undefined Application Layers

As an example of the application of Formal Methods for the development of test strategies, we sketch how the problem of undefined application layers was solved for FTC testing[7]: Conceptually – though physically residing inside the computer hardware of the system under test – the test application layer is a part of the system's test environment, the system under test itself comprises the hardware, the operating system and the application services. For FTC testing, this means that the system under test consists of the four FTC hardware lanes in conjunction with the AVI, FML and ASS software layers. We will now present

---

[7] Further examples have been described briefly in [23].

a theorem on (timed) trace refinement whose interpretation below indicates how a useful TASL should be constructed:

Theorem 2. *Let specSUT be an abstract specification process of the desired SUT behaviour. Let impSUT denote the SUT implementation and ENV the environment (including the TASL) used for testing. Then, if*

$$(ENV \parallel specSUT) \sqsubseteq_T (ENV \parallel impSUT) \text{ and } ENV \sqsubseteq_T ENV'$$

holds, $(ENV' \parallel specSUT) \sqsubseteq_T (ENV' \parallel impSUT)$ *follows.*

Proof. Let $s \in traces(ENV' \parallel impSUT)$. This implies

1. $s \in traces(ENV') \cap traces(impSUT)$ [semantics of $\parallel$]
2. $s \in traces(ENV)$ [$ENV \sqsubseteq_T ENV'$]
3. $s \in traces(ENV \parallel impSUT)$ [semantics of $\parallel$]
4. $s \in traces(ENV \parallel specSUT)$ [$(ENV \parallel specSUT) \sqsubseteq_T (ENV \parallel impSUT)$]
5. $s \in traces(specSUT)$ [semantics of $\parallel$]
6. $s \in traces(ENV') \cap traces(specSUT)$ [1. and 5.]
7. $s \in traces(ENV' \parallel specSUT)$ [semantics of $\parallel$]
8. $(ENV' \parallel specSUT) \sqsubseteq_T (ENV' \parallel impSUT)$
                                           [Definition of (timed) trace refinement.]

$\square$

In the context of FTC testing, *specSUT* denotes the specification of the system under test, *impSUT* denotes its implementation[8] and *ENV* denotes the test environment consisting of the operational FTC environment plus the TASL residing in the FTC application layer. Let *ENV'* denote a concrete operational environment plus concrete application layer. Since the operational environment is modelled equivalently in the test environment, the relation $ENV \sqsubseteq_T ENV'$ will hold if the concrete application layer is a refinement of the TASL. From the underlying testing theory we know that successful exhaustive testing according to the test strategy implemented in RT-Tester would imply the refinement relation $(ENV \parallel specSUT) \sqsubseteq_T (ENV \parallel impSUT)$ (see [21, 22]). Now the theorem above may be interpreted as follows: suppose that an exhaustive test suite has been successfully executed in the test environment *ENV*. Further suppose that the TASL has been designed in such a way that it is refined by every concrete application layer. Then the behaviour of the FTC operating in any concrete environment plus application layer *ENV'* will be a refinement of its associated specification $(ENV' \parallel specSUT)$.

The last question to be solved is how to specify and construct a TASL satisfying the above mentioned property. Now the most general admissible behaviour of

---

[8] Of course, the explicit formal representation of *impSUT* is unknown, but its existence is guaranteed.

an application layer is defined in the programmers' reference manual specifying – at least in a semi-formal way – the interfaces and restrictions for the usage of all system services available to an application. Furthermore, restrictions regarding the maximum CPU load which may be created by applications are described there. As a consequence, the most general behaviour of an admissible application can be derived from the programmers' reference manual and serve as input for the design of the TASL. Observe however, that as long as the reference manual is an informal document, the derivation of the TASL from such a manual is a process which cannot be automated and depends on the technical insight of the specialists performing this process. As a consequence, the TASL design has to be validated carefully in order to justify the claim that the possible behaviours of every concrete admissible application layer will form a subset of the TASL behaviour.

For FTC testing, the different variants of TASL behaviour were controlled by the test engine: abstract machines running in the AML used MIL bus messages to transfer commands to the TASL. As a consequence, the expected FTC behaviour was known in the test engine at every point in time, so that evaluation of observed FTC behaviour against expected behaviour could be performed automatically. The FTC TASL activities can be roughly classified as follows:

– Data transmission and reception with variable length on the various communication channels available to the FTC application layer,
– Simulation of exceptional application behaviour, such as creation of communication overloads (to test FTC robustness in overload situations), corruption of data packages and creation of timing jitters on isolated lanes (to test fault detection capabilities of the FML voters),
– Control of FTC lane re-integration after occurrence of a lane fault,
– Control of redundant bus wires.

5   Discussion

5.1   A Summary of Verification, Simulation and Test Results

In the subsequent paragraphs, an overview of results obtained during the verification, simulation and test suite described above is presented. More details may be found in [5, 6, 30].

Verification of Deadlock and Livelock Freedom. The deadlock analysis for the AVI layer was performed at the stage when the transition from detailed design to coding had just been completed and the first informal tests were carried out by the development team. In this phase, 7 deadlock situations were uncovered during our verification suite. Only two of these errors were detected by the developers' tests, since the traces leading to the other deadlock situations involved complex communication and scheduling patterns which only occurred in rare situations. As a consequence, the probability of running into these situations during informal testing was quite low. Using the FDR-generated example traces leading to the deadlocks in combination with a manual analysis of the software design, all error situations could be clearly identified and corrected.

In one situation it turned out that the original design was too complex to be verified completely, corrections of deadlock situations led to new deadlocks at other places. The problems were related to a command leading AVI processes from an operational state back into their initial states from where they would wait until a new command was given to become active again. During this "software shutdown" procedure, deadlock situations occurred frequently and were very hard to fix. It was therefore decided to use a new process shutdown protocol designed by the authors. This protocol could be formally proven to be free of deadlocks for all types of processes applying the protocol; as a consequence it was possible to omit the shutdown procedure in the model checking process.

The FML deadlock analysis was performed at a later stage on code level, after the software design had already been carefully reviewed and the developers' test had been completed. Here only one deadlock was uncovered which could only occur in a situation where several exceptions would have happened before. The livelock analysis was carried out after the deadlock analysis. About 5 livelocks were detected in the AVI layer, no errors were found in the FML software.

Simulation Results. The simulations based on Generalised Stochastic Petri Nets models produced two main results [30]: (1) The quantitative predictions of throughput to be achieved by AVI software and hardware on the MIL-STD 1553 busses were consistent with the actual values observed during preliminary throughput tests performed with the FTC engineering qualification model. Therefore the simulation helped to increase the confidence in throughput figures obtained in these preliminary tests. (2) The most important qualitative prediction was that the throughput to be achieved by the AVI is less dependent on the ratio *"number of output messages per time interval"/"number of input messages per time interval"* but on the load *profile* in a given time interval. This qualitative result influenced the test design: it was decided to use test specifications which focused on the generation of as many different load profiles as possible. If the simulation had indicated that the input/output ratio were a critical figure, we would have concentrated on tests maximising the number of different input/output patterns.

Test Results. The FTC hardware-in-the-loop test suite uncovered twelve problems. Five of them were just discrepancies between documentation in the programmers' reference manual and the FTC implementation; for example, execution time values given in the manual for some time-critical ASS functions did not hold for certain admissible load profiles in the application layer. Though this only required a change of documentation, the discovery of these problems had an important impact on the admissible scheduling techniques to be used in the application layer: designers of application layers have to reserve longer time slots for the execution of these ASS functions; during these "housekeeping phases", application tasks should not be active.

Other errors were uncovered by the exceptional behaviour tests. For example, when resuming normal operation after re-integration of a repaired lane, the re-integrated lane discarded a time telegram sent to the FTC which was already accepted and processed by the other lanes.

The most severe errors were related to load profiles, scheduling strategies and timing: certain load distributions in the application layer caused an unacceptable timing jitter between lanes, if certain priorities (which were legal according to the reference manual) were given to specific application tasks. Furthermore, it was detected that the application layers of the four lanes would occasionally run out of sync if too many (more than 90) application tasks had to be managed by the VxWorks scheduler. Under these conditions, nondeterministic scheduling discrepancies between lanes occurred which – due to the timing jitter – led to lane isolations of otherwise fully functional lanes. These test results indicate that much more restrictive scheduling techniques than the ones declared to be admissible in the reference manual should be used in the application layer: the VxWorks scheduler is not sufficiently precise for hard real-time applications with many quasi-parallel tasks sharing one CPU. Instead, the authors' recommendation is to use deterministic prioritised round-robin scheduling with cooperative multi-tasking: a main process schedules tasks as function calls from a main loop. Each task evaluates new inputs and performs the next state transition which is determined by the internal task state and the new inputs received. The state transitions may be accompanied by outputs. After recording internal state information to be evaluated at the next activation, the task returns to the main loop from where the next application is activated by a function call. A task will only be interrupted by a software watch dog if it does not return after the maximum CPU time slice assigned to this task has been used up. Otherwise each task will be allowed to keep the CPU until it returns after having completed a full transition. According to their priority, tasks will be activated in every main loop (highest priority) or every nth main loop cycle. In fact, this scheduling scheme was adopted by the Russian development team responsible for the development of safety-critical DMS-R control applications.

Finally, a load profile was detected which led to an AVI overload problem in single-lane mode, though the average bus load produced by this profile (about 60KBytes/sec) was still less than the admissible maximum load as documented in the programmers' reference manual (90KBytes/sec). The load profile leading to this AVI problem was characterised by using a high number of short messages to achieve the average bus load. Previous tests performed by the developers had only used maximum length messages, where the AVI was stable under much higher average bus loads than the one used in this test.

5.2   Assessment of Formal Techniques Applied

Formal Verification. As explained in the preceding sections, the verification steps involved a number of manual activities that were carefully reviewed but could not be checked in a mechanical way. Therefore it is necessary to assess the completeness of the verification results obtained and the test coverage achieved. Due to the usage of very simple communication patterns in the FML software design our confidence into the adequacy of the abstractions and the completeness of the verification is very high for the FML software. For technical reasons, the AVI layer could not be designed with such simple patterns. As a consequence, the deadlock and livelock analysis results obtained for the AVI should rather be regarded as a "sophisticated test suite" which after having uncovered a number of errors did not find any new ones. However, it should be emphasised that the quality of these "tests" is much higher than what could ever be achieved by systematic but informal design reviews because of the high number of states explored during the model checking process.

The verification effort was much smaller for those parts of the system where standardised design patterns had been used by the software developers.

Simulation. The simulations could not predict the existence of specific load profiles causing problems for the AVI although the average load was still below the maximum load figure. This is due to the fact that several simplifications regarding the underlying AVI hardware had to be used in the GSPN model in order to make the simulation feasible and to keep the modelling costs within acceptable bounds. In cases where the detailed behavioural specifications of specific hardware components and the source code of off-the-shelf software used in the system implementation are not available, formal simulation models can only be approximations of the true component behaviour. Therefore the simulation results should be used as indicator which throughput aspects should be tested more closely with the real system. In this respect, they provided an excellent preparation for the selection of test strategies. Furthermore, simulations can be very helpful in early design phases to decide which design variants will result in better throughput values.

Tests. The results achieved during the hardware-in-the-loop tests obviously justify the test approach. It is noteworthy that all the critical errors uncovered during tests were related to timing and synchronisation problems. Therefore we would like to emphasise that testing should be understood as a complementary activity to (formal) verification:

- The verification activities should focus on uncovering programming bugs in data transformations and design errors related to the cooperation of parallel components.
- Testing should focus on potential problems arising from the integration of software on the hardware and on those correctness aspects where a complete formal model could not be constructed.

As was to be expected for a system of such complexity, the test coverage achieved was far from being exhaustive[9]. Therefore it was important to use a test strategy

---

[9] The situation is even worse for the test of real-time systems controlling slow physical processes or systems: since it is often impossible or not advisable to increase the controller speed for testing purposes, the achievable coverage is simply limited by time it needs to execute each test. As a consequence, the theoretical results how to achieve complete coverage and how testing may "converge" to full correctness proofs are not very helpful in this context.

focusing on the aspects which were considered to be most important. This was achieved by using *application-dependent metrics*: instead of trying to maximise a standard coverage measure – such as branch coverage on specification or code level – tests focused on maximising the coverage of different load profiles and of possible interleavings of exceptions with normal behaviour executions. We are convinced that the problems listed above could not have been uncovered if test executions had been designed to maximise a standard metrical value.

With respect to the time needed to prepare the tests, it was interesting to observe that the preparation of formal test specifications did only consume a small fraction (less than 10%) of the full preparation time: the main effort was spent on programming the test application layer described above and on connecting to the MIL-STD 1553 bus driven by the frame protocol.

5.3   Future Work and Trends

Tool Support for Abstraction Techniques. Our practical experience has shown that software code verification will always remain an important issue: instead of modelling and verifying critical sections of the detailed design in a formal way right from the start, formal methods are mostly applied a *posteriori* as a re-engineering effort, when the code produced from informal design specifications has turned out to be too buggy to be trusted without special verification measures. As a consequence, preparing program code for formal verification will remain an important part of the verification suite, and the effort required for this preparation cannot be neglected. Though at first glance it might seem attractive to develop model checkers directly interpreting programming languages in order to avoid having to perform the transformation into a formal specification language, we are convinced that the formal analysis should be kept on the level of formal specification languages such as CSP or Petri Nets: programming languages do not provide sufficient support for abstraction and refinement, therefore problem simplifications by abstraction would be rarely possible on that level. As a consequence, it seems unlikely that model checkers could process complex verification problems on programming language level without running into state explosion problems. To increase the degree of automation for verification by abstraction techniques and model checking, we advocate the following approach:

- For different programming languages, front-ends transforming programs into formal specifications should be developed. To allow a high degree of automation for this step, it should not include complex abstraction techniques, but instead lift the program code nearly in one-to-one fashion into the formal specification language representation.
- The formal specification language representation obtained from the code transformation front end will in general be too complex to be managed by a model checker. However, the new representation has the advantage to be already in the domain of the formal language and its semantics. Now a library of abstraction techniques structured by different types of verification goals could be applied in order to simplify the formal representation of the original

program until model checking (in combination with compositional reasoning and generic theories) becomes feasible.

- For verification of new programming languages, it would only be necessary to develop a new front-end for transformation into the formal language; the abstraction library could remain unchanged, since it does not depend on the programming language, but on the formal specification language and its semantics only.

Design Patterns and Generic Theories. The concepts of re-usability advertised by object orientation had a very slow start in the eighties: approaches such as the Ada Generic Package were not very widely used in practice. However, today these concepts have matured and most software designers seem to have gained a better understanding of how to benefit from re-usability; for example, it is a natural thing to use class templates and other generic concepts when programming in C++ or Java. Beyond generic class concepts, *design patterns* (that is, parameterised collaborations representing a set of parameterised classifiers, relationships and behavioural specifications) and *frameworks* (that is, patterns usable in a specific application domain) are presently becoming more popular [1, 10]. The notion of patterns shifts the focus from isolated objects and their properties to re-usable architectures comprising families of *cooperating* objects.

Initially, generic classes and design patterns have been introduced with the main intention to increase software development productivity. Today, there is a growing interest in the verification aspects of classes and patterns: what are the guaranteed correctness properties which result from using an instance of a specific generic class or from deploying a certain design pattern? What will be the impact of the design decisions on the verification and test effort needed to ensure sufficient correctness of the resulting system? We believe that the correctness properties of design patterns will gradually become more important than the properties of isolated classes, since "local errors" in isolated method implementations are often less harmful and easier to fix than errors related to the cooperation between objects: fixing problems of the latter kind often means re-designing whole portions of the system.

While in the context of the Unified Modelling Language [1, 2] design patterns and frameworks have only been defined in an informal way, closer analysis shows that they may be formally interpreted as *generic theories* in the context of formal specification languages admitting generic specifications. For example, the cooperating multiplexer/concentrator processes analysed in the verification of deadlock freedom for the FML sketched above form a design pattern defined by this specific way of communication between processes. The generic theory used to derive deadlock freedom in Theorem 1 is a correctness property valid for all instantiations of this design pattern.

We believe that the efficiency of (formal) verification may be considerably increased by providing "handbooks" of formally specified design patterns and associated generic theories[10]: system designers might pick pre-defined patterns

---

[10] A good example of the "handbook style" we have in mind is given by the generic constants and associated mathematical laws of the Z Mathematical Tool-kit as defined

and instantiate them for the specific solutions to be constructed, getting a collection of guaranteed correctness properties from the associated generic theory. Using design patterns, it might be possible to develop systems in such a way that the application-independent correctness properties (such as deadlock freedom and livelock freedom) would be automatically fulfilled. As a consequence, verification could focus on the application-specific aspects. The re-usability of generic theories associated with design patterns would justify a high effort to be invested into the verification of these theories. Therefore, we recommend to verify these theories with the support of proof tools (see [3] for an example of establishing generic theories using the HOL proof tool).

The generic theories exploited in the verification suite described in this article focus on communication patterns. For the verification of real-time systems new categories of patterns related to timing behaviour should be developed; for example, it would be useful to elaborate a family of patterns and associated theories for the handling of frame protocol communication and time-frame dependent scheduling of processes.

It remains an open question whether sufficiently powerful and widely applicable generic theories for application-dependent design patterns – that is, frameworks – will be established in the future. For example, in the application domain "fault-tolerant systems" a standard design for the full Byzantine protocol might be regarded as a framework, to be applied "off-the-shelf" as soon as mechanisms for decision making among actively redundant computers are needed.

Formal Methods, Hazard and Risk Analysis. While hazard analysis methods were originally used to investigate hardware failures and their impact on system safety, it may nowadays be regarded as state-of-the-art to extend hazard analysis to software components [17, 29]. In the context of safety-critical controllers, this is only natural, since software failures are certainly just as hazardous as hardware crashes. Among the various techniques of hazard analysis, *Fault-Tree Analysis* is of greatest value, since it allows us to consider logical combinations of local faults and their impact on global system safety. Moreover, fault-trees can be mechanically transformed into safety requirements for a controller. Conversely, a formal fault-tree representation can be used to verify safety mechanisms designed for a controller: analysing the "parallel combination" of a fault-tree model and the safety mechanism, it can be shown by model checking that the root of the fault-tree – that is, the hazard – can never be reached as long as the safety-mechanism shows its specified behaviour [14, 15].

A more subtle application of hazard analysis methods – specifically, fault-tree analysis – is becoming increasingly important. Fault-tree analysis and *Failure Modes and Effects analysis* [29, pp. 33] are extremely useful for *partial* (formal) software verification [17, pp. 615] and the design of test strategies: in most real-world applications, complete software verification will be infeasible. Therefore

---

by M. Spivey [28]. However, the Z Mathematical Tool-kit corresponds to isolated generic classes and theories about them. There is nothing equivalent to design patterns in [28].

it is important to identify those software components whose malfunction may really endanger system safety. In a good controller design, these components will represent only a small subset of all software modules, so formal verification and the main testing efforts could focus on these critical modules and their interaction. Hazard analysis methods can be used to identify the critical components and to justify why other modules may be checked with less effort.

Hazard analysis is complemented by risk analysis calculating the probability of a hazardous event and its consequences to occur [29, p. 60]. In this field, there still remains an important gap to be bridged between formal specification languages and safety-critical systems engineering: while it suffices for hazard analysis to have nondeterministic constructs in the specification language – for example, in terms like

$$SERVER = request?x \rightarrow (PROCESS\_REQUEST(x) \sqcap SERVER\_FAILURE)$$

– risk analysis requires to associate nondeterministic alternatives with probabilities, but in most formal specification languages, stochastic aspects cannot be expressed. To our knowledge, only very few attempts to extend CSP semantics in the direction of stochastic models have been made (see, for example [32] for such an approach) and currently, no tool support seems to be available for such models. As a consequence, the usability of CSP cannot be extended to risk analysis, to stochastic load analysis or to the development of test strategies based on stochastic models. For these reasons, we regard stochastic extensions for Timed CSP and similar formal specification languages to be of high importance to improve their usability in the context of safety-critical systems.

5.4   A Concluding Remark About Formal Methods and Ethics

In all the industrial verification and testing projects we have performed so far, it was never the case that Formal Methods have been utilised to *increase* product quality. Instead, they were applied in situations where adequate product quality could be achieved with *less effort* – by mechanised evaluation of formal specifications for verification by model checking or automated testing – than with conventional methods. Today, cost considerations even dominate the areas of safety-critical systems development, quality assurance and operation – the ICE train catastrophe in Eschede 1998 being the most dramatic recent example of the consequences of quality control driven by an emphasis on cost minimisation. We expect that the industrial applications of tool-supported Formal Methods will continually increase with the very objective to further reduce product assessment costs. It is therefore our responsibility as scientists and practitioners not to be carried away by the enthusiasm to advertise the benefits of our favourite methods and tools, but instead to explain the project-dependent limitations of automated formal verification, validation and test suites in an unambiguous way.

Acknowledgements. The authors would like to express their gratitude to Hans Langmaack for supporting their scientific careers. His knowledge, views and philosophical attitude towards Formal Methods, Mathematics, and Computer Science have stimulated our research work in an invaluable way.

The work presented in this article summarises results that would not have been obtained without the considerable contributions of our collaborators Rachel Cardell-Oliver (University of Essex), Hans-Joachim Kolinowitz, Michel Kouvaras, and Gerd Urban (DaimlerChrysler Aerospace Bremen), Hui Shi and Holger Schlingloff (TZI-BISS at the University of Bremen).

References

1. Booch, G., Rumbaugh, J. and Jacobsen, I.: *The Unified Modeling Language User Guide.* Addison-Wesley (1998).
2. Booch, G., Rumbaugh, J. and Jacobsen, I.: *The Unified Modeling Language Reference Manual.* Addison-Wesley (1999).
3. Buth, B., Cardell-Oliver, R., Peleska, J.: Combining tools for the verification of fault-tolerant systems. In Berghammer, R., Buth, B., Peleska, J. (eds.), *Tools for Software Development and Verification*, Monographs of the Bremen Institute of Safe Systems 1, Shaker Verlag, (1998), ISBN 3-8265-3806-4.
4. Bettina Buth: PAMELA+PVS (Abstract for Tool Demo) In Michael Johnson (Ed.): Algebraic Methodology and Software Technology. Proceedings of the AMAST'97, Sidney, Australia, December 1997, Springer LNCS 1349 (1997), 560-562.
5. Buth, B., Kouvaras, M., Peleska, J., Shi, H.: Deadlock analysis for a fault-tolerant system. In Johnson, M. (ed.), *Algebraic Methodology and Software Technology. Proceedings of the AMAST'97*, number 1349 in LNCS, pages 60–75. Springer, December 1997.
6. Buth, B., Peleska, J., Shi, H.: Combining Methods for the Livelock Analysis of a Fault-Tolerant System. In A. M. Haeberer (Ed.): Algebraic Methodology and Software Technology. Proceedings of the 7th International Conference, AMAST 98, Amazonia, Brazil, January 1999. Springer LNCS 1548, pp. 124-139, 1998.
7. Buth, B., Peleska, J., Shi, H.: Combining Methods for the Analysis of a Fault-Tolerant System. CD-ROM Proceedings of the 12th International Software Quality Week, May 24-28, 1999, Software Research Institute.
8. Dierks, H.: PLC-Automata: A New Class of Implementable Real-Time Automata. In M. Bertran and T. Rus, editors, Transformation-Based Reactive Systems Development (ARTS'97), volume 1231 of Lecture Notes in Computer Science, pages 111-125. Springer-Verlag, 1997.
9. Formal Systems: *FDR2 User Manual* Formal Systems (Europe) Lts (1997). Available under `http://www.formal.demon.co.uk/fdr2manual/index.html`
10. Gamma, E., Helm, R., Johnson, R. and Vlissides, J.: Design Patterns: Elements of Reusable Object-Oriented Software Addison-Wesley (1995)
11. D. Harel, A. Pnueli, J. Pruzan-Schmidt and R. Sherman. *On the formal semantics of Statecharts.* In *Proceedings Symposium on Logic in Computer Science*, (1987) 54-64.
12. Hoare, C.A.R.: *Communicating Sequential Processes.* Prentice-Hall International (1985).

13. Lamport, L., Shostak, R., Pease, M.: *The Byzantine Generals Problem*, In: ACM Transactions on Programming Languages and Systems, Vol.4, Nr. 3, (1982)
14. Lankenau, A., Meyer, O. and Krieg-Brückner, B.: Safety in Robotics: The Bremen Autonomous Wheelchair. In: Proceedings of AMC'98 - Coimbra, 5th Int. Workshop on Advanced Motion Control, Coimbra, Portugal 1998. ISBN 0-7803-4484-7. pp. 524-529.
15. Lankenau, A., Meyer, O.: Formal Methods in Robotics: Fault Tree Based Verification. Submitted to Quality Week Europe 99.
16. R.S.Lazić: *Theories for mechanical verification of data-independent CSP*, Oxford University Computing Laboratory technical report, 1997.
17. Lyu, M. R. (ed.): *Handbook of Software Reliability Engineering*, IEEE Computer Society Press, Computing McGraw-Hill (1995).
18. Milner, R.: *Communication and Concurrency*. Prentice-Hall International (1989).
19. J. Peleska: Test Automation for Safety-Critical Systems: Industrial Application and Future Developments. In M.-C. Gaudel and J. Woodcock (Eds.): FME '96: Industrial Benefit and Advances in Formal Methods. LNCS 1051, Springer-Verlag, Berlin Heidelberg New York (1996) 39-59.
20. J. Peleska: Formal Methods and the Development of Dependable Systems. Habilitationsschrift, Bericht Nr. 9612, Dezember 1996, Institut für Informatik und Praktische Mathematik, Christian-Albrechts-Universität Kiel (1997).
21. J. Peleska and M. Siegel: Test Automation of Safety-Critical Reactive Systems. *South African Computer Jounal* (1997)19:53-77.
22. Peleska, J.: Testing Reactive Real-Time Systems. Tutorial, held at the FTRTFT '98. Denmark Technical University, Lyngby (1998).
23. J. Peleska and C. Zahlten: Test Automation for Avionic Systems and Space Technology (Extended Abstract). Softwaretechnik-Trends (1999)19:34-36.
24. Roscoe, A. W.: *The Theory and Practice of Concurrency*. Prentice-Hall International (1998).
25. Shi, H., Peleska, J.: *Daimler-Benz Aerospace – Project DMS-R, FTC Development – Fault Management Layer (FML): Verification of Byzantine Agreement Protocol Implementation*. Technical Report, JP Software-Consulting, (1998).
26. Schneider, S.: An Operational Semantics for Timed CSP. *Information and Computation*, 116:193–213, 1995.
27. Shi, H., Peleska, J. and Kouvaras, M: Combining Methods for the Analysis of a Fault-Tolerant System. Submitted to 1999 Pacific Rim International Symposium on Dependable Computing (PRDC 1999).
28. M. J. Spivey. *The Z Notation*. Prentice-Hall International, Englewood Cliffs NJ (1992).
29. Storey, N.: *Safety-Critical Computer Systems*. Addison-Wesley (1996).
30. L. Twele, H. Schlingloff, H. Szczerbicka: Performability Analysis of an Avionics-Interface; Proc. IEEE Conf. on Systems, Man and Cybernetics; San Diego, N.J., pp. 499-504, (Oct. 1998)
31. Gerd Urban, Hans-Joachim Kolinowitz and Jan Peleska: A Survivable Avionics System for Space Applications. Published in Proceedings of the FTCS-28, 28th Annual Symposium on Fault-Tolerant Computing, Munich, June 23-25, 1998, 372-381.
32. Zhiming Liu, E. V. Sørensen, A. P. Ravn and Chaochen Zhou: Towards a Calculus of System Dependability. *Journal of high integrity systems* (1994) 1: 49-65 .

METAFrame in Practice:
Design of Intelligent Network Services

Bernhard Steffen[1] and Tiziana Margaria[2]

[1] LS V, Universität Dortmund, Baroper Str.301, D-44221 Dortmund (Germany),
steffen@cs.uni-dortmund.de
[2] LS I, Universität Dortmund, Otto-Hahn Str. 16, D-44227 Dortmund (Germany),
tiziana@sunshine.cs.uni-dortmund.de

Abstract. In this paper we present METAFrame, an environment for formal methods-based, application-specific software design. Characteristic for METAFrame are the following features: *library-based development*, meaning software construction by combination of components on a *coarse granular level*, *incremental formalization*, through successive enrichment of a special-purpose development environment, and *library-based consistency checking*, allowing continuous verification of application- and purpose-specific properties by means of model checking.

These features and their impact for application developers and end users will be illustrated along an industrial application, the design of intelligent network (IN) services.

1 Motivation

With the increasing dependency of every day's life on computer-aided support, moving large portions of the needed application programming load from programming experts to application experts or even to end users becomes a major challenge. For application experts, this requires *freeing* programming activities, intrinsic to the development of applications, from their current need of *programming expertise*. For end users, taking over advanced reshapings of applications additionally requires freedom from expertise in the particular *application domain*.

Classical software engineering tools do not provide means to support the required 'programming-free' programming style. They are typically designed to support programming experts in their usual programming activities, e.g. by starting from semi-formal modelling or description languages like OMT and later UML, as in the case of ObjectGEODE [14], or from Statecharts, as for Statemate [11], or from SDL, as for SDT and more recently Tau [26], or Petri Nets, as for Design/CPN [13, 8]. This target is shared by and large also by the known formal methods-based tools, which provide support to development activities by means of refinement from specifications expressed in various specification languages (like e.g. [1, 2] or [17]). These methods and tools are better suited to design from scratch rather than for reengineering and component integration purposes, and tend to require both programming and verification skills.

E.-R. Olderog, B. Steffen (Eds.): Correct System Design, LNCS 1710, pp. 390–415, 1999.
© Springer-Verlag Berlin Heidelberg 1999

On the other hand there are industrial tools supporting a (graphical) component-based programming style, like e.g., the visual modelling in Rational's Suite [18], supporting Microsoft's Visual Studio, or the Rapid Application Development now included in Oracle's Designer [16]. But these tools do not provide any sophisticated means for consistency control.

In this paper we present our experience with METAFrame, a tool for *formal methods-based, application-specific* software design, which is designed for directly supporting the 'programming-free' programming style of applications. To our knowledge, METAFrame is unique in using formal methods to explicitly address the issue of separation of concerns between programmers, application experts, and end users.

The remainder of this section sketches the METAFrame environment, before giving some background of the application domain, the development of Intelligent Network Services, which we will use to explain our approach in more detail.

1.1 The METAFrame Environment

We provide here an overview of METAFrame in the light of the announced 'programming-free programming' paradigm of application development. This imposes to stress the following characteristics:

Behaviour-Oriented Development: Application development consists in the behaviour-oriented combination of Building Blocks (BBs)[1] on a *coarse* granular level. BBs are here identified on a functional basis, understandable to application experts, and usually encompass a number of 'classical' programming units (be they procedures, classes, modules, or functions). They are organized in application-specific collections. In contrast to (other) component-based approaches, e.g., for object-oriented program development, METAFrame focusses on the dynamic behaviour: (complex) functionalities are graphically stuck together to yield flow graph-like structures embodying the application behaviour in terms of control. This graph structure is independent of the paradigm of the underlying programming language, which, as in the application described later, may, e.g., well be an object-oriented language: here the coarse granular BBs are themselves implemented using all the object oriented features, and only their combination is organized operationally. In particular, we view this flow-graph structure as a control-oriented coordination layer on top of data-oriented communication mechanisms enforced e.g. via RMI, CORBA or (D)COM. Accordingly, the purely graphical combination of BBs' behaviours happens at a more abstract level, and can be implemented in any of these technologies.

---

[1] BBs are software components with a particularly simple interface. This kind of interface enables one to view BBs semantically just as input/output transformations. Additional interaction structure can also be modelled, but is not subject to the formal synthesis and verification methods (see Sections 3.3 and 3.6).

Incremental Formalization: The successive enrichment of the application-specific development environment is two-dimensional. Besides the library of application specific BBs, which dynamically grows whenever new functionalities are made available, METAFrame supports the dynamic growth of a hierarchically organized library of *constraints*, controlling and governing the adequate use of these BBs within application programs. This library is intended to grow with the experience gained while using the environment, e.g., detected errors, strengthened policies, and new BBs may directly impose the addition of constraints. It is the possible *looseness* of these constraints which makes the constraints highly reusable and intuitively understandable. Here we consciously privilege understandability and practicality of the specification mechanisms over their completeness.

Library-Based Consistency Checking: Throughout the behaviour-oriented development process, METAFrame offers access to mechanisms for the verification of libraries of constraints by means of model checking. The model checker individually checks hundreds of typically very small and application- and purpose-specific constraints over the flow graph structure. This allows concise and comprehensible diagnostic information in the case of a constraint violation, in particular as the information is given at the application rather than at the programming level.

These characteristics are the key towards distributing labour according to the various levels of expertise. We envisage

Programming Experts: They are responsible for the software infrastructure, the runtime-environment for the compiled services, as well as the programming of BBs. Infrastructure and BB development require advanced programming expertise. In comparison, the wrapping of existing (legacy) components to BBs, which is explicitly supported by METAFrame, is simpler, as it always follows a similar pattern.

Constraint Modelling Experts: They classify the BBs, typically according to technical criteria like their version or specific hardware or software requirements, their origin (where they were developed) and, here, most importantly, according to their intent for a given application area. The resulting classification scheme (called taxonomy, Section 2.1) is the basis for the constraint definition in terms of modal formulas. The design of the taxonomies should go hand in hand with the definition of aspect-specific views, as both are mutually supportive means to an application specific structuring of the design process.

Application Experts: They develop concrete applications, by graphically combining BBs into coarse-granular flow graphs. These graphs can be immediately executed by means of an interpreter, in order to validate the intended behaviour (rapid prototyping). Model checking (Sect. 3.3) guarantees the consistency of the constructed graph with respect to the constraint library.

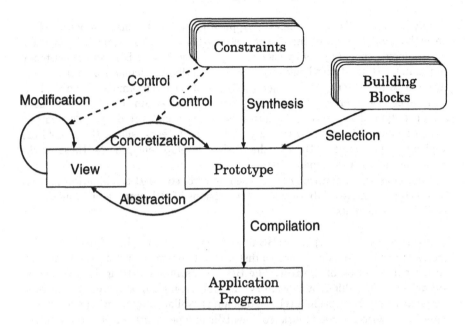

Fig. 1. Application Development Process in MᴇᴛᴀFrame

End Users: They may modify a given application program by adding requirements in terms of behavioural traces. These requirements are then 'merged' with the given program to obtain a new application program that behaves as required along the new defining traces, but still as the original program everywhere else. Section 3.6 sketches this method together with the required frame conditions.

The collection of professional profiles needed is often dictated by the application domain. The above list can of course be refined much further.

The resulting overall lifecycle for application development using MᴇᴛᴀFrame is two-dimensional: both the application and the environment can be enriched during the development process.

Application Development. Its corresponding lifecycle is summarized in Figure 1. Based on libraries of BBs and constraints, an initial application program (the prototype) is graphically constructed under model checking control, and subsequently modified in an aspect-driven fashion: the application expert chooses an aspect of interest, generates the corresponding view abstracting from all irrelevant details, and modifies it where necessary. The effect of the modification can be automatically transferred to the underlying application program in a concretization step. This cycle is iterated until all relevant aspects have been treated. Due to the on-line verification with the model checker, constraint violations are immediately detected. Current prototypes can at any time be tested, compiled, executed, and, if satisfactory, stored in a repository.

Strengthening of the Environment. Application development is superposed by an orthogonal process of incremental strengthening of the application-specific environment: this happens by successively adding further BBs and consistency constraints. Both strengthenings proceed naturally, on demand: new BBs may turn out to become necessary when the range of the environment or the application are enlarged, or when it becomes obvious that certain code fragments have a high potential for reuse. The latter situation is supported by METAFrame's macro facility [23], which essentially allows one to encapsulate (fragments of) application programs as BBs. In the further development process, these blocks can be used just as 'ordinary' BBs.

New constraints naturally arise when an erroneous BB combination pattern is detected in the test lab, or when new versions of BBs impose or induce compatibility constraints.

METAFrame explicitly separates BB implementations from their descriptions: for each application domain we have a distinct Meta-Data repository containing an abstract description of the BBs. The BBs themselves and their documentation are available in a different repository. As prototyping can start already as soon as the abstract description level of a domain is available, application experts can experiment with the combination of new BBs independently of their direct physical availability. This experimentation phase may in fact influence the choice and design of new BBs. In fact, METAFrame explicitly encourages feedback flowing from the application experts to the programming experts by allowing abstract descriptions of BBs to be associated with simulation code, in order to prototypically use new BBs before they are actually implemented.

Rather than providing a technical description of all these features and their impact, we will illustrate them along an industrial application: the design of intelligent network (IN) services. We gained experience in the area during an intense industrial cooperation in 1995/96, which led to a product that has been adopted, bought, and marketed by Siemens Nixdorf Informationssysteme AG (SNI) [20, 22, 23, 5, 21].

1.2   Intelligent Network Services

Intelligent Networks have changed the world of telecommunication in the last decade: by integrating telecommunication and computer technology, the Intelligent Network concept (see [9] for an overview) helps (network) providers to make new and flexible telecommunication services available to their customers. Concretely, complex programs steer the call handling of special telephone services, ranging from simple Free Phone services, where the called party pays the bill, to ambitious Virtual Private Network services establishing a distributed, private telephone network for a group of users within the public network.

In fact, practically everybody has already made use of IN services. Particularly widespread examples are Televoting, Personal Mobility services, or Premium Rate Services, which enable the service subscriber to supply certain in-

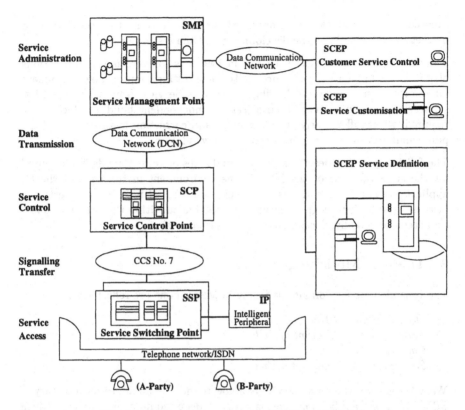

Fig. 2. Global Architecture of an Intelligent Network

formation (train schedules, stock quotes) under a unique number and against a usage fee. To satisfy the growing expectations on IN services, a flexible Service Definition Environment is a must. This need is independent of the current shift of emphasis from IN solutions towards *unified messaging* approches comprising also IP, GSM, satellite communication.

The underlying Intelligent Network Architecture (see Fig. 2) is composed of several subsystems that cooperate to implement the intended functionality. They form *complex distributed systems*, where central computers, databases, the telephone network, and a huge number of peripherals must be coordinated under real-time, availability, and performance constraints. This complex structure makes modifications and extensions difficult and error prone. In particular, the design of new services must take into account requirements imposed by the underlying intelligent network: e.g., system-dependent frame conditions must be obeyed in order to guarantee reliable execution of the new services.

Therefore, the introduction of complex services like the ones mentioned above typically still takes expert-years for development and testing. A good Service Definition Environment is intended to support a reliable service development, tailored to the specifics of the intelligent network, in order to shorten time to market by reducing both the development and the testing phase.

The challenge of the project with SNI in 1995 was to overcome the limitations of standard 'clipboard-architectures' with some testing support: an environment for the creation of advanced Intelligent Network Services from a library of basic service components called SIBs (service independent building blocks) was required, which offers early error detection and correction features beyond the pure simulation-based approaches to service validation.

The following section describes the essential steps of domain modelling required for the successful use of the METAFrame environment in the light of the IN application. The impact of this modelling is illustrated in Section 3. Section 4 discusses the major design decisions for METAFrame within the chosen application scenario. Finally, Section 5 presents our conclusions.

2   Domain Modelling

The central steps for domain modelling in METAFrame are reflected by

- *Identification of SIBs*
- *Taxonomic classification of SIBs*[2]
- *Constraint Modelling*
- *Structural and Behavioural Views*

We will not enter the discussion here of how to identify an appropriate library of SIBs for a given application. This is part of a deep requirements analysis, which is typically dominated by the application experts in cooperation with the modelling expert.[3] METAFrame allows SIBs to be implemented in different application languages (C, ML, C++) of different programming paradigms (imperative, functional, object-oriented). This is important whenever legacy components need to be addressed. In this respect, this project dealt with a pure reorganization of the application development environment on top of legacy BBs: the underlying SIB library remained untouched.

We now turn our attention to describing the use of taxonomies, models, constraints, and views in this application.

2.1   Taxonomies

SIBs have an associated abstract description in terms of a *taxonomic classification* which establishes their (coarse) application profile within METAFrame. Far from capturing their complete semantics (like e.g. algebraic specification approaches), taxonomic specifications are here intended to provide an abstract, application-specific characterization based on a collection of predicates.

---

[2] In the full setting, we taxonomically classify BBs and types.

[3] 'Historical' growth of the SIB library, like in the IN-application, may severely hinder an efficient development of applications.

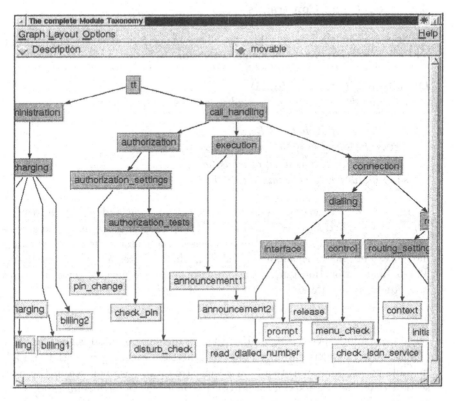

Fig. 3. Fragment of the SIB Taxonomy

Formally, taxonomies are labelled directed acyclic graphs. In this case, sinks represent concrete SIBs, the atomic entities of the taxonomy, and intermediate nodes represent groups, i.e., sets of SIBs with a particular profile. Edges reflect an *is-a* relation between their target and source node. Figure 3 shows a fragment of the SIB taxonomy as it is presented by the hypertext system. Here `pin-change` and `check-pin` are both sinks, and represent SIBs of the group `authorization`.

The development of adequate taxonomies is a crucial part of the domain modelling as it provides users with an application-specific handle to the available BBs. Thus, in general, taxonomies must be extended not only when new functionalities are integrated, but also whenever one wants to establish a new 'application-specific view' on the so far integrated functionalities: the same BB may well be taxonomically classified completely differently in different application domains. E.g. establishing a network connection is quite central in the area of telecommunication, whereas it may be regarded just as a 'commodity' in another application area.

In this project the taxonomies were defined freely, on top of an SNI-specific set of SIBs implementing the IN-functionality defined in the ITU standard.

2.2   Models and Constraints

Services are modelled as flow graphs, whose nodes represent elementary SIBs, and whose edges represent branching conditions.[4]

Definition 1 (Service Model).

A service model is defined as a quadruple $(S, Act, \rightarrow, s_0)$ where

- *S is the set of available SIBs,*
- *Act is the set of possible branching conditions,*
- *$\rightarrow \subseteq S \times Act \times S$ is a set of transitions,*
- *s_0 is the uniquely determined initial SIB.*

In METAFrame service models are subject to *local* and *global constraints* which, in conjunction, offer a means to identify critical patterns in the service graph already during the early design phase. The classification of constraints into local and global is important, as each kind requires a specific treatment. The on-line verification during the design of a new service, however, captures both kinds of constraints.

Local Constraints.

Local constraints specify single SIBs, their branching potential, as well as their admissible subsequent parameterization. Whereas branching potential and admissible parameterization require a special treatment, we will see in the next section that the loose specification of SIBs in terms of *taxonomy expressions* enters the global constraint language in form of atomic propositions.

Definition 2 (Taxonomy Expressions).

Let TAX be a taxonomy over some set. Then we can construct the corresponding set of taxonomy expressions by:

$$\text{te} ::= A \mid \neg \text{ te} \mid \text{te} \wedge \text{te} \mid \text{te} \vee \text{te}$$

where nodes $A \in TAX$ are taken as atomic propositions.

Thus local SIB specifications are formulated as simple propositional logic formulas over the respective taxonomies, which are regarded as definitions of *sets of* basic predicates (atoms).

The verification of local constraints is invoked during the global verification process. In the following we will omit details about the rather straightforward local verification and concentrate on the more interesting global constraints.

---

[4] This modelling was preferred by SNI to the standard transition system-based modelling in METAFrame, where BBs are represented by nodes and types by edges. The underlying model checking and synthesis components of METAFrame easily adapt to this modelling.

Global Constraints: The Temporal Aspect.
Global constraints allow users to specify causality, eventuality and other vital relationships between SIBs, which are necessary in order to guarantee executability and other frame conditions.

A service property is global if it does not only involve the immediate neighbourhood of a SIB in the service model[5], but also relations between SIBs which may be arbitrarily distant and separated by arbitrarily heterogeneous submodels. The treatment of global properties is required in order to capture the essence of the expertise of designers about do's and don'ts of service creation, e.g. which SIBs are incompatible, or which can or cannot occur before/after some other SIBs. Such properties are rarely straightforward, sometimes they are documented as exceptions in thick user manuals, but more often they are not documented at all, and have been discovered at a hard price as bugs of previously developed services. They are perfect examples of the kind of precious domain-specific knowledge that expert designers accumulate over the years, and which is therefore particularly worthwhile to include in the design environment for future automatic reuse.

In the presented environment such properties are gathered in a Constraint Library, which can be easily updated and which is automatically accessed by the model checker during the verification.

Besides the looseness in the specification of single BBs at the abstract level of the taxonomies, METAFrame also supports the loose specification of whole call flows in terms of abstract constraints specifying precedences, eventuality, and conditional occurrence of single taxonomy objects. Typical pattern for this kind of loose specification are

- *general ordering properties*, like

  this BB must be executed/reached some time before some other BB,

- *abstract liveness properties*, like

  a certain BB is required to be executed/reached eventually, and

- *abstract safety properties*, like

  two certain BBs must never occur within the same run of the system.

In particular, users can specify elaborate requirements concerning the interplay between the occurrences of SIBs and conditions during the run of a specified IN-service. In the following we present an according temporal logic, which comprises the taxonomic specifications of SIBs.

Definition 3 (SLTL).

The syntax of Semantic Linear-time Temporal Logic (SLTL) is given in BNF format by:

---

[5] I.e., the set of all the predecessors/successors of a SIB along all paths in the model.

$$\Phi ::= \text{ te } | \ \neg\Phi \ | \ (\Phi \wedge \Phi) \ | <c> \Phi \ | \ \mathbf{G}(\Phi) \ | \ (\Phi\mathbf{U}\Phi)$$

where te *represents a SIB constraint formulated as taxonomy expression, and c a possible condition.*

In the IN-application, SLTL formulas are interpreted over the set of all *legal call flows*, i.e. alternating sequences of SIBs and conditions[6] which start and end with SIBs. The semantics of SLTL formulas is now intuitively defined as follows:[7]

- *te* is satisfied by every call flow whose first element (a SIB) satisfies the taxonomy expression *te* .

- Negation ¬ and conjunction ∧ are interpreted in the usual fashion.

- Next-time operator < > :
  $<c> \Phi$ is satisfied by all call flows whose second element (the first condition) satisfies c and whose *continuation*[8] satisfies Φ. In particular, $<tt> \Phi$ is satisfied by every call flow whose continuation satisfies Φ.

- Generally operator $\mathbf{G}$:
  $\mathbf{G}(\Phi)$ requires that Φ is satisfied for every suffix[9].

- Until operator $\mathbf{U}$:
  $(\Phi\mathbf{U}\Psi)$ expresses that the property Φ holds at all BBs of the sequence, until a position is reached where the corresponding continuation satisfies the property Ψ. Note that $\Phi\mathbf{U}\Psi$ guarantees that the property Ψ holds eventually (strong until).

The definitions of continuation and suffix may seem complicated at first. However, thinking in terms of paths within a flow graph clarifies the situation: a subpath always starts with a node (SIB) again.

The interpretation of the logic over service models is defined path-wise: a service model satisfies a SLTL formula if all its paths do.

The introduction of *derived operators* supports a modular and intuitive formulation of complex properties. Convenient are the dual operators

$$
\begin{array}{llll}
\textit{False}: & f\!f & =_{df} \neg tt \\
\textit{Disjunction}: & \Phi \vee \Psi & =_{df} \neg(\neg\Phi \wedge \neg\Psi) \\
\textit{Box}: & [c]\Phi & =_{df} \neg <c> (\neg\Phi) \\
\textit{Eventually}: & \mathbf{F}(\Phi) & =_{df} \neg\mathbf{G}(\neg\Phi) & = & (tt \ \mathbf{U} \ \Phi)
\end{array}
$$

The following two simple examples illustrate typical loose sequencing constraints which can be conveniently specified in SLTL:

---

[6] The absence of a condition is identified with the condition **true**.

[7] A formal definition of the semantics can be found in [19].

[8] This continuation is simply the call flow starting from the second SIB.

[9] A suffix of a call flow is any subsequence arising from deleting the first 2n elements (n any natural number).

– **F** (connect)
which means 'A connect SIB is guaranteed to be reached eventually'.

– **G** (connect ⇒ **F**(charging))
which is a liveness property meaning 'Whenever a connect SIB occurs, then
a charging SIB is guaranteed to eventually occur as well'.

First-Order Extension. Our temporal logic also allows for first-order quantification over finite parameter domains [12]. Quantified formulas are expanded as
needed for the considered service so that they can be checked by our iterative
model checker. This may lead to an explosion of the number of constraints to
be checked, but in our experience this did not turn out to be a serious bottleneck. Section 3.5 illustrates the use of these constraints in our Service Definition
environment.

2.3   Views

The definition of aspect-specific views is part of the domain modelling phase,
which is itself an incremental process. *Structural Views* allow capturing a system (here, a service) at a certain level of granularity, where subsystems are
encapsulated as single SIBs. *Behavioural Views* are based on the idea of hiding
aspects, like a specific kind of SIBs or conditions. These views can be defined
explicitly by defining equivalences, i.e., visibility relations, on the set of SIBs
and conditions, together with some structural properties, like the preservation
of branching structure[10], or implicitly by means of temporal formulas.

Structural Views: Macros.
Technically, hierarchy is realized in form of a powerful mechanism for the definition, parametrization and reuse of *macros*, which is fully compatible with
both formal verification and behavioural views. The macro facility covers the
standard *stepwise refinement* approaches. This allows developers to define whole
subservices as primitive entities, which can be used just like SIBs. As macros
may be defined on-line and expanded whenever their interna become relevant,
this supports a truly incremental service construction. Moreover, as macros have
formally the same interfaces as SIBs, this enhances the reuse of already designed
(sub-) services.

Behavioural Views.
Behavioural views are *abstract* service models. As such, they show aspects of
actual, concrete models. They are used to hide any aspect of an IN model which
is irrelevant wrt. an intended operation. This is useful during the development
phase in order to concentrate on specific themes, e.g., the billing or the user-
interaction contained in a service, while abstracting from all the rest. This com-
plements the macro facility (for structural views) in order to attack the problem

---

[10] In our case this is defined in terms of bisimulation[15].

of growing size of services, which may contain several hundreds of nodes and which are in their whole unmanageable.

Most useful are *error views*, which are implicitly defined by global constraints. They reduce the service size on the basis of the so-called *model collapse* [24]. Their pragmatics is illustrated in the next section.

In their handling, views do not differ much from the actual IN models. E.g. they can be loaded and edited in the usual way, however, often with quite dramatic effects: minor modifications on views may correspond to radical structural changes of the underlying concrete model. In addition, views can be *created*, corresponding to the application of an abstraction function, and *applied* to the underlying concrete model, corresponding to the application of a concretization function (cf. Fig. 1 and 5). *Execution* of a view means execution of the underlying concrete model.

Fig. 4 shows a version of the UPT service, which has 158 nodes and 239 edges together with a comprehensible error view: just 10 nodes and 16 edges. Spotting the errors (informally explained in the pop-up window) in the original service graph is difficult, even though their location is indicated here by the thick arrows.

3   Using the METAFrame-based Service Definition

The service definition environment must be easily usable also for pure application experts: IN-service designers with hardly any programming skills. They graphically build services on top of the SIBs, usually interactively, in cooperation or even in presence of the customers, and need an intuitive tool support which does not restrict creativity.

3.1   Background

Service Definition (SD) Environments for the creation of IN-services are usually based on classical 'Clipboard-Architecture' environments, where services are graphically constructed, compiled, and successively tested. Two extreme approaches to error handling characterize the state of the art of marketed SD environments:

- The *avoidance* approach guarantees consistency by construction, but the design process is strongly limited in its flexibility to compose SIBs to new services. A representative of this category is e.g. described in [4], where the output of a Service Logic element is checked for its consumability by its successor.
- The *creative* approach allows flexible compositions of services, but provides little or no feedback on the correctness of the service under creation during the development: the validation is almost entirely located after the design is completed. Thus the resulting test phase is lengthy and costly. [27] describes an IN environment to develop, in several cycles, service logic program

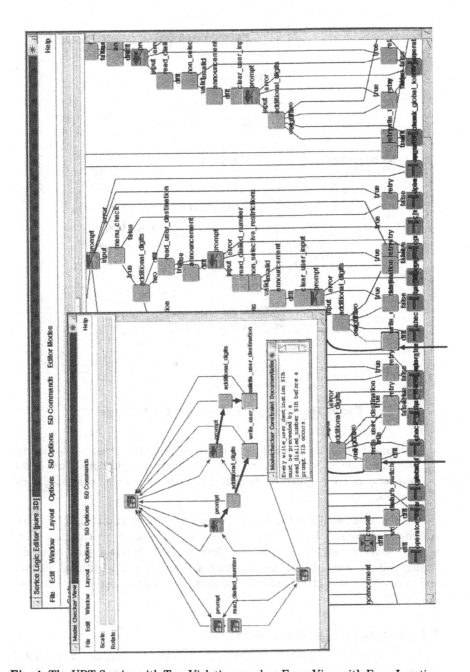

Fig. 4. The UPT Service with Two Violations, and an Error View with Error Location

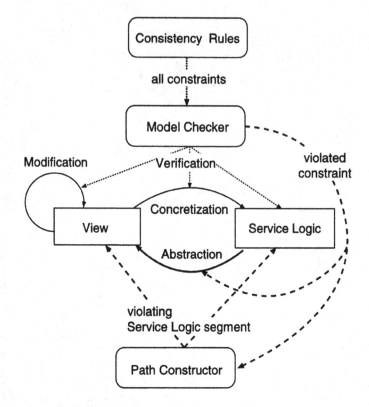

Fig. 5. The Service Design Process in IN-METAFrame

instances from SIBs. After the services have been developed in the simulation environment, with a rich execution environment, additional tests of the new services are required in the live environment replacing simulated components.

Our environment conjoins the desirable features of both approaches: the constraint-based Service Logic design restricts the liberal approach only where needed, while it provides a handle for formal methods-based early error detection and correction techniques. In combination with the traditional features and the sophisticated error correction support, this drastically reduces the 'time to market'.

3.2   The Service Design Process

Figure 5, an application-specific refinement of Figure 1, summarizes the global structure of our approach, which supports an arbitrary decomposition of the design process. This is necessary, since the same Service Design environment is shared by teams of users with completely different profiles. We offer the needed design flexibility by means of the second of the following three phases:

1. A first draft of the service is usually obtained via modification of a pre-existing service of similar application profile from the service library. A completely new design from scratch is also possible. Both design styles are supported by the macro facility and happen under model checking control.

2. The central design step consists of repeated, aspect-driven modification, implementing a *point-of-view* design strategy: the user chooses an aspect of interest, generates a corresponding view of the current service which abstracts from all details irrelevant for this point of view, and modifies it where necessary. Due to the on-line verification with the model checker, which is separately applicable also on views, constraint violations can be detected immediately. In this phase automatic expansion of macros may be required, in order to resolve 'internal errors'. The effect of view modifications can be automatically transferred to the underlying model. This 'apply' operation is automatically supervised by the model checker: modifications disrupting the service structure are rejected.

3. Current service prototypes can at any time be tested, compiled, executed, and, if satisfactory, stored in the service repository.

In combination with our concept of macros, views provide an extremely flexible service development. In addition, views support the realization of a very flexible *access control mechanism*, by enabling designers and service providers to define customer specific views with restricted modification potential. Views provide in fact a natural means to organize the central design process (step 2) into successive levels of refinement taking adequate care of role-specific areas of competences. In particular this allows us to tailor the environment for the specific needs of the service designer, the service provider, the customizer, and the user. The view-specific hiding can be used to automatically define and enforce access permissions.

3.3   Model Checking-Based Formal Verification

The service creation process is constantly accompanied by on-line verification of the *global* correctness and consistency of the service logic (Fig. 5). Vital properties concerning the *interplay* between (arbitrarily distant) SIBs of a service and the executability conditions for intermediate prototypes can be verified at any time during the design phase in a push-button fashion,via model checking. Design decisions that conflict with the constraints and consistency conditions of the intended service are thus immediately detected.

Global properties concerning the interplay between the SIBs of a service are expressed in a user-friendly specification language based on SLTL, and gathered in a constraint library that is automatically accessed by the model checker during the verification. The maintenance of the constraint library is supported by a hypertext system. Our model checker is optimized for dealing with hundreds of constraints and moderate size systems (around 10.000 nodes), in order to allow their verification in real time.

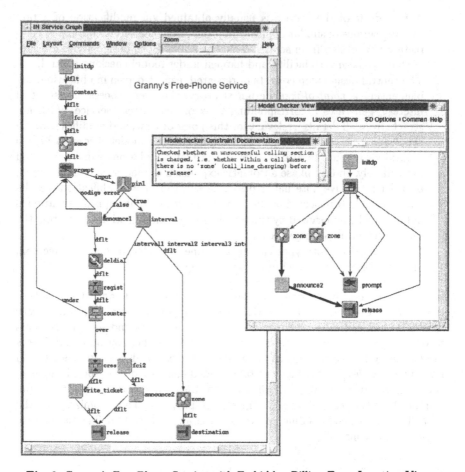

Fig. 6. Granny's Free-Phone Service with Forbidden Billing Error Location View

If the model checker detects an inconsistency, a plain text explanation of the violated constraint appears in a window as shown in Figure 6, and an *error view* is automatically generated, concentrating on the SIBs containing information relevant for the error detection, thus simplifying the location of the error. Corrections can be done directly on the error view, and the subsequent view application automatically updates the underlying concrete model.

3.4   Example: Granny's Free-Phone

The service shown in Fig. 6 presents the flow graph of a simple kind of Free-Phone (800-service). In essence, the service logic is the following: after a call initialization section common to all services, the caller dials the desired specific Free-Phone number, then a prompt requires entering a Personal Identification

Number (PIN) and, depending on the time of the day, the call is either released (in the forbidden time windows) after an announcement, or it is routed to the desired destination number.

A 'Billing Constraint'. The following Billing Constraint

Unsuccessful calling sections will not be charged

guaranteeing a property Germans are used to, can be expressed by the formula

$$\text{release} \Rightarrow (\neg\text{zone } \mathbf{BU}(\text{prompt} \vee \text{initdp}))$$

Here **BU** stands for a *backward until* modality, which is not part of SLTL, but can nevertheless be dealt with by our model checker. Intuitively, it is interpreted as the standard *until* operator on a service model, where all edges have been reverted. Intuitively the formula expresses the Billing Constraint as follows: traversing the service model backward from the release SIB, which marks unsuccessful call attempts, no zone (i.e. call segment charging) SIB should be met on the segment, which is delimited by a prompt or by an initdp SIB. The verbal formulation is shown in Fig. 6(middle).

Here we see that the logic allows expressing constraints not only along the flow of the call (forward constraints), but also in the opposite direction. Thus, a wide class of causality interactions can be elegantly and concisely formulated, successfully checked, and efficiently enforced.

In our example, model checking the Free-Phone service wrt. this constraint results in the discovery of erroneous paths in the graph. To ease its location and the correction of the error, an abstract *error view* is automatically generated, to evidence only the (usually few) relevant nodes. In order to supply a maximum of information concerning the error, error views do not touch the erroneous part, but constrain the application of the (model) collapse to the correct portion of the service. This choice also supports error correction, since the attention is immediately drawn on the (usually small) erroneous portion of the service logic, which is presented to a level of detail typically sufficient for correcting the error.

Fig. 6(right) shows the automatically generated error view with error location information for that same service and constraint.

- The error locating view has been obtained automatically after the failed model checking. Irrelevant nodes are collapsed in the unlabelled nodes. It is now easy to see that there is a constraint violation along the (unsuccessful) path between the release and the initdp SIBs: the portion evidenced by the highlighted arrows contains a zone SIB which is not allowed on this path. The location of the error is thus much more easily spotted than by inspection of the whole graph.
- The view graph can be directly edited, e.g. by deleting the zone SIB.
- The view *application* actualizes the corresponding IN-service model which is thus automatically corrected. A new verification via model checking confirms the conformance of the resulting service.

Note the precision and conciseness of the diagnostic information: the checked properties involve an interplay of several SIBs along a path, which usually describe their relative positioning in a loose fashion. Thus they leave room for several alternatives. As a consequence, legal error correction is not unique (in the example, one could insert a new call segment delimiter (prompt) at any place on the path below the zone SIBs), and a corresponding automatic selection process is not wished, as it would unnecessarily constrain the designer, who usually chooses the appropriate correction according to other (semantic) criteria. In this case, service providers may desire billings to be valid on the longest possible portion of a call segment. Thus the most convenient location for the zone SIB is immediately before the last prompt SIB on the path.

Of course this simple example service could have been still easily handled by hand, but current IN services have reached sizes and complexities which demand for automated support for error detection, diagnosis, and correction. Our environment encourages the use of the new method, as it can be introduced *incrementally*: if no formal constraints are defined, the system behaves like standard systems for service creation. However, the more constraints are added, the more reliable are the created services [21].

3.5   Typical Constraints

This section summarizes some typical constraints, which provide a good feeling for the style and common patterns in temporal constraint specification. They comprise backward modalities and examples for constraints written in our first-order extension of SLTL:

- 'All call sections (which are separated by prompt or initdp SIBs) are separatedly billed'. Billed segments are determined by an initializing billing SIB and a corresponding closing call-line-charging SIB.

$$(\text{prompt} \vee \text{initdp}) \; \Rightarrow \; (\neg\text{call-line-charging} \; \mathbf{U} \; \text{billing})$$

- 'Every pin-protected path in a service only leads to a successful connection if the final pin check was successful'. The slightly indirect modelling of this property assumes that the check_pin SIB only has two outgoing branches, marked *False* and *True*.

$$\text{check\_pin} \; \Rightarrow \; [\textit{False}] \, (\neg\text{destination} \; \mathbf{U} \; \text{check\_pin})$$

- More technical is the following constraint:

$$\text{write\_user\_destination} \; \Rightarrow \; (\neg\text{prompt} \; \mathbf{BU} \; \text{read\_dialled\_number})$$

which means that 'every write_user_destination SIB must be preceded by a read_dialled_ number SIB before a prompt SIB occurs'. This is exactly the constraint underlying the error view in Figure 4.

The following constraints make use of our first-order extension of SLTL. This extension was not part of the product delivered to SNI in 1995.

- 'counter SIBs are only allowed to appear after a corresponding init SIB', making sure that counting is always properly initialized. The parameter is only used to identify different counters within the same service.

$$\forall n.\ \mathsf{counter}(n)\ \Rightarrow\ \mathbf{BF}\,(\,\mathsf{init}(n)\,)$$

- More complicated is the following constraint guaranteeing pathwise version compatibility: 'on every path, where SIB1 occurs in version n, each subsequent occurrence of SIB2 is at least of version $n + 2$'.

$$\forall n.\ \mathsf{Version(SIB1)} = n\ \Rightarrow\ \mathbf{G}\,(\,\mathsf{Version(SIB2)} \geq n + 2\,)$$

- Finally, it is also possible to express global version consistency properties, like: 'whenever a SIB occurs in version n within a service, then all its occurrences are of version n'.

$$\forall n.\ \neg\mathbf{G}\,(\neg\mathsf{Version(SIB)} = n\,)\ \Rightarrow\ \mathbf{G}\,(\mathsf{Version(SIB)} = n\,)$$

In fact, in discussions with application experts it turned out that only very few simple patterns of constraints are required in order to express most of the desired properties. Thus application experts should be able to input their own constraints on the basis of very few corresponding templates.

3.6 Safe Service Customization

The incremental formalization approach, where (global) constraints are added online, aims at establishing a (loose) correctness filter but is far from guaranteeing correctness. Thus that responsibility remains with the programming or application expert. This approach is not applicable for customizers, subscribers or end users: they require a dual assistance, which constrains their freedom of design in order to guarantee consistency and executability. *Safe Service Customization* [6] is such a technique. It flexibly supports subscribers in their desire of modifying the *service logic* in a controlled fashion, while guaranteeing that the modified services can immediately be activated, without previous intervention of specialists like service designers or testers. Thus it goes far beyond the usual service adaptation capabilities, which either

- concern user-specific data only, like changing the PIN or modifying the time windows or the destination numbers for some routings, or
- are restricted to the combination of a small selection of Features or Service Independent Building Blocks, like e.g. those for call center functionality.

Together with its call flow-oriented user interface, our technique satisfies the following two requirements, essential for success in a competitive market:

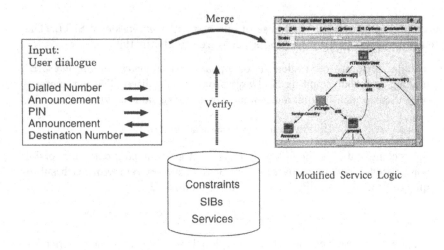

Fig. 7. The Service Modification Process

1. Ensured safety of the IN system: service modifications and definitions can only be accepted if they do not affect the reliability of the currently running system.
2. Comfortable and intuitive user's guidance: wide distribution also among non-experts requires a self-explaining tool.

As sketched in Fig. 7, our system offers service subscribers the possibility of modifying the service logic simply by giving call flow skeletons describing the desired user dialogues (left): by their nature, these do not require any advanced technical knowledge. The dialogues can then be integrated into a pre-existing (or basic) service (e.g. the off-the-shelf UPT just subscribed) by means of an advanced synthesis technique, which takes care of the vital consistency and frame conditions guaranteeing reliability. The result is a minimal running extension of the basic service that also provides all the features specified by the given call flows. An on-line testing facility allows users to validate whether all their desires are now satisfied. This safe service customization technique has been developed only after the delivery of our service definition environment to SNI.

4   Some Reflections

How practical and widely applicable is the METAFrame environment? The following reflections are dictated by considerations of 'soft' criteria, like acceptability, usability and extensibility.

4.1 Separation of Concerns

This principle is a methodological cornerstone of our environment. It plays a central role in our service definition environment e.g. for the management of teams of designers that work on several aspects of the service under development. Examples for required separation of concerns are the 'classical' distinction between environment administrators, service designers, and service customizers with their role-based responsibilities, as well as thematic-oriented separations according to the aspect currently considered, e.g. user interaction, billing, exception handling, routing and network related features. Our tool supports separation of concerns

- at the *description level*, by offering a variety of constraint languages on different abstraction levels [19], which are typically tailored for different user groups, and
- at the *presentation and operation levels*, e.g. by means of its flexible *view* mechanism, which highlights the essence of the considered design decision by hiding all the irrelevant details of the overall service graph [20].

4.2 Parameterization, Exchangeability and Reuse

Due to the abstract view of the components as coarse-grain, highly parameterized procedural entities, their use is largely independent of their concrete realization. Interchangeability of the implementing code has been exploited e.g. in order to offer mixed-mode simulation of services. A component may in fact have several implementations:

- at differents abstraction levels, from functional prototypes (adequate for service animation) to the code running on the installed Service Control Point.
- for operability in different environments (e.g., vendor-, country-, standard-dependent).

Mixed-mode simulation enables the execution of services whose components are not homogeneously realized. Obviously, correct executions are only possible if the interoperability is guaranteed. Temporal constraints provide a corresponding abstract means.

Besides the direct reuse of components in a different setting, we support a more flexible reuse policy in the prototyping phase: a flexible wrapper/adapter concept makes BBs[11] uniformly accessible for graphical, behaviour-oriented application programming, and application-specific taxonomies, which may categorize one and the same BB completely differently in different contexts, provide an application-specific view onto the content of the BB libraries. This supports the construction of complex heterogeneous application programs by providing policies for a context-dependent reuse of existing modules beyond the native application domain, as long as the patterns of usage are compatible.

---

[11] In particular also functionalities of legacy software.

4.3 Tailoring of the Visible Complexity

The described view concept provides all user groups of the development environment with a tailored representation of the system under construction. These representations, which arise as abstracted versions of the overall system representation in terms of a flow graph-like structure, are formally derived on the basis of hiding, abstract interpretation, model collapse and renaming concepts. The whole system development can be reduced to stepwise modifications of adequate role- or topic-specific views, like the error view shown in Fig. 4.

4.4 Semantics-Based Control

Systems, as well as their underlying domain model, can be loosely specified in terms of modal-logic constraints [3]. METAFrame provides a model checker for the corresponding verification, and a synthesis tool for guiding the development process [25]. Design errors like those spotted in Fig. 4 are in fact automatically detected on-line within seconds, even for libraries of hundreds of constraints. Important feature is here the full automation of these tools, which are indeed profitably used without requiring any specific knowledge of the underlying formal methods.

4.5 Incremental Formalization

The key to the acceptance of our system development method in the industrial context was its *incremental formalization* character [21, 6], ranging from 'no extra specification', resulting in the old-fashioned development style, to 'detailed specification', exploiting full tool support. In fact this property was probably psychologically most important for the acceptance of the tool within the SNI designers group and by their customers, because it builds upon familiar development habits.

4.6 'Evolutionary' Application Programming

The idea to this development style, which provides non experts with restricted programming power, first came up in connection with the ETI platform [19, 7], but turned out to be nicely applicable to the IN scenario (cf. Section 3.6). The proposed combination of inputs in terms of *user dialogues, controlled extension* by means of our synthesis feature, and *validation* in terms of animation guarantees reliability while allowing service subscribers a flexible and intuitive means to customize their services, including modifications of the Service Logic. This flexibilization and simplification of the service customization process reduces the costs for tailored intelligent network services and therefore provides a key to a service-on-demand market. Currently, we are exploring these concepts as a powerful means for personalizing internet services.

All these methods aim at making a global behaviour-oriented approach to programming applicable, essentially by reducing the apparent size of the underlying global model. The success of this approach therefore strongly depends on the existence of an adequate granularity and on the adequacy of the temporal constraint-based specification mechanism. We have a very promising experience with 'workflow-oriented' systems, which provide a flexible management and organization of collections of components, like in the IN application. On the other hand, the design of the underlying libraries of components themselves or the construction of large concurrent systems should be done by other means. E.g., we use the object-oriented approach for the design of our component libraries.

5   Conclusions

The presented approach exactly meets the demands for the emerging paradigm of *Domain Specific Formal Methods* [10]: use formal methods on a large or huge grain level rather than on elementary statements, thus support the programming with whole subroutines and modules as elementary building blocks. This is precisely what METAFrame is designed for and what the application to IN services embodies.

Still, the step towards the use of formal methods is rather big and can hardly be done at once. The METAFrame environment therefore offers a *lazy* and *incremental* use of formal methods: if no formal constraints are defined, the system behaves like standard systems for service creation. However, the more constraints are added, the better is the automatic control and the more reliable are the created services. In fact, in the extreme case of a full specification of the vital frame conditions, very few representative tests are required to guarantee the correctness of the service.

Experience shows that it is often impossible to write complete formal specifications in practice. E.g. in the case of service creation, the knowledge about the exact requirements is distributed over several groups along the development process, and it is only used implicitly during the development. Thus people need to learn that and how this knowledge should be made explicit. The incremental refinement of the formal specification, by successively adding more and more constraints, provides a 'soft' entry into the world of formal methods.

Acknowledgement

The technical development of the METAFrame environment, as well as of its instance for the IN application, was competently promoted and supervised by Volker Braun. He took over leadership of the METAFrame team from Andreas Claßen early in 1995, and made sure that the environment reaches industrial strength. We are very grateful to the whole METAFrame team, in particular to Achim Dannecker and Andreas Holzmann, who accompanied the development from the very beginning.

Finally, we would like to thank Gerhard Goos, Bengt Jonsson, Markus Müller-Olm and Perdita Stevens for their constructive feedback.

References

1. Digilog, Inc.: Atelier-b online. http://www.atelierb.societe.com/index_uk.html
2. B-Core(UK) Ltd., B-tool documentation. http://www.b-core.com/
3. M. von der Beeck, B. Steffen, T. Margaria: "*A Formal Requirements Engineering Method and an Environment for Specification, Synthesis, and Verification*", Proc. of SEE '97, 8th IEEE Conference on Software Engineering Environments, Cottbus (Germany) 8-9 April 1997.
4. P. K. Bohacek, J. N. White: "*Service Creation: The Real Key to Intelligent Network Revenue*", Proc. Workshop Intelligent Networks '94, Heidelberg, May 24-26, 1994.
5. V. Braun, T. Margaria, B. Steffen, H. Yoo: *Automatic Error Location for IN Service Definition*, Proc. AIN'97, 2nd Int. Workshop on Advanced Intelligent Networks, Cesena, 4.-5. Juli 1997, in "Services and Visualization: Towards User-Friendly Design', LNCS 1385, Springer Verlag, März 1998, pp.222-237.
6. V. Braun, T. Margaria, B. Steffen, H. Yoo, T. Rychly: *Safe Service Customization*, Proc. IN'97, IEEE Communication Soc. Workshop on Intelligent Network, Colorado Springs, CO (USA), 4-7 May 1997, IEEE Comm. Soc. Press.
7. V. Braun, T. Margaria, C. Weise: *Integrating Tools in the ETI Platform*, [25], pp.31-48.
8. Design/CPN Online. http://www.daimi.au.dk/designCPN/
9. J. Garrahan, P. Russo, K. Kitami, R. Kung: "*Intelligent Network Overview*," IEEE Communications Magazine, March 1993, pp. 30-37.
10. J.A. Goguen, Luqi: "*Formal Methods and Social Context in Software Development*," (invited talk) 6th Int. Conf. on Theory and Practice of Software Development (TAPSOFT'95), Aarhus (Denmark), May 1995, LNCS N.915, pp.62-81.
11. D. Harel, M. Politi: *Modeling Reactive Systems With Statecharts : The Statemate Approach*, McGraw Hill, October 1998, ISBN: 0070262055
12. J. Hofmann: *Program Dependent Abstract Interpretation*, Diplomarbeit, Fakultät für Mathematik und Informatik, Universität Passau, August 1997.
13. L. Kristensen, S. Christensen, K. Jensen: *The Practitioner's Guide to coloured Petri Nets*, STTT, Int. Journal on Software Tools for Technology Transfer, Vol.2, N.2, pp.98-132, December 1998, Springer Verlag, DOI 10.1007/s100099800003.
14. P. Leblanc: *OMT and SDL based techniques and tools for design, simulation and test production of distributed systems* STTT, Int. Journal on Software Tools for Technology Transfer, Volume 1 Issue 1+2 (1997) pp. 153-165, December 1997, Springer Verlag.
15. R. Milner: *Communication and Concurrency*, Prentice-Hall, 1989.
16. Oracle, Inc. Oracle Designer information page. http://www.oracle.com/tools/designer.
17. The Raise Project homepage. http://dream.dai.ed.ac.uk/raise/
18. Rational, Inc. The Rational Suite description. http://www.rational.com/products.
19. B. Steffen, T. Margaria, V. Braun: *The Electronic Tool Integration platform: concepts and design*, [25], pp. 9-30.
20. B. Steffen, T. Margaria, A. Claßen, V. Braun, M. Reitenspieß: "*An Environment for the Creation of Intelligent Network Services*", invited contribution to the book "Intelligent Networks: IN/AIN Technologies, Operations, Services, and Applications – A Comprehensive Report" Int. Engineering Consortium, Chicago IL, 1996, pp. 287-300 – also invited to the *Annual Review of Communications*, IEC, 1996, pp. 919-935.

21. B. Steffen, T. Margaria, A. Claßen, V. Braun: *Incremental Formalization: a Key to Industrial Success*, in "Software: Concepts and Tools", Vol.17(2), pp. 78-91, Springer Verlag, July 1996. Tool presentation in AMAST'96, Munich, Juli 1996, LNCS, Springer Verlag.

22. B. Steffen, T. Margaria, A. Claßen, V. Braun, M. Reitenspieß, H. Wendler: *Service Creation: Formal Verification and Abstract Views*, Proc. 4th Int. Conf. on Intelligent Networks (ICIN'96), Nov. 1996, Bordeaux (France), pp. 96-101.

23. B. Steffen, T. Margaria, V. Braun, N. Kalt: *Hierarchical Service Definition*, Annual Review of Communic., Int. Engineering Consortium, Chicago, 1997, pp.847-856.

24. C. Stirling: *Modal and Temporal Logics*, In *Handbook of Logics in Computer Science*, Vol. 2, pp. 478 – 551, Oxford Univ. Press, 1995.

25. *Special section on the Electronic Tool Integration Platform*, Int. Journal on *Software Tools for Technology Transfer*, Vol. 1, Springer Verlag, November 1997

26. Telelogic AB. Tau's description. http://www.telelogic.com/solution/tau.asp

27. Mike Wrax, Mark Syrett: "*Service Creation Using the Hewlett-Packard Service Creation Environment*", Proc. Workshop Intelligent Networks'94, Heidelberg, May 24-26, 1994.

Author Index

Lecture Notes in Computer Science

For information about Vols. 1–1622
please contact your bookseller or Springer-Verlag

Vol. 1667: J. Hlavička, E. Maehle, A. Pataricza (Eds.), Dependable Computing – EDCC-3. Proceedings, 1999. XVIII, 455 pages. 1999.

Vol. 1668: J.S. Vitter, C.D. Zaroliagis (Eds.), Algorithm Engineering. Proceedings, 1999. VIII, 361 pages. 1999.

Vol. 1670: N.A. Streitz, J. Siegel, V. Hartkopf, S. Konomi (Eds.), Cooperative Buildings. Proceedings, 1999. X, 229 pages. 1999.

Vol. 1671: D. Hochbaum, K. Jansen, J.D.P. Rolim, A. Sinclair (Eds.), Randomization, Approximation, and Combinatorial Optimization. Proceedings, 1999. IX, 289 pages. 1999.

Vol. 1672: M. Kutylowski, L. Pacholski, T. Wierzbicki (Eds.), Mathematical Foundations of Computer Science 1999. Proceedings, 1999. XII, 455 pages. 1999.

Vol. 1673: P. Lysaght, J. Irvine, R. Hartenstein (Eds.), Field Programmable Logic and Applications. Proceedings, 1999. XI, 541 pages. 1999.

Vol. 1674: D. Floreano, J.-D. Nicoud, F. Mondada (Eds.), Advances in Artificial Life. Proceedings, 1999. XVI, 737 pages. 1999. (Subseries LNAI).

Vol. 1675: J. Estublier (Ed.), System Configuration Management. Proceedings, 1999. VIII, 255 pages. 1999.

Vol. 1976: M. Mohania, A M. Tjoa (Eds.), Data Warehousing and Knowledge Discovery. Proceedings, 1999. XII, 400 pages. 1999.

Vol. 1677: T. Bench-Capon, G. Soda, A M. Tjoa (Eds.), Database and Expert Systems Applications. Proceedings, 1999. XVIII, 1105 pages. 1999.

Vol. 1678: M.H. Böhlen, C.S. Jensen, M.O. Scholl (Eds.), Spatio-Temporal Database Management. Proceedings, 1999. X, 243 pages. 1999.

Vol. 1679: C. Taylor, A. Colchester (Eds.), Medical Image Computing and Computer-Assisted Intervention – MICCAI'99. Proceedings, 1999. XXI, 1240 pages. 1999.

Vol. 1680: D. Dams, R. Gerth, S. Leue, M. Massink (Eds.), Theoretical and Practical Aspects of SPIN Model Checking. Proceedings, 1999. X, 277 pages. 1999.

Vol. 1682: M. Nielsen, P. Johansen, O.F. Olsen, J. Weickert (Eds.), Scale-Space Theories in Computer Vision. Proceedings, 1999. XII, 532 pages. 1999.

Vol. 1683: J. Flum, M. Rodríguez-Artalejo (Eds.), Computer Science Logic. Proceedings, 1999. XI, 580 pages. 1999.

Vol. 1684: G. Ciobanu, G. Păun (Eds.), Fundamentals of Computation Theory. Proceedings, 1999. XI, 570 pages. 1999.

Vol. 1685: P. Amestoy, P. Berger, M. Daydé, I. Duff, V. Frayssé, L. Giraud, D. Ruiz (Eds.), Euro-Par'99. Parallel Processing. Proceedings, 1999. XXXII, 1503 pages. 1999.

Vol. 1687: O. Nierstrasz, M. Lemoine (Eds.), Software Engineering – ESEC/FSE '99. Proceedings, 1999. XII, 529 pages. 1999.

Vol. 1688: P. Bouquet, L. Serafini, P. Brézillon, M. Benerecetti, F. Castellani (Eds.), Modeling and Using Context. Proceedings, 1999. XII, 528 pages. 1999. (Subseries LNAI).

Vol. 1689: F. Solina, A. Leonardis (Eds.), Computer Analysis of Images and Patterns. Proceedings, 1999. XIV, 650 pages. 1999.

Vol. 1690: Y. Bertot, G. Dowek, A. Hirschowitz, C. Paulin, L. Théry (Eds.), Theorem Proving in Higher Order Logics. Proceedings, 1999. VIII, 359 pages. 1999.

Vol. 1691: J. Eder, I. Rozman, T. Welzer (Eds.), Advances in Databases and Information Systems. Proceedings, 1999. XIII, 383 pages. 1999.

Vol. 1692: V. Matoušek, P. Mautner, J. Ocelíková, P. Sojka (Eds.), Text, Speech and Dialogue. Proceedings, 1999. XI, 396 pages. 1999. (Subseries LNAI).

Vol. 1693: P. Jayanti (Ed.), Distributed Computing. Proceedings, 1999. X, 357 pages. 1999.

Vol. 1694: A. Cortesi, G. Filé (Eds.), Static Analysis. Proceedings, 1999. VIII, 357 pages. 1999.

Vol. 1695: P. Barahona, J.J. Alferes (Eds.), Progress in Artificial Intelligence. Proceedings, 1999. XI, 385 pages. 1999. (Subseries LNAI).

Vol. 1696: S. Abiteboul, A.-M. Vercoustre (Eds.), Research and Advanced Technology for Digital Libraries. Proceedings, 1999. XII, 497 pages. 1999.

Vol. 1697: J. Dongarra, E. Luque, T. Margalef (Eds.), Recent Advances in Parallel Virtual Machine and Message Passing Interface. Proceedings, 1999. XVII, 551 pages. 1999.

Vol. 1698: M. Felici, K. Kanoun, A. Pasquini (Eds.), Computer Safety, Reliability and Security. Proceedings, 1999. XVIII, 482 pages. 1999.

Vol. 1699: S. Albayrak (Ed.), Intelligent Agents for Telecommunication Applications. Proceedings, 1999. IX, 191 pages. 1999. (Subseries LNAI).

Vol. 1700: R. Stadler, B. Stiller (Eds.), Active Technologies for Network and Service Management. Proceedings, 1999. XII, 299 pages. 1999.

Vol. 1701: W. Burgard, T. Christaller, A.B. Cremers (Eds.), KI-99: Advances in Artificial Intelligence. Proceedings, 1999. XI, 311 pages. 1999. (Subseries LNAI).

Vol. 1702: G. Nadathur (Ed.), Principles and Practice of Declarative Programming. Proceedings, 1999. X, 434 pages. 1999.

Vol. 1703: L. Pierre, T. Kropf (Eds.), Correct Hardware Design and Verification Methods. Proceedings, 1999. XI, 366 pages. 1999.

Vol. 1704: Jan M. Żytkow, J. Rauch (Eds.), Principles of Data Mining and Knowledge Discovery. Proceedings, 1999. XIV, 593 pages. 1999. (Subseries LNAI).

Vol. 1705: H. Ganzinger, D. McAllester, A. Voronkov (Eds.), Logic for Programming and Automated Reasoning. Proceedings, 1999. XII, 397 pages. 1999. (Subseries LNAI).

Vol. 1707: H.-W. Gellersen (Ed.), Handheld and Ubiquitous Computing. Proceedings, 1999. XII, 390 pages. 1999.

Vol. 1708: J.M. Wing, J. Woodcock, J. Davies (Eds.), FM'99 – Formal Methods. Proceedings Vol. I, 1999. XVIII, 937 pages. 1999.

Vol. 1709: J.M. Wing, J. Woodcock, J. Davies (Eds.), FM'99 – Formal Methods. Proceedings Vol. II, 1999. XVIII, 937 pages. 1999.

Vol. 1710: E.-R. Olderog, B. Steffen (Eds.), Correct System Design. XIV, 417 pages. 1999.

Vol. 1718: M. Diaz, P. Owezarski, P. Sénac (Eds.), Interactive Distributed Multimedia Systems and Telecommunication Services. Proceedings, 1999. XI, 386 pages. 1999.